Wildlife of Southern Forests: Habitat and Management

JOHN SIDELINGER

Wildlife of Southern Forests:
Habitat and Management

Compiled and Edited by

James G. Dickson

Hancock House Publishers

ISBN 978-0-88839-017-2

Third softcover printing 2017
B&W Edition

Cataloging in Publication Data

Wildlife of southern forests : habitat and management /
compiled and edited by James G. Dickson.

Includes bibliographical references and index.
Issued also in electronic format.
ISBN 978-0-88839-672-3

1. Zoology—Southern States. 2. Wildlife conservation—Southern States. 3. Wildlife management—Southern States. 4. Forest management —Southern States. 5. Forest ecology—Southern States. I. Dickson, James G.

QL157.S68W54 2008 591.975 C2008-908006-8

Printed in the USA

Editor: Compiled and edited by James G. Dickson
Production: Bob Canlas, Ingrid Luters
Line Drawings: John Sidelinger
Front cover artwork *(clockwise from top left)*: *Suspicions of Fall* by Hayden Lambson, National Wild Turkey Federation; *Wood Ducks* by John Sidelinger; *Ivory-billed Woodpecker* by George Sutton, Cornell Lab of Ornithology; *Ambush* by Mark Twain Noe, National Wild Turkey Federation
Back cover images *(from top)*: G. Smith, US Forest Service, J. Walker, John Sidelinger

Published simultaneously in Canada and the United States by

HANCOCK HOUSE PUBLISHERS LTD.
19313 Zero Avenue, Surrey, B.C. Canada V3Z 9R9
(604) 538-1114 Fax (604) 538-2262

HANCOCK HOUSE PUBLISHERS
#104-4550 Birch Bay-Lynden Rd, Blaine, WA 98230
(800) 938-1114 Fax (800) 983-2262
Website: **www.hancockhouse.com**
Email: **sales@hancockhouse.com**

Contents

List of Tables

Chapter 17 Waterfowl

Chapter 18 American Black Bear

Chapter 21 Carnivorous Furbearers

Chapter 22 Omnivorous Furbearers

List of Figures

Acknowledgments

Theresa Arnold	Richard Lancia
Celeste Baine	Gary Larson
Carl Betsill	Dan Lay
Timothy Breault	Mike Legg
Tammy Bristow	Bruce Leopold
Peter Bromley	John Lewis
Cliff Brown	Greg Linscombe
Don Burdette	Susan Loeb
Robert Cambell	Paula Malcolm
Keith Causey	Larry Marchington
Dick Conner	Billy Minser
Noel Cost	Paul Moore
Tom Darden	Rose Moore
Randy Davidson	Bob Nelson
John Dickson	Michael O'Linde
Liz Dickson	Bill Palmer
Ralph Dimmick	Mike Pelton
Richard Dolbeer	Shirley Reagan
John Edwards	Steve Rickerson
Robert Ellis	Ken Reinecke
Daniel Figert	Jay Robertson
Mel Finkenberg	Pete Roussopoulos
Dan Forster	Craig Rudolph
John Frampton	Michael Shaw
Dave Frederick	John Schoellkopf
Ernie Garcia	Tink Smith
Dave Guynn	Mike Staten
Keith Guyse	Dave Steffen
Melissa Gosdin	Cindy Swanson
Gary Graham	Jack Ward Thomas
Doug Grann	Roy Tomlinson
William Healy	Dave Urbston
Nancy Herbert	Bill Thomason
Billy Higginbotham	Mike Vaughan
David Hoge	Greg Wathen
Howard Hunt	Jim Wentworth
Rhett Johnson	David Whitehouse
Rob Keck	Bently Wigley
Brian Kelly	Howard Williamson
James Earl Kennamer	Steve N. Wilson
Noel Kinler	Mariko Yamasaki
David Krementz	Stephen Young

Preface

Wildlife are natural components of southern forests, function in various ways in the forest systems, and are important to the people of the region economically and for recreation. In *Wildlife of Southern Forests* we trace the history of southern forests and associated wildlife, detail the biology and habitat requirements of species and communities, and offer practical guidelines for habitat management on a broad scale. Information in this book should help land managers assess land suitability for various species and communities, determine how different land and forestry management practices affect wildlife, and actively manage for target species and communities.

The book is divided into 10 general sections with 31 individual chapters. The scope of this book is broad. It contains chapters on landscape ecology, sensitive plant communities, and managing forests for wildlife. Also included are chapters on classical game species such as white-tailed deer and wild turkey; an endangered species- the red-cockaded woodpecker, and nongame communities, such as bats, birds, and reptiles and amphibians. It provides an introduction, overview, and synthesis of information concerning the hundreds species of vertebrate wildlife inhabiting southern forests.

Chapters of *Wildlife of Southern Forests* are written by leading wildlife experts from universities, federal agencies, and conservation organizations of the South. The book is illustrated by renown wildlife artist John Sidelinger. The book features more than 200 black-and-white and 31 color photographs. More than 1,500 technical references will prove valuable to readers wishing to pursue particular points of interest. The book was compiled as a USDA Forest Service Southern Research Station project.

The collaborators for *Wildlife of Southern Forests* were the USDA Forest Service, National Wild Turkey Federation, Wildlife Forever, and Louisiana Tech University. The

USDA Forest Service was an early conservation leader; and continues today in the conservation and wise use of the nation's forest and rangeland systems. The USDA Forest Service manages nearly 200 million acres of public land, assists states and private landowners in applying conservation practices, and conducts research to provide information to advance management.

The National Wild Turkey Federation, headquartered in Edgefield, SC, is a natural resources conservation leader. The NWTF, with about 500,000 members, is committed to and instrumental in the conservation of the wild turkey and other wildlife, and the preservation of our hunting heritage. Since 1985, more than $200 million NWTF and cooperator dollars have been spent on over 25,000 wildlife projects. Thanks to the NWTF, working with state wildlife agencies, other conservation partners, and volunteers, now the gobble of the wild turkey can be heard throughout forested North America.

Wildlife Forever is a national non-profit organization founded to preserve America's wildlife heritage through conservation education, preservation of habitat, and management of fish and wildlife. Working with private conservation groups, state game and fish departments, and federal agencies, since 1987 Wildlife Forever has supported more than 550 projects covering every state in the union. For more information, write to Wildlife Forever at 10365 West 70th Street, Eden Prairie, MN 55344 or visit the Wildlife Forever website at *www.wildlifeforever.org*.

Louisiana Tech University, a member of the University of Louisiana System, is committed to quality in teaching, in research, and in public service. With the education of students its highest priority, the University offers a broad range of undergraduate programs as well as masters and doctoral degrees in specific areas of expertise. Forests and the wildlife that inhabit them are important ecologically, economically, and for recreational use in the North Louisiana region. And the Wildlife and Forestry Programs are integral educational offerings of the University.

All 13 southern state wildlife agencies were cooperators in the study. They provided data on estimated populations and harvest for game species.

A few people are owed a special thanks for their role in this book. Dr. James Earl Kennamer, Dr. Jack Ward Thomas, Mr. Bob Nelson, and Dr. Nancy Herbert were instrumental in the initial support of the book. Mr. Lowell Halls and Mr. Dan Lay were early biologists and mentors, whose efforts helped kindle an interest and pursuit of understanding of southern wildlife.

— James G. Dickson, Ph.D.

CHAPTER 1

Introduction

James G. Dickson[1]
US Forest Service
Southern Research Station, Nacogdoches, TX

The temperate climate, productive soils, and lush forests of the South support an abundant and diverse wildlife community. But these forests and the wildlife that inhabit them have never been stable. They have continually been molded by a variety of forces. Early, during the Pleistocene period, drastic periodic climatic shifts wrought wholesale changes to the nature of southern forests. And more recently, floods, ice and wind storms, insects and diseases, and interactions of the vertebrate species themselves have played a continual role in the dynamics of these forests.

ARRIVAL OF HUMANS

Influences on the forest communities were enhanced with the arrival of the first humans over 10,000 years ago. It appears that the first human inhabitants of the region preyed upon and eliminated megafauna of the region, such as the mastodon. Southern wildlife became primary food for people of the region. Burning of the forests by natives was common. The effects of humans on southern forest systems became even more pronounced with the invasion of European settlers in the 1700s, and became more severe in the 1800s and early 1900s, as their population swelled. With settlement came exploitation of the forests and associated wildlife with little regard for the future. Settlers cleared forests for wood products and to create openings for their crops. The vast mature upland longleaf forests were cleared, as were the bottomland cypress forests. The American chestnut was eliminated from the Appalachians by the introduced chestnut blight. And to feed the expanding pioneer families, game was harvested at will.

[1]Current Address: School of Forestry, Louisiana Tech University, Ruston, LA

The temperate climate, productive soils, and diverse forests of the South support an abundant and diverse wildlife community *(US Forest Service)*.

Southern forests have always been dynamic, and continue to be influenced by a variety of natural and anthropogenic forces. Right: Flooded bottom *(J. Neal)*, Bottom right: Wild Hogs *(J. Meyer)*.

In this era of settlement and exploitation, a few wildlife species, such as the passenger pigeon, were lost.

But later, in the 1900s, began the realization that natural resources were exhaustible and threatened, there began a conservation awakening. With this conservation movement came the initiation of regeneration, in some form, of the region's forests and restoration of important game species, such as the white-tailed deer and wild turkey.

CHANGES CONTINUE

Southern forests have always been dynamic, and there continue to be changes. Natural events, such as hurricanes, still affect southern forests. And the human population of the region and its widespread influence continue to grow. Mostly introduced pests are profoundly affecting southern forest ecosystems. Some noteworthy examples illustrate. The Chinese tallow tree continues

Several species of wildlife of southern forests, such as the wild turkey, have been successfully restored *(B. Healy)*. The status of some others is unknown.

to proliferate in the deep South. Negative effects on plant communities are being wrought by the balsam wooly adelgid on Fraser fir stands in high elevations and by the gypsy moth on Appalachian oak forests. And wild hogs and their influence continue to expand in the South and elsewhere.

THE BOOK

Wildlife are natural components of southern forests and function in various ways in the forests systems. Also, wildlife is very important to the people of the region. Wildlife hunting and viewing are important recreationally and economically. There is much interest in protecting and managing southern wildlife. Although we have developed substantial information, generally, it is piecemeal and widely dispersed. In this book we chronicle the general history of southern forests and associated wildlife to its current status, present information on habitat relationships of southern wildlife, and offer practical guidelines for habitat management. This publication should benefit wildlife. It should be helpful to forest land managers of the South for assessing forest land suitability for various species or communities, determining how various land and forestry management practices affect wildlife, and for managing land for target species or communities.

Generally, the area of coverage in this book is the 13 southeastern states; bounded to the north by Virginia and Kentucky, and to the west by the forested eastern portions of Oklahoma and Texas. We present information on landscape-scale relationships and provide relative density estimates for key species by county. Several hundred species of vertebrates inhabit southern forests. Because of that large number, space limitations, and availability of information, emphasis is given to key game species, endangered species, and species and ecosystems of concern. For individual species or species groups this book should provide an introduction to and overview of habitat relationships. More detailed information for birds is contained in Hamel (1992) and Finch and Stangel (1992), and for amphibians and reptiles in Wilson (1995). Also, this book should identify gaps in our information, such as with reptiles and amphibians, and hopefully will inspire further research.

The book is divided into 10 general sections with 31 individual chapters. Although there has been an effort to maintain consistency among chapters, there are some differences. Each chapter author(s) is an expert on their subject; and writing style, area of coverage, perspective, and conclusions vary somewhat between chapters. We hope this book helps readers to better understand, appreciate, and enjoy southern wildlife.

CHAPTER 2

Early History

James G. Dickson[1]
US Forest Service
Southern Research Station, Nacogdoches, TX

EARLY FORESTS

Primal forests.—According to fossil records from coal beds, primeval forests of the South eons ago were complex forests of club moss trees and ferns (Burdette 1995). Since that time forest composition and distribution have changed in response to natural phenomena and later, to the influences of man. Over a long period of time primeval forests evolved from club mosses and ferns to gymnosperms, related to our present-day pines, and then later to mixed gymnosperm and angiosperm (deciduous) forests. During the glacial period, tree species migrated north and south and forest composition changed as a result of climatic shifts (Burdette 1995). For example, about 20,000 years ago the northern boreal coniferous forest extended deep into the South.

Somewhere around 10,000 B.C., or perhaps before, the first humans immigrated to North America and into the South from across the Bering land bridge after the last glacier had receded to the north. Apparently they followed herds of large mammals such as mammoths, mastodons, giant bison, and ground sloths that they hunted and depended on for sustenance. In the South they found beech-maple hardwood forests. Over time,

[1]Current Address: School of Forestry, Louisiana Tech University, Ruston, LA

the forests, the archaic human inhabitants, and the faunal communities changed (Burdette 1995). By about 5,000 B.C. the climate had become warmer and drier, and oak-hickory and pine-hardwood forests had become dominate. The megafauna hunted earlier by the human inhabitants had become extinct and the people who had inhabited the South for thousands of years had switched to hunting deer, turkey, and small game animals. By 1,000 B.C. the Woodland people had developed simple agriculture and were cultivating plants, such as squash, for food. They influenced the landscape by the openings they created in the forests.

Later by about A.D. 1500, the Mississippian culture had developed extensive social, religious, and agricultural systems and fire was a common tool employed to influence forests (Burdette 1995). But for unknown reasons the culture declined.

Influence of Native Americans-1500s.—The first written records of early civilization and forests came from the Spanish explorers of the mid 1500s, such as De Soto. At that time developed cultures of Native Americans were widespread throughout the southern region; population estimates ranged up to 1.5 million natives (Cooper and Terrill 1990). They subsisted by hunting, growing crops, such as corn, beans, squash, and gourds, and gathering food and other materials (Burdette 1995). Their settlements tended to be located on better soils, but they certainly affected the drier uplands (D. Lay, pers. commun.). They used fire regularly without control to create openings in which to grow crops, to open the woods, and to drive game to facilitate harvest. Apparently substantial areas of the coastal plain were burned with high frequency and intensity, which favored pines in general and particularly longleaf pine. The burning in combination with soil conditions in some areas unsuitable for tree growth created extensive savannahs and grassland prairies. In upland mountainous areas, fires were not as frequent and hardwoods dominated. In moist bays, river floodplains, and swamps, fires usually did not occur and old-growth hardwood stands developed. It appears that the native groups moved periodically; and their influence and that of natural phenomena resulted in a wide variety of tree and forest age classes interspersed with ephemeral to longer-term openings throughout the region.

Old-growth forests-1700s.—But the extensive populations of natives encountered by the Spanish explorers of the mid 1500s were greatly diminished by the 1700s. Over half of the number of people detected earlier by the Spanish was gone by the time the next

Fire, flooding, ice and wind storms, insects, and diseases all have played a significant historic role in shaping southern forests and their fauna *(US Forest Service)*.

Old-growth forests with structural diversity, large old trees, standing snags, and down decaying logs dominated the South in the 1700s before settlement by Europeans *(J. Walker)*.

In pre-colonial southern forests there must have been openings and savannah-like habitat necessary for the herbaceous vegetation to support grazing animals and other species associated with early successional habitat.

explorers traversed the region and noted the condition of the forests and its inhabitants. Apparently the natives had little resistance to the diseases of the earliest Europeans and contact with them caused wholesale pestilence (Cooper and Terrill 1990). Native populations had been decimated, their effects on forests of the region had greatly diminished, and the forests of the region matured. Some areas, particularly hardwood bottoms, probably had not been influenced as much by earlier natives and were in an old-growth condition.

Accounts of early explorers of this era are quite variable and some should be taken with a grain of salt. But I believe we can piece together a reasonable picture of what southern pre-colonial forests of this time were like from records of early French and English explorers, such as William Bartram, an early naturalist who traveled extensively through the southeastern area in the late 1700s.

Pre-colonial old growth forests for the most part comprised a diverse landscape, with stands of varying tree ages interspersed with some openings (see Johnson 1987). In what would later become Alabama, Bartram (Van Doren 1928:318) described expansive savannahs, groves, dense cane thickets, swamps, and open pine forests. There were many big, old trees, decayed trees, standing snags, down logs, and abundant mast produced in the mature forests. Characteristics of some remnant old-growth stands that remain were described by Wharton (1977) and Walker (1991).

The Blue Ridge, Ridge and Valley, Appalachian Plateau, and Piedmont provinces were characterized by mixed forests of mostly oaks and other hardwoods with some pines on drier sites. American Chestnut was common in the mountainous areas of the Appalachian region.

Coastal Plain forests were comprised of pine and hardwoods. Fire-resistant pines dominated on upland sites where fire was common. Some stands were described as dense and others as pine savannahs with grassy understories. Longleaf pine usually dominated sandy, infertile upland sites (Johnson 1987). But contrary to most early descriptions of diverse forests, several early travelers described monotonous pine "barrens" with little vegetative variety and a paucity of wildlife in places in the southeast (Johnson 1987). William Bartram noted the forest deserts of the Georgia/Florida area where birds were uncommon (Van Doren 1928). In the southern coastal plains, hardwoods, especially oaks, were common on clayey soils. Hardwoods, particularly the shade-tolerant magnolia and beech, usually dominated on moist sites naturally excluded from fire (Delcourt and Delcourt 1974). Live oaks occupied higher ridges, which were archaic beaches, along the coast. In some areas in different regions soil conditions resulted in the development of natural prairies, which sometimes were a significant feature of the landscape.

Bottoms were occupied by oak-gum-cypress forests; particular stand composition dependent on specific site characteristics (Putnam et al. 1960). According to Bartram, about one-third of the Lower Coastal Plain of Georgia was gum-cypress or cane swamp (Johnson 1987). Other moist site forests, such as bays, pocosins, and wet prairies, occurred, particularly in the eastern portion of the region. Palmetto and cane were dominant understory species, sometimes forming extremely dense thickets. Apparently vast thickets of cane dominated ridges of southern bottoms. William Bartram made frequent reference to the thick cane in the Alabama region. President Theodore Roosevelt described cane in Louisiana so thick that human access could only be gained by cutting a path. And early settlers in East Texas noted the dense cane thickets.

Southern old-growth forests were not stable, but were dynamic, changing continually in response to numerous influences of natural phenomena and Native Americans. Natural plant succession continually affected plant communities over time; shade and competition-tolerant plants replaced intolerant pioneer species. Disturbance was a major determinant of forest composition. In the river bottoms, flooding and associated sedimentation were largely responsible for site characteristics and distribution of specific forest types and representative species. Also, insects, diseases, ice and wind storms, and fire all certainly played a role in shaping and changing the early old-growth forests. In summary, there were numerous forces affecting early forests and those forests were continually changing in response to those forces.

Fire played a major role in the composition of early southern forests. Although lightning fires were probably not very frequent because lightning usually was accompanied by rain in the South, the fires that started naturally burned unabated. Probably of much greater impact were the frequent fires set by Native Americans to create openings for crops, open up the forest, and drive game for harvest. Many native tribes used fire to drive deer for harvest (McCabe and McCabe 1984). Bartram made frequent reference in the late 1700s to the annual firing of the forests by the natives in the Southeast (Van Doren 1928). The thick bark of older pines, particularly longleaf, afford some protection from heat from fire and are more resistant to damage and mortality from fire than hardwoods with thinner bark. Repeated burnings greatly reduced hardwoods on upland sites throughout large areas of the region and hardwoods persisted on moist, unburned sites. Old, large, shade-tolerant southern magnolia and American beech observed by Bartram in the late 1700s occurred on moist sites where fire was naturally excluded or was infrequent enough to allow the hardwoods to develop (Delcourt and Delcourt 1974).

From all indications forest openings and savannahs, such as open-grown mature longleaf stands, were a regular part of the southern forest landscape. William Bartram in his journey through the region saw many of several species of animals associated with early successional stands, such as the yellow-breasted chat and blue linnet (indigo bunting). Bison, a grazing animal, were widespread throughout the region at one time. Also, he reported a super abundance of white-tailed deer and wild turkeys, that depend on early successional vegetation during some phases of their life cycle, supporting the premise of abundant grass-forb and young brushy stands in early forests.

These forest openings and savannahs were a result of numerous factors (Johnson 1987). A variety of disturbances previously discussed set back succession and created openings. Natural fires and burning by Native Americans reduced woody vegetation and favored grass-forb vegetation. Also they created openings by girdling trees to clear land for their crops on more fertile sites. The rapid oxidation of organic matter of the "new ground" and rapid leaching of nutrients from most southern soils resulted in short term fertility and encouraged natives and early settlers to move their crop fields and settlements frequently.

WILDLIFE COMMUNITIES

Early records concerning wildlife of the pre-colonial era are certainly incomplete and therefore some conclusions are speculative. I believe, however, there is sufficient information from that era to draw some conclusions, regarding species of interest during that era, such as game species and large carnivores. These wildlife communities were determined by habitat, natural factors affecting populations, and substantial influence by Native Americans. The earliest time period with sufficient documentation to describe the pre-colonial wildlife communities was about the 1700s.

Large herbivores.—The early settlers readily utilized the great herds of bison that roamed throughout the region (for example, see Lowery's (1974:504) description of bison in Louisiana in the 1700s). Apparently there were sufficient prairies and grassy savannahs to support populations of bison and also elk that were encountered in some places by the new settlers (Van Doren 1928).

White-tailed deer.—According to early travelers white- tailed deer were widespread throughout North America except the arid southwest. Native Americans and later early settlers used them extensively for food, clothing, and for trade. Based on estimated Native American populations and diet, it was calculated that pre-colonial natives consumed an estimated 4.6 to 6.4 million deer annually in what is now the United States and Canada (McCabe and McCabe 1984).

Deer hides became the major trade item of the South. Numerous deer hides representing widespread hunting in Louisiana were sold by the Caddos to the fort at Nachitoches in the early 1700s (D. Lay, pers. commun.). Deer hides were the main export item from southeastern ports in the early to mid 1700s (Johnson 1987). For example in the mid 1700s, an average of about 150,000 deer hides per year were shipped from Charleston, South Carolina, and similar numbers were shipped from other coastal ports in the South (McCabe and McCabe 1984). The number of deer hides exported at that time, not including those used domestically, was several times the number of deer harvested in recent years (Johnson 1987). Apparently the combination of mature forests and openings or savannahs with browse and forbs created by fire or other disturbance was excellent habitat for this abundant herbivore.

Wild turkey.—There were very abundant wild turkeys in the diverse forests before white settlement. Based on early reports, Native Americans harvested wild turkeys with ease, and many tribes used them for food and adornments (Mosby and Handley 1943). Kennamer and Kennamer (1992) recount several descriptions of abundant turkeys in pre-colonial America. McCabe and McCabe (1984:29) reported that turkey remains were second in abundance to deer in eastern native refuse areas. Bartram described the spring gobbling at dawn near St. Augustine as a "universal shout" for hundreds of miles around from the

Several game species, such as white-tailed deer, wild turkey, and gray squirrels, thrived in pre-colonial forests *(C. Miller)*.

turkey cocks roosting in cypress and magnolia trees (Van Doren 1928:89). Wild turkeys became a food staple for early colonists as they settled the area (Mosby and Handley 1943). The diverse forests with mature stands with hard mast as fall and winter habitat, and the openings with grass-forb vegetation and associated insects and other invertebrates as spring and summer habitat bode well for the wild turkey before exploitation by new settlers.

Squirrels.—Squirrels were abundant in pre-colonial forests. Bartram saw several color phases of fox and gray squirrels, and noted that flying squirrels were common (Van Doren 1928). Excellent gray squirrel habitat is comprised of large tracts of mature, mast producing trees with adequate dens in decayed wood (Huntley 1986); and gray squirrels probably thrived in most old growth forests before white settlement. Fox squirrels inhabit more open habitat and would have been favored in areas with pine- hardwoods, pine savannahs, openings, or agricultural crops.

Ducks.—The extensive area of mature flooded bottoms in the South with prolific acorn production and invertebrates in the oak litter was excellent winter habitat for wood ducks and mallards. They wintered by the millions in the flooded bottoms. Also, wood ducks probably were common nesters in the abundant cavities in the old-growth forests. Hooded mergansers, green-winged teal, gadwall, and American widgeon are other species of waterfowl that frequented flooded bottoms, particularly small openings, during winter.

Carnivores.—In general, large carnivores probably were abundant in pre-colonial forests where there was sufficient diversity and early successional vegetation to support prey populations. Bartram (Van Doren 1928:62) recorded numerous bears, tygers (cougar)- which preyed on calves and young colts, wolves (red wolf), and wild cats (bobcat). According to most early accounts cougars were widespread in pre-settlement forests (see Lowery 1974). In his journey from the Georgia to Alabama area, Bartram observed "tygers" regularly (Van Doren 1928). With hunting pressure they usually are intolerant of humans and have large home ranges. Cougars probably were supported by the abundant white-tailed deer. It is likely that bobcats were abundant where there was sufficient low vegetation to support adequate small mammal densities. They were sighted frequently by William Bartram in his journey through the southeast in the 1700s.

The red wolf seemed to be widespread in pre-colonial forests in the Coastal Plain and north along the Mississippi River delta (Lowery 1974, U.S. Fish and Wildlife Service 1989). As with other species, apparently there was sufficient early succession vegetation to support herbivorous prey of the wolf.

Black bears were abundant in the diverse pre-colonial forests. The combination of mature forests with large trees, interspersed with openings, and little human interaction created ideal conditions for this large omnivore. Large trees provided dens, and important food, such as mast of American chestnut and oaks. Openings provided small vertebrate and invertebrate food, and abundant soft mast, such as blackberries. In the bottoms, bears often frequented the dense cane thickets, particularly when they were hunted (Roosevelt 1908, Van Doren 1928).

Small mammals.—Early naturalists had little interest in small mammals and records are minimal. Bartram saw 3 kinds of rabbits in his travels through the southeast (Van Doren 1928). An analysis of small mammal communities in 4 southeastern regions containing wilderness areas, revealed a small mammal community that was representative of the entire eastern United States (Schmidly 1986). The Appalachian region supported the highest diversity of species and was faunistically the most distinct, but the Florida/South Georgia region had the greatest number of endemic species.

Miscellaneous mammals.—In his travels in the late 1700s, Bartram noted otter, mink, weasel, pole cat (skunk), raccoons, and opossums in great abundance (Van Doren 1928:232). Hill (1986) reviewed species inhabiting wilderness areas; noting general biological characteristics. Species inhabiting hydric habitat included the mink, muskrat, river otter, and beaver. Species inhabiting mesic habitat in pre-colonial forests included the gray fox, red fox, striped skunk, spotted skunk, long-tailed weasel, opossum, and raccoon.

Red-cockaded woodpecker.—The red-cockaded woodpecker was probably widespread in pre-colonial forests where large pines dominated; found in what was to become New Jersey southwest through Kentucky and Tennessee, to southeastern Oklahoma and East Texas (Jackson 1971). Prime habitat consists of open-grown pine stands with old trees with red heart disease used for cavities, with limited hardwoods. In the northern periphery of its range where hardwoods dominated stands, it probably was never very abundant. In the southern coastal plain where fires limited hardwoods, woodpecker populations probably thrived. The species was considered common by John James Audubon in the monotonous pine barrens described by travelers in the early 1800s in Florida, Georgia, and South Carolina (Jackson 1971).

Bird communities.—Where old-growth forests were diverse with trees and stands of different ages, there were probably abundant and diverse breeding and wintering birds. Old, diverse forests with foliage in many different layers usually support a greater abundance and diversity of birds than simpler forests (Johnston and Odum 1956, Meyers and Johnson 1978, Dickson and Segelquist 1979). Bird abundance and diversity has been shown to be related to habitat patchiness (Roth 1976) and vertical foliage diversity (MacArthur and MacArthur 1961). In a series of forest stands of different ages in the South, the highest bird community values (more than 25 species and more than 2,500 territorial males per square mile) were found in mature pine-hardwood and mature hardwood stands (Dickson 1978a, Meyers and Johnson 1978).

Although it entails some speculation, reconstructing bird species in historic old-growth stands based on current data on birds in mature stands probably is reasonable. A variety of long-legged waders and the wood stork nest and forage in flooded forests. Avian predators, such as Mississippi and American swallow-tailed kites, bald eagles, osprey, red-shouldered hawks, and barred owls are regular occupants of mature bottoms now (Dickson 1988) and historically (Van Doren 1928). Vireos and warblers that frequent mature mesic forests now probably were abundant in historic forests. Red-eyed and yellow-throated vireos inhabit mature forest canopies, and white-eyed vireos are regular inhabitants of shrubby vegetation. Mature moist riparian forests consistently harbor several species of warblers, such as the black-and-white, prothonotary, Swainson's, worm-eating, northern parula, yellow throated, ovenbird, Louisiana waterthrush, Kentucky, and hooded warbler (Dickson et al. 1980, Hamel 1992). Swainson's warblers, and Bachman's warblers which now are extinct or close to extinction, were probably regular occupants of the dense cane thickets, which were widespread on higher ridges in the bottoms.

Early notes from Bartram (Van Doren 1928) detailed abundant Carolina parakeets in the North Carolina area, where he described them eating the seeds of cypress balls. They probably were very abundant elsewhere also. Passenger pigeon nesting colonies often covered miles of forests and they wintered in southern bottoms by the millions (Truett and Lay 1984), where they fed on the abundant oak mast. Bartram described wagon loads of pigeons killed by servants with lights at night.

Cavity nesting and using birds probably were abundant in early southern forests as has been documented in European forests (Tomialojc 1991). Old-growth forests contain numerous partially-decayed trees and snags used for nest sites by primary and secondary nesters, and abundant arthropod prey used for food. Truett and Lay (1984) noted from historical records, that cavity nesting birds, such as red-headed woodpeckers, American kestrels, and great crested flycatchers, were abundant in early forests of eastern Texas. In his trips through the southern bottoms in the early 1900s, Theodore Roosevelt (1908) regarded woodpeckers as characteristic species. The ivory-billed woodpecker once thrived in southern oak-gum forests where they foraged on recently dead trees (Tanner 1942). Wood ducks nested in the abundant natural cavities in the old-growth forests and prothonotary warblers were probably abundant in the bottoms where they nested in small cavities, often in trees and shrubs killed by flooding.

The red-cockaded woodpecker probably thrived in old-growth pine forests maintained by fire *(US Forest Service)*.

Although extent of habitat and populations were likely less abundant than today, bird species associated with early successional stands probably were regular inhabitants of openings and open-grown savanna-like stands with abundant grass-forb and/or shrub vegetation. In his early travels, William Bartram made frequent reference to several species of birds associated with early successional habitat, such as the yellow-breasted chat and blue linnet (indigo bunting); and noted that he saw many more birds near habitations of men than in desert forests (Van Doren 1928). As best we can surmise, the distribution and abundance of other species associated with shrub or grass-forb vegetation probably were determined by extent of appropriate habitat in the diverse and ever-changing landscape.

Other species.—In the old-growth forests, game species associated with early successional stands, such as rabbits, mourning doves, and northern bobwhites were limited by the extent of appropriate habitat and probably were not very abundant. Early records of reptiles and amphibians were limited, although Bartram (Van Doren 1928) makes frequent reference to rattlesnakes and to numerous sightings of alligators.

SETTLEMENT AND EXPLOITATION

Colonization

The earliest European settlers had little effect on southern forests except where they settled along the Atlantic and Gulf Coasts (Burdette 1996a). However during the 1800s, America's population increased from about 5 to about 76 million people; and this growth was accompanied by greatly increased demands for natural resources. By 1819 all land east of the Mississippi River was claimed by the United States, and in the early 1800s pioneers were moving into the Southeast. There were conflicts with Native Americans from the initial colonial settlement of the eastern coast and as the colonists moved westward. Hostilities and wars resulted, and eventually most of the natives were evicted from the region by the U.S. Army along the "Trail of Tears" to Oklahoma.

White settlement increased greatly following the exodus of Native Americans from the region. New settlers were 95% rural (Burdette 1996a) and closely tied to the land. By 1860 New Orleans was the only city of over 150,000 people and by the turn of the century only about 20% of the southern populous lived in urban areas, compared to about half of the population nationwide (Cooper and Terrill 1990:332,505).

Early settlers regarded mature southern forests as wilderness to be conquered. Natural resources were considered inexhaustible and were exploited. The new settlers cleared openings in the forest to plant their crops and provide pasture for their livestock. Corn was an important staple of Native Americans which was passed on to early European settlers. Corn became an important food of the large families of early settlers throughout the region. Also, it was raised to feed their horses and mules used to plow the ground for crops and to feed their cows, pigs, and chickens.

In the 1800s before the Civil War, major commercial crops of tobacco, rice, sugar cane, and to a lesser degree wheat and hemp, were developed and exported from the region (Cooper and Terrill 1990). Tobacco was an important crop in colonial Virginia, and later in Kentucky and parts of North Carolina and Tennessee. Rice was the dominant crop of coastal South Carolina and Georgia. Sugar cane was the main commercial crop of the French settlers on the fertile alluvial soils of southern Louisiana. But cotton was king. By 1860 cotton dominated the southern coastal plains, blackland prairies, and alluvial river bottoms from North Carolina to Texas. It was not dominant only in Florida, or the mountainous areas of the northern part of the region.

Wood from the forests was used to supply settlers' needs for other purposes. Wood was used extensively as fuel for heating and cooking and by the mid 1800s wood supplied more than 90 percent of the nation's heat energy, most of it for home use. Wood also was used for building houses and barns in the growing settlements. Southern timber was used for building ships before iron replaced wood as the main material. Another main product of the southern coastal plain forest in about a 125-mile longleaf-slash pine swath along the coast was turpentine and naval stores used early for waterproofing wooden ships and for various other products (Walker 1991).

Harvesting of forests during early white settlement was piecemeal and patchy, usually around settlements and along streams and rivers. By the mid 1800s, however, demand for wood from settlers was having a substantial effect on southern forests. Railroads were built throughout the region to carry passengers, and farm and forest products (Burdette 1996b). Wood was used in railroad construction; mainly crossties for which some 2,500 were required for each mile of track and replacement needed every few years (Burdette 1996b). And by the late 1850s a timber trade had developed in the region.

By the mid 1800s there developed real differences in philosophy between the southern states and the federal government over issues such as states' rights and slavery, and in 1860 the Confederate States of the South seceded from the Union. The ravages of the Civil War from 1861 to 1865 placed heavy demands on the South's people and forest resources for fuel, equipment, supplies, and fortifications (Burdette 1996b). And after the war southern forests were tapped for products for post-war reconstruction.

During the 1800s a substantial lumber industry was developing in the nation. In this era vast landscapes were logged with no thought of reforestation before logging crews simply moved on to new areas of mature timber. Pines were an early commercial species due to their strength and light weight. The nation's early lumber industry was centered in Maine for about 200 years, but in the mid 1800s logging crews moved southerly and westerly as entire forests were eliminated (Brown and Bethel 1958:2). In the latter part of the 1800s the lumber industry moved from Maine, to New York, to Pennsylvania, then westward to the Lake States. And then, with the exhaustion of the mature forests to the north, wholesale logging moved to the flourishing forests of the South. The nation's total lumber production and that of southern pines peaked in 1909. Previously, the forests had been cut mainly to make way for the planting of crops, but then they were logged extensively for commercial products. For example, before settlement vast stately stands of longleaf pine covered some 74 million acres of the southern coastal plain (Frost 1993). But with extensive commercial logging advanced by new steam technology in logging and sawmilling virtually all of the mature longleaf forests were felled from about 1870 to 1920. After most of the mature forests in the South fell to the saw in the early 1900s, the logging crews headed west for the vast forests of large western conifers.

Also, hardwoods were in demand for a variety of products such as railroad ties and barn boards, and specialty products, such as hickory and ash for tool handles and hickory for vehicle wheels before they were made of metal. Cypress throughout the vast southern swamps was cut for shingles, boats, houses, water tanks, and other products in which the decay-resistant heartwood was needed. The commercial harvesting of hardwoods accompanied the industrial development of the nation during the nineteenth century (Brown and Bethel 1958:3). The center of hardwood logging moved from New England southerly and westerly, and then southerly down the Mississippi Valley and Appalachian Mountains.

And further losses befell the second-growth bottomland forests that regenerated. A particularly drastic loss has been the conversion to other uses of the bottomland hardwoods of the Mississippi River Delta. The first land use data analyzed in the early 1930s showed there were approximately 11.8 million acres in bottomland hardwoods in the primary delta states of Louisiana, Arkansas, and Mississippi (Sternitzke 1976). But by the early 1970s Forest Service survey results showed only a little over half (7.2 million acres) of the original forested wetland remained in the Delta in the 3 states. The cleared bottomland forest was converted mainly to soybeans, and also improved pasture and cotton. Bottoms in the western gulf coastal plain have diminished also. According to the last Forest Service survey for East Texas (USDA Forest Service 1986) bottomland hardwood types occupy 14 percent of the timberland base, a decrease of 12 percent during the last 10 year period, continuing a long-term downward trend. The main causes for the decline were the development of man-made lakes, logging of mature stands, and shifts to cropland. Apparently, bottomland hardwood forests in the southeastern portion of the region have not suffered such extensive losses as elsewhere; wetland forest area has remained relatively consistent from the 1940s through the 1970s. Recently, some bottomland in the South has been planted to hardwoods under the Conservation Reserve Program.

In summary, southern forests supplied wood for houses and other products in the South, to the north which had been cut-over earlier, and in the developing midwestern plains where there were few forest resources. In the late 1800s and early 1900s southern forests were devastated by unrestricted logging. The forests were cut with little thought for forest regeneration, often soils were seriously depleted, and wildlife communities were threatened by the wholesale logging of the forests as well as unrestricted harvest of game animals.

Wildlife Demise

Early white settlers in the South were occupied with the basics of survival and had little regard or long-term perspective for husbanding natural resources. Generally, southern pre-colonial forests were regarded as wilderness to be conquered. Plants and animals were used for food and in other ways to support the colonists. Large carnivores were regarded as threats to livestock and personal safety, and as competitors to the early settlers for game animals. Wild animals were harvested the easiest way possible for food and also sold commercially. Also inherent in the settlers attitude toward the forest and its resources was the concept of free and open access and use. The growing population of settlers and their demands on southern forest resources would take its toll on wildlife of the region. The story of a few high-profile species illustrate.

White-tailed deer were in high demand for their hides and for food, and Native Americans and later white settlers would take their toll. According to McCabe and McCabe (1984), historic deer populations nationwide went through 3 different stages and their history in the South probably was similar. From about 1500 to about 1800 as deer became the main item of sustenance and trade for Native Americans and European settlers, total estimated deer numbers were reduced by about 50%. With the expulsion of most of the natives from the area in the mid 1800s, deer populations recovered somewhat, but only temporarily. The period of greatest exploitation was the latter 1800s. Aggressive, prolific, white settlers invaded the region, and there was intense demand for deer for sustenance and for market. The repeating rifle facilitated the widespread harvest of deer and development of the railroad improved access through the region and transportation of deer for market. Although estimates are variable, by most accounts deer populations nationwide plummeted to less than a million animals by 1900 (McCabe and McCabe 1984).

A similar scenario was unfolding for the wild turkey. With expansive settlement, unrestricted harvest and market hunting, coupled with the widespread habitat degradation from wholesale logging in the 1800s and early 1900s, came the demise of the once-plentiful wild turkey. By 1920 the wild turkey had disappeared completely from 18 of the original 38 states it occupied nationwide and by the early 1940s it was reduced to about 28% of its original range, mostly in the South (Mosby and Handley 1943). In 1948, populations southwide were estimated at about 100,000 (Mosby 1949). Remnant populations were relegated to remote tracts of mostly mature timber with limited human access and impact, such as the mountains of Appalachia; the Mississippi River bottoms of Louisiana, Mississippi, and Arkansas; and large land ownerships of southwestern Alabama, Georgia, and South Carolina.

The wood duck, a characteristic waterfowl species of southern bottoms, also experienced drastic reductions. By the beginning of this century they had been reduced to precariously low populations. They are vulnerable to the gun at roost sites at dusk and probably were decimated by overharvest.

Black bears, once numerous throughout the South, also were decimated. The new settlers' crops and free-ranging livestock were easy prey for bears during lean times, and bears were regarded as predators to be eliminated. Also they were used for food and lard for cooking, and in places bear hunting was a major activity of the men. Bear and humans and their activities often were in conflict, and bear population declines continued into the twentieth century. Distribution of bears in the region was reduced to only about 5 to 10% of their former range in the South (Maehr 1984). Viable populations were mostly relegated to relatively remote areas, such as the large tracts of federal land in the Appalachian Mountains and some southern bottomlands.

The passenger pigeon once nested throughout the forested United States and into Canada. Over a billion of these birds wintered in the southern bottoms where a main food item was the abundant oak mast (Truett and Lay 1984). The clearing of southern hardwood bottoms and the ease with which the communal birds were killed for market undoubtedly led to their demise. But the decline continued after market hunting ceased, perhaps due to their social reproductive behavior. The last passenger pigeon, named Martha, died at the Cincinnati Zoo in 1914 (Ehrlich et al 1992). The Carolina parakeet was another species that did not coexist well with the new colonial settlers in the south. In natural habitat they fed on fruits of native trees, such as cypress, and other plants. But with the opening of the forest they were attracted to the settlers' crops and gardens. Their crop depredations and unwary nature rendered them vulnerable to the settlers' gun (Truett and Lay 1984).

The ivory-billed woodpecker foraged in dead trees in mature bottomland hardwoods but also in upland mature forests. The last specimen was taken in a large mature bottomland forest near Tallula, Louisiana and a small population existed there until 1943 when the last of that mature forest was cleared to make way for soybeans (Lowery 1974). Since then there have been some unverified sightings in the United States, which were probably pileated woodpeckers. But a small remnant population has been reported in the mountains of Cuba.

The Bachman's warbler, a species associated with shrub-level vegetation, especially cane thickets in the bottoms, is extinct or nearly so, probably as a result of extensive clearing of the Mississippi River and West Gulf Coastal Plains bottoms. Although there have been occasional reports, the last confirmed sighting was in 1962 (Ehrlich et al. 1992).

Although documentation is minimal, other species probably experienced serious declines during this period of exploitation. Many shore birds as well as some of the large forest birds were harvested for food and sold at market. Clearing of the bottoms likely eliminated substantial nesting areas of several colonial nesters. Also, many large colorful birds were harvested extensively for plumes for ladies' hats.

In this era the new settlers, mostly originally from Europe, expanded rapidly throughout the region. The forests and their associated wildlife were used by the rapidly-growing population of settlers to meet their needs as they moved westerly, settled new areas, cleared new ground, and planted their crops throughout the South. They used whatever the land produced to survive and be productive. There was little provision for natural resources for the long term and those resources were substantially impacted.

CHAPTER 3

Natural Resources—Into the 20th Century

James G. Dickson[1]
US Forest Service
Southern Research Station, Nacogdoches, TX

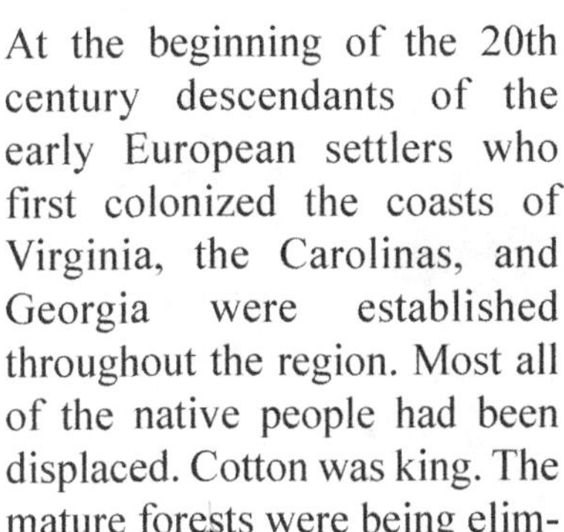

At the beginning of the 20th century descendants of the early European settlers who first colonized the coasts of Virginia, the Carolinas, and Georgia were established throughout the region. Most all of the native people had been displaced. Cotton was king. The mature forests were being eliminated. And wildlife populations had been seriously depleted by the burgeoning human population.

A few species, such as the ivory-billed woodpecker and the passenger pigeon, never recovered from exploitation and have become extinct. Game animals, such as wild turkey and white-tailed deer, had been seriously reduced and eliminated from most of their former range. Generally, because of interactions with man, the large carnivores, such as black bears and cougars, remained as viable populations only in a few places. With most other species, such as the myriad of birds, reptiles, and amphibians, there has been too little information to assess their status accurately.

In this era, land uses and the people and their distribution would affect forests and wildlife of the region. After World War I, the status of cotton, which had ruled the southern world, wavered and then toppled. Demand for the South's cotton declined due to new competition in production from parts of the western United States and foreign countries, and the development of synthetic fibers (Cooper and Terrill 1990). Also, there were problems with agricultural depressions and depaupered soil as a result of years of cultivation. Land use for crops and pasture peaked in the early 1920s and declined afterwards as farm land was abandoned (USDA Forest Service 1988). From 1929 to 1939 the main land use, cotton, decreased by about half (Cooper and Terrill 1990:671).

EARLY CONSERVATION

At the turn of the last century about 100 years ago things were bleak for southern forests and their wildlife. But the stage was being set for conservation activities which would help restore much of the southern forests in some form and some wildlife species.

Federal initiatives.—Early efforts were made to establish National Forests and manage them for multi-

[1]Current Address: School of Forestry, Louisiana Tech University, Ruston, LA

At the beginning of the 20th century most of the natives had been displaced and mature forests were being eliminated *(A. M Staten, B. Texas Parks and Wildlife)*.

Cotton was king *(J. Dickson)*.

In this era of natural resources exploitation a few species, such as the passenger pigeon, became extinct *(A. Brooks, Cornell Lab of Ornithology)*.

Wildlife populations such as the wild turkey had been seriously depleted by a burgeoning human population.

Remnant populations of exploited species, such as turkey, deer, and bear, were relegated to remote areas such as mountains and swamps.

ple resources (Dickson 1985). The forestry reserves were established in 1897 to protect timber and water, and this was interpreted quite broadly to include multiple resources. Cooperative forestry was established to assist in the forest management of private land and a research arm of the Division of Forestry was established early in this century.

The role of federal forestry expanded early in the 20th century. In 1905 the forest reserves were transferred from the Department of Interior to the Department of Agriculture, and the Bureau of Forestry became the U.S. Forest Service. Later, managing federal land for multiple products and providing multiple services was confirmed and expanded; and the guiding tenet of managing National Forests for the greatest good of the greatest number in the long run was developed (Steen 1976).

The Weeks Law of 1911 authorized the purchase of forests in watersheds of navigable streams, which was the justification for acquisition for the National Forests in the South. This legislation and the Clark-McNary Act of 1924 strengthened cooperative forestry. Protection of remnant populations of game animals was an early consideration. Between 1916 and 1948, 17 National Game Refuges totalling 514,556 acres were established on southern National Forests (B. Sanders, pers. commun.). The Pisgah Game Refuge in North Carolina became a deer research center and provided deer for stocking other areas throughout the South.

In the 1930s most land in the South had supported crops of cotton for years, and erosion and topsoil loss was a major problem throughout. To address this problem in 1935 the Soil Conservation Service was established to promote soil protection and reforestation (Cooper and Terrill 1990).

Wildlife management.—After World War I states begin taking stock of the dire status of their game populations and limited efforts were initiated to address the problems. The first significant wildlife publications were produced. In 1933, Aldo Leopold's *Game Management* established wildlife management principles and in 1932 Herbert Stoddard published a complete treatise on Bobwhite Quail from his research which still stands as the authoritative text today. A major boost to these efforts was the passage of the Federal Aid in Wildlife Restoration (or Pittman-Robertson Act) of 1937. This legislation imposed a tax on firearms and ammunition that was matched (3:1) with individual state money, and used as the main funding vehicle for state wildlife restoration programs. Wildlife management as a profession was developing at about the same time. The Wildlife Society was formed, state governments were forming agencies responsible for wildlife, universities were initiating wildlife education programs, and wildlife research was underway. Many of the first research efforts were surveys of the status of game populations. But the demands of World War II on the people of the region essentially put wildlife restoration and other natural resource programs on hold until after the major conflicts in Europe and the Pacific had been settled.

MIDCENTURY

After the War the troops returned home, interest in wildlife problems was rekindled, and management efforts were instilled with new vigor. The story of a few key species illustrates some wildlife management successes.

Wild turkey.—The first comprehensive survey of the 13 southeastern states in 1949 revealed an estimated regional population of slightly over 100,000 wild turkeys (Mosby 1949). The first efforts at restoring wild turkeys to the South, and what seemed to be the logical approach, was the raising of game farm turkeys for release in the wild. But mother nature was too harsh for the pen-raised turkeys. Predation in the wild was high and survival of adult turkeys was low. Also, the pen-raised hens were not able to pass on critical survival skills to their poults and reproductive success was minimal. What initially seemed like a good idea was a failure throughout the region. But what did work was the capture of wild turkeys from the wild and immediate transfer to the wild. Beginning about 1950 the cannon net, which had been developed for capturing waterfowl,

Adaptation of the cannon-propelled net to capture wild turkeys proved useful in restoring this species *(D. Dyke)*.

was adapted for and used to capture and release wild turkeys (Hurst and Dickson 1992). Through intensive trapping effort, better protection, and improved habitat the wild turkey has been restored throughout the South and number now some 1.5 million wild turkeys. The annual harvest now region wide is approximately 200,000, which is more than the total population several years ago (Kennamer and Kennamer 1996).

White-tailed deer.—The white-tailed deer story is similar to that of the wild turkey; restoration has been successful throughout the region. White-tailed deer populations remained at low levels until after World War II, when restoration efforts were initiated (Newsom 1984). Dramatic results were realized through trapping and transplanting deer, enhanced habitat conditions, and improved protection. By 1969, the estimated population of deer in the coastal plain states was 1.7 million, with an annual harvest of 266,000, and by 1975 the estimated population (4.3 million) and harvest (557,000) had doubled (Newsom 1984).

Environmental legislation.—Multiple use of National Forests, environmental awareness, and maintaining wildlife populations at viable levels on federal land were confirmed by legislation in the 1960s and 1970s (for example, the Multiple Use-Sustained Yield Act of 1960). The Wilderness Act of 1964 officially sanctioned the incorporation of land into the wilderness system. The National Environmental Policy Act (1969) required federal agencies to consider effects of their actions on the environment. The Endangered Species Act of 1973 mandated protection for threatened or endangered species. The National Forest Management Act (1976) provided for a coordinated land management planning process with public participation. It required that wildlife be considered in each forest plan for each administrative unit, that habitat for animals be maintained, and that management indicator species be monitored. The net result of this collective legislation on wildlife management on National Forests was that, in general, the Forest Service was charged with maintaining viable populations of plant and animal species, promoting recovery for threatened and endangered species, and providing habitat for species of high demand, such as game animals (Nelson et al. 1983).

Federal land management.—On federal land, even-aged management became practice in the 1960s and the featured species concept of wildlife management was incorporated in the 1970s (B. Sanders, pers. commun.) As a result of the National Forest Management Act of 1976 the Forest Service was required to develop Land Management Plans for each National Forest and in the 1980s integrated the use of management indicator species as indices of wildlife communities. Later in the 1990s, enhanced environmental and landscape scale concern fostered Ecosystem Management.

People and the forests.—After World War II there were significant changes in the people and their use of the land. Southerners left the farm, and what had been a

After World War II what had been a rural South became mostly an urban South. By 1980 only about 3% of southerners lived on farms. By 1952, area in timberland had increased to about 60% and has remained relatively constant since then *(C. Taylor)*.

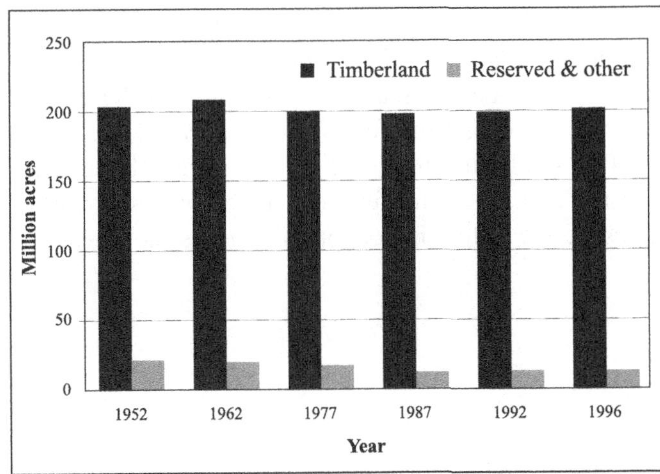

Fig. 1. Area of forestland in the South, 1952-1996.

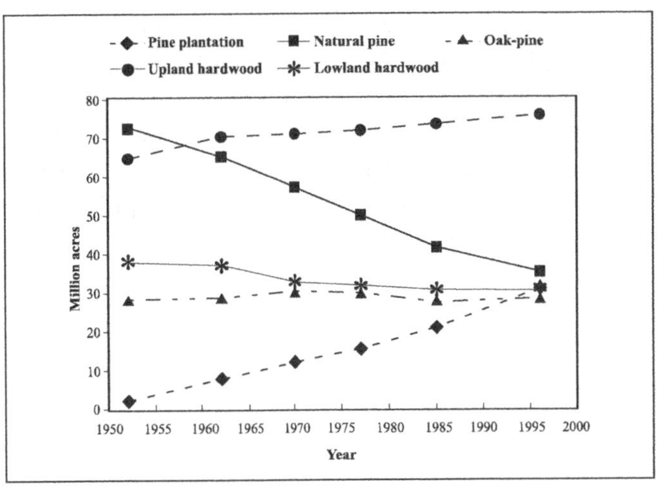

Fig. 2. Changes in extent of general forest types in the South, 1952-1996.

rural South became a mostly urban South. In 1940 40% of southerners (15.6 million) farmed, compared to only 15% for the rest of the U.S. Forty years later only 3-4% of southerners (1.6 million) farmed. From the beginning to the end of this period 14 million fewer people lived on farms and the number of farms declined from 2.9 million to 949,000 (Cooper and Terrill 1990:763). And more diverse products were being produced from the land that remained in agriculture. Beef cattle, poultry, soybeans, tobacco, and dairy products became the leading farm products (Cooper and Terrill 1990:763). The land of cotton had become the land of pines, grass, cattle, and soybeans.

After World War II as cropland in the South was abandoned, the area in timberland (forests not withdrawn from commercial timber production and capable of producing traditional wood products) increased (USDA Forest Service 1988). By 1952 about 3/5 of the land area (about 200 million acres) was classified as timberland; and the proportion of forested land has changed little since then (Fig. 1). Southern deforested land was converted mainly to crops, pasture, and urban associated uses, but at the same time other land reverted or was planted to forest. Forestland losses were the most severe in Florida where large human population increases have usurped forest land, and in Arkansas and Louisiana where large areas of bottomland hardwoods have been converted to cropland.

During the period 1952 to 1996, distribution and area occupied by forest types in the South changed also (Sheffield and Dickson 1998). The loss of bottomland hardwoods was substantial, particularly from about 1950 to 1970 in the Mississippi Delta. By 1996 area in this alluvial type had declined to 30.2 million acres. Much of this land went into soybean production.

Upland stands were undergoing changes also. Pioneering pines had invaded much of the previously abandoned cropland. Natural plant succession progresses from early successional pines to more shade-tolerant hardwoods that develop in understories of pine stands. With natural succession and harvesting, many stands of naturally-occurring pines reverted to mixed pine-hardwood or upland hardwood stands. Forest surveys from 1952 to 1996 (Sheffield and Dickson 1998) showed that area in natural pines decreased by about one half, from about 72 million acres to about 36 million acres. During this period, the total area in mixed hardwood-pine remained about the same (28-30 million acres). There was some gain in this type from natural stand development after harvesting of natural pine stands. Losses in this type were experienced from harvesting and natural hardwood succession or conversion to pine plantations. Related to this was the increase of upland hardwoods by about 15%. From 1952 to 1996 upland hardwoods increased from about 65 million acres to about 75 million acres. But the biggest proportional change in southern forestland during this period was the increase in pine plantations. Area in pine plantations increased from less than 2 million acres in 1952 to over 30 million acres in 1996 (Fig. 2).

There were changes in tree harvesting also. Between 1952 and 1962 total annual softwood harvests declined slightly. During this period annual production of softwood pulpwood increased 35%. But softwood sawlog production decreased by 30% as hundreds of large and portable small sawmills shut down as the region experienced a major shift from lumber to pulp and paper production (USDA Forest Service 1988). But during the next 2 decades (1962 to 1985) softwood harvests increased by 5.0 billion cubic feet (77%) as the pulp and paper industry expanded, the lumber industry was revitalized, and a pine plywood industry developed.

There have been changes in hardwood roundwood harvest also (USDA Forest Service 1988). Between 1952 and 1976 annual harvests varied little (1.7 -1.8 billion cubic feet). But by 1984 harvests had jumped to 2.5 million cubic feet. Hardwood pulpwood, insignificant in 1952, had become the leading hardwood product, accounting for 40% of the annual harvest. Fuelwood consumption also increased dramatically at the end of this period, accounting for 27% of hardwood use.

The southern landscape, its human inhabitants, its forests, and its wildlife, had undergone substantial changes. The following chapter describes the forests.

CHAPTER 4

Defining the Forests

James G. Dickson[1]
US Forest Service
Southern Research Station, Nacogdoches, TX

Raymond M. Sheffield
US Forest Service
Southern Research Station, Ashville, NC

Forests of the South are very diverse and productive. Included among southern forests are the boreal spruce-fir forests of the highest mountain peaks of the Blue Ridge Mountains to the lowest bottomland hardwoods on flood-deposited soil with elevations near sea level. In between are the diverse upland hardwood stands in northerly mountainous areas of the South and southern pines and hardwoods along the Coastal Plain.

Climate of the south is predominantly continental, except for the cooler Appalachian Mountains, grading to maritime along the coast (Schoeneberger 1995). Temperatures are generally mild in winter and hot in summer (USDA Forest Service 1969). Mean maximum temperatures for January vary from the 40s (degrees F) in the mountains to the 70s in Florida. Mean minimum temperatures for January range from the 20s in the mountains to the 60s in Florida. July mean minimum temperatures vary from the mid 50s in the mountains to the 70s along the Gulf Coast and Florida. Mean maximum temperatures are about 90 for most of the region and slightly lower in the mountains. Mean length of the freeze-free period varies from as few as 150 days in the

[1]Current Address: School of Forestry, Louisiana Tech University, Ruston, LA

higher eastern mountains to 300 days along the Gulf and lower Atlantic coasts, and even longer in peninsular Florida (USDA Forest Service 1969).

The region is well watered; most of the area receives upwards of 48 inches of precipitation and all of the area receives more than 40 inches of precipitation annually (USDA Forest Service 1969). An occasional mountain peak and the coastal area near the mouth of the Mississippi River both receive more than 60 inches of rainfall annually. The driest portions of the region, receiving 40 to 45 inches of annual precipitation, is an area east of the Appalachian mountains, including part of Virginia, and a portion of central South Carolina and Georgia; and the western portion of the region in eastern Oklahoma and Texas.

Soils of the region are formed primarily by climate, parent material, inhabiting organisms, topography, and time. Southern forest soils are shaped by a warm, moist environment with the exception of the cooler high mountains and the drier western edge of the region (Schoeneberger 1995). Generally, the warm, moist climate interacting with the geologic stability and moderate geologic age produced soils with considerable pedogenic alteration.

Forests of the South are diverse and productive. Included among southern forests are the boreal spruce-fir forests of the highest peaks of the Blue Ridge Mountains to the lowest bottomland hardwoods on flood-deposited soil near sea level *(Top: Upland oak-hickory, G. Smith; Above: Bottomland hardwoods, J. Dickson).*

PHYSIOGRAPHIC REGIONS

The Coastal Plain is the largest province of the physiographic diverse region, stretching along the Atlantic and Gulf coasts from Virginia to Texas (see color section). It is characterized by broad flats and nearly level uplands, and is about 54% forested.

The Lower Coastal Plain is almost level flatwoods dissected by rivers and swamps (Schoeneberger 1995). Elevations are less than 90 ft. above mean sea level and soil drainage usually is poor. Soil materials are mostly sand, silt, and clay derived from river and marine sediments. Dominant soils are Ultisols, except beach sediments which are Entisols. Forests cover about 90% of the area. Historically, the area was covered with mature longleaf pine forests. But as the valuable stands were cut, harvested areas usually were regenerated with faster-growing loblolly and slash pine plantations. Also, diminished fire favored hardwoods and pines other than longleaf.

The Upper Coastal Plain is characterized by broad uplands and low plateaus (Schoeneberger 1995). It is geologically older than the Lower Coastal Plain and has greater dissection, topographical relief, and soil development. Elevations range from about 90 to 600 ft. and dominant soils are Ultisols. Within the Upper Coastal Plain various subregions vary in forest cover from a low of about 25% in peninsular Florida to about 70% west of the Mississippi River, in Louisiana and Texas.

The Piedmont is the second largest physiographic area of the region. It stretches from Georgia to Virginia, and is bounded on the west by the Appalachian Highlands and sloping down to the east and south to the Coastal Plain. The Piedmont is characterized as a rolling upland plain, derived from diverse metamorphic and igneous rock, with minor relief and moderate elevation (300-700 ft) (Schoeneberger 1995). The stable, erosional nature of this area has produced soils dominated by Ultisols from acidic rocks, Alfisols from basic igneous rocks, and Inceptisols on steep slopes. About half of the area is forested. On both the Upper Coastal Plain and Piedmont, pine and pine-hardwood forests dominate. Loblolly pine is very common. It has been planted extensively and pioneers open land where it is found in association with shortleaf pine and hardwoods, such as white oaks, red oaks, sweetgum, and yellow poplar.

The Mississippi River Valley splits the South. Most of it is a nearly level river valley with low elevations, from sea level to 520 ft. It is composed of a complex of river terraces, meanders, and backwater swamps. Soils are a variable mixture of alluvial deposits from the Mississippi River and its tributaries overlying marine sediments (Schoeneberger 1995). Dominant soil orders include: Entisols in the active floodplain, Inceptisols on low alluvial terraces, Alfisols and Mollisols on mid-elevation terraces, and Alfisols on the older, higher terraces of northeastern Louisiana and eastern Arkansas. Only 27% of this productive alluvial area is forested. Historically, oak-gum-cypress forests predominated, and remain in portions of the area. Within this forest complex individual tree species and forest types often occur only on specific bottomland sites which were formed by flooding and siltation, and natural plant succession.

Within this general physiographic area is the loess-covered uplands east of the Mississippi River, covered by thick wind-blown silt up to 60 ft. deep. Dominant soils are Alfisols interspersed with Ultisols (Schoeneberger 1995). About half of this steep terrain is forested. Red oaks, such as Shumard, white oak, and yellow poplar are characteristic species of this productive hardwood forest.

The Blue Ridge Mountains are the highest mountains in the South, extending from the northern extremity of Virginia running southwesterly into Georgia. Elevations range from about 1,000 to 4,000 ft. with peaks almost 7,000 ft. The slopes are steep. The subsurface is predominantly igneous and metamorphic rocks. Steep slopes are dominated by Inceptisols and lesser slopes by Inceptisols and Ultisols (Schoeneberger 1995). The high mountainous region is dominated by forest (94%).

The Ridge and Valley province is a narrow belt west of and parallel to the Blue Ridge Mountains extending from Virginia into northern Alabama. The limestone and shale valleys of around 600 ft. elevation are bounded by steep-sided ridges of sedimentary rock (Schoeneberger 1995). Limestone-underlain soils are primarily Ultisols with some Alfisols. Sideslopes and steep ridges are dominated by Inceptisols. Forests cover about 3/4 of this area.

The Appalachian Plateaus west of the Ridge and Valley and occupying much of eastern Kentucky and a substantial part of Tennessee, are a series of deeply dissected plateaus with rolling topography. Most of the plateaus are from 1,000 to 2,000 ft. elevation with some areas exceeding that. Typically, plateau substrate is sandstone, with eroded shale underlying the sideslopes. Relatively flat uplands and valley floors are dominated by Ultisols; escarpments and valley slopes are also dominated by Ultisols (Schoeneberger 1995). Forests are the primary land use (72%). All 3 of these mountainous physiographic areas are dominated by various species of white and red oaks with other hardwood associates, such as hickories and yellow poplar.

The Interior Low Plateau lies west of the

Southern forests have never been static. They are dynamic as well as diverse, continually influenced by ever-changing forces. For example, Hurricane Hugo struck coastal South Carolina in 1989, with drastic impact on the people and forest ecosystems of the area *(D. Baumann)*.

Appalachian Plateaus through middle Kentucky and Tennessee, and into Alabama. It is an extensively dissected rim with moderate elevations (300-900 ft.) underlain by limestone (Schoeneberger 1995). Alfisols dominate in the plateau interior, with Ultisols and Alfisols associated with the dissected rim. Two thirds of the area is comprised of upland oak-hickory forests.

The Ouachita Uplands lies west of the Mississippi River Valley in Arkansas and eastern Oklahoma, and is composed of 2 different formations (Schoeneberger 1995). The Ouachita Mountains is similar in form to the Appalachian Plateaus. Elevations range from about 300 to 1800 ft. and topography is steep. On steep sandstone or southerly facing cherty-limestone hills or ridges the dominant soils are Ultisols. On steeper, north-facing slopes Inceptisols predominate, and valleys composed of eroded slate, shales, and sandstones are dominated by Ultisols. Oaks, such as northern red and white, are characteristic species, often found with shortleaf pine on drier sites.

North of the Ouachita Mountains is the Arkansas Valley and Ridges, composed of broad river valleys and associated ridges. Elevations and soils are similar to that of the Ouachita Mountains, except that Alfisols overly shallow limestone. Slightly over half (52%) of the area is forested.

The Ozark Plateau to the north is a deeply dissected plateau of narrow ridgetops with steep sideslopes with considerable relief and moderate elevations (500-2,500 ft.). Ridges and uplands are dominated by Ultisols. Sideslopes are dominated by Inceptisols, and valley floors overlying limestone, dolomite, and shales are dominated by Alfisols (Schoeneberger 1995). Upland forests dominate the landscape (80%). The Ozark forests are similar to those of the Ouachitas except pines are scarcer and hardwoods more dominant.

The Central Lowlands to the west of the Ouachita Uplands is a geomorphic area of broad flats and rolling hills with low elevations (400-1,200 ft.). The sandstones, shales, and clays are dominated by Mollisols and interspersed with Alfisols in alluvial areas (Schoeneberger 1995). Only 8% of the area is wooded. Characteristic species of the oak-hickory forests include post and blackjack oaks.

FOREST INFLUENCES

Southern forests have never been static. They are dynamic as well as diverse; continually changing in response to ever-changing forces. The forests have been molded and influenced by a number of natural factors as well as the different populations of people who have used the forests of the South. Some factors influencing southern forests have worked slowly and have not been apparent in the short term. Other factors shaping southern forests have been obvious and dramatic. Wind storms have played a major role in shaping southern forests. The coastal areas of the South have been subjected to severe tropical storms. For example, in September 1989 Hurricane Hugo struck coastal South Carolina near Charleston with winds over 150 mi/h, with drastic impact on the people and the forest ecosystem of the area (Baumann et al. 1996). The storm killed 35 people and caused more than $6 billion in property damage. Over 4 million acres of timberland and nearly 11 billion board feet of sawtimber were damaged or destroyed. The pine overstory of the coastal forest was virtually eliminated throughout many areas, and soon replaced by a brushy hardwood understory.

Ice storms also affect southern forests. Conifers with long persistent needles are particularly vulnerable to ice damage because precipitation accumulates and freezes. Because of its fast early growth, slash pine was planted extensively in the deep South. But it is vulnerable to breakage from ice and many plantations never reach rotation age without sustaining ice damage.

A number of diseases and insects have been a part of and helped shape southern forests. The American Chestnut was a dominant tree of the eastern mountains. The Chestnut blight was introduced, spread rapidly, and in the early 1900s the American Chestnut was eliminated from eastern forests. Roots remaining from a few trees live and resprout periodically, but the sprouts succumb to the blight as they develop. Dogwood anthracnose is a fungus that infects and can kill dogwoods. It was introduced with an Asiatic dogwood into the northeastern U. S. and has moved southerly into the southern Appalachians. The disease particularly affects plants above 3,000 ft. elevation and the full impact of the disease is yet to be determined. A large number of other fungi infect southern hardwoods.

The main widespread diseases affecting southern pines are fusiform rust, littleleaf syndrome, and annosus root rot (Meadows and Hodges 1995). Loblolly and slash pine seedlings and saplings are particularly vulnerable to fusiform rust, and annual economic losses probably exceed $100 million. Oaks are alternate hosts for the fungus. Littleleaf syndrome is the most serious disease affecting shortleaf pine in the South. Incidence usually is higher in trees growing on poorer sites. Annosus root rot is a major disease of southern pines, causing reduction in tree growth and direct mortality. Stumps and roots exposed by harvest operations provide avenue for invasion into the root systems.

Insects have evolved with southern forests and play a major role in these forested systems. A few examples illustrate their importance. The southern pine beetle is an important economic pest of southern pines (Meadows and Hodges 1995), affecting millions of acres during periodic outbreaks. Usually pines under stress and of low vigor are more vulnerable to attack, but at epidemic beetle population levels a wide variety of pine trees can be infected and killed. In mixed pine-hardwood stands pines killed by diseases and insects usually are followed by shade-tolerant hardwoods.

In the South, Frasier fir occurs only at high elevations in the Blue Ridge Mountains. It is being threatened by the balsam wooly adelgid, which feeds on the main tree bole and kills trees. The tiny insect was introduced into New England in the early 1900s and has spread south.

Currently, an insect that is substantially affecting southern upland hardwood forests is the gypsy moth. In the eastern mountains, the gypsy moth defoliates mostly oaks and reduces their vigor. Repeated defoliations eventually can result in mortality.

Man's Direct Influences

Virtually all of the South's forests today have been molded by man directly as well as indirectly. Usually, harvesting has been selective for certain species or forms of trees. Often those that remained were of lesser value or poorer form, or defective for use as wood products. For example, bald cypress of the bottoms and longleaf pine of the lower Coastal Plain are forest types that have diminished the most. Cypress was in demand for the heartwood's decay resistance and easy working properties. In the humid southern climate decay-resistant cypress was used for boats, houses, water tanks, and numerous other products. The large trees in vast stands were girdled to dry, felled, floated to mills, and sawn into boards. Also, longleaf pine was in high demand due to the light weight, large size, cylindrical shape, and sparsity of lower limbs. Vast stands of these monarchs fell to the saw. Both cypress and longleaf stands hardly ever were regenerated back to these same species when the mature stands were cut because they are relatively slow growing. Acreage in longleaf pine illustrates; where once there were some 90 million acres of mature longleaf pine only less than 3 million remain today (Landers et al. 1995). Man also affects southern forests in other ways. Flooding and soil deposition determine bottomland site characteristics and suitability for specific tree species and timber types. Man's alteration of flooding by creation of reservoirs, channelization, and other land and water manipulations has affected site characteristics and tree composition of forest stands. For example, the Atchafalaya Basin of Louisiana, constructed to accommodate floodwaters from the Mississippi River, has become higher and drier from siltation. Swamp forests have been replaced by cottonwood and willow stands, and soybean fields.

Also, pollutants can affect forest vigor. Ozone can occur in sufficient concentrations to injure trees. Ozone is the main air pollutant of concern in the South, where there are numerous sunny days and high levels of automobile and industry emissions of hydrocarbons and nitrogen oxides, precursors of ozone (Fox and Mickler 1995:9).

STATUS OF THE FORESTS

Forests continue to dominate the southern landscape, covering some 214 million acres (or a little over half) of the landscape. Commercial timberland accounts for 94% of the total, with the remainder in reserved and

Over half of the South is forested; pines and pine-hardwoods dominate on upland sites in the lower South.

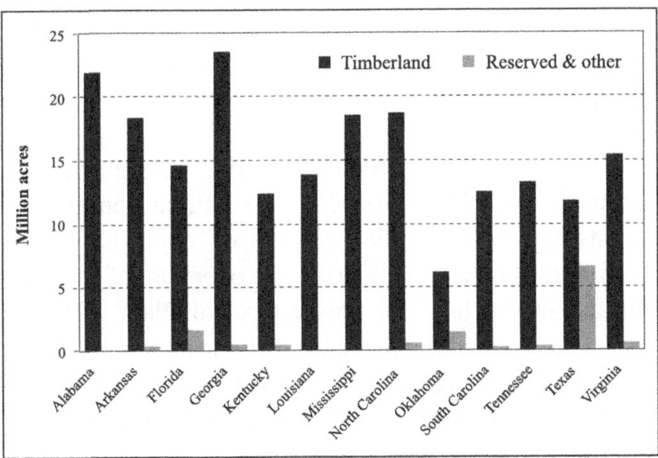

Fig 1. Area of forestland by state *(from Sheffield and Dickson 1998)*.

other forests. The most heavily forested states, each with over 15 million acres of forest and over 60% forested, include: Georgia, Alabama, Mississippi, North Carolina, and Virginia (Fig. 1). Proportion of forest land varies widely by county (Fig. 2). The least forested areas are southern Florida, the Mississippi River Delta, the western edge of the region, and local areas where urban or agriculture land dominate. Heavily forested areas are dispersed over much of the region.

Composition

Over half (52%) of the timberland of the South is classified as hardwoods (Sheffield and Dickson 1998) (see color section). Upland hardwood forests cover 75 million acres or some 37% of the timberland and has

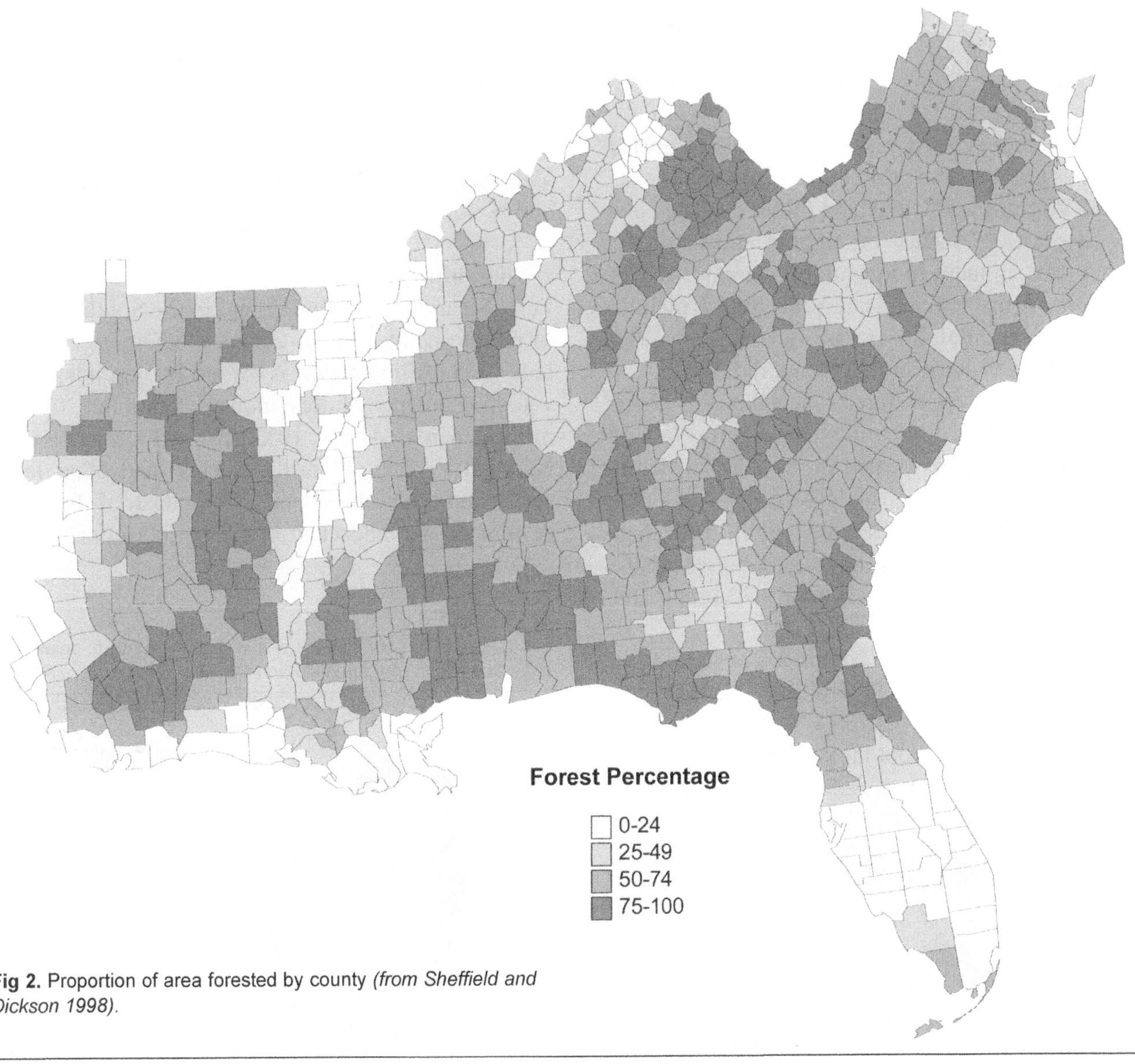

Fig 2. Proportion of area forested by county *(from Sheffield and Dickson 1998)*.

Table 1. Percentage of timberland in southern states by forest type.

State	Pine plantation	Natural pine	Oak-pine	Upland hardwood	Bottomland hardwood
Alabama	18	18	19	33	10
Arkansas	12	17	16	38	16
Florida	33	19	9	14	25
Georgia	23	26	12	25	15
Kentucky	1	5	7	82	5
Louisiana	18	21	12	15	34
Mississippi	16	15	17	32	20
North Carolina	11	22	14	38	14
Oklahoma	10	13	14	53	10
South Carolina	21	23	15	20	20
Tennessee	3	8	12	72	5
Texas	15	21	21	27	15
Virginia	10	12	13	62	4
South	15	18	14	37	15

[a]From Sheffield and Dickson (1998).

increased in recent years. Upland hardwoods comprise more than half of the timberland in Kentucky, Tennessee, Virginia, and Oklahoma (Table 1). The oak-hickory association occurs throughout most of the region, but predominates in mountainous areas, such as the southern Appalachians and Ouachita Uplands. Common species include oaks, hickories, yellow poplar, sweetgum, American beech, and red maple.

Bottomland hardwood forests account for about 15% of the timberland, or 30 million acres. Over half of these lowland forests are located in the alluvial floodplain of major rivers in Louisiana, Florida, Georgia, and Mississippi (USDA Forest Service 1988). Prevalent species include water, willow, laurel, swamp chestnut, and cherrybark oaks; tupelo, blackgum, sweetgum, and baldcypress.

Mixed oak-pine stands are comprised of more than half hardwoods and 25 to 50% pines. These stands occupy about 29 million acres, or 14% of southern timberland, and occur throughout the region.

Approximately a third of southern timberland is dominated by pine types; some 36 million acres (18%) in natural pines and 31 million acres (15%) in planted pines (Sheffield and Dickson 1998). Loblolly pine is the most common species in natural pine stands, which have declined in area significantly in recent decades. Natural stands of loblolly and associated hardwoods are especially prevalent in the Coastal Plain and Piedmont, where they have pioneered abandoned cropland and pasture. Shortleaf pine, a common associate of loblolly, is dominant at higher elevations, such as the southern Appalachian Plateau and Ridge and Valley, and the Ouachita Uplands.

Pine plantations, which have increased significantly recently, comprise some 15% of southern commercial forests region wide. Pine plantations comprise 1/3 of Florida timberland, and make up over 1/4 of the timberland in much of the lower Coastal Plain of South Carolina, Georgia, Alabama, Mississippi, Louisiana, and eastern Texas (Table 1). Loblolly pine is the species most widely planted, with slash pine planted in some southerly areas. Recently there is some effort to reestablish longleaf pine.

Age

In the last 2 decades, overall southern forests have aged. For both softwoods and hardwoods, sapling and pole-sized trees have become less abundant and conversely, sawtimber-sized trees have increased (Sheffield and Dickson 1998). The most recent data showed sawtimber-sized trees were more abundant than sapling or poletimber-sized trees in pine/pine-hardwood stands and dominant over smaller trees in upland hardwood and bottomland hardwood stands (Fig. 3).

Ownership

Forests classified as timberland in the South largely are in private hands. About 2/3 of southern forest timberland (138 million acres) is owned by nonindustrial private forest owners. Forest industry has about 20%, or 41 million acres. About 10% (21 million acres) is in National Forests (11 million acres) and other federal, state, and municipal land. Nonindustrial forest land dominates the landscape in the northern portion of the

Fig 3. Area of general forest types in seedling-sapling, poletimber, and sawtimber *(from Sheffield and Dickson 1998)*.

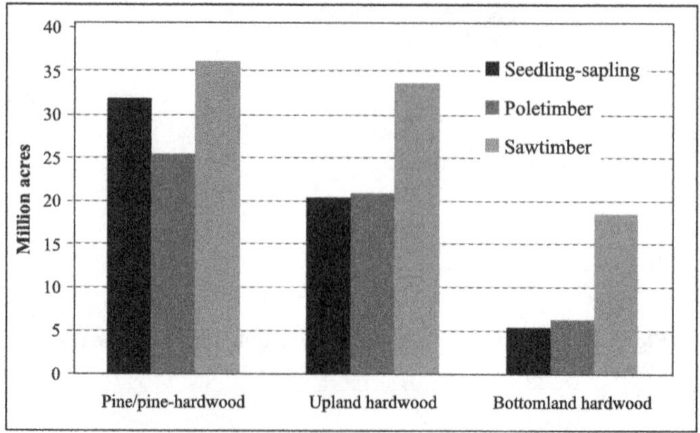

Of the 182 million acres of southern timberland, about 90% is privately owned, mostly nonindustrial owners *(J. Dickson)*.

region where upland hardwoods are most common. Over 3/4 of the timberland is in this classification in Kentucky, Tennessee, Virginia, and North Carolina. Conversely, in the deep South where the more valuable pines dominate, forest industry ownership is higher. In Louisiana, eastern Texas, Florida, Georgia, Alabama, and Arkansas, forest industry controls at least 25% of the timberland (Sheffield and Dickson 1998). Over half of the National Forest timberland is located in Arkansas, Virginia, Mississippi, and North Carolina. Upland hardwoods predominate on National Forests of the Appalachian Mountains; whereas natural pine, upland hardwoods, and mixed pine-hardwoods dominate National Forests elsewhere in the South.

Economic Value

Timber is a very important economic commodity in the South. An estimated 7.5 billion cubic feet of roundwood timber products (sawlogs,veneer logs, pulpwood, fuelwood, and other round products) were harvested from southern forests in 1984 (USDA Forest Service 1988). Of this volume, over 5 billion cubic feet came from softwood species, primarily southern pine; and almost 2.5 billion cubic feet from a variety of hardwood species. The stumpage value of the trees cut in 1984 was $2.7 billion for softwoods and $0.4 billion for hardwoods. The value added from harvesting and transportation totaled $6.1 billion in 1984; $4.5 billion for softwoods and $1.6 billion for hardwood products. The $6.1 billion product value was about twice the value of soybeans or cotton produced, and about three times the value of tobacco, wheat, or corn crops in the South.

Forest industries in the South produced about 10% of value added to the southern economy and employed about 10% of southern workers. Timber as a crop ranked among the top three agricultural crops in value in all southern states, and was first in value in 6 states: Virginia, S. Carolina, Georgia, Alabama, Mississippi, and Louisiana.

Harvesting and associated economic value has increased recently as a result of increased wood demand and harvest restrictions in the Northwest. In 1991 the South accounted for 55% of domestic growing stock removals, up from 45% in 1970 (Powell 1992).

Wood Products

Harvested trees from southern forests go into a variety of products. Most trees large enough to be cut into lumber are harvested and used mostly as sawlogs (USDA Forest Service 1988). Smaller trees and trees of lower grade are cut as pulpwood to be made into paper and reconstituted wood products. Pulpwood and sawlogs are the 2 main wood products of southern forests. Some 2.4 billion cubic feet of softwood pulpwood and 1.5 billion cubic feet of hardwood pulpwood was harvested in 1996; 41% of the total roundwood production (Fig. 4). Sawlogs comprised 38% of roundwood harvest; 2.7 billion cubic feet of softwoods and 959 million cubic feet of hardwoods (Johnson and Stratton 1998).

Relatively large, high quality logs and bolts are selected for veneer for use in furniture, cabinets, and plywood. Veneer logs comprised about 9% of the volume of roundwood products but represented a higher

Timber is a very important economic commodity in the South. Almost 10 billion cubic feet of roundwood timber products were harvested from southern forests in 1996. Timber as an agricultural crop was first in value in about half (6) of the southern states, and was among the top 3 in all states.

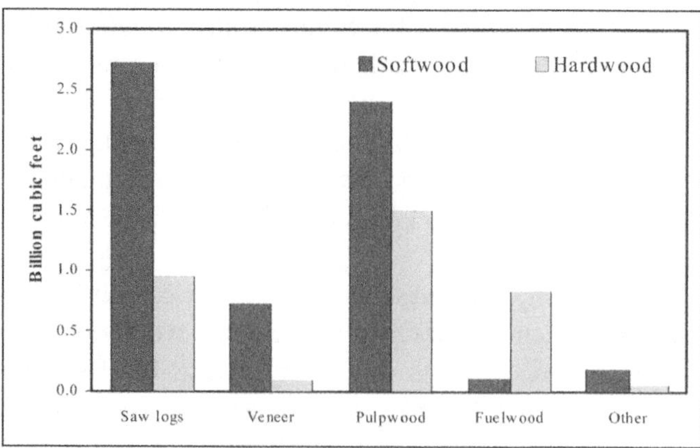

Fig 4. Volume of roundwood output in the South by product and species group, 1996 *(from Johnson and Stratton 1988).*

proportional stumpage value. There was about 8 times the volume of softwoods as hardwoods.

Southern forests also produce substantial fuelwood (Fig. 4); about 10% of the roundwood production went for fuelwood for industrial and residential use (Johnson and Stratton 1998). Hardwoods primarily were used; 24% of the hardwood harvest (839 million cubic feet) went for fuelwood, but only about 2% of the softwoods (109 million cubic feet).

A variety of other wood products produced from southern forests account collectively for about 2.5% of roundwood production and are not commercially important regionally, but individual products may be locally significant. These products include poles and pilings (softwood), fenceposts, cooperage logs and bolts, mine timbers, shingle bolts, handle bolts, wood turnings, panel products, other items, and chemical wood (USDA Forest Service 1988).

SILVICULTURE

Both even-aged and uneven-aged silvicultural systems are employed to harvest and regenerate southern forests. Even-aged stands are often maintained when intolerant to mid-tolerant species of trees are favored. Even-aged stands may be regenerated by clearcutting, in which all stems are removed; seed tree cut, in which

Both uneven-aged and even-aged silviculture systems, such as this shelterwood, are employed to regenerate southern forests (R. Mirarchi).

some mature trees (typically 8-12 per acre) are left during harvesting to seed and regenerate the stand; and shelterwood cut, in which the overstory trees are removed in a series (usually 2 or 3) of partial cuts with the harvesting effects on the residual stand moderated over time (Smith 1962). Seed tree and shelterwood systems use natural regeneration. Natural regeneration often is adequate in small clearcuts of several acres, but planting is necessary in larger clearcuts where advance regeneration of desired intolerant species is not present. Uneven-aged stands of at least 3 tree age classes can be maintained by single-tree and group selection harvesting. Intolerant southern pines are usually maintained in even-aged stands because without full light they normally are replaced by more tolerant hardwoods. Hardwoods can be maintained in even-aged or uneven-aged stands. Both upland hardwoods and bottomland hardwoods are regenerated satisfactorily with group selection or small clearcuts that are large enough (at least 2 or 3 acres) to allow full sunlight into the harvested area and where advance regeneration is present.

Site preparation is conducted in some situations to expose the seed bed, eliminate logging residue, or reduce competing vegetation. Site preparation usually is not necessary for hardwood stands with advance regeneration, but sometimes is used in regenerating pine stands. Desired results can be achieved through burning, mechanical means, or herbicides.

Thinning is an intermediate treatment in stands of longer rotations to harvest a portion of the stand, and redistribute growth on the remaining trees. Thinning normally is applied in 10 to 15 year-old and older pine stands grown on a sawtimber rotation. Pine stands often are burned when they are thinned.

Rotations, or the age of stands at harvest, are variable, depending on products or objectives. Some forests are maintained as old growth or wilderness and are not harvested. Most forests are managed for sawtimber and/or pulpwood production. It is desirable for trees grown for sawtimber to be large and free from lower lateral limbs. A typical sawtimber rotation would be 60 to 100 years for southern pines and faster-growing bottomland hardwoods on well-drained sites and somewhat longer for upland hardwoods. Pulpwood rotations typically are 20 to 30 years for fast growing pines, and somewhat longer for slower growing hardwoods.

CONCLUSIONS

Forests of the South are diverse and dynamic. Southern forests have been and continue to be shaped by a myriad of different forces. The suitability of these forests for wildlife communities and species and options for managing the forests for wildlife are detailed in the following chapters.

CHAPTER 5

Sensitive Plant Communities

Joan L. Walker
U.S. Forest Service
Southern Research Station, Clemson, SC

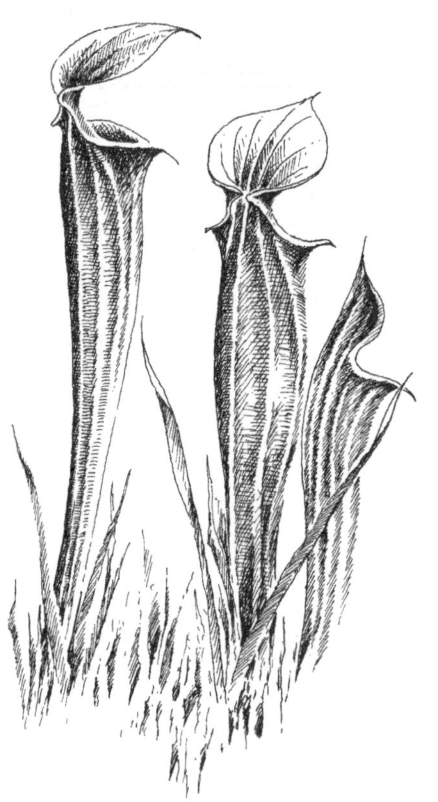

Over half of the southern landscape is forested, but nearly all of the land has been modified considerably, especially during the centuries following European settlement (See history chapters). Such extensive changes in the southern landscape have contributed to the threatened status of many plant and animal species that are now protected under the Endangered Species Act. Additionally these changes have resulted in the reduction and degradation of native plant communities. Conserving and managing communities can contribute to the conservation of natural biological diversity by protecting ecological functions and providing habitats for many individual species of concern. As targets for conservation, natural or semi-natural communities may protect rare species, especially non-vascular plants and invertebrates for which inventories are universally inadequate.

This chapter defines sensitive community and reviews assessments of southeastern sensitive communities. The chapter provides accounts of selected sensitive communities, including their distribution, composition, rare species, threats, and management. A final section summarizes factors likely to influence the success of sensitive community management.

DEFINITIONS AND CONCEPTS

"Sensitive" is a management designation for communities that are vulnerable to loss, and require special attention to insure their existence and to retain their composition (including rare species), structure, and function. The sensitivity of natural communities results from scarcity (relatively few, small locations exist) and/or vulnerability to anthropogenic changes. Communities that are likely to lose populations are considered vulnerable. Communities that are both rare and vulnerable to human disturbances constitute the group of highly sensitive types, and are candidates for the greatest management consideration and modification. Conversely, abundant and resilient types are unlikely to be adversely impacted by human activities and would not be considered for special management actions. Highly vulnerable but comparatively abundant, and scarce but not threatened communities may require special considerations, however generalizations are difficult to make.

Scarce communities include both geographically restricted (narrowly endemic) types, and those that occur over a larger area but are distributed as small, discrete patches. Natural scarcity may arise from dependence on unique and rare physical conditions, such as a specific rock type or hydrological regime, or on localized disturbances, such as fires on ridgetops. Scarcity also may be the result of losing historically abundant types. The amount of loss relative to the historical abundance has been used as an indicator of vulnerability to anthropogenic disturbances (Noss et al. 1995). Other conditions associated with the likelihood of being adversely impacted by human activities include site accessibility; suitability for other activities, such as agriculture and recreation; and proximity to other vegetation that is desirable for other uses, for example, depressions embedded in potential forest plantations.

Because of concerns about the loss of biological diversity, communities may be considered sensitive if they contain rare species. Some have numerous rare species, but because many rare species have narrow geographic ranges (narrow endemics), a general community type may have different rare species in different places.

Globally sensitive communities are of concern throughout their ranges and are therefore of national concern from a conservation perspective. But even types that are widespread may be important locally to provide habitat for target species. Managers may view locally uncommon habitats as sensitive. Though both globally and locally sensitive communities require management attention, globally sensitive habitats are the focus of this chapter.

Old growth forest, Joyce Kilmer Memorial Forest. Old growth forest remnants are rare throughout the South and they vary with forest type. Common characteristics of many old growth forests include large and old trees, a multi-layer tree canopy, a diverse ground layer, and an accumulation of standing and down dead trees *(J. Walker)*.

SENSITIVE COMMUNITY DESCRIPTIONS

Several publications describe the biodiversity of the Southeast, including threatened and endangered ecosystems. Two volumes edited by Martin et al. (1993a,b) describe biodiversity and identify threatened terrestrial vegetation types (Martin and Boyce 1993). Grossman et al. (1994) identified an initial list of imperiled community types; Noss et al. (1995) lists endangered and threatened ecosystems; and White et al. (1998) identified threats to southeastern ecosystems. Results of these assessments are somewhat difficult to compare because authors had different objectives and methods.

Based on a classification system developed by The Nature Conservancy (TNC), it is clear that the South has many different communities, a high proportion of them are considered imperiled to some degree, and sensitive habitats are found in all states and in all physiographic provinces. In TNC's system plant associations are defined by dominant species in all the vegetation layers and each community is assigned a conservation rank. Community types are ranked on a global (G) scale of 1 to 5, with 1 indicating critical imperilment due to rarity, endemism, and/or threats, and 5 indicating low risk of elimination. A rank of G1 indicates a great risk of extinction of the type worldwide. Grossman et al. (1994) listed fifty-eight G1, G2 communities in the southeast (excluding Oklahoma and Texas). A 1998 report (Grossman et al. 1998) shows no less than 100 plant associations per southeastern state, and more than 400 identified in North Carolina alone. On a per state basis, no less than 10%, and as many as 30% of the identified associations are classified as imperiled (G1, G2).

Fewer more broadly defined sensitive communities have been recognized. Boyce and Martin (1993) evaluated the sensitivity of southeastern ecosystems defined by Kuchler Potential Natural Vegetation types, which are defined broadly on vegetation physiognomy and dominant species (Kuchler 1964). Everglades, mangroves, bottomland hardwood forests, pocosins, mountain bogs, and Carolina bays were classed as *Threatened*; and longleaf pine, spruce-fir and other high elevation forests, heath balds, maritime communities, rock outcrops, glades, grasslands, and sandpine scrub as *Vulnerable*. Noss et al. (1995) listed 48 southeastern types that have experienced over 70% losses compared to estimated presettlement areas (Table 1).

Three major trends threaten biodiversity in the Southeast (White et al. 1998). First, natural areas in general, and old growth forests in particular, have been permanently lost or changed drastically. Secondly, active fire suppression has resulted in the loss and degradation of ecosystems in all areas of the Southeast. Finally, disruptions of hydrological systems have put wetlands at risk. Considering these broad trends, White et al. (1998) identified broadly defined community types considered susceptible to continued losses of biodiversity (Table 2).

The next sections describe selected sensitive communities including distribution, composition, threats, and general management. Because it is not feasible to discuss the many specific sensitive plant communities ranked G1, G2 (Weakley et al. 1998), this chapter discusses more general community types (Table 2). Each type includes multiple associations according to The Nature Conservancy Classification system, but within a general class, communities share broad ecological characteristics such as dominant species, physiognomy, controlling processes, and landscape context. General management recommendations can be made for broad community types, but in practice site-specific variations must be considered.

Notable omissions from this chapter are sub-tropical communities in peninsular Florida, maritime communities, and bottomland forests. These are widely recognized as communities that are ecologically at risk. All are discussed by Martin et al. (1993a,b) and summarized by White et al. (1998). Messina and Conner (1998) review southern wetlands.

The following community descriptions are grouped into forests, non-forested openings in forested landscapes, and non-alluvial wetlands. Federally threatened and endangered plants occur in many communities, including but not limited to the ones discussed in this chapter. When they occur in selected communities, they will be noted. Appendix 1 contains a list of all Threatened and Endangered plants in the region, their distributions by state, and brief habitat descriptions.

FORESTS

Unusual forest communities (G1,G2 communities).— Some forest communities contain unusual combinations of plant species or populations of individual rare plants, and many of these communities are ranked G1, G2 by The Nature Conservancy. Some G1, G2 forest types have always been rare because they are restricted to rare physical habitats, such as special soils. The coastal plain forests on marl or chalk outcrops, or forests on loess soils of the Mississippi alluvial plain

Table 1. Estimates of ecosystem loss from Noss et al. (1995; Appendix A) based on published papers, State Natural Heritage Programs, The Nature Conservancy, and expert opinions. Ecosystems are listed in declining order of percentage loss. Some estimates are based on more quantitative analysis than others, and not all states had data to report.

>95% loss; critically endangered

Old-growth deciduous forests	Southeast
S.App. Spruce-fir	TN, NC, VA
Longleaf pine	Coastal Plain
Rockland slash pine	FL
Loblolly-shortleaf pine	West Gulf Coastal Plain
Canebrakes	Southeast
Bluegrass-savannah-woodland	KY
Blackbelt, Jackson prairies	AL, MS
Dry prairie	FL
Wet and mesic coastal prairie	LA
Atlantic white-cedar forest	VA, NC
Native prairies	KY
Bottomland forest	WV
High quality Oak-hickory forest	Cumberland Plateau, TN

85-95% loss; endangered

Ecosystem	Location	Ecosystem	Location
Mesic limestone forest	MD	Mixed hardwood-loblolly pine	LA
Red spruce	Cntal Appalachians	Xeric sandhill	LA
Upland hardwoods	Coastal Plain, TN	Stream terrace-sandywoodland	
Old-growth oak-hickory	TN	Savannah	LA
Cedar glades	TN	Slash pine (1900-1989)	FL
Longleaf pine	TX, LA	Gulf coast pitcher plant bogs	Coastal Plain
Longleaf pine forest (1936-87)	FL	Pocosins	VA
Calcareous prairie, Fleming glades	LA	Mountain bogs	NC
Live-oak, live-oak hackberry	LA	Appalachian bogs	Blue Ridge, TN
Prairie terrace loess oak forest	LA	Upland wetlands	Highland Rim,TN
Mature forest, all types	LA	Natural barrier island beaches	MD
Shortleaf pine-oak-hickory	LA	Ultramafic glades	VA

70-84% loss; threatened

Bottomland and riparian forest	Southeast
Xeric scrub, scrubby flatwoods, sandhills	Lake Wales Ridge, FL
Tropical hardwood hammock	Florida Keys
Saline prairie	LA
Upland longleaf pine	LA
Live oak-pine-magnolia	LA
Spruce pine-hardwood flatwoods	LA
Xeric sandhill woodlands	LA
Flatwood ponds	LA
Slash pine-pond cypress-hardwood	LA
Wet hardwood-loblolly pine	LA

Table 2. Sensitive communities in the South. Communities discussed by Boyce and Martin (1993), Grossman et al. (1994), Noss et al. (1995), White et al. (1998), and in this chapter are indicated with X. Blanks indicate community is not discussed. [Table Modified from White et al. 1998]

Ecosytem/community group	Boyce & Martin	Grossman et al.	Noss et al.	White et al.	This Chapter
Widely distributed					
Upland forests	Resilient	X	X	X	X
Bottomland forests	Threatened		X	X	
Glades, barrens, prairies, outcrops	Vulnerable	X	X	X	X
Canebrakes	Threatened	X	X		X
Mountain					
Spruce-fir	Vulnerable	X	X	X	X
High-elevation deciduous forest	Vulnerable	X		X	
Heath balds	Vulnerable			X	
Pine forests	Vulnerable			X	X
Mountain bogs	Threatened	X	X	X	X
Grassy balds	Vulnerable	X		X	X
High-elevation cliffs	Vulnerable	X	X	X	X
Rocky stream gorges	Vulnerable	X		X	
Coastal Plain					
Longleaf pine	Vulnerable	X	X	X	X
Seepage, hillside, pitcher plant bogs	Vulnerable		X	X	X
Carolina bays, cypress domes, ponds	Threatened		X	X	X
Pocosin	Threatened		X	X	
Maritime communities	Vulnerable	X	X	X	
South Florida					
Tropical hardwoods	Vulnerable	X		X	
Slash pine	Vulnerable	X	X	X	
Florida sand pine scrub	Vulnerable		X	X	
Mangroves	Threatened			X	
Everglades	Threatened			X	

are examples. Although rare forest communities may contain rare plant species like Price's potato-bean, other rare species like small whorled pogonia, are found even in apparently common forests types. Rare forest communities are found throughout the region; state Natural Heritage Programs are the best sources for local information.

Threats and management.—Common threats to rare forest communities include invasions by non-indigenous species, such as Japanese honeysuckle, privet, and Chinese tallow tree; interruption of natural disturbance regimes; high concentrations of herbivores such as white-tail deer; outbreaks of forest pests; and direct impacts from modern forest management methods, for example clearcutting and intensive site preparation.

Management options and needs vary with the type of forest and the specific threats, but controlling non-indigenous species and herbivores, and choosing benign methods to accomplish these objectives are factors to consider. Management actions that mimic natural disturbances may be particularly important because natural

Table Mountain Pine, Rabun County, Georgia. Table Mountain pine forests occupy southern and southwestern slopes and ridges. They often occur as isolated islands in the southern Blue Ridge. In the absence of fire, this community is being changed by the invasions of oaks and shrubs. With hardwood invasion, the fuels available for prescribed fire change, making it very difficult to reintroduce fire and restore the community *(T. Waldrop)*.

disturbance regimes are unlikely to be intact. Where there are rare species, management should focus on providing conditions favorable to target plant species.

Old Growth Forest Remnants

Estimates of the amount of old growth forests vary with the criteria used to identify old growth, but by all definitions old growth remnants are scarce in the Southeast (Davis 1996). Many definitions of old growth include criteria for trees of great size or age (for a specific kind of site and tree species), and for degree of naturalness (lack of apparent recent human disturbance) (Leverett 1996). White and White (1996) suggest that tracts that have been continuously forested (at least since European settlement) have conservation value, and they argue that such sites should be considered and protected as old growth. Even though these continuously forested stands may have younger trees established after recent natural disturbances or have experienced some harvest or grazing, such sites have undisturbed soils with associated soil biota, and may retain locally adapted genotypes of some species. The conservation value of such sites lies in unique cryptic biota and genotypes. Fragments of the presettlement forest have survived, especially on inaccessible slopes or sites, but most large old-growth remnants occur on public land.

Old growth forest composition varies with forest type, but forest characteristics generally associated with old growth forests include large, old trees; accumulations of standing and down woody debris; and multi-layered canopies. The absolute sizes and ages of trees will vary with the types of trees. The Forest Service and The Nature Conservancy have developed a series of diagnostic descriptions for specific old growth forest types. For southern forest types the descriptions are available from the Southern Forest Research Station, Asheville, North Carolina.

Threats and management.—Threats to old growth remnants are similar to those described for rare forest communities: non-indigenous species invasions, high numbers of herbivores, modern management practices.

Management emphasis should be placed on preserving existing conditions, especially intact soil profiles and local genotypes. Avoid soil-disturbing management activities, and if species re-introductions are desired, choose seed sources from other nearby, relatively undisturbed sites. The future of existing sites may be extended if existing forested buffers are retained, or are developed over time. Small patches of old growth forests alone will not provide habitat for large-area dependent forest species, but in larger forested landscapes may provide important habitat features such as large trees and abundant woody debris.

Fire-dependent Pine Woodlands

At the time of European settlement pines dominated or shared dominance in some forests in all parts of the Southeast. Longleaf pine and longleaf mixed with slash, loblolly, and/or shortleaf pines dominated coastal plain forests (Christensen 1988). Sand pine occupied xeric ridges in peninsular Florida (Myers 1990). Virginia or pitch pine communities were common on dry slopes and ridges in the Ridge and Valley province, and shortleaf communities occupied similar sites in the Ouachita Mountains (Foti and Glenn 1991; Strausberg and Hough 1997). In the southern Appalachians shortleaf and Virginia pine communities occurred at low elevations, pitch pine at low to mid-elevations, and Table Mountain pine at mid-to high elevations (Vose et al. 1997; Williams 1998). Except on extremely xeric sites where edaphic factors helped maintain pine dominance, lightning and human-set fires prehistorically and historically maintained all of these.

Pine communities of the Southern Appalachians and longleaf pine communities are included in several assessments of sensitive communities (Table 2). Descriptions of montane pine (pitch and Table Mountain pine) communities and longleaf pine communities follow.

Pitch and Table Mountain Pine Communities.—In the South, pitch pine is widely distributed in the Ridge and Valley and Blue Ridge Provinces, and occurs occasionally in the Piedmont. In contrast, Table Mountain pine is restricted to the Blue Ridge. In the mountains pitch pine dominates at mid-elevation (2300 to 3200 feet above sea level), and is replaced by Table Mountain pine at higher elevations (2500 to 4600 feet above sea level). Site types for both include south and southwest slopes, ridgetops, and granite rock outcrops. Soils are generally shallow, acidic and low nutrient inceptisols.

With the dominant pines, the most important canopy species are oaks, especially chestnut and scarlet oaks. A dense, sometimes continuous, small tree and shrub layer develops where fire is excluded. Common shrubs include dwarf and bear huckleberries, early lowbush blueberry, sweet-fern, mountain-laurel, and Allegheny-chinkapin. The typically sparse ground layer includes trailing-arbutus, galax, eastern teaberry, spotted wintergreen, bracken, little false bluestem, goat's rue, and mountain bellwort (Williams 1998). Some species are most abundant following fire and decline with fire exclusion including Michaux's wood-aster, horseflyweed, greater tickseed, rosette grasses, American burnweed, Canadian horseweed, rabbit tobacco, oblong-fruit pinweed, hairy and creeping bush-clover, anise-scented goldenrod, and yellow Indian grass (Harrod et al., In press).

No federally listed plants are found in these communities, but there are plants of concern in some locations. Table Mountain pine has a limited distribution, and some have suggested that fire suppression has put the species at risk for long-term survival (Turrill et al. 1997).

Historically montane pine communities burned with understory-thinning fires every 5-7 years, and stand-replacing fires about every 75-100 years (Frost 1998), and fire is still important in controlling the succession of pine communities to oak-dominated communities. Fire creates the conditions required for pine reproduction: high light, exposed mineral soil. In the case of Table Mountain pine, fire opens serotinous cones to release seed onto the fire-exposed seedbed (though in some years, cones open without burning; Barden 1977). Fire also controls the invasion by fire-tender hardwoods (Williams and Johnson 1992). Where fire has been excluded, oak basal area increases; basal area and density of fire-sensitive species increase in the understory, pine reproduction declines, and the density of grasses and forbs decreases (Harmon 1982; Harmon et al. 1983; Vose et al. 1997; Williams 1998; Harrod et al. 1998). At the landscape level, fire suppression has resulted in the loss of open, low basal area stand conditions.

Threats and management.—Fire exclusion poses the dominant threat to montane communities. Overall the area occupied by pine communities has been declining since the mid-twentieth century, and without prescribed fire losses will continue (Williams 1998).

The use of fire for restoration seems a logical management choice, but exact prescriptions and schedules for re-introducing fire to long-unburned sites are not available (Vose et al. 1997). Williams (1998) suggests pulsing high- and low-intensity fires to mimic historic patterns and effects. Because hardwoods may grow to fire-resistant sizes (Harmon 1984), they may have to be removed by cutting.

Longleaf Pine Savanna Research Natural Area, Apalachicola National Forest. This area has been burned about every 3 years for decades, including fires during the growing season in recent years. The foreground shows seasonally wet woodland, which grades into a nearly treeless community with some carnivorous plants (locally known as a savanna). The savanna borders a cypress strand visible on the distant horizon. This landscape has a high diversity of grasses, sedges and herbs *(R. Costa)*.

Longleaf Pine and Associated Communities..—Historically, longleaf pine dominated coastal plain sites, and shared dominance with other pines and hardwoods on the Piedmont and on dry sites in the southern Ridge and Valley and Southern Blue Ridge provinces (Ware et al. 1993). Longleaf pine woodlands occupied a range of site conditions, grading into xeric habitats such as scrub oak forests, and into wetter seepage bogs often found in transitions to cypress strands, bayhead pocosins or baygalls, and bottomlands (Stout and Marion 1993). Remnants of this widespread forest types are still found through much of the historical range; however, good examples of natural communities on productive soils are virtually non-existent.

Although longleaf pine unifies community types in the longleaf ecosystem, the vegetation varies considerably. Community composition varies with soil moisture and geography (Peet and Allard 1993; Harcombe et al. 1993), presumably associated with soil fertility and with historical biogeography. Peet and Allard (1993) recognized four major groups of communities east of the Mississippi River: xeric woodlands, subxeric woodlands, mesic woodlands, and seasonally-wet woodlands. Similar communities occur in the west Gulf Coast region.

Xeric community types are found on deep coarse sands, especially in the fall-line sandhills, along the northeast sides of major rivers that flow into the Atlantic, and on relict dune systems in the outer coastal plain. Canopy associates include turkey oak and common persimmon. Xeric communities have scattered shrubs (blueberries, dwarf huckleberry, wax myrtle) and sparse grass and herb layers. Wiregrass (pineland three-awn or Beyrich's three-awn) is the dominant grass, and bare soil is usually present. Fire is important in these communities, however, because fuel accumulates slowly the frequency was likely lower than in other types (Christensen 1988).

Sub-xeric communities occur on well-drained sandy to silty soils from the lower coastal plain through the upper coastal plain and sandhills. Few intact examples on silty soils remain, as those sites have been mostly converted to agriculture. These woodlands have widely spaced pines, an open deciduous understory, and continuous grass and herb layer. The hardwood understory species include turkey, bluejack, and sand post oaks on sandier soils, and blackjack and post oak on clayey soils. Common shrubs include blueberries, dwarf huckleberry, yaupon, and St. Andrew's-cross. Wiregrasses dominate the ground layer except in central South Carolina, which falls between the ranges of northern and southern wiregrasses, and west of Mississippi. Bluestems dominate sites outside the ranges of wiregrass. Composites and legumes are well represented (for examples, anise-scented goldenrod, gayfeathers, flax-leaf ankle-aster, silk-grasses, milk peas, hoary-peas, tick-trefoils).

Mesic longleaf woodlands occur on relatively fertile, loamy, well-drained soils. These communities are virtually gone from the Atlantic coastal plain, but some good examples remain on the Gulf coastal plain. The ground layer is continuous with a high diversity of herbs mixed with wiregrass and bluestem. These are extremely rich in legumes. There may be as many as 100-140 species of vascular plants in 1,000 square yards, higher than any other community in North America (Peet and Allard 1993). Compared to drier community types, the diversity of trees, shrubs and herbs increase. Succession to hardwood forests in this community is rapid without fire.

Seasonally wet longleaf communities include savannahs and flatwoods. Savannahs typically have open pine canopies over graminoid-dominated and nearly shrub-free ground layers. Savannahs can be exceptionally species rich with over 40 species per 1 square yard and up to 100 species per 100 square yards. The ground layer includes a variety of grasses (bluestems, wiregrasses, toothache grass, hair-awn muhly, dropseeds), many composites (for examples honeycomb-heads, rayless-goldenrods, chaffheads, sunflowers, and goldenrods), small sedges, insectivorous species (sundews, Venus' flytrap, butterworts, pitcher-plants, bladderworts), orchids (grass-pinks, rosebud, fringed, fringeless, snake-mouth orchids), and lilies (colicroot, lilies, coastal false asphodel). Legumes are not common. Savanna communities were found throughout the coastal plains, but extensive savannahs were found in southeast North Carolina and on the Gulf coast from the central Florida panhandle west to Louisiana. Each of these regions has distinguishing endemic species. Compared to savannahs, flatwoods have denser pine canopies, sometimes have midstories with red maple, sweetgum, and water oak, have denser shrub layers, and less diverse herb layers. Typical shrubs include runner oaks (on drier sites) and many species found in bay forests and depression ponds; herb composition overlaps with savannahs.

Many species now considered rare are associated with the longleaf ecosystem (Hardin and White 1989). These include nearly 200 plant species; twenty-six are federally listed as endangered or threatened (Table 3; Walker 1998).

Relatively frequent, low intensity fires characterized the historical fire regime. Estimates of historical fire frequency range from about every 3 years on productive sites with rapid fuel accumulation to once in a decade on xeric sites. Without fire both pine and hardwood densities increase, forest floor depth increases, and light and soil moisture availability may be reduced via increased forest transpiration in wet sites and increased in xeric sites when a duff layer accumulates and holds water. Without fire, the cover and vigor of grasses and herbs decline, and ultimately species are lost.

Threats and management..—Altered fire regimes and landscape fragmentation, which interferes with large-scale fires, are major threats to the diversity of longleaf pine communities. Conversion to other uses and to other forests types, and intensive management practices also reduce longleaf ecosystem diversity.

Managing longleaf pine forests for timber production at some level is compatible with retaining values for biological diversity. If they have been burned regularly, the ground layers of many older second-growth longleaf stands contain characteristic native species and few non-indigenous species. In contrast, high-density plantations established following intensive mechanical site preparation, are often devoid of rich herb layers, and particularly lack the grasses needed to carry fire (Walker and Van Eerden 1996; unpublished data). The loss of wiregrasses, the dominant bunch grasses producing essential fine fuels in much of the longleaf range, has been attributed to intensive mechanical site preparation (Outcalt and Lewis 1990). From the perspective of maintaining biological diversity, natural regeneration methods limiting site preparation to prescribed fire are preferred. Uneven-aged management systems have been used in some areas, and researchers are investigating the feasibility of applying uneven-aged management for longleaf on a variety of sites.

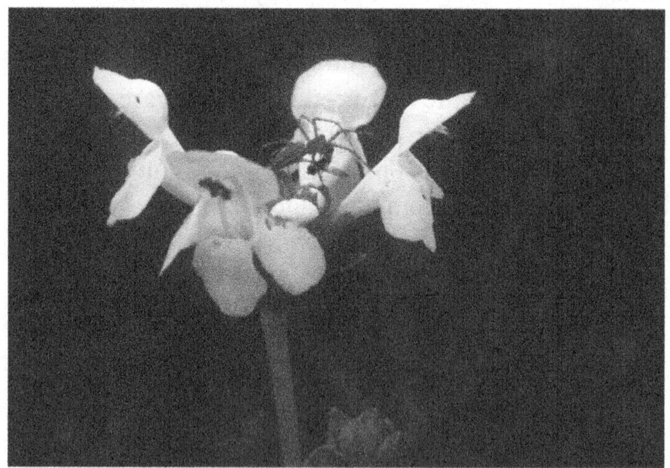

White-bird's-in-a-nest (*Macbridea alba*) is a federally threatened species endemic to 4 counties in Florida's central panhandle. It is one of over twenty federally protected plants associated with longleaf pine communities. Many of these rare species have narrow geographic distributions. For this reason conserving longleaf pine communities throughout its range is important for conserving biological diversity *(J. Walker)*.

Table 3. Federally listed species associated with longleaf pine ecosystems and direct and indirect habitat factors cited as reasons for listing. Habitat-related listing factors are coded as follows: a = drainage/fire plow lines/road work; b = silviculture activities; c = agriculture conversion; d = residential/commercial/recreational development; e = other human activities; f = fire suppression; g = herbicide/pesticide use; h = mining; i = habitat fragmentation. Trends reported by the U.S. Fish and Wildlife Service in 1990, and listing dates post-November 1990 are shown.

Common Name	Scientific Name	Status	Codes	Trend
Hairy rattleweed	*Baptisia arachnifera*	E	b	Declining
Pigeon wings	*Clitoria fragrans*	T	c,d,f	1993
Apalachicola rosemary	*Conradina glabra*	E	b,c,f,g	1993
Beautiful pawpaw	*Deeringothamnus pulchellus*	E	d,f	Declining
Rugel's pawpaw	*Deeringothamnus rugellii*	E	d,f	Declining
Scrub wild buckwheat	*Eriogonum longifolium var. gnaphalifolium*	T	c,d	1993
Telephus spurge	*Euphorbia telephiodes*	T	b,d,f,g	1992
Harper's beauty	*Harperocallis flava*	E	a,b,d,f,g	Improving
Pondberry	*Lindera melissaefolia*	E	a-d	Unknown
Roughleaf loosestrife	*Lysimachia asperulaefolia*	E	a-f	Unknown
White birds-in-a-nest	*Macbridea alba*	T	b,f	1992
Britton's beargrass	*Nolina britoniana*	E	c,d	1993
Canby's dropwort	*Oxypolis canbyi*	E	a,b,c	Declining
Texas trailing phlox	*Phlox nivalis* ssp. texensis	E	a,b,d,f	1991
Godfrey's butterwort	*Pinguicula ionantha*	T	a,b,d,f	1993
Small Lewton's milkwort	*Polygala lewtonii*	E	c,d	1993
Chapman's rhododendron	*Rhododendron chapmanii*	E	b	Declining
Michaux's sumac	*Rhus michauxii*	E	b-f	Unknown
Alabama canebrake pitcher-plant	*Sarracenia rubra* ssp. alabamensis	E	a,c,g,h	Declining
Chaffseed	*Schwalbea americana*	E	b,c,d,f	1992
Florida skullcap	*Scutellaria floridana*	T	b,f	1992
Gentian pinkroot	*Spigelia gentianoides*	E	b,c,f	1990
Cooley's meadowrue	*Thalictrum cooleyi*	E	a-c,f,g	Unknown
Wide-leaf warea	*Warea amplexifolia*	E	c,d	Declining
Carter's mustard	*Warea carteri*	E	c,d	Declining
Florida ziziphus	*Ziziphus celata*	E	c,d,f	Declining

The need for frequent burning (2-5 year intervals depending on site conditions) is widely accepted, but the timing of burning is still debated. The effects of season of burn may vary among site types and current site conditions (Rebertus et al. 1993, Glitzenstein et al. 1995). In the absence of additional information, Robbins and Myers (1992) suggest managers vary the season and interval of burning randomly. Depending on current site conditions, fire alone may not restore the plant diversity to remnant longleaf stands. Mechanical or chemical control of hardwoods may be required to facilitate the reestablishment of longleaf pines. Thinning densely stocked pine stands to restore light conditions to the understory is recommended, and locally extirpated species may have to be reintroduced.

High-elevation Conifer Forests and Associated Communities.—Red spruce-Fraser fir forests dominate 8 of the 10 high peaks areas (above 5,500 feet) in the southern Appalachians. Seven of these have well-developed spruce-fir forests (Great Smoky Mountains, Balsam Mountains, Black Mountains, Roan Mountain, Plott Balsams, Grandfather Mountain, Mt. Rogers); an eighth (Whitetop Mountain) has spruce without fir (White 1984). Excepting Grandfather Mountain, the largest remaining spruce-fir forests occur on public lands.

The composition and productivity of the canopy varies with elevation and exposure. In general, Fraser Fir achieves dominance at the highest elevations with Red Spruce increasing at lower elevations and more protected positions. Spruce forests grade into hardwood forests, northern hardwoods, or red oak forests. Forest biomass and stature increase from higher to lower elevations and from exposed ridges to protected coves.

Although southern Appalachian spruce-fir forests share species with boreal conifer forests, the flora is distinctive. Characteristic southern trees include Fraser fir, heart-leaved paper birch, red spruce, mountain maple, and mountain ash. Shrubs include catawba rosebay, skunk currant, smooth blackberry, southern mountain cranberry, and hobblebush. Bryophyte communities are well developed in closed forests, while herb diversity increases in openings. High elevation openings provide important habitats for rare herbs, including many species that also occur in granite outcrops and seeps (See granite outcrop descriptions for a rare species list).

The forests reproduce in small-scale patches resulting from local disturbances, primarily wind. Fire is not important, probably occurring less than once in a thousand years. Given these natural processes, it is not surprising that many high elevation forests never recovered after the wholesale harvest and subsequent fires in the early twentieth century.

Threats and management.—Southern Appalachian spruce-fir communities are threatened by two human-related causes: an infestation of an exotic insect and air pollution. Throughout its range, Fraser fir is suffering heavy mortality from an introduced Eurasian insect, the balsam woolly adelgid. The adelgid infects and kills adult trees, while seedlings and saplings appear to be more resistant. It is unknown whether resistant seedlings will survive to produce viable seed. As the canopy dies, the forest herbs are exposed to higher light and temperatures and drier soils. Thus, the indirect effects of the adelgid put the entire flora and dependent fauna (like the federally endangered spruce-fir moss spider (*Microhexura montivaga*) at risk. The stresses induced by insect attack are exacerbated by additional stresses of acid precipitation and air pollution.

Individual stands can be sprayed to control the adelgid, but this is not practical or particularly effective, as it is difficult to spray all the feeding sites (White et al 1998). Even if genetically resistant fir populations exist, the future is uncertain for this forest type and associated rare species.

NON-FORESTED OPENINGS

Introduction and Definitions

Openings in forested landscapes were once common throughout the Southeast (DeSelm and Murdock 1993, Quarterman et al. 1993). Natural succession to the surrounding forest vegetation was inhibited by a natural disturbance regime such as fire, and perhaps grazing, or

Mt. Mitchell, NC. Fir seedlings regenerate among the skeletons of fir trees killed by the balsam wooly adelgid. This non-indigenous insect was introduced presumably on non-native silver fir planted in experimental efforts to reforest the high peaks after logging. The adelgid was discovered in the South in the mid-1950s, but by that time had already spread through the Black Mountains. Infestations were found in the Great Smoky Mountains by the late 1950s and the Mt. Rodgers area by 1962. It is difficult to eliminate and subsequent infestations are likely. With the added stresses of acid precipitation the future of this sensitive community is uncertain *(J. Walker)*.

Stone Mountain, Georgia. Ephemeral, vernal pools in granite flatrocks hold water and remain wet during winter and early spring. The pools provide microhabitats for many granite outcrop endemic plant species. The depths of water and soil accumulation determine which plants occur and how they are arranged in the pools. This small pool has several species: the reddish Diamorpha smallii (Elf Orpine), the white-flowering *Minuartia uniflora* (One-flower Stitchwort), and the old flowering stalks of little bluestem *(J. Walker)*.

by physical conditions (soil nutrient status or depth) that limit woody species establishment and productivity. Composition varies, but typically openings support regionally unique species that cannot survive in the surrounding forests. Some types are rich in local endemics. Most types have become scarcer as a result of development or natural succession to other vegetation types after natural disturbance regimes were disrupted.

The terms to describe non-forested vegetation are not standardized and can confuse communication; therefore definitions are provided for terms used in this chapter. *Outcrop communities* are found where exposed rock surfaces comprise more than 25% surface cover. *Glades* are communities on rock or shallow soil, dominated by annual or perennial forbs, annual grasses, cryptogams, or some combination of these (Baskin et al 1994) and including less than 50% perennial grass cover. *Barrens* are herbaceous communities with greater than 50% perennial grass cover (DeSelm 1989, 1994). *Prairie* is applied most commonly to the tallgrass grasslands of the Midwest, but has been applied to some specific areas in the Southeast (Black, Jackson, and Grand Prairies). Only the coastal prairies of the West Gulf Coast are considered part of the midwestern grasslands. *Canebrake* refers to areas dominated by native giant cane. Canebrakes are not strictly herbaceous but are considered in this section because they occupy openings in forested landscapes, were once more widespread as a result of Native American land use practices, and are quickly lost to forest succession (Platt and Brantley 1997). *Grassy bald* applies to herbaceous vegetation complexes on the tops of high peaks in the Southern Appalachians.

The next three sections describe rock-associated communities; barrens and prairies; and canebrakes. In this order they generally represent a decreasing reliance on physical conditions (shallow soil, low moisture availability, high light) and an increasing dependence on disturbance, especially fire, for retaining their openness. Similarly, management needs grade from protecting and limiting mechanical disturbances of fragile communities, to actively reinstating disturbances, especially prescribed fire. Grassy balds are the last type of opening discussed.

Rock-associated Communities: Outcrops and Glades

Communities of rock outcrops are restricted to island-like, exposed or near-surface rock substrates, but outcrops themselves are scattered throughout the region (Quarterman et al. 1993). Community composition and structure vary geographically with rock type and

Cliff Tops on Mt. Leconte, Sevier County, TN. High elevation outcrops provide unique open habitats embedded in, or adjacent to, spruce-fir communities and grassy balds. This cliff community includes the state rare Tufted Leafless-Bulrush, the grass-like plant in the foreground, Rock Club-Moss, Cain's Reed Grass, and the federally endangered Appalachian Avens *(P. White)*.

with soil type and depth. Granite (or other igneous rock) outcrop communities are found in the Piedmont of Alabama, Georgia, South Carolina, North Carolina and Virginia, and on exposed cliffs and ridges at high elevations in the Blue Ridge. Sandstone outcrops and glades occur in the Cumberland Plateau (Alabama, Georgia, Tennessee), Coastal Plain (Florida, Georgia, South Carolina), and Interior Highlands (Arkansas). The most extensive rock-associated communities occur over limestone in the Interior Low Plateau (Alabama, Tennessee, Kentucky), the Ridge and Valley province in Georgia and Tennessee, and interspersed with sandstone outcrops in the Interior Highlands (Arkansas).

Rock outcrop habitats and communities share some attributes. Except waterfall spray zones in the Blue Ridge, outcrops and glades are xeric to subxeric habitats receiving high light intensities. [Compared to Piedmont sites, growing conditions in high elevation outcrops are moderated somewhat by high rainfall, fog, and reduced evapotranspiration (Wiser 1994).] Soils are thin or non-existent, and fragile plant communities are easily dislodged. Potential vegetation is primarily herbaceous, but woody species root in crevices in the outcrop or in adjacent areas with adequate soil development. The effects of woody plant encroachment are from adjacent communities, but since individual outcrops may be small, shading from the edges can change microhabitats and their suitability for outcrop species. Finally, outcrop communities have many endemic or rare plant species, which are discussed in more detail for each outcrop type.

Woodlands dominated by Eastern red-cedar are commonly associated with rock outcrops and glades of various types (Small and Wentworth 1998). Cedar-hardwood woodlands are found on steep south to southwest facing (granite) rock outcrops in the Piedmont and southern Blue Ridge (North Carolina,

Cedar glade, Shaw Arboretum, Gray Summit, Missouri. Cedar glade communities are open patches interspersed with patches of red cedar or other woodlands. Glades typically have shallow, rocky soils, which help restrict the rate of succession to woodlands. They also provide habitat for many endemic plants, most of them small herbs *(P. White)*.

Xeric limestone prairie along the Buffalo River, Arkansas. Patches of grass-dominated communities are found on hillsides and ledges in the Ozarks. To maintain the species diversity of these sensitive communities managers must control the encroachment of woody plants, cedars in this photo *(J. Walker)*.

Tennessee, South Carolina, Georgia). Eastern red cedar woodlands also border limestone cedar glades and barrens in the Low Interior Plateau (Tennessee, Kentucky, Alabama) and sandstone glades in the Cumberland Plateau. On chert or cherty limestones in the Ozarks, Ashe juniper woodlands surround xeric openings dominated by three-awn grasses, rather than bluestem. All of these communities include some species found on nearby outcrops, as well as species of local forests (Quarterman et al. 1993).

Granite outcrops.—Granite outcrop communities occur on flat to gently sloping surfaces in the Piedmont, and on exposed domes or cliffs in the southern Blue Ridge. Outcrop conditions vary from bare rock surfaces, to lichen covered patches, shallow pools that hold water and remain moist during winter and early spring, seepage areas sometimes with deeper pools, and marginal communities found in deeper soils where outcrops meet adjacent habitats. In depressions as soil accumulates, vegetation may develop through time from lichen and annual plant communities, through annual-perennial herb communities, to herb-shrub communities. Succession to woody vegetation is limited on steep surfaces.

The Central Georgia Piedmont is a center of endemism for flatrock granite outcrop species, with the number of endemic species decreasing along a northeast-southeast axis from the center (Murdy 1968). Flatrock endemics include little amphianthus (endangered), granite flat sedge, black-spore quillwort, Merlin's-grass, Georgia rush, spotted scorpion-weed, Small's purslane (endangered), Georgia oak, globe beak sedge, granite stonecrop, and confederate daisy.

A host of rare plants occur on mountain outcrops and cliffs, and in other high elevation openings such as grassy balds, heath balds, and seeps (See grassy balds discussion.). Wiser (1994) lists 17 species (out of a total of 288 species found in a study of 145 outcrops) that are restricted to high-elevation outcrops. These include federally endangered Appalachian avens, mountain bluet, and threatened Blue Ridge goldenrod, Heller's gayfeather, and mountain golden-heather. The high-elevation outcrop flora include local endemics, Cain's reed grass and mountain golden-heather; species related to northern Appalachian alpine species, Sitka alder, Greenland stichwort, highland rush, fir club-moss, and Northern bent grass; and southern Appalachian endemics, wretched sedge, Appalachian avens, Blueridge St. John's-wort, mountain dwarf-dandelion, Heller's gayfeather, and Piedmont groundsel. The more northerly species are considered to be relicts from Pleistocene alpine communities (Quarterman et al. 1993).

Unlike other outcrop habitats, waterfall spray zones are perpetually wet, providing conditions suitable for diverse non-vascular (mosses and liverworts) plant communities. Some species are common in more northerly locales, while other have their closest relatives in the tropics. These sheltered habitats may have served as refuges for species found in the Southeast before Pleistocene glaciations (Zartman and Pitillo 1998).

Sandstone outcrops and glades.—On the Cumberland Plateau in Alabama, Kentucky, and Tennessee, sandstone outcrops occur on canyon shoulders and on flats. They are mixed with limestone outcrops in northwestern Arkansas. Shallow soils support lichen and moss mats, while somewhat deeper soils support annual three-awn grasses or little false bluestem and silky wild oat grass, and a variety of forbs such as lance-leaf tickseed, Michaux's wood-aster, orange-grass, Appalachian stitchwort, and small-head gayfeather. Deeper soils support a shrub-herb community. Sandstone outcrops contain some species of granite outcrops (dense-tuft hair sedge, quill fameflower, Menges' fameflower, elf orpine), as well as unique endemics such as Little River Canyon onion, woodland tickseed, and Gulf pipewort.

Plant communities of Nuttal's rayless-goldenrod with mixed grasses and forbs, (for examples, scaly gayfeather, dissected beardtongue, and sandhill St. John's-wort) are associated with sandstone boulders, flats, and ledges in the Upper Coastal Plain in Georgia, northern Louisiana, and eastern Texas. Soils are acid sandy loams or silty clay loams that can be saturated in winter, and dry and hardened in the summer. Fires starting in surrounding longleaf-wiregrass communities may have controlled succession in these habitats, but because fuel accumulates slowly, the habitats probably burned infrequently.

Limestone outcrops and glades.—The limestone outcrops and glades of central Tennessee, northern Alabama, and northern Arkansas are extensive. Early explorers described these areas, and contemporary biologists continue to study them, attempting to document their diversity and understand their ecology (Quarterman et al. 1993).

Glades vary from site to site, which is reflected in the large number of endemic and near-endemic plant species (Table 4; Baskin and Baskin 1986, 1989), and within a given site. Cryptogams and small herbs, including many winter annuals, dominate gravelly areas; perennial herbs and grasses increase in importance, and glade communities grade into grass-dominated barrens (see below) as soil depth increases. Shrubs such as false buckthorn, rusty blackhaw, winged sumac, and maidenbush, and trees, notably Eastern red cedar, can establish in crevices that afford adequate soil and water; but mostly harsh conditions keep glades open.

The limestone glades of the Ozarks are found on hillsides, benches, and ledges. They are more prairie-like than those of the Interior Low Plateau, being dominated by perennial grasses such as little false bluestem and poverty wild oat grass. Typical herbs include prickly pear cactus, Adam's-needle, Texas stonecrop, small palafox, Michaux's gladecress, large Indian-breadroot,

Table 4. Endemic and near-endemic plant species of limestone cedar glades in the Interior Low Plateau of central Tennessee, northern Alabama, and southern Kentucky (Baskin and Baskin 1986; Kartesz and Meacham 1999). ** indicates Federally Endangered; * indicates Federally Threatened; — indicates no common name.

Scientific Name	Common Name
Species found in 3 or fewer states	
Delphinium alabamicum Kral	Alabama Larkspur
Echinacea tennesseensis (Beadle) Small**	Tennessee Purple-Coneflower
Leavenworthia alabamica var. alabamica Rollins	Alabama Gladecress
Leavenworthia alabamica var. *brachystyla* Rollins	—
Leavenworthia crassa var. *crassa* Rollins	Fleshy-Fruit Gladecress
Leavenworthia crassa var. *elongata* Rollins	—
Leavenworthia exigua var. *exigua* Rollins	Tennessee Gladecress
Leavenworthia exigua var. *laciniata* Rollins	—
Leavenworthia exigua var. *lutea* Rollins	—
Leavenworthia stylosa Gray	Cedar Gladecress
Leavenworthia torulosa Gray	Necklace Gladecress
Lesquerella lyrata Rollins*	Lyre-Leaf Bladderpod
Lobelia appendiculata var. *gattingeri* (Gray) McVaugh	Gattinger's Pale Lobelia
Pediomelum subacaule (Torr. & Gray) Rydb.	White-Rim Indian-Breadroot
Phacelia dubia var. *interior* Fern.	Small-Flower Scorpion-Weed
Phacelia dubia var. *georgiana* McVaugh	—
Solidago shortii Torr. & Gray**	Short's Goldenrod
Talinum calcaricum Ware	Limestone Fameflower
Species found in 4 or fewer states including the Ozarks	
Dalea gattingeri (Heller) Barneby	Purple-Tassels
Onosmodium molle ssp. *subsetosum* (Mackenzie & Bush)Cochrane	Soft-Hair Marbleseed
Solidago gattingeri Chapman	Gattinger's Goldenrod
Species found in 5 or fewer states including Midwestern states	
Astragalus tennesseensis Gray ex Chapman	Tennessee Milk-Vetch
Dalea foliosa (Gray) Barneby**	Leafy Prairie-Clover
Hypericum dolabriforme Vent.	Straggling St. John's-Wort
Onosmodium molle ssp. *molle* Michx.	Soft-Hair Marbleseed
Viola egglestonii Brainerd	Glade Violet

large-flower tickseed, smartweed leaf-flower, rock sandwort, and limestone adder's-tongue. Associated shrubs include upland swamp-privet, fragrant sumac, and coral-berry. To distinguish these communities from Central Basin glades, Baskin et al. (1994) described them as xeric limestone prairies. Historically, xeric limestone prairies were probably maintained by fire, drought, and grazing. Without disturbances to remove woody species, shrubs invade.

Threats and management.—Threats to all outcrop and glade communities include development (construction, quarrying), agriculture (pasture), succession resulting from fire suppression, and non-indigenous species invasions. To retain characteristic species, management must remove or prevent woody species encroachment. Managers must regulate access, perhaps identifying trails and travel corridors. Rare species should be protected and monitored.

Barrens, Prairies, and Other Perennial Grasslands

Communities discussed in this section vary from dense sod forming to bunch grass types. They generally occur as small to medium (2-20 acre) islands, separated from other openings by forested habitats. Grasses common to many barrens include little false bluestem, Indiangrass, and big bluestem. Legumes and composites are well represented. There are few endemics and few federally listed plants (e.g., endangered Schweinitz's sunflower, smooth purple-coneflower, and Tennessee purple-coneflower) associated with barrens, but most states with grassland remnants list a number of grassland species of state concern, such as Oglethorpe oak, Gattinger's pale lobelia, ridge-stem false foxglove, Heller's bird's-foot-trefoil, and Georgia American-aster (DeSelm and Murdock 1993, Deselm 1994, Webb et al. 1997, Leidolf and McDaniel 1998).

Grasslands overlap with limestone and sandstone glade distributions in the Interior Low Plateau (Big Barrens, Kentucky; Highland Rim and Central Basin, Tennessee), Ridge and Valley Section (Alabama, Tennessee), Cumberland Plateau (Kentucky, Tennessee, Alabama), and the Interior Highlands (mostly Ozarks, Arkansas, Oklahoma). They are found on nearly level to rolling sites in the Central Basin and Big Barrens, and occur on cliff tops, ledges and hillsides in the other areas. Little false bluestem and yellow Indian grass commonly dominate interior barrens. Additional species include side-oats grama, big bluestem, and a variety of composites and legumes.

Other grassland habitats are associated with special soil types, mostly developed over marl, chalk, or clayey substrates in the upper Gulf Coastal Plain and Mississippi Alluvial Plain (Alabama, Mississippi, Louisiana, Texas). Such soils (typically alfisols and vertisols) are not very permeable, and with shrink-swell clays provide difficult growing conditions that slow woody species invasions. These include the blackland prairies (Jackson Prairie, Black Prairie) (Alabama, Mississippi), the Grand Prairie of eastern Arkansas (over loess-capped alluvial deposits), grasslands on calcareous clayey soils in northern Louisiana, eastern Texas, and southwestern Arkansas. They occupy gently rolling topography and are dominated by little false bluestem, often with Indian grass and rarely with side-oats grama. Switchgrass and big bluestem may be found on wetter sites. Blackland prairies include many other grasses and a rich forb flora with such rare species as ear-leaf false foxglove, ridge-stem false foxglove, and whorled rosinweed (Leidolf and McDaniel 1998).

Remnants of a once-extensive coastal prairie are found in the lower West Gulf Coastal Plain of east Texas and southwestern Louisiana. This is the only southeastern grassland formally mapped as part of the midwest prairie ecosystem. As in other grasslands, species composition varies with site moisture: grama, switchgrass, little false bluestem, or Florida crown grass are found on wetter sites; little false bluestem and Indian grass are more common on upland sites.

Barrens with grassland species are scattered through the Southern Blue Ridge and Piedmont (South Carolina, North Carolina, Virginia), especially on soils with high concentrations of calcium and magnesium. In the absence of occasional fires, open pine canopies may develop. These barrens provide the habitats for federally endangered smooth purple-coneflower and Schweinitz's sunflower. These may be remnant from grassland habitats historically widespread in the Piedmont (Barden 1997), and evident today as populations of grassland species in managed grassy rights-of-way.

Threats and management.—In total, grass-dominated habitats have been lost rapidly, but estimates of original extent and rate of loss are difficult to make. They continue to be threatened by conversion to agriculture, recreational use, exotic species invasions, and fire exclusion. Their conservation and restoration depend on controlling the invasion of woody species from adjacent forest habitats, and probably require prescribed burning to restore (see Chester et al. 1997) and maintain the diversity of the grassland communities.

Canebrakes

Areas dominated by giant cane were once common throughout the Southeast, especially in alluvial corridors. Based on historical accounts, canebrakes were extensive, especially on the deep rich soils of the Bluegrass Region of Kentucky, an area with almost no natural vegetation remaining (Noss et al. 1995); only scattered remnants remain. Treeless or nearly treeless (Platt and Brantley 1997) canebrakes likely developed where native Americans abandoned agricultural sites, and were maintained with periodic burning by Indians and European settlers. They declined with overgrazing by domestic livestock, frequent burning to improve grazing resources, and land clearing for agriculture.

Threats and management.—Threats to canebrakes lie in the interruption of disturbance regimes. Cane invades disturbed sites such as roadsides, old fields, and cut over forest sites, and resprouts after fires, if not burned too frequently (Hughes 1966, Platt and Brantley 1997). Existing canebrakes may benefit from a combination of overstory removal, periodic burning (once every 7-10 years), and perhaps fertilization. Recent studies have shown that cane restoration is difficult because seedlings grow slowly and competition in alluvial sites is intense (Eddleman et al. 1980, Feeback and Luken 1992, Platt and Brantley 1993). Improving extant

Smooth purple coneflower, Oconee County, SC. The endangered Smooth Purple Cone-flower is found in prairie-like grassland remnants in VA, NC, SC, and GA. Related coneflowers are found in barren and glade communities throughout the Southeast. Tennessee Purple Coneflower, restricted to the limestone cedar glades of Tennessee, is also federally endangered. All species of Purple Coneflowers (*Echinacea* spp.) are collected, often illegally, for the medicinal herb market *(J. Walker)*.

Grassy balds, Roan Mountain, NC. Views are spectacular from the grassy balds of the southern Appalachians. They provide habitats for some rare plants, but they are valued as much for their cultural and historical significance. Famous displays of native rhododendrons have attracted visitors for decades. The balds are being reduced as trees and shrubs invade from adjacent communities (seen at the left in this photo). Some combination of grazing, herbicide, prescribed burning, and mechanical removal will be needed to control woody plants *(J. Walker)*.

sites may prove the best option for keeping canebrakes in the southern landscape.

Grassy Balds

Grassy balds occur on mountaintops and ridges in the southern Blue Ridge Mountains (North Carolina, Tennessee), at about 4,700-6,000 feet, especially on south and west aspects (DeSelm and Murdock 1993; Lindsay and Bratton 1979; White and Sutter 1998). Grassy balds occur on shallow acid soils on gentle to steep slopes. They are generally considered to be of anthropogenic origin, and are being lost as shrubs and trees (ericaceous shrubs, fire-cherry, blackberry, oaks and hawthorns) invade from adjacent communities. Bald vegetation is a mosaic of herbaceous and shrubby communities. Although no species are considered strictly endemic to balds, balds provide habitat for a number of federally listed plants and a dozen G1-G3 ranked species (Table 5). White and Sutter (1998) identify an additional twenty-three species of concern to the Tennessee and North Carolina state heritage programs.

Threats and management.—Woody plant encroachment and recreational use threaten bald communities. Maintenance and restoration approaches have included herbicide use, prescribed fire, mowing/hand-cutting, and grazing. A combination of these various methods will probably be most effective (Deselm and Murdock 1993).

ISOLATED WETLANDS

Among the most vulnerable wetlands are small, isolated wetlands that harbor sensitive plant communities throughout the region. They require distinct hydrological conditions to function ecologically and to retain characteristic species. Most are surrounded by lands that have been altered for agriculture or silviculture, and are affected by the practices applied to adjacent lands.

Mountain Bogs and Fens

Small wetlands occur in depressions or flats in otherwise hilly or mountainous terrain (Richardson and Gibbons, 1993; Moorhead and Rossell, 1998). Historically, mountain wetlands, locally described as bogs or seeps, probably occurred in every mountainous county in the South. They range in elevation from 1,200-1,500 ft, and overlie a variety of rock types that influence water quality. Individual sites are usually small

Table 5. Rare and endemic plants found on grassy balds (after White and Sutter 1998). Under rarity G1, G2, G3 are the top levels for globally rare plants under the Nature Conservancy ranking system. Other habitats for each species are noted. ** indicates Federally Endangered.

Scientific Name	Common Name	Distribution	Rarity	Other habitats
Carex misera Buckl.	Wretched Sedge	Endemic	G3	Outcrops
Delphinium exaltatum Ait.	Tall Larkspur	Northern	G3	Rich woods, rocky slopes
Geum geniculatum Michx.	Bent Avens	Endemic	G1	Moist, rocky woods
*Geum radiatum Michx.***	Appalachian Avens	Endemic	G3	Outcrops
Glyceria nubigena W.A. Anderson Manna Grass	Great Smoky Mtn.	Endemic	G2	Seeps, streams
Houstonia purpurea var. *montana* (Small) Terrell**	Mountain Bluet	Endemic	G1	Rocky summits
Lilium grayi S. Wats.	Gray's Lily	Endemic	G2	Forest openings, meadows, seeps
Prenanthes roanensis Chickering	Roan Mtn.Rattlesnake Root	Endemic	G3	Seeps, woods
Rhododendron cumberlandense E.L. Braun	Cumberland Rhododendron	Endemic	G2Q	Openings
Rhododendron vaseyi Gray	Pink-Shell Azalea	Endemic	G3	Seeps, swamps
Rugelia nudicaulis Shuttlw. Ex Chapman	Rugel's-Indian-Plantain	Endemic	G3	Woods
Stachys clingmanii Small	Clingman's Hedge-Nettle	Endemic	G3Q	Seeps, woods

Pitcher plants are the most visible of the carnivorous plants that can be found in the bogs of the coastal plain. They occur as dense extensive colonies in some sites, but are limited to isolated clumps in others. The insectivorous plants of the Southeast do not rely entirely on consuming insects, but captured insects may provide additional phosphorus and nitrogen to individuals growing in these extremely nutrient-poor habitats *(J. Walker)*.

(1-5 acres), and often are embedded within forested vegetation or make up part of a forest and bog complex.

The soils are saturated for extended periods during the year. Technically, the wet condition of bogs is maintained primarily by rainfall input, while groundwater seepage maintains fens. Often both precipitation and ground water influence individual sites. Wetlands predominantly supplied by groundwater, especially seeping through calcareous substrates, tend to be more nutrient-rich and less acidic.

Mountain wetlands may be forested, though often with sparse canopies, or they may be open herb-dominated communities. Acidic Appalachian and Cumberland Mountain bogs (Schafele and Weakley 1990) have raised mats or hummocks of mosses, primarily sphagnum. Along with alder and willows, members of the blueberry family dominate the shrub layer. Typically scattered trees include red maple, white pine, Canada hemlock, and red spruce. Grasses, sedges and some shrubs dominate circum-neutral wetlands in high elevation flats of northwestern North Carolina, seeps and springs in the Ouachitas, and in calcareous seeps in the southern Ridge and Valley sections of Alabama and Tennessee.

Murdock (1994) listed 21 species of state concern in mountain wetlands, including federally endangered mountain sweet pitcherplant, green pitcherplant, bunched arrowhead, and threatened swamp pink.

Threats and management.—Mountain wetland occurrences have been much reduced since European settlement. Many have been destroyed directly by grazing, logging, mining, acid mine drainage, residential

Hillside bog, Kisatchie National Forest, Louisiana. Bogs on the lower coastal plain are often flat or concave, but further inland in the geologically older marine terraces bogs may occur in seepage areas on the sides of hills (as shown in this photo). In addition to carnivorous plants, seepage bogs contain a diversity of other herbs, especially sedges, grasses and composites. Notice the young longleaf pines that have established, and the evergreen shrubs at the bottom of the slope. These communities are easily shaded out as woody species increase in the absence of fire *(R. Costa)*.

Table 6. Characteristics of three coastal plain depression habitats.

	Carolina Bays	Karst ponds	Citronelle ponds
Distribution	se NC, SC, e GA	FL panhandle w of Suwanee River and contiguous sw GA and se AL	central Gulf coastal plain-Pearl River Co.,MS to Okaloosa Co., FL
Formation process	removal of surface substrate by wind or meteoritic impact	dissolution of underlying limestone	dissolution and removal of kaolinitic clays from surface
Water source	rainfall, runoff, shallow seepage; some spring-fed	rainfall, runoff, shallow seepage; deep ground water	rainfall, runoff, shallow seepage
Profile	gradual side-slopes	gradual side slopes	abrupt slope, flat bottoms
References	Richardson and Gibbons 1993 Sharitz and Gresham 1998	Sutter and Kral 1994	Folkerts 1997

development, agriculture, inundation in artificial reservoirs, and recreational off-road vehicle use. Any activity that alters the surrounding watershed will degrade these sensitive wetlands.

Considering the scarcity of mountain fens, preservation and restoration may be the preferred management goals. Maintaining site hydrology is the primary objective. Secondarily, woody plant invasion must be controlled. The natural role of fire for controlling shrub and tree encroachment is debated, and its use may best be considered with respect to individual types (Schafale and Weakley 1990). For example, fire may be effective in sites that contain remnant populations of species associated with fire on the coastal plain, but may be inappropriate in other wetland types.

Coastal Plain Herb Bogs: Seepage Bogs, Hillside Bogs, Pitcher Plant Bogs

Thirty-nine carnivorous plant species, 85% of all carnivorous plant species that occur in North America, are found in the Southeast, and over half of those are endemic to the Atlantic and Gulf Coastal Plains. These species abound in wet habitats collectively referred to as carnivorous plant bogs. The bogs have acidic and low nutrient status soils and are found in poorly drained sites throughout the coastal plains including the fall-line sandhills regions. The largest examples occur in the lower coastal terraces in the East Gulf Coastal Plain (Folkerts 1982). They range from large poorly drained flats to small depressions in surrounding pine woodlands to narrow ecotones between upslope pines and downslope swamps or shrub bogs. On the Lower Coastal Plain, pitcher plant bogs grade into seasonally wet savannahs (See longleaf pine communities). Bogs grade down slope into shrubby or forested communities including shrub bogs and bayheads.

In addition to carnivorous species, the bog flora is known for its diversity of orchids (rosebud, fringed and fringeless, pogonia), lilies (yellow-eyed grass, featherling, rush-featherling, lilies) and graminoids, especially small sedges (beak sedge, nut-rushes, fimbry). Federally listed plants that occur near or with carnivorous species include Harper's Beauty (endangered) and rough-leaved loosestrife (threatened).

These communities are typically embedded in pine-dominated (longleaf pine or slash pine) woodlands or forests. Fires that started in the surrounding pine uplands and burned into the bogs were critical for eliminating or limiting woody species encroachments (Frost et al. 1986). Historically, coastal plain herbaceous bogs burned about as frequently as the surrounding uplands (approximately every 3-5 years), but in wet, very low productivity sites where fuels accumulate slowly less frequent fires may have maintained herbaceous bogs.

Coastal plain bogs have water at or near the surface for much of the year, the water coming from upslope seepage, precipitation, or both (Gibson 1983). Saturated soil conditions allow for some peat accumulations, but most of these sites have fine-textured mineral soils that can support pines, especially with fertilization. Planted pines shade out herbs, and as they grow, dry out the sites facilitating the establishment and growth of a different plant community. Saturated conditions help retard woody plant growth that can eventually shade out the herb community.

Threats and management.—Fire exclusion across the pinelands and bogs results in increased woody plant components and reduced species richness, and threatens carnivorous plant habitats. Ironically, in the past the use of prescribed fire contributed to the loss of these sensitive bog communities because fire control lines often were plowed through the bogs to prevent fire moving into adjacent shrub communities and swamps. Maintaining these communities requires that the water sources remain intact and that sites are burned regularly to control woody species invasion. Additionally, excluding heavy equipment that can produce long-lasting ruts in these wet soils is important. If species have been lost through time, reintroductions into isolated sites may be required.

Coastal Plain Depressions and Pond

Depression wetlands are widespread throughout the Southeast, but are especially prevalent in the Coastal Plain (Ewel 1998, Sharitz and Gresham 1998). Various overlapping types, including Carolina bays, karst ponds, lime sinks, cypress domes, Citronelle ponds, and sandhill ponds, have been described. [Note: These habitats are physiognomically and compositionally similar to shrub dominated palustrine wetlands including shrub bogs, bayheads, bayhead or bay swamps, baygalls, streamhead pocosins, and pocosins. No habitat classification clearly distinguishes among these types (Sharitz and Gresham 1998). All are defined as non-alluvial wetlands (Sutter and Kral 1997), that is, wetlands with variable hydroperiods occurring in basins or depressions, or on slopes, with no connection to above-ground stream or river systems. Water levels are not dependent on stream or river dynamics. This section describes Carolina bays, karst ponds, and citronelle ponds (Table 6). All are generally isolated, round to oval formations, which may contain open water ponds, and are completely surrounded (historically) by forested vegetation; however, origins, distributions, and water sources differ.

Within all types vegetation varies. Factors that determine the type of vegetation at a given site include hydroperiod, fire frequency, presence of organic matter, and water source (Ewel 1990). Furthermore, vegetation can vary considerably from year to year. Sustaining diversity through time depends in part on the presence of viable and diverse seed banks (Sutter and Kral 1994).

Depression wetlands provide essential habitat for reptiles and amphibians that tolerate or require variable hydroperiods (Dodd 1992, 1995; Semlitsch and Bodie 1998) and for a few rare plants including the federally endangered Canby's dropwort.

Carolina Bays.—Carolina Bays are oval-shaped and oriented with the long axis running generally northwest to southeast (Richardson and Gibbons 1993; Sharitz and Gresham 1998). Size ranges from a few acres to several thousand. Carolina Bays are associated with sandy substrates, often with underlying lenses of impervious clays that hold water in overlying layers, but surface organic layers accumulate where soil disturbances are minimal. Zoned vegetation grades from forested or shrub communities through emergent herb communities and floating and submerged aquatics in the deeper water.

Some bays are filled with predominantly evergreen shrubs and bay forest species such as fetterbush, redbay, loblolly-bay, titi, inkberry, highbush blueberry, red chokeberry, huckleberries, and wax myrtle. Others contain forest or woodland communities dominated variously by pond cypress, pond pine, tupelo, and associated species. Herb zones may ring the bays in some cases, especially where fire is used to manage the surrounding landscape. Sutter and Kral (1994) describe pond cypress savannahs. These unique communities have an open canopy of pond-cypress and a diverse herbaceous ground layer, which includes federally threatened Canby's dropwort.

Karst Ponds, Limesinks, Dolines.—Karst depression communities are reviewed by Sutter and Kral (1994). Unlike other isolated depression communities, these communities are influenced to some degree by deep ground water. Owing to a dependence on subsurface water, water levels change over decades rather than months, and the water quality depends partly on regional water quality.

The typically gently sloping sides of karst depressions result in a characteristically zoned vegetation: surrounding forest or shrubs give way to sandy beaches dominated by grasses and sedges, and finally to open water. They are embedded in sandy uplands dominated on yellow sands by longleaf pine, deciduous scrub oaks and hickories, and wiregrass; and on white sands by sand pine, evergreen scrub oaks, and heaths. The forested fringe typically has evergreen oaks, hollies and heaths; shrub zones are evergreen and influenced by the water levels. Open sandy beaches vary from site to site, seasonally and from year to year depending on water levels. Sedges are abundant and common herb genera include yellow-eyed grass, pipeworts, arrowheads, primrose-willows, and rose-gentians. Carnivorous sundews and bladderworts are common. Tall emergent and submerged species are found in deeper water. Rare and endemic plant species include panhandle meadow-beauty, smooth-bark St. John's-wort, Harper's yellow-eyed-grass, and Kral's yellow-eyed-grass. Karst ponds are important breeding habitat for flatwoods salamander (proposed for federal listing) and gopher frog.

Citronelle Ponds.—This habitat type is named for the Citronelle Formation, which defines their distribution, and is synonymous with Grady ponds so named for the soil type that typifies them (Folkerts 1997). The highest concentrations (as high as 4/mi2) occur in western Escambia County, Alabama. They range in size from 6-10 feet across to occupy areas as large as 200 acres. Ponds are rain-filled by mid-winter, remain high until mid-April, and then drop through October with some drying completely. They are typically shallow and flat-bottomed, the vegetation changing abruptly from surrounding vegetation types.

Citronelle depressions were naturally forested with pond-cypress or swamp or both. Past logging has left some ponds treeless today. Shrubs and small trees of the shallow edges include yaupon, slash pine, wax myrtle, red maple, mayhaw, Virginia willow, sweet pepperbush, and fetter bush. Spanish moss and laural-leaf greenbriar are common, but understory vegetation is never dense. Shallow water herbs include Virginia chain fern, saw-grass, pipewort, yellow-eyed grasses, Georgia tickseed, and tall pine-barren milkwort. Adjacent forests probably were mixed deciduous-broadleaf evergreen forests with longleaf pines dominating more distant uplands. There are no rare species reported from Citronelle ponds.

Threats and management.—Throughout the region, depressions are lost directly by conversion to agriculture and forestry, and are adversely affected indirectly by management in the adjacent uplands. Management in the uplands regulates both water quality and frequency of burning. Historically, depression vegetation probably burned in drought years (perhaps 1/15-20 years according to Folkerts 1997) as fire burned into them from the surrounding pyrophyllic vegetation. Fire exclusion in the uplands eliminates fire in the wetlands and results in the reduction of herbaceous community. Further, amphibians that depend on these generally fish-free environments for breeding also require nearby fire-maintained uplands to complete their life cycles. Finally, depression communities, especially in the Gulf Coastal Plain, are being lost to invasive non-indigenous plants such as privet, Japanese honeysuckle, and Chinese tallow tree.

Restoring or maintaining natural hydrology is critical for management. This may involve closing any artificial drainage ditches, as well as protecting the immediate watershed. For maintaining karst communities, protecting regional quality may be necessary to ensure sensitive community composition. Generous buffers into the uplands should be established to protect watershed quality. Fire should be used in the surrounding habitats to restore natural ecotonal patterns and habitat values. Burning may also retain habitat values for amphibians and help control non-indigenous species. To protect seedbanks, which are important in isolated wetlands, preserve natural soil dynamics and avoid large-scale disturbances that may deplete the seed bank unnaturally.

FACTORS AFFECTING SENSITIVE COMMUNITY MANAGEMENT

The goal of managing sensitive communities is to retain or restore the composition, structure and function of these communities. Given the losses of natural areas and disruptions in natural disturbance and hydrological regimes, most sensitive communities will depend on active management. Several factors are likely to influence the success of management. First, many sensitive communities are found on private lands and their persistence requires the commitment of private landowners to management. The value of small tracts for conserving diversity is sometimes overlooked, but populations of rare plants with possible unique genetic composition can persist for long times in small areas. Additionally, retaining small areas of sensitive communities may enhance larger landscape diversity.

Secondly, managers must be aware that sensitive communities often occur as inclusions in different and often highly modified landscapes, like grassland remnants in forests or forest remnants in agricultural landscapes. The integrity of sensitive communities often depends on the condition and management of surrounding lands. For example, water quality in a mountain seep may be impaired by runoff from surrounding grazed pastures. Or, the values of a coastal plain depression pond may be diminished if the surrounding uplands are not burned. Management may have to create conditions at small scales that once depended on larger scale processes (like flooding or burning), or to simulate processes (like gene flow via pollination or propagule dispersal) that once occurred at larger scales. Cooperative efforts among adjacent landowners may provide opportunities for maintaining sensitive communities on complex landscapes.

Recognizing that current landscapes are very different from conditions in which today's sensitive communities originally developed must influence the choice of management objectives. In this chapter frequent reference is made to historical conditions, but presettlement conditions are not necessarily the desired management objectives. Also, presettlement conditions may not be achievable; for example, landscape scale burning is not feasible. However, presumed historical conditions along with current conditions and observations of recent community change do provide management guidance (White and Walker 1997). Especially on small tracts, it may be more practical to identify specific conditions to be maintained or achieved. For example, where a population of rare plants occurs, management objectives may be stated in terms of providing suitable habitat conditions for that single species. Where possible, achieving those objectives with processes that more or less resemble natural ecological process is likely to sustain other ecological values.

Third, the lack of information always presents challenges to management. In the absence of information, managers may adopt an adaptive management approach of determining actions based on available information, observing outcomes, and adjusting future actions. Monitoring to learn from management actions, and communicating knowledge gained from monitoring, will enhance the likelihood of conserving biodiversity in the South.

Finally, over the long-term managers encounter unanticipated problems. Some of these may be foreseen, but not easily controlled, such as climate change, disease epidemics, insect epidemics. The ongoing loss of Fraser fir forests presents a vivid example of an unforeseen impact on a forest type that has always been rare. Though remaining fir forests are protected from logging, efforts have failed to protect the forests from an exotic insect, the balsam woolly adelgid. With unpredictable threats possible for sensitive communities, a useful strategy is to manage in a way that conserves genetic diversity, thereby protecting the capacity for plant species to evolve and adapt to changing conditions over time.

CHAPTER 6

Principles of Landscape Ecology for Conservation of Wildlife and Biodiversity

Frank R. Thompson, III
North Central Research Station
USDA Forest Service, Columbia, MO

The abundance and distribution of wildlife cannot be completely understood solely from the composition and structure of individual habitat patches. Processes occurring in the surrounding landscape, as well as larger and smaller spatial scales also affect most species. This realization has resulted in a growing interest by managers and scientists in landscape ecology and the importance of a multi-scale perspective in wildlife management. Because patches make up landscapes, I begin with a review of patch characteristics and processes. I then review terms and ideas about landscape composition, structure, and processes, and illustrate these points with examples based on some of the species in this book. I conclude by demonstrating how a landscape perspective, and a multi-scale perspective in general, is important to maintaining regional biological diversity. One chapter cannot cover landscape considerations for all southern forest wildlife; however, this short review will provide a valuable perspective that can be used with the species specific information provided in other chapters.

A landscape is a mosaic of habitat patches. Its scale or size may be a few acres to many square miles. A landscape's size is usually defined based on the organisms or ecosystems being managed or studied. Landscapes generally encompass the area in which individuals live and disperse, or the area within which processes affect individuals or populations of interest (Forman and Godron 1986, Turner 1989, Dunning et al. 1992).

PATCHES

The identification or definition of habitat patches in a landscape depends on the perception of an organism of interest. A habitat is an area with the appropriate combination of resources (food, cover, water) and environmental conditions for survival and reproduction of a species. A habitat patch is a contiguous block of habitat. Patches are relatively discrete and homogenous, and habitat quality or fitness varies among patches for the organism under consideration. A habitat patch can be a group of shrubs and saplings in a gap created by a blowdown, or a 1,000-acre island of forest surrounded by cropland. Forest stands are often treated analogously to habitat patches; this may or may not be appropriate and depends on the organisms being considered. Stands are an alternative way to define patches that

We are beginning to understand the relationships of habitat fragmentation and population phenomena of species and communities *(J. Woodward, Cornell Lab of Ornithology)*.

reflect silvicultural conditions rather than wildlife. Stands are generally defined as a contiguous group of trees sufficiently uniform in species composition, age structure, and condition to be distinguished as a management unit (Smith 1986). In practice, forest stands can be a useful definition of habitat patches, particularly if nested within a broader ecological classification system.

The origins or causative mechanisms of patches, and characteristics such as size and shape, have significant effects on the processes that occur in and around patches, as well as the wildlife species that inhabit them (Forman and Godron 1986). Important processes that occur within patches are plant succession and disturbance, and species reproduction, mortality, emigration, immigration, extinction, and colonization.

Disturbance Patches

Disturbance of a small area in a landscape creates a disturbance patch (Forman and Godron 1986). Fire, windstorms, and timber harvest or other management activities can create disturbance patches in forests. A disturbance patch is relatively small when compared to the total size of the landscape and often results in a isolated patch of habitat that differs from the surrounding landscape. Several common processes and changes in community composition and structure almost universally occur after the creation of a disturbance patch, and are sometimes referred to as post-disturbance species dynamics (Forman and Godron 1986). Immediately after a disturbance certain species become locally extinct as a result of death or emigration from the newly created disturbance patch. Some species common before the disturbance persist at reduced levels, and other species rare before the disturbance may dramatically increase after the disturbance. New species also immigrate and colonize the newly created patch. After this initial response succession continues and involves all of these processes: changes in population size, immigration, emigration, and changes in abundance and extinction in the patch.

Species dynamics in disturbance patches have been reported for forest birds and timber harvest. Timber harvest creates disturbance patches that range from single tree gaps to group selection openings and clearcuts. Birds that breed in mature forest, such as the Acadian flycatcher, Eastern wood-pewee, red-eyed vireo, and scarlet tanager, typically emigrate from recently logged habitats while early-successional species (blue-winged warblers, prairie warblers, and indigo buntings) rapidly colonize disturbance patches such as clearcuts and group selection openings. As forest succession returns the patch to mature forest habitat there are continual changes in species abundance and recolonization by mature forest species (Dickson et al. 1995, Thompson et al. 1995, Thompson et al. 1996).

Remnant Patches

Remnant patches are created when widespread changes in the surrounding landscape result in a small patch or remnant of the original habitat. Large-scale processes such as fire or conversion to agriculture or other human-dominated habitats can result in remnant patches of forest. Remnant patches are often the result of habitat fragmentation, which is the breaking up of blocks of habitat (see discussion of habitat fragmentation later in this chapter). Remnant patches are often referred to as habitat islands and many parallels have been drawn between dynamics of remnant patches and oceanic islands (reviewed by Faaborg et al. 1995).

While the mechanisms creating remnant patches are essentially the inverse of that for disturbance patches, there are similarities in their patch dynamics. Remnant patches can also have large changes in species abundance, immigration, emigration, and extinction. Remnant patches often have elevated rates of extinction and then gradually reach equilibrium. This process was first described for oceanic islands (MacArthur and Wilson 1963) and later applied to habitat patches. The species that become extinct in remnant patches are usually those with small populations, those with large territories, or those that are sensitive to interactions with the surrounding landscape which has been disturbed.

Other Types Of Patches

Disturbance and remnant patches are perhaps the two most basic types of patches but a variety of other terms are used to describe patches. Environmental resource patches are the result of naturally occurring environmental conditions dynamics (Forman and Godron 1986). For example, wetlands and glades are the result of hydrologic and geologic processes or patterns. Environmental resource patches are often more stable than disturbance patches. A variety of types of introduced patches also occur in landscapes, for example forestry plantations or agricultural fields.

Patch Characteristics

In addition to the habitat type, the most basic characteristics of patches are size and shape (Forman and Godron 1986). Patch size can be an important determinant of the suitability of a patch for a species, population viability, and as a result, species richness. Many studies have investigated the relationship between patch size and species richness, primarily for forest birds. They found the number of species increased with patch size (see Askins et al. 1990, Robinson and Wilcove 1994, Faaborg et al. 1995 for reviews). Very small disturbance patches in forest landscapes are avoided by some species like the prairie warbler, and preferred by other species like the hooded warbler (Annand and Thompson 1997). Minimum area requirements have been developed for some species (Robbins 1979), but these are generally based on species occurrence and do not address species viability and source-sink interactions (see discussion later in this chapter). Some reasons for species absence from small habitat patches are large area requirements by species, random or periodic extinction of small populations, and reduced species viability due to competition or predation from animals in adjoining habitats (Robinson and Wilcove 1994).

Edge is the border or ecotone between patches. Several patterns or processes, often referred to as edge effects, may occur at patch edges. Edge effects can include changes in animal and plant diversity or abundance, increased interactions among species from adjoining habitats, (predators, competitors, parasites, and humans), and changes in the micro-climate.

Patch shape can have similar effects on the suitability of patches or species richness. The shape of a patch influences the amount of the patch that is in close proximity to the adjoining habitat, or the ratio of patch perimeter to patch area. Species that inhabit edges or that benefit from proximity to adjoining habitats (see discussion of landscape complementation) will benefit from irregular shaped patches with a high perimeter to area ratio. Species negatively affected by edge or proximity to adjoining habitats are sometimes called edge sensitive and will benefit from larger patches with compact or circular shapes that minimize the perimeter to area ratio. The concept of core area was developed to assess the value of patches for edge-sensitive wildlife (Temple 1986). It is the area of the patch that is some minimum distance from the patch perimeter or edge (typically 50 to 200yds when considering forest birds). Core area integrates the effects of patch size and shape.

Patches also have temporal characteristics. Disturbance patches tend to be ephemeral because plant succession usually returns them to a condition similar to the surrounding habitat. Environmental resource patches tend to be more stable because geologic or hydrologic processes work very slowly. Some introduced patches also change little because of repeated disturbance or inputs by humans.

CORRIDORS

Corridors are narrow strips of land or patches that differ from the land on either side. They serve to both connect and isolate patches in a landscape (Forman and Godron 1986). Examples of corridors are wooded fencerows running through agricultural fields, powerline corridors running through forest, or roads and their rights-of-way cutting across any habitat. Corridors can function the

Figure 1. Differences in predicted numbers of some forest songbirds in 10,000 acre central hardwood landscape under different management regimes. Differences in bird abundance are the result of differences in landscape composition, as defined by forest age classes (Table 1). PRWA is prairie warbler, HOWA is hooded warbler, ACFL is Acadian flycatcher, and OVEN is ovenbird. Mature forest is an 80-year old even-aged forest; Group sel. is uneven-aged forest with group openings; Bal. eam is a landscape under even-aged management on 100 year rotation; and Group+eam is 50% Group sel. and 50% Bal. eam. Figure modified from Thompson et al. (1996).

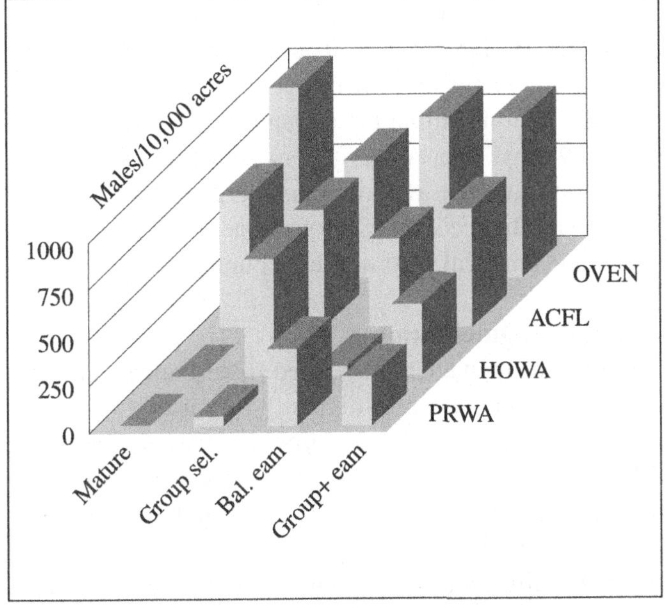

Table 1. Differences in landscape composition among forest management options. Balance even-aged regime is based on a 100-year rotation and even-aged regeneration methods. Group selection + balanced even-aged represents 50% of the landscape under each management system. Predicted differences in bird abundance among these management regimes for a Central Hardwood landscape are shown in Figure 1.

	Percent of landscape in forest age-class				
Management regime	0-10	11-20	21-40	>40	All-aged
Mature even-aged	0	0	0	100	0
Balanced even-aged	10	10	20	60	0
Group selection	0	0	0	0	100
Group selection + even-aged	5	5	10	30	50

same as patches and have similar processes and dynamics. They have, however, important additional functions. Corridors can facilitate or hamper movements of wildlife. Wooded riparian corridors or fencerows may facilitate movements of forest wildlife such as squirrels, deer, and turkeys across open habitats. Corridors can also impede movements between patches. Highway or riparian corridors may hamper movements of animals that either cannot cross them or suffer high mortality when crossing them.

LANDSCAPE STRUCTURE

The structure of a landscape affects ecological processes including species interactions and distribution (Dunning et al 1992). The relative amount of each patch type or habitat in a landscape is the landscape composition. Species composition and abundance vary among habitats; therefore, species richness and abundance in landscapes are affected by landscape composition. Measurements of landscape composition include presence, absence, relative proportion or percent, dominance, richness, and landscape diversity (Turner 1989).

In Figure 1 and Table 1 I demonstrate how landscape composition can affect densities of 4 forest birds in a central hardwood landscape. These 4 model landscapes each represent a different management regime. Landscape composition, as defined by forest age-classes, varies among the 4 landscapes as a result of even-aged and group selection methods of forest regeneration (Table 1). Because each species has different habitat preferences (see Thompson et al. 1996), bird density varies among species and management regimes (Fig. 1). It is interesting to note that the highest species diversity results from a mix of even and uneven-age silvicultural practices (see discussion of spatial heterogeneity later in this chapter).

Landscape pattern, physiognomy, or configuration is the spatial arrangement of patches or elements in the landscape. Landscape pattern also affects ecological processes and the abundance and distribution of organisms in landscapes. For example, highly fragmented landscapes consisting of small remnant patches of forest may be lacking some forest birds (Faaborg et al. 1995, Freemark et al. 1995), or species may have lower reproductive success (Robinson et al. 1995), or higher mortality rates.

Landscape structure is dynamic over time because patches are dynamic. Plant succession and disturbance are driving factors behind patch dynamics. These dynamics result in changes in species composition, abundance, and distribution in landscapes over time.

PROCESSES IN LANDSCAPES

Many different ecological processes occur in landscapes. They occur at microhabitat, patch, and landscape levels and affect individuals, populations and communities. Here I review a few that affect wildlife populations and are a function of landscape structure.

Landscape Complementation

Landscape complementation is the benefit derived by some species from the proximity of different habitats (Dunning et al. 1992). Many species require different habitats at different times in their daily or annual activities. For example, bedding and feeding habitats for white-tail deer; roosting and feeding habitats for bobwhite quail; nesting, drumming, and brood habitat for ruffed grouse; and nesting and juvenile habitat for songbirds; are often in different habitat patches. Landscape complementation occurs when landscapes support larger populations if required patch types are in close proximity than if they are farther apart. This may be because individuals can use both resources more efficiently when they are close together, or they may reduce the amount of time spent between patches where they could be exposed to predators or other unfavorable environmental conditions.

Landscape Supplementation

Landscape complementation involves the arrangement of different or non-substitutable resources. Supplementation is the benefit derived from the proximity of similar or substitutable resources or habitats. Landscape supplementation occurs when a population is larger as a result of the proximity of several similar or substitutable patches. For example, a small remnant patch of forest may be too small to support a particular species, but a cluster of remnant patches may be adequate. Some early successional songbirds such as prairie warblers and yellow-breasted chats are absent from small disturbance patches such as group selection openings (Annand and Thompson 1997), but may use a portion of a landscape where disturbance patches are clustered (F. Thompson, personal observation).

Source-Sink Interactions

Source-sink interactions occur when productive patches, called population sources, produce a surplus of offspring that emigrate and support populations in less productive patches, called population sinks (Pulliam 1988). An important consequence of this is a species may be present in a patch or landscape that could not support a population without immigration from source areas. A population may be a sink because of low reproductive success or high mortality. Populations of some Midwestern forest birds in fragmented landscapes, for example, have low reproductive success due to nest predation and brood parasitism and may be population sinks (Robinson et al. 1995, Donovan et al. 1995a).

Source-sink interactions have important consequences for wildlife management. The presence of a species or population in a habitat patch does not necessarily indicate good habitat conditions because that population could be a sink supported by immigration. Also, to maintain viable populations in or among landscapes, adequate source populations must exist to balance sink populations. For instance, if sink habitat becomes too abundant in landscapes it could drain population sources and result in a lower overall population size or even extinction (Pulliam and Danielson 1991, Donovan et al. 1995b). The conservation implications of these interactions are that wildlife managers must be aware of spatial variation in processes such as dispersal, productivity, and survival, and not just abundance.

Habitat Fragmentation

Natural and management-related disturbances, and the resulting habitats, create diversity or variety in a landscape. A diverse landscape provides habitat for many different species as well as for species that require more than one type of habitat. Too much habitat diversity, however, can reduce the quality of some habitats for some wildlife species, as habitat patches become small and fragmented. Habitat fragmentation is a process that results in increased habitat discontinuity by breaking up blocks of habitat. It ranges from the creation of small disturbance patches within a large block of habitat to widespread habitat loss resulting in small remnant patches. Habitat fragmentation can have positive or negative effects on wildlife, depending on the particular species of interest, the overall landscape composition and structure, and the level or scale of fragmentation.

Forest fragmentation is a general term that refers to the fragmentation of forest habitats by non-forest habitats. High levels of forest fragmentation have negative consequences for many forest wildlife species. For example, in southern forests large carnivores such as black bears or Florida panthers may be sensitive to habitat fragmentation by human development. Some species of forest songbirds are often absent from highly fragmented forests, and some species, while present in fragmented landscapes, have lower reproductive success there (Robinson et al. 1995). Forest fragmentation can benefit species that require both forest and non-forest habitats because it results in greater interspersion of these habitats.

Levels of forest fragmentation can be measured by landscape measures such as the percent forest cover and

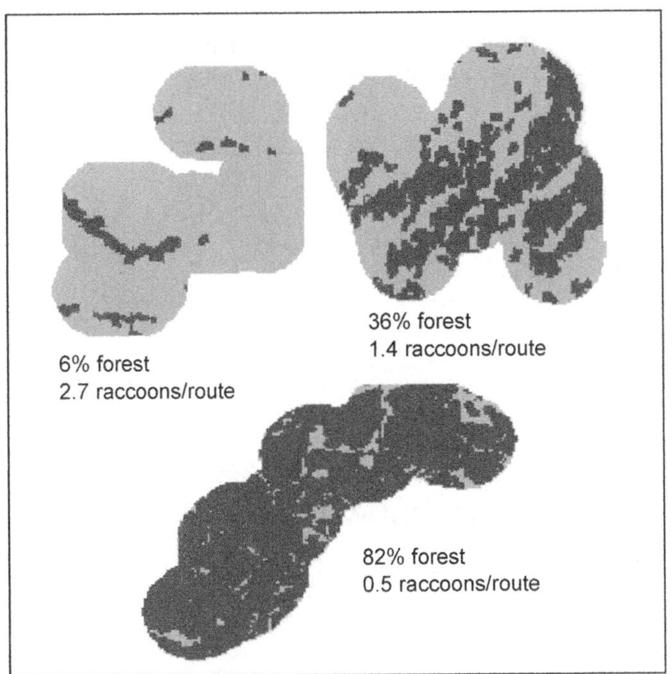

Figure 2. Three landscapes in Missouri that illustrate a positive relationship between raccoon numbers and forest fragmentation. Under each landscape we report the percentage of forest cover in the landscape and the mean number of scent stations/route visited by raccoons from 1988 to 1993 (Dijak and Thompson 2000). Landscapes are approximately 90,000 acres, dark gray=forest, light gray=pasture and cropland.

mean forest patch size. Figure 2 depicts several landscapes in Missouri that cover a range of fragmentation levels. In this example we also show how the abundance of a medium-sized, generalist predator (the raccoon) benefits from forest fragmentation (Dijak and Thompson 2000).

Forest habitat can be defined more finely to reflect differences between successional stages, forest age classes, or forest types. Forest management activities, including the regeneration of forest stands, may fragment forest habitats by creating a mosaic of forest age-classes or forest types. For example, the use of clearcutting will create patches of young forest mixed with mature forest, and forest habitats will be more fragmented than if the entire landscape were the same age. Similarly, silvicultural practices can change tree-species composition and forest type, again fragmenting forest habitats. It is this issue of habitat fragmentation resulting from the creation of early-successional forest habitats that is often controversial with the public and land managers.

Fragmentation of forest habitats by forest management practices or natural disturbances creates forest habitat diversity and can have positive and negative consequences for forest wildlife. It has positive effects for early-successional wildlife or species that require habitat diversity because it creates patches of early-successional forest amidst older forest habitats. It has negative effects on late-successional wildlife because it results in a loss of late-successional forest habitat. It is unclear whether this level and type of habitat fragmentation results in some of the other negative consequences of forest fragmentation, such as edge effects (see below). Most evidence suggests the primary effect of this type of habitat fragmentation is changes in the availability of early and late-successional forest (Thompson 1993, Thompson et al. 1996). Forest habitat fragmentation is generally ephemeral because of forest succession; forest fragmentation resulting from the conversion of forest to non-forest land uses is usually more permanent.

Edges and Edge Effects

As previously defined, edges are simply the border between patches or where two or more ecosystems meet. Edges can be an abrupt or gradual transition between the patches. Inherent edges are relatively stable features of a landscape resulting from relatively long—term processes. Induced edges are short-term edges created by changes in the vegetation due to short-term relatively rapid processes such as fires, wind, or timber harvest. These edges are often short-term because succession usually moderates the difference between the patches. The differences among these edges are important because they may result in different processes at edges that affect wildlife at the edge or in the adjacent patches.

Edges have often been considered areas with high wildlife abundance or diversity. Wildlife may be more common at edges because some species prefer the habitat structure created by edges; some species require more than one habitat type and are often found near the edge between those habitats, and some species are found in one habitat and overlap into the edge (Hunter 1990).

Edges also can be bad for wildlife. The juxtaposition of habitats and species can result in increased interactions among predator and prey, competitors, parasites and hosts; these conditions can be good for predators and parasites but bad for prey and host populations. Edges may create adverse environmental conditions resulting from increased solar radiation and wind and lower humidity.

Potential negative effects of edges on songbirds have been investigated (see Paton 1994 for review).

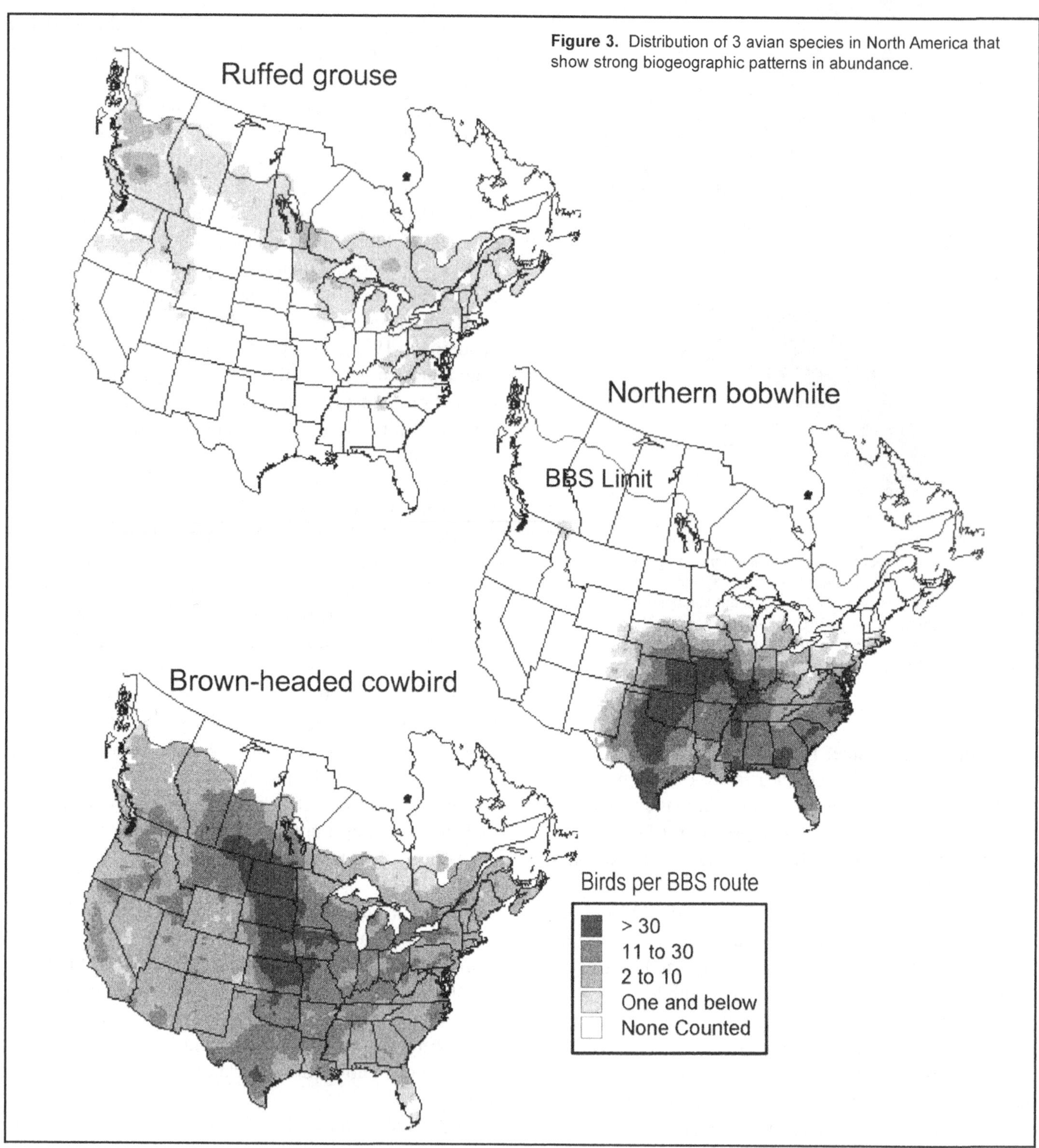

Figure 3. Distribution of 3 avian species in North America that show strong biogeographic patterns in abundance.

Results differ greatly among studies but in some landscapes songbirds nesting near edges have lower reproductive success resulting from increased nest depredation or brood parasitism. Landscape processes such as edge effects may vary as a result of landscape context. In the case of forest songbirds, edge effects occur in moderately fragmented landscapes but not in heavily forested landscapes in the Midwest (Donovan et al. 1997).

Fragmented landscapes have more edge per area of habitat than non-fragmented landscapes. Edge effects have been suggested as the mechanism that results in smaller songbird populations or lower reproductive success in fragmented landscapes (Temple and Cary 1988). Edge effects, however, may not be the mechanism causing fragmentation effects such as lower reproductive success, but simply correlated with them. Negative effects of fragmentation on songbirds could be the result of habitat juxtaposition or landscape complementation, as opposed to increased amounts of edge (Thompson et al. 1998).

CONSERVING BIODIVERSITY IN SOUTHERN FORESTS

The focus of wildlife conservation has broadened from selected species to a wide array of species, ecosystems, or biological diversity in general. This has greatly complicated the job of land managers and planners. Because there are numerous wildlife species with differing habitat requirements, no landscape, forest, or region can be managed to provide maximum benefit to all species. Some species are habitat generalists, some species require habitat diversity or unique combinations of habitats, and other species are specialists and require very specific habitats. This creates inevitable resource management conflicts. Single-species wildlife management alone cannot conserve biological diversity in southern forests because of the logistical problems of planning for hundreds of species, inadequate knowledge of some species requirements, and because some aspects of diversity require an ecosystem or landscape focus. Rather, conservation of biodiversity in southern forests requires a mix of single species management for special species, management of ecosystems and landscapes, and consideration of spatial heterogeneity at multiple spatial scales. These management approaches provide a framework for managing wildlife and biodiversity.

Importance of a Multi-Scale Perspective

The landscape scale is often the largest spatial scale land managers and planners consider, perhaps because this scale represents the largest extent of their management actions or planning. A larger-scale perspective is often needed, however, to understand abundance patterns in wildlife. A regional scale refers to geographically defined areas such as the Southeast. A biogeographic scale usually encompasses different climates, vegetation formations, and species assemblages (Wiens et al. 1986). Ecological patterns and processes at any one of the scales discussed in this chapter are often influenced by factors at scales larger than the one under consideration. These multiple spatial scales have been suggested to represent a hierarchy where larger scales may act to constrain patterns and processes at lower scales (Allen and Starr 1982). It is for this reason that a multi-scale perspective is important for land managers and planners; the outcome of actions they plan at the habitat patch or landscape scale may be constrained by regional or biogeographic patterns and processes.

Land managers commonly use a multi-scale perspective when they take into account geographic patterns in species abundance, but perhaps fail to recognize it. For example, Figure 3 shows abundance maps for three species discussed in this book. The northern bobwhite, ruffed grouse, and brown-headed cowbird all have distinct patterns in abundance across their range. These species demonstrate a general pattern in geographical ecology; species abundance, survival and productivity usually are lower near the periphery of their range (MacArthur 1972). This pattern, or other geographic patterns, may result in source-sink population interactions. A major implication of this for land management is, given the same habitat type and landscape structure, wildlife numbers may vary greatly based on geographic location. For example, land managers should not expect densities of ruffed grouse in the south to reach the levels they do in the north, even under intensive habitat management. The reverse is true for bobwhites; northern populations of quail will never be comparable to southern populations in good habitat. Similarly, brown-headed cowbirds, a brood parasite that has significant negative effects on songbird populations in the Midwest, is much less a threat in the Southeast or Northeast, even in comparable landscapes (Thompson et al. 1998).

Although large-scale, biogeographic patterns may affect local populations, important interactions also occur between habitat patches and landscapes that affect habitat quality of or the abundance, productivity, or survival of wildlife in a patch. This interaction between a habitat patch and the surrounding landscape is sometimes referred to as the landscape context of a patch or habitat. Failure to account for landscape context may result in unexplainable discrepancies between expected and actual population size. For example, reproductive success of forest and grassland songbirds is often related to the total amount of forest and grassland habitat, respectively, in the landscape. This is because the other habitats in the landscape provide resources for predators, parasites, and competitors that invade the habitat patches used by the forest or grassland birds. Local habitat factors may not always explain

Fragmentation of forest habitats occurs at different scales. The gap created by selection harvest and the clearcut opening (upper left and right, respectively) are disturbance patches that change the pattern of tree size and age classes in the landscape. The lower picture illustrates fragmentation of forest cover at a landscape scale by agricultural land use. It is this latter type of fragmentation that is usually associated with higher songbird nest predation and brood parasitism (F. Thompson).

poor productivity or survival in a wildlife population because they may be determined by landscape context.

An example of another interaction between habitats, populations, and landscapes is the effect of regional or landscape habitat availability, population size, and local abundance. For example, local population densities may be lower than expected if there is a surplus of habitat available. This can happen when a large-scale disturbance creates a surplus of habitat and it takes several years for the population to respond and fully occupy the surplus habitat. Habitat use patterns may shift also if a more preferred habitat becomes available in the landscape (Probst and Weinrich 1993).

Single-Species Management

Even with increased focus on ecosystem management and biological diversity, there is a continued need for single species management. This is because some species are "special" because they have some social value (Hunter 1990). This includes species with commercial value, ecological value, aesthetic value, game species, and endangered species. Because these species are considered special they are often considered a priority and their needs are considered before other resource values on at least some portion of the landscape.

In some ways single-species management for special species is the most traditional approach to wildlife management. Even this traditional form of wildlife management is dependent on a landscape perspective. Managers should consider how landscape composition, structure, and processes affect a species population size, productivity, and survival as well as possible effects from interactions at other spatial scales. In addition to sustaining the appropriate habitats, we now know that managers should consider their abundance and spatial arrangement in the landscape, and the larger landscape, regional, and biogeographic context in which they occur. This book includes much of this information for some special species in southern forests.

Ecosystem Conservation

Ecosystem conservation or management is a complement to species management. Protecting, managing, and restoring ecosystems protects species about which little is known. Ecosystem management often focuses on vegetation and habitat structure and ecological processes that maintain these. By not focusing on species, ecosystem management can avoid some of the potential resource management conflicts that arise from single-species management. Inevitably resource managers will be asked to make decisions about how much of this ecosystem is enough, or how large should the patch be? So ultimately, as with single-species management, some prioritization will be required.

Because ecosystems are tied to the physical characteristics of the land, the range of potential ecosystems in any landscape is constrained. The advent of hierarchical ecological classification systems, such as the National Hierarchical Framework of Ecological Units adopted by the USDA Forest Service (McNab and Avers 1994, Bailey 1998), has greatly facilitated managers' ability to identify potential ecosystems within a landscape.

Within the range of potential ecosystems that can occur within a landscape, management decisions can be made based on current vegetation and criteria ranging from economic to ecological. From the perspective of conserving biological diversity, a high priority should be to protect and restore rare ecosystems. Noss et al. (1995) defined critically endangered ecosystems in the United States and suggested they should be priorities for protection and conservation of biodiversity. In the southern U.S. these include old-growth eastern deciduous forest, longleaf pine forest and savannahs in the southeastern coastal plain, slash pine rockland habitat in South Florida, loblolly-shortleaf pine-hardwood forests in the West Gulf Coastal Plain, canebrakes, and others (Noss et al. 1995). The distribution of ecosystems prior to European settlement has sometimes been used as a guideline for current distribution of ecosystems. However, while a valuable reference point, it is only one point in a dynamic history of the distribution of ecosystems.

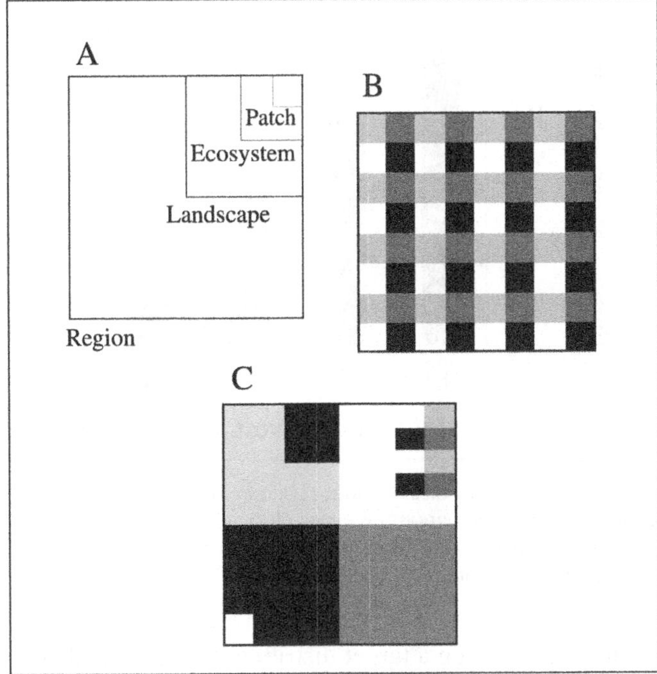

Figure 4. Graphical representation of spatial scales, A; of spatial heterogeneity maximized at a small (ecosystem) scale, B; and spatial heterogeneity at multiple scales (region, landscape, and patch), C.

Spatial Heterogeneity

A key principle to managing for multiple objectives and maintaining biological diversity is to provide spatial heterogeneity by providing ecosystem and habitat diversity. This diversity should be provided by conserving the full range of native ecosystems and habitats and by providing diversity at all spatial scales. Early efforts to manage for diversity sometimes mistakenly focused on diversity only at small scales (Robinson 1988). Providing spatial heterogeneity at multiple scales provides an inherently more diverse region (Fig. 4) and accommodates the needs of species that are area-sensitive as well as species requiring diversity at small scales. However, even within this guideline there is a large range of possible landscape configurations (specified by composition and structure).

If planning at large spatial scales addresses the question of what is the desired mix and spatial arrangement of ecosystems, potential resource conflicts at smaller or local scale will be minimized because decisions will be made within larger-scale constraints or priorities. For example, one model for the spatial distribution of ecosystems is based on the general observation that the size distribution of many different types of patches in natural landscapes has a negative slope or a reverse j-shaped distribution; that is, there are many more small patches than large patches. Hunter (1990) demonstrated that a variety of natural phenomena follow this distribution including physical and biological components of landscapes and ecosystems. He suggested how this could provide guidance for the distribution of timber cuts in a managed forest where a goal was to maximize spatial heterogeneity (Hunter 1990). Harris (1984) suggested this as a guideline for the conservation of old-growth forests.

In Figure 5, I demonstrate how this distribution could be applied to central hardwood forests. I considered a range of openings from 0.1 acre (the size of a group selection opening) to 100 acres (the size of a large

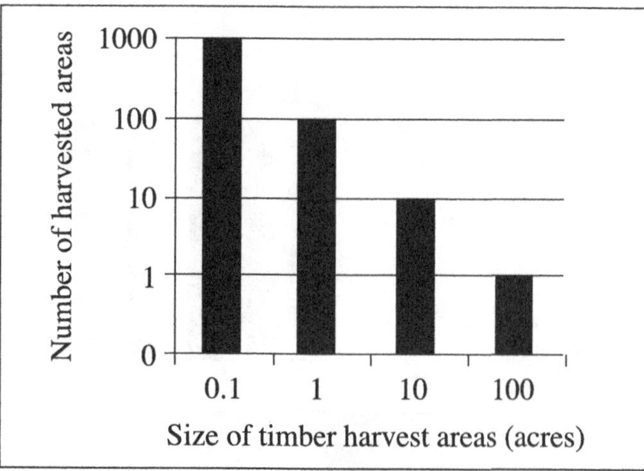

Figure 5. Frequency distribution resulting from the allocation of and equal area of timber harvest openings (100 acres) among four patch sizes that span the range from small group selection openings to large clearcuts.

clearcut). By using a target distribution of an equal area in each of four patch sizes, a negative logarithmic distribution in the frequency of opening size results (Fig. 5). Typically between 5 and 10 percent of a stand is in group openings, so to obtain 1,000 openings with a total area of 100 acres approximately 1,000 to 2,000 acres would need to be regenerated by the group selection method. This is just one model of many that can potentially be used as a guideline for spatial heterogeneity.

CONCLUSIONS

The ideas presented in this chapter such as landscape ecology, a multi-scale perspective, management of special species, ecosystem conservation, and spatial heterogeneity, provide a framework for the management and conservation of wildlife and biological diversity in southern forests. This framework is general by design but can easily be focused on real world situations once decisions are made about regional ecosystem and species priorities, and landscape level disturbance regimes or desired levels of spatial heterogeneity. Management at a local level is then a matter of identifying opportunities to meet priorities defined at a landscape or regional scale (Freemark et al. 1995, Thompson et al. 1995). By nesting local decisions and planning within land capabilities and management priorities set at regional and landscape levels, local decisions will be easier and conflicts will be minimized.

ACKNOWLEDGMENTS

I thank John R. Probst for his ideas on top down, multi-scale approaches to conservation, which greatly influenced this chapter. The USDA Forest Service North Central Research Station supported this project.

CHAPTER 7

Managing Forests for Wildlife

James G. Dickson[1]
US Forest Service
Southern Research Station, Nacogdoches, TX

T. Bently Wigley
National Council of the Paper Industry for Air and Stream Improvement, Inc.
Clemson University, Clemson, SC

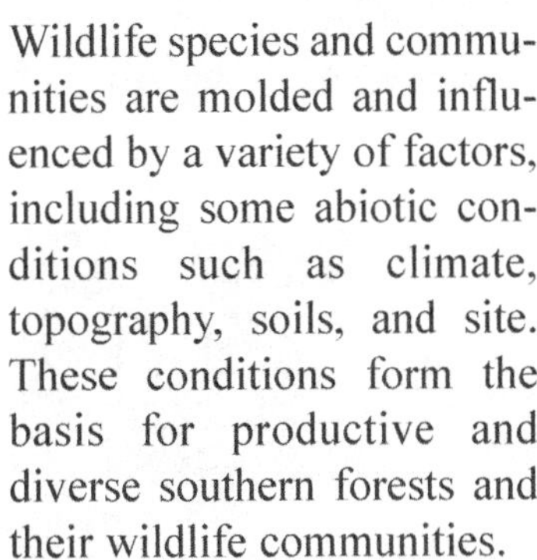

Wildlife species and communities are molded and influenced by a variety of factors, including some abiotic conditions such as climate, topography, soils, and site. These conditions form the basis for productive and diverse southern forests and their wildlife communities.

These wildlife communities are affected by habitat conditions at different scales, such as the landscape level and the smaller, stand scale. Species are very different in the scale of habitat that individual animals use. For example, some amphibians have very restricted movements and ranges. Conversely, some larger vertebrates such as white-tailed deer have relatively large home ranges.

Some migratory species may use very distant and different habitats at different seasons. For example, wood ducks that winter extensively in southern bottoms, nest throughout much of forested North America.

And probably more importantly than use by individual animals, broad-scale landscape habitat conditions affect wildlife community composition and population function of species. For example, very small pockets of forest habitat may serve as sinks for forest interior birds, where mortality exceeds productivity.

In this chapter we present some information about habitat relationships and management options at a scale broader than the stand level, such as discussion of edge and streamside zones. But we treat wildlife habitat relationships primarily at the stand level, which is the basic management unit. We approach this by treating suitability of stand structure and composition for wildlife com-

[1]Current Address: School of Forestry, Louisiana Tech University, Ruston, LA

A.

B.

C.

Wide streamside zones *(A. US Forest Service)* in southern forests are beneficial for a number of game *(B. R. Griffin)* and nongame species such as the Acadian flycatcher *(C. B. Cottrille, Cornell Lab of Ornithology)*.

munities, and present information about how common management practices affect that suitability as wildlife habitat for wildlife communities. Each species has different habitat requirements, so conditions or manipulations that favor some species likely will be negative for others.

Forest and stand suitability for wildlife should be considered in regard to alternative land uses and also how they fit into the broader landscape context. In recent years pine plantations have increased in extent in the South, there is much interest in pine plantations as wildlife habitat, and much of this chapter focuses on those relationships.

EDGE

As noted, landscape composition is important to southern wildlife communities. One factor which influences wildlife species is edge, or the juxtaposition of habitat types. The extent of edge is often determined by stand size or shape. Small stands or complex-shaped stands have large edge to area ratios. Edge has long been recognized as positive for many species (Leopold 1933). Most primary game species in the South thrive in forest edge habitat and in forest-field landscapes. For example, white-tailed deer and wild turkey thrive in forest-agriculture habitat mixes which are prime habitat for their year-round needs. Also, some other game birds, such as American woodcock and ruffed grouse, and some other species fare well in patchy habitat.

But there is concern for some forest interior birds, particularly neotropical migrants (Dickson et al. 1993). These species may be absent from small forest fragments, probably due to lower reproductive success or survival in edge-dominated forests (Faaborg 1992). While edge-related declines in reproductive success have been documented in fragmented forests in predominantly agriculture landscapes, the effects of edges created by timber harvest in predominately forested landscapes is unclear (Dickson et al. 1993). Many forest interior species remain abundant in managed forests but the status of their population viability is uncertain.

STREAMSIDE ZONES

Streamside zones (SZ) are strips of riparian and/or other mature stands maintained along intermittent or permanent streams (Wigley and Melchiors 1994). SZ usually are recommended in silvicultural Best Management Practices to protect streams from potential impacts from logging of adjacent stands, such as excessive sediment, nutrients, logging debris, chemicals, or water temperature alteration.

SZ also help maintain wildlife diversity in managed forest landscapes. Because riparian forests often predominate in SZ, they are very productive and often provide unique habitat in landscapes dominated by more xeric forest types. SZ also may provide important mature habitat attributes and may function as travel corridors and enhance connectivity within landscapes (Burk et al. 1990). SZ research in the South has documented habitat relationships for nongame birds, small mammals, herpetofauna, wild turkey, squirrels, and white-tailed deer.

Birds

Some habitat features that SZ offer birds include large trees and snags, multiple foliage layers, and open areas to forage along the land/water interface. Bird species present in SZ depend upon habitat conditions of the SZ and adjacent habitats. Thus SZ may support forest-interior species, riparian associates, early-successional species, and generalists (Murray and Stauffer 1995).

SZ width is a major consideration for many forest managers. Bird species richness usually increases with SZ or riparian zone width (Dickson et al. 1995a, Hodges and Krementz 1996). Different bird species, however, respond differently to increasing width. For example, Keller et al. (1993) found that the number of neotropical migrants increased with riparian forest width, but the number of short-distance migrants decreased, and resident species were not affected. Forest-dwelling and forest-interior species have been found to be more common in wider strips (Dickson et al. 1995a). However, data on reproductive success of forest interior species are lacking in these narrow habitats.

Game Species

SZ also can be important habitats for game species. In eastern Texas, Poteet et al. (1996) found that SZ traversing pine plantations were heavily used and an important part of deer home ranges during fall and winter, probably due to hard mast availability. Telemetry data show that SZ are heavily used by eastern wild turkeys, also primarily during fall and winter (Burk et al. 1990). Streamside zones at least 50 yards in total width appear to be necessary to provide adequate habitat for gray and fox squirrels (Dickson and Huntley 1987).

Small Mammals

Microhabitat features within SZ such as dense vegetation, fruits, seeds, down logs, and logging slash are important to small mammals (Dickson and Williamson 1988). Wider SZ may support small mammal communities associated with mature forests (Thurmond and Miller 1994). However, other studies have shown that characteristics of small mammal communities such as richness, diversity, and abundance can be similar across different SZ width-classes, or even higher in narrow strips (Dickson and Williamson 1988). Therefore, for small mammal communities, microhabitat features probably are more important than SZ width.

Herpetofauna

Obviously, SZ offer important habitat features for herpetofauna, such as pools of water, moist soils, down wood, and leaf litter. However, there are few data on these relationships, and results appear to vary. In eastern Texas, Rudolph and Dickson (1990) found the fewest amphibians and reptiles in narrow (less than 25 yards wide) strips and concluded that abundance of herpetofauna was positively related to closed-canopy conditions. But in Kentucky, Pais et al. (1988) found that herpetofaunal species richness was greatest in open, wildlife clearings while mature forest supported the fewest species. They concluded that herpetofauna richness was most affected by biomass of nonwoody vegetation and proximity to water.

Management

Retention of SZ in southern forests is positive for wildlife communities. Generally, streamside zones wider than about 50 yards total width appear beneficial for forest interior species, several important game species, and other species. Specific requirements of some species remain unknown.

Extent and management of SZ should be considered in the context of economics and adjacent land use, as well as site-specific factors, such as topography, adjacent habitats, and stream width. Management of SZ, including silvicultural operations, could enhance habitat suitability for many wildlife species. For example, hard mast-producing oaks, soft mast-producing shrubs, or cavity trees could be featured. Or species regarded as pests, such as Chinese tallow tree, could be controlled.

STAND STRUCTURE AND COMPOSITION

Within-stand structure and composition are important factors in habitat suitability for many species. Structural features, such as stand overstory, understory, leaf litter, snags, and down wood, may be important to different species. In gross aspects, composition of stands affects suitability as habitat for species. In pine stands, a few species, such as red-cockaded woodpecker, pine warbler, and brown-headed nuthatch, are associated with pines. However, many other species are associated with herbaceous and hardwood vegetation (Johnston and Odum 1956, Dickson and Segelquist 1979). Thus, practices that promote hardwoods favor species, such as red-eyed and yellow-throated vireos in canopy-level foliage, and hooded and Kentucky warblers in understory foliage.

Oak mast is an important food for a number of species, such as white-tailed deer, wild turkey, black bears, gray squirrels, chipmunks, and wild pigs. But acorn production in oak-dominated forests can be quite variable from year to year (Greenberg in press), and can

Structure is important in determining habitat suitability of forest stands. This open stand is suitable for species associated with stand canopy as well as those associated with understory *(US Fish & Wildlife Service).*

Oak mast is an important food for a number of species, such as white-tailed deer, wild turkey, black bear, chipmunk and gray squirrel. But acorn production is quite variable from year to year *(H. Williamson, US Forest Service)*.

range from several hundred pounds per acre to almost none in other years (Rogers et al. 1990). The white-oak group produces acorns in 1 growing season and red oaks in 2 growing seasons. Therefore, a variety of oaks and other hardwood species such as black gum provide diverse habitat and foods. But hardwood overstories and midstories intercept much sunlight, shading shrubs and limiting fruit production. Also, hardwood shading limits herbaceous ground vegetation (Blair and Feduccia 1977) and associated species.

HARVEST AND REGENERATION

Stand or tree harvesting can be a drastic habitat alteration (see Chapter 4, Defining the Forest). For example, bird species associated with forest canopy generally decreased and birds associated with patchy and early successional habitat increased following harvest (Webb et al. 1977). Of course, response of vegetation to harvesting depends on extent of tree, particularly overstory, removal. The more overstory removed the more profound the vegetative response, change in habitat suitability for wildlife, and change in wildlife community composition (Dickson 1981). Single-tree selection harvesting affects stands and wildlife communities the least during each harvest. With this technique, stand structure remains mostly intact. However, uneven-aged management of southern pines requires more frequent harvest cycles and hardwood control. Clearcutting alters habitat and wildlife communities the most. With complete tree removal, forage and fruiting near the ground is increased many fold over that in shaded understories (Halls and Alcaniz 1968, Blair and Enghardt 1976). Group selection, shelterwood and seed tree cuts are intermediate in effects on habitat and wildlife communities, depending on the extent of stand removal.

SITE PREPARATION

Site preparation includes measures conducted shortly before or after stand regeneration to reduce vegetation competing with pines. Moderate site treatment measures that delay development or modify non-pine vegetation can enhance vegetation diversity and wildlife habitat, particularly for early-successional species (White et al. 1975). For example, in East Texas after 3 growing seasons fruit production was lower on KG-bladed and chopped plots than on control or burned plots (Stransky and Halls 1980). But measures that severely reduce vegetation may be negative for many species of wildlife. Generally, the reduction of hardwoods in young stands favors herbaceous vegetation and species associated with that habitat type and disfavors the many species associated with the hardwood component of pine stands.

STAND DEVELOPMENT

Some species, such as white-tailed deer and northern cardinals, are tolerant of a wide range of habitat conditions. Conversely, other species have more specific habitat requirements, and respond to changes in stand structure and composition as stands age (Buckner and Landers 1980, Dickson 1981). During the first year or two of development, stands usually are dominated by grass-forb vegetation. At this stage young pine stands are suitable habitat for some bird species, such as mourning doves (Lay and Taylor 1943), eastern meadowlarks (Johnston and Odum 1956), and prairie warblers (Dickson et al. 1995). Grass-forb vegetation also provides suitable brood habitat for newly-hatched chicks of primary game birds: northern bobwhites, wild turkeys and ruffed grouse, which depend on and feed extensively on arthropods. Also, populations of herbivorous and granivorous small mammals, such as cotton rats and *Peromyscus* spp., thrive in early successional habitat (Atkeson and Johnson 1979).

Normally within a couple of years, rapidly growing vegetation invades young stands. Timing and characteristics of this vegetation depend on site quality, prior land use, and source of revegetation, as well as herbicide and other site preparation treatments. In the South, young pine stands less than about 8 years old normally are characterized by diverse, lush herbaceous and woody vegetation. Forage production often exceeds 2,000 lbs per acre (Harlow et al. 1980), and fruit (soft mast) is abundant. For example, in eastern Texas Halls and Alcaniz (1968) found 7 common browse plants produced 32 times more fruit and 7 times more twig growth in the open than in the shade beneath a sawtimber stand.

Usually there is an abundance and variety of wildlife in young brushy stands. White-tailed deer fare well in this habitat with abundant browse and soft mast (Blymyer and Mosby 1977). In this dense habitat usually there is an abundance of herbivorous small mammals (Umber and Harris 1974, Atkeson and Johnson 1979). Also, there are abundant birds (Conner and Adkisson 1975, Dickson et al. 1995); typical breeding season species include field sparrows, yellow-breasted chats, white-eyed vireos, prairie warblers, and painted and indigo buntings (Johnston and Odum 1956, Dickson and Segelquist 1979, Dickson et al. 1995).

Usually there is an abundance and variety of wildlife in young brushy stands *(A. J. Dunning, Cornell Lab of Ornithology).* Forage and soft mast production usually is high in these rapidly developing stands *(B. US Forest Service C. H. Williamson,).*

Young, dense, closed-canopy stands have little value for wildlife *(H. Williamson).*

As stands age and trees grow into the pole stage, suitability for wildlife changes. Some early successional species continue to use openings which have considerable hardwood or grass-forb vegetation. And some species associated with mature stands, such as yellow-billed cuckoos and red-eyed vireos in the canopies and hooded warblers in the understories, begin to inhabit stands with hardwood vegetation. In pine plantations about 7 to 10 years old or similar hardwood stands, pole-sized trees dominate the stand, canopies close, and shading by canopies drastically reduces vegetation beneath the canopies and fruit production of shrubs (Halls and Alcaniz 1968). Generally, habitat suitability for wildlife is reduced substantially. Usually there is little low vegetation, and bird (Dickson and Segelqist 1979) and small mammal populations (Atkeson and Johnson 1979) decline, and habitat suitability for deer and wild turkeys diminishes (e.g., Miller et al. 1999).

THINNING

Thinning is a silvicultural procedure typically conducted in stands with dense pole-sized trees. Up to ½ of the trees are removed to concentrate tree growth on the remaining crop trees. Tree removal opens up canopies and allows light into the understory. This promotes non-pine vegetation growth and fruiting, which is positive for many species.

As even-aged stands mature, some trees die and small openings develop, creating structural diversity. Also maturing trees produce mast, important to a number of species of wildlife. Generally suitability for wildlife is high in diverse mature stands, especially those with openings. For example, deer inhabit mature stands as well as stands of other ages. Gray and fox squirrels usually are abundant in mature hardwood stands. And there are high densities of breeding birds, such as yellow-billed cuckoo, tufted titmouse, red-eyed vireo, and summer tanager in mature hardwood stands, and brown-headed nuthatch, pine warbler, and red-cockaded woodpecker in mature pine stands (Dickson et al. 1995).

Logs and woody debris provide important habitat for a number of species of small mammals, amphibians, and reptiles, such as the timber rattlesnake, which hibernates in logs and also waits adjacent to logs for prey *(C. Rudolph)*.

In stands designated for old growth, as stands approach old-growth condition habitat suitability changes. Tree fall creates openings and enhances stand diversity. Tree decay increases, which provides cavity and foraging substrate for cavity-using wildlife. And down material from trees provides structure on the ground inhabited by small mammals, and a variety of amphibians, and reptiles.

SNAGS AND DOWN WOOD

Snags, dead or partially dead trees, are used by and are important to a variety of wildlife species for nesting, roosting, foraging, perching, and other uses. Woodpeckers are primary cavity nesters that excavate cavities in snags. These cavities are used for nesting and roosting by primary cavity nesters and secondary cavity nesters, such as great crested flycatchers, wood ducks, and other species, including some mammals (Conner 1978).

Availability of cavities for nesting sites may limit some populations, and leaving or creating snags or artificial nest structures may accommodate some species. For example, in Arizona the number of cavity nesting birds declined by about half after conifer snags were removed during timber harvest (Scott 1979). In young pine plantations in the South, bird populations were increased by creating snags using herbicides (Dickson et al. 1993).

Snags may result from natural phenomena such as insects, disease, lightning, or other factors; or can be created through girdling, herbicides, or other means. Dead snags do not compete with crop trees for space, nutrients, moisture, or light. Recommendations for snag size and density for different species are presented by Evans and Conner (1979). But there may be some negative aspects of snags. They may be used as perches to search for prey by brown-headed cowbirds and raptors. Also, snags may pose a safety hazard for workers.

Artificial nest structures may accomodate cavity-nesting wildlife in local situations. For example, eastern bluebirds successfully nested in artificial nest boxes in a young pine plantation (Hurst et al. 1979). But widespread application is prohibitive for all cavity-using species.

Down wood, or woody material on the ground from dead limbs, snags, or logging debris, is an important structural feature. Wood on the forest floor in varying stages of decay may be instrumental in forest nutrient cycling, supports a wide variety of invertebrates, and is important to some species of vertebrates. Logs may harbor prey for some larger species, such as black bears. Small mammal populations may be closely associated with woody material on the forest floor (see Chapter 26, Terrestrial Small Mammals). Species of small mammals, such as *Peromyscus* spp. and eastern woodrats, use woody material for protection from prey and also as a source of food. Many species of reptiles and amphibians, including snakes, lizards, frogs, and salamanders, depend on woody material and some species are only found there. An important feature of down wood to these species is the moderate environment maintained by the physical protection from weather extremes. Logs are necessary for some species as a moist environment and to avoid dessication. Down wood also affords protection from predation, appropriate sites for reproduction, and suitable habitat to support prey populations (see Chapter 28, Reptiles and Amphibians). For example, timber rattlesnakes may hibernate in logs, use logs for protection, and often wait adjacent to logs for small mammal prey. Logs also are an important feature in small streams interspersing forests. They create structure in streams which benefits some fish species. And decaying logs provide stream nutrients and invertebrate prey for fish.

PRESCRIBED BURNING

Apparently fire has been a regular part of the southern landscape since the waning of the Pleistocene Period. Southern forests and the animals that inhabit them evolved with fire, and fire has had a major influence on communities of southern flora and fauna. Lightning-set fires have been a recurring force for thousands of years (Heyward 1939). Also, natives in the region used fire to manipulate vegetation and drive game for harvest, and European settlers used fire for the same purposes and to clear new ground for planting their crops. Prescribed burning continues to be used for a variety of purposes, including wildlife management. However, recent use has declined, mainly due to liability aspects and air pollution regulations.

Obviously, fire has the potential to kill animals. However, there is little evidence of significant direct

Prescribed burning has a long history in southern forests. It has been a major technique for the enhancement of wildlife habitat *(US Forest Service)*.

mortality of vertebrates from prescribed burning (Landers 1987); and what does occur probably is insignificant on a landscape scale.

Some animals actually are attracted to the heat and smoke of fires, or to the burns shortly thereafter. Raptors, such as red-tailed hawks, kestrels, other hawks, and owls have been observed attracted to burns in search of prey (Landers 1987). Wild turkeys and mourning doves are attracted to new burns in search of exposed insects and seed. White-tailed deer are known to congregate on recent burns and lick the ash, apparently to obtain minerals.

Also, although our knowledge of fire effects is limited, arthropod populations and their interactions with vertebrates certainly are affected by fire (Landers 1987). It has been documented that parasites of wild turkey, northern bobwhite, and rabbits are reduced by burning.

Fire is commonly used to manage wildlife habitat in the South. Generally fire consumes the forest floor litter and sets back succession; usually reducing smaller hardwoods in favor of pines and herbaceous vegetation. Fire effects are quite variable because they involve condition of the area before burning and suitability for a wide variety of different communities or species; the intensity, periodicity, and seasonality of fires; landscape context and unburned areas, and numerous interactions. For example, areas burned annually for northern bobwhites are virtually devoid of hardwood shrubs, whereas areas burned occasionally with cool burns may be thick with hardwood sprouts. We approach this treatment by describing how fire may affect different forest stands or plants, and how that may affect different species of southern wildlife. Readers interested in fire effects on particular species are referred to appropriate chapters.

Prescribed burning normally is used in upland pine stands; mature pines are relatively fire resistant. Since fire causes wounds in hardwood trees it is not normally used in stands managed for quality hardwood timber. But fire affects hardwoods and their suitability for wildlife. Fire wounds on hardwood trees provide entrance for decay, that over time may become cavities used by animals such as tree squirrels. Severe fire may kill trees and create snags that are used by a variety of cavity-using wildlife. But conversely, dead snags used by cavity nesters may be consumed by fire. Fires severe enough to kill trees or cause snags to fall and produce woody debris on the ground would favor a variety of small mammals such as *Peromyscus* spp. Fires that consume woody debris on the ground, such as site preparation burns, would decrease area suitability for small mammals.

Prescribed fire is used for red-cockaded woodpeckers to reduce hardwoods and maintain a pine savannah habitat. The birds peck cavity trees to produce a resin flow around the cavity and down the tree bole. Fire may ignite the resin up the tree bole of cavity trees and may even burn out and gut the nest cavity. So surface fuel around cavity trees may need to be raked away before burning.

Typically, frequent, intense, or growing season fire reduces small hardwoods and shrubs. Numbers of small mammals and rabbits probably are reduced with the cover reduction immediately after a fire. Birds associated with shrub-level vegetation and hardwood midstory, such as northern cardinal, Carolina wren, hooded warbler, and Kentucky warbler, probably would be reduced in response to shrub hardwood reduction (Dickson 1981).

This shrub-level reduction is accompanied by a growth flush of herbaceous vegetation which usually persists for a few years. This grass-forb growth with abundant seed production favors populations of early successional breeding bird species, herbivorous and granivorous small mammals, and provides important brood habitat for northern bobwhites, wild turkeys, and ruffed grouse. And the conditions maintained by burning should favor other species such as the gopher tortoise, which burrows in sunlit sites and forages on herbaceous vegetation resulting from fire (Landers 1987).

There is some evidence that the consumption of fuel can increase temporarily the nutrient content of post-fire vegetation, such as protein and phosphorus, which generally is limited in the South. This increase in nutrient content and palatability of plants could benefit a number of species, such as deer (Stransky and Harlow 1981) and rabbits, whose reproductive success may depend on forage nutrient quality (Hill 1972).

After a couple of years the post-fire herbaceous vegetation is gradually replaced by hardwood sprouts and shrubs. This transition affects vertebrate communities as detailed in the stand composition section of this chapter. Also, fruiting of shrubs recovering from fire and those benefitting from reduction of vegetative competition from fire increase. This fruit production benefits a number of fruit-consuming species, such as white-tailed deer, wild turkey, northern bobwhites, and some omnivorous furbearers, such as coyotes, foxes, opossums, and raccoons (Landers 1987).

HERBICIDES

Herbicides are used to control plants that are exotic, noxious, competitors with crop trees, or are otherwise undesirable. Growth of crop trees is enhanced through the reduction of competition (Autter and Miller 1998). Herbicides are applied at various times during a rotation such as during site preparation or thinning, and often are effective for vegetation control. For example, mechanical site preparation involves high equipment costs and may not be suitable for all landowners or sites. Vegetation control using herbicides is increasingly common because of: (1) increased availability of more selective and environmentally compatible chemicals; (2) rising costs and less available labor for alternative control methods; and (3) other considerations, such as liability, effects on productivity, and limited number of suitable days for burning (Miller and Witt 1991).

Although there have been concerns about possible environmental and human-health effects, forest chemicals generally are a minor source of water contamination (Ice et al., 1998), and are generally not associated with cancers or genetic abnormalities in wildlife (USDA Forest Service 1984, Miller and Witt 1991). Acute and chronic doses affecting wildlife are well above those of normal herbicide applications in forestry, and chronic levels are not reached because of the low persistence of forest herbicides (Morrison and Meslow 1983). Herbicides usually degrade within days or weeks, and they pose no significant toxic hazard when applied at recommended rates (Melchiors 1991).

But herbicides affect the structure and composition of plant communities, and subsequently, wildlife habitat and associated wildlife communities. For example, Dickson et al. (1983, 1995b) found that herbicide-created snags increased the diversity and abundance of birds in young forests in eastern Texas. Increased complexity and abundance of understory vegetation following herbicide application may result in increased abundance of small mammals (McComb and Rumsey 1982). Although few data are available, amphibians likely respond to herbicide-induced changes in microclimate such as humidity and temperature of the forest floor.

Herbicide effects on plant community structure and composition, and wildlife habitat differ with the herbicide used and a host of other factors. For example, phytotoxicity of tebuthiuron has been demonstrated to vary with soil texture, precipitation, and application rates (DeFazio et al. 1988). Application methods (banded, broadcast spray, pellets, injection) also can be important. Obviously, target-specific application, such as injection or banded spraying, will have less impact on plant communities than broadcast methods.

Usually, woody vegetation is reduced and herbaceous vegetation is increased following herbicide application (Hurst and Palmer 1988, DeFazio et al. 1988). McComb and Hurst (1987) report that some wildlife foods, such as fruiting from shrubs, can be adversely affected by herbicide application, and some, such as grass seed, can be enhanced by it.

Increasing pine growth through herbicide application can decrease the time until the overstory canopy closes and understory cover is reduced from shading. Dalla-Tea and Jokela (1991) observed that 6-year-old pine plantations receiving total vegetation control intercepted about 60% of photosynthetically active radiation compared to about 30% for plantations receiving no vegetation control.

In mid-rotation or mature forests, herbicides can be used to achieve specific structural or compositional objectives for wildlife. For example, herbicides can be used to reduce overstory cover, increase cover in the lower foliage levels, or alter the litter layer (McComb and Hurst 1987). Snags for wildlife can be created using herbicides, however herbicide-created snags usually deteriorate and fall in several years in the humid South (Dickson et al. 1995b, Cain 1996).

Even though herbicides alter plant communities, those effects often are apparent for only a few growing seasons (Hurst and Blake 1987, Copeland 1989). Miller and Chapman (1995) concluded that differences occurred in plant and associated animal communities following treatment with hexazinone, imazpyr, and picloram+triclopyr, but those differences were short-lived, and treatment-related differences generally were no longer evident at 5 years post-treatment.

FERTILIZATION

Forest fertilization with nitrogen or phosphorous is increasingly common for managers seeking to increase tree growth and yield in pine and hardwood forests (Jokela and Stearn-Smith 1993). Fertilizers are commonly applied at the time of stand establishment and at mid-rotation. Of course, productivity gains vary with soils, application timing and rates, and other factors.

Fertilization with nitrogen has been shown to improve first-year survival of pine seedlings by as much as 15% (Irwin et al. 1998). In pine stands, applications of nitrogen and phosphorous produce larger growth responses than applications of either element alone. With fertilization in young stands, rapid tree growth reduces the time until canopy closure and shortens the rotation.

Most investigations of how fertilization affects wildlife have focused on responses of deer forage. On many sites in the South, nutrient content and digestibility of wildlife forage are limited (Blair et al. 1977). Although understory vegetation is affected by factors such as overstory and other conditions (Conroy et al. 1982, Blair 1982), biomass and nutrient content of understory vegetation generally increase following fertilization (Dyess et al. 1994, Haywood and Thill 1995, Hurst et al. 1982, Wood 1986). Also, studies have shown that diversity and fruit production of selected plant species groups are highest on fertilized sites (Campo and Hurst 1980). Although plant community responses to fertilization generally are positive, they usually are temporary, lasting only 2-3 growing seasons (Wood 1986). Furthermore, gains in biomass and nutrient content may be mitigated by decreased time until canopy closure.

CONCLUSION

There are abundant and diverse wildlife communities inhabiting southern forests. These communities and the species comprising them are largely determined by habitat characteristics at the landscape level and the smaller, stand scale. Natural processes, such as plant succession, and the wide variety of human activities which affect landscape composition and stand structure, play a large role in determining the composition and status of vertebrate communities of southern forests. Broad measures, such as the retention of streamside zones, benefit a number of species, and specific measures, such as species restoration, can be employed to address particular conservation concerns.

CHAPTER 8

White-tailed Deer

Karl V. Miller
D. B. Warnell School of Forest Resources
University of Georgia, Athens, GA

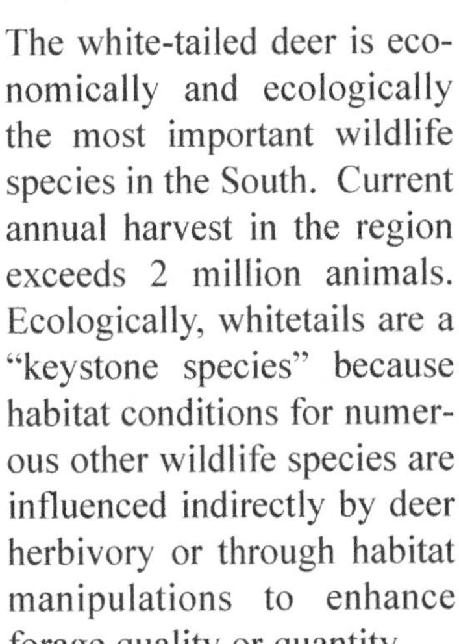
The white-tailed deer is economically and ecologically the most important wildlife species in the South. Current annual harvest in the region exceeds 2 million animals. Ecologically, whitetails are a "keystone species" because habitat conditions for numerous other wildlife species are influenced indirectly by deer herbivory or through habitat manipulations to enhance forage quality or quantity.

Of the 38 recognized subspecies in North and South America, 10 occur in the South (Whitehead 1993). The Virginia whitetail (*Odocoileus virginianus virginianus*) occupies the majority of the region east of the Mississippi and north of Florida. However, the classification of subspecies of whitetails in the South is tenuous. Restoration efforts frequently involved movement of deer from state to state which introduced or mixed subspecies from disparate areas of North America (McDonald and Miller 1993). Therefore, it is unlikely that the original description of 10 subspecies in the South is still valid.

HISTORY

Early accounts from European explorers of the North American continent make frequent mention of abundant populations of white-tailed deer (McCabe and McCabe 1984). Most tribes of Native Americans depended on deer for subsistence, fabric, and tools. Whitetails likely were particularly abundant in the South as a result of Native American agriculture and use of fire, along with lush habitats, moderate climate, and abundant hard and soft mast. Abundance in this region is reflected in records of white-tailed deer hide exports from Southern ports during the early to mid-1700s. Extensive exploitation of deer populations began shortly after arrival of European settlers. Trade in hides and venison resulted in intense hunting pressure and marked the beginning of the over-exploitation of deer populations.

Extensive clearing for agriculture, coupled with heavy exploitation, resulted in the extirpation of deer from many areas of the South by the mid- to late 1800s. Estimates of deer populations in the Southeastern states during the 1910s range from near extirpation in Georgia, Mississippi, North Carolina, South Carolina, and Tennessee, to 1,000 animals in Alabama, and to 15,000 - 20,000 animals in Louisiana. Major restoration efforts began following passage of the Pittman-Robertson Act in 1937, and most efforts to restore white-tailed deer to their former range were completed by the late 1960s and early 1970s.

DISTRIBUTION AND CURRENT POPULATIONS

Whitetails occur in virtually all habitat types throughout the region, although habitat quality varies among and within regions. Deer populations and harvests have increased dramatically since the early 1980s (Table 1). Harvest rates in some states have increased more than 400% over the past 13 years. Region-wide, harvest has more than doubled from 1982 to 1995. Currently, deer population estimates exceed one million animals in Alabama, Georgia, Louisiana, Mississippi, North Carolina, and Texas.

Of the 13 Southern states, 5 indicated that populations were continuing to grow. Population levels were stable in 6 states, and information on current trends was not available for 2 states.

BEHAVIOR

The breeding season is regulated by decreasing photoperiod length during fall. However, timing of the rut varies across the South. Generally, breeding dates become progressively later in western states. For example, peak conceptions in the Lower Coastal Plain of South Carolina occur in mid-October whereas peak breeding does not occur until early to mid-November in the Georgia Piedmont, to January - early February in Alabama and Mississippi. An exception to this trend is east Texas where peak breeding occurs in early November. Populations in Florida can have disjunct breeding dates with peak conceptions during February for populations in the Panhandle, October and November in midsections of the state, and early August in southern Florida (Richter and Labisky 1985). Most females reach sexual maturity at 1.5 years of age, although some 6-7 month old fawns may breed if habitat conditions are good. Does are in heat for 24-36 hours, and gestation averages 202 days.

Whitetail fawns are hiders, and the spotted pelage provides excellent camouflage. Does reduce the size of their home range prior to parturition, and attempt to exclude other deer from the area immediately surrounding the fawn (Ozoga et al. 1982). Fawns begin to accompany their mother at 3-4 weeks-of-age and are functionally weaned by 10 weeks.

Table 1. Estimated white-tailed deer harvest and population by state.

State	Land area (mi^2)	Deer habitat (% Total)	1970 Harvest	1982 Harvest[a]	1996-97 Harvest			Population (1996)
			Total	Total	Male	Female	Total[b]	
Alabama	51,628	93	75,000	210,000	253,092	113,708	366,800	1,500,000
Arkansas	52,609	85	26,017	42,873	104,060	48,400	152,460	900,000
Florida	51,628	57	48,624	65,000	66,055	12,391	78,446	n/a
Georgia	57,800	57	70,000	134,000	199,074	202,284	401,358	980,000
Kentucky	40,395	97	5,000	25,311	95,253	54,517	149,770	473,000
Louisiana	41,406	64	53,271	143,000	122,044	112,656	234,700	1,000,000
Mississippi	47,296	66	93,872 (76)	60,393	159,952	174,178	334,130	1,500,000
North Carolina	48,794	75	38,405	37,902	126,900	64,200	191,100	900,000
E. Oklahoma	n/a	n/a	4,093	n/a	48,367	17,519	24,000	135,000
South Carolina	30,207	73	14,000	54,321	81,981	75,873	163,758	750,000
Tennessee	42,246	61	8,630	40,370	100,972	48,658	149,630	828,000
E. Texas	n/a	n/a	13,439 (77)	n/a	n/a	n/a	54,000	583,000
Virginia	39,682	80	38,138	88,872	124,118	82,915	209,108	900,000

[a] From Stransky (1984)
[b] Total includes deer of unknown sex
n/a estimate not available

Relative densities of white-tailed deer by county for 1970 and 1996. Density categories: low <15/mi², medium 15-30/mi², high >30/mi².

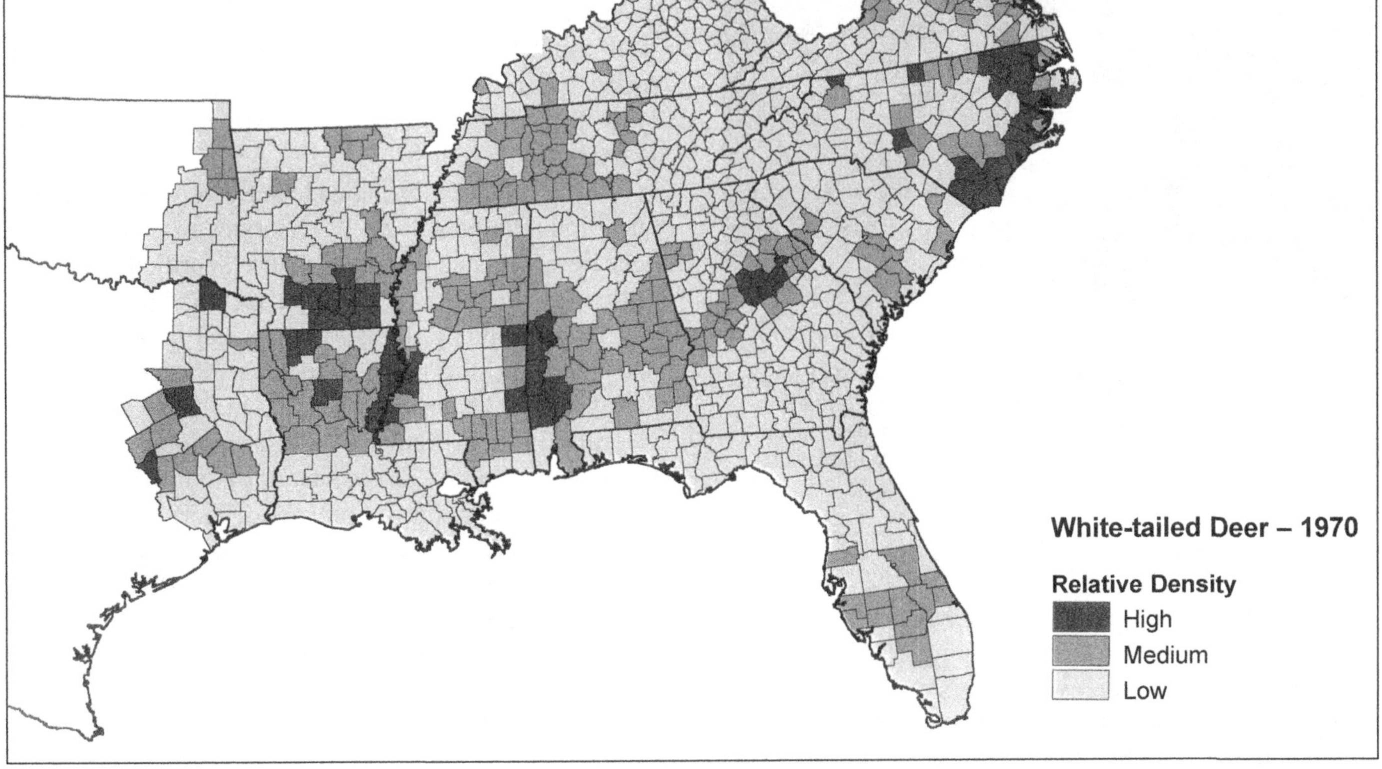

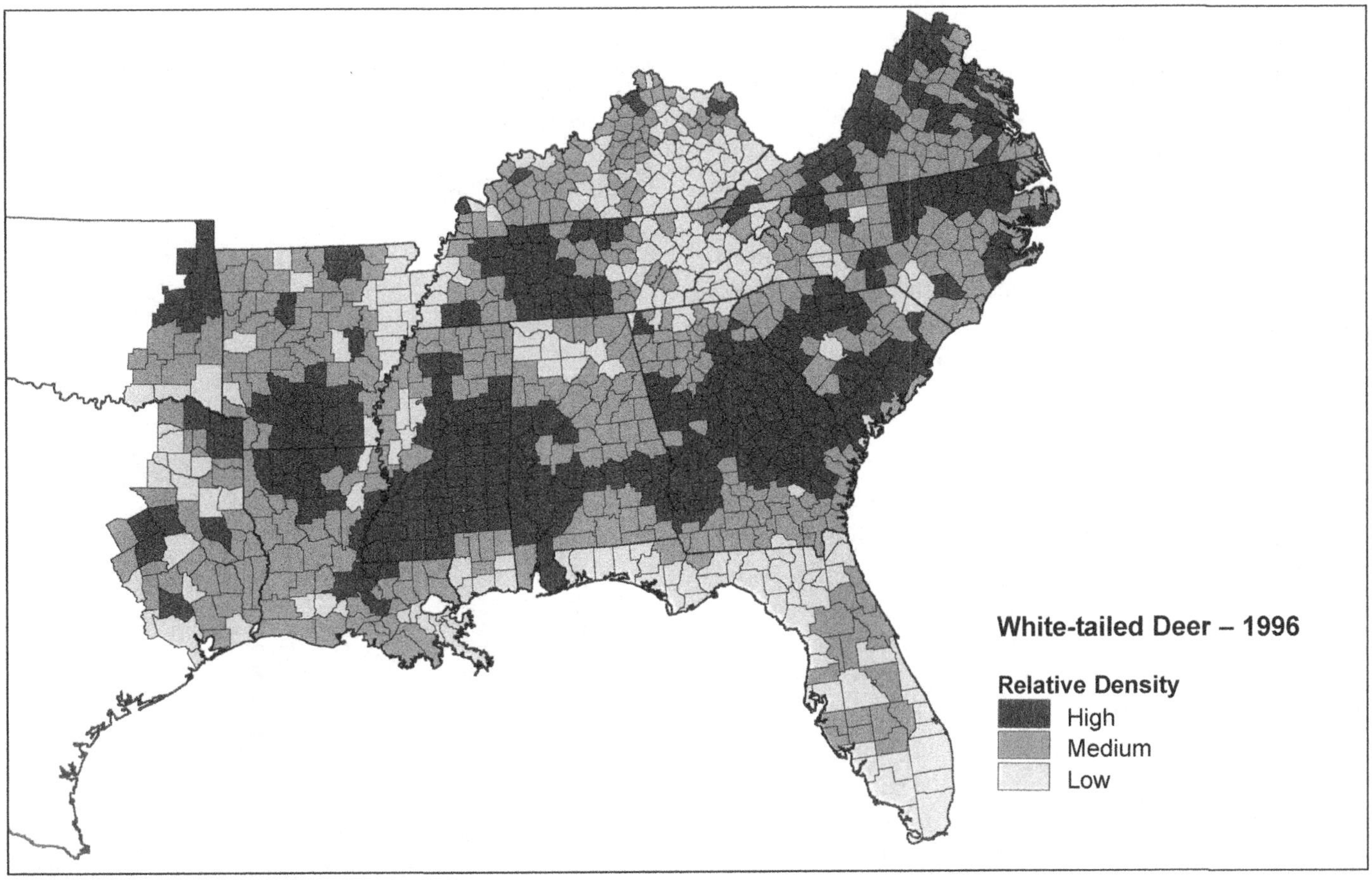

Initiation of the breeding season is triggered by changes in the photoperiod. During late summer or early fall, decreasing daylength stimulates testosterone production in males which results in shedding of the antler velvet and the development of rutting behaviors. *(Univ. Georgia, Warnell School of Forest Resources).*

The basic social unit is the matriarchal group consisting of the maternal doe, her young of the year, and female offspring from previous years. Adult males ≥1.5 years old form loose-knit bachelor groups during the nonbreeding season. During the rut, breeding privileges among males are determined though a dominance hierarchy maintained through threats, postures, sparring, and chemical signals.

Whitetails typically are crepuscular, but movement patterns vary according to weather, disturbance, habitat type, and season. In the South, deer have relatively small home ranges (200 to 1,000 acres) and typically do not migrate seasonally, although some seasonal shifts in home ranges have been reported. Home ranges tend to be smallest in areas with a good distribution of food, cover and water. Home range of adult males increases dramatically during the breeding season.

HABITAT

The most important factor affecting deer populations across the South is soil fertility and productivity. In general, the largest deer are found on the most fertile soils. In fact, Jacobson (1984) found that soil phosphorus was a useful predictor of potential physiological condition. Nevertheless, forage quality and quantity have the greatest impact on whitetail populations.

Soil fertility and productivity vary considerably across the South. The most productive soils, and therefore the best quality habitats occur in the agricultural areas of the Piedmont, Upper Coastal Plain, and agricultural areas of the Midwest, along with bottomland habitats along major rivers in other regions. An abundance of highly nutritious native and/or agricultural forages in these areas contribute to high productivity of deer populations. Even within regions of high potential productivity, habitat quality can vary and habitats largely reflect timber stand conditions and management practices.

Many other regions have lower condition indicators and productivity values. In a survey of state wildlife agencies, Shea and Osborne (1995) identified these suboptimal habitats as the Appalachian Mountains of Virginia, Kentucky, Tennessee, the Carolinas, Georgia, and Alabama, the Ozark and Ouachita Mountains of Arkansas and Oklahoma, the Coastal Plain flatwoods of Georgia, Florida, Alabama, Mississippi and Louisiana, the pocosins and Carolina bays of North and South Carolina, the dry and wet prairies of Florida, the coastal marshes of the Gulf and Atlantic Coasts, the Sandhills of the Carolinas, Georgia, Tennessee, and Florida, and the scrub oak ridges of central Florida (Fig 1). In these areas, harvest and habitat management recommendations can be quite different from those developed for higher quality habitats.

Figure 1. Distribution of poor quality habitats for white-tailed deer in the southeastern United States as reported by state wildlife agencies. *(Adapted from Shea and Osborne 1995; used with permission of Stackpole Books).*

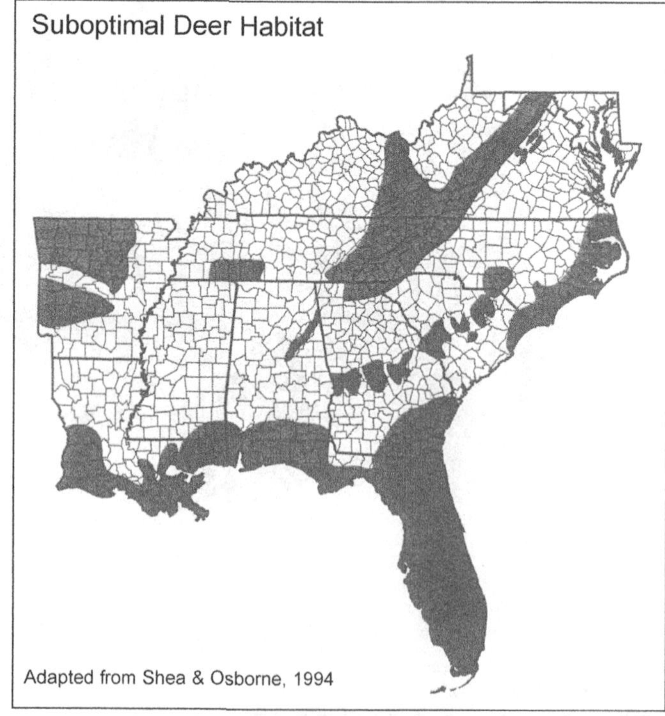

Throughout North America, winter is a nutritionally limiting season because of reduced forage quality and quantity. In the South, however, winter forage variety is greater and winter climate less extreme than in more northern deer ranges. However, unlike northern ranges, late summer can be a nutritionally stressful time for southern deer because hot dry conditions result in reduced forage quality. Summer nutritional stress may reduce lactation, fawn growth, and body weights.

FEEDING AND FOODS

Nutritional requirements of whitetails vary with age, reproductive status and season. Protein requirements for fawns after weaning are estimated to be 14 to 22%. For yearling deer, 11% is considered adequate for maintenance, whereas maintenance levels for adults are from 6-10% (Verme and Ullrey 1984). However, protein requirements during antler growth and lactation/gestation may be substantially higher.

Digestible energy requirements for pregnant does are 155 to 160 kilocalories per unit of metabolic size (kilograms of body weight$^{0.75}$). Energy requirements of fawns are somewhat greater (approx. 200 kilocalories per kilogram of body weight$^{0.75}$). Calcium requirements for growth and antler development are about 0.45%. Phosphorus requirements are less than 0.28% and even may be less than 0.12% (Grasman and Hellgren 1993), although growing or lactating deer will require more. Requirements for other minerals have not been determined, although deer use of mineral supplements suggests a physiological need for minerals that may be lacking in a deer's diet. Weeks (1995) suggested that deer use of mineral supplements was driven primarily by low sodium levels in natural forages. Sodium concentrations in natural forages may range from 35 to 70 ppm during the summer. Because these levels are well below dietary requirements, additional sodium must be obtained from sources other than forage.

Whitetails were once considered to be browsers that primarily consumed the twigs, shoots, and leaves of shrubs, trees, and vines. However, food habits studies conducted across the region have emphasized that only a moderate portion of a deer's diet consists of browse. Use of woody twigs by deer on southern ranges is insignificant, even in winter. Deer are opportunistic herbivores with a diet that includes annual and perennial forbs, fruits, hard mast, grasses, flowers, and fungi. When conditions allow, they are highly selective foragers choosing the most palatable, succulent, and nutritious plants or parts of plants.

White-tailed deer are opportunistic feeders with a diet that includes a wide variety of annual and perennial forbs, grasses, flowers, and fungi. During autumn and winter, hard mast (acorns) constitutes a significant portion of the diet when available. A wide variety of fruits such as blackberries, grapes, and persimmons also are consumed, particularly during the summer and autumn months *(R. Franz)*.

Browse quality varies among species and during different seasons. Generally, browse is adequate in protein and minerals during spring, but quality declines to near maintenance levels or below during late summer. Forbs are used most heavily during spring and early summer, and may constitute more than 50% of the diet (Fig. 2). Forage quality varies among forb species, but protein levels in some species may exceed 25% and digestion coefficients may exceed 60%.

Acorns are a major component of the whitetail's fall diet in virtually all habitat types. When abundant, they may compose >70% of the diet during November and December. They are a highly palatable concentrated source of energy, but have low protein content. In many habitat types, acorns are used heavily, but are not a critical component of the whitetail's diet. In other poor

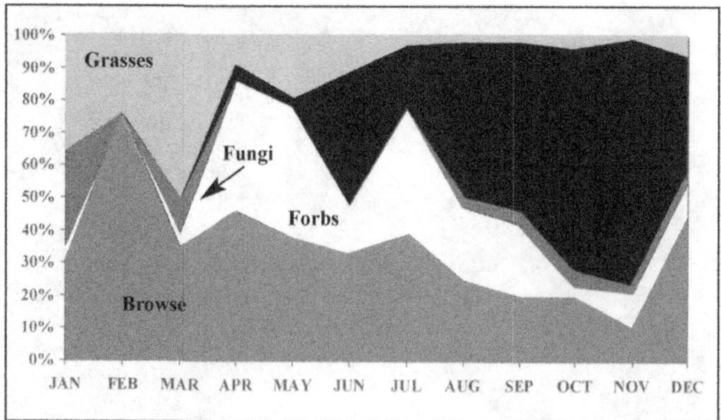

Figure 2. Generalized food habits of Southern white-tailed deer. *(Redrawn from Jacobson 1995; used with permission of Stackpole Books).*

quality habitats such as the Southern Appalachians and the coastal flatwoods, acorn mast is critical, and whitetail populations are driven by the vagaries of mast production. In these areas, body weights, reproduction, and even survival can be reduced dramatically by a poor mast crop (Rogers et al. 1990, Wentworth et al. 1992).

Since plant communities vary among regions and habitat types in the South, the whitetail's diet also must vary among regions. In Mississippi, Warren and Hurst (1981) evaluated deer use of grasses, forbs, legumes, vines, woody plants, sedges, rushes and ferns. Of 521 species of plants evaluated, 267 (51%) were rated as receiving moderate to high use. Greater than 60% of the forbs and legumes were listed as high to moderate use, whereas very few sedges, rushes, or ferns were used.

In a summary of white-tailed deer food habits from the Southeastern United States, Harlow and Guynn (1987) reported that important browse species for deer in the Coastal Plain included the leaves of greenbrier, yellow jessamine, gallberry, myrtle holly, dahoon, yaupon, blueberry, huckleberry, blackgum, blackberry, grape, sweet bay and red bay. In the Peidmont, deer make frequent use of Japanese honeysuckle along with a wide variety of herbaceous and woody plant species.

Table 2. Woody, herbaceous, and fruit-producing plants important to southern deer, and season of importance.

Woody browse species		Herbaceous species		Fruit-producing species	
Red maple	Sp, Su	Three-seeded mercuries	Su	American beautyberry	Su, Au
Rattan vine	Sp, Su	Ragweed	Su	Yaupon	Au, Wi
American beautyberry	Sp, Su	Pussytoes	Au, Wi	Hawthorn	Au, Wi
Trumpetcreeper	Sp, Su, Au	Horseweed	Su	Flowering dogwood	Au, Wi
Swamp cyrilla	Sp	Crotons	Su	Partridgeberry	Au, Wi
Strawberry bush	year-round	Tick clovers	Su	Sweetleaf	Au
Carolina jessamine	year-round	Carolina cranesbill	Sp	Yaupon	Au, Wi
Deciduous holly	Sp, Su	Lespedezas	Su	Blackberries	Sp, Su
Yaupon	Au, Wi	Sweet clovers	Sp, Su	Plums/cherries	Sp, Su
Japanese honeysuckle	year-round	White clover	Wi, Sp	Blueberries	Sp, Su
Sweetbay	year-round	Vetches	Au, Sp	Pokeberry	Su, Au
Red mulberry	Sp, Su	Vervains	Su	Coralberry	Au, Wi
Blackgum	Sp, Su	Asters	Sp, Su, Au	Grapes	Su, Au
Buffalo-nut	Sp, Su	Bedstraw	Sp, Su	Persimmon	Au, Wi
Oaks	Sp, Su	Sunflowers	Sp, Su	Fringetree	Su
Blackberries	year-round	Pokeweed	Sp	Sumac	Au, Wi
Greenbriers	year-round	Goldenrods	Sp, Su	Saw-palmetto	Au
Muscadine/grape	Sp, Su	Poison ivy	Sp, Su		
Yellow poplar	Sp, Su	Day flower	Sp, Su		
Sourwood	Sp, Su	Galax	Au, Wi		
Blueberries	Sp, Su	Wintergreen	Au, Wi		
Rhododendron	Au, Wi				
Mountain laurel	Au, Wi				
Mapleleaf viburnum	Sp, Su				
Coralberry	Au, Wi				

In the Southern Appalachian Mountains, hardwood leaves and annual and perennial forbs are important during summer.

Soft mast consumption peaks during the summer and includes a wide variety of fruits and berries (Table 2). Each species of soft mast producer constitutes a minor part of the whitetail's overall diet because they are available for a relatively short time. However, collectively they are available for considerably longer and therefore are very important.

Use of native grasses appears to be low except for young shoots which are consumed readily during early spring. Several cool season agricultural grasses (wheat, oats, rye, ryegrass) and naturalized cool season exotic grasses (orchard grass, fescue) are used commonly during the winter months throughout the South. These agricultural grasses often are planted for winter food plots.

Mushrooms also can be a significant component of the diet. Although consumed in moderate amounts throughout the year, when fungi are abundant, they may constitute more than 15% of the diet. Mushrooms are high in phosphorus and protein and likely are a very important source of phosphorus in areas such as the Coastal Plain Flatwoods which have phosphorus-deficient soils.

Unlike many other parts of the country, in some regions of the South broadleaf evergreens remain highly palatable and nutritious throughout the winter. Two escaped exotic species, Japanese honeysuckle and Chinese privet, constitute the majority of the winter diet in areas such as the Piedmont and Upper Coastal Plain where they are abundant. Broadleaf evergreens in other regions tend to be less palatable and less nutritious. Rhododendron can replace acorns in the diet of Southern Appalachian deer, but it is of very low quality. In the Coastal Plain, low to moderate quality evergreens such as yaupon, blueberry, and large gallberry are used heavily during winter.

DISEASES

Whitetails are susceptible to a number of diseases and are hosts to over 100 species of parasites. Deer tolerate most of these infections and parasitic organisms well, and in most populations, disease-related mortality is of limited importance to population dynamics. A major exception, particularly in the South, is hemorrhagic disease caused by either the EHD (epizootic hemorrhagic disease) virus or the BTV (bluetongue virus). Five serotypes of BTV and 2 serotypes of EHD have been detected in the United States. The disease was first identified during a 1955 epizootic in New Jersey, although it likely occurred well before that time. Some mortality from this disease occurs in the South every year. Mortality rates typically are low (less than 15%) although rates over 50% have been reported (Davidson and Doster 1997). Virus transmission and active infection occur during late summer or early fall in the South and coincide with peak populations of biting midges (*Culicoides* spp.) which serve as the vector. Apparently, viral exposure and serotype diversity vary inversely with latitude in the South, whereas the severity of the disease increases with latitude (Davidson and Doster 1997). Therefore, across the South, whitetail populations have different levels of risk for infection and manifestation of the disease.

As with most wildlife species, deer host a variety of parasites. Over 100 species of internal or external parasites have been reported (Samuel 1994). Although not all species of parasites occur in the South, deer in this region are host to a highly diverse fauna of protozoan, helminth, and arthropod species. Highest parasite diversity occurs in the Coastal Plain whereas diversity is lowest in the Southern Appalachians. However, heavy parasite loads are most commonly associated with nutritionally stressed herds regardless of whether the stress results from inherently poor-quality habitat or habitat degraded by overbrowsing.

Although deer may be plagued by several species of protozoans, flukes, and tapeworms, the most important groups of parasites include the internal nematodes (roundworms) and the external arthropods (ticks, lice, etc.). The large stomach worm (*Haemonchus contortus*) and the large lungworm (*Dictyocaulus viviparus*) are the two most pathogenic helminths. The large stomach worm inhabits the abomasum and occurs throughout the South but higher prevalences and intensities occur in the Coastal Plain. Deer less than 1 year old tend to have higher worm burdens than adults. The large lungworm also occurs across the South. Prevalence of infection in the Southeast is about 30% with young deer and males most susceptible to infection (Prestwood et al. 1971). Infection rates are highest during spring through fall, and lowest in winter. Other helminth parasites of importance in the South are the liver fluke (*Fascioloides magna*), the meningeal worm (*Parelaphostrongylus tenuis*), the muscle worm (*P. andersoni*), the arterial worm (*Elaeophora schneideri*), and stomach worms (*Ostertagia* spp. and *Trichostrongylus* spp.)

Parasitic arthropods include ticks, deer keds, lice, and bot flies. Ticks are the most important external parasites of deer. Tick infestation is rarely the major cause of mortality in deer, although in some areas, significant fawn mortality has been attributed to lone star tick (*Amblyomma americanum*) infestations. Ticks, however, are important because they are vectors of several pathological agents, some of which have serious human health consequences. The black-legged tick (*Ixodes scapularis*) is a vector of the agents of Lyme disease and human granulocytic ehrlichiosis whereas the lone star tick is the vector of the rickettsial disease, human monocytic ehrlichiosis. Other external arthropods are seldom of significant health consequences to whitetails.

INTERACTIONS WITH OTHER SPECIES

Other than man, coyotes and bobcats are the only significant predators of whitetails. Recent expansion of the coyote into previously unoccupied regions of the South has raised concern among many deer hunters. However, such concern most often is unwarranted. Although both bobcats and coyotes may take some deer, their primary prey species are small to medium sized mammals. Most predation by bobcats and coyotes is on young fawns or adults that are injured or otherwise predisposed to predation. Predation rates usually are low and insignificant when compared to other causes of mortality. However, this is not to say that predation cannot be an important population influence in some areas, such as poor quality habitats where productivity is naturally low.

Contrary to popular thought, dogs usually are ineffective as deer predators. Although domestic and feral dogs often chase deer, they usually have little effect unless the deer are sick, injured or otherwise debilitated, or hampered by deep snows. When pursued by dogs, whitetails use a number of escape strategies. According to Marchinton and Hirth (1984) some deer may remain bedded in thick cover in attempts to avoid detection. When pursued, deer often run a relatively straight course using speed to outdistance dogs. Others run circuitous patterns, often crossing their trail to confuse pursuing dogs. Pursued deer also use water as an escape route when accessible.

Other than competition for acorns with turkeys, squirrels, and other small mammals, white-tailed deer usually do not compete directly for forage with native wildlife species. Grazing of woodlands by domestic livestock can eliminate deer forage, reduce escape cover, and change plant species composition. However, light cattle stocking in some open pine woodlands can be of some benefit to deer habitat. In most areas of the Southeast, whitetails and wild hogs do not compete much directly, although abundant hog populations can impact forest understories, particularly in bottomland habitats. In areas where deer populations are highly dependent on acorn mast, the potential for competition is substantial in years of low mast production. Hogs also can severely impact food plot programs.

Although deer may be little affected by other wildlife species, they can have profound impacts on habitat conditions for other wildlife. Several studies have demonstrated that overabundant deer populations can have significant effects on forest regeneration. Deer are now recognized as agents of ecological change with the ability to greatly influence plant and animal communities. A survey of resource managers throughout the United States indicated that 98 species of threatened or endangered plants were affected by deer herbivory (Miller et al. 1992). Deer have even been reported to cause negative impacts on ground-nesting and shrub-nesting songbirds. Clearly, resource managers and the hunting public must appreciate that overabundant deer populations cannot be justified ecologically.

MANAGEMENT

Harvest

White-tailed deer management involves manipulation of mortality (harvest via hunting) to keep the population within the capacity of its habitat along with manipulation of the habitat itself. Harvest regimes depend on management goals, population size, and habitat productivity, but in almost all cases some harvest management is required to maintain population levels. Management programs must reflect the understanding that no 2 areas and populations are the same. This is particularly true in the South where habitat quality and deer population dynamics can vary dramatically across short distances.

Reproduction, mortality, dispersal, and movement patterns drive deer population dynamics. Important reproductive parameters include fertility rates (no. young/female), age at first breeding, timing of the rut, and adult sex ratio. On high quality range, does on average produce more offspring and many female fawns may become pregnant. Conversely, on poor range, some does do not breed until they are 2.5 years-of-age.

In many areas, white-tailed deer populations respond predictably to changes in herd density. These 'density-dependent' herds tend to occur in regions of moderate to good habitat quality. In these areas, reproductive rates, body growth and antler development are related to herd density. Therefore, harvest of female deer is necessary to maintain productivity. Questions of

Regulated annual harvests are the primary tool of scientifically-based population management. Harvest guidelines attempt to target specific sex and age classes to maintain populations within the capacity of the habitat. Across the South, differences in habitat quality necessitate region-specific harvest guidelines *(J. Hamilton)*.

how many deer to harvest in these areas are difficult to answer, but for most situations, maintaining the population at a density from 40 to 80% of carrying capacity results in similar sustained yields. If non-harvest mortality (poaching, disease, etc) is not significant, 20 to 40% of the females should be harvested annually (Jacobson and Guynn 1995).

Buck harvest guidelines depend on the goals of the landowner/manager. Maximum antler development and body size are attained when populations are maintained well below the carrying capacity of the habitat. However, antler size and body weights do not peak until bucks are 4.5 to 6.5 years old. Therefore, management strategies to produce large mature bucks will require guidelines to minimize harvest pressure on younger-aged males. Restrictive harvest regimes based on minimum antler size criteria can be used to protect 1.5 and 2.5 year-old males from harvest. Antler spread or antler beam length generally are good predictors of age while number of antler points is not. For example, in productive habitats an antler spread limit of 15" or greater will protect virtually all 1.5 year-old bucks from harvest, while protecting few 2.5+ year-olds. However, harvest criteria must be established for different regions because what works well in one area may not work in another. In some poor quality habitats, number of antler points may be a more accurate predictor of age than antler spread. In these areas, a simple regulation protecting spike animals from harvest may protect the 1.5 year-old age class from harvest. As with all harvest guidelines, establishment of regulations to increase the age structure of the bucks must be based on local data.

In some poor quality habitats of the South (see Fig. 1), adherence to the density dependence model of harvest management likely will produce dismal results. In these regions of poor inherent productivity, dramatic changes in herd density in response to management may not result in increases in deer condition or herd productivity. For example, deer forage in the Coastal Plain Flatwoods may be highly abundant, but all is low quality. Mean protein content of browse in some Florida flatwoods may be below 8%. Reducing herd density in these areas will not cause an increase in deer diet quality, and therefore herd productivity will not respond. These habitats still may have high carrying capacities although herd increases occur at much slower rates. Antlerless harvest guidelines should be conservative to avoid excessive population reduction that would take years to recover. In fact, herds in some areas can be maintained with little or no antlerless harvest.

Habitat

Because whitetails have limited home ranges, areas with a high habitat diversity will most often be higher quality habitat. Since a single forest type rarely provides all of a deer's habitat requirements, habitats can be improved by using timber harvest, prescribed fire, and/or agricultural food plots to divide large stands into smaller units.

Early successional plant communities provide abundant herbaceous forage and summer soft mast whereas later successional forests provide fall and winter mast, cover, and limited browse. Maintenance of a mixture of successional stages will provide year-round forage. The following from Kammermeyer and Thackston (1995) are general guidelines for timber stand size, shape, and distribution in the Southeast: Distribute stands so that no more than one-third of a square mile is occupied by age classes under 20 years; separate regeneration areas with older stands, buffer strips, or streamside zones of mature timber; and if younger stands must join, maintain a minimum age difference of 5 to 7 years.

Thinning forest stands can increase understory browse availability and release mast-producing trees. Oaks with large crowns should be left when hardwood stands are thinned since acorn production is directly related to canopy size. The US Forest Service recommends having at least 20% of an area in mature mast-producing hardwoods. A mixture of oaks from the red and white oak groups will help guard against a total mast failure. In poor quality habitats such as the Southern Appalachians and the Sandhills of the Upper Coastal Plain, deer populations are dependent on annual acorn crops. Because forest management such as clearcutting does not improve winter ranges in these areas, maintenance of mature hardwood stands is particularly important.

In the South, approximately 60 million acres are in pine types, many of which are managed intensively. These agricultural forests provide special problems along with special opportunities for deer habitat management. Intensive site preparation to eliminate hardwoods, short rotations, and use of prescribed fire preclude significant hard mast production in pine stands. From initial stand establishment until canopy closure at 8 to 10 years, pine plantations provide abundant forage in the form of annual and perennial forbs, soft mast, and vines. Mechanical site preparation appears to promote greater development of woody browse species, whereas herbicide site preparation may promote herbaceous growth, although the species composition depends on the chemical used. Release treatments that remove competing hardwoods also can shift forage production from woody browse to more palatable herbaceous growth.

After canopy closure, pine stands produce little forage for white-tailed deer, although they do provide excellent escape cover. Thinning pine stands as soon as commercially feasible will open the pine canopy and allow production of deer forages. As a general rule, stands should be thinned so that 30% of the forest floor is in direct sunlight. Periodic thinnings with or without prescribed fire will maintain productive deer habitat through the life of the stand.

Since forage production changes dramatically as a pine stand matures, interspersion of stands of different ages is important. Limiting clearcut sizes also will ensure that some portions of an area are in the productive stage. Mast-producing hardwoods should be maintained in streamside zones.

Prescribed burning in some timber types can be a beneficial and economical means of habitat improve-

Supplemental plantings of agricultural crops (food plots) can provide an important nutritional boost. Plantings should focus on highly nutritious, productive crops that are available during the late summer and winter periods of nutritional stress. A well-maintained food planting can produce several tons of quality forage on an annual basis. *(B. Murphy, Quality Deer Manage. Assoc.)*

ment. In pine types, fire can increase browse production, palatibility, and nutrition. Pine stands should be burned on a 3 to 5 year rotation. Best results are obtained when prescribed fire is used in concert with thinnings to allow additional sunlight to reach the forest floor.

Food plots can be important in deer habitat management. They also can increase the opportunity to observe and harvest deer. However, they should be viewed as a supplement to natural food supplies, not as a cure for poor population or habitat management. Because well maintained food plots can produce several tons of forage annually, as little as 1% of an area in high quality food plots can enhance reproduction, growth, and antler development. They can be particularly beneficial in areas where native forages are naturally low in quality or quantity.

In the South, choice of food plot plantings should target the winter and late summer nutritional stress periods. Several annual grasses such as wheat, oats, rye, and ryegrass produce an abundance of forage throughout winter and early spring. These grains are easy to establish and are used heavily by deer. Many biologists recommend using a mixture of legumes and annual grasses for cool season plantings. Annual legumes such as arrowleaf clover and Austrian winter peas can be used but a perennial clover such as ladino clover is preferred. After the first year, these plantings will revert to stands of pure ladino clover which can persist indefinitely if managed properly. Management may necessitate annual mowing, pesticide application to control grubs, and a grass-selective herbicide to eliminate weedy grasses.

Food plots that target the late summer stress period include agricultural crops such as corn and grain sorghum and legumes such as alfalfa, alyceclover, sweet clover, soybeans, cowpeas and American jointvetch. Grain sorghum may be preferred to corn as it is easier to grow and is more drought tolerant. Both are good sources of energy, but generally low in protein. Legumes are high in protein and may provide better nutrition than either corn or grain sorghum. In planting trials, alyceclover and American jointvetch have proven to be productive, nutritious, and highly preferred deer forages. Their only drawback is that they generally do not do well in droughty soils.

Artificial supplementation with corn or pelleted rations is a controversial topic but generally is not necessary for proper deer herd management. Also, it is expensive, may artificially concentrate deer, and may 'dewild' deer. Costs per ton of artificial forage consumed may be 10 to 30 times the cost of forage consumed from food plots. Additionally, corn sold as deer food may contain higher levels of aflatoxin than is allowed in livestock feeds.

No studies have demonstrated increased deer health, body size, or antler development in response to mineral supplementation. Nevertheless, the seasonal attractiveness of mineral supplements, especially salt, and the inherent low sodium levels in natural forages suggest that minerals may provide some benefits.

Sound population management in concert with proper habitat management is critical to the management of deer herds. However, no single management regime is appropriate for all areas of the South. Each area provides its own unique problems and opportunities. Identification of these conditions is a challenge and the responsibility of land managers and biologists.

HUNTING

The white-tailed deer is without question the most popular big game animal in North America. In the South, more than 3 million hunters pursued whitetails during the 1995-96 hunting season (Table 1). Regionwide, deer hunting has a tremendous economic impact. In 1991, hunting for white-tailed deer in the 13 southern states generated an estimated 2.2 billion dollars in retail sales, 59,000 jobs, and more than 200 million dollars in state and federal taxes. Bag limits are liberal and deer seasons are long (Table 3). Firearms season ranges from 9 days in Oklahoma to 140 days in some parts of South Carolina. Hunter success likewise is very high compared to other regions of the country. Success during the firearms season ranges from 27% success in Oklahoma to 60% or greater in Alabama and Mississippi. The use of dogs for hunting is a steeped tradition throughout the South, and most states permit dog hunting on at least some areas. Kentucky, Oklahoma, Tennessee, and Texas are exceptions in that dog hunting is prohibited statewide.

Most hunting in the South occurs on private lands. Percent of land area open to public hunting is low, ranging from 2% in Alabama to 16% in Florida. Hunting rights on much of the private lands are leased with lease prices ranging from $2 to $10 or more per acre.

Likely even more important than its economic impact, deer hunting has a extremely important sociological and spiritual impact. The quality of hunting experiences cannot be measured only by the number of deer harvested or the economic return generated. A quality hunting experience defies definition because the definition differs among people. Wildlife and wild

Table 3. Number of deer hunters and hunting statistics by state, 1995-1996.

State	No. deer hunters	5-Year Trend	Length of season (days) Archery	Length of season (days) Firearms	% Hunting success Archery	% Hunting success Firearms	Harvest/mi² occupied habitat	% Land area public hunting	% Land area open to dog hunting
Alabama	229,600	0	109	75	34	60	8.3	2.0	70
Arkansas	250,000	0	152	36	n/a	n/a	3.7	12.0	81
Florida	117,567	-	30	72	n/a	n/a	2.9	16.0	75
Georgia	308,342	0	35	51-79	26	61	n/a	6.0	10
Kentucky	209,000	0	109	10	13	47	2.8	8.0	0
Louisiana	181,200	0	123	14-69	21	45	8.9	7.0	80
Mississippi	166,320	+	62	47	44	65	10.7	6.0	99
North Carolina	285,000	+	24-54	18-67	n/a	49	5.9	6.0	53
E. Oklahoma	200,000	0	78	9	17	27	2.88	2.0	0
South Carolina	176,114	+	10	60-140	n/a	n/a	6.8	7.0	60
Tennessee	186,342	-	23-34	18-28	23	47	5.6	8.5	0
E. Texas	582,148	n/a	32	65	15	n/a	4.0	<5	0
Virginia	290,000	0	41-71	12-42	30	50	6.9	7.9	55

n/a not available

things (including hunting) add immeasurably to our quality of life, often in ways we cannot explain. Deer hunting reaches to the core of our evolutionary heritage as predators. It joins families, providing quality recreational time for adults and children. It maintains important traditions in a time of rapid social change. But most importantly, it maintains our connectivity with nature and natural processes in a rapidly urbanizing environment.

THE FUTURE–GOOD, BAD, AND UGLY

The future of white-tailed deer management and hunting in the South is a mixture of positive and negative trends.

Good.—Whitetail populations are at an all time high throughout the region. Recently, many states have stabilized, or even reduced populations in attempts to maintain an ecological balance. More and more landowners are appreciating the aesthetics and economics of deer.

Across the South, hunters and landowners are playing an increasingly important role in directing harvest goals and habitat management. As a result of extensive hunter-education programs and the initiation of property-based management, most hunters now view themselves as stewards of the wildlife resource. *(R. Kingsley, Quality Deer Manage. Assoc.)*

A growing trend is for hunters and landowners to play a positive (rather than negative) role in deer management. Increasingly, hunters are practicing Quality Deer Management (QDM) on the lands they hunt. QDM attempts to manage deer herds in an ecological and social balance. Hunters now view themselves as stewards of the resource, not merely consumers. Although the promise of larger bucks first attracts hunters to practice QDM, they soon learn of additional benefits including increased herd health, enhancement of hunting experiences, better knowledge of the quarry and its needs, and most importantly promotion of ethical hunting. Management strategies that promote a more natural age structure, sex ratio, and population density also can impact deer sociobiological processes. Beneficial impacts may include more synchronous reproduction and enhanced fawn survival (Miller and Ozoga 1997).

There also is a growing trend for hunters to take a positive role in the establishment of state regulations. For example, hunters in several counties of Georgia have voluntarily (through referenda) established restrictive minimum antler size requirements which will protect young antlered bucks from harvest. Other counties are following the same trend. Thus the future looks bright for deer and deer hunting.

Bad.—Concern about the negative aspects of abundant deer populations is growing. Vehicle collisions, crop depredation, urban and suburban deer damage, and negative impacts of overabundant deer populations on forest communities are important issues that must be addressed. As human populations increase in the South, conflicts will increase. Means of population control other than regulated sport hunting must be evaluated for application in localized situations where hunting is not feasible.

Another negative trend is the potential decline in hunter numbers. Nationwide, the percentage of hunters in the population is declining, and recently it appears that the absolute number of hunters has stabilized or declined slightly. In the South, hunter numbers currently appear stable (Table 3), but future declines are predicted.

Ugly.—Nationwide, well-intentioned but misinformed citizens increasingly view sport hunting as cruel and antisocial. Although most Americans view hunting for meat as a valid use of the deer resource, only a minority condone hunting for trophy specimens. Clearly, public support for hunting is eroding as we progress from a rural society to an urban society. This change increasingly estranges the public from the life and death processes of the food chain. If there is a simple answer to disputes over deer management and deer hunting, it lies in the education of everyone affected by them, particularly youth.

CHAPTER 9

Wild Turkey

James G. Dickson[1]
US Forest Service
Southern Research Station, Nacogdoches, TX

A traditional and very important game species of southern forests is the wild turkey (*Meleagris gallopavo*). The wild turkey is a truly wild creature and inspires an amazing level of admiration and devotion among turkey hunters. Wild turkeys have stout legs that support the heavy bird and are used to scratch for food, and short powerful wings associated with rapid short flight. Wild turkeys can run or fly rapidly for short distances. Of the 5 traditional subspecies of the wild turkey in North America, the 2 genetically most similar (Mock et al. 2001) are found in the South. The Florida wild turkey (*M. g. Osceola*) inhabits peninsular Florida and the eastern wild turkey (*M. g. silvestris*) is found in the remainder of the region (Pelham and Dickson 1992). Consistent with their humid southern forest habitat, both subspecies are characterized by dark tail coverts and tail tips, in contrast to the whitish tips of the western subspecies. The Rio Grande wild turkey (*M. g. intermedia*), a subspecies of the more arid west, occurs and intergrades with the eastern wild turkey in the oak-hickory forests of northeastern Oklahoma.

HISTORY

Wild turkeys were very abundant throughout the precolonial South, based on reports of early European settlers along the coast and travelers into the interior (Mosby and Handley 1943). Early explorers in the region reported numerous and often large flocks of turkeys (see Kennamer et al. 1992:10). The interspersion of mature forests and openings caused by natural phenomena, such as wind storms, and burning by the natives created ideal habitat conditions for wild turkeys.

Early settlers cleared small patches in the forest, and grew crops for sustenance for their families and livestock, with little impact on wild turkey populations. Wild turkeys remained abundant in the region through the early 1800s.

[1]Current Address: School of Forestry, Louisiana Tech University, Ruston, LA

However, settlement by the new Americans and their demands ultimately were hard on wild turkeys. In the latter half of the 1800s and early 1900s as the human population grew, the impact on wild turkey habitat and populations increased dramatically. Also, better access to southern forests and turkey flocks were provided by new roads and railroads. Wholesale cutting of the forests and indiscriminant hunting took its toll. Turkeys of both sexes and all ages were hunted year round, often attracted to bait.

With habitat reduction and intense hunting pressure remnant flocks were mostly relegated to remote areas with limited human activity or with good protection. Examples of areas in the South with remnant populations were mountainous areas of Virginia and elsewhere, remote areas in Florida that were considered

A traditional and very important game species of southern forests is the wild turkey. The wild turkey inspires an amazing level of admiration and devotion among turkey hunters *(M. Johnson)*.

Wild turkeys were exploited and populations suffered in the late 1800s as new settlers populated the region. A restoration technique that did not work was the raising of turkeys in pens and release in the wild *(B. Minser)*.

inhospitable at that time, and larger farms and river bottoms in southwestern Alabama.

Eventually people began to realize that natural resources in general and the wild turkey in particular were in critical condition and that something had to be done. Efforts to bring back wild turkeys began around the 1930s and 1940s. Money provided through the Pittman-Robertson (Federal Aid in Wildlife Restoration) Act in 1937 was a major factor in initiating wildlife management and enhanced efforts to protect wildlife populations.

The first restoration attempt was the raising of turkeys in captivity and release in the wild. Although this concept seemed reasonable at the time, it was a costly failure throughout the country. Turkeys raised in captivity were ill-suited for survival in the wild, and their offspring fared worse. Pen-raised turkeys just didn't work.

However, what did work was the trap and transfer of wild turkeys in the wild. The cannon net, which had been used successfully on waterfowl, was adapted for capturing wild turkeys about 1950, and it and the later improved rocket net proved immensely successful in capturing wild turkeys for transplanting in the South.

The technique that was immensely successful was the trapping of wild turkeys from the wild and release in the wild *(A. Cornell, D. Dyke).*

Other factors also contributed to the return of the wild turkey in the South. During and after World War II the rural human population decreased as many people left small farms for industrial employment in cities. The forests, which had been devastated in the early part of the century, were now maturing again. These maturing

Relative densities of wild turkeys by county for 1970 and 1996. Density categories: low <6/mi^2, medium 6-15/mi^2, high >15/mi^2.

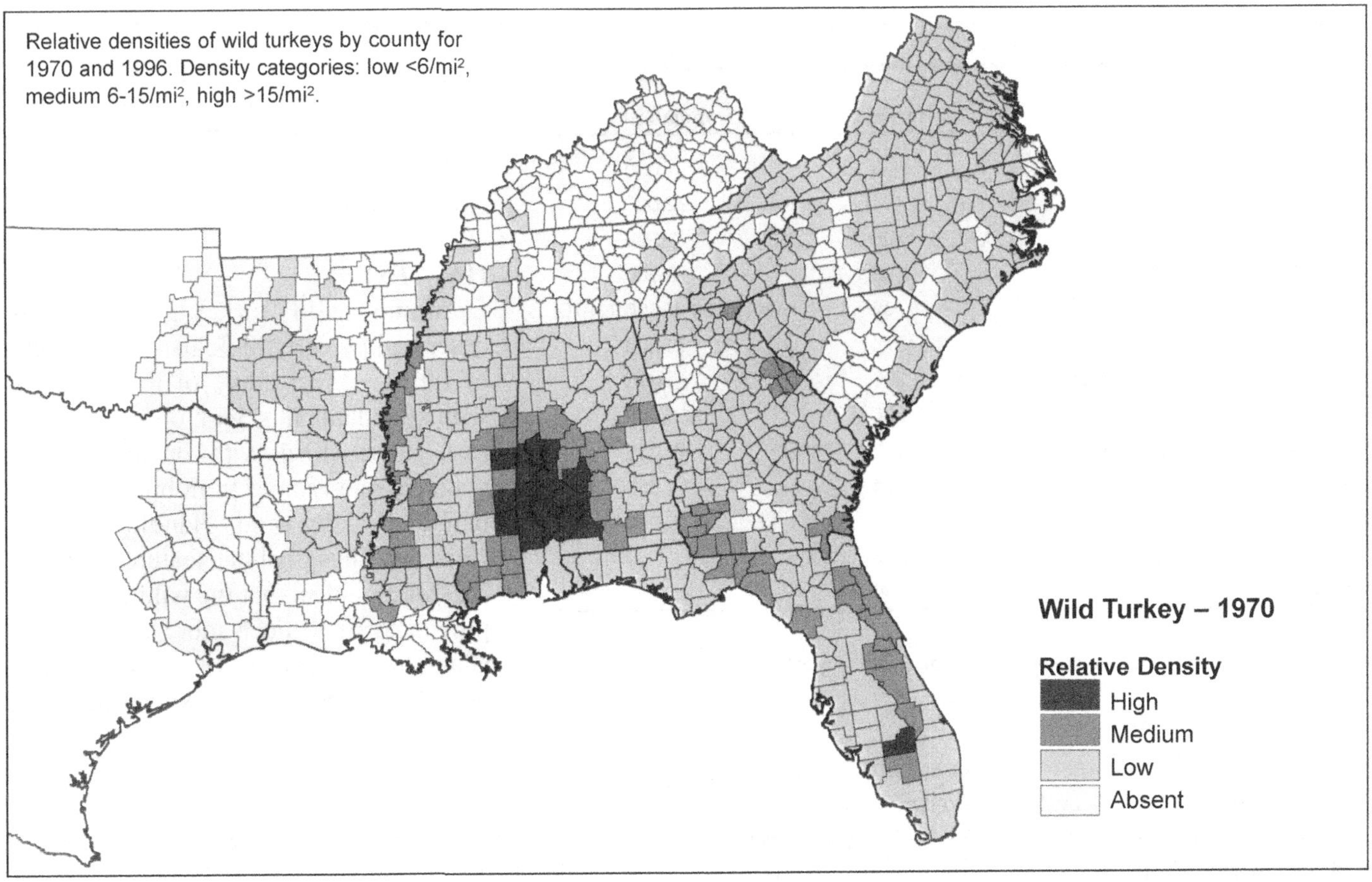

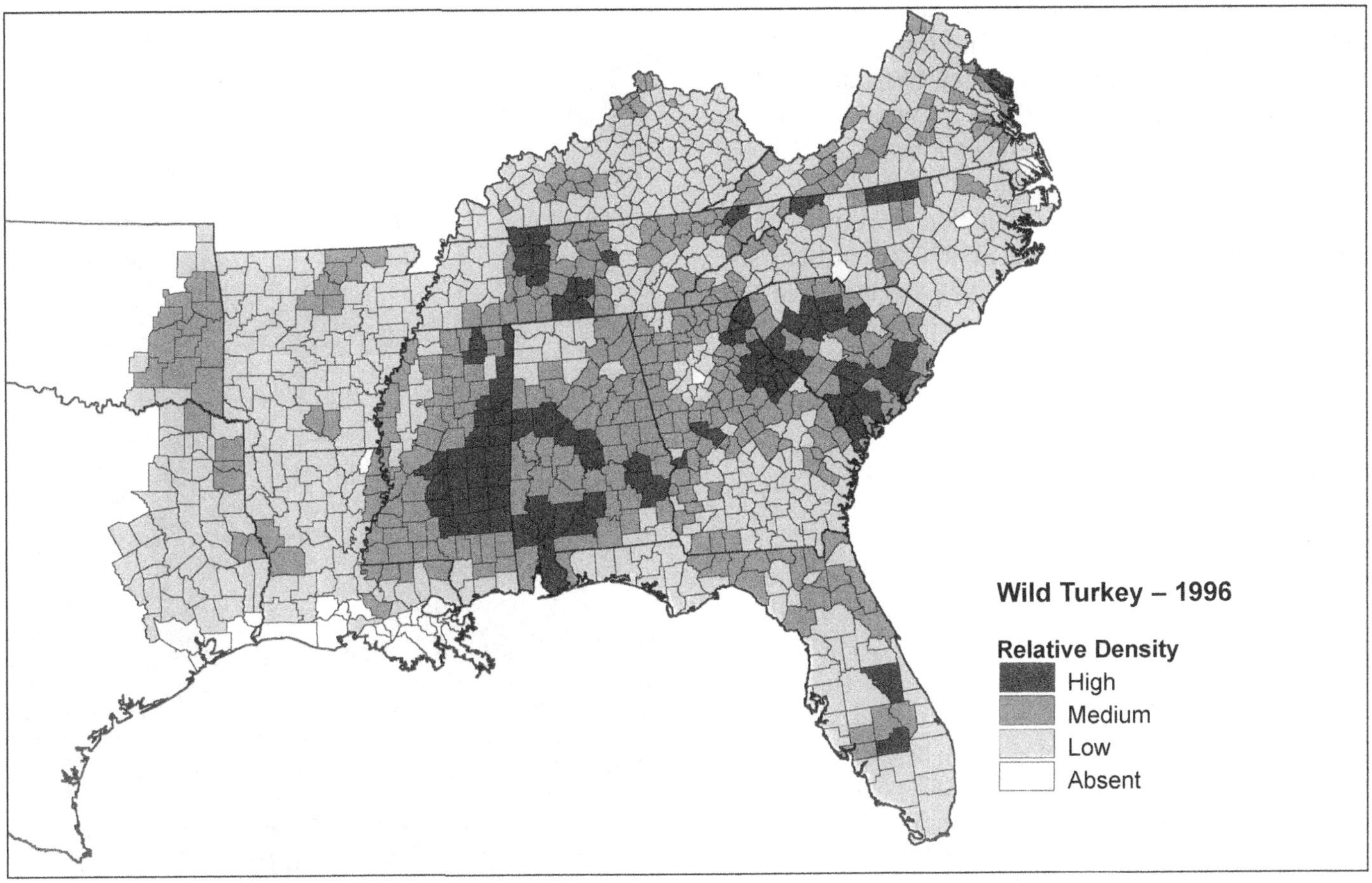

Wild Turkey – 1970

Relative Density
High
Medium
Low
Absent

Wild Turkey – 1996

Relative Density
High
Medium
Low
Absent

Table 1. Estimated wild turkey harvest and population[a] by state.

	1998-99 Harvest		1970 Harvest	1970 Population	
Kentucky	19,225		0	1,000	
Virginia	21,564		6,494	22,000	
Tennessee	16,961		206	2,500	
North Carolina	5,340		<100	2,000	
South Carolina	11,261		32	15,000-18000	(1976)
Georgia	47,000	(1998)	<675	<40,000	
Florida	35,531	(1997-98)	25,200	NA	
Alabama	56,900		28,000	200,000	
Mississippi	32,808	(1998)	19,192 (1976)	50,000	
Arkansas	15,770		1,164	15,000	
Louisiana	4,000	(1998)	3,000	25,000	
East Texas	221		0	0	
East Oklahoma	2,299		0	<1,000	

[a] Populations sometimes are generally estimated as 10 times the gobbler harvest.

forests, along with increased awareness and better protection, helped wild turkey flocks thrive.

The combination of these factors bode well for wild turkeys in the South. By 1959 there was an estimated 227,760 wild turkeys southwide. By 1970 the regional population had increased to almost half a million birds (455,430) (Kennamer et al. 1992). From 1970 to 1999 in the South the population increased from about half a million to over 2 million wild turkeys, and the estimated harvest from less than 100,000 to over 250,000 (Table 1). What a remarkable story!

Harvest and associated population in every state in the region increased during that period. Recent substantial increases have been observed particularly in the northern upland hardwood region in Tennessee and Kentucky where state populations have increased from a few thousand turkeys in 1970 to over 100,000 now.

DISTRIBUTION AND CURRENT POPULATIONS

The wild turkey currently flourishes in southern forests. Wild turkeys are found throughout the South, mostly in medium to high densities (Table 1, Tapley et al. 2001).

Currently, lowest state populations (less than 100,000) probably occur in North Carolina and Louisiana, where the recent harvest in each state was estimated at less than 6,000. Also low populations are found in the small eastern Oklahoma area (about 18,000), and the in eastern Texas (5,000) where restoration has been recent. Highest state harvests (over 30,000) were reported for Alabama, Georgia, Florida, and Mississippi, where state populations probably range from 300,000 to 600,000 wild turkeys.

HABITAT

Optimum wild turkey habitat was described by early biologists as a variety of forest stands, many of them mature with abundant oaks, with open understories, interspersed with openings, well watered, and remote from human disturbance (Mosby and Handley 1943). Currently these habitat features are still regarded as ideal, but the wild turkey has proven to be a much more flexible and adaptable species and is found in a variety of southern forests where adequate

We have been effective in developing information to successfully manage wild turkey populations, hunting, and habitat *(H. Williamson).*

Better protection has helped flocks flourish; now there are over 2 million wild turkeys region-wide *(H. Williamson)*.

Optimum habitat is mature forests interspersed with openings.

protection from humans is afforded (Hurst and Dickson 1992).

Openings have long been recognized as an important component of wild turkey habitat. Turkey foods such as green grass and forbs, seeds, soft mast, insects and other invertebrates, and planted crops may be produced in openings (Hurst and Dickson 1992).

Fall and Winter.—During fall and winter turkeys usually associate in flocks by sex and age. Finding food and avoiding predators is their program at this time of year. Winter food is important for survival and preparation for spring breeding activities. Hens, especially juveniles, need to overwinter in good physical condition for spring reproduction. At the same time, gobblers are developing their breast sponge, fatty tissue that provides energy during the spring rituals when they feed little.

During fall and into winter, immature and adult wild turkeys use a variety of field and forest habitats, often based on food availability in proximity to appropriate cover. Fields provide foods, such as insects (until cold weather limits them), succulent forbs, grass seeds, and waste grain in some agriculture fields.

Forests are used frequently in fall and especially winter. Turkey use often is associated with the foods found there, mostly in the forest floor litter. Mature hardwood stands such as hardwood or pine-hardwoods in northern mountains, bottomland hardwoods, and streamside zones provide excellent habitat. Acorns consistently show up in turkey winter diets during years of production wherever oaks occur. A variety of other food items, such as dogwood and blackgum fruit, are taken where available. Snow covering food is not the problem in the South that it is in the northern portion of the wild turkeys' range.

In Alabama, Speake et al. (1975) saw a shift in gobbler range from old fields and pastures in fall to mixed uneven-aged stands of pine and hardwood stands in winter. The authors concluded that food availability was the determining factor. In upland hardwood forests of northwestern Alabama, prime winter habitat was creek bottom hardwoods and wildlife openings. In the coastal plain in areas with substantial pine plantations, Kennamer et al. (1980) found that turkeys used natural hardwoods the most and pine plantations the least during winter. Exum et al. (1987) found that gobblers and hens used bottomland hardwoods and burned middle-aged pine plantations more frequently than at random.

Breeding and Nesting.—In late winter the winter social flocks break up and turkeys shift from winter range to spring breeding, nesting, and brood range, with associated openings, shrubby nesting sites, and herbaceous brood habitat. This may be a very limited movement, or it may be several miles.

Turkey hens nest on the ground and most first nesting attempts in the South are initiated from late March through April. After the clutch of 10 or 11 eggs has been completed (normally in April for initial nesting attempts), the hen will incubate almost continuously for about 28 days until the clutch hatches. It takes about 2 days for all the poults to hatch, dry out, imprint on the hen and other poults, and exit the nest.

During incubation when the hen sits on the nest almost continuously, the hen and her nest are particularly vulnerable to predation and disturbance. If the nest is predated or abandoned some hens will renest. Even though most hens attempt to nest at least once each year, hen success is quite variable year to year (e.g.,Vangilder et al. 2001). On average only about half of all hens are successful in hatching any poults each year (Exum et al. 1987, Everett et al. 1980).

The structure of specific turkey nest sites usually exhibits some consistent features. Nest sites usually are characterized by abundant herbaceous vegetation and some woody shrub vegetation. Often there is sparse or no overstory vegetation. Most nests are situated under or adjacent to some form of structure, such as logging slash, brush, or vines. The nest site often is located within 100 yards of an opening, such as a woods road or food plot.

Wild turkey hens nest in a variety of different general habitat types; such as pine plantations, older pine-hardwood stands, agriculture fields, rights-of-way, and miscellaneous other vegetative types. In the coastal plain, typical nest sites were described as open pine woodlands or near openings such as roads surrounded by dense ground cover which had not been burned for several years (Wheeler 1948, Stoddard 1963, Exum et al. 1987). Nest locations were determined from results from 4 different areas in Alabama and 1 in Kentucky. Speake et al. (1975) determined that 75% of the nests were situated in old field stages of succession and the remainder were located in bottomland hardwood, upland hardwood, pine-hardwood, or pine stands. Of 48 nests in south-central Alabama, a few were found in agriculture fields (6%), bottomland hardwoods (10%), and cut-over areas (10%), but most of the nests (71%) were in slash pine plantations of all ages (Exum et al. 1987). In South Carolina and Mississippi studies, pine regeneration stands were selected for nesting (Seiss et al. 1990, Still and Baumann 1990). In a mature upland hardwood forest, Everett et al. (1985) found that power

Wild turkeys are opportunistic feeders. During the warmer months a variety of insects are consumed by adults and especially young turkeys *(P. Pelham, G. Hurst).*

line rights-of-way were preferred nesting habitat; almost one third of the nests found were in rights-of-way which comprised less than one percent of the area. Upland hardwood forests were not selected as nesting habitat. The rights-of-way provided low, brushy vegetation appropriate for nesting in an area dominated by mature hardwood trees.

Broods.—Recently hatched poults follow the hen who leads them away from the nest when all are hatched and dry. The small poults are foraging soon after hatching. They grow rapidly and to satisfy their need for protein they consume large quantities of arthropods, such as grasshoppers and spiders. The hen and her young brood seek out and feed in lush herbaceous vegetation, ideally which is dense enough to produce the arthropods, but is not too dense for the young poults to get through. The best young brood foraging areas usually have vegetation tall enough (about 2 feet) to hide the poults from numerous predators, but low enough for the hen to see over. Nearby or interspersed tree or brush cover affords protection from predators (Hubbard et al. 2001).

Radio-instrumented hens and young poults have provided specific data on different habitat types used. In pine forests of eastern Texas, hens with broods selected areas of sparse overstory and midstory trees with abundant ground cover that had been burned (Campo et al. 1989). In the coastal plain of Mississippi, mature bottomland hardwoods with sparse shrub cover and moderate ground cover was preferred habitat (Seiss 1989).

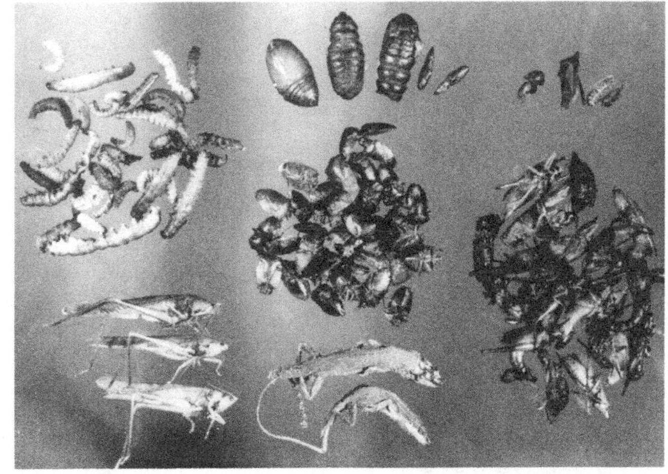

In Alabama, hens with broods (n=85) used several types of openings, such as pastures, hayfields, grainfields, and old fields (Speake et al 1975). In another study, Hillestad and Speake (1970) found that hens with new broods moved into and used a lightly-grazed old field and made regular use of the woods-pasture edge.

Mortality of young turkey poults less than 2 weeks old before they are able to fly to roost is very high; usually less than half survive (see Vangilder 1992). Studies of radio-instrumented poults have shown that poult survival is directly related to the type of brood habitat selected by brood hens (Everett et al. 1980). Hens that took their broods to small ryegrass food plots and mature hardwood forests raised only 9% of 86 poults to 2 weeks of age, whereas hens that took their poults to grazed pastures and woods' edge raised 36% of 116 poults.

Improved pastures, cutover hardwoods, wildlife openings, and rights-of-way were preferred brood habitat by 23 hens that were successful in raising their broods in northwestern Alabama (Everett et al. 1985). Upland hardwood sites were avoided by successful hens. In upland hardwood forests of northeastern Alabama (Metzler and Speake 1985), poult survival in 21 broods was greater in taller dense herbaceous vegetation which probably allowed hens with broods some visual protection from predators. Old fields afforded better cover than grazed pastures. In a recent Alabama study, hens successful in raising poults to 2 weeks of age selected brood habitat that had fewer large trees, less shrub level vegetation, and denser herbaceous vegetation than habitat selected by hens that were unsuccessful in raising their broods or random habitat (Peoples et al. 1996).

At about 2 to 3 weeks of age poults can fly and start roosting overnight in trees. Survival then is better and poults begin using more open areas, such as grazed pastures (Metzler and Speake 1985) or mowed fields (Hillstad 1973). In Georgia, broods moved to a complex of old fields, Bahia grass fields, grassy depressions, and young pine and oak stands (Hon et al. 1978). The rapidly growing poults start eating more plant food found in openings and fields (Blackburn et al. 1975, Hamrick and Davis 1971).

Roosts.—In the South where extremely cold winter weather is not normally a problem, wild turkeys roost in a variety of tree species on different sites. In areas with some topographical relief, turkeys often roost on the upper portion of slopes, just off ridge tops. Turkeys often roost in pines in uplands, and conversely, where available, turkeys roost in cypress or bottomland hardwoods over water (Still and Baumann 1990). During cold weather in winter, roost trees that provide some

Herbaceous vegetation is particularly important habitat for young poults *(G. Wunz)*.

protection, such as large pines and magnolias, have been selected (Wheeler 1948). Pine plantations frequently are selected as roost sites where they occur (Smith and Teitelbaum 1986, Exum et al. 1987). Broods particularly use pine plantations for roosting during spring and summer.

Water.— Water was long thought to be an important part of wild turkey habitat; however, recent information suggests that turkeys in the humid South can get adequate moisture from their diet, such as dew, insects, and succulent berries. In a south Alabama study, hens with their broods made no attempt to go to permanent water sources (Exum et al. 1985).

FEEDING AND FOODS

Turkeys are opportunistic feeders; a lot of how and what they eat is dependent on what is available and what they can find and consume. Wild turkeys feed in different ways. Turkeys find most of their food on or near the ground. They can dig tubers and other food from the ground with their strong feet. And, during periods when they cannot reach their normal food, such as with extended flooding or snow covered ground, turkeys will feed from trees and shrubs on buds and fruits, such as sumac.

Wild turkeys are omnivorous; they eat a wide variety of types of foods and specific items (Hurst 1992). They eat some animal matter, including insects such as grasshoppers, other arthropods such as spiders, and some small vertebrates such as tadpoles and anoles. But the main food for adult turkeys is plant material. Turkeys feed directly on grass and forbs, consume grass seed such as Panicum and Paspalum, and take large amounts of soft fruits and berries such as blackberries and American beautyberry when they are available during the growing season. They consume large quantities of hard mast, such as oak acorns and beech mast, during fall and winter when it is available. Turkeys also consume cultivated crops, such as corn, soybeans, and wheat. Food habits vary by season and by life stage, summarized as follows.

Poults.—Young poults feed voraciously, grow fast, and consume mostly insects and other arthropods early in life. The diet of a young poult the first week of life usually is about 90% animal matter (Hurst 1992). It has been said that young poults will eat anything slow enough to catch and small enough to swallow.

Poults imprinted to turkeys or chickens feeding in fields or forest stands ate beetles, true bugs, grasshoppers, and leafhoppers; along with dewberry fruits and seeds of sedges, nut rushes, and panic grasses (Hurst and Stringer 1975). In middle-aged slash pine plantations in south Alabama, dropping analyses showed 60 percent insects and 40 percent fruits of blackberry, blueberry, and huckleberry, and nozeburn seed (Exum et al. 1985,1987). But at least in some situations poults eat mostly plant material. In a 2-year-old pine plantation where insects were scarce and seeds were abundant, 94% of the diet of chicken-imprinted poults was seeds of nut-rush, sedge, panic grass, and blackberry fruits (Hurst 1992).

Juveniles.—Within about a month of age, the diet of young turkeys has changed from predominantly animal matter to predominantly plant material and is similar to adults (Hurst 1992). Several food habits studies conducted in Alabama in mid-to-late summer showed that a variety of grass and forbs, grass seed, fruits, and some insects were consumed. Hamrick and Davis (1971) found that in forest/field habitat the dominant food item of juvenile turkeys was Bahia grass seed, and grasshoppers were the most important animal food. Blackburn et al. (1975) found that foods in grassland habitats were consumed in proportion to their abundance. The most important foods were carpet, Bahia, and crabgrass seed; and blackberries. Primary foods of juvenile turkeys in south Alabama were determined to be insects, fruits, green vegetation, and *Paspalum* and crabgrass seed (Exum et al. 1987).

Adults.—As with juveniles, adult turkeys consume a wide variety of many different food items, mainly dependent on availability (Hurst 1992). They feed on green forage and grass seed, such as wood sorrel, panic grass, and *Paspalum*, including domestic forages such as oats, wheat, and ryegrass. They eat fruits of shrubs, such as dogwood, saw palmetto, blackberry, American beautyberry, and huckleberry. They eat fruits of vines, such as poison ivy, pepper vine, and grape. Seed of trees, such as oaks, pecan, hackberry, blackgum, and pines are relished. Turkeys feed on domestic crops, such as corn, soybeans, and chufas. Adult turkeys also eat a variety of invertebrates wherever they are easily found.

DISEASES

The wild turkey can be infected with many different diseases, but not much is known about direct mortality from diseases and even less is known about long-term effects of diseases on turkey populations. Two of the more important diseases of wild turkeys in the South are avian pox and histomoniasis.

Avian pox, also known as fowlpox, is a contagious virus that infects both wild and domestic turkeys. It has been commonly diagnosed from sick and dead turkeys in the southeastern states. The most obvious symptom is wartlike-like growths, particularly on unfeathered body parts, such as the head, legs, and feet. The disease normally is not fatal unless the eyes are obstructed and the bird starves or is predated. Mosquitos can be vectors, or turkeys can be infected directly from other turkeys.

Histomoniasis, also known as blackhead disease, is caused by a protozoan which is carried by a cecal nematode worm. The disease is characterized by necrosis of the ceca and liver. The disease may be transmitted by the nematode through turkey feces or by consumption by turkeys of earthworms which have ingested the infected nematodes. It has been diagnosed in turkeys in the South and can be carried by other gallinaceous birds, such as pheasants and barnyard chickens. More information on these and other diseases can be found in Davidson and Wentworth (1992).

INTERACTION WITH OTHER SPECIES

Wild turkeys are part of complex ecosystems that are continually changing over time and interact with a number of other animals. Wild turkeys have evolved with predators and predation is part of what makes them wild. Predation helps insure that unfit individuals are culled and populations are fit. We know generally which animals prey on wild turkeys, but we don't know what long-term effects predators have on wild turkey populations at different predator and turkey densities in a variety of habitats.

Nest and Poult Predators.—Turkey nests and flightless young poults are predated heavily by a number of animals. Raccoons and skunks have been consistent nest and young poult predators, and opossums, dogs, crows, foxes, hawks, owls, and snakes have been implicated as well.

Adult Predators.—Overall wild turkey mortality is substantial; very generally about one half of all hens and a third of all gobblers die each year (Vangilder 1992). Mortality for hens is highest during the nesting and brooding season and predators are mainly responsible. Although predators kill some gobblers, usually adult gobblers are pretty hardy and hunting is the main mortality factor. A number of animals, including bobcats, coyotes, dogs, foxes, owls, and other species, prey on grown turkeys.

Wild turkeys can be impacted by human-related disturbances and harassment by dogs can be a problem. Also, free ranging dogs have been implicated as a substantial nest predator (Speake 1980). Coyote populations have expanded throughout the South, and while coyotes do kill an occasional turkey they are not thought to be a serious turkey predator. Previously, bobcats have not been regarded as a substantial predator. However, recent studies elsewhere (for example in Missouri, Vangilder 1996) have shown that bobcats were a significant predator of adult turkeys. Bobcats currently may have an impact on turkeys in the South with bobcat populations apparently higher now than previously.

Predator control may enhance turkey survival in the short term and on a local basis. But specific control of predator populations is difficult, costly, and not a good long-term solution. Creating high quality habitat helps turkeys withstand predation and reproduce more consistently.

Feral Hogs.—Hogs are widespread and potentially affect turkeys and management activities. Although on a local basis hogs may consume or trample some nests, generally throughout the South I do not think wild hogs are a significant predator.

Hogs, and probably deer also, compete with turkeys for some cultivated foods, such as chufa or grain crops, and natural foods as well. For example, acorn production in mixed hardwood forests is quite variable year to year (Dickson 1990). In years of very low production where hog densities are high they compete with turkeys and other native wildlife for a limited acorn supply. On the other hand hogs may uncover some foods which turkeys find; turkey scratchings are observed in hog rootings. Also, hogs may promote some small spots of grass-forb growth with their rootings, which may be beneficial to young poults.

But hogs certainly can be a problem with management activities, such as maintaining food plots. It is recommended not to release hogs into new areas and where they are established to keep hog numbers at a modest level, which is difficult to accomplish.

MANAGEMENT

People.—People and their activities are a primary factor in wild turkey management. Wild turkey populations usually will tolerate some interactions with people, but turkey populations do not prosper in areas of intense unrestricted hunting. If populations are viable and normal reproduction and recruitment is occurring, gobbler hunting during spring in a sporting manner will not jeopardize turkey populations. However, year-round illegal hunting, such as hunting hens and poults in the fall or turkeys over bait, can suppress populations.

Limiting Factors.—Habitat can be manipulated to minimize the effects of limiting factors and benefit turkeys in a number of ways. But the manager should be cautious not to create an attractant to turkeys, such as food plots adjacent to roads, where they could be exploited by illegal hunting.

Studies have shown that wild turkeys in the South may use anywhere from a few hundred to a couple of thousand acres of range annually. Also, flocks use different habitat types which may be quite different during different seasons. So an inspection and assessment of total turkey habitat suitability is necessary to determine what habitat features may be limiting for wild turkey year-round needs. For example, in the hardwood mountains of the Appalachians or the extensive bottomland hardwoods along major rivers, mast-producing hardwoods may provide good winter habitat, but grass-forb vegetation in openings suitable for brood habitat probably is limited. In such situations, openings with herbaceous vegetation, such as small fallow fields, could benefit poults and enhance population recruitment. Throughout much of the South it appears that the extent of grass-forb vegetation appropriate as brood range may be a widespread and important limitation. Most forest stands lack adequate herbaceous vegetation and small patch farming has diminished drastically.

Nesting and Brood Habitat.—Low dense vegetation, such as that found in fallow fields, power and pipeline rights-of-way, and small young clearcuts or partial cuts can be provided as nesting habitat. Areas with grass-forb vegetation with abundant arthropod populations, such as fallow fields, idle crop fields, wildlife openings, and unimproved pastures can be provided for brood range. Nesting and herbaceous brood habitat should be widespread and in close proximity to each other in order to help limit predation. Limited nesting and brood habitat may concentrate predators and result in high predation rates. Also, after hatching, hens take their broods from the nest site to appropriate early brood range. If this is some distance from the nest site these movements may result in substantial poult mortality.

Fall and Winter Habitat.—Improvement and maintenance of turkey habitat can be accomplished in silvicultural manipulations. Trees or stands particularly valuable for wildlife can be favored, and nesting and brood habitat can be created by harvesting (Swanson et al. 1996).

Particular habitats used at this time of year and desired habitat conditions, often keyed to foods available, are explained in previous sections. The best wild turkey winter habitat contains a variety of stand ages from early to late successional, particularly mature stands, interspersed with openings. Acorn production is quite variable so a variety of red and white oaks and trees other than oaks, such as sweet pecan and black gum, are important for adequate winter habitat.

Pine Stands.—Generally, mature pine or pine-hardwood stands are good turkey habitat. When these stands are harvested wild turkeys use the cut over area for a couple of years, especially if some residual mature trees or mature adjacent stands are left unharvested. Because of overstory removal and increased sunlight to the ground recently harvested stands quickly develop abundant herbaceous vegetation and soft mast, such as blackberries and American beautyberry. However, within 2 or 3 years vegetation normally becomes too dense for wild turkey use except for hens, which will nest around the edges of young stands. Pine plantations usually remain too dense for general turkey use until plantations are about 10 years old when canopies of the rapidly growing pine trees are closing and shading out understory grass, forbs, and shrubs.

When pine canopies close in young pine stands, understories normally are sparse enough for some wild turkey use, but shaded understories usually are mostly devoid of turkey food items, such as grass seed, forbs, and fruits of shrubs. In middle-age pine plantations from 10 to 20 years-old, thinning of the stand, especially in conjunction with burning, opens up dense stands to sunlight which enhances understory growth valuable for turkeys.

But older pine and pine-hardwood stands grown for sawtimber products are better wild turkey habitat. Mature pines are used for roosting and produce some seed consumed by turkeys. The combination of mature pines or pine-hardwoods, and openings can comprise good turkey habitat. Mature pine stands which have an open understory with some herbaceous vegetation and some fruit producing shrubs, such as dogwood or American beautyberry, in a landscape with mature hardwoods and small agricultural fields, or herbaceous fallow fields usually are good turkey habitat. The mature hardwoods can be distributed throughout pine-hardwood stands, in distinct hardwood stands, or in streamside zones or hardwood corridors traversing pine stands.

Burning.—Many important wild turkey foods such as native legumes are fire adapted and promoted by fire.

Today in the South as turkey flocks flourish, many youngsters and women as well as traditional male hunters are enjoying the tremendous sport of turkey hunting *(J. Dickson, J. Langston, J. Robertson)*.

Prescribed burning is an important land management practice conducted in middle-aged to older pine stands which can control the development of dense understories and helps promote understory grass, forbs, and shrubs, all important for wild turkeys. In pine plantations burning is particularly useful after a thinning. Light is increased, and understory vegetation develops. Prescribed fires have to be hot enough and frequent enough to kill small woody vegetation. Air pollution and the threat of litigation are two problems with burning.

Wildlife Openings.—Planting of wildlife openings can enhance wild turkey habitat suitability. An obvious benefit is that turkeys feed directly on foods produced. Plots can be planted to produce during the cool season or growing season, or both. Chufa, a nut sedge, is a favorite food of wild turkeys. It grows best in a sandy loam soil and the tuber is readily scratched and eaten by wild turkeys. It is also relished by several other species, including hogs and raccoons. Clovers are an excellent choice for turkeys. There are a number of particular varieties suited for local conditions, and available to wildlife at different times of the year. Clovers have a high vitamin A content, valuable to pre-nesting hens. Also, clovers may contain a high density of arthropods valuable for young turkey poults. Wheat and oats plots, normally planted for deer, can be useful to wild turkeys. The seeds or young succulent plants may be consumed and fallow plots with arthropods may be used by hens with broods. Small grains, such as millet, milo, and Egyptian wheat may provide supplemental food during the growing season.

Feeding.—The direct provision of supplemental foods has limited value in sound turkey management. Feeding may concentrate human or natural predators. Also, there may be problems with disease transmission, such as histomoniasis, at long term feeding sites. Corn feeding in many areas has been a tradition. While it is high in carbohydrates and provides energy, it has little of the other essential nutrients needed by animals. Aflatoxin is a fungus that sometimes develops in corn and other grains grown under droughty conditions. It may debilitate or impair turkeys that feed regularly on infected grain. Birds are more susceptible to Aflatoxin than mammals. The problem is that some corn which may have higher levels of Aflatoxin than the USDA standards permissible for livestock food is sold as deer corn and consumed by wild turkeys.

HUNTING

Turkey hunting is important in the South. Most of the southern states have a limited fall hunting season. But the fall harvest southwide is small (only 12% of the total harvest in 1994) and substantial only in Florida (48% of total state harvest) and Virginia (55%) (Kennamer and Kennamer 1996). In the South the main hunting season and harvest occurs during spring.

The sport of hunting the wild turkey by calling is a well-steeped tradition in places in the South where there have been turkey populations historically and has become a tremendous new sport in areas where new turkey flocks flourish. There is no other excitement like hunting the wild turkey!

Spring turkey seasons and bag limits in the South generally are liberal (Kennamer et al. 1992), but they are more restrictive where populations are low, such as eastern Texas. Spring seasons start in March in some southernmost states and in April in the others. Spring seasons in most states extend more than a month. Bag limits for states range from a low of 1 on some areas with newly established populations to a high of 5 or 6 for some states. Hunting wild turkeys over bait is illegal in all southern states. Decoys are legal in all states except Alabama. Hunting turkeys with rifles is legal only in Virginia, Florida, Mississippi, and Oklahoma in the fall.

CONCLUSION

The wild turkey was very abundant in the precolonial South, was reduced drastically by the early 1900s, and has been restored in remarkable fashion throughout. Turkey populations now thrive in southern forests; estimates surpass 2 million Southwide. Turkey hunting has become a tremendously popular sport and spring ritual throughout the region. The gobble of old long beards greeting spring dawns is a welcome sound thrilling southern hunters. The future also looks bright; the main obstacles will probably come in the form of challenges to hunting and management, and loss of habitat.

CHAPTER 10

Northern Bobwhite

L. Wes Burger, Jr.
Department of Wildlife and Fisheries
Mississippi State University, Mississippi State, MS

Throughout its range, the northern bobwhite provides important ecological, social, aesthetic, recreational, and economic values. Hunting of bobwhite is rich in tradition, particularly in the southeastern United States. In recent decades, bobwhite populations and hunting have declined throughout the range. Bobwhite population declines have been attributed to changing land use associated with modern agricultural and silvicultural practices. However, bobwhite have tremendous reproductive potential and exhibit dramatic population responses to creation of favorable habitat conditions. This chapter will provide an overview of bobwhite taxonomy and morphology, summarize historic and current distribution and abundance, characterize population and habitat ecology, and describe management practices that enhance habitat quality. The intent is to provide habitat managers with the basic knowledge required to create conditions favorable for the maintenance and increase of bobwhite populations.

SPECIES DESCRIPTION

Taxonomy

Taxonomically, the northern bobwhite is in the class Aves, order Galliformes, family Odontophoridae, genus *Colinus*, species *virginianus*. The northern bobwhite is the only living representative of the genus *Colinus* occurring in North America and the only member of the quail family (Odontophoridae) indigenous to the southeastern U.S. Bones of the modern bobwhite from Florida have been dated to the Pleistocene (ca. 15,000 years before present) (Holman 1961).

Various authors have identified 5-7 subspecies including *C. v. floridanus*, Florida bobwhite; *C. v. virginianus*, southeastern bobwhite; *C. v. taylori*, plains bobwhite; *C. v. texanus*, Texas bobwhite; *C. v. ridgwayi*, masked bobwhite; *C. v. marylandicus*, northeastern bobwhite; *C. v. mexicanus*, midwestern bobwhite. Aldrich (1946) identified the previously listed 7 subspecies. Rosene (1969) suggested that *C. v. virginianus*, *C. v.*

The northern bobwhite is a traditional southern game bird. Populations have declined in recent decades as early successional habitat has dwindled *(J. MacHudspeth)*.

mexicanus, and *C. v. marylandicus* are all simply a single subspecies *C. v. virginianus*, eastern bobwhite. Although little genetics work has been conducted on the bobwhite, Nedbal et al. (1997) demonstrated that 2 subspecies (*mexicanus* and *texanus*) are genetically distinct and uniquely adapted to the physiographic regions in which they occur.

Morphology

Like other galliformes, the bobwhite has a compact, somewhat rotund body with short, rounded wings and well developed breast muscles. Bobwhite are rapid flyers for short distances with measured velocities varying from 28-38 miles/hr (Stoddard 1931:51). However, they prefer to walk and typically fly only when threatened or when flying to roosting locations. Their legs are strong with feet adapted to walking and scratching through light litter for weed seeds. The adult plumage varies from chestnut to gray with rich browns on the back, white to buff on the breast and belly, and gray in the primaries, secondaries, and coverts. Males have a distinctive white mask and throat, whereas that of the females is buff. Both sexes have a prominent black eye stripe. The beak is black and downturned, adapted to pecking and picking up seeds. Bobwhite exhibit latitudinal variation in size with southern birds being smallest and northern birds being largest. Mean winter body mass varies from 5.8 oz for southernmost states to 7.3 oz for northern states. Mean length of 1152 birds from across the range varied from 9.5 to 10.8" in length (Rosene 1969:37).

DISTRIBUTION AND ABUNDANCE

Current Distribution and Abundance

The broad geographic distribution of the bobwhite (Fig. 1.) reflects its ability to inhabit a wide variety of ecosystems ranging from pine/grassland in the southeast, to rangeland in Texas/Oklahoma, to tallgrass prairie in Missouri and Kansas, to agricultural lands in the Midwest. Wherever it occurs, the bobwhite typically occupies early successional seral stages and frequently colonizes those plant communities that follow some form of natural or man-induced disturbance such as, fire, tornado, timber harvest, or agriculture.

Bobwhite density varies considerably both temporally and spatially. Leopold (1933:51-52) suggested an upper threshold density, which he referred to as a "saturation point" of 1 bird/acre. More recent studies have reported bobwhite densities in excess of 1 bird/acre (Kellogg et al. 1970, Kellogg et al. 1972, Rice et al. 1993, Guthery 1986:130). Clearly, bobwhite densities in optimum habitat can exceed 1 bird/acre, however, 1 bird/acre is considered an excellent density throughout most of the bobwhite's range. Fig. 1 illustrates the relative abundance of bobwhite throughout the southeast as indexed by the North American Breeding Bird Survey. Under current land use practices, bobwhite are most abundant in an irregular crescent that runs from south Texas north through central Oklahoma, northeast through eastern Kansas and northern Missouri, southeast through southern Illinois and western Kentucky, and south to northern Mississippi. Bobwhite are also abundant in southwest Georgia and northern Florida on lands specifically managed as quail plantations.

Presettlement – Early 1900's

Historically, the bobwhite was probably patchily distributed over some portion of its current range. The contiguous eastern hardwood forest did not provide the annual weed communities on which the bobwhite depended for food, insects, nesting, and brood rearing habitat. Bobwhite likely persisted at low densities in pockets of habitat across the landscape, erupting in local population explosions where natural disturbances such as fire or tornados created early successional communities. During the early 1800s European settlers cleared much of the eastern forest for agriculture, burned the woods for pasture and created a mosaic of woods, croplands, grasslands, and annual weed communities. As primitive agriculture spread north and westward during the early 19th century, the bobwhite expanded it range (Schorger 1944). Clearing of forest in

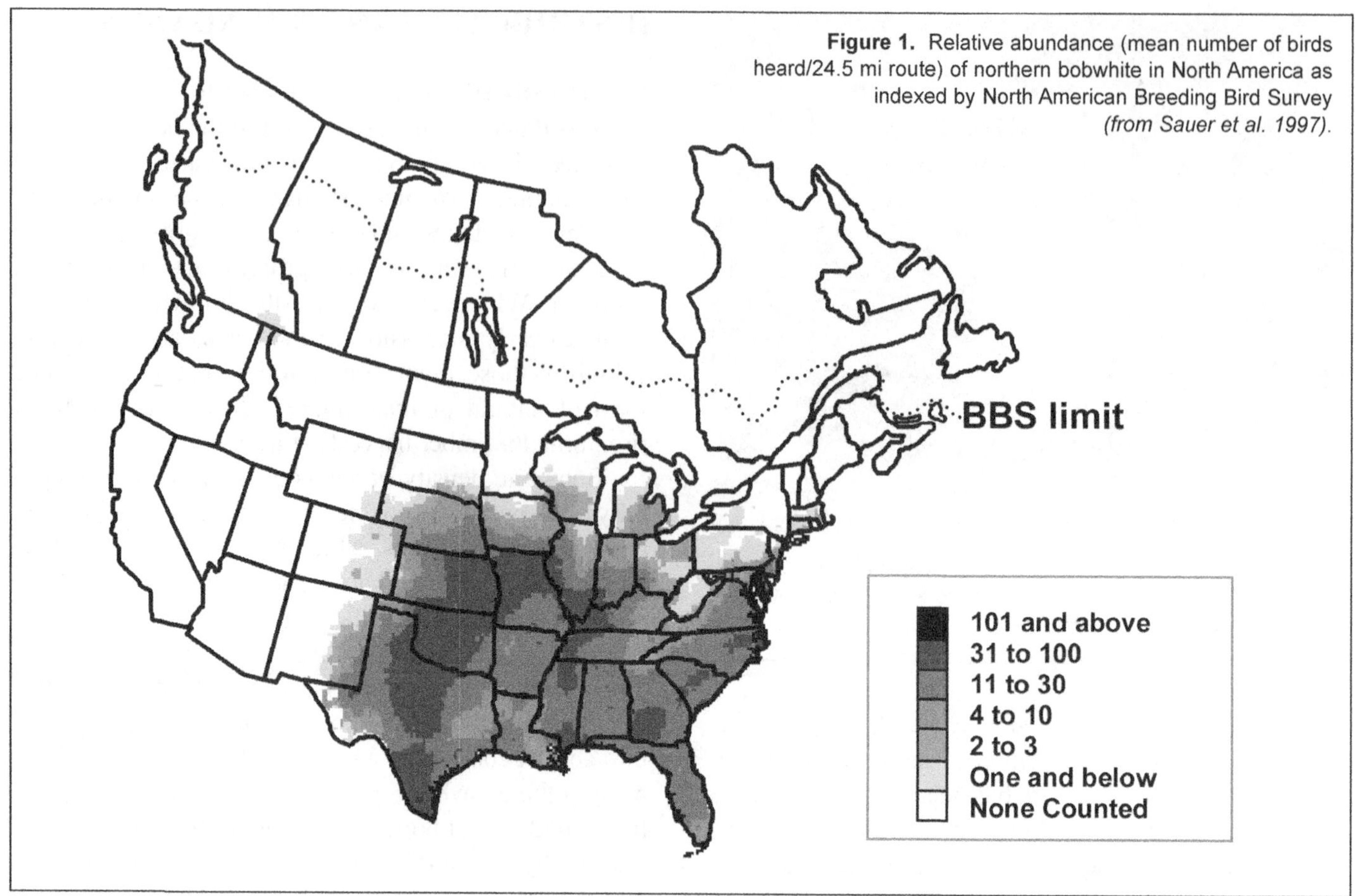

Figure 1. Relative abundance (mean number of birds heard/24.5 mi route) of northern bobwhite in North America as indexed by North American Breeding Bird Survey *(from Sauer et al. 1997).*

the South and the East and plowing of prairie sod in the Northern Plains and Midwest increased winter food resources and early successional habitats (Rosene 1969:15). Summarizing numerous historical accounts, Rosene (1969:14) suggested that bobwhite increased throughout the northern portion of their range until about 1860 and in the southern portion until about 1890, then remained relatively high throughout the range until about 1940, after which a downward trend began.

High bobwhite populations throughout the Southeast from the mid-1800s through the early 1900s were an accidental by-product of diverse land use practices. As forests were cleared and burned, small patch farms were established with small, irregularly-shaped fields. Primitive rotational cropping systems, annual burning, and low-intensity grazing of native pastures created a mosaic of row crop, grasslands, fallow, and forested lands to which bobwhite were ideally suited. And they flourished. As human uses of the land once accidentally created optimal quail habitat, changes in land use practices also contributed to declining habitat quality and subsequent population declines. As early as 1931, Stoddard (1931) noted that the tide was turning against the quail in the Southeast. During the period 1939-1948, Goodrum (1949) attributed range-wide declines in quail populations to "clean farming" and increased livestock production. Rosene (1969:15) attributed declining populations in the south to pasture development (replacement of native grasses with improved exotic forage grasses and replacement of row-crops with pasturelands) and reduction in burning which caused the forest understory to change from herbaceous dominated to hardwood dominated.

1966 – Present

From 1966 through the present, the North American Breeding Bird Survey (BBS) conducted by the U.S.G.S., Patuxent Environmental Science Center provides the most consistent range wide measure of bobwhite relative abundance and population trends. BBS are conducted during June which corresponds to the peak of calling and nesting activity for bobwhite over much of the Southeast. BBS routes are randomly located in order to sample habitats that are representative of the entire region. Each route is 24.5 miles long, with a total of fifty stops located at 0.5 mile intervals along the route. A three-minute point count is conducted at each stop, during which the observer records all birds heard

Table 1. Decline of northern bobwhite populations (percentage/year) in the southeastern United States, 1966-1996 (based on North American Breeding Bird Surveys, Sauer et al.1997).

State	1966-1996	1966-1979	1980-1996
Alabama	-3.9	-1.4	-6.4
Arkansas	-2.9	0.2[a]	-5.2
Florida	-2.7	-1.4[a]	-4.2
Georgia	-4.1	-1.7[a]	-4.9
Kentucky	-2.4	-3.2	-2.3
Louisiana	-4.7	-2.4	-4.3
Mississippi	-3.6	-1.7[a]	-4.5
North Carolina	-4.0	-3.4	-6.2
South Carolina	-4.1	-3.1	-4.7
Tennessee	-3.1	-1.5	-4.4
Texas	-2.0	3.3	-4.7
Virginia	-3.8	-2.5	-5.2

Trends marked with superscript[a] not significantly different from 0 ($P > 0.05$)

or seen within 0.25 mile of the stop. The index represents the mean number of birds heard calling/24.5 mile route. Throughout the southeast (U.S.F.W.S. Region 4) from 1966-1996, bobwhite populations have declined at a rate of 3.5%/year (Sauer et al. 1997). The rate of decline has increased over the last 17 years of the survey, changing from -1.8%/year during the period 1966-1979 to -4.9%/year during 1980-1996. All states within the southeast have experienced a significant decline over the entire survey period and during the past 17 years (Table 1).

Although these declines have been attributed to a variety of factors including coyotes, nest predators, fire ants, pesticides, and avian predators, the primary cause has been the cumulative effects of large-scale deterioration of quail habitat quality associated with advanced succession (Roseberry et al. 1979, Fies et al. 1992), intensive monoculture farming (Vance 1976, Exum et al. 1982, Roseberry 1993), and intensive timber management (Brennan 1991). Specific factors that have contributed to population declines vary regionally. In agricultural systems, farming practices have changed from diverse rotational cropping of row crops, small grains, hay, and legumes to intensive monocultural production of cotton, corn, soybeans, and rice. In intensively cultivated regions, lack of suitable grassy cover for nesting, weedy areas for brood rearing, and woody fencerows for winter and escape cover has reduced the overall capability of the land to support bobwhite (Kabat and Thompson 1963). In forested regions of the southeast, reduction in extent and frequency of fire, increasing forest coverage, loss of small agricultural fields to natural succession and reforestation, expansion of densely planted pine plantations, and increasing use of total vegetation control in clearcuts and regeneration stands have reduced availability of grassy and weedy areas required for nesting, foraging, and brood-rearing (Fies et al. 1992). Modern land use practices which strive to maximize food, fiber, and forest products have the net effect of simplifying the landscape. This reduction in landscape complexity, or heterogeneity, has simply reduced the proportion of the landscape in usable space for bobwhite (Guthery 1997)and the population size which a given location is able to support. In the face of diminishing habitat quantity and widely distributed habitat patches, isolated bobwhite populations may be more vulnerable to demographic and regional stochastic processes (random, regionally correlated catastrophic events such as weather) that increase the probability of local population extinctions, reduce recolonization rates, and contribute to regional population declines (Roseberry 1993). Declining bobwhite populations may be more vulnerable to harvest and concomitantly increasing predator populations (Hurst et al. 1996).

HARVEST TRENDS

As bobwhite populations have declined, harvest of bobwhite in 10 southeastern states declined from an estimated 17.1 million birds in 1970 to 3.5 million in 1995 (Table 2). The rate of decline in harvest (-6.4%/year) exceeds the rate of population decline (-3.8%/year) during the same period (Sauer et al. 1997) reflecting a reduction in hunter participation (Table 2). Five southeastern states with continuous hunter participation data experienced a -6.9%/year mean rate of hunter attrition from 1980 to 1995 (Burger et al. 1999). As northern bobwhite populations continue to decline this pattern will continue. Conversely, management activities and programs that create bobwhite habitat and contribute to population increases will likely reduce hunter attrition, increase recruitment, and generate economic activity associated with quail hunting.

POPULATION ECOLOGY

Survival

Seasonal and annual survival of bobwhite have typically been estimated by differences between fall and spring surveys, covey counts, or age-ratio information. Only

Table 2. Number of hunters, hunter days, and harvest of northern bobwhite for Southeast states based on state-level hunter mail surveys, 1980-95. No data were available for Arkansas.

Year	Parameter	Alabama	Florida	Georgia	Kentucky	Louisiana	Mississippi	N. Carolina	S. Carolina	Tennessee	Virginia
1970	Harvest	2,240,000	2,423,520	2,639,806	1,139,250	1,680,000	2,173,500	1,993,616	2,082,406	2,364,927	1,178,720
1980	No. hunters	66,288	53,588	73,000	NA	NA	65,084	NA	NA	81,293	NA
	Hunter days	509,384	360,160	559,000	NA	NA	449,740	NA	NA	558,932	NA
	Harvest	1,382,800	824,238	1,229,000	NA	NA	1,504,599	NA	NA	1,498,250	NA
1981	No. hunters	56,064	45,504	57,500	NA	38,300	56,248	NA	NA	77,136	NA
	Hunter days	427,408	333,046	436,900	NA	237,700	424,676	NA	NA	566,646	NA
	Harvest	1,081,340	633,380	1,011,000	NA	407,200	1,284,291	NA	NA	1,381,682	NA
1982	No. hunters	45,780	37,876	56,500	67,000	42,000	57,562	NA	58,736	79,469	NA
	Hunter days	331,482	288,193	403,000	597,191	NA	412,475	NA	475,567	588,754	NA
	Harvest	1,010,940	619,327	970,000	953,723	660,000	1,226,987	NA	1,402,909	1,417,340	NA
1983	No. hunters	44,365	32,811	52,800	NA	36,000	51,849	70,120	NA	77,477	40,086
	Hunter days	342,679	233,214	383,000	NA	NA	406,151	469,803	NA	573,375	213,759
	Harvest	1,033,480	542,897	983,000	NA	480,000	1,260,278	816,204	NA	1,366,590	346,354
1984	No. hunters	45,873	30,603	53,600	89,133	32,000	45,651	NA	NA	75,485	NA
	Hunter days	416,788	210,355	389,000	953,723	NA	298,529	NA	NA	557,997	NA
	Harvest	930,746	457,802	908,000	597,191	465,000	854,804	NA	NA	1,315,840	NA
1985	No.hunters	40,906	30,206	48,900	NA	29,000	40,748	NA	48,248	81,363	NA
	Hunter days	342,966	228,392	371,000	NA	NA	275,086	NA	376,472	398,679	NA
	Harvest	754,152	588,398	961,000	NA	405,000	708,449	NA	882,488	1,275,773	NA
1986	No. hunters	37,333	27,291	50,400	NA	23,000	39,995	56,301	NA	87,241	NA
	Hunter days	274,860	221,121	329,000	NA	NA	228,568	426,403	NA	427,481	NA
	Harvest	678,251	519,666	714,000	NA	336,000	617,893	698,079	NA	1,265,344	NA
1987	No. hunters	31,611	28,532	NA	NA	19,000	42,949	NA	NA	80,369	NA
	Hunter days	226,708	217,137	NA	NA	NA	225,762	NA	NA	415,508	NA
	Harvest	676,566	534,185	NA	NA	203,000	604,346	NA	NA	1,346,246	NA
1988	No. hunters	28,050	23,000	NA	NA	NA	NA	NA	NA	80,506	NA
	Hunter days	251,726	180,349	NA	NA	NA	NA	NA	NA	305,118	NA
	Harvest	560,722	378,539	NA	NA	NA	NA	NA	NA	527,854	NA
1989	No. hunters	25,549	18,424	52,000	53,650	NA	42,183	46,644	NA	81,557	28,249
	Hunter days	227,397	114,096	366,000	772,562	NA	134,089	283,696	NA	359,666	155,558
	Harvest	381,964	230,837	1,009,000	423,835	NA	383,209	409,358	NA	823,635	188,680
1990	No. hunters	26,200	13,424	NA	NA	11,900	25,706	NA	NA	NA	NA
	Hunter days	235,400	102,669	NA	NA	NA	152,762	NA	NA	NA	NA
	Harvest	544,300	149,598	NA	NA	114,800	429,882	NA	NA	NA	NA
1991	No. hunters	23,200	14,850	NA	NA	8,900	18,580	NA	NA	NA	NA
	Hunter days	179,500	100,727	NA	NA	46,000	101,888	NA	NA	NA	NA
	Harvest	389,200	177,856	NA	NA	70,300	220,474	NA	NA	NA	NA
1992	No. hunters	23,100	13,132	31,409	NA	8,800	19,634	35,447	32,282	58,825	NA
	Hunter days	144,200	87,916	215,413	NA	43,000	104,297	284,181	215,248	394,127	NA
	Harvest	379,600	186,446	321,991	NA	90,800	215,093	323,227	511,935	906,492	NA
1993	No. hunters	23,100	16,149	NA	NA	7,000	14,507	NA	NA	70,385	30,621
	Hunter days	169,700	110,676	NA	NA	34,500	87,633	NA	NA	351,925	190,677
	Harvest	407,500	173,057	NA	NA	43,100	194,622	NA	NA	827,024	258,738
1994	No. hunters	17,800	16,888	NA	NA	5,200	13,446	NA	28,575	49,504	27,765
	Hunter days	148,100	113,886	NA	NA	23,500	98,673	NA	180,195	267,321	141,026
	Harvest	342,300	161,305	NA	NA	48,100	230,721	NA	532,856	462,465	185,136
1995	No. hunters	NA	14,667	41,998	NA	3,800	12,998	28,407	NA	NA	25,287
	Hunter days	NA	109,792	245,436	NA	9,200	62,361	135,208	NA	NA	128,704
	Harvest	NA	161,048	630,138	NA	22,200	156,319	225,305	NA	NA	202,307

Table 3. Seasonal and annual survival of northern bobwhite from studies throughout the range.

State	Fall-spring survival	Spring-fall survival	Annual survival	Citation
Illinois	0.300[c]	0.607[car]	0.188[ar]	Roseberry and Klimstra (1984:89)
Illinois	0.50[c]	0.411[c]	0.205[c]	Roseberry et al. (1979)
Wisconsin	0.50[c]	0.307[c]	0.154[c]	Kabat and Thompson (1963)
			0.161[ar]	
Missouri	0.159[rt]	0.332[rt]	0.053[rt]	Burger et al. (1995)
Missouri			0.180[c]	Marsden and Baskett (1958)
South Texas			0.300[ar]	Lehman (1984:133)
Alabama			0.323[ar]	Rosene (1969:380)
South Carolina			0.250[ar]	Brennan et al. (1997)
South Carolina			0.205[ar]	Rosene (1969:383)
Mississippi		0.343[rt]		Taylor and Burger (1998)
North Carolina	0.185[rt]	0.328[rt]	0.061[rt]	Curtis et al. (1988)
North Carolina		0.330[rt]		Puckett et al. (1996)
Florida	0.644[rt]	0.400[rt]	0.257[rt]	Curtis et al. (1988)
Florida			0.167[b]	Pollock et al (1989)
Georgia	0.472[rt]	0.438[rt]	0.201[rt]	Burger et al. (1998)

[c] Survival estimate derived by sequential fall and spring censuses
[ar] Survival estimate derived by fall age ratios
[rt] Survival estimate derived by radio-telemetry
[b] Survival estimate derived by mark-recapture

recently have individual-based seasonal and annual survival, and cause-specific mortality been reported for any bobwhite populations (Curtis et al 1988; Pollock 1989, DeVos and Mueller 1993; Suchy and Munkel 1993; Burger et al. 1994b, 1995a). These individual-based estimates are determined by uniquely marking individuals with numbered legbands or radio-transmitters. Each of these methods have their own assumptions and biases which are beyond the scope of this text. Consequently, estimates derived by different methods may not be directly comparable. However, all techniques indicate that throughout their range bobwhite experience high annual mortality (70-95% Table 3). Based on age ratio information, Guthery (1997) hypothesized that bobwhite exhibit latitudinal variation in mean demographic patterns with populations in northern regions generally exhibiting higher annual mortality (80-85%) and greater productivity (greater than 4 juveniles/adult), whereas southern populations experience about 70% annual mortality and produce about 2.33 juveniles/adult. In general, in northern regions most mortality (both harvest and natural) occurs during the fall-spring period (Roseberry and Klimstra 1984:49, Burger et al. 1995a) and in southern locals the breeding season is the period of highest mortality (Curtis et al. 1989, Burger et al. 1998). In plantation environments of south Georgia, where both habitat and nest predators are intensively managed, mortality is approximately equitably distributed between breeding and non-breeding season (Burger et al. 1998. Hunted populations experience proportionately more of their mortality prior to the breeding season, relative to unhunted populations which experience greater mortality during the breeding season (Roseberry and Klimstra 1984). This is illustrated in the 2 Illinois populations reported in Table 3. Both studies were conducted during the same time period and in close proximity, yet the population reported in Roseberry and Klimstra (1984:141) sustained a mean annual harvest of 42.5% whereas, the population reported in Roseberry et al. (1979) was unhunted.

Numerous researchers have reported a male-bias in bobwhite fall sex ratios, particularly among adults. Although male-bias has been attributed to greater female mortality associated with incubation (Leopold 1945, Buss et al. 1947, Bennitt 1951) this bias most likely arises from higher overwinter mortality of females (Stoddard 1931:94, Roseberry and Klimstra 1984:136). In Missouri, breeding season survival was similar between sexes but females had higher overwinter mortality supporting the hypothesis that males biased sex ratios arise primarily from differential mortality outside of the breeding season (Burger et al. 1995a). During the breeding season, parental involvement in reproduction reduces survival for both male and female bobwhite. Predation associated with incubation and brood-rearing may reduce survival of reproductively active birds by 16% (Burger et al. 1995a). Kabat and Thompson (1963) suggested that the physiological stress of reproduction was the primary factor affecting late summer mortality; however, increased predation while accompanying flightless chicks reduces survival during brood-rearing, likely contributing to late summer mortality (Burger et al. 1995a).

During the breeding season male bobwhite advertise for females by calling from elevated singing posts. During this period they may be particularly vulnerable to avian predators *(W. Burger)*.

Mortality factors

Predation.—Past studies have presented conflicting views regarding the relative importance of predation in regulating bobwhite populations. Stoddard (1931) stated that the importance of predation as a limiting factor varies with range-wide habitat quality and quantity, bobwhite harvest rate, and harvest rate of furbearing predators, but in general, specific bobwhite predators must be controlled if a harvestable surplus is to be sustained. In contrast, Errington (1934) proposed that predators had no measurable impact on carrying capacity and that vulnerability to predators was largely a function of security of winter covey ranges. Leopold (1933:251-252) recognized that predation may be affected by prey density, buffer prey species, and habitat quality. Recent studies have quantified seasonal and annual patterns in cause-specific mortality throughout the bobwhite's range. These studies suggest that predation can have substantial effects on bobwhite populations and that the relative importance of specific predators varies with sex, life stage, biological processes (mate acquisition, nesting, brood rearing) and local predator community structure. Several authors have suggested that some bobwhite populations may not be self-sustaining under existing habitat conditions, depredation regimes, and harvest levels and that former paradigms regarding mechanisms of bobwhite population regulation need to be re-examined in the context of current landscape patterns (Robel 1993, Roseberry 1993, Church et al. 1993, Burger et al. 1994a, Hurst et al. 1996).

In studies of radio-marked bobwhite in Missouri (Burger et al. 1994b, 1995a), Mississippi (Taylor et al. 2000), North Carolina (Curtis et al. 1988, Robinette and Doerr 1993), and Florida (Curtis et al. 1988) predation was the primary cause of mortality. However, the relative importance of specific predators varies regionally and seasonally. As a group, avian predators account for a substantial amount of total bobwhite mortality. In North Carolina and Florida, avian predators accounted for 60-65% of total mortalities of radio-marked bobwhite. In Missouri, avian predators killed 28.7% of the fall population with avian cause-specific mortality rates being approximately equal between fall-spring and spring-fall intervals (Burger et al. 1995a). In the southeastern United States, Cooper's hawks and sharp-shinned hawks are the dominant avian predators with depredation concentrated during migration (Feb.-Mar.) and nesting (Jun.-Jul.). However, in Missouri, bobwhite populations experienced sustained high avian depredation from December-April, primarily attributable to resident great-horned owls (Burger et al 1995a).

Within seasons, vulnerability of bobwhite to specific predator groups varies temporally in relation to biological processes and activities of bobwhite. As an example, during the peak of the nesting season, male bobwhite are more vulnerable to avian predation than females (Burger et al. 1994b). Male bobwhite calling from exposed perches may be vulnerable to predators that hunt by sight (Burger et al. 1995a).

In contrast to avian-related mortality, mammalian mortality is often high during midwinter then again during the peak of the nesting season (Burger et al. 1994b, Burger et al. 1998). Increased mammalian-related mortality during this period likely reflects vulnerability of incubating and brood-rearing birds to predators that hunt by scent. Important mammalian predators for nonbreeding bobwhite likely include feral cats, red and gray fox, and bobcat and these in addition to mink, weasel, coyote, raccoon, and skunk may prey on incubating or brood-rearing bobwhite (Roseberry and Klimstra 1984:66).

Diseases, parasites, and pathogens.—Like all wildlife, bobwhite are subject to numerous diseases, parasites and other pathogens. However, the role of diseases and parasites in population regulation is poorly understood. The majority of literature concerning diseases and parasites of bobwhite is in relation to pen-reared birds with limited information available concerning wild populations. The most comprehensive surveys of diseases and parasites of bobwhite are detailed in Stoddard 1931, Kellogg and Doster (1972), Davidson et al. (1982a), and Lehman 1984.

Diseases.—Bobwhite are subject to more than 30 viral, bacterial, mycotic, and protozoan diseases (Kellogg and Doster 1972, Davidson et al. 1982a). At least 4 viral diseases have been reported in bobwhite including equine encephalitis, avian pox, Newcastle disease, and quail bronchitis. Among these, avian pox is the most frequently encountered. Bacterial diseases reported in bobwhite include avian tuberculosis, botulism, chronic respiratory disease, Erysipelas, fowl cholera, fowl typhoid, paratyphoids, psuedotuberculosis, pullorum, tularemia, and ulcerative enteritis. Two mycotic diseases, Aspergillosis and crop mycosis have been reported in bobwhite. At least 13 protozoan diseases have been reported in bobwhite including those caused by one or more species of the following genera: *Chilomastix* sp., *Eimeria* spp., *Haemoproteus* sp., *Hexamita* sp., *Histomonis meleagridis*, *Plasmodium* spp., and *Trichomonas* spp. Although many of these infectious agents commonly occur when bobwhite are held at high density for propagation, their occurrence in wild populations is much rarer. In a review of infectious agents encountered in wild bobwhite in the southeast, Davidson et al (1982a) reported 3 viral agents (quail bronchitis virus, TR-59 adenovirus, and avian pox), 1 bacterial agent (*Bacillus* sp.), and 3 mycotic agents (*Aspergillus* sp., *Mucor* sp. and *Candida albicans*). Protozoan induced diseases reported in wild bobwhite in the Southeast included Coccidia (*Eimeria* spp., *Eimeria dispersa*), blood-born parasites (*Haemoproteus* sp, *Plasmodium* spp.), and flagellates (*Trichimonas* spp., *Histomonas meleagridis*). As wild bobwhite populations decline, landowners increasingly rely on release of pen-reared birds to supplement wild stocks for hunting. Release of pen-reared birds, although common, continues to be controversial because of concerns regarding transmission of disease from released birds to wild populations. Although most diseases and parasites common to bobwhite tend to reach problem levels only under the high-density conditions of propagation, two diseases, avian pox and histomoniasis, may pose substantial risk to wild populations (Davidson et al. 1982a).

Avian pox is a viral infection of birds characterized by wart-like lesions on the skin of the feet, eyes, and mucous membranes of the mouth and upper respiratory tract (Davidson et al. 1982b). The virus may be transmitted by contact with or ingestion of infectious scabs, inhalation of viral particles, or blood-sucking arthropods, especially mosquitos. Avian pox occurs in 2 forms. The cutaneous form, or "dry pox" is characterized by lesions on the legs, feet, eyelids and head. Dry pox is usually not serious unless vision is obscured by lesions around the eyes. The more debilitating form is "wet pox" characterized by lesions on the mucous membranes of the mouth, nasal passage, and upper respiratory tract which may impair feeding or respiration. Avian pox is the only infectious disease of wild bobwhite demonstrated to cause substantial annual mortality. Mortality rates from avian pox are influenced by a myriad of environmental and population factors and may range from 0 to more than 50% of a local population. Bobwhite infected with "wet pox" may have much lower survival than birds with dry pox or uninfected birds (Mueller et al. 1993). Avian pox has occurred at low levels (<2%) in wild bobwhite populations throughout the Southeast since the 1920s. A region-wide outbreak of avian pox with a 12-fold increase in prevalence (12.1% infected) occurred in 1978-79 (Davidson et al. 1982b). Since the outbreak, avian pox has regularly occurred at low to moderate levels (3-5%) in wild populations throughout the South and has periodically been a significant disease (10-40% infected) in local areas (Davidson et al. 1982a).

Histomoniasis, also called "blackhead", is a disease caused by the flagellate *Histomonas meleagridis*. The Histomonas flagellate is carried and transmitted by the cecal worm, *Heterakis gallinarum*. Histomoniasis is characterized by both cecal and liver lesions. Mortality rates associated with histomoniasis may range from 30-70% (Davidson 1982a). Although histomoniasis occasionally occurs in wild bobwhites, it is far more prevalent in pen-reared birds. Thus, release of Histomonas-infected pen birds poses risks of disease transmission to both wild bobwhite populations and other galliforms, particularly wild turkeys.

In addition to the protozoan parasites discussed in the previous section, wild bobwhite are subject to numerous helminthid parasites. A study of 937 wild bobwhite collected from throughout the Southeast documented occurrence of 23 helminthid species (Davidson et al. 1982a). Two trematode species (flukes) occurred in the intestine (*Brachylaima* sp.) and liver (*Brachylecithum nanum*). Four Cestode species (tapeworms) (*Hymenolepis* sp., *Raillietina cesticillus*, *R. colinia*, and *Rhabdometra odiosa*) and one Acanthocephalan (*Mediorhynchus papillosis*) were observed in the intestine. Sixteen species of Nematodes (roundworms) were isolated from the eye (*Oxyspirura matogrosensis*), air sacs (*Aproctella stoddardi*), crop (*Capillaria contora*), esophagus (*Gongylonema ingluvicola*), proventriculus (*Cyrnea colini*, *Dispharynx nasuta*, *Tetrameres pattersoni*), gizzard (*Cheilospirura spinosa*), intestine (*Ascaridia lineata*, *Capillaria* sp., *Strongyloides avium*), and ceca (*Heterakis banasae*, *H. gallinum*, *Subulara* sp., *Subulara brumpti*, *Trichostrongylus tenuis*). Although, bobwhite are subject to parasitic infestation, parasitism in wild bobwhites typically produces limited pathogenicity and is probably not an important factor in population regulation (Davidson et al. 1982a).

Similar to endoparasites, ectoparasites are common in wild bobwhite, however, typically pose little pathogenic problems. Vulnerability to ectoparasites may vary in relation to environmental conditions and stress. Lehman (1984) reported that bobwhite in southwestern Texas had remarkable few external parasites, however; as range conditions worsened, prevalence and intensity of infestation by fleas, ticks, and lice increased. A study of 481 wild bobwhite in the Southeast documented infestation by ticks (*Amblyoma americanus*, *A. maculatum*, *Haemaphysalis chordeilis*, *H. leporispaulstris*, *Ixodes minor*), chiggers (*Eutrombicula alfreddugesi*, *Neoschoengastia americana*, *Neotrombicula whartoni*), nasal mites (*Boydaia colini*, *Colinoptes cubanensis*), feather mites (*Pterolichus* sp., *megninia* sp.), shaft mites (*Coliniphilus wilsoni*, *Dermoglyphus* sp., *Apionacarus wilsoni*), skin mites (*Microlichus* sp., *Rivoltasia* sp.) and lice (*Menacanthus pricei*, *Colinicola numidiana*, *Gonoides ortygis*, *Oxylipeurus clavatus*) (Davidson et al. 1982a).

Harvest.—The effect of hunter harvest on bobwhite populations has been the source of considerable debate. Biologists have traditionally assumed that, below some threshold, harvest has little effect on bobwhite overwinter survival and breeding densities (Errington and Hamerstrom 1935, Baumgartner 1944, Parmalee 1953, Marsden and Baskett 1958). This harvest model, termed the "annual surplus harvest model" assumes that: 1) more bobwhites are produced each year than can survive overwinter, 2) the spring breeding population size is relatively invariant, fixed by local habitat conditions, and 3) this doomed surplus can be harvested without affecting spring breeding density. The annual surplus harvest model implicitly assumes that up to some harvest level, hunting mortality is completely compensatory with natural mortality through density dependent mechanisms (Burger et al. 1994a). Alternatively, under the sustained yield harvest model, partial compensation is assumed and reductions in breeding density are an expected consequence of harvest (Roseberry and Klimstra 1984:149, Robertson and Rosenberg 1988). If survivors of the hunting season have enhanced survival and the population exhibits density-dependent reproduction, the annual growth increment can be harvested on a sustained basis with little appreciable effect on fall density (Roseberry and Klimstra 1984).

In evaluating the applicability of these 2 competing harvest models, increasing evidence demonstrates that harvest mortality, particularly late season harvest, is not completely compensatory but contributes additively to natural mortality (Roseberry and Klimstra 1984, Pollock et al. 1989). Roseberry (1979) modeled the effects of varying levels of harvest on breeding densities of a southern Illinois population and demonstrated that harvest at any level depressed breeding density to some degree, although the effect was slight (less than 14%) at harvest rates below 40%. Harvest became increasingly additive as the time of harvest occurred later in the season (i.e. January-February). A fifteen year study in Florida, demonstrated that a mean harvest rate of 23% taken in February was largely additive to natural mortality (Pollock et al. 1989). It should be noted that this study was atypical of normal southeastern harvest regimes in that the entire harvest was compressed into a 10-day period in mid-February. Concurrent studies (Curtis et al. 1988) demonstrated that the period of high natural mortality for this population was January-March. With the harvest occurring during the period of high natural mortality there is little opportunity for compensation. However, if harvest ended before the period of high natural mortality a reduction in natural mortality through density-dependent mechanisms could have occurred (Pollock et al. 1989). A North Carolina study demonstrated that hunted (~5-10% harvest rate) bobwhite populations exhibited lower overwinter survival than unhunted populations, suggesting that harvest mortality was not completely compensated for by a reduction in post-harvest natural mortality (Robinette and Doerr 1993). As expected, this study demonstrated lower breeding densities in the hunted populations. However, a reduction in overwinter survival, and consequently breeding density, does not necessarily imply overharvest. In fact, some reduction in breeding density is consistent with the production of a harvestable surplus under the sustained yield model (Roseberry and Klimstra 1984:149). Additional compensation occurs through density-dependent reproduction. The study in North Carolina did not monitor reproductive effort and success to determine if compensation occurred through density-dependent reproduction. Thus the net effect of harvest on fall populations was unknown.

Our understanding of the relationships among harvest, natural mortality, and population density are largely based on anecdotal evidence, unreplicated "experiments", and computer simulation. Thus, it is not surprising that little consensus exists on what constitutes acceptable harvest levels. Early harvest recommendations, based largely on northern populations, ranged from 30-55% of fall densities. Harvest rates as high as 70% have been suggested as sustainable on public wildlife management areas in Illinois (Vance and Ellis 1972). However, Rosene (1969:207) suggested that overwinter mortality from all causes including harvest should not exceed 45%. Maximum sustained yield for a southern Illinois population, was estimated to be 55%, although a more conservative harvest was suggested as an optimum sustained yield (Roseberry 1979).

Increasing evidence suggests that complete compensation is unrealistic, the traditional "annual surplus" view is an inadequate basis for scientific management of bobwhite populations, and a sustained yield approach to harvest management will likely more accurately model true population processes (Roseberry and Klimstra 1984:145, Burger et al. 1994a). Under the sustained yield harvest model, it is recognized that exploited populations in relatively constant habitat conditions will ultimately stabilize under a wide range of harvest levels. However, the equilibrium population level will vary in relation to harvest level. Optimal harvest levels for any given area must be selected in the context of specific management objectives for population density, hunting opportunity, and sustained yield. Furthermore, optimal sustained harvest levels may vary in relation to latitude, habitat quality (Stoddard 1931:226), landscape context (Roseberry 1993), and predator communities (Stoddard 1931:226, Robertson and Rosenberg 1988).

Reproduction

Mating system.—To compensate for high natural mortality, bobwhite exhibit a flexible and highly productive reproductive ecology characterized by ambisexual mating system, high reproductive effort, repeated renesting, and male-incubation (Curtis et al. 1993, Burger et al. 1995b). Although bobwhite have historically been considered monogamous (Stoddard 1931), recent work has demonstrated that bobwhite have a complex mating system combining elements of monogamy with substantial polygamy (Curtis et al. 1993, Burger et al. 1995b). Both male and female bobwhite participate in incubation and brood-rearing. Either the male or the female will incubate a nest, but they rarely alternate incubation duties.

Usually, female bobwhite incubate the first clutch. If this nest is destroyed, the female may lay a second clutch that is incubated by a male or she may incubate this renest. If incubation of a second clutch is assumed by a male, the female may lay and incubate a third clutch. Females will renest multiple times in an effort to successfully hatch a clutch. If the first nest successfully hatches, the female may attempt to produce a second clutch, called double-clutching. Females can double-clutch by turning parental care responsibilities for the first brood over to a male or by raising the brood to 3-6 weeks of age then abandoning the brood and laying and incubating a second clutch (Sermon and Speake 1987, Suchy and Munkel 1993, Burger et al. 1995b). In studies conducted in Missouri, Alabama, North Carolina, and Iowa, 25-33% of those females that were successful on their initial nest attempted double-clutches (Sermon and Speake 1987, Suchy and Munkel 1993, Burger et al. 1995b). Although double-clutching is seemingly a regular reproductive strategy throughout the range, numerically it accounts for a relatively small (0-7%) proportion of total production (Burger et al.

1995b, Guthery and Kuvlesky 1998). The extent of double-clutching in any given year will be, in part, a function of first nest success and length of breeding season.

Throughout the range, numerous authors have reported that male bobwhite incubate 13-27% of nests (Stoddard 1931, Klimstra and Roseberry 1975, Curtis et al. 1993, Suchy and Munkel 1993). Stoddard (1931:31) suggested that males might assume incubation after death of the female. Burger et al. (1995b) proposed that male incubation is an alternative strategy that maximizes reproduction. Breeding opportunities for males become increasingly limited as the breeding season progresses and the number of available females/male becomes more skewed as females become unavailable during incubation. Although incubation and brood rearing reduce survival (Burger et al. 1995a), males that would otherwise be unmated because of the skewed sex ratio could increase their reproduction by assuming parental care. Male incubation obviously benefits females because they are free to nest again (Burger et al. 1995b).

Total production is maximized through renests, second clutches, and male-incubated nests. In Missouri, female-incubated first nests represented 45.9%, female-incubated renests 20.1%, female double-clutch attempts 5.7%, and male-incubated nests 28.3% of all nest production (Burger et al. 1995b).

Clutch size.—Bobwhite have high physiological capacity for egg production with mean clutch sizes ranging from 11.9 to 14.4 (Missouri 13.8, Burger et al. 1995b; Illinois 13.7, Roseberry and Klimstra 1984:72; Tennessee 11.9, Dimmick 1974; Georgia 12.0, 11.8, Simpson 1976:34; Georgia/Florida 14.4, Stoddard 1931:28; Florida 12.8, DeVos and Mueller 1993; Texas 11.9, Lehman 1946). Mean clutch size exhibits latitudinal variation with larger clutches in the North than South (Rosene 1969:68, Roseberry and Klimstra 1984:72). Mean clutch size declines over the breeding season throughout the range (Rosene 1969:68, Lehman 1984, Roseberry and Klimstra 1984:74, Burger et al. 1995b).

Nest success.—Bobwhite experience low average nest success ranging from 32-44% (Illinois 32.7%, Roseberry and Klimstra 1984:77; Tennessee 38.8%, Dimmick 1974; Missouri 43.7%, Burger et al. 1995b, Mississippi 40%, Taylor and Burger 1997; Florida-Georgia 36%, Stoddard 1931:134). In a study of 602 bobwhite nests in northern Florida depredation was the primary cause of nest failure (Stoddard 1931:134). Stoddard estimated that 11% of nests were destroyed by skunks, 4% by ants, and 1-3% by each of numerous other predators. In southwestern Georgia, from 1967-1971, Simpson (1976) reported that on one intensively managed plantation, 17% of nests (n = 1,412) and on a second plantation 21% (n = 313) of nests were successful. Predation was the primary cause of nest failure. Simpson (1976) reported that skunks (19.9% of all nests), rodents (11.5%), opossums (4.7%), snakes (2.1%), foxes (1.6%) and raccoons (1.3%) were the primary nest predators. More recently in south Georgia/north Florida, 45% (n = 51) of nests were successful and predation on nests or females accounted for 89% of nest failures (DeVos and Mueller 1993). In this study, 52% of depredations were attributed to mammalian predators, 28% to reptiles, 10% to unknown predators, and 10% to mortality of the attending adult. In Tennessee, 23% of all nests showing evidence of use by quail (n = 766) were successful and 38.8% of nests that were active when located (n = 232) were successful (Dimmick 1974). In southern Illinois, from 1952-1966, Klimstra and Roseberry (1975) reported that 33.7% of 863 nests were successful and 36.7% depredated (55.4% of nest failures). The attending adult was killed at 4% of nests (11% of depredated nests). They attributed 70.7% of nest predation to mammals, 11.7% to snakes, 1% to birds, and 16.7% to unknown animals. Known predators in rank order of importance were house cats, striped skunks, snakes, fox, feral dogs, birds, weasel, and opossum. In an agricultural landscape in northern Missouri, 43.7% of 157 nests were successful (Burger et al. 1995b). Thirty-eight percent of nests were depredated and an additional 13.4% were lost from mortality of the attending adult. Nest predation was distributed among mammals (31.7% of depredated nests), snakes (43.3%), birds (11.7%) and unknown predators (13.3%). Sixty-eight percent of nest failures in which the adult was killed were attributed to mammals, 32% to raptors. In an intensive agricultural landscape in North Carolina, Puckett et al. (1995) observed 33.9% nest success. Predation accounted for 83% of nest failures. Mammalian predators caused 29% of nest losses, snakes 43%, and unknown predators 11%.

Seasonal patterns of nest predation vary latitudinally. In the northern portion of the range, early season nesting attempts may be more successful, whereas, in the southern portion of the range, late season nests seem more successful. In studies conducted in Iowa (Suchy and Munkel 1993), Missouri (Burger et al. 1995b), and Illinois (Klimstra and Roseberry 1975), nest success declined as the nesting season progressed. In North Carolina (Puckett et al. 1995), Tennessee (Dimmick

1974), Florida (Stoddard 1931, DeVos and Mueller 1993), and Georgia (Simpson 1972, 1976), nest success increased as the season progresses.

Reproductive effort.—One factor contributing to the bobwhite's high reproductive capacity is the long interval over which it nests. Bobwhite begin laying in April and may continue nesting through September if weather permits. The primary nesting season across most of the range extends from mid-June through mid-August (Simpson 1972, Stanford 1972, Roseberry and Klimstra 1984:84). In Illinois, the length of the laying season (date of first clutch started to last clutch started) varied from 78 to 128 days with a mean length of 112 days (Roseberry and Klimstra 1984:84). In Illinois, 90% of the variation in length of laying season was associated with ending date rather than beginning date. In hotter southern latitudes, heat stress may cause premature termination of the nesting season, influencing overall reproductive effort and success (Guthery 1997).

Although individual nest success is low, for females that survive until the end of the breeding season the probability of producing at least one brood is high because of repeated renesting. In Missouri, 74% of females surviving until 1 September hatched at least 1 nest. Similar success rates have been reported in Iowa (76%; Suchy and Munkel 1993) and Florida (72%; Devos and Mueller 1993). Roseberry and Klimstra (1984:83) suggested that the bobwhite's high annual rate of female success, in relation to average nest success (34%), would require that females initiate 2-3 nests/season. In Missouri, most females (58%) that failed on an initial nesting attempt, renested one or more times (Burger et al. 1995b). The average number of nesting attempts for birds that survived the breeding season was 1.8 nests/female and 1.0 nests/male.

Over a 25 year study in Illinois, Roseberry and Klimstra (1984:83) observed a mean percent summer gain of 205%, which would require a production of 5.2 chicks/female alive at the start of the nesting season. Similarly, mean parameter estimates in Missouri from Burger et al. (1995b) resulted in production of 5.4 chicks/female alive at the start of the nesting season. In Illinois, variation in clutch size or egg hatchability did not account for a significant proportion of annual variation in productivity (Roseberry and Klimstra 1984:80). Instead, the ratio of chicks hatched to females in the spring breeding population was the reproductive index most closely associated with recruitment. They observed that two thirds of the annual variation in percent summer gain was associated with the number of chicks that hatched per hen in the spring population.

Bobwhite chicks are born precocial and are active soon after hatching. During the first 6 weeks chicks eat insects almost exclusively. Characteristics of good brood habitat include 25-75% bare ground, abundant insects, and herbaceous canopy *(J. MacHudpeth)*.

Based on this information they suggested that large variation in chick survival did not occur and may not contribute much to variation in recruitment. Similarly, in Tennessee, Dimmick (1974) reported that the total number of nests built per season was the best predictor of recruitment and fall density. These studies suggest that factors influencing reproductive effort (female body condition, sex ratio, % of hens participating in reproduction, length of breeding season, etc.) may have the greatest impact on fall population size.

Brood ecology.—Brood ecology is the least understood component of bobwhite population ecology. Because the chicks are precocial and forage in resource rich habitats, bobwhite broods do not require biparental care. Therefore, broods may be attended by a male, a female, or both. Parental care is most critical during the first 12-14 days. During this period chicks are growing rapidly and developing contour feathers essential for thermoregulation and wing feathers needed for flight. Parental care is less critical after 14 days and brood abandonment may occur after the chicks have attained thermoregulatory independence and flight. Studies in Iowa, Missouri, North Carolina, Florida, and Georgia have reported abandonment of broods 14-42 days of age, after which the female may mate again and renest (Sermon and Speak 1987, Curtis et al. 1993, DeVos and Mueller 1993, Suchy and Munkel 1993, Burger et al. 1995b). In Florida, Mueller and DeVos (1993) observed that 80% of broods had at least 1 chick surviving to 2 weeks of age. Thirty-eight percent of chicks survived to 2 weeks and 29% to 4 weeks. In western Oklahoma, chick survival from hatch to 20 days was 37.9% and hatch to 39 days was 36.7% (DeMaso et al. 1997). Thus,

Table 4. Forty-five most important bobwhite foods in the Southeast as measured by frequency of occurrence and percent volume in 27 food habits studies reviewed by Landers and Johnson (1976).

Food type	Scientific name
Beggar weeds	*Desmodium* spp.
Ragweeds	*Ambrosia* spp.
Common lespedeza	*Lespedeza* striata
Corn	*Zea mays*
Korean clover	*Lespedeza stipulacea*
Partridge peas	*Cassia* spp.
Oaks	*Quercus* spp.
Milk peas	*Galactia* spp.
Sumacs	*Rhus* spp.
Bush clovers	*Lespedeza virginica*
Pines	*Pinus* spp.
Soybean	*Glycine max*
Cowpeas	*Vigna unguiculata*
Jewel-weeds	*Impatiens* spp.
Dogwoods	*Cornus* spp.
Sweet-gum	*Liquidambar styraciflua*
Wild-beans	*Strophostyles* spp.
Sorghum	*Sorghum* spp.
Hog peanut	*Amphicarpa bracteata*
Panic grasses	*Panicuum* spp.
Black locust	*Robinia pseudoacacia*
Johnson grass	*Sorghum halepense*
Wheat	*Triticum aestivum*
Honeysuckles	*Lonicera* spp.
Sassafras	*Sassafras albidum*
Smartweeds	*Polygonum* spp.
Vetches	*Vicia* spp.
Crab grass	*Digitaria* spp.
Paspalums	*Paspalum* spp.
Ash	*Fraxinus* spp.
Poor Joe	*Diodia* teres
Bull grass	*Paspalum boscianum*
Spurred butterfly peas	*Centrosema virginianum*
Grapes	*Vitus rotundifolia*
Dove weeds	*Croton* spp.
Foxtail grasses	*Seteria* spp.
Cranesbill	*Geranium carolinianum*
Wood sorrels	*Oxalis stricta*
Sericea	*Lespedeza cuneata*
Nut rushes	*Scleria* spp.
Bicolor	*Lespedeza bicolor*
Blackberries	*Rubus* spp.
Nightshades	*Solanum* spp.
Beggar ticks	*Bidens frondosa*
Ground nut	*Apios americana*

most chick mortality occurred during the first 14 days, prior to flight and thermal-independence. Chick survival was similar between broods raised by males and those raised by females (DeMaso et al. 1997). In Iowa, survival of abandoned broods was similar to that of broods accompanied by an adult (Suchy and Munkel 1993).

FEEDING HABITS

Fall and Winter

In general, bobwhite are opportunistic granivores foraging on a wide variety of weed seeds and cultivated grains. The most comprehensive treatment of bobwhite foods was compiled by Landers and Johnson (1976) who summarized the results of 27 major studies from throughout the Southeast representing nearly 20,000 birds and more than 650 different seed foods. However, 23 of these studies were based completely on crop contents collected during the fall and winter. Although bobwhite ingest a tremendous variety of seed types, only 78 plant species (12% of total reported kinds of quail seed foods) comprised more than 1% of the food volume in 1 or more of the studies. The relative importance of specific food types varied among physiographic regions and over time as land management practices changed throughout the region. Landers and Johnson (1976) developed a relative importance score (1-16 increasing with increasing importance) for each food type based on frequency of occurrence and percent volume. The 45 most important food types reported in these 27 studies are listed in Table 4.

Spring and Summer

During the breeding season bobwhite consume primarily seeds, fruits, and hard mast. However, invertebrates account for a greater portion of the diet during summer than winter, particularly among females. Invertebrates are an important source of protein for reproductively active females physiologically preparing for egg production or restoring protein balance. In Georgia, fruits (primarily blueberry and huckleberry) accounted for 15% and seeds 50% of the summer diet (Harshbarger and Buckner 1971). In northern Florida, blackberries were the most important food during June, and black cherry during July (McRae et al. 1979). In North Carolina, seeds and fruits (rye, red bay, acorns, shrub lespedeza, red maple, and corn) accounted for approximately 70% of the summer diet of male bobwhite (Curtis et al. 1990). Animal matter made up only 7-8% of the summer diet of males. During the breeding season in Mississippi, female bobwhite consumed greater biomass and numbers of animal matter than did males (Brennan and Hurst 1995). Animal biomass accounted for 20% of the crop contents of females, whereas in males it was 4%. The most important animal foods consumed by females were snails, short-horned grasshoppers, crickets, stinkbugs, spittlebugs, beetles, and spiders (Brennan and Hurst 1995).

Chick Foods

For optimum growth and survival bobwhite chicks require a high protein diet (~28%) during the first 10 weeks post hatch (Nestler et al. 1942). Additionally, protein content of the diet may affect immune response of young chicks (Lochmiller et al. 1993). In the wild, bobwhite chicks meet their protein requirements primarily through consumption of invertebrates (Handley 1931, Hurst 1972, Jackson et al. 1987). Handley (1931:160) reported that during the first 2 weeks after hatching virtually all (84%) of the food consumed by bobwhite chicks was some type of animal matter, consisting of (in order of importance) beetles, grasshoppers/crickets, caterpillars and moths, and other insects. In Mississippi, the most important insects consumed by bobwhite chicks less than 20 days old were beetles, leafhoppers, ants, spiders, larval forms, true bugs (hemiptera), grasshoppers, and flies (Hurst 1972). Similarly, Jackson et al. (1987) observed that bobwhite chicks 1-28 days old preferred beetles, lepidoptera larva, and true bugs.

HOME RANGE

Leopold (1933:77) referred to bobwhite as the least mobile of North American game species. His inferences were based on banding studies conducted by Stoddard (1931:175) in South Georgia in which 70-81% of banded birds were recovered within ½ mile of where they were banded. More recently, reliable estimates of mobility and seasonal and annual range of bobwhite have come from studies of radio-marked birds. Leopold (1933:74) suggested that annual mobility of bobwhite may increase toward the edges of the geographic range. Recent studies throughout the range seemingly support Leopold's supposition in that radio-marked birds in the southeast tend to be more sedentary, whereas studies conducted in Missouri (Burger unpubl. data), Iowa (W. Suchey pers. comm.) and Oklahoma (DeMaso pers. comm.) have observed seasonal movements of 7-32 miles. Spring dispersal is the period of greatest movements. Magnitude of movements is likely influenced by habitat quality and landscape structure.

Fall-Winter Home Range

The distribution, size, and specific location of winter covey ranges is a function of the distribution of winter food and cover (Rosene 1969:88). In agricultural systems of Missouri, the distribution of woody cover and the amount and complexity of rowcrop and grassland edge were important determinants of the distribution of winter covey ranges (Burger unpubl. data). Permanent wooded habitats provide essential escape cover for bobwhite and most foraging activity occurs within 22-55 yards of these components (Bell et al. 1985, Kassinis and Guthery 1996, Burger unpubl. data). Given the affinity of bobwhite for woody escape habitats, the distribution of permanent woody cover likely determines the proportion of the landscape in "usable space" during fall and winter (Guthery 1997) and the location of potential winter ranges. However, woody cover need not be large, mature trees, nor does it need to be extensive. Shrubby cover 4-10' tall, such as wild plum, provides suitable cover.

Although individuals within a population exhibit high annual turnover resulting from low survival, winter coveys tend to occupy the same covey ranges year to year. Given covey ranges tend to be occupied on a regular basis because the juxtaposition and characteristics of resources within the range are usable to quail in general and not because they are repeatedly inhabited by the same individuals (Roseberry and Klimstra 1984:23). In Illinois, annual occupancy rates of specific winter ranges varied from 27-80%. It has commonly been assumed that habitat quality or security varies among covey ranges, with high occupancy reflecting high quality ranges. A long held assumption of bobwhite population ecology is that at low densities only the most optimal ranges will be occupied and as density increases, increasingly marginal ranges will be occupied. Negative correlations between average occupancy rates and population densities have been taken as evidence to support the hypothesis "that individual and collective security declines as population density increases" (Roseberry and Klimstra 1984:30). This obviously provides a mechanism for density dependent overwinter survival. This hypothesis assumes that survival varies among covey ranges and that security within a covey range (range specific survival rate) is a function of habitat characteristics.

Estimates of mean winter covey range size vary throughout the distributional range from 7.4-94 ac. Estimates of winter ranges based on telemetry tend to be larger than those based on visual observations (Maytag plantation, South Carolina, 8.2 ac.; Oakland

Bobwhite nests usually are constructed from residual litter remaining from the previous growing season. Management practices such as disking and prescribed fire affect the amount and distribution of residual cover and hence nesting habitat. Perennial grass communities such as broomsedge are important nesting habitats and typically are optimal the second growing season following fire (*W. Burger*).

Club, South Carolina, 18.3, Rosene 1969:88) and ranges in forest land (Louisiana, 90.2 ac, calculated from Table 1. Bell et al. 1985) and agricultural systems (Illinois, 37 ac., Bartholomew 1967; Missouri, 94 ac, Burger unpub. data) larger than those on managed plantations (Ames Plantation, Tennessee, 16.8 ac., Yoho and Dimmick 1972; South Carolina, 27.4 ac, Dixon et al. 1996).

Breeding Season Home Range

During the breeding season, bobwhite allocate most of their time to habitats that provide either high quality nesting or brood-rearing resources. Nesting and brood-rearing habitats differ structurally (Burger et al. 1994*c*) and bobwhite often exhibit distinct shifts in location and habitat use between nesting and brood-rearing activities. In the Southeast, bobwhite typically nest in perennial grasses (often broomsedge) associated with old field or unburned pine/grassland habitats (1-2 years post-burn). Brood-rearing habitat typically is characterized as broad-leaved herbaceous vegetation with 20-50% bare ground, an abundance of insects, and scattered shrubs or brush for thermal cover (Lehman 1984, DeVos and Mueller 1993, Burger 1994b, Taylor and Guthery 1994b, Taylor 1996). Breeding season ranges must provide both nesting and brood rearing habitat within the range of mobility of newly hatched chicks.

Throughout the South, estimates of breeding season ranges of adult bobwhite vary from 54.4-153.2 ac. On Tall Timbers Research Station, Florida, breeding season ranges of adult bobwhite averaged 64.2 ac. (DeVos and Mueller 1993). Mean breeding season ranges for bobwhite in pine habitats of east Texas was 153.0 ac. (Liu 1995). In managed old field habitats in Mississippi, mean breeding season range was 56.3 and 75.9 ac. for male and females respectively (Manley 1994). In managed old field and forested habitats in South Mississippi, Lee (1994) reported mean breeding season range of 153.2 ac.

Like other galliforms, mobility of bobwhite broods increases with age (Taylor and Guthery 1994a). In

Florida, brood ranges averaged 16.1 ac. during the first 2 weeks and 24.7 ac. during first month post hatch (DeVos and Mueller 1993). In south Texas, Taylor and Guthery (1994a) reported mean brood ranges of 1.7 for prefledging and 3.5 ac. for postfledging broods.

HABITAT USE

Bobwhite tend to be associated with early successional plant communities, however, the appropriate seral stage for bobwhite depends on the primary productivity of the site (Spears et al. 1993). Furthermore, it is the plant community at the ground level that proximately determines the utility for bobwhite. Therefore, bobwhite may be associated with a climax community (such as mature longleaf pine/grassland) if frequent disturbance (fire) maintains an early successional, grass/forb ground cover. In forested landscapes the midstory and overstory influence habitat suitability because these components affect groundcover composition through interception of light, water, and nutrients. Bobwhite depend on multiple cover types to meet different biological needs within daily, seasonal, and annual intervals. Therefore, the interspersion of micro- and macro-habitats imposes a limiting condition that influences potential habitat quality.

Two theoretical frameworks of habitat quality have been proposed for bobwhite. One model views habitat quality at a point in space as a continuous variable ranging from low to high (0-1), (Guthery 1997). Under this continuum model, habitat quality is a function of habitat characteristics that affect individual survival and reproductive success (VanHorne 1983, Schroeder 1985). It follows from this model that density increases as mean habitat quality increases (Guthery 1997). Guthery (1997) proposed an alternative "usable space-in-time" model of habitat for northern bobwhite. He suggested that if a landscape is viewed as a set of points surrounded by an environment with various features, a point in space would be usable if it is associated with habitat characteristics compatible with the behavioral, morphological, and physiological adaptations of bobwhite. Under this model, points are either usable (quality = 1) or unusable (quality = 0) and quality of a landscape can be expressed as the proportion of points usable to bobwhite, but quality of individual points do not follow a continuum. Empirical evidence supports elements of each of these theoretical models. Under either model, one must recognize that bobwhite habitat requirements and use will vary throughout the annual cycle in relation to resource availability, thermal conditions, and specific biological processes unique to the season.

Winter habitat use

Woody escape and thermal cover.—During winter, bobwhite require 3 essential habitat components; 1) woody or brushy cover, 2) adequate and accessible food resources, and 3) grassland or annual weed communities (Roseberry and Klimstra 1984). Woody or brushy cover, with some dense understory, provides refuge cover used for midday loafing coverts, predator escape cover, and severe weather roosting habitats (Roseberry 1964, Bartholomew 1967, Yoho and Dimmick 1972, Roseberry and Klimstra 1984). In Illinois, woody winter covey "headquarters" were at least 0.5 ac. (Roseberry and Klimstra 1984:30).

The presence of dense understory vegetation, specifically honeysuckle, is a consistently reported component of winter covey headquarters in the central and northern portion of the range. During periods of severe winter weather, dense upright vegetation such as honeysuckle is increasingly used for roosting and loafing (Roseberry 1964, Bartholomew 1967, Yoho and Dimmick 1972). Robust shrubby vegetation retains its vertical structure, even during periods of snow and ice. The vertical structure of dense woody cover reduces wind speed at ground level. This property, combined with the radiant properties of dense vegetation mitigate both forced convective and radiant heat loss, thereby reducing thermoregulatory costs during winter.

Additionally, brushy vegetation cover provides important escape cover for bobwhite. Bobwhite are morphologically and physiologically adapted to short, rapid bursts of flight. It seemingly, therefore, would be adaptive for bobwhite to forage within a short flight range of suitable predator escape cover. In Texas, mean length of bobwhite escape flights was 162' and 88% of flights were less than 246' (Kassinis and Guthery 1996). In this study, bobwhite typically flew to sites that had more woody cover than random locations. Similarly, in Missouri, mean distance from winter diurnal locations to some form of woody escape cover was 69 feet.

The association of bobwhite with "edge" has long been recognized and was immortalized in Leopold's (1933:132) "Law of Interspersion". Bobwhite require some minimal degree of interspersion because of their dependence on multiple cover types. However, Guthery and Bingham (1992) recognized that below some threshold level, an increase in the amount of edge would increase usable space and subsequently, population density. However, edge in excess of population requirements is redundant and above some threshold, further increases in amount of edge or interspersion will have neutral or negative effects on bobwhite habitat quality. Thus, because of its importance in providing both escape and thermal cover, the distribution of permanent woody vegetation and associated edge and interspersion, likely set a limiting condition on usable space in a landscape during winter (Guthery 1997).

Roosting habitat.—Bobwhite typically night roost in sparse stands of grasses and annual or perennial forbs. In Illinois, Klimstra and Ziccardi (1963) reported that most roosts were on bare ground or light duff in herbaceous vegetation with a mean height of 23". Eighty percent of roosts were in vegetation 12-36" tall. They described roosting habitat as low, sparse herbaceous vegetation with open canopy and bare ground. Similarly, in Oklahoma, most roosts were in grasses or forbs with a mean height of 27" (Wiseman and Lewis 1981). In Missouri, winter nocturnal roosts had a mean 34% perennial grass canopy cover, 27% broad-leaved forb canopy cover, 23% bare ground, and 53% litter cover. Most roosts were on bare ground in open stands of grasses or forbs (Burger et al. 1994*c*). Stoddard (1931) reported that bobwhite in Georgia roosted in relatively open areas of herbaceous vegetation, open pine woods, broomsedge, or fallow fields. Rosene (1969) described winter roosting habitat as scattered herbaceous vegetation about 24" tall, open at ground level and open above. Plant species frequently associated with roosting habitat include blackberry, ragweeds, bluestems (including broomsedge), asters, and lespedezas (Stoddard 1931, Yoho and Dimmick 1972, Klimstra and Ziccardi 1963, Wiseman and Lewis 1981). Rain, snow, ice, and wind cause vegetation to deteriorate, fall over, and lodge as winter progresses. Roost sites may shift to denser woody vegetation during severe weather or in late winter as herbaceous vegetation deteriorates. Thus, bobwhite exhibit a preference for roosting in sparse herbaceous vegetation with vertical structure, open canopy, and bare ground, but will shift to more robust cover as the preferred structure becomes less available.

Foraging.—Bobwhite live, roost, and forage on the ground, thus the stratum within 8" of the ground must provide all essential resources. Bobwhite eat a tremendous variety of annual grass and weed seeds, hard and soft mast, and cultivated grains. In agricultural landscapes bobwhite may heavily utilize waste grains during winter; however, seeds of annual grasses, forbs, and legumes comprise much of the diet throughout the range. Bobwhite can find these resources in croplands, woodlands, fallow fields, grasslands, and oldfield habitats. However, if seeds are to be available to birds they must fall to bare ground where they can be seen or fall in litter light enough that birds can scratch through to find them. Additionally, the structure of the vegetation must be sparse enough to allow free movement. This association with bare ground during both the breeding and the non-breeding seasons has been recognized by numerous authors as essential for making resources available to birds (Stoddard 1931:406, Rosene 1969:122, Roseberry and Klimstra 1984:32). Bare ground in the range of 25-75% has been suggested as optimal for bobwhite (Schroeder 1985, Guthery 1986:115, Rice et al. 1992). Early successional plant communities are important for bobwhite because they simultaneously provide the seed-producing annual plants and a structure (vegetation density and bare ground) consistent with the bobwhite's foraging strategy and morphological adaptations. Finally, to be consistent with the behavioral adaptations of bobwhite, food resources must be distributed in close proximity to escape cover. Even abundant food resources, such as waste grain, located in the middle of a large open field are essentially unavailable to birds if not in close proximity to secure escape cover. Roosting, foraging, and escape cover must be in close proximity so as to meet minimum daily requirements and minimize energetic costs of foraging and exposure to predators (Roseberry and Klimstra 1984:33).

Breeding Season

Nesting.—Bobwhite nests are domed, spherical structures built on the ground of dead grass, pine needles, or other stems. Nests often have a woven canopy although they may simply have overhanging vegetation or, rarely, be open from above. In Illinois, over 88% of the materials used in nest construction were grasses. Bobwhite nests are typically constructed of the dead residual material from the previous growing season or in the case of early maturing species, senescent material from the current growing season. In Georgia, 89% of nests were constructed in standing residual growth of the previous season (Stoddard 1931:22). Stoddard (1931:21) reported that 82% of nests were in growth sufficiently open at the bird's level for them to move about freely. Bobwhite in Missouri nested in sites that were predominantly perennial grasses (74% perennial grass canopy cover), with 26% canopy cover of broad-leaved forbs, 71% litter cover, and 6% bare ground (Burger et al. 1994*c*). Roseberry and Klimstra (1984:21) characterized prime nesting cover as "scattered shrubs and brambles interspersed with a moderately dense stand of herbaceous and grassy vegetation". In Georgia, 56% of nests were in broomsedge fields, 16% in open pine woodland, 15% in first or second year fallow fields, and 4% in cultivated fields (Stoddard 1931). In Tennessee, bobwhite nested primarily in broomsedge dominated oldfields with residual grasses 12"-24" tall (Dimmick 1968). Bobwhite have a propensity to construct nests in locations that have access to open ground. In Georgia, 74% of nests were within 50' of some break in cover such as a road, path, or field edge (Stoddard 1931:21).

Breeding season ranges tend to be more open and herbaceous dominated compared to brushier winter ranges (Roseberry and Klimstra 1984:35). Urban (1972) reported that bobwhite whose winter ranges were devoid of nesting cover shifted to more weedy areas in April, whereas coveys whose winter ranges contained nesting habitat simply began using that portion more intensively. Although winter and breeding season habitats must be available within the range of the bobwhite's seasonal mobility, it may not be necessary to have nesting cover closely interspersed with winter cover. Roseberry and Klimstra (1984:35) reported numerous well-used winter ranges that were more than 2/3 mile from intensively used nesting cover. However, the amount and interspersion of breeding and wintering habitat in the landscape will influence the amount of usable space-in-time, thereby potentially influencing mean density (Guthery 1997).

Brood-rearing.—When a clutch hatches, the attending adult leads the chicks to habitat that is structurally distinct from nesting habitat. Newly hatched chicks require an abundance of insects to meet daily protein requirements. Insects must be available in a vegetation structure that is open at ground level to facilitate free movement of chicks. Brood-rearing habitat is characterized as broad-leaved herbaceous vegetation with 20-50% bare ground, an abundance of insects, and scattered shrubs or brush for thermal cover (Lehman 1984, DeVos and Mueller 1993, Burger et al. 1994*c*, Taylor and Guthery 1994b, Taylor 1996). Fallow agricultural fields provide superior brood habitat. In forested landscapes in southern Georgia, 77% of 75 radio-marked bobwhite broods used fall-disked, fallow agricultural fields in greater proportion than their availability (Yates et al. 1995). During the breeding season, these fallow fields were characterized by lush stands of ragweed and partridge pea with an abundance of bare ground. Fallow agricultural fields had a 2.6 times greater volume of insects than any other available habitat (Yates et al. 1995). In Florida, sites used by radio-marked broods had a higher occurrence of composites, grasses, legumes, roses, and shrubs than random plots (DeVos and Mueller 1993). They described brood habitat as fallow agricultural fields, burned during the previous 2 years with scattered patches of shrubby thickets, 50% bare ground, 50% herbaceous canopy cover, within 131" of an ecotone. Brood foraging sites had higher insect abundance than random plots and size of brood range was inversely correlated with insect abundance (DeVos and Mueller 1993). In Texas, Taylor and Guthery (1994b) reported that the structural characteristics of sites used by bobwhite broods varied in relation to time of day or activity. Moisture content of vegetation was greatest at brood foraging sites and brush canopy cover was greatest at midday loafing sites (Taylor and Guthery 1994b). The more succulent vegetation at brood foraging sites might support higher invertebrate populations and the greater shrub canopy at brood loafing sites likely creates a thermally favorable microclimate. In Mississippi, diurnal locations of radio-marked broods were characterized by 32% grass canopy, 38% forb canopy, 37% woody canopy, 21% bare ground, and 65% litter cover (Taylor 1996).

MANAGEMENT

Throughout the distributional range, bobwhite flourish in a wide range of ecosystems including rangeland in Texas and Oklahoma, tall grass prairie in Kansas, agricultural systems in the Midwest, and pine forests in the Southeast. Bobwhite habitat requirements are functionally the same throughout, however, the specific seral stages and plant communities with which they are associated will vary regionally in relation to rainfall, site productivity, length of growing season, and disturbance regime. Consequently, the management practices and disturbance regimes required to create and maintain appropriate habitat structure will vary regionally. Furthermore, because every property or landscape is unique in its resources and limitations, there is not a fixed formula for bobwhite habitat management that is applicable in every situation. However, the descriptions of seasonal habitat use provided previously identify the structural components required by bobwhite on an annual basis. These descriptions, when interpreted in the context of seasonal biological processes, will assist wildlife managers in prioritizing management objectives for a specific location.

Fire is integral in the creation and maintenance of many southeastern ecosystems, such as prairies, pine/grasslands, and old field habitats. Fire sets back succession, recycles nutrients, reduces litter accumulation, exposes bare ground, stimulates germination of native legumes, and controls hardwood invasion. The frequency, timing (dormant vs. growing season), and intensity of fire determines the effects on plant communies and associated fauna *(W. Burger)*.

Habitat Evaluation

Guthery (1997) suggested that "The goal of a habitat management program for bobwhite should be to make all points on an area usable for bobwhite at all times." The first step in any management program is to evaluate existing habitat quality and distribution. The conceptual model of "usable space-in-time" can serve as a formal basis for evaluating the quality (proportion of landscape in usable space over time) of an area or identifying habitat deficiencies in time and space (Guthery 1997). Other habitat evaluation procedures treat habitat quality as a continuous variable and can be used to rate sites from unsuitable to optimal (Baxter and Wolfe 1972, Bidwell et al. 1991, Rice et al. 1992, Schroeder 1985). Year-round habitat quality will be a function of the availability and distribution of resources required to meet all essential seasonal habitat needs. In summary, these requirements are: nesting habitat-2-3 year idle grasslands; brood rearing habitat- 1-2 year fallow annual weed community, bare ground, insects; roosting cover-annual or perennial weed community, bare ground, shrubby woody cover; fall and winter food resources- abundant and diverse mixture of grain crops, annual weeds, and mast; escape cover- woody shrubby cover. Specific management practices should then be formulated to provide each of these seasonal habitat components in a distribution that maximizes proportion of a landscape that is usable throughout the annual cycle.

Disturbance

Bobwhite in the Southeast are disturbance-dependent. Bobwhite are adapted to early successional habitats, which by their very nature are ephemeral. In pristine landscapes, early successional plant communities and bobwhite populations likely existed in a dynamic mosaic landscape. Historically, natural disturbances such as tornados, hurricanes, and fire created patches of early successional habitat. These patches were colonized by dispersing bobwhite, fully occupied by rapidly growing

Prescribed fire and fall disking stimulate germination of lush stands of native legumes such as partridge pea, which provide quality brood rearing habitat and winter food resources *(W. Burger)*.

Strip disking on a 2-3 year rotation creates a mosaic of annual and perennial weed communities which enhance plant diversity, insect abundance, bare ground, and brood habitat quality *(W. Burger)*.

Pine forests maintained in an open structure with a herbaceous ground cover can support moderate to high density bobwhite populations. Thinning and hardwood midstory management using some combination of selective herbicide, mechanical disturbance, and prescribed fire are necessary to maintain this condition *(W. Burger)*.

populations, then abandoned as plant communities matured through natural succession. Disturbance and succession governed colonization and extinction processes and every population was subject to extinction if succession progressed unabated. Thus, disturbance regimes and habitat dynamics drove the spatial and temporal population dynamics of bobwhite.

In modern landscapes, bobwhite are no less dependent on disturbance regimes. Much of the habitat loss and population decline throughout the South is attributable to advanced natural succession associated with lack of disturbance. Disturbance is not just desirable, but essential for maintenance of bobwhite populations. Prescribed fire, rotational agriculture, disking, and herbicide are the modern equivalents of natural catastrophic events. Each of these different disturbance tools results in a unique plant community response. Thus, comprehensive bobwhite habitat management uses combinations of these practices to achieve the desired mosaic of early successional communities in a cost-effective manner. Although disturbance is always a part of bobwhite management, the timing and frequency of disturbance will vary among locations in relation to the rate of ecological succession. In general, the rate of natural succession is influenced by temperature, moisture regime, fertility, and length of growing season. Thus, succession advances more rapidly as you move from northern to southern latitudes, drier to wetter sites, and low fertility to high fertility sites. In locations such as Tennessee, northern Mississippi, and Virginia a 3-year disking or prescribed fire regime may be appropriate. In the relatively infertile Sandhills region of North Carolina 2-3 year fire regimes may control hardwood encroachment and maintain herbaceous ground cover. Whereas, in the lower coastal plain, or on more fertile sites, annual or biennial fire and/or disking will be required. The key is to select a disturbance regime that maintains an annual and perennial grass/forb community in the context of the site-specific successional conditions.

Forested Landscapes

High density bobwhite populations can be maintained in pine-forested landscapes if forest structure and landscape composition are consistent with the morphological and behavioral adaptations of bobwhite. The southern pine ecosystem is a fire created and maintained community. The bobwhite evolved with fire in this system and is dependent on the effects of fire on the plant community. A fire-maintained southern pine forest is characterized by an open canopy, sparse scattered shrubs, and a grass/forb ground cover. In the absence of frequent fire (every 1-3 years), southern pine forests develop a dense hardwood under- and mid-story that shades out the herbaceous ground cover on which bobwhite depend. Thus, prescribed fire is an essential management tool for bobwhite in pine forested systems. Prescribed fire should be applied annually on 33 to 70%

of upland pine habitats. Rotate burn units so that each unit is burned on a 1-3 year rotation. Sites with higher productivity or greater rainfall will require more frequent fire to maintain an appropriate structure. In any given year, at least 30% of pine/grassland habitats should remain unburned to provide nesting habitat. In Georgia, the most preferred nesting habitat was 1 year (second growing season) post-burn (Simpson 1976). Patches of nesting habitat should be larger than 1 ac and well distributed (Simpson 1976). Clumps of brushy or woody escape cover should be preserved at approximately 300' intervals. This can be accomplished with disked "ring-arounds" (Rosene 1969). Historically, pine forests were managed for bobwhite using dormant season (winter) prescribed fire. However, dormant season fires may simply top-kill hardwood understory resulting in prolific resprouting. Periodic growing season fires (April-May) may be required to maintain control over hardwood understory.

When tree canopies close, insufficient sunlight reaches the forest floor for grasses and herbaceous seed-producing plants to germinate. It is essential to maintain forests as open as economically feasible. Thinning, coupled with fire, are the 2 most important forest management tools. However, the level of thinning that is optimal for forest management is still too dense for optimal quail production. For quail, 30-50% canopy closure is optimal. Optimal thinning regimes will vary regionally in relation to fertility, soil type, and moisture regimes. Low fertility, exceptionally well-drained, or sandy soils may require a more severe thinning to elicit a given level of response from the herbaceous community. Various authors have suggested that pole and sawtimber stands should be thinned to 25 ft^2/ac less than site index to achieve a compromise between timber and bobwhite management objectives. Thinning regimes with bobwhite as the priority would further reduce basal area to less than 40ft^2/ac. Young pine stands should be thinned as early as commercially feasible (usually 12-18 years). Clumps of mast producing hardwoods or naturally occurring hardwoods in drains should be left. However, dense, wide hardwood drains will harbor avian and mammalian predators and may reduce population performance in the surrounding uplands. Low quality or non-mast producing hardwoods should be removed.

Clearcuts can provide quality bobwhite habitat during the first 2-4 years following harvest. However, the choice of site preparation methods following clearcutting substantially influences potential habitat quality for bobwhite. Site preparation using prescribed fire and mechanical disturbance brings to the soil surface and scarifies seeds of annual weeds and native legumes, producing a herbaceous plant community suitable for use by bobwhite. Herbicide site preparation using selective hardwood herbicides such as Arsenal® can also create a desirable herbaceous community by controlling hardwood resprouting and releasing desirable native grasses and legumes. However, herbicidal site preparation with tank mixes designed to suppress all vegetation ("total control") dramatically reduces potential habitat quality of regenerating clearcuts. Regardless of site preparation method, quail habitat exists for only a short window of time in a developing pine stand. As natural succession advances or artificially regenerated stands develop, quail habitat rapidly deteriorates. Some habitat value can be preserved in a pine plantation landscape by maintaining 10-30% of harvested areas in permanent openings. Prescribed fire or disking should be used to maintain openings in early successional plant communities.

In forest dominated systems, 10-30% of the landscape should be maintained in small (2-5 ac) fallow/agricultural rotation fields. These fields provide fall and winter food resources and high quality brood rearing habitat (Yates et al. 1994). Fields should be maintained in a mosaic of grain crop, previous year's fallow stubble, and fall-disked annual weed communities. In open pine forests, roller-chopping or disking can be used in a strip or checkerboard pattern to improve access, control woody regeneration, and create soil disturbance. Soil disturbance associated with roller-chopping and disking increases bare ground and stimulates germination of native legumes and annuals, producing quality brood rearing habitat. However, long-term application of roller-chopping, disking, or dormant season fire may merely top-kill hardwood regeneration and result in copious resprouting. Selective herbicides, such as Arsenal® can be used to cost-effectively gain long term control of hardwood understory.

Agricultural Landscapes

Habitat quality in agricultural systems will be affected by crops grown, field size and shape, extent and type of chemicals used, tillage and residue management practices, distribution of woody habitats, and amount and condition of grasslands and idle areas. Smaller, irregularly-shaped fields increase interspersion, improve juxtaposition, and generally result in a greater proportion of the landscape usable throughout the annual cycle. Grain crops such as corn, soybeans, and wheat are better than fiber crops such as cotton. Outer rows of grain crops left standing adjacent to roosting or escape cover

In contrast to sod forming forage grasses such as fescue and Bermuda grass, native bunch grasses including broomsedge, big bluestem, little bluestem, and Indian grasses have a clumped distribution, leaving spaces of bare ground important for travel. During the first growing season following fire, litter accumulation is light and bare ground abundant, which is ideal for foraging by bobwhite chicks and adults *(W. Burger)*.

provide important winter food resources. Crop residue should be left undisturbed. Standing crop stubble provides roosting habitat, secure foraging habitat, and waste grain. Agrichemicals with lethal or sublethal effects on bobwhite should be avoided (Palmer et al. 1998). Field borders and adjacent crop rows should not be sprayed with herbicide or insecticides. No-till cropping systems can increase usable space and improve habitat quality by increasing available foods, retaining residual cover for nesting and increasing insect availability for chicks. Brood habitat can be further enhanced by leaving a 15-30' fallow field border (Puckett et al. 1995). Although hay fields generally provide poor quality nesting and brood rearing habitat, they can be enhanced by leaving a 15-30' border unmowed. Rowcrop and hayfield borders should be disked or burned on a 3 year rotation to inhibit woody invasion. In agricultural landscapes, the distribution of woody cover largely determines the amount of usable space, and therefore habitat quality, during winter. In large agricultural fields wooded hedgerows should be preserved or added so that every point within the field is within 300' of woody cover.

Grasslands within an agricultural landscape must be disturbed periodically to maintain an appropriate vegetation structure and composition. In the absence of disturbance, grasslands succeed to dense stands of perennial grasses and forbs, litter accumulates, and bare ground declines. Periodic disturbance such as disking or burning reduces litter, increases bareground, inhibits woody invasion, and stimulates germination of seed-producing annuals and native legumes. The desired grassland composition is a mosaic of perennial grasses, perennial forbs, and annuals. Rotational strip disking and prescribed fire (2-3 year rotation) can be used to encourage legumes, annual weeds and insects and maintain grasslands in a mosaic of early successional plant species.

Supplemental Food Management

Both cultivated grain crops (corn, beans, sorghum, Egyptian wheat, etc.) and annual native weeds (pigweed, ragweed, foxtail, bidens, croton) and legumes (partridge pea, lespedezas, desmodiums) provide important fall and winter foods for bobwhites. Frequently, natural vegetative response to management practices is sufficient to provide ample food resources. However, many factors, including moisture, management practice, timing of management, soil fertility, and soil seed bank affect production of native seed plants. In agricultural landscapes fall and winter food is generally abundant in the form of waste grain. However, fall tillage practices significantly affect availability of waste grain. The primary objective should be to manage availability of the food to birds. Crops in edge rows or corners can be left unharvested to increase availability. The distribution of woody cover can be manipulated to increase access to food resources. Crop residue can be left undisturbed to maximize residual waste grain.

In grassland or forest dominated landscapes, native foods can be supplemented with food plots. Although the value of supplemental feed has not be unequivocally demonstrated (Guthery 1997), food management may increase winter body condition, survival, and reproductive success. The goal of a comprehensive food management program is to provide a superabundant and continuous food supply from September through April. A food management program should provide each potential covey range with 2-4 different food resources (in addition to native seeds) so as to ensure a continuous and reliable food supply throughout the fall and winter in all years. It is important to recognize that different food resources become available to birds at different times in the annual cycle and persist for varying lengths of time. For example, millets and sunflowers mature in late summer (August) and provide a good but short-term food resource that is mostly exhausted by late October or early November. Soybeans mature somewhat later (October) and persist through December or

Bobwhite hunting with bird dogs in the South is steeped in tradition. Declining bobwhite populations throughout the southeast have resulted in declining hunter participation and loss of economic benefits to rural communities *(W. Burger)*.

January, but are typically shattered and deteriorated by February and March. Grain sorghums like milo and Egyptian wheat mature in September or October but typically persist through January or February because they tend to stand up and are rot resistant. The hard seed coat of partridge pea allows it to remain sound and available to birds well into March. Additionally, annual variation in weather conditions will result in some crops producing better than others in any given year. Foodplots should be rotationally cropped so as to create a mosaic of food plots and annual weed patches.

Predation Management

Historically, predator management was viewed as an effective, if not essential part of bobwhite habitat management. In fact, Stoddard (1931:415) devoted an entire chapter to "Control of natural enemies of the bobwhite". Attitudes among professional biologists concerning the effectiveness and ethical legitimacy of predator management have varied over the last 70 years. Stoddard (1931:416) denounced indiscriminate "vermin killing", but maintained that selective control of specific predators on lands devoted primarily to game production was legitimate and necessary under certain circumstances if a considerable surplus of birds was to be available for a sustainable harvest. In contrast, Errington (1934) stated that the "kinds and numbers of wild predators, migrant or resident, had no measurable impact on carrying capacity". With regard to effectiveness, Stoddard (1931) reported that over a 4 year period, moderate trapping and night hunting of skunks "materially and progressively" reduced skunk populations and total nest depredation. Little rigorous scientific information exists on the effects of predator communities, density, and control on bobwhite population processes in modern landscapes. However, the effect of predator removal has been thoroughly investigated for numerous other ground-nesting galliforms and waterfowl. A recent meta-analysis of 20 published predator removal studies reported that overall, predator removal had a large positive effect on nest success and fall densities (Cote and Sutherland 1997). But the effects of predator removal on breeding densities varied widely. They concluded that predator removal often fulfills the goal of game management by enhancing harvestable post-breeding populations, but is less consistent in increasing breeding populations (Cote and Sutherland 1997). The effect of predators on bobwhite populations, and therefore the efficacy of predator removal, will likely vary in relation to landscape context, predator density and diversity, and habitat quality. Often bobwhite populations show dramatic response to habitat management alone. However, in some situations, local predator densities may limit or curtail bobwhite population response to habitat management and predation management may be warranted. If predator management is to be implemented, it must be conducted using legal means within the legal time frame specified by pertinent state & federal regulations and laws. Selective predator removal that focuses on predators of nests and chicks would likely be more effective and palatable than indiscriminate removal of all bobwhite predators.

SUMMARY

Abundant bobwhite populations of the past were an accidental by-product of broadly applied, diverse, land use practices that maintained a heterogenous mosaic of early and mid-successional plant communities, forests, and agricultural lands. Bobwhite populations have declined precipitously throughout the Southeast during the last half century. Factors contributing to bobwhite population declines are complex and cumulative, attributable to changes in how we utilize our natural resources. Bobwhite population trends are not isolated but indicative of changes in an entire ecosystem. Loss of early successional communities and reduction in landscape heterogeneity associated with large scale, intensive, and monocultural production of agricultural and forest products is the direct cause of region-wide population declines. In modern landscapes, a return to previously favorable conditions is unlikely and thus prospects for a regional recovery of bobwhite populations are dim. However, on a local basis population declines can be remedied by proactive habitat management efforts. Local populations can be maintained and increased by managing early successional habitats through fire, mechanical, and chemical treatments. Habitat management and monitoring programs have demonstrated the efficacy of habitat management, producing local population increases of 100-600% in 2-5 years while broad scale populations continue to decline. However, because bobwhite are adapted to dynamic early successional systems, annual disturbance is essential to maintain the plant community in a suitable stage.

CHAPTER 11

Ruffed Grouse

Daniel R. Dessecker
Ruffed Grouse Society

The ruffed grouse is of particular interest to a dedicated corps of upland bird hunters in the southern United States. Although ruffed grouse typically receive only limited interest from state resource management agencies and the general public, their heart-stopping flush and the dense forest stands in which they reside combine to provide sportsmen with a unique challenge. In addition, their relatively precise habitat requirements and the fact that breeding males readily advertise their presence by "drumming" in the spring allow ruffed grouse to be used as an indicator of the status of other wildlife species of young forest stands and early-successional communities.

Ruffed grouse in the south differ physically from northern birds in both body weight and coloration. The general trend in warm-blooded animals is that body weight increases as mean environmental temperature decreases (Bergmann's rule). Therefore, individuals from northern latitudes are larger than those from the South. However, ruffed grouse don't adhere to this rule, southern birds are larger than their northern counterparts. In the aspen forests of northern Minnesota, adult males average approximately 22.6 oz. (Dessecker, unpubl. data) while adult males in North Carolina and Georgia tip the scales at 24.1 oz. (Seehorn, unpubl. data). Adult male ruffed grouse from southern Ohio are similar in weight to birds in the southern Appalachians (Stoll and McClain 1988).

Ruffed grouse exhibit a host of color variations from a light silver-gray to a deep red-brown. Color phase is genetically controlled and any number of color combinations may appear in the same brood. However, gray-phase ruffed grouse are more common at northern latitudes while red birds predominate toward the southern edge of the bird's range.

The likely explanation for this phenomenon is that a red-brown bird is better camouflaged on a forest floor covered with oak leaves than would be a gray bird. In

The Ruffed Grouse is a bird of the southern Appalachian Mountain region whose populations have declined in recent years (P. Carson).

contrast, the gray coloration common in the north blends quite well with the lightly-colored fallen leaves and the pale tree trunks of aspen, birch and maple.

DISTRIBUTION AND STATUS

The ruffed grouse is North America's most widely distributed Tetraonid. The southern boundary of the ruffed grouse range is consistent with the southern edge of the Appalachians in northern Georgia and extreme northeast Alabama. Although some locales can support relatively high ruffed grouse numbers at lower elevations, grouse are generally more common above 1,500 feet in elevation throughout the southeast United States, even though habitats that appear suitable exist in the Piedmont from Georgia north through Virginia. The effect of elevation on ruffed grouse distribution is largely nonexistent in the central Appalachians and further north, suggesting that warm southern climates are inhospitable to ruffed grouse.

Ruffed grouse are generally found only where forest comprises a significant proportion of the landscape. Highly fragmented landscapes with only scattered woodlots typically support only small, isolated populations of ruffed grouse.

References to ruffed grouse in the writings of early explorers and settlers are rare for the South, whereas mention of important food species such as white-tailed deer and wild turkey are relatively common. However, numerous authors (Rostlund 1957, Goodwin 1977, and others) suggest that forest disturbance from fires set by native Americans was likely significant prior to the 16th Century. It is likely that ruffed grouse populations were maintained on the landscape in reasonable numbers as a result of this disturbance.

Widespread logging of hardwood and mixed pine and hardwood forests of the South in the late 19th and early 20th centuries provided ruffed grouse with abundant habitat as these cutover lands regenerated to dense, young forest communities. In addition, the abandonment of family farms in the early 20th century and the resulting establishment of young forest stands on these retired agricultural lands provided quality habitat for grouse.

Relative densities of ruffed grouse by county for 1970 and 1996. Density categories: low $<5/mi^2$, medium 5-10/mi^2, high $>10/mi^2$.

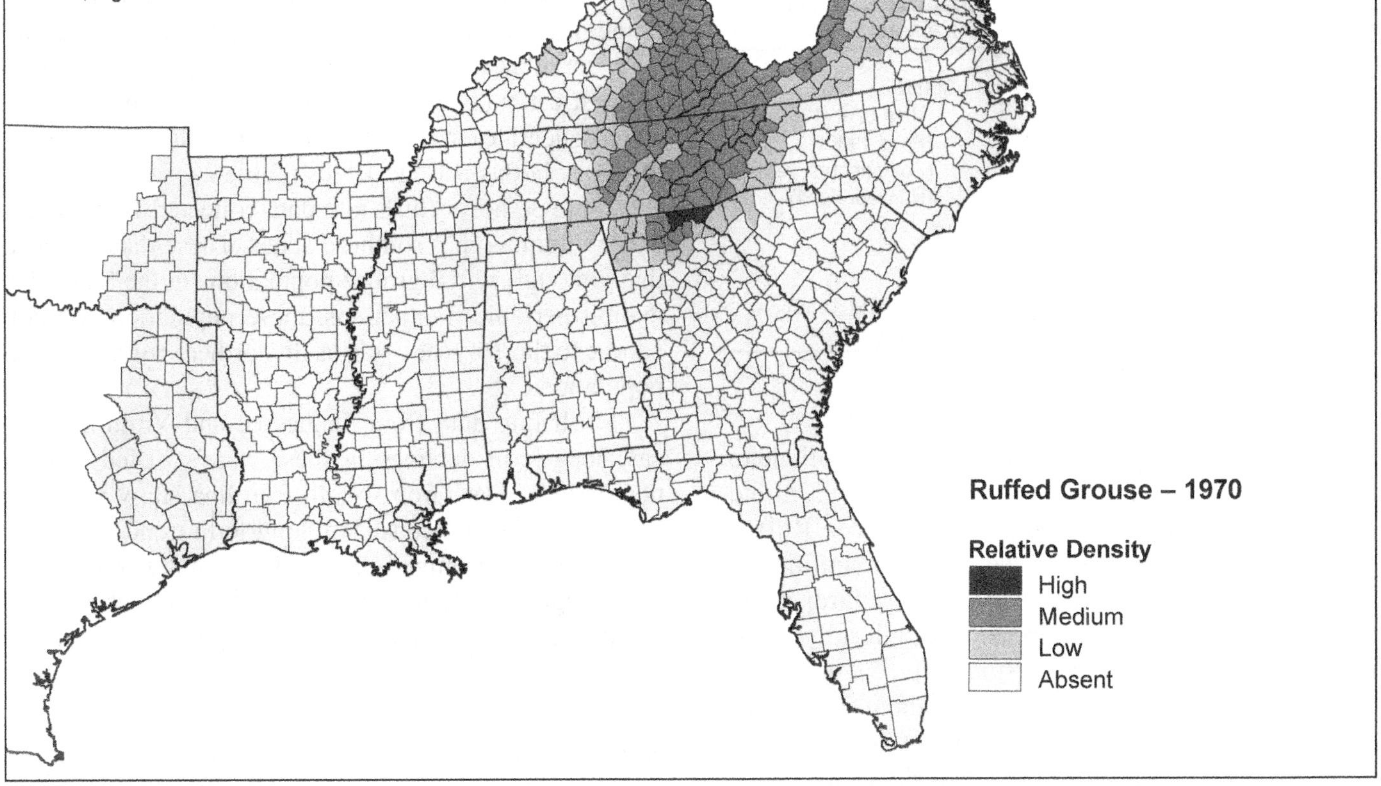

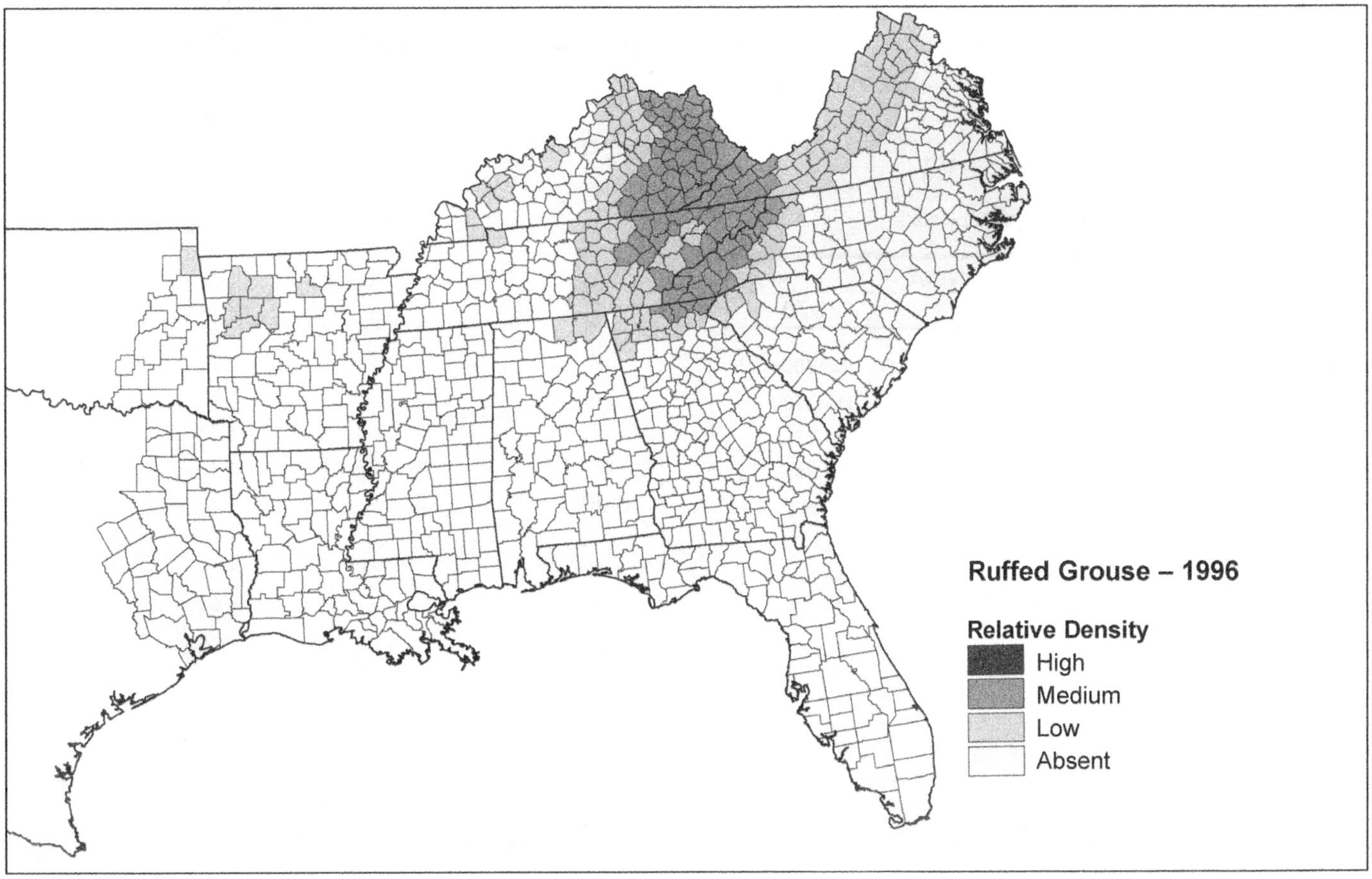

Ruffed Grouse – 1970

Relative Density

High
Medium
Low
Absent

Ruffed Grouse – 1996

Relative Density

High
Medium
Low
Absent

Table 1. Drumming male ruffed grouse densities in the southern United States and, for comparison, in aspen communities of the Great Lakes region.

Drumming males / 100 acres		
	Southern United States	
Northern Georgia	0.7 - 1.0	(Hale et al. 1982)
Eastern Tennessee	0.1 - 0.9	(Boyd 1990)
Northeast Kentucky	1.1 - 1.5	(Sole, unpubl. data)
Central Missouri	0.7 - 1.8	(Hunyadi 1984)
	Aspen forest	
Central Wisconsin	2.2 - 6.4	(Kubisiak 1985)
Northern Minnesota	3.9 - 9.1	(Gullion 1984)

Today, as the region's deciduous forests continue to mature, ruffed grouse habitat and, therefore, ruffed grouse, are becoming increasingly scarce. Ruffed grouse population densities in the South are significantly lower than in the northern portion of the birds range (Table 1). However, ruffed grouse can be locally abundant where quality habitats exist in sufficient quantity.

Throughout the 1980s, several southern states reintroduced ruffed grouse to portions of their historic range: Arkansas (Pharris 1983); Kentucky (Sole 1991); Missouri (Hunyadi 1984); and Tennessee (Gudlin and Dimmick 1984). These efforts often appeared successful in the short-term. However, typically these populations experienced long-term declines after initial apparent success.

Table 2. Estimated Ruffed Grouse harvest by state.

State	Harvest 1996/97		Harvest 1970	
Kentucky	63,800	(95/96)	63,600	
Virginia	46,519		112,278	
Tennessee	24,370		64,766	
North Carolina	11,758	(95/96)	30,843	(72)
South Carolina	<100		NA[a]	
Georgia	2,000-3,000		5,000-10,000	
Florida	0		0	
Alabama	0		0	
Mississippi	0		0	
Arkansas	0		0	
Louisiana	0		0	
East Texas	0		0	
East Oklahoma	0		0	

[a] Estimate not available.

As for most species of wildlife, definitive site and time-specific population data for ruffed grouse are seldom available. Although a game species throughout its range in the South, most states collect data that can, at best, serve as a long-term index to population trends. Harvest estimates for southern states are imprecise but suggest declines in ruffed grouse population size, hunter effort, or both since the 1970s (Table 2).

Table 3 shows flush rate data collected from cooperating hunters in 3 southern states. These data suggest that although ruffed grouse populations in the South do exhibit periodic fluctuations, these populations do not adhere to the 10-year cycle as do northern ruffed grouse populations.

Flush rate data from Tennessee and Virginia indicate long-term declines in these state's ruffed grouse populations. Data from North Carolina show periodic fluctuations but no consistent long-term trend.

The ratio of immatures to adult females in the harvest is significantly lower in the South than in the northern portion of the ruffed grouse range. The immature

Table 3. Cooperating hunter flush rates, Tennessee, Virginia and North Carolina.

Year	Flushes/hour TN	Flushes/hour VA	Flushes/hour NC
1973		1.31	
74		1.00	
75		0.98	
76		0.72	
77	1.44	0.90	
78	1.43	1.21	
79	1.41	1.21	
80	1.64	1.44	
81	1.20	1.36	
82		1.57	
83	1.04	1.17	
84	0.85	1.17	0.55
85	0.83	1.18	0.52
86	1.07	1.40	0.64
87	1.28	1.19	0.64
88	0.81	0.83	0.59
89	1.08	1.05	0.74
90	0.96	1.03	0.73
91	0.81	0.98	0.62
92	0.97	1.01	0.52
93	0.75	1.10	0.58
94	0.96	1.05	0.71

adult female ratio averaged 3.5 based on 9 years of data from Kentucky and Virginia collected during the late 1980s and early 1990s. Kubisiak (1985) and Gullion (1988) found this ratio to be 7.3 in Wisconsin, and 6.8 in Minnesota, respectively. These data suggest that productivity is lower in southern ruffed grouse populations than in those at northern latitudes.

FOOD HABITS

Southern ruffed grouse feed upon herbaceous vegetation throughout the year. Succulent broad-leaf herbs are readily available from mid spring through late fall. Although less available during the winter, grouse still rely heavily upon succulent herbaceous vegetation, supplementing this important food with fruits from grape, greenbrier, hawthorn and dogwood, ferns, and the leaves from evergreen broad-leaf plants, such as wintergreen and mountain laurel (Norman and Kirkpatrick 1984). Servello and Kirkpatrick (1987) suggest that low quality winter foods might be one reason that ruffed grouse recruitment and population densities in the South are low compared to northern populations, where trees and shrubs preferred for budding, such as aspen, birch and hazel can be common.

Hard mast is eaten by ruffed grouse but this food source is not often found in dense, young forest stands. Therefore, to utilize these foods, ruffed grouse must forage in relatively open, mature stands which can increase their exposure to potential predators.

Insects comprise the majority of the diet of ruffed grouse chicks during their first 4-6 weeks of life, after which time plants become increasingly important to their diet. As the summer progresses, both immature and adult grouse will consume fleshy fruits.

HABITAT REQUIREMENTS

The correlation between tall shrub and tree regeneration stem densities and ruffed grouse habitat quality has been well documented in numerous studies across the ruffed grouse range (Gullion 1984 and others). Young forest stands from 5-15 years of age that support high densities of woody stems are a critical component of quality ruffed grouse habitat. Optimum habitat supports 8,000-10,000 stems greater than 6 feet tall/acre. This dense, almost impenetrable cover affords grouse protection from their principal predators, hawks and owls. However, research in the central Appalachians has found higher mammalian predation rates than previously documented.

Dense stands of understory shrubs in mature forest stands or on partially reforested old-field sites can provide ruffed grouse with quality protective cover. These shrubs commonly include greenbrier, honeysuckle, grape, rhododendron and mountain laurel. However, small discrete patches of dense shrubs likely provide only minimal security for grouse.

Dense, young forest stands are especially important to breeding males in the spring as these birds "drum" to advertise their presence to nearby females (Hale et al. 1982, Boyd 1990). The visual and auditory displays of a performing male are designed to draw attention to the bird. This necessitates that the male select the most secure portion of his home range as the location for his breeding activity. Indeed, a male's activity center, which is the area that encompasses his drumming platform(s), is typically the most structurally dense and, therefore, secure site available.

Preferred drumming platforms are typically large-diameter, partially decayed fallen logs greater than 10 feet in length. Rocks, stone fences, upturned roots and other elevated perches are also used as drumming platforms. In hilly terrain, logs oriented along the contour provide a relatively level platform and are most likely to be used by performing males. Although ruffed grouse activity centers can be located anywhere on a hillside, males often select benches or positions near the top or the base of the ridge where the slope is less than 25 degrees (Rodgers 1981).

Nest site characteristics can be quite variable. Hens seem to prefer forest stands that are older and more open than those selected by males for activity centers. Suitable nesting habitat is not considered a potential limiting factor.

Hens with broods are seldom far from dense, young forests or shrub-dominated, overgrown agricultural fields. The physical protection provided by high stem densities is critical to brood survival. Indeed, densely-structured habitats are an essential component of quality ruffed grouse habitat throughout the year.

Ruffed grouse populations in the South are not often confronted by prolonged, severe winter weather conditions characteristic of northern latitudes. However, brief periods of ice, snow and extreme cold can be expected during most winters.

Conifers with a dense canopy such as spruce, fir or red cedar can provide thermal protection for ruffed grouse, as can evergreen shrubs-rhododendron and mountain laurel. Thompson and Fritzell (1988) documented far greater than expected use of red cedar for roosting during winter in Missouri. Unfortunately,

Ruffed Grouse thrive in early successional forest stands created by tree harvest *(Ruffed Grouse Society)*.

spruce and fir are uncommon in the South and red cedar is most often found in abandoned pastures.

Mature white pine and eastern hemlock, the 2 most common conifers throughout the higher elevations of the South provide only limited protection from inclement weather due to their relatively open canopies. Dense young stands of pine or hemlock can impede wind penetration and afford grouse protection from adverse weather.

Insect abundance is greater in open habitats dominated by herbaceous vegetation than on the forest floor beneath a closed canopy (Hollifield and Dimmick 1995). These herbaceous openings can provide an abundant source of insects for young chicks. Unfortunately, foraging in an opening is an inherently unsafe situation for ruffed grouse and the potential benefits of herbaceous openings must be weighed against the likelihood of increased predation.

North and east facing hillsides receive less direct sunlight and are cooler and more moist than south and west facing slopes. Cool, moist sites on north and east slopes are preferred by ruffed grouse, possibly due to microclimate and the increased availability of succulent herbaceous vegetation. However, dense thickets of mountain laurel or other shrubs on dry, south and west slopes or ridge tops can provide ruffed grouse with quality cover.

HABITAT MANAGEMENT

Silvicultural Options

Ruffed Grouse are habitat specialists. Although they can survive in various forest communities, they are most common on extensively forested landscapes that include numerous young (less than 15 years old), even-age hardwood stands. Optimum ruffed grouse habitat is created through the drastic disturbance of existing, mature forest stands, or through the establishment of dense, old-field communities resulting from succession on abandoned agricultural lands.

Historically, the disturbance required to maintain ruffed grouse habitat was provided by fire, wind, ice damage, insect infestation and diseases. Fire was the predominant agent of disturbance throughout much of the ruffed grouse range.

Today, the effects of natural disturbance have been greatly diminished by man's efforts to control fire in forest communities. However, this absence of fire is partially offset by man-made disturbance, most notably silvicultural treatments. Although no silvicultural treatment perfectly mimics fire, such treatments are effective in establishing early-successional communities.

Because ruffed grouse require high woody stem densities characteristic of early-successional communities and young forest stands, habitat availability is determined by the extent of even-age silvicultural treatments within the previous two decades. Even-age management prescriptions, which include clearcut, seed-tree and shelterwood regeneration treatments, can produce the stem densities required by ruffed grouse. Uneven-age management prescriptions such as thinning and single-tree selection treatments seldom remove enough overstory to allow the development of dense woody vegetation. Group selection treatments can produce stem densities comparable to clearcuts, but patches are generally too small and isolated to provide secure habitat for ruffed grouse. Uneven-age management should not be prescribed where ruffed grouse habitat development is a primary management objective.

In general, the greatest amount of overstory removal will yield the greatest degree of understory development. However, the maintenance of a limited amount of residual basal area can yield regeneration stem densities similar to what would be expected after a clearcut treatment or some other drastic disturbance. Smith et al. (1989) found similar regeneration stem densities 5 years post treatment in stands that had been clearcut and stands where less than 20 sq. ft./acre of residual basal area had been maintained. Treatments where these low levels of basal area are maintained have been called deferment cuts or modified shelterwood harvests and typically lead to a stand dominated by 2 distinct age classes.

The diameter distribution of residual overstory trees can have a significant impact on regeneration stem densities. For example, 20 sq. ft. of residual basal area is provided by retaining approximately 16 15-inch diameter trees or approximately 150 5-inch diameter trees. Although the crowns of the larger diameter trees are far more expansive than the 5-inch trees, the latter would quickly respond to release and the shade cast by the combined crowns of these small-diameter trees would likely have a greater effect on the developing regeneration than would the shade cast by the larger trees.

The spatial distribution of residual trees within a harvest unit can also have a significant impact on regeneration stem densities. Residual basal area maintained in discrete patches can minimize shading of regenerating hardwoods and, therefore, the effects of this shade on regeneration stem densities.

Residual basal areas greater than 20 sq. ft./acre can significantly reduce regeneration stem densities and should not be maintained within harvest units designed to provide quality habitat for ruffed grouse. In addition, residual basal area levels less than 20 sq. ft./acre can under some circumstances reduce stem densities and habitat quality for ruffed grouse. Likely eventual crop trees exhibit dominance and can be identified as early as 5 years after the parent stand has been regenerated (Marquis and Jacobs 1989). The growth of these crop trees can be enhanced by felling all adjacent stems. Initial crop tree release typically is conducted in stands less than 15 years old. This 10-year window from age 5 to age 15 is precisely that period in stand development when habitat quality for ruffed grouse is optimal. The release of crop trees in 5 to 15-year-old stands can significantly reduce stem densities and greatly diminish the protection afforded ruffed grouse by these stands. Such treatments are inconsistent with ruffed grouse management and should not be prescribed where the development of quality habitat for ruffed grouse is a primary objective.

Extensive grape vine control can eliminate areas of suitable grouse habitat and an important food source for grouse and many other species of wildlife. The negative effects of these control efforts should be weighed against the potential silvicultural benefits.

Size of Treatment Unit

Scattered small-block harvest units on landscapes dominated by mature forest stands can provide quality habitat for ruffed grouse but these isolated islands likely provide only limited security. On such landscapes, large cutting units, perhaps 10-40 acres in size may best provide long-term security for local ruffed grouse populations. Research conducted in the aspen forests of the great lakes region shows that small harvest units (3-5 acres) are of greater benefit to ruffed grouse than are larger units on landscapes where approximately 25% of the forest is 1-10 years of age (Gullion 1984). The juxtaposition of small harvest units is designed to provide local ruffed grouse populations with abundant protective cover, afforded by 10 to 15-year-old stands, interspersed with their principal winter food, the flower buds from male aspen trees in nearby mature stands. The small cutting unit size ensures that stands of varying ages are available in close proximity to one another, thereby promoting maximum ruffed grouse densities. Because there is in the South no single, universally-available source of quality winter forage as is found in aspen forests, the interspersion of varying age classes through a pattern of small-block timber harvests is not likely as beneficial to ruffed grouse.

Site Selection

In hilly or mountainous terrain, clearcut regeneration harvests on north and east-facing slopes are more likely to provide quality forage for ruffed grouse than are similar treatments on south or west exposures. However, the availability of dense woody vegetation on relatively warm south and west exposures can benefit ruffed grouse, particularly during inclement winter weather.

Habitats positioned at or near the base of a slope typically provide a more cool, moist microclimate than those near the top of a ridge and can be important to ruffed grouse. Restrictions on silvicultural treatments near riparian corridors conflict with efforts to establish early-successional communities on these inherently productive sites. Clearly, riparian corridors warrant special consideration, but partial overstory removal can promote understory vegetation and provide at least marginal habitats for ruffed grouse and other early-successional wildlife.

Old Field Habitats

Ruffed grouse habitat can develop as agricultural cropland or pasture is retired from production and allowed to undergo natural succession. Old field habitats that support dense shrubs and young trees can be maintained in this "transitional" stage by removing individual stems likely to advance into a canopy position.

A dense sod layer on some abandoned land can limit seed germination and seedling development. The thick humus layer and the interwoven root systems of densely-matted herbaceous vegetation can physically preclude seeds from shrubs or trees from germinating on moist mineral soils. Mineral soil can be exposed by physically disrupting the humus and the established root systems. A shallow-running plow or disk can provide the physical disturbance required but such mechanical treatments can be expensive and they are impractical on steep terrain.

Soft Mast

The establishment of soft mast-producing trees and shrubs can benefit ruffed grouse but the costs associated with such efforts need to be considered. Species selected for planting should be well suited to local soil and climatic conditions. These include hawthorn and dogwood, among others.

Soft mast-producing plants should be maintained. Fruiting trees and shrubs and grape arbors can be released from the competition of surrounding overstory trees. These food sources are most beneficial to ruffed grouse when they are located in close proximity to dense protective cover. Deciduous plantings often are susceptible to browsing pressure but can be protected with fencing or tree shelters.

Herbaceous Openings

Maintained herbaceous openings can provide ruffed grouse with a readily available source of quality forage. These openings also support greater arthropod densities than do habitats dominated by woody vegetation (Hollifield and Dimmick 1995). Arthropods can be an important source of protein-rich food for developing chicks. Seed mixtures for openings vary but typically contain a combination of grasses and legumes (clover or trefoil). Legumes remain relatively succulent throughout much of the year and provide ruffed grouse with a nutritious source of forage during winter when little other herbaceous vegetation is available. Annual mowing helps to maintain the legume component of these openings.

The high-contrast edge formed by the maintenance of herbaceous openings adjacent to forested habitats can lead to increased predation over what would be expected in the absence of openings. The potential for increased predation can be minimized by locating maintained herbaceous openings adjacent to dense, young forest habitats.

Conifers

The establishment of small patches of conifers can provide ruffed grouse with protection from inclement winter weather. Densely-needled conifers such as white or Norway spruce are preferred due to their ability to impede wind penetration. Norway spruce is relatively unpalatable to white-tailed deer and is the easiest to establish in areas that support high deer densities.

Plantings should be greater than 0.5 acres in size to provide an effective refuge from inclement weather. This refuge effect can be enhanced by using a relatively tight spacing (6 ft. X 6 ft.) during planting.

HUNTING

Aldo Leopold (1966) stated: "There are two kinds of hunting: ordinary hunting, and ruffed grouse hunting." As a general rule, hunters who pursue ruffed grouse in the South are quite dedicated to their sport. Relatively low grouse population densities and difficult terrain make the pursuit of ruffed grouse most challenging.

Southern states that support huntable populations of ruffed grouse typically have an open season from mid-October through January or February. Although not consistent throughout the South, limited data suggest that the majority of the hunter effort and the harvest occurs during the last half of the season. Warm weather precludes significant hunter effort during the early season. Available data also suggest that hunter numbers and harvest appear to be declining throughout the South.

LIKELY FUTURE TRENDS

Historically, fire was the principal agent of forest disturbance throughout much of the South (Christensen 1981, Komarek 1974). Today, fires have been largely precluded from the landscape and commercial timber harvest has replaced fire as the principal agent of forest disturbance. Unfortunately, commercial timber harvest is currently viewed by some publics as "the problem," rather than "the solution."

Some 70% of the timberland in the southern United States is in non-industrial private forest (NIPF) ownership. Forest management treatments on NIPF lands typically maintain residual basal areas in excess of levels that allow the development of optimum-quality ruffed grouse habitat.

Approximately 10% of the timberland in the southern United States is in public ownership (Powell et al. 1992). Public land management agencies have responded to public concerns over active forest management by proposing significant reductions in such management and, particularly, clearcut regeneration treatments (U.S. Forest Service 1995).

Ruffed grouse populations are declining throughout much of the southern United States as a direct result of habitat loss. Given ongoing changes in land ownership patterns and the impacts of current societal attitudes towards forest management on land management policy, these declines are likely to continue.

C H A P T E R 1 2

Mourning Dove

Ralph E. Mirarchi
Center for Forest Sustainability
School of Forestry and Wildlife Sciences, Auburn University, AL

Mourning doves are well known throughout the South because they nest close to humans and they frequent our bird feeders. They also have become woven into the cultural fabric of southern hunting because they traditionally are the species that opens the fall hunting season each year. They are among the most abundant and widespread terrestrial birds found in middle and North America, and are the leading game bird in North America in terms of numbers harvested, easily eclipsing all other migratory game birds combined (Baskett and Sayre 1993).

The scientific literature on the biology, ecology, and management of the mourning dove is extensive and has most recently been summarized by Baskett et al. (1993), Mirarchi and Baskett (1994), and Tomlinson et al. (1994). The author refers readers to these accounts for more specific information, because only the most important aspects of mourning dove habitat use and management in southern forests are detailed here.

DESCRIPTION

Aldrich (1993) described the distinguishing physical characteristics of the species. Adult mourning doves are streamlined, mid-sized columbids (roughly 12 inches long, 4 ounces in weight; males larger and heavier than females), with small heads and long pointed tails. They are grayish-blue or grayish-brown above and buffy below, with the males being more colorful than the females, particularly in spring. They have black spots on the wings and behind the eye; tail feathers other than the elongated central pair have black-bordered gray-white tips. The bill is black and the legs and feet are dull red. Wing coverts of immature birds have white or buffy edging, which gives them a somewhat mottled appearance. The mournful, crooning vocalization, which is heard in spring and summer accounts for the species' common name. A larger, grayish-brown eastern subspecies, and a slightly smaller, paler western subspecies occupy parts of southern Canada and most of the continental United

Mourning doves can produce multiple broods at about 35 day intervals during a prolonged breeding season. These 10-day -old nestlings will fledge in few days *(AL Coop. Wildl. Res. Unit)*.

Mourning doves usually lay 2 white eggs in a shallow nest *(K. Hudson)*.

States into temperate Mexico. The eastern subspecies predominates in the South, although some overlap of the subspecies occurs in eastern Oklahoma and Texas and western Arkansas and Louisiana.

Mourning doves can produce multiple broods at about 35-day intervals during their prolonged breeding season. In the South, 4 to 6 broods may be raised during a breeding season that spans February through September. Both parents care for the 2-egg clutch and young, and feed them a unique substance called "crop milk" (Mirarchi 1993a). After the young leave the nest at 12-15 days of age, the adult male is primarily responsible for their care and aids in their dispersal from the nesting area via a variety of behavioral interactions. The average life span for a wild mourning dove is about 1 year for immatures and 1.5 years for adults, but the longevity record is 19.3 yr for a free-living bird (Baskett and Sayre 1993). More details on nesting and production, reproductive strategy, growth and development, molt, physiology, and behavior are provided by Sayre and Silvy (1993), Blockstein and Westmoreland (1993), Mirarchi (1993b,c), and Sayre et al. (1993), respectively.

HISTORY AND IMPORTANCE

Reeves and McCabe (1993) provide a detailed historical perspective of the mourning dove relative to the settlement of North America. Unlike many other birds, mourning doves generally have benefitted from human changes to the North American landscape, and they have expanded their geographical distribution and greatly increased in numbers since European man settled the continent. Although mourning doves were killed and eaten by native Americans, early explorers, and early European immigrants, they did not originally occur in numbers large or concentrated enough to make them an important commodity in early game markets. In the South, as well as the rest of the eastern portion of the continent, the species was originally observed in and around the edges of openings created in the forest canopy by natural forces such as lightning-caused fires, hurricanes and tornadoes, and densely packed roosting sites of passenger pigeons that killed extensive patches of hardwoods with thick layers of droppings. Native Americans further improved habitat conditions for mourning doves in southern forests by clearing areas for villages and farming. They also purposely set fires to maintain these openings for agriculture and berry production, to allow easy travel, to protect themselves from warlike tribes and animal pests, or to attract game. These activities set the stage for the larger scale changes in the forested habitats of the South wrought by European man. Early settlers opened up more forests, and introduced exotic weeds and cultivated crops that mourning doves readily used. Cattle grazing maintained openings containing various seed producing forbs and grasses used by doves. More recently, ornamental plantings and bird feeding associated with an increasingly suburban and urban South have p[illegible]ed additional habitats that continue to sust[illegible] mourning dove population.

Today, in addition to recreational and aesthetic pleasures, mourning doves contribute significant financial benefits to local economies and wildlife conservation through hunting. Dove hunters expended an estimated $500 million in pursuit of doves in 1985 (Baskett and Sayre 1993). More importantly, the number of shotgun shells expended annually by dove hunters adds significant monies to federal and state conservation coffers. Mourning dove hunting is estimated to return $7-$14 million a year to the Federal Aid in Wildlife Restoration (Pittman-Robertson) Program via an 11% excise tax on ammunition sales alone.

DISTRIBUTION AND CURRENT POPULATIONS

The breeding and wintering distributions of mourning doves overlap broadly (Fig. 1); most birds overwinter considerably south of the Mason-Dixon line, but small groups will spend the winter as far north as Canada, where food is available. Most populations are migratory, but migratory and nonmigratory individuals coexist in many breeding areas of the South, and some nonmigratory or resident populations are found at mid- and higher latitudes. Nonmigratory populations seem to be associated with suburban and urban areas where food from bird feeders is abundant year round. Nonmigratory populations appear to be more numerous in the South probably because of the milder climate and the year-round availability and accessability of food and water.

A detailed description of mourning dove migratory chronology and movements is presented by Tomlinson (1993). Briefly, migratory pathways of both subspecies generally are contained in three flyways or "Management Units" (MU): Eastern (EMU), Central (CMU), and Western (WMU). Banding data indicates doves from the EMU, which contains most of the southern states, generally migrate south and southwestward from northern areas and overwinter within the Unit. Banded doves recovered in the Carolinas generally are produced in New England and mid-Atlantic states, whereas Alabama, Georgia, Florida, Louisiana, and Texas are major recovery areas for doves banded in the north-central states. Most doves from Kentucky, Tennessee, and the Carolinas overwinter in these states, although some will drift farther south; doves in the remaining southern states migrate very little with only limited movement southeastward and southwestward (Tomlinson et al. 1994). Some doves from the CMU also migrate southeastward into the southern states of the EMU.

Figure 1. Mourning dove distribution in North America *(after Mirarchi and Baskett 1994).*

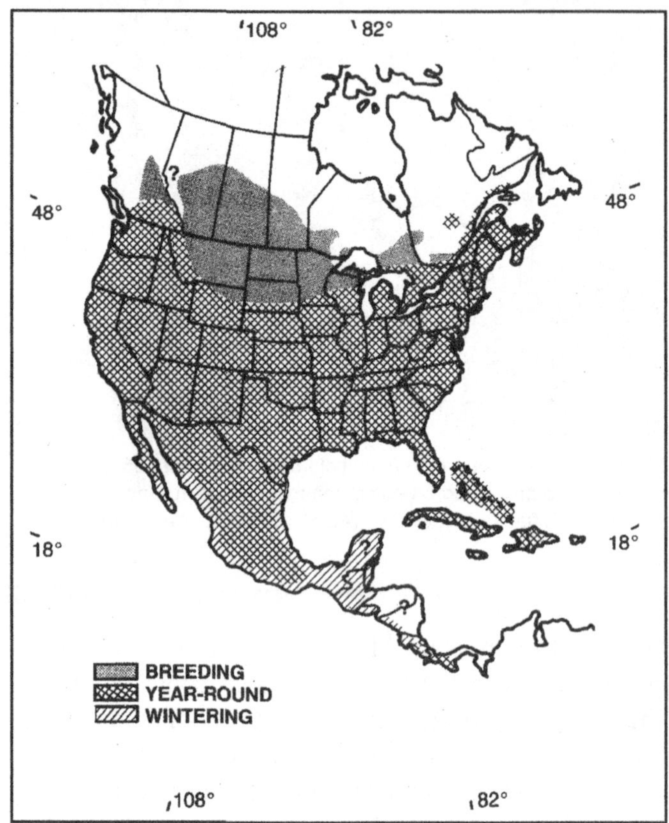

Call-count surveys of cooing males have been used to index breeding population trends for decades (Dolton 1993; T.S. Baskett 1993) and their analyses are detailed by Martin and Sauer (1993), Tomlinson and Dunks (1993), and Reeves et al. (1993). Population trends by management unit, region of the country, and by state are published annually (see Dolton and Smith 1999). Most recently, the highest densities of breeding birds were in Kansas, Nebraska, North Dakota, and North Carolina, with North Carolina and Georgia having the greatest breeding densities in the South (Dolton and Smith 1999).

Breeding EMU populations have declined from 1989-1999 in hunting and non-hunting states; however, this population decline was mirrored over the long term (1966-1999) only in the hunting states (Dolton and Smith 1999). Mourning dove populations in the eastern and mid- CMU, which includes at least portions of some southern states (Arkansas, eastern Oklahoma and eastern Texas), have experienced slight long-term (1966-1999) downward population trends (Dolton and Smith 1999).

Mourning dove populations normally increase from spring through late summer and peak populations normally are reached in September and October just before migration. The current estimated fall population of mourning doves in the United States is about 475 million birds (Tomlinson et al. 1994).

FOODS AND FEEDING

The detailed review of Lewis (1993) is briefly summarized here. Mourning doves normally feed on the ground, but occasionally will perch on stiff erect plants or feeders to feed. Doves are primarily (99% of diet) seed-eaters, with insignificant amounts of animal matter and green forage occasionally taken (possibly incidentally). Grit also is ingested and retained in the gizzard to help grind hardened seeds. Mourning doves usually feed on sparsely vegetated ground. They do not scratch or probe the ground, but will use their bills to whisk away light ground litter.

A large variety of small to medium sized seeds are eaten, although a high percentage of the volume of foods eaten often consists of only a few species. Some commonly ingested seeds of non-agricultural crops plants include a variety of grasses, crotons, lambsquarter, saltbushes, sunflowers, ragweeds, pokeweed, pricklypoppies, pigweeds, smartweeds, hemp, mustards, and pines. The principal food items eaten vary by region and immediate locale. Agricultural crops, particularly cereal grains, are avidly sought wherever available. In the South, choice agricultural grains include wheat, millets, corn, sunflowers, rye, grain sorghum, soybeans, and hulled peanuts.

DISEASES AND CONTAMINANTS

A detailed examination of the diseases, parasites, and contaminants that affect mourning doves is presented by Conti (1993). The two most important diseases found in the species are avian pox (viral) and trichomoniasis (protozoan). Avian pox, which is usually characterized by wart-like nodules on the bare areas of the body (feet, eyes, bill), generally is not fatal unless it impairs vision or develops into the diphtheritic form that invades the mouth and prevents feeding. In the South, pox outbreaks are fairly common in areas where and when densities are high, particularly in late summer. Once the lesions disappear the birds acquire at least partial immunity. Trichomoniasis causes yellowish lesions in the mouth and esophagus and is transmitted through contaminated food and water, billing, and regurgitive feeding. Mortality usually is very high, particularly in squabs. A large-scale epizootic resulting in tens of thousands of mortalities occurred in the South during the early 1950s. Today, mostly smaller outbreaks and die-offs are reported usually where feral pigeons and mourning doves interact at feeding sites, such as grain elevators, or in conjunction with poorly maintained backyard bird feeders and baths.

Mourning doves are infected with nematodes (roundworms), cestodes (tapeworms), and trematodes (flukes), and also a variety of mites and lice. The effects on populations probably are minimal. The blood sucking species potentially may have the most important effect on populations as vectors of diseases like avian pox.

Residues of several contaminants have been reported in tissues of mourning doves, with some resulting in fairly large die-offs (Conti 1993). Of the organochlorines, dieldrin and aldrin were the most acutely toxic. Die-offs also have resulted from the organophosphates parathion and methyl parathion, and the carbamates carbofuran and oxamyl. Polychlorinated biphenyls (PCBs) have been reported to reduce metabolic rates and body temperatures, and adversely affect courtship behavior and hormone levels. No contaminated dove tissues have caused known health problems in humans, or resulted in warnings against their consumption.

Lead poisoning may have the most widespread potential for contaminant-caused mortality in mourning doves (see Conti 1993). Lead shot is ingested primarily from shooting ranges and fields planted to attract doves for hunting. Ingestion rates vary from 0.2 to 6.4% depending on locale. Ingestion of 1 to 4 lead shot can result in mortality rates of up to 60% of experimentally treated birds on corn diets, and also appears to increase embryonic mortality in eggs laid by females that have ingested lead shot and survived. A field study of wild doves also suggests lower survival of lead-dosed birds. Discing or plowing feeding fields after hunting seasons considerably reduces the availability of shot considerably at the surface. Certain sizes of steel shot may be as effective as lead in harvesting doves and its use should be encouraged in heavily hunted areas. However, until some form of inexpensive non-toxic shot becomes more readily available in sizes appropriate to minimize crippling, its widespread use will remain problematic.

INTERACTIONS WITH OTHER SPECIES

Adult and young mourning doves are heavily preyed upon by raptors, mammals, and reptiles (Sadler 1993a). For example, in Alabama predation accounted for 30%

Rat snakes are primary predators of eggs and young of doves and other small birds. This one ate a young fledgling dove *(R. Mirarchi)*.

(18% avian, 8% mammalian, 4% reptilian) of known mortalities of nestlings and fledglings (Grand et al. 1984). In the South, swift and agile peregrine falcons, merlins, Cooper's, and sharp-shinned hawks probably are the most effective avian predators. Raccoons, domestic cats, and dogs are common mammalian predators, and rat snakes are the most likely reptilian predator.

HABITAT REQUIREMENTS

Mourning doves nest in a wide variety of habitats throughout southern Canada, the 48 conterminous United States, north central Mexico, and the Greater Antilles (Sayre and Silvy 1993). A great deal of variability occurs in the nesting habitats used in rural, urban, and suburban situations, but extensive, heavily forested areas generally are avoided. Mourning doves select more open woodlands and the edges between forests and prairies for nesting (Tomlinson et al. 1994). The highest breeding densities occur in the agricultural areas of the mid-western, southeastern, and southwestern United States (Sayre and Silvy 1993).

Mourning doves frequently nest in trees and shrubs close to human habitation. They will nest in a variety of coniferous and deciduous tree species and shrubs, on the ground, in vine tangles, on building ledges, and in other less typical locations (Sayre and Silvy 1993). In the rural South, most nests are constructed on horizontal substrates with conifers and occasionally ground sites preferred early in the year before deciduous trees and shrubs develop leaves. In more urban and suburban areas, any flat substrate that affords some type of protection from the elements may be selected. Dense tree or ground cover within 150 feet of nesting sites provide ideal locations for interaction between parents and young after they leave the nest (Grand and Mirarchi 1988). Such sites are invaluable in helping the young disperse from nesting sites and to develop feeding skills. In all situations, abundant food and water must be

Mourning doves nest in trees, shrubs, and a variety of other locations. Both parents incubate the eggs. *(R. Mirarchi)*.

available within 12-18 miles of nesting areas (Tomlinson et al. 1994).

Specific habitats used during the fall and spring migrations probably are similar to those used at other times of year. They appear to be determined primarily by food availability, and roosting and loafing cover. In the South, locally produced mourning doves regularly move between roosting and loafing sites (wooded areas) and specific feeding sites such as harvested grain fields in late summer and early fall (Losito et al. 1990). During this time they move substantial distances (0.6-5 miles per flight, 3-11 linear miles per day), and may range over 500 acres daily and 6,000 acres within a few weeks while searching for new feeding areas (Losito and Mirarchi 1991). Winter roost sites appear to consist of small to medium sized woodlots where suitable protection from elements is available (Tomlinson et al. 1994).

Recent declines in mourning dove populations in certain areas of the United States may be due to changes in land use that affect reproduction, recruitment, and survival. More intensive and cleaner farming, such as expansion of extensive improved pasture and loss of shelter belts, fencerows, and isolated trees or clumps of trees, tends to be detrimental to mourning dove habitat. In the South, extensive plantings of pine monocultures also are detrimental, especially during the early dense brushy and closed canopy period that ranges from 3-12 years after planting. Increases of large, single-aged stands have been predicted to result in decreases in breeding populations of doves (Amend 1969). However, new clear cuts before dense vegetation develops, or young pine plantations treated with herbicides that prevent development of dense vegetation, are suitable habitat. Also, older thinned pine stands receive some dove use for nesting, roosting, and/or foraging. Of course, any changes in the availability of small agricultural grains can result in local changes in dove abundance. Because mourning doves are highly mobile and can move over several thousand acres while foraging (Losito and Mirarchi 1991), dove populations probably will respond most to changes in habitat that occur at the landscape rather than the stand level.

MANAGEMENT

Human Impacts — Harvest

The most obvious impact of humans on mourning dove populations is through hunting. Specific recommendations to improve population and harvest management have been outlined recently (Tomlinson et al. 1994). Mourning doves are hunted in 37 of 48 conterminous states in the United States, including all of the South. They are considered a songbird in 11 northeastern and north central states where hunting is not allowed. Survival rates are lower in selected hunting states than in non-hunting states (Martin and Sauer 1993); thus, while dove populations are not adversely impacted long term by hunting, they do turn over faster in hunted versus unhunted areas. Hunting kill and crippling losses are estimated at 70 million birds annually in North America, or about 15% of the fall population (Sadler 1993b).

The estimated national harvest of mourning doves increased linearly for decades beginning in the 1940s reaching approximately 50 million birds by the early 1980s. However, it appeared that the harvest had declined to about 41 million birds by the late 1980s (Tomlinson et al. 1994). Harvests in the South were among the highest nationally, with eight states (Texas, Tennessee, Georgia, South Carolina, Alabama, Mississippi, North Carolina, and Louisiana) harvesting over two million doves annually, and comprising about 50% of the national harvest (Tomlinson et al. 1994; Table 1). The decreased harvests in the last decade or so probably are reflective of the general decrease in hunters in general, and fewer dove hunters and lower harvests in the central and western portions of the country as dove populations there have declined.

Table 1. Mourning dove harvests, number of hunters, and average seasonal bag of states in the South, 1988-89. Modified from Tomlinson et al. (1994).

State	No. hunters	No. doves harvested	Ave. seasonal bag
Texas	393,259	5,207,490	13.24
Tennessee	139,514	3,183,702	22.82
Georgia	107,191	3,155,452	29.94
South Carolina	111,996	3,148,336	28.11
Alabama	98,264	3,029,572	30.83
Mississippi	112,597	2,933,571	26.05
North Carolina	116,895	2,498,555	21.37
Louisiana	110,600	2,497,000	22.58
Kentucky	85,994	1,930,005	22.44
Oklahoma	75,002	1,859,041	24.72
Florida	107,428	1,655,199	15.22
Virginia	62,588	931,776	14.89
Arkansas	42,918	813,251	18.95

Management of hunting pressure on mourning dove populations involves the interplay of many biological and political factors, and the interaction of many different government agencies (Tomlinson et al. 1994). Trends in call-count surveys, annual harvest estimates, and knowledge obtained from quantitative analyses of band recoveries and survival rates (Nichols and Tomlinson 1993), are used to make recommendations for annual hunting seasons and bag limits within each of the 3 management units (also see Reeves 1993). Even more complete information on mourning dove harvests from mail questionnaires are becoming available as data from the National Migratory Bird Harvest Information Program (HIP), which was fully implemented nationally in 1998, are now being analyzed and presented. The HIP is a cooperative venture between the federal government and the individual states that was begun on a trial basis in 1994.

Because it is a migratory species, regulation of mourning dove hunting falls primarily within the domain of the federal government, which cooperates with the various states in establishing hunting seasons, bag limits, and other regulations. The federal government outlines a basic season framework that protects dove populations while allowing sport hunting. The individual states can set seasons and bag limits within these guidelines to coincide with seasonal population abundance and migration chronology. In the South, "split seasons" often are established at different times to take advantage of peak populations of locally raised doves early and migrants later on.

In general, southern mourning dove populations have maintained their numbers with regulated harvests that have included 10-18 bird daily bag limits (Hayne and Geissler 1977). However, populations can experience temporary "burn-outs" once the surplus of birds produced locally is exhausted by heavy hunting pressure, and before migratory birds move back into an area (Losito and Mirarchi 1991). Hunters need to be made aware that intensive shooting over dove fields within 10 miles of each other can lead to these temporarily depleted local populations. While mourning doves are extremely prolific reproducers, it doesn't take many dove shoots where hundreds and maybe even thousands of birds are harvested to deplete local surpluses.

Human Impacts — Habitat

Although hunting may seem the most obvious human impact on dove populations to the casual observer, habitat changes wrought by humans have the greatest long term potential to affect dove populations positively or negatively. Specific recommendations to improve habitat management for mourning doves have been outlined (Tomlinson et al. 1994). The greatest threat to the species appears to be loss of breeding habitats as a result of various land use changes and practices. Remember, mourning doves are ecotonal species so they must have a good mix of openings and forested areas to provide adequate nesting and foraging opportunities.

Land management practices in the South differ from other regions of the country in that those detrimental to mourning doves have come about as a result of adding, not removing, vegetation. Edges are being eliminated by filling in openings in the forest canopy via the conversion of many pasture and farming areas into extensive pine plantations. Such practices have proven more profitable for landowners than farming or raising cattle in recent years because of rising timber prices and increasing federal subsidies for tree planting. These extensive even-aged pine plantations provide little used dove habitat of any type during the 3-12 year period after planting. Despite such setbacks in the South, the prospects for the species appear to be fairly good. Populations will ebb in more rural areas as more nesting and foraging sites are lost when farming/cattle operations give way to intensive timber production, but populations probably will increase in suburban and urban areas as these habitats expand. However, expanded suburban and urban dove populations may not provide additional hunting opportunities because suburban and urban doves appear reluctant to leave these areas to forage, or during migration (D. P. Scott, Ohio Div. Wildl., unpubl. data).

Details on mourning dove nesting habitats have been provided by Sayre and Silvy (1993). In the South, ideal nesting habitat generally is associated with the presence of edges and clearings and the absence of understory within continuous forests (Grue et al. 1983), but there is good evidence that dense tree or ground cover near nest trees is beneficial to recently fledged doves for approximately 12-15 days after they leave the nest (Grand and Mirarchi 1988).

Balanced year-round habitat meant to produce as well as attract doves has been described previously (Russell 1974, Madson 1978), and has been modified and updated for southern forests here. Ideal habitat should include about 70% of the landscape in openings that consist of agricultural crops (wheat, millets, corn, sunflowers, sorghum, etc.), pasture land, and old field succession. Random conifers and hardwoods should be present within openings in the landscape to provide nesting and loafing sites. One could obtain a similar

Open grown pines and ground cover pictured above provide ideal nesting and fledging areas for doves in the South *(K. Hudson)*.

effect by planting widely spaced conifers (loblolly pine and eastern red-cedar) and hardwoods, such as water oaks, along roads through open areas, or scattered among naturally vegetated fencerows around pastures. Habitats beneath such nesting trees should be maintained in 1-2 year old natural vegetation to provide ideal habitat where recently fledged doves can interact with their parents while learning to feed on their own. Any scattered dead snags (particularly hardwoods) should be retained because they also seem to attract mourning doves as loafing and congregation sites.

Approximately 28% of the entire landscape should remain wooded to provide roosting, loafing, and additional nesting opportunities. The greatest proportion of the wooded areas should be in stands greater than 20 years of age. Mixed pine-hardwood stands, or thinned pine stands are probably best. Pine stands should be thinned similarly to what is recommended for bobwhite quail (approx. 45-60 sq.ft. basal area), and burned regularly (every 2 years) to provide good nesting and foraging areas. Prescribed burning is beneficial to a variety of forest wildlife species, and mourning doves are known to be attracted to recently burned areas for nesting (Soutiere and Bolen 1972) and foraging (Bock and Bock 1992). Young, densely-stocked pine or hardwood stands are not good dove habitat.

The remaining 2% of the landscape should be in free-standing water sources to satisfy the mourning doves' daily requirement for water. Water for doves can often be provided coincidentally with water maintained for cattle (via ponds or stock tanks, or limited access to streams), irrigation, fish farming, or recreational fishing and swimming. Watering areas provided for mourning doves should have access via gently sloping banks that are kept free of thick vegetation.

Feeding fields can be managed to attract mourning doves (R. K. Baskett 1993). Mourning doves apparently locate food visually and by observation of other birds feeding. Doves prefer to alight, walk, and feed on ground relatively free of dense vegetation. They can be attracted in large numbers by harvesting agricultural crops and manipulating the residues to make them

Doves feed on small seeds of naturally-occurring plants and agricultural crops. Foraging areas are sparsely vegetated.

attractive, or by planting and manipulating certain crops to serve as "dove fields." So, fields most heavily used are those with an abundance of small seeds scattered on bare soil and having very little horizontal cover. Removal of excess vegetation by burning or light discing may be necessary.

In the old South, small sesame and hemp fields grown for other purposes were original "hot spots" that attracted doves. More recently, southern dove fields are most often specifically prepared using various millets, wheat, sunflowers, corn, and grain sorghum. Attractive feeding areas also can be prepared by machine mowing/shredding fields that have been allowed to go fallow for a growing season or two. Such fields often develop natural plant communities that include croton, ragweed, pigweed, and pokeweed, which are attractive to doves.

Good concentrations of doves frequently are drawn to "hogged-down" (introduction of cattle and pigs into fields to feed on unharvested grain crops) corn and peanut fields, and to fields from which wheat, corn, millet, sunflowers, grain sorghum, soybeans, or peanuts have been harvested. For example, in different regions of Alabama harvested fields of brown-top millet, corn, and peanuts often provide excellent shooting opportunities.

Size and the method of field preparation are considerations in attracting doves for hunting. Five acres generally is considered to be the lower limit in size. Recent legal rulings on baiting have changed some previously favored methods of field preparation in certain regions of the South. For example, top sowing of wheat on a freshly prepared seed bed as an attractant in the fall is now considered baiting in Alabama and Georgia, but not in Texas. To counteract the loss of top-sown wheat as a fall attractant in certain areas, one must now plan planting, harvesting, and/or mowing schedules to provide a variety of crop/weed seed throughout the summer and into the fall hunting season. Such a well-planned, longer term strategy works well in maintaining dove fields for use by resident and migrant doves throughout the year.

To maximize seed production and availability, and to ensure that there is seed on the ground at all times, some crops may be planted together in the same field. For example, in corn fields browntop millet may be broadcast between rows following the last cultivation treatment. In some southern states such as Alabama, it has been recommended that fields be divided into early season, late season, and combination season fields based on anticipated shooting times and the types of foods planted (Waters 1983). Browntop and proso millets, sunflowers (small oil varieties), and wheat are recommended for early season (September to November) fields, corn and grain sorghum for late season (November through January), and a mix of crops from the early and late season choices are recommended for the combination fields (September through January). If questions arise with regard to planting times and methods; seeding, liming, and fertilization rates, etc., southern dove managers should refer to specific sources of such information (Mahan 1978, Waters 1983, Bourne 1991, R. K. Baskett 1993a) and/or call their county extension agent for details.

Mourning doves may respond to heavy and consistent hunting pressure in the same feeding areas by moving elsewhere. Hence, many managers feel it beneficial to voluntarily regulate hunting pressure on selected areas by restricting the number of hunts allowed within a given time frame, restricting the location and number of hunters on a dove field, and/or the duration of hunting on individual hunts. To manage pressure and to ensure safety, no more than one hunter per acre should be allowed on a dove field. Some dove managers allow hunters to only "ring" such fields, preferring to keep the centers of fields as refugia where any doves that safely arrive are allowed to alight, feed, and survive for the next hunt (Bourne 1991). Many managers hunt only a half day if they have morning hunts, cease all hunting about an hour and a half before dark to allow doves to enter the fields to feed without harassment, and restrict hunts to once or twice a week until they learn how much pressure the birds can take. If a large number of doves is harvested off of a given area, it is probably wise to let it rest for at least a week before hunting again. Some southern dove hunting clubs lease a number of areas to hunt, and rotate their hunts among the different leases to minimize hunting pressure and to prolong their hunting opportunities. Planned experimentation and cooperative efforts by landowners in an area should provide plentiful recreational opportunities without overshooting.

Landowners and hunters need to remember that baiting mourning doves is illegal, and is one of the most frequently cited game violations. They should check with federal and state conservation officers with regard to baiting regulations prior to hunting over fields prepared for mourning doves. They may even want conservation officers to inspect their fields prior to hunting to ensure that they are legal.

Other specific management needs for mourning doves have been reviewed in detail by Braun et al. (1993) and Tomlinson et al. (1994). They considered the 2 most important issues for mourning dove management to be correction of population declines where they occur, and institution of a standardized nationwide harvest survey (now implemented via the Harvest Information Program). They also recommended establishment of an extension-like network to improve mourning dove habitat on public and private lands, and to improve cooperation of natural resource agencies nationwide. Also, opportunities for mourning dove habitat improvement through long term contracts such as the Conservation Reserve Program (CRP), Wetland Reserve Program (WRP), Agricultural Conservation Program (ACP), Environmental Quality Incentive Program (EQIP), and the Wildlife Habitat Incentives Program (WHIP) should be explored. Development of habitat management manuals for different regions of the country were recommended to educate landowners and conservation agencies about dove nesting and foraging needs, and techniques to attract doves.

HUNTING

Liberal bag limits, rapid (up to 55 mph) and erratic flight patterns that make them elusive targets, and their excellence as table fare have assured the popularity of mourning doves as game birds over the years. The specific techniques and traditions associated with mourning dove hunting in the South have been detailed by Russell (1974, 1993), and mourning dove hunting there has best been summarized by Madson (1978:46) as a "blend of family reunion, lodge picnic, an old-style barbecue, and a Juarez election." Mourning dove "shoots" have become the traditional "kick-off" of the southern fall hunting seasons, and as such often are associated with some type of social gathering. Many shoots are preceded or followed by a barbecue or fish fry where stories of previous hunting seasons and plans for the upcoming season abound. The number of hunters involved may range from parties of 1 to 5 that "tailgate" on the back of a pick-up to 50 or more, who attend a well-planned affair complete with designated cookers, beverage suppliers, and bird-dog handlers. Dove hunts may contain a diverse mix of races, gender, and socio-economic groups, and include every day working folks, high-ranking government officials, and university presidents.

Temperatures during early season afternoon hunts (September) in the South often reach into the 90's, so hunters often socialize or rest in the shade until 3:00 or 4:00 p.m. before taking up their shooting positions. Mourning doves often are loafing in surrounding wooded areas during the heat of the day, waiting until later afternoon to feed and water as temperatures begin to cool. Doves usually begin flying into fields to feed shortly after sunrise.

Favored hunting sites usually include recently harvested grain or hayfields, specially prepared dove fields, farm ponds, and stock tanks. Flight lines leading to such areas, such as power or gas line rights-of-way, also can be productive. Doves are shot on the wing as they approach, pass over, or circle such areas. Hunters typically dress in camouflage clothing and station themselves to break their outline, preferably in the shade, in fencerows, or behind hay bales. Sites adjacent to lone trees, snags, or power lines in or near feeding fields also are favored locations because doves often fly to these areas to alight prior to going to the ground to feed. Some hunters mark off known distances around their chosen blind site with stakes or flagging to better judge shooting distances. Decoys may be placed in trees or on fences to attract doves within shooting range. Retrieving dogs often are helpful in locating downed birds. They should be kept cool and well-watered.

Typical of other migratory birds, the breast meat of mourning doves is dark; however, most find it less strong than American woodcock or duck, and excellent table fare. A wide variety of recipes is available that includes frying, grilling, roasting, baking, and use in casseroles. The reader is referred to Madson (1978), Stribling and Mikel (1991), and Russell (1993) for a good sampling of southern style recipes.

CHAPTER 13

American Woodcock

R. Montague Whiting, Jr.
Arthur Temple College of Forestry
Stephen F. Austin State University, Nacogdoches, TX

The American woodcock is a shorebird (Family Scolopacidae) that has adapted to forested habitats. There are no recognized subspecies in North America. Its closest relative is the Eurasian woodcock, which is found throughout much of Europe and Asia; in North America, the woodcock's closest relative is the common snipe. Although the 2 species occupy different diurnal habitats and are colored differently, they often are confused. One of the many colloquial names of the American woodcock in the southern United States is snipe; other colloquial names include timberdoodle, bog sucker, *pec noir*, and *becasse*.

HISTORY

The status and distribution of the American woodcock before the arrival of Europeans are unknown. However, woodcock were definitely in the diet of American Indians. Woodcock hunting in North America was first described in *The Sportsman's Companion* in 1783. By the 1830s, woodcock had come into its own as a game bird and were harvested in remarkable numbers. Population declines were noted shortly before the Civil War, and were widespread by the turn of the century (Sheldon 1971).

Although several eastern states established closed seasons earlier, it was not until the Migratory Bird Treaty Act of 1918 that the species was provided widespread protection, especially from spring shooting and market hunting. That act placed woodcock and all other migratory bird species under the authority of the federal government.

BIOLOGY

Physical description.—The basic color of the woodcock is mottled brown, a color pattern that blends well with the forest floor. In hand, a distinguishing color pattern is the transverse bars on the head. The species has

The American Woodcock is a shorebird that has adapted to forested habitat. Hens nest on the ground and most clutches are completed in late winter *(H. Williamson)*.

Four eggs are the normal clutch. Eggs are grayish brown to grayish green with blotches *(H. Williamson)*.

short, rounded wings and when flushed, can produce a quavering whistle-like sound similar to that of a northern bobwhite; it also can flush silently. The woodcock has relatively short legs, large eyes set high and back on the head, and a long (2.25-2.75 in.), narrow beak which is prehensile at the tip.

Sexes are similar, but adult females are significantly larger (5.9-8.5 oz.) than adult males (4.3-6.4 oz.). In hand, size differential makes sexing woodcock relatively easy. For females, combined width of the outer 3 primary feathers, measured 0.79 inches from the tip, is greater than or equal to 0.50 inches whereas that for males is less than 0.50 inches. Beak lengths of females range 2.75-3.00 inches while those of males range 2.32-2.72 inches. A simple method of determining sex is to insert a dollar bill crosswise into the beak of the woodcock. If the bird's beak extends completely across the dollar, it is a female. If the beak is not as long the dollar is wide, it is a male.

Subadults and adults are similar in appearance but can be distinguished by secondary and tertial wing feathers. The inner secondaries of subadults have a light tip with a dark subterminal band below the tip. Adults lack the dark subterminal band, and the light tip is slightly darker than that of subadults. Also, on adults the color patterns on the outer portions of the secondaries grade smoothly into those on the tertials. On subadults, there usually is an abrupt change in color patterns between adjacent or near-adjacent feathers.

Breeding biology.—Woodcock are polygamous; males have an elaborate courtship display which begins on the ground with an insect- or frog-like noise called a "peent". The peent is preceded by a burp-like sound called a "tuko" which is audible when the observer is very close to the bird. After several minutes of peenting, the bird flushes, spiraling upward with twittering wings to perform its unique "skydance". At heights of 100-200 yards, the courting male flies in a circle with melodious chirping which increases in rapidity until the chirping suddenly stops and the bird silently dives back to the same opening on the ground to resume peenting. Females either fly or walk to the courtship site where breeding occurs.

In the lower Coastal Plain, regular courtship flights begin about the first of January. The peak of courtship activity is mid-February in eastern Texas (Whiting and Boggus 1982) and mid-March in Tennessee (Roberts and Dimmick 1978) and central Missouri (Murphy and Thompson 1993). Courting males generally are no longer present a month after the activity peak.

Clutch initiation begins in early February in the lower Coastal Plain (Causey et al. 1974, Whiting et al. 1985). Although nest initiation extends into early April, most clutches are completed in February and early March (Roboski and Causey 1981). Nest initiation peaks in early March in Tennessee (Roberts and Dimmick 1978) and North Carolina (Stamps and Doerr 1977) and in mid-March in Missouri (Murphy and Thompson 1993).

The hen builds a simple nest on the ground which is constructed primarily of hardwood leaves and pine needles. The nest usually is at the base of a small sapling and within about 150 yards of a singing ground. Four eggs normally are laid. Eggs are grayish brown to grayish green with darker spots and blotches. Color pattern of the eggs blends well with leaves and straw of the nest; when the hen leaves the nest to feed, she covers the eggs with such material.

The chicks are precocial; mud on their beak suggests they start probing within 3 or 4 days after hatching *(H. Williamson)*.

Incubation takes 21 days, and the chicks are precocial. Although chicks probably require maternal feeding for a week (Greg 1984), mud on the beak suggests that they begin probing within 3 or 4 days of hatching. Chicks are able to make short flights by 14 days and sustained flight by 18 days, and are independent of the hen by 38 days (Horton and Causey 1982).

Predators.—In the southern United States, woodcock probably are subjected to much the same predator community as are other ground- or shrub-dwelling birds that thrive in early successional habitats. Krementz et al. (1994) found relatively low woodcock survival during winter in Georgia and South Carolina and attributed all woodcock deaths to predation. Mammalian predators included bobcats, gray foxes, raccoons, and house cats. Barred owls, great horned owls, short-eared owls, barn owls, and red-shouldered hawks were probable avian predators. No doubt some woodcock also are taken by red foxes, free-ranging dogs, and various other southern hawks.

Nesting hens probably are subjected to the same types of predators; during the chick-rearing periods, hens probably are very susceptible to avian predators. There are no data on woodcock nest depredation, but studies of nesting northern bobwhite in the South indicate that raccoons and snakes are important nest predators. However, late-winter nesting by woodcock probably limits nest depredation by snakes. Skunks, Virginia opossums, squirrels, blue jays, and American crows surely depredate some nests.

Wiley and Causey (1987) found that prefledgling survival of woodcock chicks was higher than post-fledgling survival. Of 10 chick mortalities, 8 were attributed to predation with avian, mammalian, and unknown predators taking 4, 2, and 2 chicks, respectively.

Diseases and parasites.—Little is known about diseases of American woodcock. Some birds have been reported with bumblefoot and tumors. Malaria, gregarine infection, and a reovirus have been reported, but each was restricted to 1 or very few birds (Keppie and Whiting 1994).

Pursglove (1973) recorded 49 types of parasites on 275 woodcock from the southern United States. The most common parasite groups were Protozoa,

Trematoda, Cestoda, Acanthocephala, Nematoda, Mullophaga, Diptera, and Acarina.

FOODS

The primary food item of the American woodcock throughout its range and its life cycle is earthworms. The bird's long beak with its flexible upper mandible is specialized for capturing earthworms. Data from 12 studies and 1,446 digestive tracts showed percent frequency of earthworm occurrence was 77. Other regularly-occurring invertebrates included ants (24%), beetles (50%), flies (23%), and millipedes (27%). Plant materials, primarily seeds of grasses (11%), roses (12%), sedges (11%), and smartweeds (13%), occurred in 38% of the digestive tracts (Keppie and Whiting 1994).

Studies in the southern United States demonstrate that earthworms comprise 63-99% of the volume of foods consumed and vegetation makes up 5-16%. However, at least 2 southern studies (Miller and Causey 1985, Gregory 1987) reported that earthworms were consumed in proportion to their abundance. Those studies suggested that centipedes were the most-preferred food items. Other preferred invertebrates included beetle, fly, and butterfly larva. Millipedes were avoided in both studies.

Drought and frozen soil both impede foraging and are very detrimental to woodcock. During drought, birds will move into mixed pine-hardwood forests with old-growth characteristics[1] and scratch in the litter in a manner similar to brown thrashers. Birds also will concentrate around springs, marshes, lakes, and ponds, and may seek insects under cow manure in pastures. Frozen soil concentrates woodcock around springs and sometimes above septic tanks. Birds also have been recorded feeding in salt marshes, on watered lawns, and around feed troughs. Extended hard freezes in the southern United States have, on occasion, caused extensive woodcock mortality (Sheldon 1971).

DISTRIBUTION

Woodcock occur throughout the eastern United States and southeastern Canada. In both countries, woodcock are managed in 2 population segments, the Eastern and Central Regions; the Appalachian Mountains generally separate the regions (Bruggink 1997). The species is migratory and most birds winter in the Gulf and Atlantic Coastal Plains. Severity of winter weather may dictate how far south the birds winter. In mild winters, large numbers of woodcock may remain in the upper Coastal Plain and Piedmont Regions (Sheldon 1971). In severe winters, woodcock often are concentrated in coastal marshes of the lower Coastal Plain (Lynch 1951, Glasgow 1958). Although woodcock are usually recorded in the Rio Grande Valley of Texas during Christmas Bird Counts, higher numbers are noted during severe winters (G. Waggerman, Texas Parks and Wildlife Department, pers. commu.).

Wintering woodcock also have been recorded near San Luis Potosi, Mexico, in Bermuda, and on the Dry Tortugas. Westwardly, wintering birds are common in central Texas and central Oklahoma. During migration, birds have been recorded as far west as Albuquerque, New Mexico, eastern Colorado, and eastern Montana (Keppie and Whiting 1994). However, an attempt to introduce woodcock into California in the early 1970s failed.

Breeding range of the species almost entirely overlaps the wintering range. Although nesting woodcock are rare in coastal areas and the Atchafalaya River Basin of Louisiana, birds regularly nest in the remainder of the South. Nests have been recorded as far south as central Florida and near Corpus Christi, Texas, and as far west as Austin, Texas, central Oklahoma, and eastern Nebraska and South Dakota (Keppie and Whiting 1994).

The northern edge of the species' breeding range is not well known, but it extends into Manitoba to perhaps 51°N, 100°W, then east to the northern shores of the Bay of St. Lawrence. Northern limits of the range may be expanding due to forest management activities, primarily clearcutting, which create favorable nesting habitat.

HABITAT

As the primary component of the woodcock's diet is earthworms, the most critical aspect of its habitat is soil type. Woodcock capture earthworms by probing the soil with their beak to a depth of about 3.1 inches. Therefore, soils with high earthworm densities are favored by woodcock. In southern forests, such soils are usually calcareous with relatively high pH values. On bottomland areas, especially the Mississippi Alluvial Valley, calcareous clay soils are widely used by wood-

[1]Editor's Note: American Woodcock probably use old-growth stands wherever they occur in the South, but the extent of these stands is very limited. Woodcock use pine, pine-hardwood, and hardwood stands of a variety of different ages, development, and structure.

Woodcock prefer early successional vegetation as habitat *(M. Whiting)*.

cock. On upland sites, sandy loams and loamy sands with high organic matter often are favored (Boggus and Whiting 1982); sands or clays are usually avoided. However, sands with high organic matter and soil moisture may be used (Kroll and Whiting 1977). In fact, soil moisture is an important aspect of woodcock habitat. Soils which are too dry are not used and low soil moisture may account for the absence of woodcock on the Coastal Plain during summer.

Woodcock prefer early successional vegetation made up of a mixture of hardwoods, conifers, and vines (Keppie and Whiting 1994). The species also utilizes mixed pine-hardwood and hardwood forests with old-growth characteristics (i.e., lacking midstory vegetation and containing dense understory thickets), especially when such stands are near early successional stands. Provided soil conditions are correct, plant species assemblages usually are not important. However, a knowledge of soil/plant associations is important in recognizing woodcock habitat.

In the stratum that extends to about 12 inches above ground level, the woodcock needs sparse vegetation to facilitate mobility and visibility. Conversely, it needs overhead vegetation for protection from avian predators. In 5-year-old plantations, dense overhead vegetation is most important in the 12 to 33- inch stratum (Boggus and Whiting 1982). Britt (1971) described the

Open fields are used at night by woodcock *(T.Boggus)*.

Courtship sites where males do their dance are small openings *(T. Boggus)*.

preferred vegetation structure as "...picket fence-like in appearance..." with "...erect and spreading life forms."

Fall and winter.—In the southern United States, wintering woodcock may use different habitats for diurnal and nocturnal cover. Woodcock will feed in both habitats and many birds will not move from diurnal habitat to nocturnal habitat each day (Horton and Causey 1979). Nocturnal habitat often is referred to as roosting habitat; however, wintering woodcock may feed much more actively in such habitat than in diurnal habitat (Glasgow 1958).

Woodcock use a wide variety of diurnal habitat types. In bottomland complexes, diurnal cover often is comprised of dense switch cane and blackberry thickets in both recently regenerated stands and in hardwood forests with old-growth characteristics; other understory species indicative of good woodcock habitat include greenbrier, Alabama supplejack, hawthorn, and swamp dogwood (Glasgow 1958, Britt 1971, Dyer and Hamilton 1977, Straw et al. 1994).

On upland sites, a good indicator of diurnal woodcock habitat is southern waxmyrtle; other indicator species include hawthorns, blackberries, blueberries, yaupon, devil's walking-stick, American beautyberry, flowering dogwood, and oak seedlings (Kroll and Whiting 1977, Johnson and Causey 1982, Straw et al. 1994).

Small, low-growing evergreens also are very important. On bright winter days, woodcock may seek shade (Dyer and Hamilton 1977). On such days that are hot, the birds often will be found beneath evergreens with spreading branches that extend to the ground. When snow occurs, the birds will use the same type of cover or seek refuge under pine saplings bent by the weight of the snow.

When woodcock seek nocturnal cover, it often is in the form of open fields, including both improved and unimproved pastures, harvested croplands, and very young pine plantations (Horton and Causey 1979, Straw et al. 1994). The birds move to and from nocturnal cover at dawn and dusk. Use of open roosting fields may be greater on cold, rainy nights than on warm, clear nights (Glasgow 1958). Overhead cover may be lacking, or may be provided by weeds, grasses, sedges, woody vines and seedlings, persistent stalks of crops, and/or the row troughs (Straw et al. 1994). Dense grass which restricts movement limits use of openings, for woodcock may feed upon arrival and before leaving nocturnal fields.

Nocturnal fields usually are within 1.25 miles of diurnal habitat (Straw et al. 1994). The distance moved between diurnal and nocturnal habitat may be dependent on broadscale habitat features. In Alabama, it averaged approximately 0.11 miles (Horton and Causey 1979) whereas in Georgia and Virginia, that value was about 0.45 miles (Krementz et al. 1995). Woodcock that remain in diurnal habitat throughout the night often walk or fly to openings within the habitat; birds regularly roost in roads and trails through young pine plantations and other such thickets.

Breeding and nesting.—Males may use both diurnal and nocturnal habitats for courtship displays. Without exception, the courtship site is a small opening; it may be a log deck or a food plot in a mixed pine-hardwood forest with old-growth characteristics or a small area where woody plants are absent in an extensive young plantation. Young plantations and other such large-scale habitats may be used by numerous males; Pettingill (1977) described such sites as leks. Preferred singing grounds consist of early successional habitats. On upland sites, seedling/sapling mixed pine-hardwood stands which serve as both diurnal and nocturnal cover often are favored. Such stands provide clearings for courting and thickets for nesting. Open roosting fields such as grazed pastures and agriculture fields usually are lightly used by courting males (Tappe and Whiting 1989).

Woodcock that nest in the South use habitats similar to those used for diurnal cover. Nests regularly are recorded in early successional thickets as well as mixed pine-hardwood stands with old-growth characteristics and have been noted in overgrown pastures (Roboski and Causey 1981, Keppie and Whiting 1994). The birds normally do not nest in bottomland hardwood types which are prone to flooding.

Probably the 2 most important aspects of brood habitat are ground cover and soil moisture. For chicks to move about and forage, the ground surface must be relatively open; dense grass and large debris will impede chick movement. In order to probe, chicks must have access to soils that are nearly saturated with water. Hens usually select nest sites which reflect these requirements. However, drought conditions after nest initiation probably result in significant chick mortality.

CURRENT PROBLEMS

Trends in woodcock populations are assessed annually from approximately 800 singing-ground survey transects in the northern United States and Canada (Bruggink 1997). Analyses of survey data suggest long-term (1968-1996) downward trends in the numbers of courting males. Numbers have declined an average of 2.5% per year in the Eastern Region and 1.7% per year in the Central Region (Bruggink 1997). Recent reductions in season lengths and bag limits were implemented in response to these data.

Although these values are based on courting males only, there seems little doubt that woodcock populations have declined. However, hunting probably has negligible impact on populations. Band recovery rates generally are low (2.5-4.7%) (Straw et al. 1994). Even considering illegal harvest, unreported bands, and crippling loss, hunters probably account for less than 10% of annual woodcock mortality.

Loss of habitat is the greatest threat facing woodcock. Urbanization and drainage of forested wetlands permanently eliminates woodcock habitat. Conversion of forest lands on rich soils to agricultural and rural suburban uses decreases woodcock habitat suitability. Broadscale, however, the public's negative attitude toward even-age forest regeneration systems may be the most important threat. The woodcock is a scrub/shrub species that thrives in young forests. Local, state, and federal laws which may require forest landowners to regenerate their forests using uneven-aged management could have severe negative impacts on woodcock.

A second major problem involves a paucity of knowledge about woodcock breeding biology, especially in the southern portions of its range. Prior to the mid-1970s, virtually all research on breeding biology took place in the northern portions of the species range; in the South, research concentrated on winter habitat. Since the mid-1970s, however, research has suggested that woodcock regularly court and nest in the South (Roboski and Causey 1981, Walker and Causey 1982, Whiting et al. 1985, Causey et al. 1987). However, singing-ground surveys are not conducted in the South and the contribution of woodcock produced in the southern United States to the continental population is unknown. Likewise, the dispersion of southern-nesting hens and their chicks has not been studied thoroughly. However, it is doubtful that the birds remain on the Coastal Plain; it is extremely rare to see a woodcock in that area during late summer. Probably both hens and chicks move north (Causey et al. 1987).

MANAGEMENT

Unfortunately, woodcock management in the southern United States consists primarily of harvest restrictions. In managing habitat for woodcock, soil conditions and stage of vegetational succession are critical. On unsuitable soils, woodcock habitat management is ineffective. However, on suitable soils, forest management which promotes early successional vegetation is effective woodcock management.

Forest regeneration systems.—On upland pine sites, clearcutting and planting, when done properly on the proper soils, creates excellent woodcock habitat. Clearcuts should be at least 10 acres, although smaller clearcuts may provide habitat for a few birds.

Woodcock concentrate in and around large clearcuts, especially in mid-winter after regular courtship activity has begun; as noted, such areas may function as leks.

After merchantable timber has been removed, residual stems should be sheared then windrowed along with logging debris. Shearing residual hardwoods promotes sprouting and increases the hardwood component in the resulting stand; windrowing removes large debris which impedes woodcock movement, especially by flightless chicks. The windrows rapidly become dominated by blackberries and a multitude of hardwood species, thus serving as protective cover. When planting, seedlings should be in widely spaced rows to delay crown closure by pines.

Pine plantations managed in such a manner provide courtship, nocturnal, diurnal, and brood-rearing habitat for woodcock until canopy closure. Thereafter, suitability and usage declines because the closed canopy impedes flight by the bird and excludes hardwoods and thus hardwood litter which provides food for earthworms.

Clearcuts which are regenerated naturally and seedtree and shelterwood regeneration areas can provide excellent woodcock habitat. However, in both pine and hardwood stands, density of the desired species of seedlings is difficult to control. If regeneration is so dense as to exclude hardwood vegetation in pine stands or to preclude use by woodcock, the area should be precommercially thinned. Conversely, in understocked stands, crown closure is delayed and woodcock habitat suitability may be extended several years.

Riparian zones which originate in clearcuts can provide excellent woodcock habitat. Riparian zones should not be site prepared or planted. However, they should be of sufficient size to contain manageable stands. This will allow for regular entry and hardwood management. If the overstory canopy is closed, some large-crowned trees should be harvested, especially at the upper ends and along edges of the zones. This allows for rapid development of thickets in areas that often are moist during winter, thus providing excellent foraging and diurnal habitat. In all situations, areas adjacent to streams should be protected to prevent siltation.

In bottomland areas, naturally regenerated hardwood clearcuts often are too dense for woodcock. In such areas, seed tree (with high numbers of residual trees) and shelterwood regeneration systems are appropriate when woodcock are a consideration. These systems reduce understory density and increase edge. If understory vegetation is too dense, suitability for woodcock may be improved by mowing lanes through it. Hardwood regeneration areas interspersed with stands of sawtimber-size trees may provide excellent woodcock habitat.

Regardless of the regeneration technique, as even-age stands progress into the stem exclusion stage (canopy closure), woodcock habitat suitability declines (Kroll and Whiting 1977, Roberts et al. 1984). If stands are carried into the understory reintroduction stage, woodcock habitat may improve. As stands progress through this stage, overstory canopy closure breaks up and understory thickets develop. In pine stands, hardwoods reoccupy the understory, thus both improving earthworm habitat and providing diurnal cover for woodcock. The lack of midstory in such stands provides flight lanes for woodcock moving to and from nocturnal habitat.

In pine stands, single tree selection regeneration, applied properly, would discriminate against woodcock. Hardwoods would be eliminated, early successional vegetation would occur in clumps too small to be of value to woodcock, and the dense midstory would impede flight. In hardwood stands, the latter 2 conditions would be present and if timber values were a consideration, maintaining composition of desirable tree species would require expensive timber stand improvement.

In both pine and hardwood areas, group selection may be appropriate, especially if the groups are relatively large (greater than 2.0 acres), dispersed throughout the forest, and if the male woodcock are not using the area for courtship. In both pine and hardwood stands, 2 acres is not large enough to support several-to-many courting males in a lek-type situation.

Intermediate operations.—There is a wide variety of intermediate operations available to the resource manager which may impact woodcock habitat suitability. Probably the most important are chemical applications, thinnings, prescribed fires, and salvage operations.

The direct impact of herbicides on woodcock is unknown. Indirectly, however, herbicides which hasten crown closure in young pine plantations will shorten the length of time that the plantations provide suitable habitat. Likewise, herbicides that severely reduce the hardwood component in a stand probably negatively impact earthworms and thus woodcock.

In most cases, thinnings probably benefit woodcock. Thinnings in pine stands promote understory hardwood vegetation, thus benefiting woodcock. Pine plantations which are thinned at an early age and at regular intervals should provide at least marginal woodcock habitat throughout the rotation. Recently, forest industry has begun to thin and prune in 8- to 12-year old pine plantations to promote rapid growth of crop trees. These activities open the canopy, allow development of hardwood understory, and should benefit woodcock.

Salvage operations, especially for southern pine beetles, benefit woodcock in much the same manner as do small clearcuts. Woodcock probably are more abundant in southern pine beetle spots in which the merchantable timber was removed than in cut-and-leave spots.

Prescribed burning definitely is a 2-edged sword for woodcock. Burning which reduces grasses in stands of any age benefits woodcock. Burning is especially beneficial in mixed pine-hardwood stands with old-growth characteristics. Such stands that have a grassy ground cover provide marginal diurnal cover. However, after burning, birds often will be concentrated in such stands during the day (Johnson and Causey 1982). Burning also increases nocturnal use of pastures and fallow fields (Glasgow 1958), and perhaps clearcuts.

The negative aspect of prescribed burning is that in the southern United States, most of it takes place in late winter and early spring, during the nesting season. If possible, winter burns should be made in January before nesting begins. In any case, within the area to be burned, moist soil early-successional vegetation areas should be protected.

On the proper soils, red-cockaded woodpecker management which limits midstory development provides suitable woodcock habitat, particularly if woody vegetation and vines are abundant and grasses are limited. Woodcock hens will nest in woodpecker colonies if soil conditions are appropriate.

HUNTING

Historically, woodcock hunting in Europe predates the settlement of North America as well as the advent of the shotgun. Shakespeare uses "Springes to catch the woodcocks" in Hamlet and makes several other references to the species (Hall 1946).

In North America, true sport hunting of woodcock probably began in the mid-1700s, but did not really become popular until after the Civil War. During that period, hunters used spaniels and young boys to flush the birds from thickets. The preferred dog was a cocking (cocker) spaniel, which was developed for woodcock hunting (Woolner 1974).

After the passage of the Migratory Bird Treaty Act, hunting was restricted to fall and early winter and bag limits were established. Between 1918 and the mid-1960s, season lengths ranged 15-60 days and daily bag limits 4-6 birds. From the mid-1960s to mid-1980s, regulations were stabilized at 65 days and 5 birds per day. Since then, due to declines in population indices, the daily bag limit has been reduced to 3 birds and season lengths to 30 and 45 days in the Eastern and Central Regions, respectively.

Estimates of the numbers of woodcock harvested annually vary widely, depending on how the data are collected. State estimates generally are much higher than federal estimates (Whiting et al. 1985). By any measure, total harvest has declined since about 1980. Straw et al. (1994) estimated the 1991 harvest to be approximately 1.1 million woodcock, with most of the southern harvest occurring in Louisiana. In 1995, average bags in the Eastern and Central Regions were 1.2 birds and 1.6 birds per day and 6.8 and 10.2 birds per season, respectively (Bruggink 1997).

Obviously, woodcock hunters do not pursue the species in anticipation of a full freezer. Because of the thick habitat in which they normally hunt, some would classify woodcock hunters as masochist. Certainly the birds make excellent table fare. Recipes for cooking the woodcock range from simply grilling the breast and legs to aging, picking, and cooking the whole bird, then using the entrails and brains to make a sauce.

Although the woodcock is considered a minor game species in the South, there is a dedicated cadre of woodcock enthusiasts. Some are frustrated bobwhite hunters, others have only recently been introduced to the sport. However, virtually all woodcock hunters are dog enthusiasts. The excitement of the hunt is watching an English setter catch a faint aroma, then work upwind until it slams on brakes at the edge of a thicket or, in a similar thicket, hearing the steady tinkling of the bell on a Brittany suddenly go quiet. The shot, the kill, and the meal are a bonus; the joy is in the dog work.

CHAPTER 14

Squirrels

Jacob L. Bowman[1] and Michael J. Chamberlain[2]
Department of Wildlife and Fisheries
Mississippi State University, Mississippi State, MS

Fox and gray squirrels are popular small game animals throughout the southeastern United States (Flyger and Gates 1982a) and squirrel hunting effort is second only to white-tailed deer hunting in some areas. Additionally, fox and gray squirrels are enjoyed by many nonconsumptive users as readily observed wildlife species in many urban areas. Although these 2 species are prevalent in most of the Southeast, concern for some subspecies of fox squirrels has led managers to restoration and conservation programs designed to ensure persistence of threatened populations. The importance of fox and gray squirrels to southeastern ecosystems requires an understanding of ecological requirements and population management strategies.

Red squirrels, northern flying squirrels, and southern flying squirrels are less conspicuous than fox and gray squirrels and are rarely harvested. Red squirrels have a limited distribution in the Southeast. Although southern flying squirrels are abundant in many areas, they are rarely seen because of their secretive, nocturnal activities. Northern flying squirrels are rarely seen and have declined in many areas of the Southeast, prompting concern for this species.

Together, these species generate considerable revenue and sport, provide aesthetic enjoyment, and serve as a recognizable or noteworthy wildlife species to many people. Squirrels provide the main source of mammalian wildlife viewing opportunities in most

[1]Current Address: Department of Entomology and Applied Ecology, University of Delaware, Newark, DE
[2]Current Address: School of Forestry, Wildlife, and Fisheries, Louisiana State University, Baton Rouge, LA

There are several species of tree-dwelling squirrels in the South, including the gray squirrel *(R. Griffin)*.

urban settings. Additionally, recent declines in local or landscape-wide populations of particular species or subspecies increases the importance of understanding ecological relationships, habitat requirements and developing management strategies. Thus, it is important to understand the ecology of the southeastern squirrels, including general habits, diets, habitat use and management schemes directed at ensuring continued existence of these species.

GENERAL SPECIES DESCRIPTIONS

The 5 species of squirrels discussed in this chapter are all part of the Order Rodentia and Family Sciuridae. All members of this family have specialized incisors, large eyes, and a densely furred tail (Linzey 1998). Sciuridae is divided into 2 subfamilies: Sciurinae (tree squirrels) and Petauristinae (flying squirrels). Tree squirrels include the eastern gray squirrel, fox squirrel, and red squirrel, whereas flying squirrels include northern flying squirrel and southern flying squirrel. Tree squirrels are primarily diurnal, whereas flying squirrels are primarily nocturnal. All 5 species are arboreal, although fox squirrels are considered to be the least arboreal. Additionally, all species den in cavities (natural or artificial) or leaf nests. Fox squirrels are the largest of this group and southern flying squirrels the smallest. None of these squirrel species are sexually dimorphic.

The eastern gray squirrel is a medium-sized tree squirrel. As its name implies, gray squirrels appear gray, but are really salt-and-pepper colored because of alternating bands of black, brown, and white on their hairs (Flyger and Gates 1982a). Melanism is common and colors vary from black to dark gray. Additionally, colonies of albino squirrels have been documented in urban areas (Flyger and Gates 1982a). Gray squirrels range in weight from 0.75-1.70 lbs and total length from 15-22 in. (Flyger and Gates 1982a, Linzey 1998).

Six subspecies of southeastern fox squirrels are recognized. Three of these subspecies have locally reduced populations and are of management concern (Loeb and Moncrief 1993). The Delmarva fox squirrel (*S. n. cinereus*) of Virginia and Maryland is listed as federally threatened (Loeb and Moncrief 1993). The Big Cypress (*S. n. avicennia*) and Sherman's (*S. n. shermani*) fox squirrels of Florida are state listed (Loeb and Moncrief 1993). Fox squirrel pelage varies more than gray squirrels with extensive variation within the same area common (Flyger and Gates 1982a). Common color patterns include: pale gray back with a black head (east coast); brownish orange with pale orange to yellow-orange belly (west of Mississippi); and white ears, feet, and white face or nose (deep south) (Choate et al. 1994). Fox squirrels range in weight from 1.3-3.3 lbs and total length from 17.9-27.6 in (Flyger and Gates 1982b, Linzey 1998).

Red squirrels are often referred to as pine squirrels. Their pelage is reddish brown dorsally, white ventrally, with a black lateral stripe separating dorsal and ventral coloration. They also have a distinctive white eye ring (Flyger and Gates 1982b). Melanism is uncommon in this species. Red squirrels range in weight from 0.3-0.6 lbs and total length from 9.8-15.2 in (Flyger and Gates 1982a, Linzey 1998).

The northern flying squirrel and southern flying squirrel are similar in appearance; however, northern flying squirrels are slightly larger (Linzey 1998). The northern flying squirrel's pelage is brownish dorsally and grayish ventrally, whereas the southern flying squirrel is brownish dorsally, but white or cream ventrally (Linzey 1998). Additionally, the bases of the northern flying squirrel belly hair are gray in contrast to the southern flying squirrel, which has white bases on its belly hair (Linzey 1998). Their tail is long and densely furred (Linzey 1998). The flying squirrel's most obvious diagnostic characteristic is the loose fold of skin between the wrist of the fore and hind legs, used to glide, not fly, as its name implies (Linzey 1998). Northern and southern flying squirrels range in weight from 0.2-0.3 lbs and 0.1-0.2 lbs, respectively (Linzey 1998). Additionally, their total body length ranges from 10.0-10.8 in and 7.9-10.4 in, respectively.

Density estimates vary by species and geographic location. Sherman's fox squirrel density was estimated at 0.30 squirrels/acre (Kantola 1986), whereas fox squirrel densities average 0.12 squirrels/acre and ranged from 0.02-0.42 squirrels/acre for an 8 year period in coastal North Carolina (Weigl et al. 1989). Gray squirrel densities in an unexploited population in North Carolina were 0.84-1.49 squirrels/acre (Barkalow et al. 1970). In Mississippi, squirrel densities were 7-16 squirrels/acre in pine-hardwood forests; however, fox and gray squirrels were not separated for this estimate, and 95% of the squirrels counted were gray squirrels (Warren and Hurst 1980). Reported densities of red squirrels across their geographic range are 2-12 squirrels/acre (Steele 1998). Southern flying squirrel numbers in southeastern Virginia were 77-94 squirrels/acre (Sawyer and Rose 1985), whereas in central Virginia densities were 7-35 squirrels/acre (Sonenshine et al. 1979). Northern flying squirrels occur in isolated populations of very low numbers and no density estimates are available in the Southeast. Densities from other parts of their range are 1-25 squirrels/acre (Wells-Gosling and Heaney 1984).

DISTRIBUTION AND ABUNDANCE

Historically, gray, fox, and southern flying squirrels were found throughout the southeastern U.S. Red and northern flying squirrels were found from Virginia, down the Appalachian Mountains to northern Georgia. All species have declined from colonial times, likely because of habitat alteration or destruction.

Fox squirrels in the southeast have continued to decline over the past 100 years in the southeastern coastal plain, presumably because of the destruction of the open mature, pine-oak forest (Loeb and Moncrief 1993). However, populations of fox squirrels along the Mississippi River, west of the Mississippi River, north of Tennessee, and west of the Appalachian Mountains are considered stable. Gray squirrel numbers have stabilized or increased across the Southeast. Reforestation has increased habitat for gray squirrels throughout their range, and in most areas, gray squirrels are considered common. They can be found in nearly all forested environments, except extremely hydric sites. Red squirrel numbers are stable or increasing throughout their range. In the Southeast, red squirrels are found in the Appalachian Mountains as far south as northern Georgia. Additionally, they are found in the Piedmont of Virginia, but are considered rare or uncommon. In the Southeast they generally occur in mixed hardwoods and conifer stands with a preference for hemlocks (Brown 1997). Northern flying squirrels are found in the Appalachian Mountains south to the Great Smoky Mountains. Their populations continue to decline for unknown reasons (Brown 1997). This species generally occurs above 3,200 ft in spruce-fir and mixed conifer-hardwood stands (Linzey 1998). Only isolated populations remain and their outlook is uncertain. Southern flying squirrel numbers are stable or increasing across the Southeast. They are common in most areas, although they are rarely observed. Nearly all forested areas have populations of this squirrel, although they prefer hardwood forests.

REPRODUCTION

Reproductive characteristics of squirrel species are similar. Most are capable of producing 2 litters per year, but evidence of 2 litters per year is not available for the flying squirrels. Generally, mating occurs in winter and summer, with young born during late-winter to spring and late-summer. Sex ratios are even at birth. Young develop slowly compared to other rodents, with young born naked, pink, and eyes closed. Eyes typically open at approximately 4 weeks and young are weaned at 6-9 weeks (Dolan and Carter 1977; Flyger and Gates 1982a,b; Wells-Gosling and Heaney 1984; Steele 1998).

Fox Squirrel

Fox squirrels can mate throughout the year, but most mating occurs from November to February (peaking in December) and April to July (peaking in June) (Colin 1957, Koprowski 1994b). Females are capable of reproduction at 8-11 months of age, but most will not mate until older than 15 months of age (Flyger and Gates 1982a, Koprowski 1994b). Females born in win-

Hard mast, such as oak acorns and hickory nuts, are important fall and winter squirrel foods *(R. Griffin).*

Squirrels readily eat fungi, particularly during the spring when hard mast is scarce *(R. Griffin).*

ter do not mate until the following winter and typically produce only 1 litter that year (Flyger and Gates 1982a). Females remain reproductively viable to 12+ years of age (Koprowski 1994b). Gestation is 44-45 days. Females may produce 2 litters per year, ranging from 1-5 and averaging 3 young per litter (Weigl et al. 1989, Koprowski 1994b). Males are reproductively viable at 10-12 months of age (Flyger and Gates 1982a).

Gray Squirrel

Gray squirrels mate from December to March (peaking in February) and May to August (peaking in July) (Kirkpatrick et al. 1976). Females are capable of reproduction at 5.5-11 months of age, but most will not mate until older than 15 months of age (Koprowski 1994a). Females born in winter will not breed until the following winter, and typically produce only 1 litter that year (Flyger and Gates 1982a). Females remain reproductively viable to 8+ years of age. Gestation is 44 days (Koprowski 1994a), and most females produce 2 litters per year, averaging 3 young per litter (Kirkpatrick et al. 1976). Males are reproductively viable at 10-11 months of age (Cordes 1965).

Red Squirrel

Red squirrels mate from February to March and June to July (Steele 1998). They are capable of reproduction at 10-11 months of age, but most will not mate until older than 15 months of age (Flyger and Gates 1982b). Gestation is 32-38 days (Lair 1985), and most females produce 2 litters per year with 2-7 young per litter (Linzey 1998).

Northern Flying Squirrel

Northern flying squirrels are born during spring and mid-summer after a 30-37 day gestation period. Litters range from 2-5 and average 2.3 young (Linzey 1998). Similar to other sciurids, they are likely capable of reproduction at 10-11 months of age.

Southern Flying Squirrel

Southern flying squirrels mate from December to March and June to July. They are capable of reproduction at 6-8 months of age, but many will not mate until 10-11 months of age (Linzey and Linzey 1979, Sawyer and Rose 1985). Gestation is 40 days (Sonenshine et al. 1979); litters average 1-4 young and range from 1 to 5 (Dolan and Carter 1977, Linzey and Linzey 1979)

DIETARY PATTERNS

Squirrels are primarily herbivores, but invertebrates and other animal matter are occasionally consumed. Predation on birds, their nestlings and eggs, and small mammals has been documented. Flying squirrels are believed to be more carnivorous than the other squirrels. Generally, nuts and seeds are important in squirrel diets, especially during fall and winter. Invertebrates are usually consumed during summer to supplement a diet of berries, buds, fruits, and seeds. Squirrels in the Southeast have very diverse diets, including agricultural crops, such as corn or soybeans.

Fox Squirrel

Fox squirrel diets are very diverse. Fall hard mast is important throughout the Southeast; but fox squirrels consume a variety of other food items to supplement their diet throughout the year. Common items in their diets include hard mast, pine buds, staminate cones, berries, fungi, insects, and longleaf pine seeds. Fruits of

Soft mast is an important food when hard mast is unavailable *(J. Bowman)*.

woody species consumed included maple, chinquapin, pignut hickory, sweet gum, longleaf pine, and a wide variety of oak species (Loeb and Moncrief 1993). Greslin (1970) found that mockernut hickory and post oak were important food resources for fox squirrels in east Texas. Live oaks were a major food resource for Sherman's fox squirrels in Florida (Kantola and Humphrey 1990). The most common items in Big Cypress fox squirrels in Florida diets were cabbage palm fruit, seeds from cypress cones, figs, flowers of silk oak and bottlebrush, seeds from slash pine cones, and queen palm fruit (Jodice 1992).

Gray Squirrel

Gray squirrels, like fox squirrels, are primarily herbivores, but insects, bird eggs, and nestlings are consumed. Insects are an important part of juvenile squirrel diets during summer (Koprowski 1994a). Oaks, hickories, walnuts, and beech account for most of their diet (Flyger and Gates 1982a). In Missouri, oak and hickory mast were documented as being more important in the diet of gray squirrels than in fox squirrels (Korschgen 1981). Fruits, seeds, buds, and flowers of numerous species are important when hard mast is unavailable. For example, fruit of the southern magnolia is important to squirrels of the Everglades in Florida. Also, fungi is an important year-round food source (Flyger and Gates 1982*a*). Additionally, bones, deer antlers, and turtle shells are consumed for calcium and other minerals (Flyger and Gates 1982*a*).

Red Squirrel

Red squirrels are typically associated with coniferous forests and are specially adapted to feeding on serotinous cones (Flyger and Gates 1982b). Their populations have been documented to fluctuate with cone crops in more northern latitudes (Flyger and Gates 1982b). Their diet is more diverse in southern latitudes, and includes berries, buds, catkins, fruits, fungi, seeds, and nuts (Linzey 1998). Additionally, they are specially adapted to feeding on fungi, often consuming species that are poisonous to other mammalian species. Birds' eggs and nestlings also are part of their diet, as well as some invertebrates (Flyger and Gates 1982b, Steele 1998). Red squirrels are known for their habit of caching seeds and nuts in middens for later consumption.

Northern Flying Squirrel

Northern flying squirrel diets are not well documented. Food items which have been documented include nuts and seeds of hardwoods and conifers, buds, catkins, fruit, and insects. They are also believed to prey on birds and their eggs (Wells-Gosling and Heaney 1984).

Southern Flying Squirrel

Southern flying squirrels are thought to be the most carnivorous of the squirrels, however sometimes animal matter consumption is minuscule (Harlow and Doyle 1990). Their diet includes some birds and nestlings, eggs, carrion, and invertebrates. Invertebrate consumption is highest during summer, with plant matter comprising a large percentage of their diet in other seasons (Dolan and Carter 1977, Linzey 1998). Typical diet includes buds, fruits, mushrooms, nuts, and seeds. They are known for nut storing (caching) which appears to be associated with fall photoperiod (Dolan and Carter 1977, Linzey 1998).

HOME RANGE AND HABITAT USE

Fox, gray, and southern flying squirrels inhabit a wide variety of habitats, but the importance of hardwoods can not be over emphasized. Removing hardwoods from mixed stands is detrimental to all 3 species. Streamside zones in intensively managed pine forests also are important to these 3 species, because these areas provide hardwoods. Red and northern flying squirrels are more dependent on northern conifer habitat types. The northern flying squirrel is associated with relict communities of conifers and hardwoods in the southern Appalachians and can be considered a relict itself. Allen (1942) hypothesized that squirrel populations were affected by mast availability more than harvest rate. Mast crops have been linked to tree squirrel reproductive success in northern climates (Barkalow et al. 1970).

Fox Squirrel

Habitat conditions for southeastern fox squirrels are variable. Typically habitat is xeric upland forest or fragmented forests with open understories maintained by fire (Taylor 1973). A notable exception is *S. n. subauratus* which inhabits bottomland hardwood forests of the Mississippi Alluvial Valley. Typically, southeastern fox squirrels are thought to be associated with the longleaf pine-turkey oak systems. Fox squirrels in North Carolina preferred open, mature, pine-oak habitats. However, hardwoods and forested wetlands were preferred during summer (Weigl et al. 1989). In Alabama hardwood habitats were used by fox squirrels more than expected, pine habitats were used less than expected, and pine regeneration areas were avoided (Powers 1993). Additionally, in coastal South Carolina, hardwoods, mixed pine-hardwoods, and pines with hardwood midstories were preferred (Edwards et al. 1989). Recent research documented that understory density was not a significant predictor for fox and gray squirrel distribution; thus, the current paradigm of fox squirrels needing areas with open understories may need to be reevaluated (Brown and Batzli 1984).

Denning sites are an important component of fox squirrel habitat. Both natural cavities and leaf nests are used. Fox squirrels use leaf nests more than cavities and use leaf nests more than gray squirrels (Kantola and Humphrey 1990). Cavities are used more in fall and winter, and pines, oaks, and gum species more than 8 in dbh are preferred for denning (Edwards and Guynn 1995, Edwards et al. 1989). However, trees greater than 16 in dbh will provide more dens than trees 8-16 in dbh.

Home ranges for southeastern fox squirrels vary by habitat and subspecies ranging from 3-106 acres (Greslin 1970, Kantola and Humphrey 1990), but typically home ranges are 32-67 acres (Ha 1983, Weigl et al. 1989, Powers 1993). In addition to changes in seasonal home ranges, shifting of home ranges has been documented during food shortages, and home ranges and movements varied with food abundance in coastal North Carolina (Kantola and Humphrey 1990). Home ranges and movement rates were lowest when food supplies were at their highest and lowest levels, whereas home ranges and movements were highest with moderate food supplies (Ha 1983). Squirrels likely reduce movements during food shortages to reduce energy expenditures and low movement rates during high food abundance likely result from short search time and effort required to acquire resources necessary to meet energy demands.

Gray Squirrel

Gray squirrel habitat is typically considered hardwood forests with dense woody understories. However, gray squirrels live in nearly all forested habitats in the Southeast. Gray squirrels use natural cavities and leaf nests for denning, but prefer cavities in the fall and winter; particularly pines and oaks (Edwards and Guynn 1995). In the Atchafalaya Basin, Louisiana, bottomland hardwoods (*Celtis-Fraxinus-Liquidambar-Ulmus*) were preferred over cypress-tupelo or cottonwood-willow. However, squirrels are found in cypress-tupelo stands when overstories and midstories are dense enough to allow movements during high water (Heuer and Perry 1976). Gray squirrels in Alabama preferred hardwood streamside zones in even-aged pine and mixed pine-hardwood stands. Additionally, squirrel abundance was greater in hardwood and mixed pine-hardwood stands than in even-aged pine stands (Fischer and Holler 1991). In the Appalachian mountains, mixed hardwood stands are preferred. Sugar maples are selected for natural cavities, whereas hickories, yellow poplar, and maples larger than 16 cm dbh are preferred for nests (Sanderson et al. 1975). Male gray squirrels typically move more and have larger home ranges than females (Cordes and Barkalow 1972). In Virginia, average home range size was 1.2 acres (Doebel and McGinnes 1974). Across their range, home range sizes varied from 1.2-15.0 acres (Flyger and Gates 1982*a*).

Red Squirrel

In more northern latitudes, red squirrels primarily inhabit coniferous forests. However, in the Southeast they inhabit conifers and mixed stands of conifers and hardwoods, usually at higher elevations. A notable exception is in Virginia where they occupy the northern half of the state and can be found in mixed stands at any elevation (Linzey 1998). Unlike fox and gray squirrels, red squirrels are territorial. In British Columbia, their home range averaged 1.2-2.2 acres, and varied with food supply. Territoriality is believed to allow more successful defense of middens, which are extremely important to red squirrels (Smith 1968).

Northern Flying Squirrel

Northern flying squirrels are typically found at higher elevations (>3,200 ft) of the Southern Appalachian Mountains, and elevations where squirrels occur are greater at more southerly latitudes (Linzey 1998). Populations persist only in isolated patches of relict habitats. Preferred habitats are mixed stands of red spruce and birch, and Fraser fir and American beech, with variable understories (Payne et al. 1989). Home range estimates from across the species range vary from 2.0-31.1 acres (Wells- Gosling and Heaney 1984, Weigl and Osgood 1974).

Southern Flying Squirrel

Southern flying squirrels prefer mature hardwood forest, but are found in most forested habitats (Linzey 1998). In central Virginia, they prefer oak or mixed stands with a dense midstory. Mixed lowland forests are preferred if they are not dominated by pine (Sonenshine and Levy 1981). Use of nest boxes increases in fall and winter at low temperatures, and it is common to find groups of more than 6 individuals using the same nest box. Additionally, nest boxes are often used as food caches which indicates that boxes are used as feeding stations (Sonenshine et al. 1979). Home range estimates range from 4.0-19.0 acres (Dolan and Carter 1977, Sawyer and Rose 1985).

DISEASES AND PARASITES

Although fox and gray squirrels are susceptible to numerous diseases and parasites, the most notable is cutaneous warbles (popularly known as "wolves"), caused by larvae of flies from the genus *Cuterebra* (Davidson and Nettles 1988). Larvae are located in swellings under the skin with a small opening at the center through which the larvae breathe. Once the larvae emerge from the skin, the lesion heals. *Cuterebra* larvae are not considered to negatively impact squirrel populations, but do have a significant impact on management strategies. Presence of larvae often causes hunters to discard harvested squirrels that are infected; however, lesions are restricted to the skin and do not damage the flesh (Jacobson et al. 1979). Hence, squirrel hunting seasons in many areas of the Southeast are set after most larvae have emerged from their hosts (Jacobson et a. 1979).

Fox and gray squirrels have been reported to be infected with encephalitis (Masterson et al. 1971); however, confirmation of these afflictions in the Southeast is lacking. Similarly, plague has been reported in western fox squirrels, but not in the Southeast. Gray squirrels may become infected with squirrel fibroma, caused by a poxvirus related to Shope's fibroma virus in rabbits. Additionally, ringworm (*Trichophyton mentagrophytes*) and other fungi have been reported in gray squirrels (Lewis et al. 1975), and *Leptospira* and tularemia have been reported in fox and gray squirrels.

Red squirrels are susceptible to a variety of parasites, including protozoa, cestodes, nematodes, and acarina (mites). Additionally, red squirrels may be infected by tularemia (Burroughs et al. 1945) and the encephalitis virus has been detected in western populations. Other infectious agents reported in red squirrel populations include *Haplosporangium* and *Adiaspiromycosis* (Flyger and Gates 1982b). Southern flying squirrels have been infected with osteomalacia and rabies has been reported for 1 individual in Florida (Dolan and Carter 1977). Both flying squirrel species are affected by nematodes, cestodes, and protozoa. All squirrels are hosts to numerous ectoparasites, including fleas, ticks, and lice. A common malady in many squirrels is mange caused by the mite *Cnemidoptes* spp. that frequently results in hair loss. Fleas may become a serious problem in tree cavities or den boxes, but appear to be less of a problem when squirrels inhabit leaf nests (Flyger and Gates 1982b).

INTERSPECIES INTERACTIONS

A great deal of speculation exists concerning competition between tree squirrel species. Whereas these species are known to coexist, examples of possible competitive exclusions led to theories about niche overlap or partitioning. Niche differences in gray and fox squirrels are related to foraging and predator escape behavior, and habitat differences (Brown and Batzli 1985, Sexton 1990). However, Armitage and Harris (1982) reported no exclusion or territoriality between the 2 species. Although home ranges overlapped, centers of activity were separated and grouped by species and heterospecific feeding aggregations were observed (Armitage and Harris 1982). Additionally, Armitage and Harris (1982) documented that each species was more likely to have a conspecific as its nearest neighbor, and concluded that gray squirrels are more social than fox squirrels. Another way fox and gray squirrels reduce competition is by differences in nest site selection (Edwards and Guynn 1995, Edwards et al. 1998).

Northern flying and red squirrels are limited more by food resources than interspecific competition (Ransome and Sullivan 1997). Habitat specialization, not interspecific aggression, influenced the distribution of gray and red squirrels in Wisconsin (Riege 1991). Red squirrels prefer areas dominated by conifers, whereas gray squirrels prefer areas dominated by hardwoods, both a result of food preferences (Riege 1991). Northern and southern flying squirrel niches are partitioned by habitat (Weigl 1978). Northern flying squirrels prefer conifer forests, whereas southern flying squirrels prefer hardwood dominated forest (Weigl 1978). Niche partitioning also occurs for den sites, with southern flying squirrels preferring natural cavities, whereas northern flying squirrels frequently nest in natural cavities or leaf nests (Weigl 1978).

MANAGEMENT

Squirrel populations can be manipulated through timber harvest. For example, in Alabama, squirrel abundance was not affected by removing about 1/3 of the volume of trees greater than 12 inches dbh, but abundance decreased if over half of the volume was removed (Colin 1957). Thus, if squirrel management is an objective, 6-8 oaks per acre and 6-8 hickories per acre greater than 10 inches dbh should be protected in harvested stands (Nixon et al. 1980). This management scheme will provide habitat for 0.8-1.2 squirrels per acre. Consistently good hard mast producing, trees should be identified and protected from harvest (Nixon et al. 1980). Although protection of smaller size hardwoods is beneficial for squirrels, timber rotations of 100+ years will produce more squirrels than shorter rotation lengths.

Censusing

Complete enumeration of squirrel populations is difficult. However, several researchers have documented high positive correlations ($r > 0.80$) between squirrel harvest and density (Nixon et al. 1974, 1975; Shugars 1986). Mark recapture, plot-removal method, time-area counts, and response-to-call method have been used (Bouffard and Hein 1978). However, mark recapture is expensive and logistically unfeasible in most cases. Bouffard and Hein (1978) determined that plot-removal, time-area counts, and response-to-call methods were not satisfactory for application to squirrel management. Relative abundances or indices can be obtained and are useful tools for squirrel management. Line transects are an effective way to monitor tree squirrel populations. Density estimates can be obtained if>1.5 squirrels/mile are sighted and relative abundance can be estimated when fewer are sighted (Healy and Welsh 1992). Flying squirrels are more difficult to census because of their nocturnal habits. The most common way to census flying squirrels is using nest box surveys (Sonenshine and Levy 1981). Additionally, smoke plates have been used to census northern flying squirrels (Raphael et al. 1986).

Harvest

Several studies have examined the effect of exploitation on fox and gray squirrels (Mosby 1969, Shugars 1986, Rhodes 1989). Conclusions suggest that harvest is mostly compensatory for squirrels. Early research suggested that harvest was not detrimental to gray squirrel populations, even when harvest levels reached 40% of the fall population (Mosby 1969). Additionally, Mosby et al. (1977) described a "law of diminishing returns", where hunter effort was positively correlated to squirrel densities, thus, hunter effort would diminish before populations were impacted negatively. Some research has suggested that gray squirrels are under-harvested (Shugars 1986). In Maryland, Shugars (1986) reported a 7-9% annual mortality attributed to harvest with an annual mortality rate of 48-54%. Similar mortality rates were documented in an unexploited gray squirrel

Table 1. Estimated gray and fox squirrel harvest by state.

State	Harvest 1996-97	Harvest 1970-71
Kentucky	1,627,787	1,187,000
Tennessee	2,881,900	1,850,000
North Carolina	532,387 (1995-96)	2,760,804
South Carolina	504,493	854,800
Georgia	1,204,906 (1995-96)	1,491,645
Florida	334,210[a]	1,630,060
Alabama	700,000[a]	1,980,000[a]
Mississippi	904,228	3,320,510 (1976-77)
Arkansas	3,335,821 (1994-95)	3,287,648
Louisiana	2,051,400	3,200,000
East Texas	236,727	961,366 (1981-82)
East Oklahoma	460,684	286,472

[a] Gray squirrels only.

population in North Carolina (Barkalow et al. 1970). Nixon et al. (1975) documented annual mast crops were extremely important to squirrel populations and harvest may be detrimental during poor mast crop years. However, southern squirrel populations, especially fox squirrels, may not be as greatly affected by mast failures because of their more diverse diets (Weigl et al. 1989, Loeb and Moncrief 1993). Compared to gray squirrels, over-harvest of fox squirrels may occur. An unexploited fox squirrel population in Illinois had an annual adult survival rate of greater than 60% (Nixon et al. 1986). However, in small habitat pockets Nixon et al. (1974) reported detrimental effects of exploitation on fox squirrels with an average annual hunting mortality of 75% in a 54-acre woodlot in Ohio. In contrast to Nixon et al. (1974), Jordan (1971) documented no detrimental effects of an intensive fox squirrel harvest in a small 68-acre woodlot in Pennsylvania.

SPECIES-SPECIFIC ACCOUNTS

Fox Squirrel

Fox squirrel management should focus on forest manipulations which favor food producers. A hardwood component is paramount, especially in pine-dominated forests. Increasing hard mast producing species in pine dominated forests benefits the fox squirrel. Prescribed burning to reduce understory vegetation is recommended for Delmarva fox squirrel management (Lusting and Flyger 1975) and for most pine-dominated forests. Nest boxes are used to increase the density and survival of fox squirrels. Boxes should be placed at heights of 49-82 ft (Edwards and Guynn 1995). Translocations are another tool used in fox squirrel management, which has been used successfully for Delmarva fox squirrels (Bendel and Therres 1994). Habitat conditions at the release site including food availability must be optimal or the translocated fox squirrels will disperse from the release area, causing increased mortality (Jodice and Humphrey 1993). Fox squirrel have been known to damage crops such as corn and pecans, but damage is generally not considered problematic (Flyger and Gates 1982a).

Gray and fox squirrel hunting historically has been a popular sport in the South *(R. Griffin)*.

Gray Squirrel

Gray squirrel management should emphasize a variety of oaks and hickories which are consistent food producers, and trees used for dens. Large contiguous forest blocks will benefit gray squirrels more than small habitat patches (Brown and Batzli 1984). Streamside zones are an important part of forest management in pine and pine-hardwood stands, because these areas should include abundant mast producing species (Fischer and Holler 1991). Cavities are important for squirrel survival and 2 dens per acre is recommended to achieve a density of 1 squirrel per acre, and artificial dens are recommended when natural cavities are limited (Sanderson et al. 1975). Gray squirrels have been known to cause extensive damage to corn and pecans in the Southeast (Flyger and Gates 1982a). Shooting and trapping are the most common solutions to damage situations.

Red Squirrel

Red squirrels are not a target of management in the Southeast. However, any technique to improve pine seed production should benefit this species. Additionally, red squirrel numbers can be enhanced by providing artificial nest boxes (Flyger and Gates 1982b). Red squirrels cause extensive damage to ponderosa pines in the West, but no major damage has been documented in the Southeast (Flyger and Gates 1982b).

Northern Flying Squirrel

Currently, management of the northern flying squirrel is protection of isolated pockets of suitable habitat. Additionally, nest boxes have been erected in some areas to increase survival and to aid in monitoring populations.

Southern Flying Squirrel

Effects of timber harvest are buffered when there are adjacent stands of mature hardwoods, adequate streamside zones, overstory hardwoods left unharvested, and snags. Seed-tree management without retaining overstory hardwoods will cause the loss of flying squirrels in those stands (Taulman et al. 1998). Nest boxes can be placed in areas where cavities are limited (Taulman et al. 1998). They are readily used and may increase numbers of flying squirrels (Goertz et al. 1975). Southern flying squirrels can be problematic to red-cockaded woodpecker (RCW) management because they have been implicated as nest predators of RCWs and often occupy cavities which prevents use by RCWs (Loeb 1996). However, Loeb (1996) found that squirrel excluder devices were effective at preventing cavity use by southern flying squirrels.

SUMMARY

Squirrels are integral components of ecosystems of the southeastern United States. These species provide considerable revenue, recreational and aesthetic enjoyment; and can be enjoyed in many urban and suburban environments. Although fox, gray, and red squirrel populations are stable in many areas, the range of the southeastern fox squirrel has declined in recent years, and one subspecies is listed as endangered. Additionally, red squirrel distribution is limited in the Southeast, a function of limited habitat in the region. Sound habitat management, such as retention of mature hardwoods, will ensure the persistence of these species. Flying squirrels are rarely observed, hence management schemes are not often directed at improving habitat for these species. However, the continued decline in northern flying squirrel populations in the region suggests that management practices for these populations are warranted.

ACKNOWLEDGMENTS

We would like to thank the Department of Wildlife and Fisheries and the Forest and Wildlife Research Center at Mississippi State University for funding to complete this chapter. Special thanks to Bobby Bond, Bruce Leopold, and Bronson Strickland for comments on earlier drafts of this manuscript. We greatly appreciate the contributions of the biologists, researchers and technicians responsible for collecting the information synthesized within this chapter. Approved for publication as Journal Article WF-136 of the Forest and Wildlife Research Center, Mississippi State University.

CHAPTER 15

Rabbits

James G. Dickson[1]
US Forest Service
Southern Research Station, Nacogdoches, TX

Rabbits, or lagomorphs, resemble rodents. But unlike rodents they have relatively large hind legs, large ears, a short fluffy tail, and 2 sets of upper incisors. Like rodents their incisors grow continually. They can either walk or hop, and are fleet and elusive when evading predators. They normally are silent but are capable of several different vocalizations. Rabbits of the genus *Silvilagus* are widely distributed throughout the South, occurring in every county.

Several species of rabbits occur in southern forests wherever there is sufficient low vegetation to provide adequate food, and cover as protection from predators. The eastern cottontail, distinguishable by a rusty nape patch, is a regular inhabitant of a wide variety of habitats throughout the entire region (Hall 1981), from the highest mountains to marshes and bottoms. The Appalachian cottontail is a similar species, but slightly smaller and darker because of its dark guard hairs. It is found from Pennsylvania southwesterly down the Appalachian Mountains into northeastern Georgia.

Two other rabbit species occupy moist habitat mostly in the southerly portions of the South. The dark brown marsh rabbit is found from coastal Virginia southerly along the Coastal Plain to about the western boundary of peninsular Florida. The species is normally associated with Coastal Plain swamps and marshes. Another species, the swamp rabbit, is found north and west of the range of the marsh rabbit. Swamp rabbits are darker than eastern cottontails, and larger than either cottontails or marsh rabbits. They usually occupy riparian zones, swamps, and marshes.

Two true hares are found only in limited portions of the South. The snowshoe rabbit is found in the northern portions of the United States and Canada, and only rarely into the South at higher elevations along the eastern mountains (Hall 1981). The black-tailed jack rabbit,

[1]Current Address: School of Forestry, Louisiana Tech University, Ruston, LA

a species of the western United States open savannah and grassland habitat, extends into eastern Texas and Oklahoma and northwestern Arkansas. Apparently it has expanded its range into previously forested areas as stands have been harvested and habitat is opened and converted to pasture. It feeds on grass, forbs, and sometimes crops. The species is longer lived and less fecund than the cottontail or swamp rabbit (Schmidly 1983).

STATUS

Eastern cottontails and swamp rabbits are the 2 species for which substantial information is available and are the main focus of this chapter. They have been widespread and primary game species throughout the South (Table 1). Estimated harvest for southern states for the 1996/97 hunting season was lowest for Florida (20,833) and East Texas (41,244); and conversely was highest in Tennessee and Arkansas, each with close to a million rabbits harvested.

Due to a variety of ecological factors, rabbit densities frequently fluctuate widely over time. But southern rabbit populations appear to have declined substantially in the last 25 years. Every state but Georgia reported major reductions in rabbits harvested from 1970 to 1995 (Table 1). There probably are fewer rabbit hunters and rabbit hunting opportunities now than in the past. But the main cause of the decline is attributed to loss of early successional habitat such as fields and very young forest stands. Specifically, swamp rabbit populations have decreased in Kentucky and southwide due to diminishing wetland habitat, such as bottomland and riparian hardwoods (Sole 1994).

Table 1. Estimated rabbit[a] harvest by state.

State	Harvest 1996-97	Harvest 1970-71
Kentucky	755,625	837,400
Virginia	494,372	1,421,620
Tennessee	1,066,200	1,032,122
North Carolina	348,504 (1995-96)	1,707,030
South Carolina	285,919	854,800
Georgia	366,428 (1995-96)	798,357
Florida	20,833	429,734
Alabama	217,100	1,062,000
Mississippi	386,921	1,281,138 (1976-77)
Arkansas	969,046 (1994-95)	1,175,351 (1983-84)
Louisiana	721,500	850,000
East Texas	41,244	326,000 (1981-82)
East Oklahoma	155,216	117,454

[a]Mostly eastern cottontail rabbits, but includes some swamp rabbits, Appalachian cottontails, and marsh rabbits.

There are several species of rabbits throughout the South. The cottontail is the most abundant and widespread.

LIFE HISTORY

Rabbits are mainly active at night but will forage during daylight especially during periods of low light. Normally during the day, cottontails rest in a shallow depression in the ground, called a form. Both species can swim well, but the swamp rabbit readily takes to water to escape predators.

Foods.—Rabbits consume an extremely wide variety of predominantly plant matter. During the warm growing season mostly herbaceous grass and forbs are consumed. For example, sedges, grasses, and forbs, among a wide variety of other types of plants were summarized as important swamp rabbit foods (Allen 1985). During winter when succulent material is not readily available, dry herbaceous material is eaten by rabbits, as well as bark, buds, and twigs. Agricultural crops, such as corn, clover, alfalfa, and soy beans, also are consumed where available (DeCalesta 1971). Rabbits can be a problem by damaging crops, orchards, or ornamental plants. Stems and twigs are neatly clipped at a 45% angle by rabbits but bark is consumed in an irregular pattern. Lagomorphs are noted for reingesting the greenish soft fecal pellets produced in the cecum. Free water usually is not consumed; adequate moisture is obtained from succulent foods.

Predators and parasites.—A number of mammals, such as coyotes, bobcats, foxes, weasels, raccoons, house cats, and dogs are significant predators. And several avian predators, such as red-tailed, red-shouldered, and broad-winged hawks; barred and great-horned owls; and crows prey on rabbits. In a study analyzing food habitats of crows with a sample of several thousand, young cottontails were found to be the most frequent food item (Kirkpatrick 1950). A variety of snakes take mostly young rabbits. Additionally, hunting can be a significant mortality factor.

Rabbits may harbor ectoparasites, such as ticks, fleas, and mites; and endoparasites, such as flukes, tapeworms, or roundworms (Lowry 1974). Several other parasites and diseases infect rabbits. Rabbits are parasitized by botfly larvae, usually located around the neck and chest area. The egg of the fly is laid in the hair of the rabbit, hatches into a maggot, and the maggot penetrates the skin and develops between the skin and muscle. Afterwards they exit and pupate before becoming an adult fly (Madson 1963). Some 25% of sampled rabbits in an area in Kentucky were infected with botfly larvae (Bruna 1951). Rabbits can be host for the larval form of the canine tapeworm. Rabbits also can be infected with coccidiosis, caused by a protozoan. Tularemia is a bacterial disease usually transmitted by ticks or fleas which can infect rabbits and other mammals, and previously has decimated some rabbit populations. It is transmissible to humans, such as this author. Rabbit carcasses intended for human consumption should always be fully cooked to kill any possible pathogens.

Reproduction/Mortality.—Gestation for cottontails is 27-32 days. Females excavate a shallow depression for a nest, usually in dense and often grassy cover on a well-drained site. They line the nest with vegetation and then with body fur (Casteel 1966) and place a cover over the nest. Litter sizes are variable. In a study in Kentucky (Bruna 1951), there were 3 to 6 young in 104 of the total 108 litters, 7 young in 3 nests, and 9 young in a single nest. Further south in Georgia, 3 or 4 young are typical (Pelton and Jenkins 1971). Female cottontails sometimes vigorously attempt to defend their nest from predators.

Dawn and dusk are usual feeding times for recently-born litters. The mother cottontail removes the nest cover and crouches over the nest while the young suckle. Young cottontails develop and mature rapidly. Their eyes are open within a week of birth and they are weaned and independent at 3 or 4 weeks of age. They may reproduce during the same year in which they are born.

Cottontails are very prolific. Females are in estrus immediately after giving birth and usually mate then. Several litters each year are typical and up to 6 litters may be produced by a single female in one breeding season (Lowry 1974).

Productivity of swamp rabbits is less than cottontails. Gestation is somewhat longer (36-38 days), litters are smaller (average of 2 in a study area in Mississippi) (Palmer et al 1991), and juveniles normally don't breed (Martinson et al. 1961).

Nest success rate and survival of young and adult rabbits usually is low. For example, in the Kentucky study only 10% of 36 nests were successful. Nests were lost to farm operations including spring burning of broomsedge fields, adverse weather such as heavy rain, and predation (Bruna 1951). In the midwest it was concluded that on average only about half of all young cottontails survived long enough to leave the nest (Madson 1963). And adult rabbits also suffer high losses. In an Illinois study, average annual mortality was 79% and was higher during years when the population was hunted (Rose 1977).

Spring is the main reproductive period, although cottontail reproduction has been documented during much of the year in the South. In Kentucky, documented breeding occurred from January to September, but 68% of the nests were found March through May (Bruna 1951). A similar pattern was documented in Georgia, where annual reproduction started in February and peaked in March, April, and May when 80 to 100% of females collected were pregnant. None of the females collected from November through January were pregnant (Pelton and Jenkins 1971). A similar mainly early spring reproductive period was documented for swamp rabbits in Mississippi (Palmer et al. 1991).

Due to seasonal patterns of natality and mortality cottontail populations undergo fluctuations of large magnitude each year. For example, in Kentucky cottontail summer densities after the primary spring reproduction period were several times higher than those of late winter (Giuliano et al. 1993).

HABITAT

Rabbits are found in a wide variety of general habitats from fields to forests, but specifically are associated with early successional grass/forb and brushy vegetation. Generally, rabbits fare well in areas of high habitat diversity with early successional habitat such as small crop fields, fallow fields, and forest regeneration stands. Dense forest stands with closed canopies, little light penetration through the canopy, and sparse low vegetation are poor rabbit habitat. Large pastures or crop monocultures also are poor rabbit habitat. Much of the decline of cottontail populations in the midwestern U.S.

is attributed to the expansion of clean farming and reduced weed and brush patches (Allen 1984). And swamp rabbit habitat throughout the South has been drastically diminished from conversion of riparian forests to agricultural land and reservoirs.

Several studies have documented specific habitat preferences. In North Carolina, radio-instrumented eastern cottontails preferred brushy areas to woodlots or open crop fields (Allen et al. 1982). In the Coastal Plains of Georgia, more than 4 times the number of cottontails were captured in the tall weeds-broomsedge habitat type than in cultivated areas or forest types (pine, pine-hardwood, upland hardwood, or bottomland hardwoods) (McKeever 1959). Cottontails nest in a variety of habitats with dense low vegetation. In a Kentucky study, broomsedge was the best early nesting cover but grass was preferred later in the season (Bruna 1951).

The Appalachian cottontail typically is associated with conifer forests with ericaceous understory vegetation at high elevations, but recently also has been found at moderate elevations in Kentucky. Although the eastern cottontail and swamp rabbit may occur together, the cottontail usually is associated with herbaceous vegetation in upland habitat. The swamp rabbit is associated more with woody cover in moist habitat; such as riparian areas along streams and rivers (Taylor and Lay 1944). In the Atchafalaya Floodplain of Louisiana, location of pellets deposited reflected habitat use. Swamp rabbits deposited pellets on 24% of logs in the bottomland hardwood type, but only 6% of logs in the cottonwood-willow type and less than 1% in the cypress-tupelo type (Heuer and Perry 1976).

Cover interspersed with or very near food sources is important for adequate rabbit habitat. Key areas which are important for rabbits include brushy thickets such as abandoned home sites, railroad rights-of-way; and blackberry, cane, briar, or honeysuckle patches. Thickets and other escape cover, such as mammal burrows and brushy fencerows appear to be particularly important to rabbits during winter after frosts have substantially reduced vegetation density.

Overall, good habitat can support up to 3 cottontails per acre and somewhat fewer swamp rabbits. In Kentucky, estimated cottontail populations varied from 0.1 to 2.3 per acre on 5 different areas (Giuliano et al. 1993).

MANAGEMENT

Silvicultural activities which set back plant succession and reduce forest overstory and midstory are positive for rabbits, which benefit from grass/forb and brush level vegetation, such as blackberry or plum thickets. Stand or tree harvesting increases light penetration to the ground, promotes growth of low vegetation, and benefits rabbits. For example, several studies have noted the beneficial effects of natural tree fall or tree harvest on habitat suitability for swamp rabbits (Allen 1985).

Rabbits are associated with early successional habitat, with abundant food and cover *(J. Dickson)*.

Prescribed fire is a practice that normally benefits rabbit populations. For example, in a pine-hardwood forest in the Piedmont of Alabama, eastern cottontail rabbit pellet counts were higher in areas which had been burned 1 and 2 years before than in unburned areas (King et al. 1991). Fire kills the exposed parts of low vegetation and promotes resprouting of small woody vegetation and grass/forb growth.

Some land management activities, such as burning or haying, during spring may destroy rabbit nests. Delaying these practices until after the main spring reproductive period should increase nest success.

Succulent vegetation normally is limited after frost during winter. Small fields of winter forage crops or wildlife food plots, with plantings such as winter grasses or clover, interspersed with appropriate cover will benefit winter rabbit populations.

Dense cover is very important to rabbits for hiding and escape from predators (Anderson and Pelton 1977). Where fall crops have been harvested or escape cover is limited, maintaining dense thickets or creating substantial artificial brush piles can help protect rabbit populations from predators during winter (Madson 1963). Brush piles will decay and diminish after a few years and will need to be replenished.

Rabbit hunting has been a popular activity in the South. Participation has wained as forests have matured and deer hunting has become more popular *(Outdoor Oklahoma)*.

HUNTING

Rabbit hunting has been a long-term tradition in the South. Historically, cottontails and swamp rabbits have provided more hunting recreation than any other game species for southern sportsmen, and fried rabbit has been a welcome staple of many southern meals. Historically, in the South and elsewhere many youngsters began their first hunting with rabbits. Usually shotguns with low velocity loads are used for the fleet, elusive quarry. Rabbits are not hard to kill. Rabbits may be hunted by jumping them from their form. They usually flush more readily from sparse cover than dense cover where apparently they feel safer. They are flushed more readily by slow and erratic hunter movements than by faster and more steady movements (Anderson and Pelton 1977).

A popular and traditional hunting technique is to use dogs to flush and usually also to trail rabbits. When trailed by hounds, rabbits will stay within their home range and usually eventually will run within range of the hunters, often near where they were first jumped. The cry of the trailing hounds adds to the excitement of the hunt. Beagles are a popular choice for this widespread sport; their small size, and scenting and trailing abilities make them well suited for running rabbits. And their pleasing nature makes them good pets. As with hunts for many other species, often the social aspects of the hunt are very important. A typical rabbit hunt in Tennessee consisted of 3 hunters with dogs, hunting 4 hours, jumping 6 rabbits, and harvesting 3.3 rabbits per party trip (Tennessee Wildlife Resources Agency 1996).

There can be conflicts between rabbit hunting and other hunting and trapping activities. A recent problem is the increase of white-tailed deer throughout the region resulting in rabbit hunter interactions with deer hunters, and the propensity of rabbit hounds to trail deer. Another problem sometimes encountered in trapping season is rabbit dogs getting caught in traps set for furbearers.

CHAPTER 16

Wild Hogs

James G. Dickson[1]
US Forest Service
Southern Research Station,
Nacogdoches, TX

John J. Mayer
Westinghouse
Savannah River Company,
Aiken, SC

John D. Dickson[2]
Texas Wings
Austin, TX

Wild hogs or swine are medium to large-sized, stout-bodied, and proportionately short-legged hoofed mammals with thick skin covered with sparse to dense coats of coarse bristles. These animals have elongated heads and snouts ending in a disc-like pad through which the external nares open. The only other species in the southern United States that resembles the wild hog is the collared peccary or javelina, found in Texas, New Mexico and Arizona.

Two primary types of wild hogs, Eurasian wild boar and feral swine (wild hogs solely of domestic ancestry), have been established in the southern United States. These 2 types are conspecifics and will readily hybridize (Wood and Barrett 1979, Mayer and Brisbin 1991). At present, there are only populations of feral swine and wild boar x feral swine hybrids found in the South. No pure populations of Eurasian wild boar are known or have been documented to exist in this region of the country at present (Mayer and Brisbin 1991). In this chapter, these different types of wild hogs will be treated together unless otherwise noted.

Feral hogs resemble domestic hogs, but usually are leaner, and generations in the wild have honed adaptations for life in the wild. Eurasian wild boar, also known as European wild hogs or Russian boars, are about the same size as feral hogs, but have a grizzled, sleeker appearance, with light tipped hair, and longer legs and snout. Specifically, there are both physical and molecular differences among the 3 types of wild hogs. Of these, the morphological differences are the most useful in differentiation. Variation in coloration patterns, cranial differences, and snout and hind foot length have been used to tell the different types of wild hogs apart with a far degree of accuracy. In addition, mitochondrial DNA techniques are beginning to show promise in identifications (Mayer and Brisbin 1993). In contrast to

[1]Current Address: School of Forestry, Louisiana Tech University, Ruston, LA
[2]Current Address: Texas Parks and Wildlife, Austin, TX

Recently, wild hogs have become a more prominent part of the southern landscape *(J. Mayer)*.

earlier beliefs, the presence of striped coloration patterns in piglets is not a reliable character for identifying either Eurasian wild boar or hybrids (Mayer and Brisbin 1993).

In general, male wild hogs are somewhat larger than females. This size relationship is true for both external physical dimensions and total body mass. These differences are initially evident at about 15 months of age, and increase with age. Average adult males are about 5 feet from the snout to the end of the tail, stand 3 feet at the shoulder, and weigh between 180 and 200 pounds. Exceptional animals can weigh in excess of 500 pounds. Wild hogs have an excellent sense of smell and fair to good senses of hearing and vision. Tusks or canine teeth in males are much larger than in females (Mayer and Brisbin 1988), and have trophy value to some hunters.

In many areas of the southern United States, wild hogs are considered to be an important recreational resource as a big game animal (Mayer and Brisbin 1991), with recreational sport hunting having substantial economic impact. In Florida alone, this has annually represented a multi-million dollar industry (Degner 1989). Particularly in Florida, North Carolina, Tennessee, and Texas, the opportunity to hunt wild hogs has attracted large numbers of nonresident hunters and has an economic impact (Conley et al. 1972, Degner 1989).

HISTORY

Being a non-native or exotic species, the origin of wild hogs in the western hemisphere is attributable solely to either the intentional or accidental release of these animals by man. The earliest presence of this species in the southern United States can be traced back to the introduction of domestic swine into Florida by Hernando De Soto in 1539. Along De Soto's route through 13 states, domestic swine escaped into the wild. Subsequent Spanish and French colonies in the South introduced more domestic swine. By the 1700s, feral populations of swine were established throughout the region (Towne and Wentworth 1950, Mayer and Brisbin 1991).

In addition to these early introductions, colonial settlers in the South released domestic swine into unfenced woods to fend for themselves, foraging on mast and other foods. Whenever the settlers wanted pork, the animals were either caught with dogs, trapped, or shot.

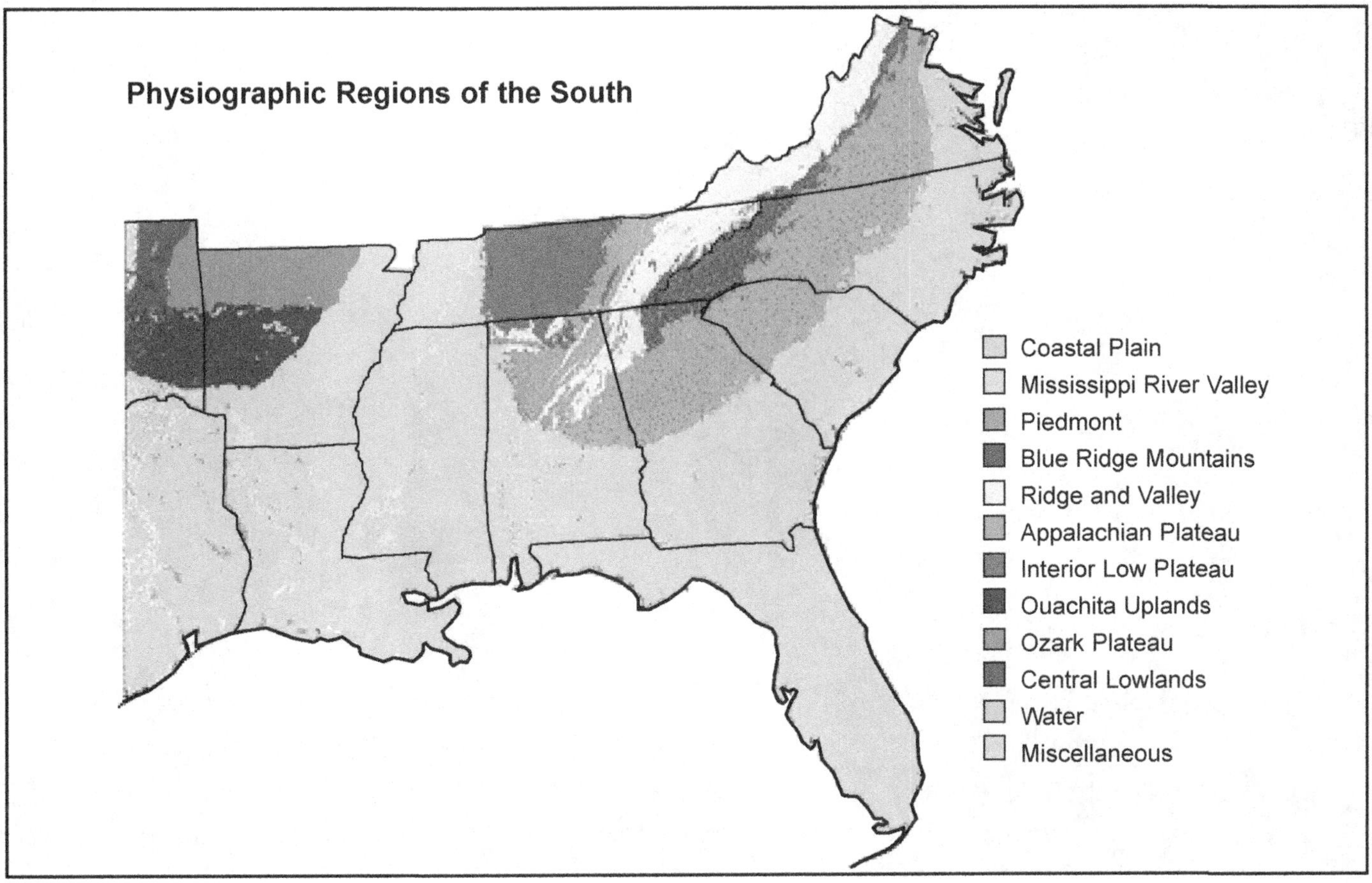

Physiographic Regions of the South

- Coastal Plain
- Mississippi River Valley
- Piedmont
- Blue Ridge Mountains
- Ridge and Valley
- Appalachian Plateau
- Interior Low Plateau
- Ouachita Uplands
- Ozark Plateau
- Central Lowlands
- Water
- Miscellaneous

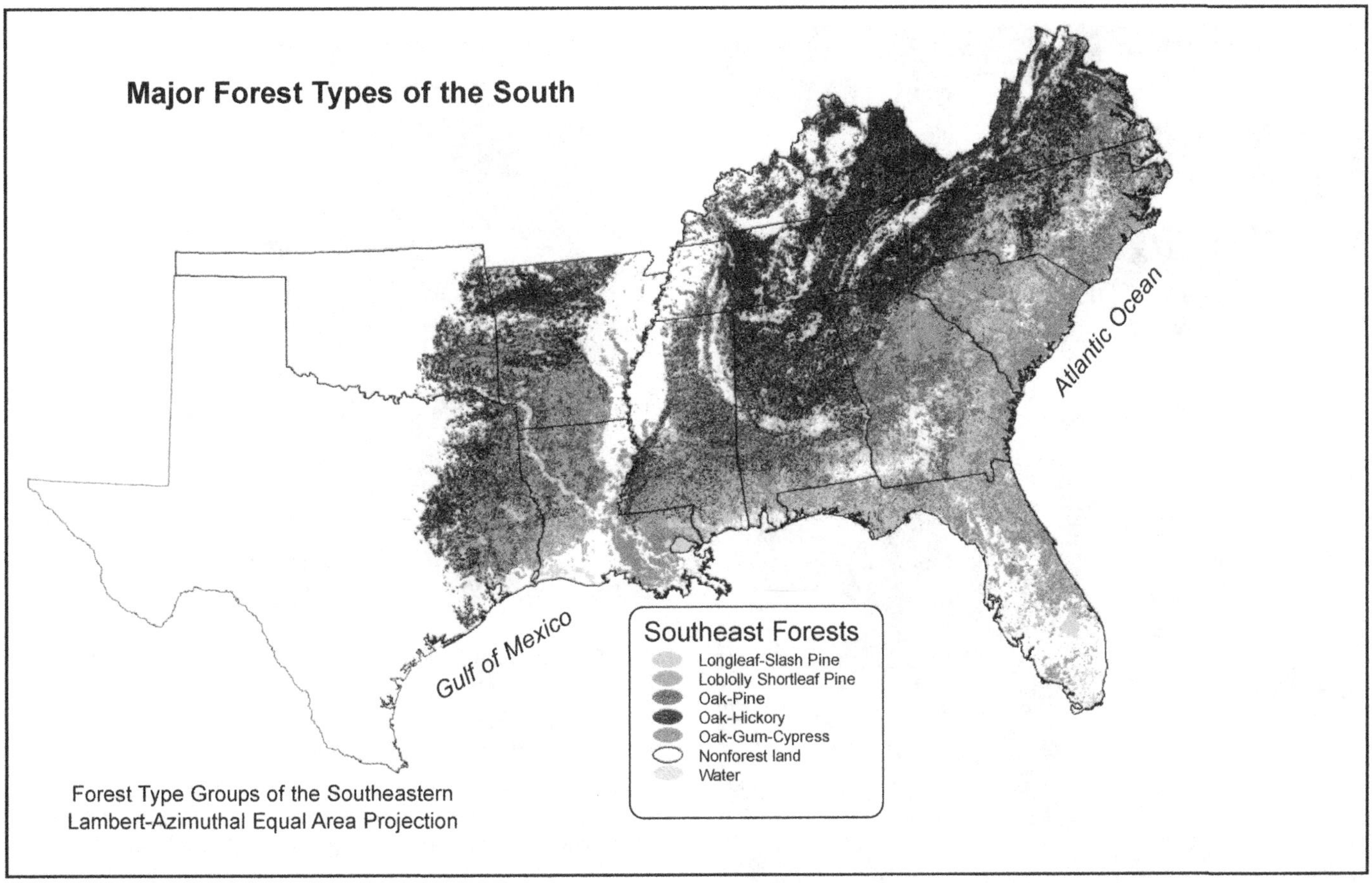

Major Forest Types of the South

Atlantic Ocean

Gulf of Mexico

Southeast Forests

- Longleaf-Slash Pine
- Loblolly Shortleaf Pine
- Oak-Pine
- Oak-Hickory
- Oak-Gum-Cypress
- Nonforest land
- Water

Forest Type Groups of the Southeastern
Lambert-Azimuthal Equal Area Projection

Top: Forests of the South have always been diverse as well as dynamic *(G. Smith).*

Left: Southern forests have been continually molded by a variety of diverse natural and anthropogenic forces (J. Walker).

Above: In the era of exploitation in the late 1800s and early 1900s a few species, such as this ivory-billed woodpecker, apparently were eliminated from southern forests *(G. Sutton, Cornell Lab of Ornithology).*

A number of species whose future once was in doubt have been successfully restored to southern forests.

The black bear—With pressure from humans it was once found only in remote swamps and mountains. Now populations are expanding where there is extensive habitat in the Appalachian and Ozark mountains *(D. Hancock).*

The white-tailed deer, a premier game species. Populations were once decimated by the new southern settlers and relegated to a few locations. Now it thrives throughout the South and is found in every county *(B. Lea).*

The bald eagle, is now making a remarkable recovery nationwide *(L. P. Brown, Cornell Lab of Ornithology).*

The gobble of the wild turkey once again resounds throughout the South. What a tremendous conservation success story. Where once there were mere 10s of thousands now there are over 2 million southwide *(G. Smith).*

The wood duck—What a beautiful creature and appropriately named. It has returned to prominence in southern forested wetlands. It is the only species of waterfowl that nests in cavities throughout the South *(J. Dickson)*

Man and wildlife continue to interact in many different ways.

Mourning doves may have declined from the loss of traditional habitat, but seem to be doing well in suburban situations with ample nesting sites and bird feeders *(R. Mirarchi)*.

Top and above: The beaver is widespread today. It's capability to flood forests and crop fields often puts it at odds with man and his land use objectives *(J. Dickson, Outdoor Oklahoma)*.

Ruffed grouse populations in the southern Appalachians appear to have dwindled due to the loss of early successional habitat *(Ruffed Grouse Society)*.

The northern bobwhite was once a very popular game bird in the South. But as small weedy fields disappeared and southern forests aged the call of the bobwhite has become increasingly rare *(J. MacHudspeth)*.

Red-cockaded woodpecker populations declined as old- growth pine stands were harvested. Now there are substantial efforts, particularly on federal land, in behalf of this species *(P. Moore, OK Dep. Wildlife)*.

Several species and groups of southern wildlife are the focus of special interest.

Population viability of some forest interior species may be negatively impacted by forest fragmentation *(M. Hopiak, Cornell Lab of Ornithology)*.

We don't know very much about the life history or habitat requirements of some vertebrates, such as bats, reptiles, and amphibians. The Rafinesque's big eared bat shown here is a species of special concern. Originally it hibernated and reproduced in large cavity trees. Now it uses man-made structures such as buildings and wells *(D. Saugey)*.

Sandhill crane chick and egg. There is some concern for a few species of birds such as the sandhill crane *(D. Hancock)*.

Wildlife foods

Oak acorns wherever they occur are a principle food in fall and winter for a number of wildlife species. Parent nutrition, and production and survival of young often depend on the previous season's acorns. However annual production is very erratic *(US Forest Service)*.

Fruits from shrubs are important wildlife food for a number of species in summer and fall *(US Forest Service, H. Holbrook, J. Dickson)*.

During spring and summer insects are primary food for a wide variety of adult and young game and nongame birds *(J. Dickson)*.

Protection and particular management is needed for some sensitive plant species and communities. Coastal plain bogs and seasonally wet longleaf pine flatwoods are among the most diverse communities in the world, supporting many different plants, *top*. Among the plants of interest found here are a variety of orchids, such as this rosebud orchid, *left (J. Walker)*.

Big-leaf geranium, *above*. The rich cove forests of the southern Appalachians are renown for displays of spring wild flowers. Many are ephemeral, growing and flowering each season before the canopy leafs out *(J. Walker)*.

The nature of the South's people and their relationship with the forest continue to change. One of the biggest challenges will be to manage for varied products, while protecting and allowing use of southern forests. It is important to help an increasingly urban population understand natural resources and their management *(K. Cordell, S. Thompkins, M. Staten).*

Smokehouses to cure pork were a common feature of early rural southern settlements. Many of these swine drifted away from the farms and eventually became feral, or wild-living (Towne and Wentworth 1950, Hanson and Karstad 1959, Mayer and Brisbin 1991). Free-ranging domestic hogs in the South were widespread in the early 1900s. But with the increasing human population in the region, open range was largely eliminated in the mid 1900s when most southern states legislated closed range laws (Mayer and Brisbin 1991).

Eurasian wild boar were introduced in the South in the early 1900s to provide new huntable big game animals. The earliest documented introduction of wild boar was into a fenced shooting preserve located on Hooper Bald, Graham County, North Carolina in 1912. Following a period of about 10 years of confinement, these animals escaped during a large-scale hunt. The wild boar dispersed into the surrounding mountainous terrain and over time interbred with local feral hogs. Hybrid stock from this area have either spread or were live-trapped and relocated into portions of California, Texas, Georgia, Florida, Kentucky, North Carolina, South Carolina, and Tennessee (Mayer and Brisbin 1991).

Additional stockings of hybrid animals of unknown origin have reportedly taken place in Arkansas, Mississippi, and Louisiana. Although prohibited by both federal and state regulations, the additional introduction or release of feral hogs and hybrids continues in many areas of the South today (Mayer and Brisbin 1991). Also, wild hogs have been introduced and populations have become established in numerous areas across the central United States.

Wild hogs currently are found in scattered populations and varying densities in all of the southern states. Most populations are found in the Coastal Plain region, however, substantial populations are also found in some portions of the Appalachian Mountains. They are widespread in eastern Texas, Louisiana, and Florida. The current regional population estimate for this species in the southern United States is between 1 and 2 million animals (Mayer and Brisbin 1991, Miller 1993).

HABITAT

Throughout the southern states, wild hogs use a variety of habitat types. The most commonly used habitat in the South is riparian forest associated with a year-round water source (Sweeney and Sweeney 1982). However, the types of habitats successfully occupied by this species range from the mountainous hardwood forests of the southern Appalachians; to the bottomland forests

With adequate nutrition sows are very prolific, producing several litters each year *(J. Mayer)*.

along rivers in South Carolina, Georgia, and eastern Texas; to the marshy palmetto and oak flats of central and south Florida, (Mayer and Brisbin 1991).

The general habitat requirements for this species include a mast-producing cover type during the fall and winter months, and both well-distributed water and escape cover on a year-round basis (USDA 1981). Both hard and soft mast play an important role in the nutritional status and reproductive biology of this introduced species. The importance of hardwoods, particularly oaks, to wild hogs is evident wherever these animals are found. For example, in the Appalachians Eurasian wild hogs used mixed oak stands during fall and winter of years of high mast production, but used other hardwood stands when little mast was available (Singer et al. 1981).

Wild hogs are found only in areas that are associated with either permanent drainages or widespread mesic habitats. The absence of water in an area will effectively preclude establishment of this species. Habitat use by wild hogs is related to cover density (Barrett 1978). Cover habitat also functions as a preferred bedding location for this species. In cooler weather wild hogs usually make beds where they will get warmth from the morning sun. In the southern Appalachians, most beds are found on slopes or areas with a south, east, or southeastern exposure. In addition, dense cover affords wild hogs some measure of protection from hunting (Conley et al. 1972).

Seasonal changes in habitat use are related to food availability and dietary shifts (Sweeney 1970, Kurz and Marchinton 1972, Graves and Graves 1977). For example in South Carolina, an abundant mast crop in the fall concentrated feral hog activity in bottomland hardwoods, but they moved to upland pine plantations around thickets of ripe plums during summer (Kurz and Marchinton 1972).

Movements of wild hogs are variable and dependent, to some extent, on food availability and sexual activity. In general, males travel more than females, and sexually active males traveled more than sexually inactive males. Also, movements were least during years and season of high acorn production; hogs moved more to find food during periods of food shortage (Singer et al. 1981).

REPRODUCTION

Compared to all other native or introduced big game species found in North America, wild hogs have the highest reproductive potential. This species sexually matures at an early age, produces the largest litters of any ungulate, can farrow 2 litters within a twelve-month period, and breeds throughout the year. Reproductive success in wild hog populations depends on food availability, particularly the annual mast crop (Matschke 1964, Scott and Pelton 1975).

Sexual maturity in wild hogs can be reached as young as 5 months in males and 6 months in females. Excluding unusual circumstances or pathological conditions, all individuals of both sexes become sexually mature before the end of the first year of life (Sweeney 1970, Barrett 1978). Wild hogs in the South are sexually active and will breed throughout the year. Although variable by area, there are usually 2 peaks in the annual reproduction among wild hogs, a major one in late fall to early winter and one in late spring to early summer (Sweeney 1970, Conley et al. 1972, Johnson et al. 1982).

The gestation period of wild hogs ranges from 110 to 140 days, with an average of 114-116. Estrous cycles are resumed and sows may breed soon after their young are weaned at about 3 to 5 months of age (Asdell 1964, Barrett 1978).

The fetal litter size in wild hogs varies from 1 to 16, with a mean of between 5 and 6. The observed intrauterine mortality varies from 23-40 % (Asdell 1964, Baber and Coblenz 1986, Hellgren 1993).

The pregnant sow builds a farrowing nest approximately 2 to 3 days before giving birth. These nests tend to be shallow depressions lined with grasses, leaves or other plant material. After the litter of piglets is born, the young stay in or near the nest for about a week, even while their dam leaves to forage. The basic social group among wild hogs is a sow with her offspring; mature boars are usually solitary except when breeding. Juvenile mortality in wild hogs can be high, with observations varying from 9 to over 90 % in any given year (Crouch 1983, Barrett 1978).

FOODS

Wild hogs are both omnivorous and opportunistic in their dietary preferences (Sweeney and Sweeney 1982). In general, however, most recent studies have shown that wild hogs consume far more plant than animal material on an annual basis. The specific diet of a wild hog population is largely dependent upon what foods are available in a local area at any one time of the year (Barrett 1978, Belden and Frankenberger 1990), and can change as new forage species become available.

The list of plant material eaten by wild hogs includes a wide variety of both above and below ground stems, leaves, fruits, roots/tubers, forbs, fungi, and woody vegetation. Hard mast such as acorns and hickory nuts is important and preferred food when it is available (Henry and Conley 1972, Scott and Pelton 1975, Matschke 1964). In general, wild hogs feed on grasses and forbs in the spring, fruits in summer and fall, and roots and tubers throughout the year (Hellgren 1993). The opportunistic food habits of this introduced species also often result in the depredation of a variety of commercial grain and vegetable crops.

Although typically low in volume and frequency (both less than 10%), the consistent use of and apparent determined searching for high protein animal food resources may indicate the importance of this component within the diet of wild hogs (Barrett 1978, Scott and Pelton 1975). On islands where food resources are more limited, the seasonal volume of animal material in wild hog diets has been documented to be as high as 26% (Baron 1979). Wild hogs eat a variety of animal matter, such as insects, crustaceans, mollusks, worms, fish, amphibians, reptiles, birds, and mammals. This component of the wild hog's diet includes consumption of both predated animals and carrion that is found. Eggs of a number of vertebrate species are also consumed opportunistically.

Wild hogs feed mostly at night, but also may feed during daylight hours. For example, in the Appalachians radio-instrumented Eurasian wild hogs were more active during twilight and at night than during the day in all seasons (Singer et al. 1981).

DISEASES AND PARASITES

Wild hogs are susceptible to a wide range of diseases and parasites. Some of these diseases are specific to swine, while others are shared by other wild and domestic mammals as well as by man. In general, wild hogs have the potential to contract and transmit all of the viral, bacterial, and fungal diseases of domestic swine (Payeur 1989). In some cases, wild hogs may carry and be resistant to diseases, but are capable of infecting domestic livestock, native game species such as white-tailed deer, or hunters. For this reason there is concern over the potential of wild hogs functioning as disease reservoirs in areas where they are abundant (Nettles 1989, Davis 1993).

The list of diseases which can infect wild hogs includes but is not limited to the following: psuedorabies, hog cholera, swine brucellosis, bovine tuberculosis, vesicular stomatitis, vesicular exanthema, trichinosis, foot-and-mouth disease, African swine fever, leptospirosis, bubonic plague, anthrax, transmissible gastroenteritis, rinderpest, porcine encephalomyelitis, porcine enterovirus, reovirus, swine influenza, and Venezuelan equine encephalitis (Davis 1993, Mebus 1989, Nettles 1989). Of particular concern are swine brucellosis and psuedorabies because these diseases are a threat to the domestic swine industry and are subjects of major control programs by both federal and state agricultural agencies.

Brucellosis is an infectious bacterial disease of animals and humans caused by members of the genus *Brucella*. The effects of this disease are generally limited to abortions and reproductive organ infections. In humans brucellosis may clinically mimic severe flu and may resemble crippling arthritis or meningitis. There is no cure for brucellosis in either animals or humans (Davis 1993). The occurrence of brucellosis infections in wild hogs in the South has been found to vary from 6 to 53% of animals tested (Becker et al. 1978, Zygmont et al. 1982). The areas of highest brucellosis incidence in the South have been in Florida (Becker et al. 1978). Bigler et al. (1977) reported that 22% of human cases of brucellosis in Florida were attributable to hunter contact with wild hogs.

Psuedorabies is an infectious, alphaherpes viral disease of the central nervous system in wild hogs that is also found in domestic livestock, cats and dogs (Davis 1993). Transmission is through animal to animal contact or contact with contaminated media such as food and water. Most swine remain latently infected following clinical recovery. Except for swine, the disease is almost always fatal (Payeur 1989). Small pigs are more severely affected, but more virulent strains have recently developed and fatalities among adult swine have been observed (Davis 1993).

A variety of parasites infect wild hogs, but typically do not cause direct mortality. Endoparasites that appear to be well-established in wild hog populations include lungworms, kidney worms, liver flukes, thorny-headed worms, stomach worms, intestinal round worms, hookworms, nodular worms, coccidia (*Sarcocystis* spp.) and threadworms (Smith 1981, Nettles 1989). Kidney worms and lung worms are known to cause severe debilitation in domestic swine; and in conjunction with other unfavorable conditions could represent significant morbidity/mortality factors to wild hogs (Smith 1981). Dog ticks, hog lice, and mites (*Sarcoptes scabiei*) are the most typical ectoparasites found on wild hogs. With the exception of sarcoptic mange, none of these

Wild hog rootings are a problem in disrupting plant communities *(J. Mayer)*.

ectoparasites constitutes a public health threat (Smith 1981).

INTERACTIONS

Although considered beneficial in some areas, abundant wild hogs usually are regarded as a significant liability (Lucas 1977, Tisdell 1982). Federal and state agricultural and environmental agencies and interest groups consider wild hogs to be serious economic pests and an undesirable exotic species that causes ecological damage.

In this species sebaceous glands do not function as sweat glands, so hogs cannot cool themselves physiologically. Therefore wild hogs need to wallow throughout the year, especially during hot weather. Wallowing serves to reduce their body temperature and provides a protective coating of mud that functions to either exclude or immobilize ectoparasites. Wild hog wallows can be found in almost any type of low-lying, wet area, and can be found in either isolated sites or in association with bottomland drainages and streams (Conley et al. 1972, Belden and Pelton 1975). Wallowing can degrade water quality of riparian streams. In the Appalachians, siltation and contamination of streams from rooting and wallowing are suspected of being detrimental to the native brook trout populations (Howe et al. 1981).

Another common activity of wild hogs is rubbing. This behavior involves an animal rubbing or scratching against a tree trunk, post, or other stable vertical structure. Rubs appear to provide comfort, remove excess mud obtained during wallowing, and to mechanically rid the body of ectoparasites. However, not all rubbing is associated with mud wallows. Wild hogs also will rub against pines and creosoted telephone poles, whose pine resin or creosote seems to serve as a repellant for lice and ticks.

Rooting is the most obvious and widespread damage caused by wild hogs in areas where these animals occur. Hog rooting is most often observed in the winter and early spring months when other food resources are not plentiful (Baron 1979). The location of wild hog rooting in different habitat types appears to be related to seasonal movement, food availability, and reproductive activities (Belden and Pelton 1975). Excessive hog rooting can destabilize surface soils and increase soil erosion that can be particularly damaging to stream channels, roads, rail beds (Lucas 1977). Singer et al. (1982) found that rooting mixed the top two soil horizons and reduced ground vegetative cover and leaf litter. In some areas, the entire herb understory was removed by rooting activity (Bratton 1977). Rooting has also been shown to damage tree roots and increase the amount of sprouting and root suckers (Huff 1977). Although claimed by some to benefit in forest regeneration, disturbances caused by rooting may enable the establishment of undesirable weed species in some areas. Extreme rooting by wild hogs can also influence nutrient cycling within the forest floor (Lacki and Lancia 1983).

Wild hogs may negatively affect native plant communities (Wood and Barrett 1979), from both rooting and direct foraging. These animals have been an especially difficult problem with respect to protecting fragile plant communities in high elevation ecosystems in the Great Smoky Mountains National Park. Wild hog rooting reduces ground cover and negatively affects some sensitive herbaceous species. Within the park, over 50 non-woody species are known to be eaten, uprooted, or trampled. Hog activities change plant species composition in favor of plants with deep or poisonous roots (Bratton 1977). In contrast to other studies, Baron (1982) concluded that the feral hog rooting and foraging did not disrupt a barrier island's plant communities.

Wild hogs have long been known for their depredations to both agricultural crops and forest plantations. The list of crops impacted by foraging wild hogs includes corn, milo, rice, watermelons, peanuts, hay, turf, wheat and other grains. Wild hog-caused damage to these crops results from feeding and related trampling and rooting. Wild hogs on national wildlife refuges also damage crops specifically planted for waterfowl (Thompson 1977). Wild hogs have been a problem in their damage to pines (Wakely 1954). They root up and chew the roots of planted loblolly and slash pine seedlings, sometimes destroying entire pine regeneration areas (Lucas 1977). Wild hogs also feed on the grass stage of longleaf pine, and chew on the lateral roots of mature pines (Conley et al. 1972, Lucas 1977). They also root up and consume newly-planted cherrybark and swamp chestnut oak seedlings, and probably other hardwoods where available.

A number of vertebrate species are preyed on by the omnivorous wild hog. Typically this predation is directed at young animals and less mobile species, but the effects on populations are unknown (Wood and Barrett 1979). Adult hogs can also be effective predators of both domestic livestock and ungulate game species. While hogs will readily prey on healthy newborn lambs, kids, calves, and fawns, it should also be noted that wild hogs will also attack, kill, and eat adult sheep and goats (Beach 1993). Wild hogs also opportunistically prey on the eggs of ground-nesting bird species, such as the ruffed grouse, wild turkey, and northern bobwhite (Conley et al. 1972, Hanson and Karstad 1959, Stegeman 1938), particularly where wild hog densities are high (Henry 1969, Matchske 1965). Recent observations in eastern Texas suggest that high densities of hogs may preclude wild turkey nesting success (J. Burk: pers. commu.). Wild hogs inhabiting the coastal barrier islands of the southeastern United States have also been found to be a significant predator of both the eggs and hatchlings of loggerhead and green sea turtles (Hanson and Karstad 1959, Thompson 1977, Baron 1982, Mayer and Brisbin 1995).

Although man is the most significant predator of wild hogs in the United States (Sweeney and Sweeney 1982), other species of wildlife prey on wild hogs. Documented predators of wild hogs include black bear and cougar for all age classes, and coyote and bobcat for immature individuals (Stegeman 1938, Young 1958, Conley et al. 1972). American alligators will also opportunistically prey on wild hogs (Shoop and Ruckdeschel 1990).

One of the concerns about the introduced species has been competition with native species for available food, particularly mast. Acorns are a primary diet item of wild hogs as well as several species of native southern wildlife, such as white-tailed deer, black bear, gray and fox squirrels, wild turkeys, and woodrats. Studies have shown annual acorn production is highly variable and in some years is very low. It has been demonstrated that low acorn production can negatively affect deer overwinter survival and subsequent fawn survival (Rogers et al. 1990); and other species are probably negatively affected as well. During these years of minimal acorn production, wild hog consumption of acorns probably negatively affects mast-consuming species in oak forests.

A general dietary overlap also suggests some competition between wild hogs and other species, such as range cattle, striped skunks, common opossums, red and gray foxes, raccoons, bobcats, muskrats, nutria, eastern cottontails, swamp rabbits, hawks, owls, and waterfowl (Conley et al. 1972, Bratton 1974, Thompson 1977, Baron 1979).

CONTROL

Because wild hogs are very prolific and become wary with hunting pressure, once populations are established they usually are difficult to control. To be effective, control efforts must be intensive and continuous (Wood et al. 1992). Control techniques include fencing, snares, trapping, shooting, and hunting with trained dogs. Although inexpensive and widely used in Australia (Hone and Pedersen 1980), poisons or toxicants such as Compound 1080 or Warfarin for controlling wild hogs have not been approved for use in the United States (Littauer 1993).

A variety of fence designs have been described for restricting wild hog access into crop fields and lambing pastures (Littauer 1993). Electric fence designs in Australia have been shown to exclude hogs 94% of the time (Hone and Atkinson 1983). Nonelectric fence must be of net wire or diamond mesh construction with a spacing of vertical wires of 6 inches or less to be hog proof (Hone and Atkinson 1983, Littauer 1993). In addition, these fences must be at least 3 feet tall and buried beneath the ground at the bottom to be effective (Littauer 1993). However, hog-proof fencing is difficult to erect and maintain in uneven terrain (Littauer 1993), and generally, is not economically feasible in most situations.

The use of snares can be effective in controlling wild hogs. For example, in the last decade over half of the wild hogs removed by the Texas Animal Damage Control Service were accounted for by the use of snares. Snares consist of a loop of steel cable that is attached to a secure object so that the loop catches the hog as it passes through a small area or opening. Snares for taking wild hogs are typically placed over holes in fences that hogs have been using (Littauer 1993). Although of relatively low cost compared to other control methods, snaring has several disadvantages including the ability to capture only one animal at a time, being inappropriate to use in some situations, the ability of very large hogs to occasionally break snares and escape, and the capture of nontarget species (Littauer 1993). In addition, the use of snares for controlling wild hogs in some areas has met with public opposition (Anderson and Stone 1993).

Large cage or pen/corral traps can be a very effective method for controlling wild hogs. Traps are available or can be constructed in a variety of designs. Some designs are made of takedown panels that are easily moved and set up. Trapping is usually more effective during winter when food is in short supply, and before spring green vegetation is available. Corn is one of the most common baits used for trapping wild hogs; soured

Controlling hog populations is a frequent problem; one method is trapping *(J. Mayer)*.

Hunting wild hogs with dogs is a popular activity and can be an effective control method *(J. Mayer)*.

or mash corn has been found to be especially attractive to hogs. The primary advantage of using traps is that more than one hog can be captured at a time (Belden and Frankenberger 1977, Littauer 1993). The drawbacks of using traps are: traps are cumbersome, require some effort to set up, hogs can become trap shy, and trapping generally is less effective during summer months when there usually is ample food (Littauer 1993).

Shooting wild hogs can be a very useful control method. This method can be carried out through pedestrian, vehicular or aerial means, and typically uses either a high-powered rifle or shotgun. Opportunistic shooting of hogs on the ground is less expensive than most other means of control, but it is typically less successful in removing large numbers of animals (Fox and Pelton 1977). In some situations large numbers of hogs can be removed through aerial shooting from a fixed wing aircraft or helicopter, but it is expensive (Littauer 1993). The primary advantage of shooting is the ability to select specific target animals for removal. Disadvantages of shooting include both a potential for wounding animals and safety concerns associated with the discharging of firearms in some areas.

The use of experienced hog dogs for removing wild hogs is an age-old technique that is still very effective. This control method also allows the hunter the option of selecting individual animals, and of killing or carrying captured hogs out alive. An advantage of using trained dogs is that many hogs can be taken in a relatively short time. However, experienced hog dogs are very expensive and dog casualties from hunting hogs may be high (Littauer 1993).

HUNTING

Wild hog hunting is a popular pastime in many areas of the South. In some states (North Carolina, Tennessee, and West Virginia), they are considered game animals with associated seasons and bag limits. However, in most other states they can be hunted at all times of the year on private land and can be taken in ways that are illegal for game animals (Mayer and Brisbin 1991). Wild hogs can be located by scouting for rootings, tracks, rubs, wallows, and scat. If not limited by state regulations, wild hogs may be still-hunted, stalked, hunted over bait such as corn, and hunted at night with lights.

Wild hogs can be located by wallows in the ground or rubs on trees *(J. Mayer)*.

A popular form of hunting in the South is with hog dogs. It is an exciting activity and has a dedicated following. Dogs, such as Catahoulas or blackmouth curs, can function as both trail and bay dogs. Other breeds of dogs, such as pit bulls or pit bull/cur crosses, are used to catch and hold the hogs. Hogs are killed or caught, thrown and tied up after they have been bayed. Captured hogs often are held in pens to be fattened for later consumption. In hunting wild hogs with dogs, a variety of weapons are employed, including guns, bows, knives, and even spears.

In still hunting, standard centerfire rifle calibers of .243 or larger that are adequate for deer are normally used. Shotguns loaded with either buckshot or slugs may also be used for both still and drive hunts. Because wild hogs are often easier to stalk than white-tailed deer, many hunters in the South hunt hogs with either handguns or archery gear. Hog hide and the subcutaneous gristle pad on the shoulders and upper sides of mature boars are thick and can be difficult to penetrate.

Care should be taken when dressing wild hogs to avoid infection with swine brucellosis. It is advisable to wear disposable plastic or rubber gloves, to avoid direct contact with blood or reproductive organs (especially the uterus and uterine fluid from mature sows), and to wash hands thoroughly when completed.

Feral hogs are very good to eat. The meat is tasty and has more natural fat than native game animals, such as deer, but normally is not as fatty as domestic hogs. Care should be taken to fully cook the meat to kill any possible pathogens.

CONCLUSION

Because of their trophy and table qualities, wild hogs have been introduced throughout much of the South. But there are substantial problems associated with these animals. Wild hogs may negatively impact natural ecosystems and vegetation. They compete with native species for food when these forage resources are in limited supply. They harbor diseases, which may be a threat to both man and domestic livestock. They are a problem in a variety of land management activities. Populations of wild hogs are very difficult to control once they are established. Because of these problems, it is recommended not to introduce wild hogs into new areas, and to control populations where they and related problems are excessive.

CHAPTER 17

Waterfowl

Mickey E. Heitmeyer
Gaylord Memorial Laboratory
University of Missouri-Columbia, Puxico, MO

Twelve species of waterfowl are common in southern forests of the United States. Two species, wood duck and hooded merganser, are residents year round and breed locally. Mallard, black duck, northern pintail, gadwall, American wigeon, green-winged teal, northern shoveler, ring-necked duck, and Canada goose (both large *Branta canadensis maxima* and medium-sized *B. c. interior* subspecies) migrate from northern breeding areas to spend the winter in or near southern forests. Many blue-winged teal use forested wetlands during fall and spring migration when they travel between northern breeding areas and southern winter destinations along the Gulf Coast, in Mexico, and in Central and South America. Another nine species occasionally are present in southern forests but their primary range and habitat use is elsewhere. These species include canvasback, redhead, lesser scaup, bufflehead, ruddy duck, mottled duck, white-fronted goose, lesser snow goose, and trumpeter swan. Rare sightings of common goldeneye, red-breasted and common merganser, oldsquaw, white-winged scoter, and Ross' goose also occur in specific forested locations, usually along large rivers and in open basins.

Waterfowl use of southern forests is mostly confined to bottomland hardwood forests and associated wetlands and agricultural lands that are seasonally flooded by on-site precipitation and flooding from rivers and streams. Rarely, mallards, black ducks, and wood ducks forage in dry upland forests. Wood ducks and hooded mergansers nest in tree cavities, mostly in bottomland hardwood stands, but occasionally in non-hardwood trees such as pine. Waterfowl use a variety of habitats throughout the annual cycle and many species rely on resources in southern forests during specific events. The timing of waterfowl migration to, and use of resources in, southern forests coincides with seasonal and annual periodicities of precipitation and flooding and food availability.

Waterfowl are highly prized game birds and hunters harvest large numbers of duck and geese each year in the southern U.S. Hunting waterfowl in flooded bottomland forests is a traditional pursuit of southern

The once vast bottomland hardwoods of the South have been largely replaced by crops and reservoirs, such as Sam Rayburn Reservoir in eastern Texas shown here. This conversion has had substantial effects on waterfowl in the South *(US Forest Service).*

sportsmen and extensive efforts are made to manage and protect important forested habitats on which waterfowl rely.

HISTORY

The number and distribution of waterfowl present in southern forests in pre-settlement times is unknown. Even today, surveys of waterfowl in forests are difficult because dense vegetation and extensive lowland areas restrict visibility and easily hide secretive species such as hooded merganser and wood duck. Historic populations of the most common species, mallard and wood duck, certainly were greater than today (Bellrose 1980). Photographs and accounts of early settlers and travelers indicate many million birds in winter; as many as five million mallards were counted on one oxbow lake in Arkansas in the early 1930s (Queeny 1946). During pre-settlement times, wood ducks may have been the most abundant duck east of the Mississippi River and their numbers certainly were in the millions (Bellrose and Holm 1994).

Historically, at least some waterfowl were present in bottomland forests in all seasons. Bottomland forests occur in each southeastern state (Fig. 1) and the relative

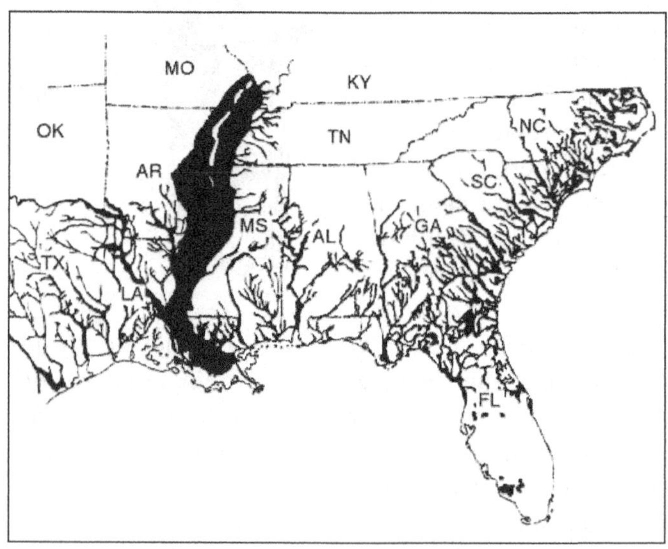

Figure 1. Distribution of bottomland hardwood forests in the southeastern United States *(after Putnam et al. 1960, MacDonald et al. 1979, and U.S. Fish and Wildlife Service unpublished satellite imagery maps).*

abundance of waterfowl, especially in winter, likely coincided with areas of forest and local weather conditions. The extent and composition of bottomland forests has changed dramatically during the past century. The best documented changes are in the Mississippi Alluvial

Scattered large open basins have been created in southern bottomland hardwood forests as a result of earthquakes, historic meander scars of major rivers, and coastal relief. These basins such as Monopoly Lake in Mingo NWR, MO *(shown above)* have been traditional roost, staging, and stopover areas for huge concentrations of migrating and wintering waterfowl in the southern U.S. *(M. Heitmeyer).*

Valley (MAV) where bottomland forests covered over 25 million acres at the turn of the 20th century. Today, less than five million acres of MAV forests remain; remnants are highly fragmented and have greatly altered hydrology (MacDonald et al. 1979). Loss of bottomland forest is as great as 75-95% in northern areas of the MAV (Korte and Fredrickson 1977).

Drainage, channelization, levees, dams and reservoirs, and deforestation have altered timing and extent of flooding and waterfowl distribution and habitat use. Significant clearing of bottomland forests in the MAV occurred in the late 1800s and early 1900s, but the most rapid loss occurred from 1950-1970 (MacDonald et al. 1979). Most lands were cleared for agricultural production. Clearing of forests in the 1950s-60s was stimulated by relatively dry periods (compared to the 1940s and 1970s), high prices for soybeans, agricultural subsidies, and improved equipment that could dredge, ditch, and clear forests efficiently. Forest sites that were cleared first, and to the greatest extent, were higher-elevation areas that typically were only seasonally flooded. These higher sites were dominated by red oak species that produced large quantities of acorns favored by wintering ducks, especially mallards. As higher-elevation forests were cleared, food supplies to waterfowl decreased and birds were more confined to lower more permanently flooded areas, and redistributed to crop fields that replaced forests.

Rivers and streams are interspersed within southern forests and meandering channels, flood events, and earthquakes periodically altered topography and hydrology of forests over historic times (Messina and Conner 1998). These geological factors and extreme climatic events such as tornados and fire, created a heterogeneous landscape that provided diverse resources to waterfowl. These events also created many low elevation open areas in southern forests, including numerous oxbows, river scours, and large natural basins such as Catahoula Lake in Louisiana, Reelfoot and Open Lakes in Tennessee, Big Lake in Arkansas, and Monopoly Lake in Missouri. These large open areas were heavily used by waterfowl as roost, loafing and staging areas and became traditional waterfowl hunting sites.

From 1940-1970, many large reservoirs were built on southern rivers. Reservoirs destroyed thousands of acres of bottomland forest and dams altered downstream hydrology and seasonal flooding of bottomland flood plains. While these losses were detrimental to forested ecosystems and seasonal waterfowl habitats, many waterfowl use reservoirs, especially in Texas,

Oklahoma, Kansas, and Missouri (Buller 1975, Ringelman et al. 1989). Species that benefitted from increased lacustrine habitats in reservoirs include many diving duck species such as bufflehead, common merganser, common goldeneye, canvasback, redhead, ruddy duck, and lesser scaup. Mallards and Canada geese concentrate on reservoirs that are near agricultural crops and use of lakes is highest during cold weather when shallow wetlands near reservoirs are frozen. Many reservoirs now have refuges that restrict hunting and disturbance and this has maintained waterfowl use of many areas over time. In general, use of lakes by waterfowl has declined as lake productivity has decreased, disturbance increased, and nearby floodplain forests and regional wetlands have been destroyed (Ringelman et al. 1989).

Another man-made habitat type that has been created on former forested land is aquaculture ponds. Most of these ponds are managed for catfish production, and they are shallowly flooded and have little emergent or submergent vegetation. Certain duck species, especially ruddy ducks, shoveler, and lesser scaup frequent aquaculture ponds. Some regions such as western Mississippi have large areas of catfish ponds and they overwinter relatively large numbers of ducks.

State and federal conservation agencies began to protect and manage many southern bottomland forests beginning in the 1930s. Large contiguous blocks of protected floodplain forests that historically were used by large concentrations of waterfowl include the White River and Cache River National Wildlife Refuges (NWR) in Arkansas, Yazoo NWR and Delta National Forest in Mississippi, Catahoula and Tensas NWRs and Saline wildlife management area in Louisiana, and Mingo NWR in Missouri. Management of these and other forested sites usually included establishing sanctuaries that restricted hunting and disturbance and provided a "core area" from which birds moved to use surrounding lands. These sites also slowed deforestation and alterations of hydrology at local scales. Refuges undoubtedly helped maintain waterfowl populations and traditional distributions in certain regions of southern forests. In contrast, western Tennessee and Kentucky, southern Illinois, the bootheel of Missouri, northeast Arkansas, northern Alabama, and eastern Texas did not have large protected areas of forest, and deforestation and hydrological alteration reduced regional waterfowl populations over the past several decades. Wildlife management areas and refuges now are present in many of these latter areas, but most are small and protect mere remnants of once-extensive forests.

Small numbers of large Canada geese and trumpeter swans formerly bred in open areas of southern forested wetlands (Fredrickson and Heitmeyer 1988). Swans no longer breed in the South and attempts to reintroduce breeding swans have failed to date. By the 1950s, only a few scattered pairs of Canada geese nested in southern forests, but recent increases in large Canada goose populations throughout North America, and reintroduction in specific locations, have increased breeding populations in the South (Rusch et al. 1996). Large Canada geese now commonly nest throughout the South.

DISTRIBUTION AND CURRENT POPULATIONS

The status of waterfowl populations in North America is monitored annually by surveys in breeding and wintering locations, banding and marking programs, samples of harvested birds, and special inventories and research studies (Martin et al. 1979). Aerial surveys of ducks on northern breeding areas have been the most consistent and systematic assessment of populations. These surveys cover midcontinent and Alaskan regions and have been conducted in May and July of each year since 1955. They provide estimates of the most common duck species and index long term population and habitat changes. Breeding duck numbers fluctuate over time as water and habitat conditions change across North America; populations have been highest during the 1950s, 1970s and 1990s and lowest during 1960s and

Figure 2. Breeding population estimates for ducks in traditional survey areas in North America, 1955-97 *(from U.S. Fish and Wildlife Service 1998).*

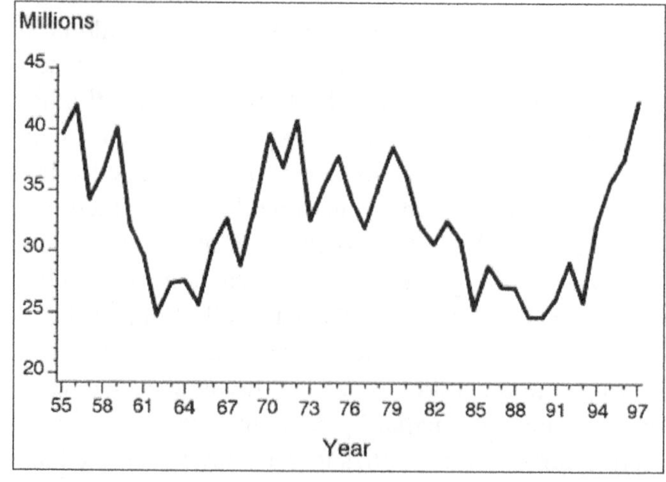

Table 1. Average breeding population estimates (in thousands) of the 10 most common duck species from traditional survey areas during the 1950s to 1990s[a] *(data from U.S. Fish and Wildlife Service 1999).*

Species	1950s[a]	1960s	1970s	1980s	1990s
Mallard	9757	6704	8199	6129	7616
Gadwall	637	1212	1518	1438	2606
American wigeon	3124	2460	2974	2462	2454
Green-winged teal	1687	1410	1858	1784	2095
Blue-winged teal	5032	3812	4653	3827	4990
Northern shoveler	1572	1732	1990	1888	2788
Northern pintail	7733	4378	5596	3017	2581
Redhead	552	545	639	592	728
Canvasback	630	531	542	510	622
Scaup	5954	4966	6302	5631	4346

[a]Data for 1950s include 1955-59.

1980s (Fig. 2). Populations of midcontinent geese also have been relatively high during the last decade. Canada goose populations are at high numbers, with the exception of the southern James Bay population of Canada geese which nest mainly on Akimiski Island in southern James Bay and migrate through Ohio and Tennessee to a former terminus in northern Alabama. Numbers of lesser snow geese are at the highest number in recorded history (Abraham et al. 1996) and mid-continent populations of white-fronted geese also are near record numbers.

Current populations of most migrant ducks that use southern forests are relatively high, however, numbers of pintail and scaup are well below long-term averages and numbers of both species continued to decline in the 1990s despite a marked improvement in prairie breeding water conditions during this decade (Table 1). In contrast to pintail and scaup, numbers of gadwall, shoveler, and blue-winged teal are at or near the highest number estimated since surveys began in 1955 (U.S. Fish and Wildlife Service 1998).

While aerial surveys in northern breeding areas have provided good population estimates for many duck species, comparable surveys and estimates do not exist for species breeding in southern forested areas and in northern boreal, tundra, and arctic regions. Many survey and population estimation techniques have been used for wood ducks breeding in southern areas, but estimates remain crude and locally variable (Brakhage 1990).

Attempts to determine numbers and distribution of waterfowl during migration and winter have not been as consistent or systematic as breeding surveys. The oldest survey of wintering waterfowl is an annual mid-winter inventory conducted by state and federal wildlife agencies. This mid-winter inventory is conducted in January and estimates numbers of birds on key concentration sites such as wildlife management areas, NWRs, hunting clubs, reservoirs, and river flood plains. Few attempts are made to estimate total winter populations within states or to separate distribution by habitat type. Consequently, the number of waterfowl present in forested habitats in each state in winter is unknown. In addition to the mid-winter inventory, a mid-December survey has been conducted during the past two decades specifically to count geese. Some states conduct surveys of waterfowl present during fall and winter to determine distribution and chronology of migration. These surveys vary considerably in extent and timing and seldom record habitat associations. Few studies or surveys have been conducted to determine distribution and habitat use in spring (Heitmeyer and Vohs 1984).

Despite the limitations of migration and winter surveys, the distribution of waterfowl in southern states in winter does suggest relative use of forested habitats. Among southern states, recent mid-winter surveys find most ducks and geese in Louisiana, Arkansas, Texas, Mississippi, Tennessee, and Missouri. Most ducks and geese present in Arkansas, Mississippi, Alabama, Tennessee, and Kentucky in winter are in or near forested regions. Approximately 40-50% of the ducks in Louisiana, Florida, Missouri, Oklahoma, and Georgia in winter are in forested regions. Less than 25% of wintering waterfowl in Texas, South and North Carolina, and Kansas are in forested areas. Typically, more ducks than geese occur in forested areas; for example few geese, but over 40% of ducks in Louisiana are in forested sections of that state.

Distribution of waterfowl in southern habitats, especially large-bodied ducks and Canada geese, varies among years in relation to temperature, precipitation, and flooding. In years when winter temperatures are mild and wetlands and flooded croplands remain unfrozen in northern latitudes, migration to southern areas is delayed and many birds never reach southern areas (Nichols et al. 1983). In contrast, when winters are cold and early, only a few ducks winter in the northern states of Missouri, Illinois, Kentucky, and Oklahoma. Winter distribution also is influenced strongly by regional precipitation and flooding. Birds readily respond to newly flooded areas, and if flood waters remain for extended periods, regional distribution can be altered considerably from traditional patterns and sites.

The distribution of breeding wood ducks in southern states closely reflects the extent of bottomland forest. Although estimates of breeding wood ducks are not consistent or precise, existing data suggest highest populations in Arkansas, Louisiana, Mississippi, Alabama, and Florida (Sauer and Droege 1990, Bellrose and Holm 1994).

HABITAT

Waterfowl use a variety of habitat types in southern forested regions (Fredrickson and Heitmeyer 1988). Birds are highly mobile, especially during fall and winter, and they readily move within and among regions. Habitat preferences among species generally reflect niche and food segregation (Fig. 3). Habitat changes within species during winter reflect changing nutritional and social requirements associated with changing annual cycle events. For migrants, annual cycle events undertaken while in southern regions include migration to and from the region, completion of the prealternate molt in fall and early winter, pairing, prebasic molt by females in late winter and spring, and reserve deposition prior to spring migration. Wood ducks and hooded mergansers that breed in southern forests also undergo egg laying, incubation, brood rearing, and summer wing molt.

Habitats in southern bottomland forests vary along an elevation and flooding continuum from low more permanently flooded sites to higher elevations where bottomland forests grade into uplands (Fredrickson 1980, Wharton et al. 1982, Heitmeyer et al. 1989). The normal pattern of annual precipitation and flooding is characterized by dry periods during summer and early fall, increasing precipitation starting in October and November, and wet conditions in late winter and spring. In the lowest elevations, habitats are flooded much of the year and include rivers and drainages, open water areas with dense submergent vegetation, and scrub/shrub vegetation dominated by buttonbush, planertree, bald cypress and water tupelo. Sites that are flooded for several months of the year, typically from fall through early summer, are mostly forested and have dominant stands of black willow, water and overcup oak, swamp privet, red maple, water locust, and scattered bald cypress and tupelo. Higher sites that typically flood for only a few months during the dormant season of winter and early spring contain mainly red oaks, American elm, and sweetgum; understory trees include possum haw and winged elm. High elevations that transition bottomlands to uplands include hickory and other trees relatively intolerant to prolonged flooding.

Figure 3. Trophic-level feeding niches of waterfowl species in southern forested wetlands.

CARNIVORE	
HOODED MERGANSER	Diver for large inverts, small fish, amphibians
NORTHERN SHOVELER	Surface dabbler for zooplankton, small seeds, small aquatic insects.
HERBIVORE	
CANADA GOOSE	Grazer on sedges, grasses, aquatic plants
AMERICAN WIGEON	Dabbler for aquatic plants and seeds, grazer on sedges and grasses
GADWALL	Dabbler for algae, aquatic plants, moist-soil seeds
NORTHERN PINTAIL	Subsurface dabbler for large moist-soil seeds, marsh inverts
GREEN-WINGED TEAL	Dabbler for small moist-soil seeds, marsh inverts
RING-NECKED DUCKS	Diver for seeds of floating leaved and aquatic plants
OMNIVORE	
MALLARD	Subsurface dabbler for acorns, moist-soil seeds, detrital inverts
WOOD DUCK	Surface feeder for acorns, small seeds, drupes, samaras, aquatic insects

Tree gaps are present throughout bottomland forests where individual (or small groups) trees fall due to wind storms, senescence, and disease. Creation of tree gaps releases shade intolerant plants and these gaps become colonized by grasses, forbs, sedges, and newly germinated trees. Herbaceous vegetation in the gaps, often referred to as moist-soil plants, produces many waterfowl foods including seeds, roots, tubers, browse, and invertebrates.

Cavities in bottomland forests are formed by many processes and are used as nest sites by wood ducks and hooded mergansers. Abundance and distribution of cavities in bottomland forests varies depending on age and composition of the stand. Typically, older stands dominated by overcup oak, bald cypress, and other long-lived species have the highest densities of cavities.

Fall Migration and Prealternate Molt.—In early fall, the only habitats typically flooded in southern forests are rivers, open sumps, tupelo/cypress brakes, and intensively managed sites (Heitmeyer et al. 1989). Early migrant ducks, such as blue-winged teal, pintail, shoveler, and gadwall concentrate on open habitats where moist-soil seeds and invertebrates are abundant. Wood ducks and hooded mergansers prefer wooded areas and riverine habitats at this time. Later migrants such as mallard, wigeon, black duck, ring-necked duck and Canada geese use open areas upon arrival, but mallards and black ducks quickly move into flooded forests if they are available (Heitmeyer 1985).

Habitats used by waterfowl in fall provide resources needed during migration and the prealternate molt. Migrants, new to an area, initially settle in open sites where they have good visibility to observe other birds, predators, and disturbance. Once familiar with an area, birds disperse to forested and densely vegetated areas depending on availability of foods and disturbance. Migration and molt are nutritionally costly and birds rely on abundant foods to replenish fat stores metabolized in flight and to grow the alternate plumage (Fredrickson and Drobney 1979).

Flooded agricultural fields are used by waterfowl in fall if available. Most crop fields in southern areas are not harvested until late fall and precipitation generally is not sufficient to flood fields until November-December in most areas. By late fall, however, many crop fields become flooded, especially rice fields that have levees and water control structures that trap on-site rainfall and runoff.

Midwinter and Pairing.—The chronology of pairing varies among waterfowl species, but most ducks and geese establish pair bonds during winter and spring. Ducks form pairs annually, while geese mate for life. Pair formation and mate selection involves elaborate courtship displays and behaviors that "test" potential fitness of prospective mates. Considerable time is invested in mate selection by individuals. During this time, birds use habitats that provide access to other birds in similar social status, optimize food intake, and provide escape cover from predators and disturbance.

Species such as wigeon, green-winged teal, and pintail have extensive aerial courtship repertoires and they use open basins, sloughs, and lakes within forests. Ring-necked ducks also use open areas, but select deeper water that has abundant aquatic vegetation such as watershield and water lily. In contrast to species that use open areas, mallards, black ducks, gadwall, hooded merganser, and wood ducks use densely vegetated and forested sites during courtship and pairing. Favored sites include scrub/shrub habitats where low tangled branches of buttonbush and swamp privet provide protection from avian predators such as goshawks and peregrine falcons. These sites also provide abundant algae and aquatic vegetation that are consumed by gadwall and crayfish which are consumed by hooded mergansers. Sites used for foraging by mallards and black ducks in midwinter include flooded forests that have abundant red oak acorns and surrounding flooded agricultural fields. Daily foraging flights between forests and crop fields in early morning and late afternoon are notable occurrences in many southern areas.

Most geese do not form pair bonds until age 2 or 3 and a mate is retained for life unless one member dies, upon which the surviving bird may repair. The timing and site of pair formation varies in geese, but often occurs in fall and winter preceding the first breeding season. Most geese do not use forested habitats during winter, except for open sloughs and lakes used as roost and loafing areas. Geese use both flooded and dry agricultural fields extensively for foraging at this time.

Disturbance and hunting pressure greatly influences habitat use and distribution of waterfowl in winter. During hunting seasons, birds quickly learn the locations of refuges and they use these sites as "core" habitats for loafing and roosting. Birds disperse from refuges for daily foraging and courtship activities. Huge concentrations of birds commonly occur on southern refuges and regional distribution of waterfowl generally reflects location of refuges.

Prebasic Molt.—Females of most dabbling ducks and some diving ducks undergo a complete prebasic body molt in late winter and spring. The basic plumage acquired from this molt is darker and more streaked than the preceding alternate plumage which is worn from late summer until late winter. Most females do not initiate the prebasic molt until after they have become paired. Pairing and initiation of the prebasic molt represent the first steps in a gradual transition of birds from a nonbreeding to a breeding status.

The prebasic molt typically takes 7 weeks to complete and daily protein demands for feather production are high (Heitmeyer 1988a). Pairs seek habitats that provide abundant high-protein foods such as invertebrates, certain seeds, roots and tubers, and new-growth grasses and sedges. Species such as mallards, wood ducks, and black ducks use flooded forests extensively during this molt where they consume primarily small crustacean invertebrates such as isopods. Gadwall and wigeon also use forested wetlands during this molt period, but they consume mainly sedges and aquatic plants. Pintail, teal, and shovelers rely on shallow wetlands where moist-soil vegetation provides seeds and marsh invertebrates. Geese forage heavily on new-growth grasses, sedges, and tubers in wetlands and on residual grain and winter wheat in agricultural fields.

Spring Migration and Reserve Deposition.—By late winter and spring most waterfowl are preparing to migrate to northern breeding areas. Birds seek habitats that provide abundant food to complete the prebasic molt and to store nutrient reserves for migration and eventual reproduction. Large-bodied species such as geese, mallard, black duck, pintail, and wigeon store large amounts of fat at this time that ultimately influences reproductive potential (Heitmeyer 1988b, Alisauskas and Ankney 1992). In dry winters, flood plains are not flooded as extensively or for long periods and other wetlands also are limited. Consequently, birds are more concentrated on limited flooded habitat or marginal habitats in these years and foods often are depleted by spring, causing birds to be in poorer body condition by winter's end. In contrast, in wet winters, southern flood plains are gradually flooded throughout winter and spring and birds have continuous access to new and abundant foods. In these wet years, birds are fatter and winter survival and reproductive potential are higher (Heitmeyer and Fredrickson 1981, Kaminski and Gluesing 1987).

Waterfowl migrating through southern forests in spring are attracted to most habitats that are shallowly flooded, especially sites that have just become flooded by spring rains and floods. Like fall migrants, birds often settle first in open sites where visibility is good and other birds are present. Migrants then follow other birds that are more familiar with the area to more densely vegetated habitats or they sample local habitats until they find favorable foraging and loafing sites.

Wood Duck and Hooded Merganser Reproduction.—Wood ducks and hooded mergansers begin egg laying as early as late January in southern latitudes (Bellrose and Holm 1994, Dugger et al. 1994). Both species nest in tree cavities and artificial nesting structures, such as boxes. Natural cavities must be large enough to allow entry by females and suitable sites usually are in older trees. Most cavities used are within ½ mile of water (Soulliere 1990).

Wood ducks and hooded mergansers lay an average of 10-12 eggs/clutch and they rely heavily on foods high in protein such as aquatic invertebrates (Drobney 1980). Mergansers also consume many small fish and

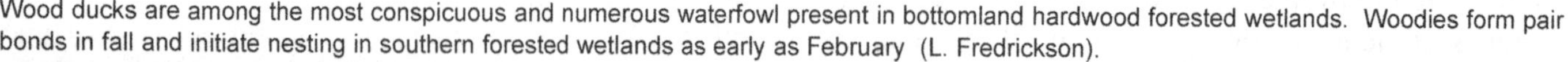

Wood ducks are among the most conspicuous and numerous waterfowl present in bottomland hardwood forested wetlands. Woodies form pair bonds in fall and initiate nesting in southern forested wetlands as early as February (L. Fredrickson).

crayfish during egg laying. In the deep South, wood ducks may lay and hatch 2 clutches in a single breeding season if water and food are abundant (Fredrickson and Hansen 1983). While both species use flooded forests during breeding, wood ducks use primarily higher elevation sites that are shallowly flooded. Here they consume large quantities of insects and crustacean invertebrates associated with detrital litter of red oaks. Hooded mergansers use deeper sites where they specialize in foraging on small crayfish and fish.

After hatching a clutch, female wood ducks and hooded mergansers take ducklings to densely vegetated sites including scrub/shrub, emergent vegetation, and watershield patches. These sites provide protection from avian and mammalian predators and usually are in areas too shallow for predatory fish such as gar, bowfin, and black bass. As ducklings grow they use many forested habitats wherever flooding occurs. Wood ducks often form roosting aggregations in summer and fall where up to several hundreds of birds spend the night in a single location. Roost sites often are characterized by scrub/shrub vegetation and within larger blocks of bottomland forest.

Low elevation sites in southern forests are flooded for extended periods and are characterized by bald cypress and tupelo trees. Old mature cypress trees have numerous natural cavities that are used as nest sites by wood ducks and hooded mergansers. In many locations, artificial nesting structures such as these wood duck boxes have been erected to supplement natural cavities and increase nesting opportunities *(L. Fredrickson).*

FEEDING AND FOODS

Waterfowl consume a wide variety of foods within southern forests. Timing of annual events described above coincides with seasonal flooding and availability of certain foods and behavioral and physiological patterns of birds reflect social and nutritional adaptations. Species tend to segregate according to trophic level food niches (Fig. 3).

Two species, hooded merganser and shoveler, are primarily carnivorous. Hooded mergansers forage extensively on crayfish, fingernail clams, frogs, salamanders and small fish. Their bill morphology facilitates capture of these animal foods and birds regularly dive to 6 feet to obtain food. Shovelers consume primarily zooplankton, aquatic insects, and snails. Their fine lamallaed bill and social foraging behaviors allow birds to stir up wetland sediments and filter small animal foods. Shovelers foraging in open marsh habitats also consume small seeds of moist-soil plants, especially in fall.

Six species are primarily herbivorous in southern forests. Gadwall and wigeon eat mainly aquatic vegetation such as coontail, water milfoil, and pondweeds. Both species eat moist-soil seeds and aquatic invertebrates where available and gadwall eat large quantities of algae during winter. Wigeon shift habitat use and foraging behavior in late winter and spring and begin to graze on new-growth sedges and grasses at the edges of wetlands and in adjacent wet uplands. The bill morphology of wigeon is similar to that of a small goose and is adapted to clip aquatic and emergent/upland plants. Ring-necked ducks consume mainly large seeds of aquatic vegetation such as watershield, water lily, and pondweeds. They also eat vegetative parts of these plants and associated aquatic insects and snails. Ring-necks regularly forage in water up to 6 feet deep and usually occur in large foraging flocks that can maintain vigilance to predators.

Canada geese, and historically, trumpeter swans, forage on roots, tubers, and plant stems in open forested wetlands. The large stout bill of geese and swans allows birds to grub and dig in the soft bottoms of these emergent wetlands. In late winter and spring, geese graze extensively on new-growth sedges, grasses, and rushes.

Two species, mallard and wood duck, are omnivorous and food selection changes from fall to spring in relation to the annual cycle event in which individual birds are engaged. Both species are opportunistic foragers when flood waters inundate floodplain forests (Heitmeyer and Fredrickson 1990a, Bellrose and Holm 1994). In general, however, mallards forage primarily beneath the water surface and on bottoms of wetlands, tend to use somewhat larger foods, and have a more northern distribution in winter than do wood ducks which tend to pick food items from the water surface, eat smaller foods, and spend winters farther south.

When mallards arrive in the South in fall they use low sites that are flooded at that time and eat large quantities of moist-soil seeds (Fig. 4). Common seeds in their fall diet include smartweed, millet, sprangletop, beggarticks, rice cutgrass, and panic grass. Many insects and aquatic invertebrates associated with herbaceous vegetation also are consumed by mallards in fall. As mallards begin courtship activities and foods in moist-soil habitats become depleted, birds move to flooded forests and crop fields (if available) where they eat high-energy acorns and waste grains. Normally, acorns do not become available until early winter when rain and river overflows flood forests. Mallard prefer the small acorns of red oaks, especially pin, cherrybark, willow, water, and Nuttall oak. During midwinter mallards eat little animal matter, but as birds become paired and initiate the prebasic molt, consumption of invertebrates increases, especially among females. By late winter, most forest habitat is flooded in most years and detrital decomposition has accelerated and produced large quantities of crustacean grazers and shredders such as amphipods, isopods, and crayfish. Mallards readily forage on these foods at this time. Floods also trap many terrestrial insects and mallard readily eat beetles, fly larvae and spiders in flood waters. Animal foods eaten by mallards in late winter provide protein needed for feather growth during the prebasic molt and also enhance catabolism and storage of lipids prior to spring migration (Heitmeyer and Fredrickson 1990b).

Figure 4. Relationships of seasonal food and habitat use of mallards in bottomland hardwood wetlands during the nonbreeding season *(modified from Heitmeyer 1985)*.

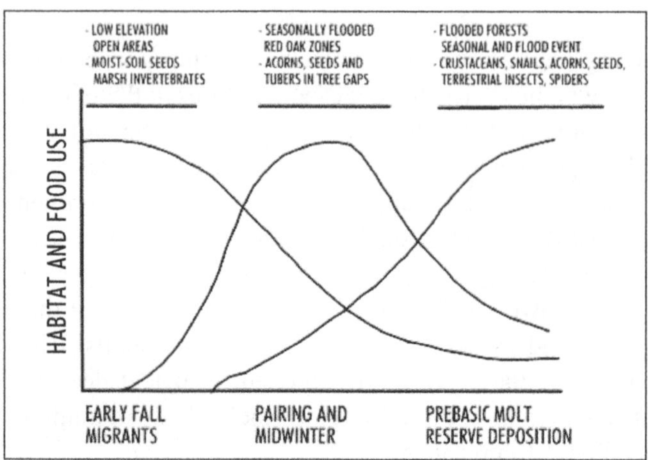

Wood ducks primarily eat foods found in flooded forests, although they occasionally will forage in herbaceous wetlands (Drobney and Fredrickson 1979, Delnicki and Reinecke 1986). Favored foods of wood ducks in winter are small acorns, drupes from tupelo trees, small crustaceans, and snails. Egg production and molt require large amounts of protein and wood ducks forage extensively on invertebrates during reproduction. Other high protein foods that wood ducks eat include maple samaras.

DISEASES

Many diseases, some of which can be lethal, have population-level impacts on waterfowl (Wobeser 1981, Friend 1987). Four diseases, avian botulism, avian cholera, lead poisoning, and duck virus enteritis (DVE) can kill large numbers of waterfowl. Other common, usually non-lethal, diseases include avian influenza, Newcastle disease, aspergillosis, and Leucocytozoon and Sarcocystis parasitic infections.

Outbreaks of botulism and cholera occur almost every year somewhere in the range of waterfowl. Botulism causes death or severe sickness in birds and the toxin of *Clostridium botulinum* type C is consumed by birds in the carcasses of maggots. Outbreaks usually occur in mid-late summer when waters warm, oxygen in the water column decreases, and water levels fluctuate. Major outbreaks and mortality are most common in large terminal basins of western North America including the Bear River marshes in Utah, Whitewater Lake in Manitoba, Old Wives Lake in Saskatchewan, and Pakoki Lake in Alberta. Botulism in southern wetlands, especially in forested systems, is rare.

Avian cholera is a bacterial infection caused by the bacterium *Pasturella multicoda*. Before 1950, cholera outbreaks in wild waterfowl were rare, but frequency of the disease and geographical distribution are increasing. Once birds contract the disease, death is rapid. Certain species such as snow geese seem especially vulnerable to cholera. DVE occurs commonly in semi-tame ducks but its status in the wild is unclear. Major DVE outbreaks have occurred in the Northern Plains, the New York finger lakes region, and certain western areas.

Sarcocystis infection is one of the more common and conspicuous parasitic conditions of ducks. The large white or yellow rice-grain like macrocysts in the breast and leg muscles of waterfowl are frequently observed by hunters. Ducks are intermediate hosts for the parasite and incidence of the disease is most common in fall among duck species consuming large quantities of invertebrates. Dabbling ducks are more prone to contract sarcocystis than are diving ducks or geese.

Waterfowl sometimes are exposed to large amounts of contaminants including lead and other heavy metals, pesticide and herbicide residues, and PCBs. Waterfowl obtain lead primarily by ingesting spent lead shot pellets (Sanderson and Bellrose 1986). Prior to the 1980s, lead shot was legally used for waterfowl hunting, and large amounts of pellets were deposited in the sediments of wetlands where duck and goose hunting occurred. Many southern wetlands, including forested types, have heavy clay soils that retard movement of pellets to lower soil layers and certain traditional hunting areas, such as Catahoula Lake, continue to have large amounts of lead in soil sediments even though lead shot has not been used for many years. In these locations, waterfowl still die or have reduced body mass from consumption of lead pellets (Hohman et al. 1990). Legal restriction on use of lead shot for waterfowl hunting began in the late 1970s, and by the mid 1980s lead shot was illegal for waterfowl hunting in the U.S. Recently, lead shot also has been banned for waterfowl hunting in Canada. Now, only alternative shot such as steel, tungsten, and bismuth is used for waterfowl hunting.

Waterfowl are exposed to other contaminants by consuming benthic invertebrates and plants that contain high concentration of chemicals. For example, bivalves such as zebra mussels that are readily consumed by some ducks filter large amounts of water and biomagnify contaminant residues. Rice seeds often are coated, or mixed, with pesticides and herbicides when seeded in spring and waterfowl migrating through rice production areas in late spring occasionally are exposed to heavy concentrations of insecticides. Formerly, birds were exposed to very toxic substances used in agricultural production including aldrin, dieldrin, DDT, and carbofuran. Labeling and distribution restrictions on these chemicals has eliminated or greatly reduced agricultural use and subsequent exposure to waterfowl.

INTERACTION WITH OTHER SPECIES

Many birds and mammals, and a few fish and reptiles, prey on waterfowl in southern forests. Predation on ducks and geese is relatively low during the nonbreeding season, but high during nesting and brood rearing periods.

Primary avian predators on waterfowl from fall through spring include large buteos, accipiters, falcons, owls, and eagles. Small ducks such as teal and shoveler often are caught by birds of prey, but even large species such as mallard, wigeon, gadwall, and black duck occasionally are caught by goshawk, peregrine falcon, great horned owl, and golden eagle. Harriers and red-tailed hawks usually only prey on injured or sick waterfowl and bald eagles primarily scavenge carcasses and injured ducks and geese. Mammals including red and gray fox, bobcat, coyote, mink, and raccoon occasionally prey on waterfowl in winter, but they are not adept at catching birds and predation is mostly opportunistic. Alligators occasionally catch waterfowl, but predation is limited during colder winter months when gators are relatively torpid.

In contrast to nonbreeding periods and migrant species, breeding wood ducks and hooded mergansers are exposed to numerous predators in the South. Nests and eggs of both species are actively sought by black rat snake, raccoon, mink and certain avian predators. In spring and summer many potential nest predators forage in the forest floor and ground nesting birds experience high nest loss. Consequently, wood ducks and hooded mergansers escape much nest predation by nesting in tree cavities. Even Canada geese, which seldom leave nests during incubation and are large enough to fend off most predators, historically avoided nesting on the ground and selected nest sites over water in stumps and on islands and hummocks.

Ducklings and goslings are favored food of many predators including alligators, snapping turtles, black bass, chain pickerel, gar, bowfin, great blue heron, hawks, owls, otter, mink, raccoon, fox, and coyote. Most predation on ducklings occurs during the first 2 weeks after hatch; by the time ducklings are a month old they are larger, more mobile, and have learned escape behaviors and safe habitats. Nonetheless, larger

Waterfowl forage on a diverse array of natural foods in southern forests including acorns, invertebrates, and seeds from annual and perennial "moist-soil" plants such as this wild millet and sprangletop. Mallards use small openings in southern forests extensively for foraging sites, and also as thermal cover and courtship locations *(M. Heitmeyer)*.

ducklings are caught by several animals especially owls.

Waterfowl also interact with other animals in southern forests in many indirect, non-predatory ways. Tree cavities used by nesting ducks are formed from the actions of insects, woodpeckers, raccoons, and squirrels. Beavers alter hydrology of bottomland drainage and can significantly change habitats and waterfowl use in an area. In many locations, beaver dams restrict water flow and inundate drier forest sites which then become heavily used by ducks in fall and winter. Over time and continued flooding by beaver dams, however, trees such as red oaks that are not highly water-tolerant in the growing season die. These "beaver ponds" become relatively open and dominated by water-tolerant trees and shrubs such as bald cypress, water privet, and buttonbush. Reduced shading and more permanent water stimulates growth of aquatic plants and algae and beaver ponds become especially attractive to gadwall and wigeon. Beaver lodges also are used as nest sites by Canada geese in scattered locations.

A variety of birds, wild hogs, deer, squirrel, and other species consume certain foods that also are eaten by waterfowl in southern forests. Foods such as acorns often are abundant and competition between species usually is minimal. Furthermore, waterfowl seldom forage for acorns on dry ground and they consume acorns when bottomlands are flooded; a time when these habitats are not heavily used by other animals. In open habitats, seeds and invertebrates associated with annual and perennial plants are usually abundant in fall and competition among rails, herons, shorebirds, and waterfowl is probably minimal. However, when seed or acorn production is low and few sites are flooded in fall and winter, competition for food probably occurs to some degree among waterfowl and other species. Gadwall and wigeon also occasionally will steal aquatic plants brought to the water surface by coots.

MANAGEMENT

Because most waterfowl in North America are migratory and they use habitats that are distributed throughout the continent, management of populations necessarily occurs at broad geographic scales. Traditionally, waterfowl conservation has concentrated on: 1) protecting, restoring, and managing habitats; 2) regulating sport harvest; 3) managing disease outbreaks; 4) regulating pollution of habitats; 5) managing predators; and 6) propagating and translocating rarer species (Sanderson and Bellrose 1969, Sanderson 1980).

Many agencies and entities affect management of waterfowl and their habitats. In 1986, a North American Waterfowl Management Plan (NAWMP) was developed by U.S. and Canadian governments. This plan established population goals for species and advocated habitat-based programs using private-public partnerships (Canadian Wildlife Service and U.S. Fish and Wildlife Service 1986). Recent updates to the NAWMP refined population and habitat goals and included Mexico as a signatory. A series of "Joint Ventures" comprised of state, federal, and private conservation groups have been formed in priority geographical areas. The principal Joint Venture covering southern forested wetlands is the Lower Mississippi Valley Joint Venture which includes states from Illinois to Louisiana and Texas to Alabama. Forested wetlands along the Atlantic Coast are part of the Atlantic Coast Joint Venture.

Harvest management is a primary means used to control annual survival of waterfowl. Waterfowl hunting regulations in the U.S. are under federal jurisdiction in accordance with the Migratory Bird Treaty Act of 1917. State laws define specific regulations within federal constraints. In the U.S., Flyway Councils representing states of the four major migration corridors used by waterfowl (Atlantic, Mississippi, Central, Pacific) meet each year to review status of populations and habitats, harvest rates, and other management considerations. The Councils recommend hunting regulations to a national regulations committee comprised of representatives from the U.S. Fish and Wildlife Service which makes final regulations recommendations published in the Federal Register. Upon receipt and consideration of public comment, these regulations are promulgated into laws governing bag limits, season length, frameworks for season periods, and special considerations. Currently harvest recommendations are developed in an "adaptive harvest management" context (Johnson et al. 1997).

Habitat management for waterfowl attempts to secure resources needed by populations throughout the annual cycle. Conservation of broad regional wetland complexes throughout North America is key to sustaining populations. Active management is often needed to restore or protect ecological processes and functions, maintain complexes of diverse habitats and foods, and integrate multiple species considerations (Laubhan and Fredrickson 1993, Heitmeyer et al. 1996). In southern forests, habitat management includes protection of remnant forest tracts, restoration of degraded or deforested areas, and enhancement of existing resources with timber, water, and food manipulations.

Restoration of bottomland forests is accomplished by encouraging natural regeneration with timber stand improvements, direct seeding of acorns or planting seedlings, and manipulating water with levees and water control structures and conveyances (Newling 1990). Opportunities for reforestation typically are best where hydric soils are present, in lower sites conducive to seasonal flooding, and where remnant forest patches are adjacent or nearby. Because there has been substantial reduction of red oak stands on higher bottomland sites, there are efforts to establish new red oak stands (especially pin, willow, Nuttall and water oaks). Also, restoration efforts prioritize areas where forest stands are sparse and "gaps" in riparian or interior forest corridors are present (Haynes et al. 1995).

Water management is fundamental to managing southern forests for waterfowl. Unfortunately, extensive alterations to forest hydrology have been caused by levees, land leveling, water diversions and channelization of rivers, bank stabilization, dredging, and agricultural pumping and runoff. Management of regional forested basins must address these serious and often large-scale problems. Where possible, cooperative agreements to manage rivers, reservoirs, ditches, and levees for seasonal flooding of southern forests for waterfowl have been developed with levee and drainage districts, the U.S. Army Corps of Engineers, and other water authorities. However, in most sites managers cannot control large-scale regional hydrology and they must use on-site manipulations including construction of levees and water control structures, trapping and releasing of water, and pumping or diversion of water (Reinecke et al. 1989, Nassar et al. 1993).

Greentree reservoirs (GTR) are a special type of southern forest managed for waterfowl. In a GTR, bottomland forests are purposefully flooded from fall through late winter or spring to increase habitat availability for migrating and wintering ducks, especially

Duck hunting is an important activity in the South. Annually, about half of the U.S. total harvest comes from about ½ million southern hunters *(J. Dickson)*.

wood ducks and mallards (Fredrickson and Batema 1993). Usually, a levee surrounds part or all of the forest patch in a GTR and water control structures allow water manipulation. In GTRs, tree clearing, mowing, strip planting of certain foods, and timber stand improvement are used to enhance food production. In most areas, management of GTRs seeks to maximize red oak stands and small acorn production from pin, cherrybark, willow, Nuttall, and water oaks. Gradual flooding of GTRs in fall and removal of water in late winter is used to provide shallow foraging zones for ducks and make foods most available during critical times.

In southern forests managed for waterfowl habitats, many practices are used to improve regeneration of desirable tree species, increase acorn production, enhance moist-soil plants and seeds in open gaps, improve stand vigor and sustain desirable tree and understory composition. Southern forests are dynamic ecosystems and flooding and drying cycles occur naturally. Consequently, management seeks to emulate hydrological periodicities and dynamics. By avoiding prolonged flooding, naturally occurring tree composition can be maintained and stand decadence averted. Maintaining some old-age stands of oaks is desirable to maintain detrital bases, cavities for nesting, and acorn production.

Open areas in forests often are managed as seasonally flooded "moist-soil" impoundments (Fredrickson and Taylor 1982). Moist-soil impoundments typically have low levees and water control structures that allow manipulation of water to establish desirable annual and perennial plants that produce foods for waterfowl. Herbaceous vegetation in impoundments is periodically manipulated by discing, mowing, burning, rolling, and flooding. By varying timing of water removal in spring and flooding in summer and fall, managers can establish dense stands of high food production plants like millet, smartweed, sprangletop, panic grass, rice cutgrass, chufa, spikerush, and beggarticks. Water and soil manipulation is also used to control succession of woody invasive and problem plants like cottonwood, Chinese tallow tree, salt cedar, willow, sesbania, marsh mallow, cocklebur, aster, thistle, and joint vetch.

Agricultural fields often are managed for waterfowl in the South. Harvested fields can be flooded by building small levees and dikes to trap flood and rain waters or by pumping. Rice fields often can be flooded more easily than other crop fields because rice levees and drainage controls are present. Crop vegetation and soils can be manipulated to increase food availability to waterfowl by burning, rolling, and discing prior to flooding. Federal laws govern manipulation of agricultural vegetation and seeds, and normal production practices must be used to avoid "baiting" violations (Elkins 1996).

HUNTING

Large numbers of sportsmen avidly hunt waterfowl in the southern U.S. The traditions of duck hunting in the South run deep and are often symbolized by the sight of a flock of mallards banking to a hunters high-ball call and falling through flooded timber on a clear crisp winter day.

In the 14 southern states of North and South Carolina, Florida, Georgia, Alabama, Mississippi, Tennessee, Kentucky, Illinois, Missouri, Arkansas, Louisiana, Texas, and Oklahoma where the majority of forested wetlands occur, approximately 460,000 adult hunters pursued waterfowl in the 1995-96 season (Martin and Padding 1996). These hunters represented 34% of the 1.34 million total U.S. adult hunters in that year. Southern waterfowl hunters spent 4.6 million days afield for an average of 10 days/afield per season for each hunter in 1995-96. Total days afield by U.S. waterfowl hunters in that year was almost 12 million days.

Not only do southern hunters spend many days afield hunting waterfowl, but they also are highly successful. In 1995-96, hunters in the 14 southern states harvested approximately 6.3 million ducks and 830,000 geese (Martin and Padding 1996). These numbers represented 50% and 35% of the total U.S. harvest of ducks (12.6 million) and geese (2.3 million), respectively. Mallards were the most commonly harvested duck in 8 of the 14 states. Wood ducks were the most harvested species in Georgia and North and South Carolina. Ring-necked ducks, gadwall, and blue-winged teal were the most harvested species in Florida, Alabama, and Texas, respectively. Green-winged teal were among the top 3 species in the harvest in 7 states. Most goose harvest occurred in Arkansas, Illinois, Louisiana, and Texas. Canada geese were the most harvested goose in Illinois while lesser snow geese comprised the majority of the goose harvest in Arkansas, Louisiana, and Texas.

CHAPTER 18

American Black Bear

Michael R. Pelton (retired)
Department of Forestry, Wildlife, & Fisheries
University of Tennessee, Knoxville, TN

The American black bear is the most common of the 8 bear species of the world. The North American population exceeds 600,000, with most states and provinces currently reporting stable to increasing numbers (Pelton et al. 1994). Previously, significant land use changes, primarily in the lower 48 states, have resulted in shrinkage of occupied range to approximately 62% of the historic continental range (Pelton and van Manen 1994). The species has been extirpated from some Midwestern and eastern states, and other states have only remnant populations (Pelton 1982). In the South, over 90% of the species' historic range has disappeared, primarily due to intensive agricultural activities (Wooding et al. 1994). Hall (1981) lists 16 subspecies, of which 3 occur in the South. Because of fragmented habitats in the southeastern coastal plain, 2 of the 3 subspecies are listed or proposed for listing, (*Ursus a. luteous* and *U. a. floridanus*), by the U.S. Fish and Wildlife Service (USFWS) under the federal Endangered Species Act (Wooding et al. 1994). In addition, the U.S. Forest Service has designated black bears as a potential management indicator species (MIS) on most national forests in the southern Appalachians.

HISTORY

Human attitudes toward bears have varied from mortal fear, hate, and caution to respect and even reverence

(Cahalane 1947, Raybourne 1987). Because they are plantigrade (walks on soles of feet), bears were often described as "the beast that walks like a man" (Kolenosky and Strathearn 1987). Their intelligence, size, secretive behavior, strength, speed, and imagined ferocity are other attributes that have attracted the interest of humans for thousands of years. Most Native Americans treated black bears with great respect. Many tribes accorded human attributes to them. Black bears often were incorporated into rituals and ceremonies, or made into effigies or objects of respect and worship. However, the species was used for practical purposes as well, such as meat for food, fur for clothing, bones as tools, and fat for cooking, tanning hides, and waterproofing (Raybourne 1987).

The onslaught of white settlers into the South changed the picture for both Native Americans and black bears (Shropshire 1996). The first settlers in the 1700s, like Native Americans, hunted black bears for their meat and skins. As more settlers poured into the region, bears and bear habitat receded quickly. As the once occasional small slash and burn clearings became too numerous and extensive, black bears began to disappear. Instead of a respected provider of food and other amenities, the species was quickly relegated to pest status as a competitor for space and food such as corn fields, gardens, and livestock. Its vermin status persisted well into the 20th century. The first areas to be heavily settled and cleared for agriculture were the Piedmont and Ridge and Valley physiographic provinces. In the Piedmont, because of relatively fertile soils and flatter terrain, most of the region was cleared for cotton. The settlement of fertile valleys of Tennessee, Virginia, Kentucky and other states closely followed. By the early 1900s bears were present only in the more remote mountain and swamp habitats of the South. Not only did the species suffer from extensive land clearing and overharvest, the chestnut blight removed a prime source of fall food in mountain areas. Fortunately, the creation of national parks, forests, and wildlife refuges in the early 1900s was the turning point for recovery of this species. Today, black bears in the South are regarded as a game animal, charismatic megafauna, or landscape/management indicator species.

Even as adults, black bears are excellent tree climbers. Whether feeding on serviceberry and catkins of a variety of tree species in spring, cherries in summer, or oak mast in fall, they spend considerable time and energy climbing trees *(M. Pelton)*.

DESCRIPTION

Although black bears exhibit a variety of colors ranging from solid black to brown and even white (coastal British Columbia), the southeastern black bear is normally solid black with a brownish muzzle and an occasional white chest blaze. Within the South there is considerable phenotypic variability in terms of body size, depending on location and seasonal or annual food supplies (Eason 1995). Average summer weights of adult females range from less than 100 pounds in the southern Appalachian mountains to greater than 150 pounds on the North Carolina coast (Maddrey 1995, McLean and Pelton 1990). Variability in summer weights of adult males can be even more dramatic, ranging from less than 200 pounds to greater than 400 pounds. Fall weights can increase by 30% or greater. Black bears are omnivorous; are plantigrade; have a keen sense of smell and hearing; are intelligent; have a compact body structure; and have strong, short recurved claws (Pelton 1982, Kolenosky and Strathearn 1987). All of these adaptations benefit the species in negotiating typical southern habitats, in enabling them to feed, to den or take refuge in large trees, or to escape into thick pocosin swamps or mountain laurel thickets.

DISTRIBUTION AND STATUS

Because the Piedmont and Ridge and Valley provinces became so heavily developed in the late 1700s and early 1800s, and largely have remained so, black bears still do not inhabit these regions; only occasionally dispersing bears pass through from occupied habitats of the Coastal Plain or Mountains. Consequently, since the 19th century, the South has had two relatively disjunct bear ranges, split by the Piedmont. In the Mountains, 9 national forests (Jefferson, Cherokee, Pisgah, Nantahala, Chattahoochee, Sumpter, Ouachita, and Ozark) and 2 national parks, (Shenandoah and Great Smoky Mountains) make up the bulk of the occupied habitat (over 70% of all bear range is on public land). Coastal habitats are predominantly private lands (76%) with interspersed public lands serving as reservoir populations and playing an important stabilizing role (for example, Great Dismal Swamp, Alligator River, White River, Tensas River, and Okefenokee National Wildlife Refuges and Oseola, Ocala, and Appalachicola National Forests) (Wooding et al. 1994). Healthy and expanding populations are currently found in the mountains: the Allegany and Blue Ridge Mountains of Virginia, the southern Appalachians of Tennessee, North Carolina, Georgia, and South Carolina, the Ouachita and Ozark mountains of Arkansas, and in the coastal areas of North Carolina and Southeast Virginia. Range expansion has been noted on the fringes of these populations. For example, eastern Oklahoma and southern Missouri are reporting increased numbers of bears immigrating from Arkansas populations. Kentucky and Ohio report more bears dispersing into their states from Virginia and West Virginia. North Carolina and Virginia report increased numbers of bears moving along river corridors from the mountains and coastal plain into Piedmont habitats.

Bear populations are not doing as well in the Coastal Plain due to extreme habitat fragmentation (Hellgren and Vaughan 1994, Pelton and van Manen 1994). Black bears in East Texas, Louisiana, Mississippi, Alabama, Georgia, and Florida are regarded to be in jeopardy by the USFWS. A Recovery Plan is currently being implemented for the Louisiana black bear (Bullock 1993, USDI 1995).

One of the most successful efforts to reintroduce a carnivore was the reintroduction of 254 black bears from Minnesota and Canada into the Ozark and Ouachita mountains of Arkansas (Smith and Clark 1994). The success of this effort has given hope for reintroducing the species into other southern habitats. An experimental reintroduction is currently underway on the Big South Fork National River and Recreation Area and adjacent Daniel Boone National Forest in the Appalachian Highlands of Tennessee and Kentucky (Eastridge and Clark 1998). The Virginia Game Commission also introduced more than 100 bears into the Mt. Rogers area of Southwest Virginia to reestablish a population.

In 1970, a regional estimate of bear numbers from all southern states was less than 4,000, with Virginia estimating a high of 1,300 bears and Kentucky reporting an estimate of only 25 animals (Pelton and Nichols 1972) (Table 1). At that time Virginia was the only state attempting to census their bear population in a quantitative manner and North Carolina was the only state collecting data other than harvest information. However, 5 states (North Carolina, Georgia, Tennessee, Virginia, and Florida) had initiated research projects on their respective bear populations. In 1996, the regional population estimate of black bears was approximately 20,000. All 11 states currently have active bear management programs, which include the collection of baseline harvest data, the development of population management strategies, preparation of information—education materials, and research (Pelton et al. 1994).

HARVEST

Legal annual harvest of black bears in North America exceeds 42,000; this represents less than 10% of the known continental population (Vaughan and Pelton 1995). Bear hunting occurs in 6 of the 11 southern states (Virginia, Tennessee, North Carolina, South Carolina, Georgia, and Arkansas). Seasons vary but are restricted to the fall and start as early as 19 September (Georgia) and occur as late as 1 January (North Carolina and Virginia). The most restrictive season is in South Carolina lasting only 12 days. North Carolina has the most lengthy season, occurring from 9 November to 1 January in various parts of the state. Arkansas and North Georgia allow still hunting only. The other 4 states (Tennessee, Virginia, North Carolina, and South Carolina) and south Georgia allow the use of dogs. Baiting is prohibited in all 6 states (Pelton et al. 1994). The level of harvest increased from 628 in 1970 to 2,018 in 1996, about 10% of the total estimated population of black bears in the South (Table 1). Although

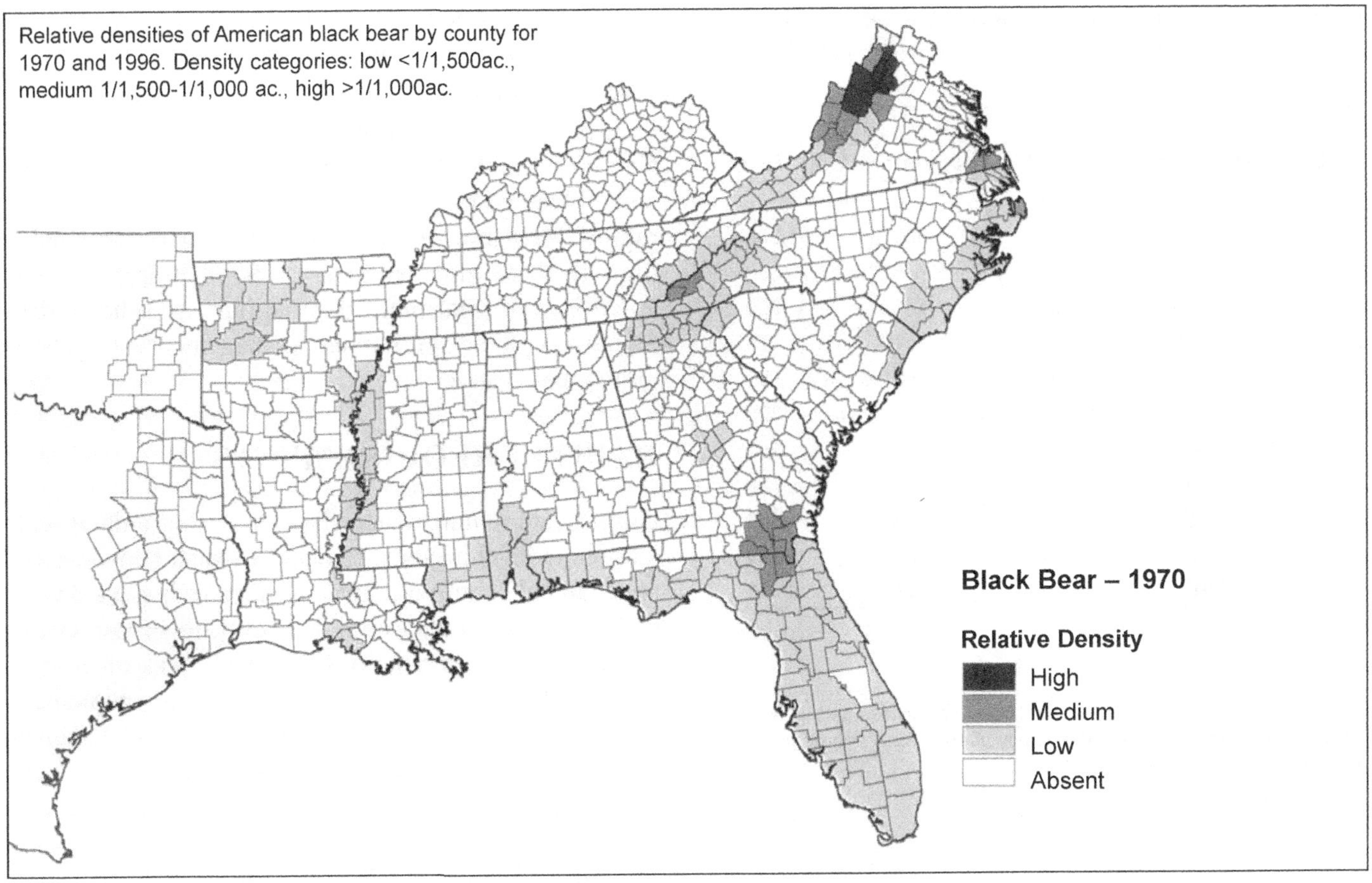

Relative densities of American black bear by county for 1970 and 1996. Density categories: low <1/1,500ac., medium 1/1,500-1/1,000 ac., high >1/1,000ac.

Black Bear – 1970

Relative Density
High
Medium
Low
Absent

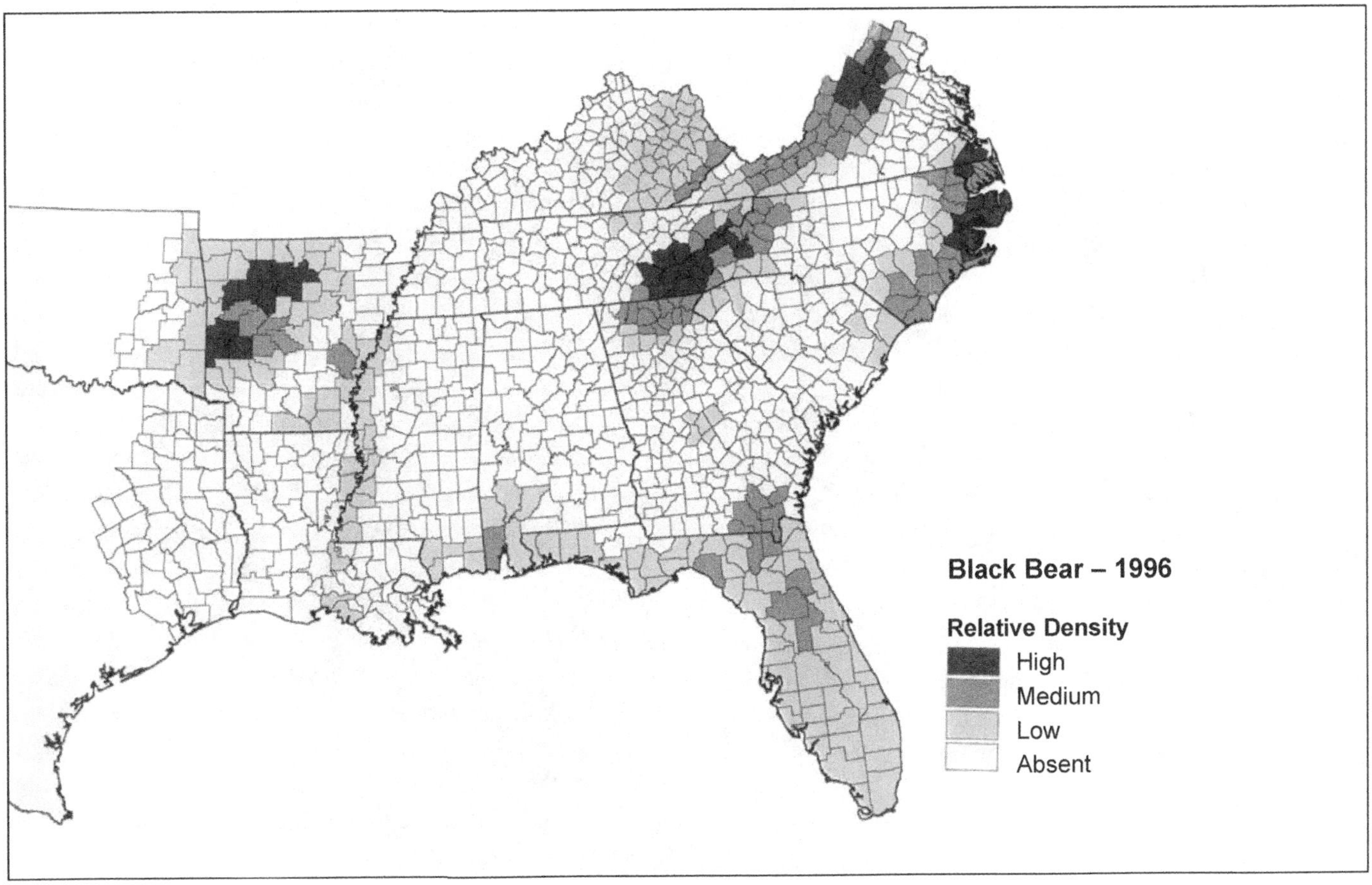

Black Bear – 1996

Relative Density
High
Medium
Low
Absent

Table 1. Population estimates and harvest of black bears in the South, 1970 and 1996 (From Nichols and Pelton (1972) and other sources).

State	1996 Harvest	1996 Pop. Est.	1970 Harvest	1970 Pop. Est.
KY	0	100	0	25
VA	602	4,000	326	1,300
TN	81	900	0	350
NC	1,000	8,000	171	900
SC	12	300	1	75
GA	0	1,500	50	500
FL	0	300	0	300
AL	0	50	0	150
MS	0	20	0	50
AR	133	2,500	0	50
LA	190	2,150	80	295
Totals:	**2,018**	**19,820**	**628**	**3,995**

Female black bears generally select large tree cavities as a preferred winter denning site. The security of such sites affords good protection for newborn cubs *(F. VanManen)*.

black bear populations vary in their sensitivity to harvest (Vaughan and Pelton 1995), populations in Virginia, most of the southern Appalachians (Tennessee, North Carolina, Georgia), coastal North Carolina, and the Arkansas mountains can likely sustain annual harvest rates from 20 to 25% as long as the sex ratio of the harvest is approximately equal. For populations that are more vulnerable (South Carolina), and emerging or marginal populations in other areas (Kentucky, Florida) harvest management should be more conservative.

HABITAT REQUIREMENTS

Black bears require space. They are a big animal with landscape-level needs in terms of food and cover. They are adaptable omnivores and can survive in a wide variety of habitats in the South. However, to sustain viable and harvestable populations, forested areas of at least 150 to 300 square miles with low to no permanent human populations are needed (Hellgren and Vaughan 1994, Rudis and Tansey 1995). In the mountains, vari-

Cavities in large trees offer the best winter denning locations for black bears. Such sites are usually dry, well-insulated, and protected from disturbances *(M. Pelton)*.

ous succulent herbaceous plants, catkins, and buds in diverse mesic to semiaquatic habitats are important in Spring. Squawroot, a parasitic plant growing on the roots of oak trees, is an important food consumed in spring (Beeman and Pelton 1977). Colonial insects such as ants, and other invertebrates found under rocks or rotten logs also are important. During summer more open and drier sites provide a wide variety of berry crops, such as blueberry, blackberry, huckleberry and raspberry. Yellowjackets also can be an important source of summer protein. Hardwood stands dominated by red and white oak are important in fall along with secondary species such as wild cherry, grapes, and pokeweed.

Coastal habitats are highly variable and range from pocosins (Hellgren et al. 1991), to bottomland hardwoods (Weaver et al. 1990), to Carolina bays (Landers et al. 1979), to cypress gum and mixed bay swamps (Mykytka and Pelton 1990), to pine flatwoods and sand pine scrub (Wooding and Hardisky 1994), and finally to mesic stands of various oak species (Hellgren and Vaughan 1994). Berry and nut crops also are the most important foods in the coastal plain and include tupelo, pawpaw, palmetto berries, greenbriar, pokeweed, and various species of gallberry. An occasional armadillo adds protein to their diet. In some locales bears feed on and sometimes are dependent on agricultural crops such as corn, wheat or soybeans (Maddrey 1995).

Black bears need thick, almost impenetrable, understory cover as a component of their habitat. The combined effects of steep terrain and laurel thickets provide such cover in the mountains. Swampy environments and various understory species such as greenbriar, or titi forming thick, vegetation provide similar refuge cover in the coastal plain.

Winter denning habitat also is important to black bears in the South where lack of snow cover makes concealment more difficult. Female bears, particularly pregnant females, den for longer periods and are more selective of the den they choose; they prefer cavities in large trees (Pelton et al. 1977). When old trees are not available, bears are flexible enough to den on the ground; however, they still prefer the cover afforded by the root masses, logs or stumps of downed large trees. Where no large trees or other permanent objects (rock crevices) are present, they typically choose thick understory cover and build a nest (Hamilton and Marchinton 1980). If the female is pregnant and has the security of a cavity in an old tree, she may den for over 4 months (Johnson and Pelton 1981). This period of relative inactivity is critical, particularly for females and cubs because they are more susceptible to disturbance. In Arkansas, south Georgia, Louisiana, and Florida, females den for shorter periods and some males move from one nest site to another, never settling down (Weaver and Pelton 1992). Whatever their sex, age or reproductive status, adequate denning cover in the form of large, old trees; rock outcroppings; or secure, impenetrable thickets is a necessary component of black bear habitat in the South.

Black bears need secure corridors to make seasonal movements for food, for dispersal movements of younger animals, or for movements by males during the breeding season (Anderson 1997). Corridors need to be uninterrupted by human activities or developments and adequate in width and understory vegetation to conceal the movements of animals (Weaver et al. 1990).

ECOLOGICAL RELATIONSHIPS

The long growing season and warm and humid climate of the South provide black bears with a luxurious and diverse plant life for food and cover. However, these necessities vary both in quantity and quality, by season and region. Although they are taxonomically carnivores and functionally omnivores, in reality black bears exist primarily as herbivores. They depend on berries and nuts to provide the nutrition and energy necessary for maintenance and growth. Most of their movements and activities center around food searching and gathering and use of cover to do so. The seasonal and annual variation in nut and berry crops dictates the dynamics of bear populations in the South. Fall is the most critical period when physiological, behavioral, and ecological adaptations occur. Their ability to digest high energy foods efficiently, their focus on specific energy rich foods, and their shift in home range to accommodate such foods allows them to gain weight in the form of fat prior to winter denning (Pelton 1989). During periods of food scarcity, bears are stimulated to move more and, therefore, become more vulnerable to mortality via road kills, nuisance control, or illegal hunting. Also, during years of low food production or failure, female black bears may not successfully reproduce (Eiler et al. 1989). The fertilized eggs may not implant, or the fetuses are resorbed, aborted, or neonates die (Vaughan, per. comm.). If food is adequate, pregnant females give birth in mid-January to mid February while in dens. Without substantial fat, younger animals and females nursing cubs may become malnourished to the point of starvation. The normal litter size is 2 (range 1-5), age of first reproduction is 4, and litters are produced every 2 years. However, this scenario can be disrupted by a poor year of food production and result in a decrease or delay in these events. Survival rates are high if energy needs are met (Eiler et al. 1989).

Females are relatively sedentary compared to males. Sizes of home ranges vary according to habitat quality. Home ranges of females range from 2 to 15 square miles; male ranges are 3 to 5 times larger than this (Hellgren and Vaughan 1990, Kasbohm, et al. 1997, Wooding and Hardisky 1994, Smith and Pelton 1989, Garshelis and Pelton 1981, Warburton and Powell 1985). The home range of one adult male can encompass the home ranges of several females. A dominant adult is capable of breeding with several females in an area. It is not unusual to find fresh battle wounds on males during the summer breeding season when they are competing for females in estrus. Dominant adult males may play a role in causing the dispersal of subadult males. Thus, a form of population regulation and genetic and demographic mixing is assured. Black bears normally are crepuscular but can adjust their activity patterns to local conditions such as human activities and food sources (Garshelis and Pelton 1980).

Black bears are opportunistic predators, only occasionally taking advantage of easily available prey such as deer fawns or newborn domestic livestock. They are more likely to feed on the carrion of these and other species. Black bears have few non-human predators. Females are protective of their cubs until dispersal occurs at 1½ years of age. Most mortality in a black bear population takes place in this subadult age group or until they are 4-5 years old. Predation by older male bears and malnutrition are the 2 most common forms of natural mortality. During years of scarce fall foods, young bears may not consume enough calories for both growth and maintenance and consequently succumb to starvation, or be predisposed to other kinds of mortality due to their poor condition. Very old black bears (over 15-20 years old) may become malnourished due to extreme tooth wear and deterioration, thus preventing them from foraging efficiently in fall prior to denning. Few significant diseases have been reported for black bears. They have their usual array of ecto and endo parasites, none of which cause serious problems (Crum 1977, Cook and Pelton 1979). Severe cases of mange (demodicosis) have been reported in a small number of bears from Florida (Forrester et al. 1993). Heart worms occur in a high percentage of black bears but apparently are no serious hazard to the species (Cook and Pelton 1979). Most mortality is caused by humans in the form of hunting, poaching, depredation control, and road kills.

SPECIAL CONSIDERATIONS

The primary threat to black bears is habitat degradation or loss. On private lands, conversion of forests to agriculture or other more permanent developments, such as subdivisions and golf courses, obviously decreases available bear habitat. Fragmentation of large blocks of forests into separate and smaller parcels with associated permanent human occupation ultimately results in extirpation of the species. Consequently, black bears can be a sensitive indicator of these, often cumulative, habitat changes. In areas where the species occurs in a mosaic of forest and farm lands, conversion of agricultural crops from corn, wheat or soybeans to cotton, and conversion of forest lands to pine monocultures can result

Where adequate escape cover is available, some agriculture crops such as wheat and corn are an attraction to black bears *(D. Martorello)*.

in significant population declines. The species needs a mosaic of diverse forest habitat types on a landscape scale with limited human intrusions. Agricultural crops integrated into the forest system can be a positive factor if the crops are edible and not too extensive. Access management is extremely important for this species. Some form of a sanctuary can have a stabilizing influence on the population by protecting a nucleus of breeding age females. Some "sanctuaries" are created defacto naturally and simply by topographic features of the landscape; rough, steep mountain slopes and thick pocosin swamps are 2 good examples. Artificial sanctuaries can either be officially designated tracts of land as in Tennessee and North Carolina (Sanders 1978, Warburton 1984) or unofficial designations by gating roads.

As human populations increase and expand into or around occupied bear habitat, roads become a problem for bears (Brandenburg 1996). Increased incidents of road kills are being reported in North Carolina, Tennessee, and Florida (Wooding and Brady 1987, Warburton et al. 1993). Advances in hunting techniques (4-wheel drive vehicles, CB radios or car phones, radio collared hunting dogs), combined with increased access capabilities can result in over-exploitation. As the gypsy moth moves southward through the Appalachians, oaks are being killed (Kasbohm et al. 1994). The short-term impacts of this pest invasion do not seem to be too detri-

Increasing human populations and the concomitant road network to accommodate expanding developments has led to road kills as an increasing cause of direct mortality and indirectly decreases the carrying capacity of an area for black bears *(T. Allen)*.

mental to bears but the long-term impacts may lower the carrying capacity for bears in the southern Appalachians (Kasbohm et al. 1996).

MANAGEMENT

There are 8 basic components to good black bear management: human access, habitat, protection, nuisance control, information- education, harvest, monitoring, and research.

1) Human Access-Through road gating, designation of no-hunt zones, or perpetuation of natural escape cover, black bears are provided refugia. 2) Habitat-Habitat management can be broken into 3 subunits: oak forests, old growth, and forest openings. Because of the dependence of black bears on oak mast in fall, silvicultural manipulations should promote the perpetuation, regeneration and maintenance of diverse and mature oak forests. Secure dens in the form of large old trees should also be available; this means old growth management, leaving what old trees are presently in the system and providing for future old trees. Also, thinning in closed canopy forests or small clear-cut should be used to enhance production of berries. 3) Protection-Whether for prestige or monetary gain, illegal hunting of black bears is a reality, and an insidious and continuing problem in the South. Because of the potential for overharvest, this species needs the constant attention of law enforcement. Operation Smoky in 1988 in the Smoky Mountains resulted in the arrest of over 40 individuals involved in the illegal killing of bears or sale of bear parts. 4) Nuisance control-As black bear populations grow in response to positive management actions, nuisance control becomes more important. Damage to agricultural crops (corn and wheat) or apiaries is an historical problem in or near black bear habitat in the South (Wooding et al. 1988, Clark et al. 1991). Too often, at the same time the bear population is increasing, more people also are moving into bear habitat or along its fringes. Concomitant with this increasing human population is an increase in backyard birdfeeders, dogfeeders, and motel dumpsters. Dealing with nuisance bears becomes a critical and important part of bear management because it is highly visible to the public. The proper disposition of a nuisance animal is not an easy or pleasant task. 5) Information-education-A big part of the success of any bear program depends on an educated public through information-education. Historically, a lot of misinformation has been perpetuated about black bears. This species evokes a lot of emotions in people, both positive and negative. Therefore, a strong information - education program is essential for a successful nuisance control program. 6) Harvest-Black bear populations can be affected quickly by changes in harvest regulations. Season length, harvest limits, and timing of seasons are critical. Later fall seasons, light hunting

As black bear populations grow and expand, a few individuals cause problems where garbage or other foods are not secured in bearproof containers *(J. Clark)*.

pressure, and still hunting all tend to protect a larger portion of females in a population (Kolenosky and Strathearn 1987). With increased access and hunting pressure, females become more vulnerable. Overharvest can occur if too many adult females are removed. However, this technique can also be used for population control, but management agencies should be aware that overharvested populations may take years to recover. 7) Monitoring-This species requires some form of annual monitoring, particularly marginal or vulnerable populations. As an example, the Southern Appalachian Black Bear Study Group (a consortium of state and federal wildlife agencies) is currently monitoring black bears using a variety of annual indicators: harvest records, bait stations, nuisance complaints, road kills, and soft and hard mast surveys. All of these records are compiled annually to assess the status of populations and potential responses of the populations to habitat changes. 8) Research-Information from research is necessary for management of this species. Long-term data can prove useful in making rational management decisions, developing more refined and sensitive models, fine tuning and improving monitoring programs, and providing more accurate predictions of population responses to various perturbations (Pelton and van Manen 1996).

HUNTING

The South is rich in the tradition of bear hunting. The tales of Daniel Boone and Davy Crockett and black bears are legendary. These famous frontiersmen were followed into the early 20th century by the exploits of Ben Lilly and Teddy Roosevelts now famous bear hunt in the bottomland hardwoods of Mississippi and Louisiana. The famous writer William Faulkner helped immortalize bear hunting in the South with his story The Bear. The tradition of hunting black bears in the mountains and swamps of the South continues today. In recent years some methods of hunting, such as spring hunting, baiting, and use of hounds, have come under increasing criticism in other parts of the United States. Baiting and spring hunting are not controversial since neither is legal in any southern state. Dog hunting is legal in Virginia, Tennessee, North Carolina, South Carolina, and south Georgia. To date use of hounds for bear hunting in these states has not been an issue. In fact Tennessee and Virginia have recently legalized an early chase (training) season for bears; North Carolina, and Georgia already have this practice in place.

CONCLUSIONS/PROSPECTS FOR FUTURE

All the southern states report stable or increasing bear populations (Pelton and van Manen 1997). In general, current harvest rates in hunted populations are conservative and below levels of sustained yield (Vaughan and Pelton 1995). In light of future demographic or genetic viability, most concern is with the fragmented habitats and low bear populations in the Coastal Plain (Hellgren and Vaughan 1994). Recent organizations like the Black Bear Conservation Committee and Alabama Black Bear Alliance illustrate the broad-based interest and support to "recover" black bears and their habitat in coastal areas (Bullock 1993). Protecting, stabilizing, and creating viable corridors and reintroducing bears into unoccupied bear habitat are 2 important steps toward sustainable and huntable populations. There is growing interest in reestablishing bears in the Piedmont region spawned by the current existence of relatively large blocks of forests with low human population densities, occasional dispersal of bears through river corridors into the region from established populations in mountain or coastal populations, and the preliminary reintroduction effort into the Appalachian Highlands of Tennessee and Kentucky (Eastridge and Clark 1998).

Future success of range expansions or restoration efforts will depend as much on cultural carrying capacities as biological carrying capacities. Local communities must be willing to accept the presence of black bears and understand the necessity of dealing with an occasional nuisance animal. To be successful, state fish and wildlife agencies must develop proactive information-education programs that educate people and teach them how to live and interact with bears. Even without range expansions and restoration efforts, more people are moving into established bear range and more human-bear interactions are inevitable. Developing humane, efficient, and acceptable ways to deal with these issues should be a high priority for state fish and wildlife agencies. The high profile nature of the species demands that agencies develop detailed nuisance protocols and train personnel to handle nuisance control activities in a professional manner.

Population estimates for black bears over the past 30 years have increased 6-fold in the South and harvest has increased by over 3-fold. With proactive and cooperative conservation strategies involving all stakeholders, both private and public, the future for black bears in the South is bright.

CHAPTER 19

Florida Panther

Joseph D. Clark
Southern Appalachian Field Laboratory
Biological Resources Division
USGS, Knoxville, TN

The Florida panther (*Puma concolor coryi*) is a medium-sized subspecies of mountain lion characterized by a skull with a slightly convex profile, a distinctive whorl of fur located on the mid-back or base of the neck, and a kink at the tip of the tail. Individual animals may or may not exhibit all these morphological traits. The pelage of Florida panthers is darker and more reddish in color than inland mountain lion subspecies in North America but is less red than animals from South America. In addition, the fur is commonly dotted with light-colored flecks, thought to be due to scarring from tick bites rather than an inherent morphological feature. Adult male Florida panthers typically weigh from 100 to 150 lbs and females weigh from 70 to 100 lbs.

DISTRIBUTION AND STATUS

The Florida panther was discovered and described by the naturalist Charles Cory in 1896. Historically, the subspecies ranged from Arkansas and Louisiana east to the Carolinas and south to Florida. Due to large-scale habitat destruction and unregulated hunting, this animal had been extirpated throughout most of its range by the early 1900s.

Even though mountain lions have the most widespread natural distribution of any wild mammal in the western hemisphere, this species is currently represented in the eastern United States only by the Florida panther. At one time, there was considerable opinion that the Florida panther was extinct. During the early 1970s, the Florida Game and Fresh Water Fish Commission (FGFWFC) initiated an aggressive search for evidence of panthers in south Florida. Its existence was finally confirmed when a panther was treed by hounds in 1976. Some 20 years later, the Florida panther remains one of the rarest mammals in the world.

The current distribution of the Florida panther is restricted to the south Florida peninsula (Fig. 1). In this area, large interconnected blocks of poorly accessible forested and wetland habitats act as refugia which enabled a few animals to persist. Current population trends of Florida panthers are poorly understood. In 1990, no more than 50 individual panthers were thought to exist on about 2.1 million acres of land (Maehr 1990) although the population may have increased slightly since that time. Due to agricultural and suburban conversion of lands in south Florida, however, panther habitat continues to be slowly reduced.

HABITAT REQUIREMENTS

Most of what we know about the habitat requirements of this subspecies comes from south Florida. There, panthers use sawgrass prairies, cypress strands, pinelands, and hardwood hammocks. In the northern portion of the range where feral hogs are more abundant, these animals constitute the bulk of the diet, whereas white-tailed deer are more important in the south where hogs are largely absent. Panthers readily take raccoons, armadillos, and other small animals when opportunities arise.

In south Florida, soils are thin and infertile, and white-tailed deer densities are low. The occurrence of

The Florida panther was extirpated throughout its range in the South by the early 1900s, and now only about 50 individual panthers survive *(J. Clark)*.

The current distribution of the Florida panther is restricted to southern Florida, where they use sawgrass prairies, cypress strands, pinelands, and hardwood hammock habitat. Due to agriculture and suburban encroachment, panther habitat continues to decline *(J. Clark)*.

Figure 1. Distribution of resident breeding population of Florida panthers.

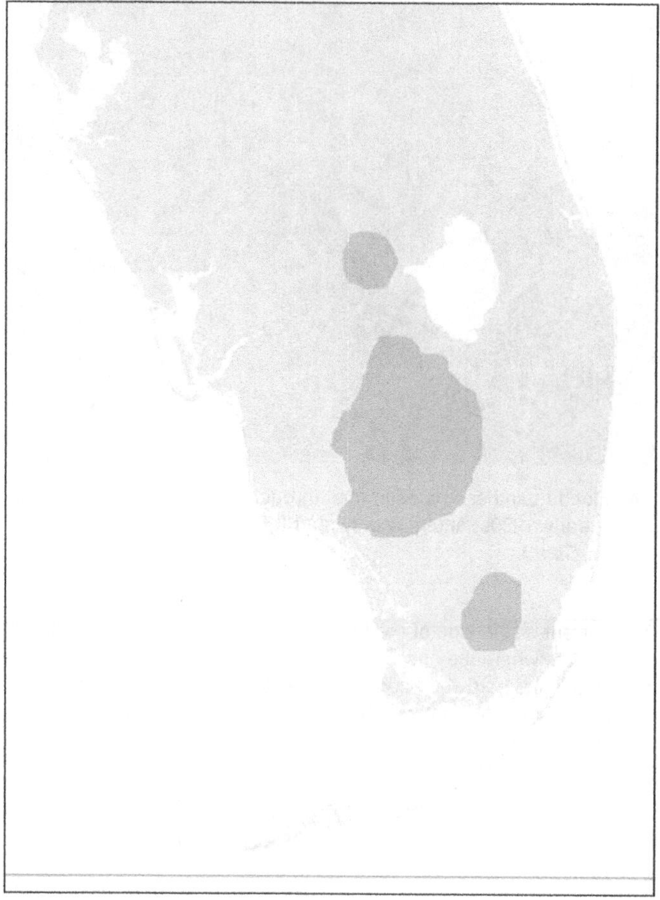

panthers there is largely by default; panthers have been able to persist because of the immense size of the area and poor human access. Hardwood hammocks and pine flatwoods, the preferred habitats in south Florida, are more commonly found in the northern extremities of the current range. These drier and more fertile areas, unfortunately, are the most sought-after for conversion to citrus, cattle, and vegetable production; activities that can be incompatible with panther conservation.

ECOLOGICAL RELATIONSHIPS

Radio telemetry research on Florida panthers began in the early 1980s with efforts to learn more about the basic life history and habitat requirements of this species. Researchers discovered that panthers can travel 20 miles in a night; females have home ranges between 50 and 100 square miles in size whereas males can range over 200 square miles. Annual mortality rates for adults are about 20%. There have been an inordinate number of road mortalities and, consequently, state officials have reduced nighttime speed limits within much of panther range and have installed underpasses along I-75 and SR 29. Since that time, panther mortalities from automobile collisions have declined. Another major mortality factor is intraspecific aggression between males, accounting for up to 33% of all mortality during past years (Land 1994).

Florida panthers give birth year round, but most parturition occurs from March through July. Females first reproduce at 2 to 3 years of age. Panthers typically give birth every other year and produce an average of 2.3 kittens per litter. The kittens accompany the adult female for a little over a year. Recruitment of female offspring is high, but is lower for males.

LIMITING FACTORS, THREATS

Florida panthers exhibit low genetic diversity and the population likely is suffering from inbreeding depression, which can cause reproductive abnormalities (Roelke et al. 1993). It has been speculated that many of the morphological traits that characterize Florida panthers may actually result from inbreeding. This is due partly to the peninsular shape of Florida, which naturally limits ingress and gene exchange. More recently, however, gene flow has been restricted because of the small effective size of the panther population. This is evidenced by the fact that, although the peculiar fur whorl or "cow lick" common to panthers can be traced back to museum specimens obtained during the late 1800s; it occurred less frequently than today, thereby suggesting recent changes in the genotypic composition of the cats. Also, a dramatic increase in lethal cardiac defects is suggestive of an increase in inbreeding and genetic depression. These animals have less mDNA variation than any similarly studied feline population in the world, including cheetahs.

Despite recent evidence that a slight increase in panther numbers may have recently occurred in south Florida, the small population size and limited genetic variability subject this subspecies to a high theoretical risk of extinction in the next few decades. As an example of the vulnerability of the population, the death of 1 adult male south of I-75 or "alligator alley" resulted in a 2-year period in which the 4 female cats that resided there did not reproduce. Thus, relatively minor stochastic events can have dramatic effects on the demographics of the panther population. Demographics aside, analyses indicate that the present panther population is losing genetic diversity by about 3-7% per generation and, at that rate, extinction is probable within 25-40 years (Seal et al. 1992).

Panther habitat conservation benefits other species as well *(J. Clark)*.

Florida panthers are subjected to a whole host of contaminants and disease pathogens. The most serious appears to be chronic exposure to mercury and to estrogenic chemicals, both of which may lower immunity and reproductive potential. The exotic hookworm (*Ancylostoma pluridentatum*) is prevalent and can cause mortality in kittens.

Habitat loss is the single most important threat to the future of panthers in south Florida. Florida leads the nation in citrus production and is second only to California in vegetable production. There is intense interest in agricultural and urban development on private lands in south Florida. For example, Hendry county has climbed from no intensive agriculture in 1900 to over 48% of the land in crops in 1973 (De Bellevue 1976). The remaining forested tracts of Collier, Glades, Highlands, and Hendry counties are threatened by continued expansion of agricultural and urban development. Since 1980, citrus alone has doubled in southwest Florida to nearly 150,000 acres and is projected to soon reach nearly 200,000 acres (Pearlstine et al. 1995). Panthers are sensitive to habitat fragmentation due to their large home ranges and extensive movement patterns. If this development continues unchecked, a concomitant decrease in the panther population would almost certainly result in extinction.

Besides the direct effects of habitat loss, there are also indirect impacts. Although intraspecific mortality occurs in mountain lion populations elsewhere in North America, mortalities due to conspecific aggression between Florida panthers are inordinately high. Problems due to fighting, as well as inbreeding and highway mortality, are exacerbated by shrinking habitats. Panthers are territorial and subadults are often either killed by other panthers or die while trying to disperse in an increasingly fragmented environment.

MANAGEMENT

Because panther ranges typically include multiple public and private land ownerships, coordination of management efforts is essential. About half the panther population occurs on 1.2 million acres of land consisting of an Indian reservation, a national park, a national preserve, a national wildlife refuge, and a state reserve. The remaining panthers are found on private lands. The large home ranges of the cats and this mixture of ownerships and management responsibilities creates a significant management challenge and, as a result, the Florida Panther Interagency Committee (FPIC) was formed in 1986 to provide a forum for a coordinated, unified recovery program. The principal duty of this group is to develop and implement a recovery plan. Objectives of the Florida Panther Recovery Plan are to 1) protect, monitor, and enhance the existing south Florida panther population, associated habitats, and prey resources; 2) take action to address population health; 3) reestablish panther populations; 4) expand public information, education, and outreach; and 5) coordinate recovery activities, monitor, and evaluate progress. Although much has been accomplished, the overall effectiveness of this group has been criticized (Alvarez 1993).

In 1989, FPIC determined that establishment of a captive population was essential to recovery of the Florida panther. Objectives for maintaining a captive population were to provide security against extinction, preserve and manage genetic resources, and provide a source of animals for population reestablishment. The captive breeding program has achieved only limited success, however, because wild stock is difficult to obtain, captive breeding has not been particularly successful, and procedures to successfully acclimate captive-born panthers into the wild have not been fully developed. As a result, the future of this program is uncertain.

A specific goal listed in the Recovery Plan is to achieve 3 viable populations within the species' historic range. Twenty-four candidate release sites across the Southeast have been evaluated using biological and sociological criteria; 14 of those were selected as potential reestablishment sites (Jordan 1994). Sites in the lower Gulf Coastal Plain of Alabama and Mississippi, along the Arkansas/Louisiana state line, and the Lower Apalachicola River (Florida) were deemed the 3 best reestablishment areas.

The FGFWFC recently completed an experiment to assess the biological feasibility of repatriating panthers to northern Florida. Nineteen sterilized Texas mountain lions (*P. c. stanleyana*) were released into northeastern Florida during 1993 and 1994 and were radiotracked to determine if they could survive, thereby giving biologists some indication about the possible success of releasing true Florida panthers there in the future. The first group of lions that were released dispersed dramatically when the deer hunting season began and some poaching was documented (Belden and Hagedorn 1993). Subsequent releases, however, were more successful. Most of those cats did not disperse, apparently establishing a social structure. However, there has been significant local public opposition to the project. The biggest obstacle to future repatriation may be obtaining public approval for the release of these large, potentially dangerous carnivores.

In the 1950s and 1960s, a private wildlife enthusiast illegally released a number of South American panthers in the Everglades. These animals, called "Piper stock," have distinct genetic markers and animals with this remnant genetic material can readily be distinguished using DNA analytical techniques. Due to the small population size and inbreeding problems, this influx of new genes may have actually been beneficial to the remnant population by increasing genetic heterozygosity; however, genetic problems remain. A workshop on panther genetics was held in 1992 and, as a result, FPIC recommended and obtained approval from the U.S. Fish and Wildlife Service to release several female mountain lions from Texas into the south Florida population for genetic augmentation purposes. Eight adult females have been released and, after an initial period of exploratory movements, the females eventually settled into areas of suitable habitat frequented by native panthers. Of the 8 released during 1996 and 1997, 1 was killed by an automobile, but 5 of the remaining 7 have produced at least 1 litter of kittens. No evidence exists to indicate that native panthers have been displaced by the Texas females.

Finally, 2 male Florida panthers captured in the wild in 1991 and reared in captivity were released at Big Cypress National Preserve in 1997. These animals were released as prospective mates for the 4 solitary females located in the area where the lone adult male had died previously. Although both released males died shortly thereafter, one was suspected to have bred a wild female. This supposition was later supported when one of the females gave birth some 3 months later, the average gestation period for Florida panthers. The cause of death of the 2 released males has not been determined.

FUTURE OUTLOOK

The Florida panther population is geographically isolated, few in number, and fairly contiguous. Consequently, it is susceptible to unforeseen catastrophic events such as disease or a die-off of its prey base. This could result in rapid extinction of all remaining wild panthers. Therefore, it is imperative that satellite populations be established as quickly as possible.

Although the proposed panther repatriation efforts have broad-based public support, there is opposition at local levels. The panther has been adopted as Florida's state mammal and millions of dollars have been generated from the sale of panther automobile license plates. More research and public education on the sociological implications of repatriation is warranted.

Although we have learned much about this species in the last 2 decades, much of panther biology remains a mystery. The vast majority of the radio telemetry data, for example, has been collected by airplane dur-

The future of the Florida panther in the wild remains uncertain *(J. Clark)*.

ing daylight hours. Consequently, panther habitat use and behavior at night, when they are most active, is poorly understood. Rapidly developing technologies relating to the use of Global Positioning Systems for tracking wildlife could greatly increase our ability to learn what these animals do at night, when conventional aerial telemetry is not possible. Furthermore, most panther data have been collected on public lands. Due to public fears of government intervention and land use restrictions, biologists are not allowed on some private lands to search for panthers. More incentives are needed to encourage private landowners to conserve panthers on their property.

The key to Florida panther conservation is habitat protection. Most problems that panthers face (such as inbreeding, intraspecific strife, highway mortalities) are direct or indirect results of habitat loss and fragmentation. A Habitat Preservation Plan was developed in 1993, which identifies panther habitat and threats to those habitats and provides options for protection. Although progress has been slow, conservation easements are being created and land acquisition efforts are ongoing, both by state and federal authorities. The state of Florida has recently established the Picayune Strand State Forest in what formerly was a proposed housing development. Also, the National Park Service recently added over 146,000 acres of critical panther habitat to Big Cypress National Preserve.

Probably the most promising recent development concerning the future of Florida panthers is the success of the Texas mountain lion releases into south Florida. These females have adjusted to the climate, successfully reproduced, and integrated themselves into the social hierarchy of the native panthers, apparently without displacing them. This experiment not only will improve the genetic vigor of Florida panthers, but because of successful reproduction of the Texas females, also suggests that male Florida panthers may be more reproductively viable than was once thought (Barone et al. 1994). Also, the Texas females established home ranges without displacing native cats indicating that at least some areas where panthers presently reside are not at carrying capacity but are capable of supporting higher densities.

CHAPTER 20

Red Wolf

Barron A. Crawford[1]
U. S. Fish and Wildlife Service, Chincoteague, VA

Christopher F. Lucash
U. S. Fish and Wildlife Service, Creswell, NC

V. Gary Henry
U. S. Fish and Wildlife Service, Asheville, NC

Red wolves are one of the three species of wild *Canis* found in North America Red wolves are intermediate in size between coyotes and gray wolves with males weighing 50 to 84 pounds and females weighing 42 to 74 pounds. Pelt coloration varies from all black to almost all blond with most animals having a tawny color with a rufus tint found on the head and ears.

Numerous theories have been proposed regarding the evolution of the genus *Canis* in North America. In 1979, Nowak postulated that modern day wolves and coyotes diverged from ancestral coyotes (*C. lepophagus*) sometime during the late Pliocene or early Pleistocene period and spread across the Northern Hemisphere during favorable environmental conditions. At some point gray wolves evolved in Eurasia and moved back into North America in a series of waves following the development and withdrawal of glaciers. The current theory proposed by Nowak (Henry per. comm. 1999) suggests that a small, primitive wolf invaded North America and evolved towards modern day red wolves and Algonquin gray wolves. Later a larger and more evolved species of *C. lupus* migrated into North America and forced the smaller wolves to the east and southeast. However, human persecution and habitat manipulation virtually eliminated all wolves from most areas in the United States. By 1980, the red wolf was declared biologically extinct in the wild and current free ranging populations today are a result of restoration efforts.

HISTORY

Red wolves historically ranged throughout the southeastern United States from central Texas to the Atlantic coast and from the Gulf of Mexico northward into the Ohio River Valley, southern Pennsylvania, and southeastern Kansas (Nowak 1979). Early explorers to the southeastern United States mentioned wolves; however,

[1]Current Address: Prime Hook NWR, Milton, DE

Audubon and Bachman (1851) were the first to publish a valid scientific name for the red wolf. Goldman (1944) examined key cranial and dental features of *Canis* specimens from across the southeastern United States and determined that all wolves of the Southeast should be classified as one species, *Canis rufus*.

Red wolves were extirpated from most of their former range primarily due to European settlers' deep hatred and fear of wolves. These fears lead to indiscriminate killing and bounties on wolves. From the early 1800s through the early 1900s, habitat destruction caused by the clear-cutting of forests, increased human settlement and agricultural practices, mineral exploitation, road development, and declining prey populations all contributed to the demise of the red wolf. Also, these changes to the landscape broke down habitat barriers that had separated red wolves and coyotes for centuries and as red wolf numbers decreased, coyotes moved eastward into the vacated areas. As a result, hybridization between coyotes and red wolves increased and thus red wolves found it increasingly difficult to locate conspecifics. By 1972, the range of the red wolf had been diminished to the forested bottoms and coastal marshes of southeastern Texas and southwestern Louisiana (Riley and McBride 1972).

In 1967, the red wolf was declared an endangered species by the U. S. Fish and Wildlife Service (FWS) under the provisions of the Endangered Species Preservation Act of 1966. With the passage of the Endangered Species Act in December of 1973, the Red Wolf Recovery Program developed and began implementation of the Red Wolf Recovery Plan. The objectives of the recovery program were to preserve local populations by responding to all *Canis* damage complaints and to reduce human persecution. However, research indicated that hybrids of red wolf/coyote intercross had formed and were moving eastward and thus the red wolf was in danger of extinction (Carley 1975). As a result, the recovery program changed objectives from local preservation to long-term preservation by removing individuals from the wild, developing methods for identifying "pure" red wolves, establishing a captive breeding program, propagating red wolves in captivity, developing and dispersing public information, evaluating potential restoration areas, and developing procedures for restoring the species back into the wild (U. S. Fish and Wildlife Service 1990).

In 1969, the Point Defiance Zoo and Aquarium (PDZA) in Tacoma, Washington was initiated as the red wolf captive breeding center with the arrival of the first red wolf. From the fall of 1973 to July 1980, more than 400 wild *Canis* were captured in southwestern Louisiana and southeastern Texas and examined by recovery personnel to identify "pure" red wolves for the captive-breeding program. Of the 400 individuals examined, only 43 met the morphological standards for the species and were admitted to the breeding certification program as probable red wolves (McCarley and Carley 1979). Morphological measurements of offspring produced from breeding these 43 individuals identified only 14 "pure" red wolves. Due to a lack of breeding, the current population is descended from 12 of the original 14 founders.

The red wolf is 1 of 3 species of wild Canis in North America, intermediate in size between the coyote and gray wolf *(B. Crawford)*.

In the fall of 1984, the red wolf was accepted by the American Zoo and Aquarium Association (AZA) to participate in the Species Survival Plan (SSP©). The goal of the Red Wolf Recovery/SSP Plan is to maintain 80 to 85 percent of the genetic diversity from the founder stock

By 1980, the red wolf was declared biologically extinct in the wild. Red wolves are maintained in captivity in several locations *(B. Crawford)*.

for at least 150 years. It was thought that this goal could be achieved with a minimum captive population of 330 animals and a minimum wild population of 220 animals at three mainland restoration sites (U. S. Fish and Wildlife Service 1990).

RESTORATION PROJECTS

With the species saved from extinction in captivity, the program shifted emphasis toward developing restoration techniques to determine the feasibility of restoring the species back to parts of its former range. Experimental releases into a controlled environment were conducted on Bulls Island, Cape Romain National Wildlife Refuge in South Carolina during 1976 and 1978 to test acclimation periods, release strategies, management techniques, and public information dispersal. These releases were considered successful and were valuable in developing release techniques and providing information for future restorations.

The Tennessee Valley Authority (TVA) invited the FWS to evaluate TVA's Land Between the Lakes (LBL) as a possible red wolf restoration area and in October of 1983, a formal proposal to restore red wolves to LBL was published (Carley and Mechler 1983). However, there was substantial public opposition to the proposed restoration. The Tennessee Wildlife Resources Agency and the Kentucky Department of Fish and Wildlife Resources then rejected the LBL proposal, and it was withdrawn by the FWS. Although the LBL proposal was biologically well planned and coordinated, sufficient effort was not allocated to public education. However, lessons learned from this experience helped in future restoration efforts such as at Alligator River National Wildlife Refuge (ARNWR) in northeastern North Carolina.

In 1987, the FWS proposed restoring red wolves to the 118,000 acre ARNWR after favorable biological studies of the refuge and local public support indicated that the project was feasible. In the fall of 1987, 4 pairs of red wolves, all born and raised in captivity, were released into ARNWR. Six of the eight wolves released either died or were returned to captivity for leaving the refuge within 9 months of release. However, during 1988, the program was able to maintain wolves in the wild for a period longer than a year, and the first litter of wild born pups was produced in the spring of 1988 (Phillips 1994). The population continued to grow slowly as a result of additional releases and reproduction in the wild. From the fall of 1987 through September of 1999, approximately 250 individuals were released or born in the wild in northeastern North Carolina. One hundred and five wolves have died due to a variety of causes including vehicle strikes, intraspecific strife, and natural causes.

Free ranging populations today are the result of restoration efforts *(B. Crawford)*.

Continued success has established northeastern North Carolina as the first permanent red wolf recovery site. This project denotes the first time an endangered carnivore that was extirpated from the wild has been restored to a part of its former range, and launched the second mainland red wolf restoration project in the southern Appalachians.

The FWS in cooperation with the National Park Service developed a proposal to restore red wolves to the Great Smoky Mountains National Park (GSMNP), and while doing so, assess the feasibility of restoring red wolves to other areas within the southern Appalachians. To address questions from the local citizens about red wolves, a 1 year experimental release was initiated to delineate movements, determine food habits, assess interactions with livestock in order to determine preventive and compensatory strategies, assess interactions with resident coyotes, and develop strategies for prevention of conflicts with public use.

The FWS conducted a 1 year experimental release of a family of 4 wolves into Cades Cove during the Fall of 1991 to the Fall of 1992. All 4 wolves were returned to captivity at the end of the experiment. The information collected was evaluated and the decision was made to proceed with a full attempt at restoration. However, the recovery project in GSMNP encountered numerous setbacks. From fall 1991 through December 1998, 39 wolves were released a total of 66 times. Eight litters of pups totaling 33 were born in the wild; however, only 4 survived to 6 months of age. Five pups have been confirmed dead and the remainder presumed dead. Sixteen wolves are known to have died of various causes including disease, inter and intra-specific aggression, and antifreeze poisoning. Seventeen wolves have been captured and returned to captivity due to a variety of problems such as leaving GSMNP and causing concern for local citizens, cattle depredation, consorting with coyotes, and frequenting campgrounds or picnic areas in and around GSMNP. Due to these problems, the FWS reevaluated the GSMNP project and decided to remove the remaining free ranging wolves from GSMNP in January 1999 and discontinue the restoration efforts in the southern Appalachians at this time.

CURRENT POPULATIONS

Currently red wolves exist in the wild as experimental populations on the ARNWR, Pocosin Lakes NWR, and Mattamuskeet NWR and adjacent private property in Beaufort, Dare, Hyde, Tyrrell, and Washington Counties of northeastern North Carolina; and as an endangered species on 3 islands: Bulls Island in South Carolina, St. Vincent Island in Florida, and Cape St. George Island in Florida. As of October 1, 1999 in northeastern North Carolina, approximately 42 red wolves were monitored with radio-collars, and approximately another 80 red wolves had fates that were unknown. Red wolves with unknown fates include individuals with non-functioning radio-collars and pups seen but never captured. All free ranging wolves were removed from GSMNP in early 1999. As of October 1, 1999, 31 institutions housed a captive population of approximately 161 animals.

ECOLOGY

Little is known about the ecology of the red wolf due to the species being extirpated by the 1900s from most of its historic range. Information concerning the ecology of red wolves is limited to a few studies in the coastal marshes of Texas and Louisiana during the 1960s and 1970s and observations by field personnel at current restoration projects.

Reproduction

Based on field observations at restoration projects, red wolves appear to have a well-developed social structure; they maintain extended family groups or small packs usually consisting of an adult pair and previous offspring up to 36 months of age. All members of the group appear to participate in pup rearing. Field personnel have recorded red wolves dispersing between 18 and 36 months of age. Red wolves, like other wild Canis, are seasonally monoestrous. Females are receptive to copulation during the 3 to 5 days of estrous sometime between January and mid March. Gestation lasts 63 days and the pups (1 to 8 normally) are born blind and helpless.

Food habits

Basically, red wolves are opportunistic predators and will take prey items that are available. Scat analysis from ARNWR and GSMNP indicate that white-tailed deer, raccoon, rabbit, and small rodents make up approximately 90% of red wolves diet. Frequencies of occurrence of food items consumed between both restoration areas are comparable, with white-tailed deer occurring in approximately 40% and raccoon occurring in approximately 30% of scats collected. During the first red wolf releases on Horn Island, Mississippi from 1989 to 1992, in depth food habits analyses were conducted. During this period, scat analysis for frequency of occurrence indicated that red wolves preyed heavily on and adversely affected populations of raccoon and nutria but had no impact on rabbit populations (Weller 1995).

Home Range

Information concerning home range sizes for red wolves are limited to a few studies in the coastal marshes of Texas and Louisiana and recent results from northeastern North Carolina and GSMNP. Shaw (1975) reported an average home range size of 17 mi^2 in Chambers County, Texas. Home ranges from northeastern North Carolina range from 19 mi^2 to 38 mi^2 depending upon habitat and prey densities (Phillips et al. 1995). The same pattern was evident in GSMNP where home ranges ranged from 8 mi^2 to more than 100 mi^2 (Lucash and Crawford 1995). In areas of high prey densities such as the open fields of Cades Cove with deer densities greater than 30/mi^2, wolves had considerably smaller home ranges than the wolves occupying the forested mountains with a deer density of less than 15/mi^2.

Habitat Requirements

Red wolves do not seem to prefer a particular habitat. Generally, red wolves require large tracts of land relatively free of human development, paved roads, livestock, and coyotes; with adequate densities of varied prey; and public support. Red wolves require large tracts of land protected from human development in order to avoid conflicts with humans. A diversity and abundance of prey items are necessary for sustaining adults and ensuring that pups survive. Project personnel in northeastern North Carolina have noticed larger litters, higher survival rates, and larger pups born in areas with higher prey densities. Red wolves require secured areas from humans and other predators for den sites.

Diseases

Red wolves are susceptible to numerous infectious and parasitic diseases. Viral diseases include rabies, canine distemper, canine parvovirus, and canine hepatitis. Only rabies has the potential to be a human health threat. Currently all captive raised red wolves released in the wild and all wild born wolves that are captured are vaccinated against these viral diseases. Commonly occurring helminths found in red wolves include canine heartworm, canine hookworm, liver fluke, and hydatid tapeworm. Currently in northeastern North Carolina, all free-ranging red wolves are infected with canine heartworm, however, this parasite does not appear to be impacting the animals' ability to survive in the wild and produce pups. Ectoparasites, such as fleas, ticks, and mites, are prevalent throughout the southeastern United States and are commonly found on red wolves. Fleas do not appear to present a major problem for red wolves. However, in areas with high densities of ticks, tick paralysis may lead to death due to secondary causes. Sarcoptic and demodectic mange mites are probably the most significant ectoparasite of red wolves. In northeastern North Carolina, 4 red wolves have died of demodectic mange, and 9 others have been treated for mange and released back into the wild.

FACTORS LIMITING RESTORATION

Potential factors limiting the successful restoration of red wolves to parts of its former range include conflicts with humans, political opposition, potential livestock depredation, increasing coyote populations, and uncertain taxonomic status (Van Manen et al. 2000).

Human Elements

Restoring a large, endangered carnivore requires a great deal of cooperation among all parties potentially involved, including resource management agencies, special interest organizations, and local citizens. Wolf restoration is a sensitive issue involving biological, socio-economical, political, and emotional considerations, and thus cannot be adequately addressed without the support of impacted groups. The greatest obstacle to overcome is local public resistance to red wolf restoration. Myth, misunderstanding, exaggeration of historical accounts, and livestock depredation give the wolf a larger-than-life reputation as a vicious and evil killer, devoid of redeeming qualities. Opposition to the project in northeastern North Carolina by CROWN (Citizens Rights Over Wolves Now) has resulted in lawsuits against the FWS and demonstrates the need for aggressive public education and consultation throughout the life of the project. Education of the public with sound biological information focusing on predator/prey relationships and general wolf ecology is necessary to overcome the ignorance-based fear and hatred still present in the general populace. Effective education can be achieved through school systems, hunting/outdoor clubs, business and agriculture organizations, and public forums. Public acceptance by the majority of impacted residents should result in favorable political support for restoration efforts.

Livestock Depredation

The perceived economic threat of a large predator to livestock operations is perhaps the greatest political barrier to restoring viable red wolf populations. The major concerns from livestock operators are depredations of livestock and the project's financial responsibility to the farmer. Other issues of concern are repercussions for accidentally killing a wolf, private landowners' legal ability to protect domestic animals against wolf attacks, and the ability of wildlife personnel to monitor and manage errant wolves.

To alleviate these concerns, project officials classified all free-ranging wolves in both restoration areas as experimental/nonessential. The experimental classification means that the animals are treated as a threatened species, for which regulations are customized to fit the specific needs of the release areas.

The 1991 regulations under the experimental/nonessential designation provided that incidental taking of red wolves during lawful recreational activities would not be a violation, provided that the taking is reported. In all cases, takings are investigated for compliance with the regulations. In addition, input from the Tennessee Farm Bureau resulted in the addition of a harassment provision that enabled landowners to harass unwanted wolves from their property using methods that were non-injurious to the wolves (Henry 1991). In response to requests from the North Carolina and Tennessee Farm Bureaus to be given the legal right to kill red wolves on private property, the 1991 rule package was revised in 1995 to allow any private landowner or person having the landowner's permission to take red wolves found on his or her property (1) when the wolves are in the act of killing livestock or pets, provided that physical evidence of attempted predation is evident, and (2) after attempts by project personnel to remove unwanted wolves are abandoned, providing that such taking is approved in writing by the FWS project personnel and is reported. Also, the incidental taking provision was changed for private lands so that only willful or intentional taking of red wolves will be a violation (Henry 1995). To date, neither restoration project has encountered a situation where the harassment of a red wolf by private landowners has resulted in the animal being injured or killed on private property or approval has been given to private landowners to take animals that could not be captured.

Coyotes

Coyotes expanded into the Southeast in the last 30 years due to landscape changes and extirpation of red wolves. The Southeast offers the adaptable coyote ideal conditions for continued population growth which presents a considerable challenge to red wolf restoration. Project personnel have observed paired wolves excluding coyotes from a portion of their home range and two or more coyotes acting aggressively to individual wolves and killing wolf pups. Red wolves may prefer conspecific mates, but unpaired wolves will consort and breed with coyotes if no conspecific is available. As a result, project personnel recommend a restoration strategy that maximizes bonded red wolf pairs and saturation of restoration areas with released wolves. Limited removal of coyotes may be necessary to allow newly released wolves to establish territories. Intensive management of

The future of the red wolf remains uncertain (*B. Crawford*).

the red wolf populations is necessary to insure that dispersing red wolves have conspecifics to mate within new areas.

Taxonomic Integrity

The taxonomic status of red wolves has been the subject of much recent controversy. The presence of a large Canis taxon in the southern United States has been documented in several historical publications (Audubon and Bachman 1851, Goldman 1944). The first extensive scientific work to determine taxonomic status of the red wolf was performed by Nowak (1979). In that study, he measured a number of cranial characteristics of red wolves, coyotes, and gray wolves and concluded, based on multivariate analyses, that the red wolf was a distinct species. The finding of a unique electrophoretically determined allele with a distribution congruent with geographical distribution of the remaining red wolf population by Ferrell et al. (1980) further supported the species status.

Based on mitochondrial DNA analyses, however, Wayne and Jenks (1991) challenged Nowak's (1979) conclusions. Wayne and Jenks (1991) and Roy et al. (1996) were unable to find segments of red wolf mitochondrial DNA or nuclear DNA markers that would distinguish it from gray wolves or coyotes, yet they found gene sequences that were characteristic of both coyotes and gray wolves. From that analysis, Wayne and Jenks (1991) and Roy et al. (1996) concluded that the red wolf was a hybrid between coyotes and gray wolves and was not a distinct species. However, after reviewing all the information available (historical, archaeological, fossil, morphological, behavioral, ecological, electrophoretic, mitochondrial DNA, and nuclear DNA analysis) the hybrid interpretation appears untenable, but no definitive conclusion has been reached on the taxonomic status. Thus the exact taxonomic position of the red wolf remains an academic question that will continue to be debated.

Project personnel believe that these taxonomic questions are largely moot within the larger arena of conservation biology. It is undisputed that a large Canis taxon was originally present in the southeastern United States that has been extirpated and that modern day red wolves are the descendants of those animals and do occupy a different niche and ecological role than that of the coyote (Phillips and Henry 1992). From an ecological standpoint, the loss of natural predators of white-tailed deer, raccoons, and other large and medium-sized mammals in the southeastern United States has had significant ecological consequences in some areas. Project personnel believe that the status of endangered species should not be judged based on taxonomic status alone, but the ecological role the animal fulfills in the ecosystem. Interpretation of the Endangered Species Act supports this as evidenced by recent genetic augmentation efforts on behalf of the Florida panther. The Endangered Species Act defines a species to include any subspecies and any distinct population segment that interbreeds when mature. The red wolf currently fits this definition and therefore is entitled to protection under Section 4 (15) of the Endangered Species Act.

CONCLUSIONS

Red wolves historically ranged throughout the southeastern United States but were virtually eliminated due to human persecution, habitat manipulation, and integration into the expanding coyote population. Little is known about red wolf ecology due to the species being extirpated by the 1900s from most of its historic range. Recent efforts to restore red wolves have encountered mixed results. Red wolf restoration is a sensitive issue involving biological, socio-economical, political, and emotional considerations. Efforts should be concentrated on collecting basic ecological data on free-ranging red wolves to address the challenges of restoring a large endangered carnivore to the southeastern United States.

Interactions between red wolves and humans, coyotes, livestock, prey species, and other wildlife need to be well understood to ensure restored red wolf populations will continue to exist. However, the financial burden of restoring and researching red wolves may exceed the means of a single agency. Thus, red wolf recovery will probably require multiple-agency funding at the federal and state levels, as well as assistance from private sources. Free-ranging red wolves do not recognize arbitrary land and political boundaries. These boundaries will need to be philosophically dismantled and the landscape managed as an ecosystem for the red wolf to be fully restored.

CHAPTER 21

Carnivorous Furbearers

Bruce D. Leopold and Michael J. Chamberlain[1]
Department of Wildlife and Fisheries
Mississippi State University, Mississippi State, MS

Wildlife species classified as carnivorous furbearers include the bobcat, coyote, red fox, gray fox, river otter, long-tailed weasel, least weasel, and mink. Carnivorous furbearers are important ecologically, and also are important to wildlife managers for several reasons, some positive, some negative. They are controversial (liked as well as disliked) because of their meat-eating habits. These carnivores consume large numbers of rodents. These rodents, without control, may impact plant growth, especially tree and shrub seedlings, destroy grain crops, which results in great economic losses, or be nuisances to humans, by promoting or transmitting diseases. Many carnivores are game animals themselves, such as bobcat, red and gray foxes. Lastly, many carnivores remove sick and injured individuals from the environment and the sooner a diseased animal is removed, the better the chances that other animals will not be exposed to the disease.

The carnivores also become controversial, nationally and in the southeastern United States, because of their importance as furbearers, and their proficiency in hunting and killing other animals, especially if their prey are important game animals. Effective programs by animal rights organizations within the past 2 decades have diminished the prominence of natural fur products within the market, with a subsequent decrease in trapping (Vangilder and Hamilton 1992). Concerns about furtrapping have resulted in increased alternative materials (greater diversity of synthetic fibers) which has further reduced the demand on these animals. Additionally, these carnivorous species have been cited as important predators of many game species, including the wild turkey by red and gray foxes (Miller and Leopold 1992, Peoples et al. 1995), white-tailed deer by coyote and bobcat (Connolly 1978a:369-394, Mech 1984:189-200), Northern bobwhite by red and gray foxes and coyote (Rosene 1969, Roseberry and Klimstra 1984), and waterfowl by foxes and mink (Sargeant and Raveling 1992, Greenwood et al. 1995, Beauchamp et al. 1996). The least controversial species is probably the river

[1]Current Address: School of Forestry, Wildlife, and Fisheries, Louisiana State University, Baton Rouge, LA

Table 1. Morphological characteristics of adult male and female bobcats in the southeastern United States.

State	Sex	Mass (lbs)	Lengths (in) Total Body	Tail	Hind Foot	Ear	Height at shoulder	Neck girth	Chest girth	Sample size	Citation
Alabama	Female	13.9	33.4	5.2	6.0	N/A	N/A	N/A	N/A	9	Miller 1980
	Male	17.4	34.5	5.4	6.5	N/A	N/A	N/A	N/A	11	
Arkansas	Female	14.8	34.1	5.7	6.0	2.6	N/A	N/A	N/A	3	Rucker and Tumlinson 1985
	Male	20.7	38.4	5.9	6.5	2.5	N/A	N/A	N/A	3	
Louisiana	Female	13.2	31.9	5.4	5.8	N/A	14.5	N/A	N/A	25	Hall 1973
	Male	17.9	35.1	6.0	6.4	N/A	15.8	N/A	N/A	24	
Mississippi	Female	13.9	32.3	5.0	6.0	2.3	N/A	8.4	14.5	38	Sullivan 1995, Edwards1996
	Male	20.9	35.5	5.5	6.7	2.4	N/A	9.9	16.9	28	
Mississippi	Female	13.0	32.5	5.6	6.1	N/A	N/A	N/A	N/A	29	Davis 1981
	Male	16.8	34.7	6.2	6.7	N/A	N/A	N/A	N/A	58	
N. Carolina	Female	16.5	28.7	4.8	5.7	2.0	N/A	N/A	N/A	51	Progulske 1952
	Male	20.1	32.4	5.4	6.3	2.2	N/A	N/A	N/A	37	
Virginia	Female	13.0	29.0	5.0	5.6	2.3	N/A	N/A	N/A	7	Progulske 1952
	Male	22.9	33.0	5.2	6.1	2.4	N/A	N/A	N/A	15	
Range[a]	N/A	9.0-33.7	29.9-42.1	4.3	7.5	N/A	17.7-22.8	N/A	N/A	?	Nowak and Paradiso 1983:1073
Range[a]	Female	8.4-33.1	30.9	5.4	6.1	2.5	N/A	N/A	N/A	?	McCord and Cardoza 1983:730-731
	Male	16.5-56.9	34.2	5.8	5.8	2.6	N/A	N/A	N/A	?	

[a] Measurements summarized for species throughout its range.

otter, although it probably has significant impacts on fish populations in some situations.

Obviously, furbearers of the southeastern United States are important and play a critical role in our ecosystems. Consequently, it is important to discuss their ecology and management, especially in the context of how they interact with other wildlife species.

GENERAL SPECIES DESCRIPTIONS (TAXONOMY, MORPHOLOGY, GENERAL HABITS, DENSITY)

The group of furbearers covered in this chapter taxonomically represent one order, Carnivora, and three families including Felidae (bobcat), Canidae (coyote, red fox, gray fox), and Mustelidae (river otter, least and long-tailed weasels, mink). Bobcats and the 3 mustelids are true carnivores with over 95% of their diet as meat, whereas the canids (coyote, red fox, gray fox) also eat plant material. No species is federally listed as threatened or endangered, although the river otter is protected by varying degrees in several states, such as Kentucky and Tennessee. However, 2 species (bobcat, river otter) are protected under the Convention for the International Trade of Endangered Species of Fauna and Flora (CITES) by being listed in Appendix II and thus must be monitored more closely by states allowing harvest of these 2 species. Consequently, they were afforded additional protection regarding detriment from harvest. The river otter was listed because of concerns regarding banning trade in European otter. The bobcat was listed because of concerns that bans in trade of spotted cats would result in the fur industry relying on North American cats [bobcat and lynx] to "replace" those spotted cats protected by their listing in Appendix I.

For the animal species covered in this group, males are generally larger than females (Tables 1-7). However, the gray fox is the least dimorphic of the carnivorous furbearers (Table 4).

One species, the river otter, is aquatic, although the semi-aquatic mink is seldom found far from water. Of the three canids, the coyote and red fox are more grassland species, whereas the gray fox is typically a woodland-dwelling animal. However, the coyote has expanded into almost all vegetation communities in the United States. The gray fox is arboreal, and uses trees for escape cover. Many biologists believe that this arboreal nature allows the gray fox to avoid coyote predation, and thus has permitted the 2 species to coexist.

The 3 terrestrial mustelids have a reputation of being efficient and effective carnivores. This is particularly true for the mink, which has developed a reputation as a vicious predator, due to its propensity to kill more prey than it can use. Mink also are notorious for

The gray fox is abundant in the South. It can evade coyotes by climbing trees *(B. Sloan)*.

being able to kill prey larger than themselves, supporting evidence that the mink is indeed a formidable carnivore for its size. Of the mustelids, the mink is considered the most valuable furbearer. Of the North American weasels, the long-tailed weasel is the largest, whereas the least weasel is the smallest, as well as being the smallest member of the order Carnivora found in the southeastern United States.

Density estimates vary for furbearers, not only by species, but by geographic location because of differing land management practices, productivity of the soils, etc. There are few reliable density estimates for furbearers because they are secretive and difficult to census. Additionally, carnivore densities are generally low because of their higher position in the food chain, (for example, there are more insects than mice, more mice than bobcats). Bobcat density has been reported to be between 0.23 and 0.39 bobcats/mi^2 in Arkansas (Rucker et al. 1989), 0.26-0.36 in Florida (Guenther 1980), 0.34 in Louisiana (Hall and Newsom 1976), 0.25 in Mississippi (Conner et al. 1992), 0.23 in Oklahoma (Rolley 1983), and 0.28 in Tennessee (Kitchings and Story 1984). Greater bobcat density estimates include 2.0 to 3.0 bobcats/mi^2 in Alabama (Miller and Speake 1978), 1.5 in South Carolina (Marshall 1969) and 1.5-7.1 in east Texas (Brownlee 1977).

Density of the canids is slightly greater than for the bobcat, and may exceed 5.18 animals/mi^2. Based on limited data, coyote densities generally range from 2.33 to 5.96 coyotes/mi^2 (Knowlton 1972); however, Babb and Kennedy (1988) estimated coyote density in western Tennessee as 0.91 coyotes/mi^2. Gray fox densities generally range from 3.11 to 5.44 fox/mi^2 (Fritzell and Haroldson 1982), and in Florida, Lord (1961) estimated fox density as 3.11 to 3.88 fox/mi^2. Density of red fox is slightly less than for gray fox, with 2.6-5.2 fox/mi^2.

Density for river otter and mink are not derivable in the context of animals/mi^2, because of the linear nature of their environment (streams or rivers), although most densities reported in the literature are expressed as a function of area. One study of river otter in Texas estimated density as approximately 1 otter/175-262 ac (Foy 1984). Density throughout the river otter's distribution

Table 2. Morphological characteristics of adult male and female coyote in the southeastern United States.

State	Sex	Mass (lbs)	Lengths (in) Total Body	Tail	Hind Foot	Ear	Neck girth	Chest girth	Sample size	Citation
Arkansas[a]	N/A	19.8-35.3	39.4-53.1	10.5-17.3	6.5-8.7	3.6-4.7	N/A	N/A	?	Sealander and Heidt (1990)
Arkansas[a]	Female	28.4	40.5-49.8	11.5-13.9	N/A	N/A	N/A	N/A	62	Gipson 1978
	Male	34.4	42.2-54.1	12.0-15.0	N/A	N/A	N/A	N/A	113	
Louisiana	N/A	18.1-30.0	47.0	14.0	7.8	4.3	N/A	N/A	5	Lowery 1974
Mississippi	Female	28.2	49.5	12.9	N/A	4.1	12.5	21.6	23	Edwards 1996
	Male	31.5	50.5	12.8	N/A	4.2	13.2	22.7	18	
Mississippi/ Alabama	Female	26.5	47.0	13.5	7.4	5.1	N/A	N/A	5	Sumner 1984
	Male	27.3	48.0	12.7	7.4	4.6	N/A	N/A	6	
Oaklahoma	N/A	24.0-28.0	40.0-50.0	N/A	N/A	N/A	N/A	N/A	?	Caire et al. 1989
Texas	Female	28.9	47.2	N/A	7.8	4.3	N/A	N/A	?	Davis and Schmidly 1994
	Male	33.1	50.0	N/A	8.1	4.6	N/A	N/A	?	
Range[b]	N/A	15.4-44.1	41.3-55.1	11.8-15.7	N/A	N/A	N/A	N/A	?	Nowak and Paradiso (1983:949)
Range[b]	N/A	21.6-37.0	39.4-59.1	15.7	N/A	N/A	N/A	N/A	?	Bekoff (1984)

[a]Range of values given for some measurements rather than averages.;
[b]Measurements summarized for species throughout its range.

Table 3. Morphological characteristics of adult male and female red fox in the southeastern United States.

State	Sex	Mass (lbs)	Lengths (in) Total Body	Tail	Hind Foot	Ear	Neck girth	Chest girth	Sample size	Citation
Arkansas[a]	N/A	6.0-19.0	35.4-44.9	11.8-17.0	5.1-6.9	3.0-4.3	N/A	N/A	?	Sealander and Heidt (1990)
AR/LA/MS	N/A	11.9-19.0	38.4	12.2	5.9	3.3	N/A	N/A	7	Lowery 1974
Georgia	N/A	6.6	30.6	11.1	5.2	N/A	N/A	N/A	3	Golley 1962
Mississippi	Female	8.4	38.8	12.7	N/A	3.3	8.2	12.7	2	Lovell 1996
	Male	9.5	43.3	13.4	6.1	2.8	8.3	14.6	1	
Texas	N/A	6.6-11.0	38.3	14.6	6.4	N/A	N/A	N/A	?	Davis and Schmidly
Oaklahoma	N/A	7.9-11.0	40.0	N/A	N/A	N/A	N/A	N/A	?	Caire et al. 1989
Range[a]	N/A	9.0-11.9	29.7-57.3	11.8-21.9	N/A	N/A	N/A	N/A	?	Nowak and Paradiso (1983:932)
Range[b]	N/A	6.6-15.4	32.6-43.2	11.5-17.9	4.9-7.2	2.6-4.0	N/A	N/A	?	Samuel and Nelson 1983:475

[a] Range of values given for some measurements rather than averages.
[b] Measurements summarized for species throughout its range.

Table 4. Morphological characteristics of adult male and female gray fox in the southeastern United States.

State	Sex	Mass (lbs)	Lengths (in) Total Body	Tail	Hind Foot	Ear	Neck girth	Chest girth	Sample size	Citation
Alabama	Female	7.7	35.2	13.1	5.2	2.7	N/A	N/A	34	Sullivan 1956
	Male	8.2	36.3	13.2	5.4	2.7	N/A	N/A	37	
Arkansas[a]	N/A	5.5-14.1	31.5-44.3	10.8-17.4	3.9-5.9	2.4-3.3	N/A	N/A	?	Sealander and Heidt 1990
Georgia	N/A	7.5	36.8	12.7	5.2	N/A	N/A	N/A	4	Golley 1962
Georgia	Female	8.6	N/A	N/A	N/A	N/A	N/A	N/A	78	Wood 1958
	Male	9.0	N/A	N/A	N/A	N/A	N/A	N/A	93	
Louisiana	N/A	14.1	34.9	12.7	5.1	2.7	N/A	N/A	16	Lowery 1974
Mississippi	Female	8.6	36.1	14.3	4.6	2.6	7.6	13.3	18	Edwards 1996
	Male	10.1	38.5	13.9	5.4	2.8	7.8	13.1	12	Chamberlain (unpubl. data)
Texas	N/A	6.6-11.0	38.2	13.7	5.6	N/A	N/A	N/A	?	Davis and Schmidly 1994
Range[a]	N/A	5.5-15.4	29.8-44.5	10.8-17.5	N/A	N/A	N/A	N/A	?	Nowak and Paradiso 1983:939
Range[b]	N/A	6.6-15.4	31.5-44.3	10.8-17.4	3.9-5.9	N/A	N/A	N/A	?	Fritzell and Haroldson 1982

[a]Range of values given for some measurements rather than averages.
[b]Measurements summarized for species throughout its range.

range from 0.1 to 1.37 otter/mi of waterway (Melquist and Dronkert 1987). As with otter, densities of mink throughout the Southeast also are poorly understood; however, some information exists for mink in parts of Louisiana. Density estimates were calculated using trapping harvest statistics in several areas of Louisiana. Linscombe et al. (1982) reported that mink densities were highest in swamps and marshes of Louisiana. Densities of 1 mink/4.9-9.9 ac were reported by Palmisano (1971) in Louisiana swamps whereas freshwater marshes had lower mink densities. The applicability of these densities to other southeastern states should be applied cautiously.

Information on density of long-tailed weasel populations in the Southeast is scarce. In Kentucky, DeVan (1982) found that densities ranged from 5.18 to 46.6/mi^2. Densities of long-tailed weasels show different trends than do densities of least weasels. Long-tailed weasel densities predominately do not fluctuate with environmental conditions to the extent of least weasels. However, generally least weasel population densities are considered to be less than those of long-

Table 5. Morphological characteristics of adult male and female river otter in the southeastern United States.

State	Sex	Mass (lbs)	Lengths (in) Total Body	Tail	Hind Foot	Ear	Neck girth	Chest girth	Sample size	Citation
Alabama/ Georgia	Female	14.8	40.2	14.6	N/A	N/A	N/A	N/A	106	Lauhachinda (1978)
	Male	17.9	42.4	15.4	N/A	N/A	N/A	N/A	235	
Arkansas[a]	N/A	9.9-30.9	35.0-51.2	11.8-20.0	3.9-5.7	0.7-1.0	N/A	N/A	?	Sealander and Heidt 1990
Louisiana	Female	N/A	38.5	14.1	4.4	0.9	N/A	N/A	3	Lowery 1974
	Male	N/A	44.4	17.5	5.1	0.9	N/A	N/A	3	
Florida	N/A	15.0	43.4	16.7	4.7	0.7	N/A	N/A	72	McDaniel 1963
Georgia	N/A	11.9-15.0	35.4-43.3	11.8-15.7	3.9	N/A	N/A	N/A	?	Golley 1962
N. Carolina	Female	10.4(97)	43.9	16.5	N/A	N/A	N/A	N/A	6	Wilson 1959
	Male	17.9(131)	46.3	17.1	N/A	N/A	N/A	N/A	12	
Texas	Female	19.3	45.8	17.5	4.8	0.7	N/A	N/A	5	Foy 1984
	Male	17.9	49.0	18.5	5.0	0.8	N/A	N/A	3	
Range[b]	N/A	6.6-30.9	29.9-52.0	11.8-19.7	N/A	N/A	N/A	N/A	?	Nowak and Paradiso(1983:1015)

[a]Range of values given for some measurements rather than averages.
[b]Measurements summarized for species throughout its range.

Table 6. Morphological characteristics of adult male and female long-tailed weasels in the southeastern United States.

State	Sex	Mass (lbs)	Lengths (in) Total Body	Tail	Hind Foot	Ear	Neck girth	Chest girth	Sample size	Citation
Arkansas[a]	N/A	0.2-0.7	11.4-19.5	3.1-6.0	1.0-2.0	0.6-1.1	N/A	N/A	?	Sealander and Heidt 1990
Kentucky	Female	0.2-0.3	11.2-13.4	3.3-4.8	1.4	N/A	N/A	N/A	?	Barbour and Davis 1974
	Male	0.4-0.6	13.8-17.0	4.5-5.9	1.8	N/A	N/A	N/A	?	
Louisiana	Male	N/A	17.8	5.6	1.9	0.9	N/A	N/A	4	Lowery 1974
Oklahoma[a]	Female	0.5	13.8-15.7	N/A	N/A	N/A	N/A	N/A	?	Caire et al. 1989
	Male	0.2	15.7-17.7	N/A	N/A	N/A	N/A	N/A	?	
Texas	Female	0.7-1.1	17.2	7.4	1.7	N/A	N/A	N/A	?	Davis and Schmidly 1994
	Male	0.4-0.9	19.2	7.6	2.0	N/A	N/A	N/A	?	
Virginia, Carolinas	Female	0.2-0.4	9.8-16.1	3.1-5.5	N/A	N/A	N/A	N/A	?	Webster et al. 1985
	Male	0.5-0.8	12.6-20.1	3.9-5.9	N/A	N/A	N/A	N/A	?	
South-central States	N/A	0.2-0.6	11.2-16.9	3.3-5.5	1.2-2.0	0.7-1.0	N/A	N/A	?	Choate et al. 1994

[a]Range of values given for some measurements rather than averages.

tailed weasels. Least weasels are considered rare, even well within certified areas of their range. No data exists on densities of least weasels in the Southeast.

DISTRIBUTION AND ABUNDANCE

All furbearer species discussed in this chapter are currently found in all southeastern states, except the least weasel. Restoration efforts during the 1980s and 1990s have assisted in restoring some species such as the river otter that were extirpated or nearly so. However, some differences exist regarding their distribution within the states, their status (rare, common, endangered) and their origin (native or introduced) and current status.

Bobcat

Bobcats are found throughout the southeastern states with the following exceptions. In Kentucky, the bobcat is absent or rare within the north-central part of the state in the Inner Bluegrass region. Additionally, the

Table 7. Morphological characteristics of adult male and female mink in the southeastern United States.

State	Sex	Mass (lbs)	Lengths (in) Total Body	Tail	Hind Foot	Ear	Neck girth	Chest girth	Sample size	Citation
Arkansas[a]	N/A	0.6-1.6	16.7-27.6	5.1-9.1	2.0-3.1	0.7-1.1	N/A	N/A	?	Sealander and Heidt 1990
Kentucky[a]	Female	0.68-1.08	18.1-22.6	5.9-7.5	2.6	N/A	N/A	N/A	?	Barbour and Davis 1974
	Male	0.85-1.62	22.8-27.6	7.5-9.1	2.9	N/A	N/A	N/A	?	
Louisiana	Female	N/A	20.4	6.8	2.0	0.9	N/A	N/A	5	Lowery 1974
	Male	N/A	22.4	7.2	2.7	0.9	N/A	N/A	29	
Oklahoma[a]	Male	1.0	24.0	N/A	N/A	N/A	N/A	N/A	?	Caire et al. 1989
Texas	Female	0.45-0.7	21.3	7.1	2.4	N/A	N/A	N/A	?	Davis and Schmidly 1994
	Male	0.68-1.3	22.0	7.5	2.6	N/A	N/A	N/A	?	
Virginia, Carolinas	Male	1.2-1.5	22.0-26.8	7.1-9.1	N/A	N/A	N/A	N/A	?	Webster et al. 1985
South-central States	N/A	0.7-1.6	20.0-26.8	5.3-8.3	2.0-3.0	0.7-1.1	N/A	N/A	?	Choate et al. 1994

[a] Range of values given for some measurements rather than averages.

bobcat is absent within the lower coastal areas of Louisiana (Lowery 1974, Choate et al. 1994). In Virginia, the bobcat is relatively common in the western part of the state, but uncommon to rare in the eastern third (Handley 1991). Regardless, where present, bobcat populations throughout the southeastern states are stable to increasing.

Coyote

Of all of the furbearers, the coyote has shown the greatest range expansion east of the Mississippi River in recent years. Prior to 1970, coyotes were not found east of the Mississippi River, instead, red wolves were common throughout the Southeast (Hamilton 1943), until trapping and poisoning eliminated free-ranging populations. Additionally, gray wolves were once found in Kentucky and Tennessee (Choate et al. 1994), and perhaps other southeastern states, including Virginia and North Carolina (Handley and Patton 1947, Webster et al. 1985). Removal of these large canids and subsequent introductions of coyote into the Southeast, enhanced by excellent habitat conditions, partially explains the observed expasion of the coyote after the 1970s.

Since the 1970s, the coyote has shown a remarkable range expansion. Based on reports from Hill et al. (1987), coyotes were statewide in Louisiana, Arkansas, Mississippi, and Alabama; mostly statewide (present in over 50% of the state) in Kentucky, Tennessee, Florida, and Georgia; and were present and expanding in Virginia, North and South Carolina. Texas and Oklahoma were not surveyed by Hill et al. (1987), but coyotes have historically been

The coyote is now found throughout the South. It is an extremely adaptable canid, with diverse habitat and diet *(M. Chamberlain)*.

statewide in both states (Caire et al. 1989, Davis and Schmidly 1994). More recent accounts (post-1989) indicate that the coyote populations have further expanded throughout the Southeast, except for the southernmost part of the peninsula of Florida (Brown 1997, Moore and Parker 1992).

Expansion of coyotes into the southeastern United States was not all natural. Hill et al. (1987) identified at least 20 sites where coyotes were released by private individuals or groups of individuals (primarily hunting clubs). These sites included all southeastern states except South Carolina and Kentucky, excluding Texas and Oklahoma as southeastern states. Most releases were either accidental or intentional releases of coyotes in pens established for hunting. The coyote's rapid expansion has been aided by conducive land management practices, such as widespread timber harvesting and subsequent regeneration.

Red Fox

The red fox is found throughout the southeastern states. However, the red fox is not actually a native of the United States, being introduced by colonists during the 1700s who "missed" the joys of fox hunting in the New World. Although very common and accepted as part of the landscape, some states still consider the red fox as not native including Texas (Davis and Schmidly 1994), eastern Oklahoma (Caire et al. 1989), and Florida (Brown 1997). Introduction of red fox in these states was primarily from individuals promoting fox hunting. Red fox are not found in the far southern tip of the Florida peninsula, nor along the coastal areas of Georgia or Louisiana (Lowery 1974, Choate et al. 1994).

Red fox populations are generally stable or decreasing in southeastern states. However, in locations outside of the southeastern United States, where coyotes are abundant, red fox tend to be displaced by the coyote (Voigt and Earle 1983, Sargeant et al. 1987, Gese et al. 1989). This displacement also is occurring in many locations within the Southeast. For example, the decline in red fox populations in Arkansas during the past 20 years has been attributed to increasing coyote populations (Sealander and Heidt 1990). However, red fox can be sympatric with coyotes, but at lower densities than would normally occur if coyotes were absent.

Gray Fox

The gray fox is native to all southeastern states; however, populations are lacking along Coastal Louisiana and the Florida Keys. Numbers are currently stable to increasing. However, as with the red fox, there is concern regarding impacts of expanding coyote populations.

River Otter

River otter populations significantly declined prior to 1970. For those states with severely reduced populations, restoration efforts have resulted in stable or expanding populations including Kentucky (source Louisiana), Oklahoma (source Louisiana) and Tennessee (source Louisiana and North Carolina) (Melquist and Dronkert 1987).

The current status and distribution of the river otter varies across the southeastern states. River otter populations are statewide in distribution and stable to increasing in Alabama, Arkansas, Florida (except in the Keys), Georgia, Louisiana, Mississippi, eastern Texas, North Carolina, and South Carolina. In Kentucky, although being considered rare prior to 1970 (Barbour and Davis 1974), restoration efforts since 1970 have resulted in rebounding river otter populations, with otters common in the far western part of the state, infrequent in central Kentucky, and being restored in the eastern half of the state, with 355 otter released between 1991-1995 (Kentucky Game and Fish, unpubl. data). In western Tennessee and eastern Oklahoma, the river otter is listed as endangered or threatened (Natural Heritage Program, 1996-97 database), although restoration programs are or were in effect (Melquist and Dronkert 1987). Although not listed as threatened or endangered in Virginia, otter are protected from harvest (closed season) west of the Blue Ridge Mountains, with limited harvest elsewhere.

Long-tailed and Least Weasels

The long-tailed weasel has the broadest distribution of North American weasels and is found throughout the Southeast, except for southern portions of Louisiana and Florida. However, populations are considered locally variable throughout the Southeast, and often rare in many areas. In contrast, least weasels are less widely distributed in the Southeast. Populations are found in the Appalachian mountains in western Virginia and North Carolina, and far eastern Tennessee. Based on historical records, least weasels occurred in eastern Kentucky and northwestern Georgia (Choate et al. 1994). The least weasel has historically not been very abundant throughout the southeastern United States, and thus trapping also did not seriously impact its numbers.

Table 8. Number of bobcat harvested in the southeastern United States from 1970-1991 (adopted from Linscombe 1993).

		STATE												
Year	Average price ($)	Alabama	Arkansas	Florida	Georgia	Kentucky	Louisiana	Mississippi	Oklahoma	N. Carolina	S. Carolina	Tennessee	Texas	Virginia
1970/71			185	0	0	0	55		45	179				59
1971/72			190	0	0	6	136		49	299				82
1972/73			348	27	0	10	481		199	462			1393	255
1973/74			520	71	0	1	953		725	745	248		7045	232
1974/75	16.80		761	32	0	0	775		1458	712	371	607	11874	370
1975/76	33.72		1026	517	422	0	1269		2302	867	661	736	9454	451
1976/77	48.01		2783	619	2577	0	2997	4517	3548	1101	0	736	27485	965
1977/78	41.42	3100	1838	983	2772	0	3718	3273	2244	593	0	608	22900	201
1978/79	72.51	3155	3278	1698	4410	0	5672	3263	2902	861	507	692	18262	321
1979/80	54.82	4875	2964	1132	3607	0	4645	3066	2214	727	540	741	17994	389
1980/81	55.09	3642	2352	1702	4365	0	3466	2230	2782	874	843	753	13581	394
1981/82	39.85	1700	1604	1031	2000	0	3161	1942	1822	514	758	351	13962	313
1982/83	38.81	1505	1869	1142	2267	0	1696	1270	2323	625	969	496	14546	339
1983/84	35.90	1349	1281	796	2406	0	1441	1276	2233	825	1203	488	17026	269
1984/85	42.45	2105	1629	787	3345	0	1397	1371	3066	678	1380	553	18005	265
1985/86	38.67	1956	1747	709	2451	0	1432	1254	3367	748	1121	599	17686	296
1986/87	52.66	2566	2067	926	3165	0	2395	1944	4515	673	1279	944	21154	290
1987/88	47.72	2968	2399	1069	4045	39	1971	2521	3452	460	1505	734	27031	263
1988/89	26.57	837	938	375	1743	34	874	1686	2372	174	496	387	13807	345
1989/90	14.84	280	627	93	1115	18	419	568	822	155	190	176	7817	44
1990/91	11.43	22	199	8	494	122	138	362	291	10	155	28	3226	15
1991/92	11.47	97	501	13	704	47	434	361	654	97	224	109	4415	46

Mink

Mink are distributed throughout the southeastern U.S., with the exception of central Florida. However, stable and thus harvestable populations of mink are only known to occur in Louisiana. In Texas, mink occur only in eastern portions of the state (Davis and Schmidly 1994). Generally, mink are most abundant in areas with stable supplies of water, either in streams, ponds, or rivers.

HARVEST TRENDS

In general, harvest of furbearers in the southeastern United States varied greatly during the period 1970/71 to 1991/92 (Tables 8-14)(Linscombe 1993). This annual variation in fur harvest varies with the species of interest and may be a function of fur prices and the national and international fur market demand, public sentiment (effectiveness of anti-trapping activities), species ecology (coyote expansion into the Southeast), and/or national and/or international policy (such as with the river otter and bobcat and CITES), and environmental conditions. Additionally, legislation or policies concerning trapping such as banning use of foothold traps, as in Florida, or methods of reporting harvest, respectively, has influenced reported trapping harvest.

All southeastern states were intensively monitoring furbearer harvest by 1977/78. Furbearer harvest was diminishing significantly by the late 1980s when fur prices significantly decreased because of public sentiment, unusually warm winters and reduced consumer demand, overstocked warehouses, lower overall fur prices, development of improved synthetic fibers, and increased use of wool.

Reported bobcat harvest (Table 8) reflects the impact of CITES on harvest reporting rates in and around 1973/74 when the bobcat was listed. Consequently, bobcat harvest increased with a corresponding increase in pelt price. However, by the late 1980s, harvest and prices had diminished. Regarding specific states, Kentucky had only a limited harvest in the early 1970s, followed by no harvest until 1987/88 when trapping resumed. Remarkably, harvest levels for Kentucky in the early 1990s resemble those of 20 years previous.

Table 9. Number of coyote harvested in the southeastern United States from 1970-1991 (adopted from Linscombe 1993).

		STATE												
Year	**Average price ($)**	**Alabama**	**Arkansas**	**Florida**	**Georgia**	**Kentucky**	**Louisiana**	**Mississippi**	**Oklahoma**	**N. Carolina**	**S. Carolina**	**Tennessee**	**Texas**	**Virginia**
1970/71			132	0	0	0	0		1097	0				0
1971/72			161	0	0	0	11		959	0				0
1972/73			274	0	0	0	112		2598	0			1479	0
1973/74			739	0	0	0	382		6935	0	0		19251	0
1974/75	7.36		686	0	0	0	342		6601	0	0	0	33774	0
1975/76	11.41		687	0	0	0	570		8514	0	0	169	19804	0
1976/77	18.78		2522	0	78	0	1086	469	13949	0	0	22	79013	0
1977/78	12.77	214	2653	0	75	0	2785	395	11366	0	0	90	94482	0
1978/79	23.49	260	3047	0	409	55	3297	779	13389	0	0	292	91258	0
1979/80	15.53	395	3233	0	416	137	3921	1151	5426	0	0	413	105797	0
1980/81	13.99	203	2342	0	415	163	1737	947	9771	0	0	128	64989	0
1981/82	19.23	203	2232	52	414	391	2188	1104	9948	0	0	210	60356	0
1982/83	9.66	145	2119	5	376	429	1603	1073	7141	0	0	315	60129	0
1983/84	6.46	129	817	4	214	602	432	1108	4624	0	0	0	42029	0
1984/85	6.39	226	854	9	520	1020	633	1680	5424	0	0	206	50841	0
1985/86	5.87	209	1039	1	309	1519	434	1306	4495	0	1	201	42811	0
1986/87	8.08	302	1129	10	332	783	937	1804	7599	0	5	500	62476	0
1987/88	6.76	393	1229	0	4680	1469	1212	2707	5890	0	8	409	68083	0
1988/89	3.83	30	493	1	2111	1722	1327	2941	2171	0	6	69	27385	0
1989/90	2.10	15	90	0	1961	1147	12	1535	603	0	16	32	19975	0
1990/91	2.76	2	39	0	11988	695	21	1146	253	0	25	45	15972	0
1991/92	13.92	2	161	0	1656	860	66	1584	1617	0	30	105	23334	0

Harvest of the coyote (Table 9) reflects its expansion into the eastern United States and supports the contention that significant range expansion of the coyote began around the early to mid-1970s. By the 1991/92 season, harvest remained relatively low for Florida, N. Carolina, S. Carolina, and Virginia. Harvest of coyotes in Kentucky showed the greatest increase with levels exceeding Louisiana by the late 1980s. This is in contrast to states west of the Mississippi River (Oklahoma and Texas), where large numbers of coyotes were harvested; however, even in these western states, coyote harvest has significantly declined since the late 1980s.

Trends in reported fox harvest (both red and gray) are similar to those of coyote and bobcat (Tables 10, 11), maximal harvest by the mid-1980s with diminishing harvest thereafter. However, differences exist between these 2 canid species. The concern of diminishing red fox populations in the Southeast is supported by harvest trends. Harvest of red fox in Arkansas and Oklahoma essentially ceased by 1974/75. Although pelt prices were increasing, significant declines in harvest to very low levels occurred in Tennessee, N. Carolina, Louisiana, Georgia, Mississippi, and Alabama, whereas stable or slightly decreasing trends exist for Virginia, Texas, S. Carolina, and Kentucky. Similar conclusions may be drawn for the gray fox with the exception that Georgia harvests are low but not excessively so, and Alabama and Oklahoma maintain some level of gray fox harvest. For both red and gray fox, harvest in Florida is non-existent.

The river otter, like the bobcat, is listed in Appendix II of CITES and exhibited similar harvest patterns and pelt prices as the bobcat: increased harvest from mid-1970s to mid-1980s, with a corresponding trend in pelt prices (Table 12). River otter harvest in many southeastern states is marginal, reflecting states' such as Oklahoma, Kentucky, and Tennessee restoring otter. Arkansas, Virginia, and Louisiana otter harvests remained relatively stable, whereas the remaining states showed significant declines. Texas otter harvest has been quite variable.

Weasels rank last among southeastern furbearers in commercial value of pelts. Long-tailed weasel harvests in the Southeast are typically very low (Table 13) and

Table 10. Number of red fox harvested in the southeastern United States from 1970-1991 (adopted from Linscombe 1993).

Year	Average price ($)	STATE												
		Alabama	Arkansas	Florida	Georgia	Kentucky	Louisiana	Mississippi	Oklahoma	N. Carolina	S. Carolina	Tennessee	Texas	Virginia
1970/71			102	0	248	636	73		15	464		32	0	1102
1971/72			162	0	122	749	143		0	483				1687
1972/73			242	0	401	1113	570		7	841			654	4101
1973/74			355	0	416	1936	994		59	1210	63		1863	2771
1974/75	15.24		552	0	842	2466	1041		75	1727	432	717	3128	3077
1975/76	28.13		0	0	3002	3475	1411		90	425	169	169	2210	3734
1976/77	37.74		0	0	2756	5684	3128	6301	0	2901	0	124	15775	4164
1977/78	38.27	3439	0	0	3026	6194	1032	4090	0	2046	235	0	16146	4991
1978/79	50.38	4825	87	0	4529	9339	1746	4667	0	2142	585	837	10342	6244
1979/80	38.97	5790	0	0	5230	8963	1877	4415	0	2637	559	173	6955	7782
1980/81	37.87	3395	0	0	4183	9968	1598	2487	0	1885	1646	244	7226	11038
1981/82	38.96	1809	0	0	2880	8098	1841	2026	0	58	1964	348	6849	8854
1982/83	27.72	1721	0	0	3123	7828	1341	1640	0	44	2452	1366	5526	9136
1983/84	30.06	1072	0	0	3014	10534	465	1165	0	460	2256	509	4511	7319
1984/85	18.40	1580	0	0	3840	9633	803	1500	0	420	2056	1470	5911	9527
1985/86	23.85	1236	0	0	2285	8551	560	887	0	1105	1479	992	6230	6470
1986/87	23.55	1233	0	0	3121	6292	396	921	0	971	1781	2000	7298	6673
1987/88	14.28	1570	0	0	3687	7628	456	1115	0	627	1917	1350	10263	5319
1988/89	8.55	404	0	0	1969	4365	76	853	0	216	1227	356	4217	0
1989/90	7.11	82	0	0	917	2202	18	269	0	87	914	149	2549	913
1990/91	6.86	16	0	0	581	1713	18	236	0	16	1039	52	1340	930
1991/92	9.99	46	0	0	679	2755	36	199	0	26	1362	170	1400	1376

have declined, reflecting decreases in commercial fur trapping. Generally, long-tailed weasels are captured in sets for mink, thus declines in harvest of long-tailed weasels may reflect declines in harvest effort for mink. Least weasels are not generally harvested for their fur, as their small size limits pelt value.

Greatest mink harvests occur in Louisiana, Mississippi, and Arkansas (Table 14), and least for Florida, S. Carolina, and Oklahoma. Harvest for N. Carolina, Virginia, Texas, Georgia, and Alabama, have declined significantly since the 1989/90 trapping season.

REPRODUCTION

Reproductive characteristics of southeastern carnivorous furbearers generally are similar. Generally, furbearers mate during late winter to early spring, with young born in mid-spring to early summer. Gestation is similar for all species, although the observed gestation for river otter, long-tailed weasel, and mink is considerably longer because of delayed implantation. Interestingly, the least weasel does not exhibit delayed implantation. All of the canids and minks are monestrous; all other species are polyestrous, meaning that estrous in females may cycle until she is bred. Age of sexual maturity varies among the furbearers, many breeding their first year, others usually their second. However, many individuals, although capable of breeding their first year, may not because of social constraints. For example, male river otters may not breed until they are 5 to 7 years old. There is no trend in type of pair-bonding between males and females for southeastern furbearers. Some furbearers are monogamous, others polygamous, and this may vary within a taxonomic group.

Bobcat

One remarkable aspect of bobcat reproduction is that males are incapable of breeding their first year, whereas females are. However, Stys and Leopold (1993) and Jackson and Jacobson (1987) have indicated that most females may not have a successful litter until their second year. Litter sizes for bobcat are relatively small

Table 11. Number of gray fox harvested in the southeastern United States from 1970-1991 (adopted from Linscombe 1993).

		STATE												
Year	**Average price ($)**	**Alabama**	**Arkansas**	**Florida**	**Georgia**	**Kentucky**	**Louisiana**	**Mississippi**	**Oklahoma**	**N. Carolina**	**S. Carolina**	**Tennessee**	**Texas**	**Virginia**
1970/71			644	0	829	1355	169		15	1857		799		1758
1971/72			734		752	1297	333		5	1854				2640
1972/73			1751	0	1113	2798	1329		0	3442			7518	4627
1973/74			2502	0	1893	6257	2318		442	5568	420		21248	7352
1974/75	10.55		4235	0	2986	6316	2430		722	8132	1094	6965	35973	9076
1975/76	18.59		3765	0	3003	8414	3293		1839	8262	1157	5040	25077	11479
1976/77	25.69		8333	0	21748	10848	3217	6454	2812	11605	0	7945	47325	9688
1977/78	29.45	18215	5547	0	22477	11944	4127	13616	1619	8182	991	8036	48439	11572
1978/79	43.49	45635	6648	25	23762	18682	5936	13051	1902	8569	1744	12724	49589	13820
1979/80	43.02	25290	8977	0	28909	19232	6284	12475	1631	10548	2336	11459	44330	16864
1980/81	35.52	16650	7109	0	22541	19259	3104	7965	1693	3542	6822	9098	29778	26063
1981/82	26.84	8306	4945	0	12531	14745	3035	5936	949	164	6641	5296	31407	15193
1982/83	28.14	8425	5301	0	12680	13196	2849	5090	1027	72	7779	12365	44927	16901
1983/84	31.62	5330	3434	0	13200	9717	988	3383	1105	946	7933	7726	37270	13701
1984/85	24.30	9971	4459	0	20391	8369	1487	3702	1382	1412	6665	7061	40320	14630
1985/86	19.11	6149	4193	0	9462	7105	1639	2468	1491	3087	5756	6078	39594	12945
1986/87	29.36	9824	5911	0	14681	5332	2405	4192	1718	2772	7860	9816	50458	14934
1987/88	26.16	11223	7865	0	17962	8039	3164	5670	1547	2246	11290	7879	52766	13081
1988/89	10.09	2440	3566	0	6586	4348	879	3980	1091	889	4285	1991	26167	0
1989/90	5.16	628	1096	0	3013	2029	169	1511	329	412	2741	733	12293	1783
1990/91	4.61	142	502	0	2007	1143	90	839	84	48	2724	245	5373	819
1991/92	8.05	212	790	0	2764	2292	279	1092	192	161	3392	1112	7402	2090

The bobcat is a common felid of the South. Bobcat kittens begin eating meat when they are about 5-6 weeks old *(Texas Parks and Wildlife Dep., D. Miller)*.

Table 12. Number of river otter harvested in the southeastern United States from 1970-1991 (adopted from Linscombe 1993).

		STATE												
Year	Average price ($)	Alabama	Arkansas	Florida	Georgia	Kentucky	Louisiana	Mississippi	Oklahoma	N. Carolina	S. Carolina	Tennessee	Texas	Virginia
1970/71			56	414	670	0	4808		0				0	890
1971/72			38		222	0	5440		0	1606				648
1972/73			76	288	585	0	7668		0	1407			0	642
1973/74			25	408	453	0	5989		0	968	526		60	602
1974/75	24.34		37	372	624	0	6118		0	893	699	0	3	661
1975/76	25.25		123	1662	495	0	5730		0	878	783	0	62	594
1976/77	41.85		363	2987	3187	0	11900	1482	0	1390	0	8	201	550
1977/78	29.79	2251	419	3326	2995	0	6597	973	0	927	560	3	190	941
1978/79	37.45	2040	749	2112	3643	0	9745	1045	0	1357	535	45	0	820
1979/80	42.44	3050	400	2100	3417	0	9324	1532	0	1618	537	0	0	1318
1980/81	28.86	1569	693	3459	4622	0	10411	1044	0	1679	864	0	0	1164
1981/82	23.47	919	503	1912	1916	0	5905	833	0	870	701	0	585	807
1982/83	15.97	425	448	804	1001	0	3126	535	0	919	602	0	359	419
1983/84	15.48	352	581	855	1624	0	4122	444	0	869	622	0	770	649
1984/85	16.53	892	499	1512	3117	0	5727	648	0	630	648	0	434	610
1985/86	14.64	1017	668	757	1474	0	3529	733	0	685	589	0	594	709
1986/87	14.93	982	776	1052	1912	0	5074	955	0	785	637	0	796	769
1987/88	15.48	961	998	1692	1666	0	4021	1064	0	689	601	0	855	785
1988/89	13.26	358	683	398	680	0	1924	532	0	367	291	0	335	495
1989/90	12.94	169	498	151	725	0	1365	425	0	408	140	126	378	182
1990/91	11.52	20	482	19	224	0	1203	199	0	247	113	0	67	136
1991/92	16.48	30	642	190	433	0	1779	302	0	321	169	64	319	436

compared to other carnivorous furbearers being less than 3 young/litter. Multiple litters/year are possible because of the bobcat's polyestrous reproductive cycle; however, usually a second litter occurs, only if the first litter is not successful (Stys and Leopold 1993). Many trappers have noted capturing kittens during late fall. This is likely a result of a female either not being bred early in the season, or loss of a previous litter.

Coyote

The coyote has the greatest reproductive potential of all southeastern furbearers, with the potential to produce up to 12 pups, although the average is 6 pups. Such a reproductive capacity explains the ability of the coyote to respond so rigorously to removal efforts, and its ability to expand its range throughout the southeastern United States within 25 years. As with most carnivores, the coyote's reproduction is density-dependent (Storm and Tzilkowski 1982). This is supported by a study in Texas which demonstrated that under intensive coyote control, the remaining coyotes produced litters averaging 7.2 pups, under moderate control, 4.5 pups, and under light control, 3.5 pups (Knowlton 1972). Thus, under intensive predator control, the high reproductive potential of the coyote is such that they will produce more young to balance losses from their harvest.

Coyotes will breed with domestic canids. Although coyote-domestic dog interbreeding produces fertile offspring (Kennelly and Roberts 1969, Silver and Silver 1969), the offspring have significantly reduced fecundity (Mengel 1971). Smith and Kennedy (1983) and Lydeard et al. (1988) evaluated skulls of canids collected in the southeastern United States and found that hybridization was minimal, with most suspected hybrids being coyotes.

Red Fox

The red fox is listed as weakly monogamous because there is some uncertainty as to the role of the male in rearing pups, although it has been reported that the red fox is seasonally monogamous and the male assists in pup rearing (Lariviere and Pasitschniak-Arts 1996). Females generally are hostile toward males, but males have been observed bringing food to nursing females (Ables 1975). Henry (1996) states that the large litter size of 5 whelps requires both male and female cooper-

Table 13. Number of weasels harvested in the southeastern United States from 1970-1991 (adopted from Linscombe 1993).

Year	Average price ($)	STATE												
		Alabama	Arkansas	Florida	Georgia	Kentucky	Louisiana	Mississippi	Oklahoma	N. Carolina	S. Carolina	Tennessee	Texas	Virginia
1970/71			4	0	0	27	0		0	38		4	0	45
1971/72			6		0	43	0		0	75				62
1972/73			3	0	0	123	0		0	112			0	242
1973/74			4	0	0	164	0		0	116	0		0	260
1974/75	0.68		6	0	0	219	0		0	116	0	61	0	224
1975/76	0.69	10	10	0	0	222	0		0	43	0	27	0	138
1976/77	0.75		5	0	64	157	0	274	0	124	0	51	0	128
1977/78	1.04	62	10	0	20	222	0	68	0	60	0	82	0	103
1978/79	1.41	55	19	0	127	271	0	94	1	125	0	117	0	141
1979/80	0.91	150	34	0	48	382	0	111	0	137	0	104	0	134
1980/81	0.67	0	13	0	30	389	0	22	0	89	0	43	0	239
1981/82	0.94	2	11	0	13	161	0	44	0	24	0	0	0	65
1982/83	0.42	5	19	0	2	167	0	10	0	11	4	83	0	100
1983/84	0.45	3	0	0	3	286	0	10	0	22	0	25	0	16
1984/85	0.82	5	168	0	9	168	0	10	0	17	2	15	0	16
1985/86	0.64	3	1	0	6	72	0	7	0	6	1	26	0	16
1986/87	0.68	1	2	0	3	78	0	15	0	3	3	11	0	12
1987/88	0.50	3	3	0	0	78	0	17	3	18	0	4	26	12
1988/89	0.65	0	2	0	0	68	0	9	0	3	1	5	0	0
1989/90	0.50	0	1	0	0	9	0	0	0	0	0	1	0	0
1990/91	1.00	0	0	0	0	29	0	0	0	0	0	0	0	0
1991/92	0.50	0	1	0	0	87	0	0	0	1	0	2	0	0

ation in feeding the young. However, radio-tracking studies have shown little contact of the male with the nursing female (Ables 1975).

Gray Fox

The gray fox is very much like the red fox in reproductive characteristics, except that average litter sizes for gray foxes are smaller (3.8 pups versus 5.0) (Table 15). Gray fox are strongly monogamous and both parents care for young. However, Sheldon (1949) in New York suggested that gray fox rarely may be polygamous, with multiple litters found in the den.

River Otter

The river otter exhibits delayed implantation of the blastocyst, which is typical of most members of the weasel family. Consequently, observed gestation may last up to 1 year, whereas actual gestation (time of development of the feti) ranges between 60-63 days. Otter are polygamous, with only the female caring for young. Additionally, females may mate within 1 month of giving birth. Females generally do not reach sexual maturity until their second year. Males, although capable of breeding their second year, may not breed until they are 5 to 7 years old. This is primarily because males do not attain the size to become dominant and subsequently defend a territory.

Long-tailed and Least Weasels

Reproductive characteristics of the weasels differ. Long-tailed weasels exhibit delayed implantation, after which gestation occurs. Breeding occurs during July and August; however, eggs are not implanted until spring. Gestation lasts from 23 to 27 days with litters born in April and May (Fagerstone 1987). Litter sizes generally average about 5 to 8. Long-tailed weasels produce only one litter per year. Unlike the long-tailed weasel, the least weasel breeds throughout the year (Fagerstone 1987), may produce multiple litters and does not have delayed implantation. Reproduction in the least weasel appears to be controlled by prey availability, in that litter sizes and number of litters produced can fluctuate drastically with changes in prey. Generally, least weasels may produce from 1 to 3 litters annually, with litter sizes ranging from 1 to 10 and averaging 5 (Heidt 1970).

Table 14. Number of mink harvested in the southeastern United States from 1970-1991 (adopted from Linscombe 1993).

		STATE												
Year	**Average price ($)**	**Alabama**	**Arkansas**	**Florida**	**Georgia**	**Kentucky**	**Louisiana**	**Mississippi**	**Oklahoma**	**N. Carolina**	**S. Carolina**	**Tennessee**	**Texas**	**Virginia**
1970/71			2068	0	2101	2490	21648		8	4386		2537	0	1899
1971/72			2836		1551	2620	24299		70	3270				2146
1972/73			3692	1	2015	4845	44062		140	5331			979	3685
1973/74			5747	2	1657	6297	38940		218	3647	61		1951	2883
1974/75	5.55		7129	4	2101	6824	32319		356	3643	30	7731	2249	3965
1975/76	7.45	0	9584	4	1748	6635	36268		595	3608	137	2624	1438	5072
1976/77	12.42		15206	27	4124	8969	54858	22105	860	4843	0	7680	3157	3417
1977/78	11.02	8220	9870	12	2829	6364	28101	15791	676	2176	53	5556	480	2787
1978/79	13.88	9460	9773	55	2513	6985	51731	12879	727	2232	105	6727	3036	2488
1979/80	18.19	11275	20774	142	3658	11288	41598	20259	704	2607	101	6713	2459	3890
1980/81	15.31	7703	20647	104	2650	14959	59497	16754	1025	3817	348	7908	4330	5835
1981/82	14.87	3813	17115	52	2053	9327	32078	15064	752	1692	312	5684	2754	3053
1982/83	12.84	2406	18687	0	1835	6681	33150	9911	1126	1757	350	6758	4599	2480
1983/84	13.02	2352	11964	51	1608	8509	24147	8776	671	1367	283	4730	3906	2604
1984/85	13.55	3230	16466	135	1950	6635	34497	8682	679	1150	236	4032	3932	2333
1985/86	11.39	2784	20920	9	1163	5586	27948	7642	826	928	267	4158	3361	2208
1986/87	15.46	2795	18220	29	1347	5964	35045	8881	1021	1021	258	6085	4719	2358
1987/88	16.63	2318	11748	39	1016	5792	33365	6201	932	861	258	4246	1607	1646
1988/89	17.15	918	9766	6	517	2984	25782	5291	478	312	116	1795	1142	0
1989/90	13.66	408	3534	0	221	2539	10267	2106	258	250	40	883	0	400
1990/91	11.43	425	4659	0	212	783	4358	917	54	118	23	442	367	384
1991/92	15.89	509	4435	0	254	2554	7736	1424	0	227	63	2148	812	647

Mink

Mink are similar to most other mustelids in having delayed implantation. Breeding occurs from January to March in most sections of the Southeast, but may breed as early as November in southern Florida (Humphrey and Zinn 1982). Females that are bred later in the breeding season do not delay egg implantation after copulation (Mead 1981). Breeding patterns in mink appear to be controlled by changes in photoperiod (Eagle and Whitman 1987). Mink are polyestrous throughout the relatively short breeding period. Gestation averages 51 days, but may last as long as 75 days with litter sizes averaging 4 to 5. Mink are sexually mature within 1 year.

DIET

The furbearers in this chapter are primarily carnivores, with over 60% of their annual diet composed of meat, although amount of plant material (especially fruits, berries, and seeds) consumed varies. Bobcat, river otter, least and long-tailed weasel and mink are true carnivores, with a diet of animal material exceeding 95% (Tables 16, 19). The three canids may vary greatly in the ratio of plant to animal matter (Tables 17, 18); however, diet of these carnivores may vary seasonally with availability. One common component regarding the diet of southeastern furbearers is the diversity of foods available to individuals. The mild climate, even during winter, and the greater abundance of prey species, affords most furbearers ample food year round. Consequently, food caching as may be found with the red fox in the northern states, is not very common in the Southeast.

Bobcat

The bobcat is undoubtedly the most carnivorous of the southeastern United States' furbearers (Table 16). Most plant material reported in its diet is incidental to consuming flesh, although plant material may be consumed intentionally to supplement the diet. Small terrestrial rodents, such as cottonrats, *Peromyscus* spp. and rabbits constitute the bulk of the bobcat diet. Other mammalian species reported in bobcat diet include squirrels, raccoon, opossum, beaver, chipmunks, weasels (Mustelidae), gophers (Geomyidae), red fox, muskrat,

Table 15. Reproductive characteristics of furbearers in the southeastern United States.

Species	Breeding season	Peak birth	Litter size	Pair bond	Estrus cycles	Litters/ year	Gestation (days)	Delayed implant.	Age at sexual maturity (years)	Literature cited
Bobcat	Dec.-June	Apr.-May	1-6 $\bar{x}$=2.8	polygamous	polyestrous	1.0	62-70, x=65.8	No	Male = 1.5 Female = 0.5	Stys and Leopold 1993, Lariviere & Walton 1997, Fritts 1973
Coyote	Jan.-May.	Apr.-May	2-12 $\bar{x}$=6.0	monogamous	monestrous	1.0	58-65, x=63	No	2.0 (some 1.0)	Knowlton 1972, Bekoff 1982, Kennelly 1978
Red Fox	Dec.-Mar.	Apr.-May	1-11 $\bar{x}$=5.0	weakly monogamous	monestrous	1.0	49-55, x=52	No	1.0	Asdell 1964, Ables 1975, Samuel and Nelson 1982
Gray Fox	Dec.-Apr.	Apr.-May	1-6 $\bar{x}$=3.8	monogamous	monestrous	1.0	51-63, x=59	No	1.0	Fritzell 1987, Trapp & Hallberg 1975, Samuel & Nelson 1982
River Otter	Dec.-Apr.	Mar.-Apr.	1-6 $\bar{x}$=2.9	polygamous	polyestrous	1.0	288-375 (60-63)[a]	Yes	2.0 males (breed 5-7)	Nowak & Paradiso 1963, Melquist & Dronkert 1987, Toweill & Tabor 1982
Long-tailed weasel	Mar.-Aug.	Apr.-May	4-9 $\bar{x}$=6.8	polygamous[b]	polyestrous	1.0	205-337 23-27 x=25[a]	Yes	15 months (males) 4 months (females)	Fagerstone 1987, Heidt 1970, Svendsen 1982, Sheffield & Thomas, 1997
Least weasel	Year-round	Mar.-May Oct.-Nov.	1-10 $\bar{x}$=4.5	polygamous	polyestrous	1.0	30-40 x=35	No	female=16 weeks male=32 weeks	Fagerstone 1987, Hall 1951, Hayssen et al. 1993
Mink	Feb.-Apr.	Apr.-May	1-8 $\bar{x}$=4.5	polygamous	monestrous	1.0	40-75, x=51 (28-30)[a]	Yes	10 months	Eagle & Whitman 1987, Linscombe et al. 1982

[a] when corrected for delayed implantation.
[b] mated pairs do exist.
[c] when prey abundant.

woodchuck, and striped skunk. Other animal groups consumed by bobcats include reptiles (primarily snakes), a diverse array of songbirds, and insects. Obviously, the bobcat is capable of subduing and killing most prey species less than 20 pounds. Deer consumed by bobcats may be from direct predation or hunter-killed but not recovered animals. Bobcats will scavenge animal matter if the animal has been dead less than 24-48 hours.

Coyote

The diet of the coyote is very diverse including animal and plant material. Additionally, the coyote, although capable of killing prey, is frequently a scavenger, making it difficult to ascertain if items found within its diet were killed by the coyote or scavenged. The coyote's diet is a mixture of rodents, rabbits, insects, and fruits. Obviously, occurrence of insects and fruits such as persimmon and berries, is seasonal. Fruits are eaten during summer and fall and insects during spring, summer and fall. Although frequently found in coyote scats and stomachs, livestock and deer are believed to be mostly obtained by scavenging rather than direct predation (Bekoff 1984). However, coyote damage to livestock may be substantial (Connolly 1992). Also, studies reflect an increased incidence of deer in coyote diets during fawning periods (Lee and Kennedy 1986, Edwards 1996, and others), but impact to deer populations is uncertain.

Red Fox and Gray Fox

There is little published information regarding diet of southeastern foxes, especially for the red fox. However, some generalizations are possible. Both fox species

Table 16. Composition (percentage occurrence)[a] of diet of bobcat in the southeastern United States.

	Dietary item																
	Mammal									Avian							
State	Rat[b]	Mice[c,d]	Sciurid	Rabbit	Deer	Racc.	Oposs.	Other	Reptile	Turkey	Other	Inver-tebrate	Plant	Method	Time period	N	Citation
Alabama	39.0	5.8	5.1	30.1	8.8	0.7	5.9	41.2	0.0	0.0	11.7	1.4	0.0	Stom.	Annual	136	Miller and Speake 1978
Arkansas	12.0	9.0	22.0	39.0	7.0	5.0	9.0	10.0	2.0	0.0	2.0	0.0	0.0	Stom.	Annual	150	Fritts and Sealander 1978
Florida	28.0	3.5	3.5	25.0	2.0	0.5	1.0	9.5	1.0	0.0	16.0	0.0	11.0	Stom.	Annual	413	Maehr and Brady 1986
Mississippi	46.3	29.9	1.5	32.8	20.9	1.5	3.0	6.0	0.0	6.0	6.0	1.5	13.5	Scat	Annual	67	Edwards 1996
N. Carolina/ Virginia	0.4	15.5	43.8	37.3	17.2	2.1	6.5	17.9	1.3	0.0	9.0	2.5	3.4	Scat/ Stom.	Annual	233	Progulske 1955
S. Carolina	64.0	1.9	3.2	43.8	0.0	0.6	0.9	3.8	2.2	0.0	21.8	0.3	18.0	Scat	Annual	317	Kight 1960
Tennessee	8.0	34.7	9.1	21.1	16.5	2.3	15.3	27.8	0.6	0.0	13.1	0.0	0.0	Scat	Annual	176	Story et al. 1982
Virginia	0.9	11.2	33.4	54.6	9.9	0.0	2.6	17.8	1.9	0.0	12.0	2.9	4.5	Scat	Annual	124	Progulske 1955

[a] Expressed as percentage of all scats or stomachs containing that food item. Percentages will not sum to 100% as scats or stomachs may contain more than one food item.
[b] includes the genera Sigmodon, and Rattus
[c] Includes all rodents, not partitioned by rodent species.
[d] Includes voles when present.

Table 17. Composition (percentage occurrence)[a] of diet of coyote in the southeastern United States.

	Dietary item																
	Mammal							Avian			Plant						
State	Rat[b]	Mice[c,d]	Sciurid	Rabbit	Deer	Other	Live stock	Reptile	Turkey	Other	Inver-tebrate	Fruit	Other	Method	Time period	N	Citation
Alabama	44.7	21.3		36.3	37.6		0.0	0.0		10.2	13.3	16.7	0.0	Scat	Annual	292	Hoerath and Causey 1991
Alabama/	29.9	18.0	2.8	35.1	27.0	9.3	4.3	4.3	0.0	23.7	39.3	51.2	13.3	Scat	Winter/	211	Wooding et al. 1984
Mississippi	21.0	23.0	6.0	34.0	30.0	11.0	24.0	4.0	0.0	28.0	41.0	17.9	18.0	Stomach	Spring	100	
Arkansas	9.0[c]		0.0	7.0	5.0	5.0	47.0	0.0	0.0	10.0	12.0	36.0[g]	2.0	Stomach	Annual	168	Gipson 1974
Kentucky	0.0	60.0	0.0	22.0	3.0	53.0[e]	28.0	0.0	0.0	10.0	0.0	0.0	3.0	Stomach	Winter	60	Crossett and Elliott 1991
Mississippi	25.6	9.8	3.7	34.5	45.1	11.0	1.2	1.2	1.2	2.4	2.4	18.3	33.0	Scat	Annual	82	Edwards 1996
Oklahoma	45.0	8.0	0.0	11.0	20.0	10.0	6.0	4.0	0.0	19.0	19.0	32.0	0.0	Scat	Annual	361	Litvaitis and Shaw 1980
Tennessee	39.2[c]			28.8	27.0	1.9	16.7	1.8	4.5[d]	10.8	12.6	32.4	46.8	Stomach	Annual	262	Lee and Kennedy 1986
Regional (Mississippi, Alabama, Kentucky, Tennessee)	5.5	13.5	2.1	31.6	30.8	13.6	0.0	0.0	0.0	10.3	41.2	40.0	14.5	Scat/ Stom.	Summer	532	Blanton and Hill 1989

[a] Expressed as percentage of all scats or stomachs containing that food item. Percentages will not sum to 100% as scats or stomachs may contain more than one food item.
[b] includes the genera Sigmodon, and Rattus
[c] Includes all rodents, not partitioned by rodent species.
[d] Cited as gamebird so would include quail, etc.
[e] Includes 10% striped skunk.
[f] Includes poultry.
[g] Includes domestic fruits, such as watermelon.

consume a diversity of foods including rodents (mice and rats), squirrels, rabbits, birds, insects as well as some plant material (fruits and vegetation) (Table 18). Another noteworthy observation is that fox diet is extremely diverse and often scats or stomachs commonly contain greater than 2, often 3 prey categories.

River Otter

Diet studies show the river otter as a specialist in capturing fish, which usually represents over 75% of the diet, followed by crustaceans, primarily crayfish (Table 19). The otter is opportunistic and capable of capturing most fish species. However, slower moving fishes, including suckers (Catostomidae) and carp (Cyprinidae), are obviously more vulnerable. For example, Lauhachinda and Hill (1977), studying otter in Alabama and Georgia, found 12 families of fish consumed including bass (Centrarchidae), bowfin, minnows (Cyprinidae), and perch (Percidae). Additional prey items include frogs (Ranidae), salamanders, and mollusks. Mammalian prey include muskrats, rodents, mink, and nutria. Turtles, although

Table 18. Composition (percentage occurrence)[a] of diet of red and gray foxes in the southeastern United States.

	Dietary item															
	Mammal							Avian			Plant					
State	Cottonrat	Mice	Sciurid	Rabbit	Deer	Other	Reptile	Turkey	Other	Invertebrate	Fruit	Other	Method	Time period	N	Citation
Red Fox																
Kentucky	0.0	100.0	3.0	18.0	1.0	44.0	0.0	0.0	19.0	11.0	10.0	3.0	Stomach	Winter	72	Crossett and Elliott 1991
Virginia	40.0[b]		6.7	53.3	0.0	26.7	0.0	0.0	26.7[e]	6.7	33.3	0.0	Stomach	Winter	15	Nelson 1933
Gray Fox																
Georgia	49.5[d]						1.0	0.0	8.5	24.5	21.0	14.0	Stomach	Annual	171	Golley 1962
Mississippi	52.8[b]		0.0	19.5	22.2	0.0	0.0	0.0	8.3	0.0	0.0	11.1	Scat	Winter	26	Tucker 1987
Tennessee	33.5[d]			47.0			0.0	0.0	24.5	48.0	0.0	10.0	Stomach	Annual	24	Yoho and Henry 1972
Texas	46.7[b,c]				0.0	0.0	0.0	0.0	17.3	24.7	10.0	0.0	Stomach	Annual	42	Davis and Schmidly 1994
Texas	77.7[d]						<1.0	0.0	9.5	4.1	??	7.8	Scat/Stom.	Annual	34	Wood 1954
Virginia	70.4	0.0		23.2	0.0	0.0	6.2	0.0	0.5	10.1	15.9	6.4	Scat	Annual	224	Hensley and Fisher 1975
Virginia	50.0[b]	1.2		41.5	0.0	3.7	2.4	0.0	42.7[e]	26.8	62.2	0.0	Stomach	Winter	82	Nelson 1933

[a]Expressed as percentage of all scats or stomachs containing that food item. Percentages will not sum to 100% as scats or stomachs may contain more than one food item.
[b]Includes all rodents, not partitioned by rodent species.
[c]Includes rabbits.
[d]Includes all mammalian prey.
[e]Includes poultry.

Table 19. Composition (percentage occurrence)[a] of diet of river otter in the southeastern United States.

	Dietary item											
State	Fish	Crustacean	Invertebrate	Amphibians	Mollusks	Mammal	Avian	Plant	Method	Time period	N	Citation
Alabama/Georgia	83.2	62.6	10.8	5.4	2.5	1.0	0.3	3.8	Stomach	Winter	315	Lauhachinda and Hill 1977
Arkansas	96.0	0.0	<1.0	<1.0	0.0	<1.0	0.0	0.0	Scat	Spring	240	Melquist and Dronkert 1987
Florida	83.3	33.3	0.0	5.6	0.0	0.0	0.0	0.0	Stomach	Winter	18	McDaniel 1963
Florida	87.0	75.0	41.0	20.0	0.0	25.0	2.0	0.0	Stomach	Winter	187	Cooley 1983
Louisiana (saltmarsh)	83.3	24.6	0.0	0.0	1.6	7.9	2.4	0.0	Stomach	Winter	126	Chabreck et al. 1982
Louisiana (swamp)	83.0	41.5	0.0	5.7	3.8	7.5	0.0	0.0	Stomach	Winter	53	Chabreck et al. 1982
Mississippi	100.0	90.9	0.0	0.0	0.0	0.0	0.0	6.1	Stomach	Winter	66	Davis 1981
N. Carolina	91.0	39.0	6.0	0.0	1.0	1.0	3.0	0.0	Stomach	??	??	Wilson 1954

[a]Expressed as percentage of all scats or stomachs containing that food item. Percentages will not sum to 100% as scats or stomachs may contain more than one food item.

abundant in the aquatic environments inhabited by river otter, rarely are found as a dietary item (Toweill and Tabor 1984).

Long-tailed and Least Weasels

Information on weasel diets in the Southeast is very limited. Weasels often kill more prey than they immediately consume and may cache prey for later use. However, caching is less common in the South where warm temperatures enhance decomposition rates. In general, the long-tailed weasel is more of a dietary generalist than is the least weasel (Sheffield and Thomas 1997). Long-tailed weasels prey on mice, rabbits, snakes, frogs, birds, and insects. Males tend to prey on larger items than do females (Errington 1936).

There are no published studies of least weasel diets in the Southeast; however, generally least weasels prey on mice, insects, and voles throughout their range (Erlinge 1975, Fagerstone 1987). Least weasels feed on small prey such as mice (Criddle 1947) and are adapted to hunt rodent runways and burrows.

Mink

Mink are strongly carnivorous, but utilize a wide variety of prey, including rabbits, mice, frogs and insects. In areas with high muskrat densities, mink may feed extensively on muskrat (Sealander 1943, Wilson 1954). Cotton rats, a locally abundant prey item in the Southeast, are often prey of mink in its southern range (Schnell 1964). Evidence also suggests that mink prey on particularly vulnerable individuals in prey populations (Sargeant et al. 1973).

HOME RANGE AND HABITAT USE

Home range and habitat use among the furbearers in the southeastern United States is a function of species, location, sex, age, season, land management practices, and population status. The home range of an animal also may vary with local conditions, including density of the furbearer population, or of prey species, variations in weather patterns, and social status of the animal. Habitat use is more variable than home range size, primarily a function of the same variables that affect home range and because a diversity of habitats exist throughout the southeastern United States. Additionally, extensive and intensive forest and agricultural activities provide a diversity of habitats and habitat conditions that favor or disfavor furbearer populations.

Bobcat

Home ranges of bobcats throughout the southeastern United States range from less than 740 ac to 17,830 ac (Table 20). There is no apparent geographic pattern of home range size for bobcats across the southeastern states. Home ranges are as small in Alabama (approximately 494 ac) as in South Carolina. Home ranges of females are significantly less than those for males. The larger home ranges of males are generally attributed to the polygamous nature of bobcats and males moving in search for multiple mates.

The prey species preferred by the bobcat (rodents and rabbits) are most abundant in early successional stages of southern forests (Chamberlain et al. 1996). Consequently, habitats used extensively by bobcats in the Southeast are primarily the early seral stages of pine or mixed pine-hardwood (Kitchings and Story 1979, Heller and Fendley 1982, Rucker et al. 1989, Conner et al. 1992) or hardwood stands (Hall and Newsome 1976). Often, these habitats are a result of timber harvest or timber stand improvement (thinning, burning, etc.). Female bobcats are more selective in habitat use than males (Edwards 1996, Lovell 1996), probably because females are more focused on securing food and raising young (Conner et al. 1992). Lastly, other habitats are used by bobcats including hardwood stands (Hall and Newsome 1976), mature pine stands (Edwards 1996, Lovell 1996), and agricultural fields

Table 20. Home range sizes (ac) of male and female bobcats in the southeastern United States.

	Home range (ac)					
State	**Male**	**N**	**Female**	**N**	**Method**	**Citation**
Alabama	650	6	277	6	100% convex	Miller and Speake 1979
Arkansas	15,864	1	6,054	3	100% convex	Rucker et al. 1989
Kentucky	11,046	5	1,161	4	95% convex	Whitaker et al. 1987
Louisiana	1,221	3	240	3	100% convex	Hall and Newsom 1976
Mississippi	4,942	18	2,773	31	95% convex	Edwards 1996, Lovell 1996
S. Carolina	15,360	2	3,482	3	100% convex	Griffith and Fendley 1982
Tennessee	10,601	1	2,842	2	100% convex	Kitchens and Story 1979
Texas	863	3	287	1	95% harmonic	Bradley and Fagre 1988

Table 21. Home range sizes (ac) of male and female coyotes in the southeastern United States.

	Home range (ac)					
State	**Male**	**N**	**Female**	**N**	**Method**	**Citation**
Alabama/Mississippi	4,942	5	10,181	3	100% convex	Sumner et al. 1984
Arkansas	8,192	7	3,264	4	100% ellipse	Gipson and Sealander 1972
Georgia	1,878	3	6,894	2	95% ellipse	Holzman et al. 1992
Mississippi	3,632	8	9,654	5	100% convex	Edwards 1996, Lovell 1996
Oklahoma	7,734	5	16,976	6	100% convex	Litvaitis and Shaw 1980
Tennessee	7,660	3	14,826	2	100% convex	Babb and Kennedy 1988
Texas	813	3	744	2	95% harmonic	Bradley and Fagre 1988

and pastures if edges and fencerows adjacent to these areas are maintained (Conner and Leopold 1996).

Coyote

Home ranges of coyotes range from 1,880 ac to over 14,830 ac (Table 21). Unlike the bobcat, male home ranges generally are smaller than those of females (Edwards 1996, Lovell 1996).

Habitat use by coyotes in the Southeast is diverse, and reflects the opportunistic nature of coyotes regarding feeding habits. Although early to mid-successional habitats of pine and hardwood forests are used frequently, all stages of forests are used (Wooding 1984, Sumner 1984, Holzman et al. 1992, Edwards 1996, Lovell 1996) including pine plantations, cedar woodlots, fencerows, edges of cultivated fields, and lake edges. In Texas, coyote habitat use was non-selective, but thickets and drainages were frequently used (Bradley and Fagre 1988). Additionally, because of its generalist nature of habitat use, male and female habitat use does not significantly differ (Bradley and Fagre 1988, Edwards 1996, Lovell 1996).

Red Fox

No published studies of home ranges or habitat use for red fox were found for southeastern states. It is generally recognized that the red fox prefers more open habitats including cropland, especially with hedgerows, shrublands, pastures, mixed hardwood stands, and the associated habitat edges (Samuel and Nelson 1984). Samuel and Nelson (1984) stated that both red and gray foxes prefer intermixed forest types rather than large tracts of homogeneous forest.

Gray Fox

Home range size for gray fox has been reported to be from 590 ac to over 4,943 ac (Table 22). Home range sizes for males and females are similar, which is expected, given the gray foxes' monogamous nature and the strong pair bond formed by a breeding pair. However, there are exceptions where male home ranges were less than those of females (Alabama and Mississippi). Conversely, home ranges of unpaired males may exceed those of paired males and/or females (Chamberlain and Leopold, unpubl. data).

In general, the gray fox is more of a woodland species compared to the red fox. Wood et al. (1958) in Georgia, Wooding (1984) in Alabama, and Edwards (1996) and Lovell (1996) in Mississippi all found that mature mixed pine-hardwood and young and mature pine stands were used most frequently by gray fox. However, in Louisiana, Foote (1984) found that early successional habitats were preferred. Sawyer and Fendley (1994) reported that males and females frequently use 5-14 year old pine stands, although all habitats including bottomland and upland hardwood, mixed pine hardwood, and all ages of pine forests were used to some degree. They also reported that habitat use differed between sexes as a function of changing food habits, cover requirements and reproductive behaviors. However, Lovell (1996) and Edwards (1996) did not find habitat usage significantly different in mated pairs participating in pup rearing. Lastly, authors have cited diel differences in habitat preferences by gray fox (Progulske 1982, Sawyer and Fendley 1994).

River Otter

Given the linear nature of its environment, home ranges of river otters are not easily determined and there are few studies. However, Foy (1984) in Texas reported a use area by river otter between 455 to 1,139 ac.

Habitat use by river otter has not been well documented for southeastern states. Humphrey and Zinn (1982) in Florida evaluated usage of 9 wetland habitats

Table 22. Home range sizes (ac) of male and female gray fox in the southeastern United States.

	Home range (ac)							
State	Male	N	Female	N	Pooled	N	Method	Citation(s)
Alabama	1,114	2	2,560	9	1,564	20	100% convex	Nicholson 1984
Alabama/ Mississippi	1,260	3	1,013	5	1,218	11	100% convex	Wooding 1984
Florida					2,011	18	Capture radius	Lord 1961
Florida					1,137	5	100% convex	Progulske 1982
Mississippi	885	2	5,286	2	3,086	4	100% convex	Edwards 1996, Lovell 1996
Mississippi	768	8	749	9	759	17	100% convex	Tucker and Jacobson 1986
S. Carolina	623	7	566	6	596	13	100% convex	Griffith and Fendley 1982

used by river otter. Otter showed greater usage of virgin cypress swamp, willow swamp, and recently burned swamp forest, although all habitats, except freshwater marsh with cypress were used. Seasonal differences in habitat use were observed. In general, river otters will use aquatic habitats as long as human disturbance is not excessive and pollution levels are low (Toweill and Tabor 1984).

Long-tailed and Least Weasels
Home range sizes of long-tailed weasels are poorly understood throughout the Southeast. Generally, home ranges of long-tailed weasels are larger than those of least weasels (Svendsen 1982). Males have larger home ranges than do females (Fagerstone 1987). In Kentucky, DeVan (1982) reported home ranges varying from 25 to 59 ac. Home ranges were larger in summer than during winter.

Long-tailed weasels use a wide variety of habitats, reflecting their ability to exploit many types of prey. Long-tailed weasels can be found in deciduous and coniferous woodlands, fencerows, rocky mountainous areas, and brushy areas surrounding agricultural fields. In some parts of its range, long-tailed weasels are limited by availability of free-standing water (Hall 1951).

There is no published information on home range sizes or habitat use patterns of least weasels in the Southeast. Home ranges of least weasels have ranged from 2 to 37 ac in other parts of their range (King 1975). Least weasels occupy a variety of habitats including open woodlands, marshes, fencerows and brushy or abandoned agricultural fields.

Mink
There are no published data on mink home ranges or habitat use patterns for the southeastern states. However, using research findings from other areas, generalizations regarding mink home range sizes and dynamics can be made. Male mink have larger home ranges than females, with adult mink of both sexes having larger home ranges than juveniles. Often, habitat usage and movement is associated with aquatic habitats.

Habitat use patterns in mink vary by geographic area, season, and often by sex. The one habitat component that is consistently required is a permanent water source, as mink are seldom found far from water. Generally, mink can be found in various kinds of wetlands, such as marshes, swamps and along the banks of rivers and streams. In Louisiana, Arthur (1931) found that mink often used coastal marshes and cypress swamps. In coastal areas of Louisiana, mink often use bottomland swamps which are high in numbers of crayfish (Lowery 1974). In Florida, Humphrey and Zinn (1982) found highest use of swamp forest and lowest use in freshwater swamps.

DISEASES AND PARASITES

Diseases rarely regulate (maintain numbers consistent with available resources) a population, primarily because density of the species must be high for the disease or parasite to become effective in regulating animal numbers. Many of the southeastern furbearers are solitary or reclusive (excluding family groups), and thus few diseases reach critical levels. However, there are some exceptions and sometimes population numbers of southeastern furbearers are controlled (are cyclic) by diseases. The diseases and parasites below are those that are most commonly found for each species, and not a comprehensive list. Much of the material presented below follows Davidson and Nettles (1988).

Bobcat
Relatively speaking, bobcats are not susceptible to many parasites or diseases and most populations are relatively "healthy" in this regard (McCord and Cardoza 1984). However, some viruses are noteworthy. The most commonly discussed disease is feline panleukopenia, also known as feline distemper. It is very infectious, but little information exists regarding its prominence in wild bobcat populations (Davidson and Nettles 1988). Other diseases of bobcats include rabies, toxoplasmosis (protozoan parasite) in which the bobcat serves as a host, and *Spirometra*, a tapeworm, with the bobcat as a definitive host. Additionally, the bobcat is a reservoir host for *Cytauxzoon felis*. However, it has not been documented to cause disease in wild felids, although it is very common in domestic cats throughout the southeastern United States.

Ectoparasites are extremely uncommon on bobcats, although various species of fleas have been reported. Other parasites found in specific studies include roundworms and hookworms (McCord and Cardoza 1984).

Coyote
Coyotes, as with most canids, are susceptible to a diverse array of diseases, and some may have debilitating effects on populations. The most common disease of coyotes in the southeastern United States is canine distemper (virus) which has been found throughout the southeastern United States (Davidson and Nettles 1988). Another disease of coyotes is parvoviral enteri-

tis, although its prominence is unknown. Diseases found in Texas coyotes included rabies and brucellosis, although cases are rare. However, recently (early 1990s) Mexican dog rabies has been found in coyote and gray fox prompting federal and state authorities to initiate a more rigorous rabies control program.

Coyotes are susceptible to a variety of parasites including roundworms, tapeworms, hookworms, whipworms, heartworms, and thorny-headed worms (Bekoff 1977). Ectoparasites include numerous species of fleas, ticks and lice. Sarcoptic mange may be locally common in some coyote populations and may result in significantly reduced fecundity and increased mortality rates (Pence and Windberg 1994).

Red Fox

Sarcoptic mange is the most prevalent disease of red fox in the southeastern United States, and it is the most significant disease-related mortality factor (Samuel and Nelson 1984, Davidson and Nettles 1988). Other uncommon diseases of red fox in the southeastern United States include rabies, leptospirosis, canine heartworm, and the subcutaneous nematode *Dracunculus insignis*. One reported disease common to red foxes on fox farms is infectious canine hepatitis. Additionally, *Echinococcus multilocularis* has been detected in translocated foxes from the midwest. Notably, canine distemper, although prevalent in the gray fox, is relatively uncommon to the red fox (Davidson and Nettles 1988). Additionally, Chomel (1993) has stated that the red fox represents the most widespread reservoir of rabies in the world.

Numerous parasites typically common to canids are common to red fox including numerous species of fleas, ticks, roundworms and hookworms.

Gray Fox

Canine distemper is the major disease of gray fox, which may occur locally or regionally (Nicholson and Hill 1984, Davidson and Nettles 1988). Often, this disease may result in reduction of local populations of gray fox, in addition to other furbearers, especially the raccoon. Other diseases of gray fox, although uncommon, include rabies, leptospirosis, canine heartworm, and infectious canine hepatitis.

External parasites of the gray fox are those found for most canids: several species of fleas and ticks.

River Otter

Disease prevalence and relevance regarding river otter ecology is little known. Davidson and Nettles (1988) stated that canine distemper, stress-induced salmonellosis and the subcutaneous nematode *Dracunculus lutrae* may occur but are very uncommon. Toweill and Tabor (1984) cite numerous helminth parasites for river otter in southeastern states, including 4 species of trematodes, 1 species of tapeworm, 7 species of nematodes, and 4 species of thorny-headed worms from otter collected in Alabama, Georgia, and N. Carolina.

Long-tailed and Least Weasels

Information on diseases in weasels is extremely limited. Long-tailed weasels can be affected by canine distemper (Goss 1948) and tularemia. Additionally, long-tailed weasels are affected by the nasal nematode (*Dracunculus medinensis*) that causes damage to sinuses, as well as some cestodes and trematodes (Davis and Anderson 1971). Similar to other furbearers, long-tailed weasels are host to numerous ectoparasites including ticks, fleas, lice, and mites. Canine distemper affects least weasels and tularemia and nasal nematodes are found in least weasels (Parker 1934). Also, least weasels carry external parasites including ticks, fleas and mites.

Mink

The mink is host to many internal parasites, including many trematodes, cestodes, and nematodes. Mink virus enteritis and kidney worms may significantly affect mink. Virus enteritis has not been documented in wild mink, but can decimate ranch mink populations. Kidney worms are not fatal in wild mink unless both kidneys are infected (Davidson and Nettles 1988). As are other southeastern furbearers, mink are host to numerous ectoparasites such as ticks, mites, lice, and fleas.

INTERSPECIES INTERACTIONS

Interactions Among Furbearers

Home range and habitat use of terrestrial furbearers overlap and interactions occur (Wooding 1984, Edwards 1996). Also, carnivores are generally territorial and thus intraspecific and interspecific aggression is likely in defense of resources. With the exception of family groups, terrestrial furbearers are generally solitary and chance meetings among conspecifics may result in aggressive behavior. Lastly, because of territoriality, resident animals may be frequently challenged by subordinate conspecifics in hopes of acquiring the territory. However, it is likely that most carnivores, with olfactory cues they use regarding scent marking (using urine, excretions from scent glands, and feces), minimize encounters through mutual avoidance reaction (Hornocker 1969). This reaction is simply that animals move away from an area that is being used by a conspecific (and for an individual of another species), thereby minimizing chances for contact socially, temporally, and spatially.

Both coyote and the red fox prefer open grassland habitat and interactions occur. Evidence suggests that where coyotes are numerous, red fox populations are sparse, or strong avoidance occurs (Dekker 1983, Voigt and Earle 1983, Sargeant et al. 1987, Gese et al. 1989, Harrison et al. 1989, Theberge and Wedeles 1989). Additionally, where coyotes and red fox are sympatric, home ranges do not overlap. There is less potential interaction of the coyote with gray fox because the gray fox generally prefers wooded habitats and is semi-arboreal and thus can escape any coyote attacks.

Studies have shown that bobcat, coyote and fox will minimize interactions. The most frequent interaction assessed is between bobcat and coyote, usually with avoidance observed (Witmer and DeCalesta 1986, Litvaitis and Harrison 1989). Edwards (1996) found minimal interaction among coyote, bobcat and gray fox.

The degree of interaction between river otter and mink with the terrestrial carnivores is minimal because of the aquatic nature and feeding habitats of these 2 species. Otter and mink interactions are minimal given that they are not competitors for resources (mink primarily non-piscivorous and otter primarily piscivorus). However, otter who venture on land are vulnerable to predation by coyote (Young and Jackson 1951) and bobcats; however, it is not believed to significantly impact otter populations (Toweill and Tabor 1984).

Weasels are fierce predators, thus interactions with other small weasels are likely rare. No published information is available on interactions among weasels and other furbearers, or of weasels and other game species. However, long-tailed weasels are preyed upon by red foxes, gray foxes, and coyotes (Fagerstone 1987). Interactions between least weasels and long-tailed weasels are likely rare, but least weasels may be preyed upon by long-tailed weasels. Declines in weasel populations have been attributed to depredation by foxes in northern parts of their range (Latham 1952, Sheffield and Thomas 1997). Weasels also are preyed upon by bobcats, rattlesnakes, hawks and barred owls.

Other than mating encounters, documented interactions between individual mink are rare. Errington (1943) speculated that encounters among mink could result in substantial mink deaths. Further, information on predators of mink is limited and often based on speculation. Depredation of mink may result from coyotes, bobcats, and great-horned owls throughout the southeastern United States. However, given the aggressive disposition of mink, intentional encounters between mink and other carnivores are likely rare.

Interactions Between Furbearers and Other Wildlife Species

There is interest in effects of furbearers, especially bobcat, red and gray fox, and mink on other wildlife species and the coyote, with its range expansion throughout the southeastern United States, has caused concern by wildlife biologists that its addition to the landscape may seriously impact game populations. Blanton and Hill (1989) examined summer coyote diet in 4 southeastern states to assess coyote predation of deer fawns. They found that in areas of high deer density and during peak fawn drop, incidence of deer in scats significantly increased. However, although consumption of deer fawns increased during the fawning season, the impact of this predation on the deer herd was not assessed. Wagner and Hill (1994) examined coyote diet in multiple study areas during the reproductive and non-reproductive period of the eastern wild turkey. They found a very low incidence of turkey in coyote scats in good turkey habitat.

Studies in Texas by Beasom (1974a) and Alabama by Speake (1980) specifically examined the impacts of carnivores (many furbearers) on game populations. Beasom (1974a) removed a diverse group of carnivores including coyote (n = 188), bobcat (n = 120), raccoon (n = 65), 3 species of skunk (n = 49), badger (n = 18), and opossum (n = 17). Population numbers of turkeys and white-tailed deer responded significantly, with quail increasing to a lessor extent. However, Beasom (1974a) was unable to ascertain which species of carnivore most significantly impacted game populations. Similarly, Speake (1980) in Alabama assessed carnivore removal (opossums, raccoons, feral and free-ranging dogs, gray foxes, and skunks), but concluded that the net effect of the removal was not an appreciable gain in turkey numbers. These studies indicated that the coyote does not seem to be a significant threat to game populations at its current density levels in the southeastern United States. However, Beasom (1974b) found that deer populations may be increased with intensive coyote and bobcat removal, but also warned that the subsequent increase in deer would have to be maintained within carrying capacity.

The study by Beasom (1974a) demonstrated that predators impact game populations. Although species-specific assessments were not made, the most likely candidates are raccoon, opossum, and red and gray fox. Both the bobcat and coyote can, and do, kill adult and juvenile game animals including squirrel, deer, turkey, rabbit and quail. However, the coyote's diverse and omnivorous feeding habits and the bobcat's keen ability to capture rodents and rabbits, preclude these 2 furbearers from having any significant impact on most game populations. In contrast, studies have shown that the medium-sized carnivores (mink, foxes) may have a significant impact on some other species, especially ground-nesting game birds (Beasom 1974b, Guthery and Beasom 1977, Miller and Leopold 1992, and others).

The above discussion has dealt with the negative effects of the terrestrial furbearers on game and nongame wildlife. However, it should be noted that coyote, bobcat, mink, weasels, and red and gray fox consume many small mammals (rats and mice) and rabbits. For example, in Colorado, Quick (1951) estimated that on an area of approximately 3,954 mi^2, approximately 8,000 long-tailed weasels inhabited the area and consumed approximately 30,000 small mammals/day! This may be beneficial in that these species may impact plant regeneration (seed consumption), seedling and sapling survival (girdling during winter), transmit diseases, and affect grain crops. Hensley and Fisher (1975) studied the effects of intensively removing gray fox from upland Virginia sites. They found that removal of gray fox resulted in a corresponding increase in long-tailed weasel and that the increased weasel population impacted small mammals more than the fox population. Obviously, this study showed the importance of gray fox in animal community dynamics. A study by Henke and Bryant (1999) in Texas grasslands found that the coyote served as a "keystone predator" by maintaining increased biodiversity, especially of rodents and other carnivores, on sites were coyotes were not trapped.

Because the river otter is an aquatic mammal, impacts on all terrestrial species are minimal. It is proficient at capturing fish and may affect fish populations. However, diet studies show that the otter feeds primarily on non-game fish species and may be beneficial by reducing competition for resources by preferred game fish (Toweill and Tabor 1984).

Mink prey on ground-nesting birds, particularly waterfowl (Sargeant et al. 1973); however, no evidence suggests that mink depredation limits populations of any wildlife species in the Southeast. Mink also prey on fish, but the extent to which mink prey on particular fish species is undocumented. Evidence suggests that in Louisiana, mink populations may rely heavily on muskrat populations and may actually track muskrat population fluctuations.

MANAGEMENT

Managing furbearers is challenging. Furbearers such as bobcat, gray fox, red fox, mink, weasels and coyote are wary, solitary and, nocturnal or crepuscular. Furbearer management is controversial because of the method of harvesting furbearers: using foot-gripping traps (for terrestrial furbearers), snares (for terrestrial and aquatic furbearers) and body-gripping traps (primarily for the aquatic furbearers, otter and beaver). A survey by Messmer et al. (1999), assessing U.S. households concerning knowledge and attitudes toward predators, predation and predator management, provides an interesting perspective. Based on survey results, most respondents felt that predators 1) have a right to exist, 2) should be reintroduced to former ranges, 3) do need to be managed, but with conditions, 4) should not be hunted or trapped unconditionally, 5) are not the cause of game population declines, and 6) play an important role in maintaining balanced natural systems. Most furbearers are carnivores and thus must be managed both within an ecological and a utilitarian (use) context. Given public perceptions, a thorough assessment of the animal population, impact on the resources in question and the resulting management requires an accurate assessment of population numbers, methods of control (or enhancement), and public perception and response to the management decisions and activities.

Censusing

Censusing the southeastern furbearers discussed in this chapter is very difficult because they are either solitary, crepuscular or nocturnal, secretive and/or very wary of man, or are aquatic and thus difficult to observe. Most census procedures are based on indirect counts because of the difficulty in direct observation. In most cases, indirect counts that allow managers to monitor trends in population numbers are adequate for effective furbearer management.

The primary indirect censusing methods commonly used in southeastern states include scent stations (Johnson and Pelton 1981), track counts, and predator calling. Scent stations are commonly used and involve clearing of a specified area (usually 1 m^2) and using some form of scent to attract the furbearer to the site so that tracks may be counted. Common tracking media include sifted soil from the site, agricultural lime or sand. Commonly used scents include a fatty acid scent

(FAS), or bobcat, coyote or fox urine. Various media are used to hold the scent, such as cotton balls or plaster-of-paris diskettes. The experimental design is usually a transect line with 10 to 20 stations spaced equally apart. Spacing should be linked to the mobility of the animal being censused to ensure that the same animal does not visit multiple stations (Roughton and Sweeny 1982). Distances between stations range from 0.124 mi to as high as 1 mi. Stations are usually sampled for one night, and percentage of stations visited, rather than number of tracks/station, is used as the index of abundance.

Numerous studies have examined the effectiveness of scent stations to monitor coyotes (Crawford et al. 1993), bobcats (Diefenbach et al. 1994, Gabor et al. 1994), river otter (Clark et al. 1987) or furbearers in general (Linscombe et al. 1983, Stapper et al. 1989, Morrison et al. 1981, Sumner and Hill 1980, Roughton and Sweeney 1982, Conner et al. 1983). Many of these evaluations also included assessments of track counts and predator calling. In general, scent stations have been effective for coyotes, bobcats, and foxes, but poor for river otter, mink and weasels. Mangrum (1994) examined variations in station monitoring by evaluating stations with scent (olfactory stimulus), hanging disks (visual stimulus), and a rabbit predator calling unit (auditory), as well as track counts, to evaluate response by bobcats. All methods were similar in visitation response by bobcat, and Mangrum (1994) suggested that track count plots were more effective than scent, visual or auditory stations. Humphrey and Zinn (1982) indicated that scent stations were effective to monitor otter abundance, but other studies have questioned their utility, especially when populations are low (Nottingham et al. 1982). Melquist and Hornocker (1979) stated that there is not any single method that effectively censuses river otter, and suggested a combination of using sign such as scat and tracks and visual observations to determine presence.

Roughton and Sweeny (1982) suggested the following regarding scent station methodology: 1) operate lines of 10 stations, 1 night; 2) ensure that scent station is properly graded; 3) timing of surveys is important; 4) distance between stations scaled to species of interest to minimize multiple visits by the same animal; 5) FAS is the best canid attractant and works well with other carnivores; and 6) plaster disks should be used to house the attractant. Although census techniques have been developed and evaluated, tremendous variation exists regarding visitation rates by furbearers and prior to implementing a monitoring program, numerous variables should be considered including density of the animal population of interest, species, man-power allocations, access to the management unit, type of road system, and frequency and intensity of road use by motor vehicles.

Several methodologies have been applied to conduct track counts. One method is to drive a specified length of road, usually following a rain shower to ensure that all old tracks were removed, and counting all fresh tracks. The index is usually expressed as animals/mi of road driven. Another derivation of this method is removing old tracks from a section of road and then counting number of animals that cross the transect.

The third frequently used method is predator calling. Sirens (Okoniewski and Chambers 1984), predator calls or tape recordings of animals are used at specified stations located at distances far enough apart to preclude repeated responses by individuals, usually at least 0.5 mi. This technique is used primarily for coyotes, and also for red fox and gray fox (Sumner and Hill 1980).

Another procedure that shows promise for indexing furbearer abundance is smoke plates, originally developed for small mammals (Mayer 1957), and later adapted for carnivores (Barrett 1983). The procedure uses a 1 m^2, 0.06 cm thick aluminum plate with one surface covered with a tracking surface (such as the soot from a kerosene lamp). Bait such as cat-food or jack mackerel is secured to the center of the plate. The plate is checked for tracks as with scent station so tracks are clearly shown on the smoked surface. It has been found effective for raccoon (Leopold and Chamberlain 1997), but less so for coyote and bobcat because of their wariness of the plate. Zielinski (1995) provides an excellent review of this procedure, including its variations in methodology.

There are numerous other census techniques to index furbearers. Those used most commonly by state management agencies include trapper questionnaires, and fur dealer reports. Because of CITES requirements, in all states, a mandatory tagging system for exported pelts is in place for river otter and bobcat. Other survey techniques include harvest reports, road mortality samples, spotlight samples (especially for raccoon), depredation indices, and field personnel reports (Clark and Andrews 1982).

General Management Concepts—Trapping and Hunting

In the South, favorable environmental conditions, such as temperate climate, long growing season and extensive area in early successional habitat, have been productive for carnivorous furbearer prey. The abundance

Early successional habitats are important areas for carnivores to secure prey such as small rodents *(M. Chamberlain)*.

of prey has resulted in high furbearer reproductive rates and population densities. Consequently, except for river otter, trapping and harvest has not been restricted for furbearers. One exception is Kentucky for the bobcat, but populations there are rebounding. In contrast, trapping for bobcat is prohibited in many mid-western states such as Ohio, Iowa, Illinois, and Indiana.

Southeastern furbearers may be managed in a variety of ways. Management for the river otter may be restoration of severely reduced populations as is the case for Kentucky, Tennessee, and North Carolina. Two species (bobcat and river otter) are managed through fur harvest, but with more intensive monitoring of that harvest (such as mandatory tagging at fur sales) to ensure compliance with CITES (non-detrimental impact to the populations from trapping). Artificial stocking also may occur as with foxes to supplement native populations for hunting. As stated previously, this activity of releasing coyotes for hunting accelerated the coyote's expansion throughout the southeastern United States.

If harvest is the primary goal, either for commercial fur or damage and nuisance control, then trapping has been the most commonly used management technique, but, also the most controversial. Carnivores may be trapped to control their numbers because of a real or perceived impact on game or non-game species, crops such as watermelon, and livestock such as poultry and cattle. Harvest of furbearers may be regulated by 1) length of harvest season, 2) permits to regulate trapper numbers, 3) restrictions of methods of capture, bag limits (both seasonal and daily), 4) establishing quotas regarding exporting pelts, and 5) ensuring an authority for emergency season closure (Rolley 1987). Harvest is conducted under the auspices of state wildlife management agencies. These species may be classified as "predator" with no restrictions on take, as a "game animal" with restrictions, or "threatened or endangered" species with very restrictive or no harvest options.

There is a wide variety of trap types (Novak 1987), including livetraps, wire cable snares, foothold, suitcase-type traps (such as Hancock or Bailey), and body-gripping traps (such as the conibear-type), as well as their modifications. Each is available in differing sizes to match the species desired, weather, and soil conditions, etc., such as number 2, 3 or 4 footholds. Some traps are more suited for specific species (such as conibears for capturing otter) or can be very general, such as snares, used for fox, river otter, and even coyote (Table 23). Lastly, trap modifications have been developed to make traps more humane. For foothold traps, this includes rubber pads on the jaws which reduces damage to skin, chain swivels which minimize dislocation of forelegs, in-line shock springs to minimize dislocation, and specialized pans and tension devices to reduce non-target species.

Trapping requires some expertise, which differs with the species, geographic location, climate, etc. and is an art as much as a science. Trapping is not just plac-

Forest stands open enough to allow development of ground cover may afford some protection from predation to ground-nesting birds *(M. Chamberlain)*.

Table 23. Recommended trapping methods for southeastern furbearers[a].

Species	Trapping method						
	Livetrap	Snares[b]	Leghold	Suitcase type	Conibear	Chemical	Other
Bobcat	15x15x40 to 24x24x48	3/32 inch	#2, #3 or #4 offset or padded	N/A	No. 330	None approved	Predator calling, shooting, hounds
Coyote	N/A	3/32 inch	#3 and #4 offset or padded	N/A	N/A	M-44 ejector (NaCn)[c] Protection collars (1080)[d]	Shooting, predator calling
Red and Gray Fox	N/A	1/16	#1.5, # 1.75 or #2 coil spring offset or padded	N/A	N/A	M-44 ejector (NaCn)[c]	Shooting, predator calling
River Otter	N/A	N/A	#1.5 padded or #11 double coil spring	Yes to live-trap	No.220 & 330	None approved	Selective shooting
Mink	8x8x22	N/A	#1 padded or offset	N/A	No. 110	None approved	None
Weasel	8x8x22	N/A	#1 padded offset	N/A	No. 110	None approved	None

[a]Adapted following Hygnstrom et al. (1994).
[b]Aircraft and cable.
[c]To protect livestock, threatened and endangered species, and human health and safety.
[d]To protect sheep and goats.

ing some type of trap in a location and hoping that an animal is captured; it requires an understanding of the ecology of the animal and the special techniques involved in animal capture.

Managers can not rely on harvest from trappers to control furbearer populations. This is particularly true now when the fur industry and trapping has dwindled and many furbearer populations are increasing (Lovell et al. 1998). Reduced trapping has necessitated cooperative programs between federal and state agencies to address damage questions. One example is in Mississippi and other states where USDA APHIS Wildlife Services is working with federal, state and county governments to address beaver control issues (Mastrangelo 1995), the same may be soon needed for carnivorous furbearers. It is ironic that the anti-trapping movement has resulted in a situation in which the taxpayer must now pay for control of a group of animals that, in the past, a group of individuals would be willing to pay for (trappers paying for a trapping license).

Publications regarding animal damage control are available such as that by Hygnstrom et al. (1984). Additionally, state cooperative extension programs and their respective county agents may have informative and useful publications to assist in furbearer management and harvest (for example, Hill and Jones 1986). This also is true for federal agencies such as U.S.D.A. Wildlife Services.

Predator Control Issues

Furbearer management is essentially predator management. Consequently, issues surrounding predator control merit discussion, as the western United States has faced this issue regarding predators and livestock. Therefore, lessons learned from the West apply directly to the southeastern United States.

The topic of predators usually centers around how carnivores impact prey populations. Few will argue that with decreased trapping and our current land use practices, many predator populations have increased. In fact, management practices including cutting of smaller tracts, making clearcuts irregularly shaped, planting logging roads in grasses, and developing food plots may enhance predation rates on game and non-game wildlife. Thus, the manner in which we have changed the landscape has, in part, increased predation. Unfortunately, numerous misconceptions, many potentially harmful to wildlife populations, exist and it is important that we, as stewards of our land and its wildlife, understand the process of predation and how it relates to game and non-game populations.

Predators are as much a part of the ecosystem as are their prey, and they often serve important functions in the environment. For example, one of the most respected game birds is the wild turkey, because of its wariness and the challenge it provides hunters. But, the reason this bird is so wary is because of turkey predators, and turkeys developed ways to evade predators (coevolution) long before man recognized them as a premier gamebird. Secondly, many of the southeastern predators such as fox, bobcat and coyote, consume large numbers of rats and mice. These animals, without control, may impact plants and plant communities, destroy valuable grain crops, or may be nuisances to humans, by promoting or transmitting diseases. Many predators such as red and gray fox are game animals themselves, and others, such as otter, provide fur and meat. It is doubtful many fox hunting clubs, with dogs valued at thousands of dollars each, would advocate substantial reductions in the animals that provide countless hours of recreational hunting. Another good thing about the carnivorous predators is that they remove sick and injured individuals from the environment. The sooner a diseased animal is removed from the population, the better the chances that other animals will not catch the disease!

Some studies have shown that predator removal may enhance short-term productivity of target species such as waterfowl, deer, turkeys, quail, and pheasant. But, carnivore control should only be conducted in an ecologically and environmentally sound manner. The Wildlife Society supports predator control in special circumstances such as to re-introduce a species if land management activities have somehow enhanced carnivore populations, or if wildlife populations (especially endangered species) are being seriously impacted by predators.

Any predator control must be carefully conducted. The target species should be identified and a plan developed that ensures a systematic and intensive removal of predators over a considerable time. Carnivore control is a labor-intensive activity that must be performed annually, intensively for the first 3-4 years, then moderately to lightly, thereafter. Short term control is ineffective. An excellent example of the results of such a removal program is with the coyote. Knowlton's (1972) study in Texas demonstrated that under intensive coyote control, the remaining coyotes produced litters of 7.2 pups, under moderate control, 4.5 pups, and under light control, 3.5 pups. Short-term predator control may result in greater carnivore productivity: when animals are removed from a population, the remaining animals now have more food, and thus are able to produce larger litter sizes.

Poisons are not acceptable for predator control. Most poisons are not selective for target species and thus may kill people's pets, and even the game animals that are trying to be enhanced. Additionally, poisons are not environmentally acceptable. One exception is a 1080 collar which is being used in the Southeast (placed on livestock) and is a very selective control method for "problem" coyotes.

Another consideration is that predator removal may not necessarily result in large increases in prey populations. Each habitat may have its own capacity to support a particular population level for wildlife species. Also, most carnivore species may compete and regulate other carnivore species. For example, the coyote tends to displace red foxes which are primary predators of ground-nesting birds such as turkey and quail. Therefore, coyote removal from an area could promote red foxes which may be detrimental to ground-nesting birds.

Also, now there is support for restoring predators previously extirpated from native habitat, such as river otters and red wolves in the South, timber wolves in Yellowstone National Park, and lynx in the northeastern United States. Consequently, prior to any predator removal program, long-term impacts of that removal must be considered, and the potential for societal demands to restore these populations.

Predator management is not simple and varies with circumstances. Many factors play a role in the process of predation such as weather, quantity and quality of habitat, land use practices, prey abundance, number and type of other carnivore species in the area, and human attitudes (Leopold and Hurst 1994). Also, the U.S. population has become more sensitive to animal welfare, which should be considered in wildlife, including predator management. We must remember that many prey species have existed with predators for thousands of years. We also must remember that promoting the removal of a group of organisms from the landscape (predators) to benefit another group (game animals) may not be well received by a public who like predators as much as other wildlife. Predator management has long been recognized as a viable management tool, but only under specific circumstances and with consideration of public opinion and input.

Species-specific Accounts

Bobcat.—The primary activity of bobcat management is monitoring populations, specifically harvest through tagging to ensure non-detriment. Throughout the Southeast, the bobcat is doing well, although there has been some concern in Kentucky. Optimal landscape and habitat configuration for bobcats in the southeastern United States is one with a mixture of mature forested (pine, pine-hardwood and hardwood) habitats intermixed with early-successional habitats such as clearcuts and agricultural lands. The bobcat's habitat and dietary preferences go well with some early-successional habitats such as young pine stands, that are important for rodent production (Conner et al. 1992). As long as forests remain dominant in the Southeast, bobcat populations can be maintained. However, concerns about clearcutting and the response by federal land management agencies such as the U.S. Forest Service, may result in reduced carrying capacity for bobcats. This is currently true for National Forests in Arkansas, where clearcutting is not used as a harvest and regeneration method. Also, Conner et al. (1992) and others have found that "clean-farming", does not result in the highest quality bobcat habitat. However, the Conservation Reserve Program (CRP) and its contemporary programs within the U.S. Farm Bill, should be helpful.

Coyote.—Although the coyote has long been considered a predator that required control (Young and Jackson 1951), its reputation as a predator of big game and livestock is not substantiated (Bekoff 1977, 1984). Early et al. (1974) found that only 23% of losses of sheep were from predators, the remaining 77% was attributed to disease (43%) and unknown causes (41%). Consequently, caution should be exercised in the decision to start coyote control. Millions of dollars are spent annually in this effort with often unknown long-term results (Bekoff 1984).

Red Fox.—There is little direct red fox management in the United States (Samuel and Nelson 1984). However, red foxes may be displaced by coyotes and fox hunting affects fox populations. In some areas, red foxes have declined or become locally extinct, apparently primarily from coyote competition/predation. Management efforts may have to address this interspecific interaction if viable red fox populations are to remain. Unfortunately, most actions necessary to control coyotes are not successful or may result in red fox capture. Fox hunting may be negative for red fox populations. Fox hunters and hunting are not determined by pelt prices, and there may be excessive pressure on the fox populations. This problem of depletion of fox populations through hunting may be confounded by the importation of red or gray fox, or even coyotes which may harbor and transmit disease. Because of the disease implications, state agencies should regulate importation of animals across state boundaries, including vaccination and/or quarantine of animals.

Gray Fox.—The gray fox, as the red fox, is not intensely managed. Although gray fox populations are not as threatened by coyotes, there are the same concerns regarding fox hunting. The gray fox also is valued for fox hunting. Consequently, many private clubs enhance habitat to favor gray fox populations by increasing cover by planting blackberry or honeysuckle, and increasing food by planting fruiting trees and shrubs (Fritzell 1987). Other management activities include prescribed burning to maintain fields and forests in desirable condition, although soft- and hard-mast producing trees and shrubs should be protected (Fritzell 1987). Mature forests mixed with an early-successional component is ideal habitat.

River Otter.—The river otter is susceptible to overharvest and intolerant of polluted aquatic environments. As evidenced by its listing in Appendix II of CITES and consequently, the river otter is a species of special consideration. It is being restored in the northern part of the Southeast (Kentucky, North Carolina, Oklahoma, Tennessee) and is protected from harvest there. Other states allow harvest, but monitor it through tagging and/or trapper surveys. However, it should be noted that monitoring does not ensure non-detriment from harvest.

Direct management of river otter through habitat enhancement is difficult because of the linear nature of its environment, and the nature of streams and rivers. Otter will not be found in polluted aquatic systems, and thus a broad range of environmental issues regarding pesticide use, water quality, and stream and river modification for flood control must be weighed to ensure viable otter populations. Lastly, the relatively low reproductive potential of the otter and the restricted nature of the ecosystem it prefers, makes the otter highly susceptible to overharvest. Consequently, strict population monitoring is needed, as well as the need to monitor harvest. Unfortunately, accurate and reliable census procedures for the river otter have not been developed.

Long-tailed and Least Weasels.—Because the reproductive potential of long-tailed weasels is limited, long-tailed weasels could potentially be negatively impacted by high harvest or trapping pressure. Also, habitat management to protect preferred foraging areas adjacent to water sources would be beneficial.

Little is known about least weasel ecology and this limits the sound management of this species throughout its southern range. However, least weasel populations often mimic local rodent populations. Consequently, knowledge of local prey abundance may allow management schemes to be developed to prevent drastic population fluctuations in least weasels.

Mink.—Successful management of mink populations requires a combination of habitat and harvest management. Mink are most abundant in wetland areas which are beneficial to many species of wildlife, particularly waterfowl, so maintaining and enhancing available wetland habitats is crucial to ensure viable mink populations. Mink are particularly vulnerable to environmental contaminants. In particular, mercury poisoning and pesticide residues in fish and muskrats may cause significant mortality of mink (Linscombe et al. 1982). Preventing high levels of environmental contaminants is needed to ensure high habitat quality.

Mink have long been harvested for their pelts in all southeastern states. Harvest should be monitored to prevent overexploitation; however, mink harvest will likely decline.

SUMMARY

The southeastern United States contains a diversity of carnivorous furbearers who inhabit all environments available within this region. However, current status of these species varies. Although populations of many species including bobcat, coyote, and gray fox are increasing, restoration efforts are necessary for other species such as the river otter if populations are to become viable and self-sustaining. The expansion of the coyote throughout the Southeast may impact the abundance of the red fox, and perhaps other wildlife species. However, of greatest concern are the Southeast's smaller mustelids (mink and weasels), as their ecology and thus management is poorly understood.

Furbearer management in the United States has changed significantly over the past century. Enhanced awareness of animal welfare combined with reduced demands for fur has created challenges for wildlife managers. The past perception that carnivores must be eliminated from the landscape has been replaced by one which acknowledges that carnivores are a viable component of the ecosystem. Reduced levels of trapping and hunting may eventually result in increased populations of furbearers and other problems associated with damage that furbearers may cause. However, public support of widespread control programs is unlikely, as non-economic values (ecological, aesthetic) may equal or exceed utilitarian values (hunting and trapping).

Management for several of the Southeast's carnivorous furbearers will be challenging for wildlife biologists. The paucity of knowledge concerning weasels and the mink will exacerbate management goals for these species. Additionally, the need to restore the river otter attests to the fact that this aquatic species is vulnerable to overharvest and habitat degradation, and must be monitored to ensure population viability. Expanding populations of coyotes and the potential impact on red fox also will challenge wildlife biologists, as efforts to control coyotes, regardless of their intensity, have proven unsuccessful in the western United States. Consequently, methods to ensure coexistence of these two carnivores, perhaps through habitat manipulation and management, must be developed. In contrast, the stable or growing populations of bobcat and gray fox also may intensify interspecific interactions, and thus potentially increase concerns regarding their impacts to game and non-game wildlife species.

Harvest will remain a prominent feature in the population ecology of southeastern furbearers, whether it is for sport hunting with dogs, meat, fur, or minimizing damage. As landscapes change, these populations may require manipulation to ensure their continued existence as well as existence of commensurate animal and plant species. However, this group of wildlife species provides additional benefits regarding ecosystem function and stability including control of rodents, interacting amongst themselves to suppress their respective populations, reducing probability of disease transmission by removing sick and injured animals, or providing recreational viewing opportunities. Therefore, management activities that involve harvest must be tempered with these non-utilitarian values.

Lastly, our knowledge concerning carnivorous furbearer ecology and thus management is profoundly lacking for many species, especially in the southeastern United States. This lack of knowledge on even the most basic aspects of mink, weasel and fox ecology limits the ability of wildlife biologists to effectively manage these species through harvest and habitat management. Consequently, research is certainly warranted on many of the southeastern carnivorous furbearers.

ACKNOWLEDGMENTS

We would like to thank the Department of Wildlife and Fisheries and the Forest and Wildlife Research Center for providing funding to write this chapter. Special thanks to Bobby Bond, Jake Bowman, Jason Burton, Chrissie Henner, Kurt Hodges, Darren Miller, Bruce Plowman, and Phil Mastrangelo for reviewing earlier drafts of this manuscript. Lastly, we would like to thank all of the biologists who captured, tracked, collected and synthesized the data that this chapter is based on. This is Forest & Wildlife Research Center Publication Number WF080.

CHAPTER 22

Omnivorous Furbearers

Michael J. Chamberlain[1] and Bruce D. Leopold
Department of Wildlife and Fisheries
Mississippi State University, Mississippi State, MS

In the southeastern United States, furbearers generate considerable interest from sportsmen, biologists, and laymen. Throughout the Southeast, furbearers are an integral part of the ecosystem and are found in a variety of forested and urban settings. Furbearers are pursued by sportsmen for their fur and meat, enjoyed and viewed by the public, and monitored by scientists to provide information on ecological processes within southern ecosystems. Although furbearers are valuable economically, increasing public concern over harvest of furbearers and recent declines in fur markets have created habitat and sociological conditions conducive to furbearer population increases throughout the Southeast.

The medium-sized omnivorous furbearers, the raccoon, opossum, and skunks, are readily identified and familiar to most persons, whether urban or rural, throughout the Southeast. Within rural, forested environments these furbearers are characterized in various ways. Raccoons provide sport for hunters and trappers, and aesthetic opportunities for scientists and laymen. However, raccoons have adapted well to urban settings, increasing encounters with humans and in some instances providing opportunities for conflict. Although not valued as highly for sport, opossums and skunks are notable furbearers, readily observed in rural and urban environments. In the last decade, urbanization has altered considerable wildlife habitat throughout the southeastern United States. Population levels of raccoons, opossums and skunks have increased in many urban and suburban areas. Population increases, coupled with increasing loss of habitat, have created furbearer/human conflicts, particularly concerning property damage and disease transmission. Specifically, raccoons and skunks are 2 major carriers of rabies, a definite human disease concern.

In many aspects, omnivorous furbearers contribute toward ecosystem stability. Omnivorous furbearers consume large numbers of insects and insect larvae, pro-

[1]Current Address: School of Forestry, Wildlife, and Fisheries, Louisiana State University, Baton Rouge, LA

viding benefits in many urban and agricultural situations. Additionally, these furbearers, particularly raccoons, are valued as game animals, providing considerable sport and income throughout the southeastern United States. Consequently, it is important to understand the ecology of omnivorous furbearers, including general habits, diets, habitat use, and management strategies to ensure continued existence of these furbearers.

GENERAL SPECIES DESCRIPTIONS (TAXONOMY, MORPHOLOGY, GENERAL HABITS, DENSITY)

The furbearers discussed in this chapter taxonomically represent 2 orders including Carnivora and Marsupialia, and 3 families including Mustelidae (skunks), Procyonidae (raccoon) and Didelphidae (opossum). Similar to larger carnivorous furbearers, omnivorous

Right: Medium-sized furbearers, the opossum, raccoon, and skunks, are readily identifiable, and familiar to most people, whether urban or rural, throughout the South *(J. Jones)*.

Below: Raccoons thrive throughout the South today. They are trapped and provide sport for hunters; but are a primary predator of ground nesting birds and can be a problem in interactions with humans *(J. Dickson)*.

Table 1. Morphological characteristics of adult male and female raccoon in the southeastern United States.

			Lengths (in)							
State	**Sex**	**Mass (lb)**	**Total Body**	**Tail**	**Hind Foot**	**Ear**	**Neck Girth**	**Chest Girth**	**Sample Size**	**Citation**
Alabama (East-central)	Female	8.2[a]	28.9	8.7	3.9	2.3	N/A	N/A	20-46	Johnson 1970
	Male	9.5	29.9	9.4	4.1	2.4	N/A	N/A	17-33	
Alabama (Southwest)	Female	N/A	28.7	9.4	3.8	2.2	N/A	N/A	40-51	Johnson 1970
	Male	N/A	29.3	9.3	4.0	2.2	N/A	N/A	58-79	
Georgia	N/A	N/A	28.4	8.2	3.9	N/A	N/A	N/A	7	Golley 1962
Louisiana	Female	N/A	28.2	9.3	3.8	2.0	N/A	N/A	11	Lowery 1974
	Male	N/A	29.6	10.1	4.2	2.2	N/A	N/A	23	
Mississippi	Female	7.1	30.9	9.7	4.1	1.9	8.3	12.7	17	Wilson 1996
	Male	9.9	32.8	9.7	4.2	2.1	9.2	14.0	62	
Tennessee	Female	7.7	N/A	N/A	N/A	N/A	N/A	N/A	26	Cantrell 1989
	Male	7.3	N/A	N/A	N/A	N/A	N/A	N/A	66	
Tennessee	Female	9.7	30.1	9.3	3.9	2.2	N/A	N/A	494	Glass 1991
	Male	11.3	31.4	9.6	4.2	2.3	N/A	N/A	543	
Texas	Female	8.8-28.7	33.4	9.7	4.9	N/A	N/A	N/A	?	Davis and Schmidly 1994
	Male	8.8-28.7	35.2	10.6	5.0	N/A	N/A	N/A	?	
Distribution[b,c]	Female	5.3-13.0	24.1-36.4	7.7-13.6	3.3-5.2	N/A	N/A	N/A	?	Lotze and Anderson (1979)
	Male	4.4-15.0	25.4-38.0	8-16.2	3.8-5.5	N/A	N/A	N/A	?	

[a] Weights provided are for Alabama statewide.
[b] Measurements summarized for species throughout its range.
[c] Range of values given rather than averages.

Table 2. Morphological characteristics of adult male and female opossum in the southeastern United States.

			Lengths (in)							
State	**Sex**	**Mass (lb)**	**Total Body**	**Tail**	**Hind Foot**	**Ear**	**Neck Girth**	**Chest Girth**	**Sample Size**	**Citation**
Arkansas[a]	Female	N/A	26.4	10.9	2.2	1.9	N/A	N/A	?	Sealander (1979)
	Male	N/A	27.8	11.2	2.3	2.0	N/A	N/A	11	
Georgia	Female	2.4	23.3	10.4	2.3	N/A	N/A	N/A	5	Golley 1962[a]
	Male	N/A	22.4	10.2	2.1	N/A	N/A	N/A	6	
Kentucky[b]	N/A	6.6-13.3	26-33.4	11-14	2.4-2.9	N/A	N/A	N/A	?	Barbour and Davis 1974
Louisiana	Female	2.7-4.9[b]	29.3	12.1	2.4	2.0	N/A	N/A	22	Lowery 1974
	Male	5.9-10.4	32.8	12.4	2.5	2.0	N/A	N/A	22	
Louisiana	Female	3.9	N/A	N/A	N/A	N/A	N/A	N/A	74	Edmunds et al. 1978
	Male	4.4	N/A	N/A	N/A	N/A	N/A	N/A	105	
Mississippi	Female	3.9	30.4	12.3	N/A	1.8	6.9	9.9	111	Chamberlain and Leopold unpubl. data
	Male	5.1	30.8	12.5	N/A	1.9	7.6	10.8	66	
Texas	Female	N/A	28.4	12.8	2.5	N/A	N/A	N/A	?	Davis and Schmidly 1994
	Male	N/A	31.3	12.9	2.6	N/A	N/A	N/A	?	
Virginia	Female	3.9	27.8	12.0	2.5	1.9	N/A	N/A	40-128[c]	Seidensticker et al. 1987
	Male	5.5	29.2	12.1	2.7	1.9	N/A	N/A	39-164[c]	

[a] Not all adults
[b] Range of values given rather than averages.
[c] Sample sizes vary by measurement, thus range included.

Table 3. Morphological characteristics of adult male and female striped skunks in the southeastern United States.

State	Sex	Mass (lb)	Lengths (in)			Ear	Neck Girth	Chest Girth	Sample Size	Citation
			Total Body	Tail	Hind Foot					
Arkansas[a]	N/A	1.1-11.9	21.6-30.4	8-11.2	2.3-3.3	0.7-1.2	N/A	N/A	?	Sealander and Heidt 1990
Kentucky[a]	N/A	3.1-11.9	21.6-30.4	8-11.2	2.8-3.3	N/A	N/A	N/A	?	Barbour and Davis 1974
Louisiana	N/A	3.1-5.1	23.7	10.6	2.4	1.0	N/A	N/A	12	Lowery 1974
Louisiana	Female	3.5	N/A	N/A	N/A	N/A	N/A	N/A	105	Adams et al. 1964
	Male	3.8	N/A	N/A	N/A	N/A	N/A	N/A	137	
Mississippi	Female	3.5	29.0	13.1	2.8	0.72	7.0	10.7	6	Chamberlain and Leopold unpubl. data
	Male	3.8	27.8	12.7	2.6	0.8	7.2	11.0	4	
Oklahoma	N/A	2.7-5.4	20-30.4	N/A	N/A	N/A	N/A	N/A	?	Caire et al. 1989
Texas	Female	3.1-14.6	24.4	9	2.6	N/A	N/A	N/A	?	Davis and Schmidly 1994
	Male	3.1-14.6	27.2	10	3.6	N/A	N/A	N/A	?	
Virginia,[a] Carolinas	N/A	2.7-11.7	21.2-28.0	9.2-14	N/A	N/A	N/A	N/A	?	Webster et al. 1985
South-central states[a]	N/A	2.7-12.2	20.8-30.8	6.8-11.2	2.6-3.4	1-1.2	N/A	N/A	?	Choate et al. 1994

[a] Range of values given for some measurements rather than averages.

furbearers are sexually dimorphic with males generally larger than females (Tables 1-3). Raccoons are generally the largest of the omnivorous furbearers, whereas body size and morphology of opossums and skunks are very similar (Tables 2,3).

Two species exhibit arboreal tendencies. The raccoon spends considerable time in trees, especially during the reproductive period when young are often kept in tree dens. Raccoons also use trees for escape cover. Opossums display some arboreal tendencies, particularly during young-rearing periods, although the young are not necessarily born and kept in true dens.

Raccoon.—The raccoon is a member of the family Procyonidae and is distinguished by its black facial mask and ringed tail. Raccoons are well known for their food-handling behaviors as well as their curiosity and intelligence.

Raccoon densities range from 30.3 raccoon/mi^2 in Alabama (Johnson 1970), 3.6 to 46.9 raccoon/mi^2 in numerous locations in Tennessee (Keeler 1978, Nottingham et al. 1982, Leberg and Kennedy 1988), and 44.9 raccoon/mi^2 in Virginia (Sonenshine and Winslow 1972). Highest reported raccoon densities occurred in South Carolina, with 64 raccoon/mi^2 (Cunningham 1962).

Opossum.—The Virginia opossum is the only native member of the family Didelphidae and the sole native marsupial found in North America. Opossums are perhaps best known for their tendency to carry young on their backs after their development in the female's pouch or marsupium.

Densities of opossums vary greatly by habitat type and availability of den sites. In eastern Texas, Lay (1942) estimated an average density of 1 opossum/3.9 ac. In Virginia, Stout and Sonenshine (1974*a*) reported an average density of 1 opossum/49.9 ac. Densities ranged from a low of 0.0 to a high of 1.0 opossum/13.8 ac. Seidensticker et al. (1987) reported similar population levels in western Virginia. They hypothesized that environmental events including drought may dictate opossum population densities. In Tennessee, Leberg et al. (1983) determined densities of 1.0 opossum/38.5 ac. Generally, opossum populations follow a predictable annual cycle with lowest densities in winter and highest densities during early to late fall (Seidensticker et al. 1987).

Skunks.—Skunks are members of the Mustelidae family with two groups occurring in the southeastern United States; the genus *Mephitis* (striped skunks) and the genus *Spilogale* (spotted skunks). Skunks are best known for their highly developed musk glands which can dispel a strong and long-lasting odiferous liquid when they become alarmed. Striped skunks are more important furbearers in terms of distribution and abun-

Table 4. Harvest (number of animals) of raccoon in the southeastern United States from 1970-1991 (adapted from Linscombe 1993).

		State												
Year	Ave. price	Alabama	Arkansas	Florida	Georgia	Kentucky	Louisiana	Mississippi	Oklahoma	N. Carolina	S. Carolina	Tennessee	Texas	Virginia
1970/71			11538		3667	9146	55726		385	41318		5616		22181
1971/72			13934		3277	11666	80632		882	36840				28877
1972/73			21818	3357	5937	21355	149274		2539	62446			150362	46428
1973/74			31135	9087	7174	37082	184688		12834	77710	18213		304273	39019
1974/75	5.92		43262	5753	6953	39714	160863		24749	77718	20843	28010	372377	50699
1975/76	6.98		65698	10661	8693	43658	181031		43499	77471	23763	18983	353444	70418
1976/77	12.07		109287	34772	83788	52502	254435	61528	47460	86307		38299	685314	54671
1977/78	10.42	42950	89194	30364	85801	51482	192845	52780	39165	52780	19405	43368	569492	63472
1978/79	15.99	68265	100690	39884	111342	64708	231747	59200	52205	88774	19433	56213	518593	75014
1979/80	12.43	85620	149405	42840	129416	86812	240088	72053	52288	98968	18728	58702	465145	87678
1980/81	10.76	94001	119065	45177	127727	71750	214687	49594	45698	112420	27854	46479	402864	118950
1981/82	13.96	55248	120007	38076	69366	73016	191161	46320	36293	88122	29481	37060	403464	85657
1982/83	11.21	71405	113827	41187	64115	82666	217660	35247	39285	115032	31946	51182	409119	85987
1983/84	9.83	36336	69808	29296	85174	25033	127929	27427	26669	91971	29702	30176	287022	74917
1984/85	11.15	94222	130192	38826	131904	28378	192616	38696	41785	81326	30049	36216	365459	68990
1985/86	10.76	57111	139181	20436	77743	21707	169645	34572	56208	70966	22591	37768	303410	62260
1986/87	11.99	57511	167458	29763	66975	17158	240396	41400	67749	70525	29505	52711	461365	72449
1987/88	7.11	54667	138793	40049	42202	26677	164184	41898	43399	63445	32292	35249	419848	65065
1988/89	3.74	12037	49041	9111	14465	12037	34987	17901	22663	19633	9472	7263	149195	
1989/90	2.58	2956	22273	3793	6305	7616	27940	7893	6452	18456	2559	6598	69767	9125
1990/91	2.12	416	18939	407	2886	3511	12018	4232	2506	8515	1707	1971	48077	4184
1991/92	2.89	806	28719	1450	4150	8608	30657	5443	7938	9301	2079	7301	57901	5254

dance than are spotted skunks. Eastern spotted skunks are somewhat smaller than striped skunks, yet tend to be similar in many ecological aspects.

Densities of striped skunks in the southeast also depend greatly on den site availability and habitat configuration. Little published research exists regarding striped skunk densities in the southeast with the exception of estimates based on trapper/hunter harvest and observations. In Tennessee, Goldsmith (1981) reported relatively high striped skunk densities (1 skunk/12 ac). According to trapper information, highest densities of striped skunks occur in Mississippi, Texas, and Kentucky, with lowest densities in Florida. Densities of striped skunks vary seasonally and geographically. No density estimates are available for eastern spotted skunks in the southeastern United States, but population levels appear to be relatively low.

DISTRIBUTION AND ABUNDANCE

On a regional basis, raccoon populations have remained relatively stable, although variations in population sizes occur locally. Consequently, raccoons, although trapped and hunted extensively, were not reduced in numbers such that statewide or regional restocking was necessary in most states. However, raccoon numbers in the southern Appalachians were low prior to 1970 and translocations did occur. Numbers of opossums and skunks have remained stable or increased in many areas, often dependent more on habitat conditions than on harvest or exploitation.

The omnivorous furbearers occur throughout the southeastern states. Although raccoons, opossums and striped skunks are widely distributed, spotted skunks are local in distribution. However, differences exist regarding distribution within the states for all species and their current status.

The raccoon is probably the most common and widely distributed furbearer of the southeastern states because of its ability to use a diverse array of habitats (see Habitat Use section). It is found in all states and populations are stable to increasing. Opossums continue to expand their range southward into Central America and northward past the Great Lakes (Gardner 1982). In the southeastern states, opossums can be found in all habitat types and elevations, except

Table 5. Harvest (number of animals) of opossums in the southeastern United States from 1970-1991 (adapted from Linscombe 1993).

		State												
Year	Ave. price	Alabama	Arkansas	Florida	Georgia	Kentucky	Louisiana	Mississippi	Oklahoma	N. Carolina	S. Carolina	Tennessee	Texas	Virginia
1970/71	0.45		4960		1708	3341	3563		323	6228		3692		7468
1971/72			6686		1519	3724	8310		639	4558				5885
1972/73			11795	58	3180	9355	17065		1518	11934			23396	13178
1973/74			21575	187	5555	25108	33676		7884	20194	1142		60545	21760
1974/75	1.31		35392	37	6643	31034	30447		23393	44407	2807	34732	153091	34789
1975/76	1.23		38600	727	7776	25397	34682		34333	16088	1758	15569	75380	25034
1976/77	1.87		63013	2038	35272	28192	44851	49098	35282	21423	0	26009	209721	22802
1977/78	2.13	39951	52429	1529	34757	25177	37208	36972	35106	16450	1310	30110	200285	18161
1978/79	3.42	62328	89078	5402	64133	27631	63303	53310	52910	21512	2251	43805	238437	21832
1979/80	3.38	88060	143979	8081	98241	68514	94341	58088	55818	33637	2336	56702	401340	35483
1980/81	1.68	28636	65436	2989	37640	53759	39591	27235	40533	16413	2116	25302	261087	40261
1981/82	1.33	12195	62988	2706	18302	38533	25682	26186	41509	8090	1671	15469	184960	18274
1982/83	1.23	9915	63989	2098	10386	26086	2770	24151	28951	6885	1731	27169	175972	18841
1983/84	1.19	4529	20099	866	4912	21976	5957	15619	18500	2869	1477	12138	118687	10852
1984/85	1.19	7328	30940	926	6064	20728	15543	15573	12222	3377	896	9196	105126	9854
1985/86	1.33	5028	39892	405	3103	20090	11810	11775	16866	2866	1313	6713	94497	7308
1986/87	1.40	8834	50183	1575	4413	19913	20376	20078	32729	3703	2241	12167	158755	9151
1987/88	1.07	5619	30635	952	32417	25606	18440	16632	17706	1635	1301	8530	151327	5714
1988/89	0.55	741	9461	62	11019	7212	1052	7209	5191	208	1384	1373	54496	0
1989/90	0.51	192	2160	17	5441	3758	1416	3969	1148	380	896	604	16048	680
1990/91	0.83	101	1720	0	3364	3139	360	2008	1451	145	1171	308	12686	384
1991/92	1.16	190	2792	6	4271	6539	1014	1424	1933	233	2090	1203	12638	1369

extremely hydric sites, such as marshes and estuaries. With increased forest disturbance (silvicultural activities) and harvest, striped skunks have actually expanded their range. However, cleaner farming practices have resulted in reduced skunk populations in some areas. In contrast to striped skunks, spotted skunks are not as widely distributed in the southeast; however, in many areas, the 2 species are sympatric. Spotted skunks are found in all the southeastern states, but are very rare in coastal and piedmont areas of Virginia, North Carolina, South Carolina and Georgia, as well as western Kentucky, and are found only in isolated habitats in Tennessee.

HARVEST TRENDS

Harvest of furbearers has fluctuated during the past 20 years (Linscombe 1993), likely a function of fur prices, public sentiment, and changes in resource users. Specifically, harvest has decreased significantly since the mid-1980s. Low fur prices and reductions in demand for pelts worldwide have precipitated the overall decline in trapping and subsequent harvest of all furbearers, including raccoons, opossums and skunks.

Raccoon.—The raccoon is the southeastern United States' primary furbearer, based on number of animals annually harvested (Table 4), with some states (Texas and Louisiana) harvesting over 250,000 animals annually. Harvest for most southeastern states generally exceeds 20,000 animals annually. As with other furbearers, pelt prices and subsequent harvests have declined steadily since 1984/85.

Opossum.—Opossums are harvested for their fur; however, pelts of opossums are less valuable than those of raccoon. Generally, opossum harvests have declined since 1980 and appear to reflect decreasing trends in furbearer trapping effort (Table 5). Harvest generally exceeds 1,000 opossums annually for southeastern states, except for Florida, where harvest is practically non-existent.

Skunks.—Striped skunk pelts are the most valuable of the skunks. This, coupled with the wide distribution of striped skunks, makes them relatively important furbearers economically. Prior to 1970, striped skunk harvest peaked around 1940, but has since

Table 6. Harvest (number of animals) of skunk in the southeastern United States from 1970-1991 (adapted from Linscombe 1993).

		State												
Year	Ave. price	Alabama	Arkansas	Florida	Georgia	Kentucky	Louisiana	Mississippi	Oklahoma	N. Carolina	S. Carolina	Tennessee	Texas	Virginia
1970/71			327	0	176	173	6		103	276		150		547
1971/72			304		73	193	114		109	91				249
1972/73			473	0	181	248	405		481	264			1011	1236
1973/74			1139	0	359	646	747		1604	474	0		6100	2789
1974/75	1.68		1362	0	700	705	298		3102	430	0	1043	12679	2704
1975/76	1.75	0	1905	3	938	562	445		2793	72	0	814	3136	2138
1976/77	3.29		2943	0	1396	619	513	4452	5780	420	0	1829	13346	2380
1977/78	4.44	2975	2033	6	1507	547	376	2965	3601	447	0	1407	14859	1677
1978/79	6.03	4080	2988	8	1172	1131	635	5451	4611	856	0	2192	98472	1886
1979/80	4.40	4265	3391	1	1079	1813	418	4310	2899	716	0	1735	114710	2377
1980/81	3.82	348	1493	2	1486	601	560	3917	2235	390	0	679	98695	3221
1981/82	2.45	65	868	0	53	357	315	3364	3070	91	60	877	82045	996
1982/83	1.66	52	538	0	47	253	27	2574	659	65	53	537	81691	550
1983/84	2.10	18	226	0	11	2293	10	2012	167	59	322	112	65382	84
1984/85	2.48	26	272	0	51	2024	6	1627	135	41	88	84	43927	70
1985/86	1.62	40	194	0	20	2695	1	1524	211	50	191	72	44348	70
1986/87	1.26	43	175	0	64	2047	8	1870	413	57	82	119	66728	27
1987/88	1.37	40	104	0	2139	2606	25	1832	114	22	183	77	55383	54
1988/89	1.50	5	49	0	929	1174	0	1031	50	1	132	2	23549	0
1989/90	2.80	4	10	0	500	737	0	386	13	6	103	11	11077	17
1990/91	0.97	5	6	0	220	562	0	177	22	0	126	0	6039	1
1991/92	1.15	1	10	0	294	1034	0	300	24	10	147	0	8816	2

declined drastically. Post 1970, greatest harvest, based on pelt sales, occurred during 1979-80 (Table 6). Harvest of skunks in the Southeast is generally permitted throughout the year except in Florida, which has a specified take season on skunks (Rosatte 1987).

Spotted skunks are occasionally harvested for their fur; however, their pelts are less valuable than pelts of striped skunks. Spotted skunks were harvested for their pelts to some extent during the 1940's. However, pelts of spotted skunks are seldom present at fur sales (Obbard et al. 1987). Thus, spotted skunks are economically insignificant as a southeastern furbearer.

REPRODUCTION

Reproductive characteristics (Table 7) of raccoons, opossums, and skunks differ to some degree, especially in litter sizes and gestation. Generally, these furbearers mate during late winter to early summer, with parturition in spring to early summer. Gestation is shortest in opossums, primarily because most development of young occurs in the marsupium following parturition. Delayed implantation in skunks results in longer observed gestation; however, corrected gestation is similar to that of raccoons. All species are polyestrous, meaning that a female may cycle until she is bred; however, some skunks do exhibit monestrous tendencies. Age of sexual maturity varies among these furbearers, but most breed their first year. All these furbearers are polygamous.

Raccoon.—Raccoons have the lowest litter sizes, between 1-6 young. Females may breed their first year, whereas males do not breed until their second year (Kaufman 1982). Only the female cares for the young. The raccoon is the only southeastern furbearer that frequently occupies dens elevated from the ground in tree cavities. Although raccoons usually breed from March to June, breeding may extend into July and August. Raccoons produce 1 litter per year (Nowak and Paradiso 1983).

Opossum.—The opossum is the only marsupial found north of Mexico. Thus, it exhibits non-typical breeding and reproduction, compared to raccoons and skunks. Reproduction in marsupials is characterized by short gestation (<15 days) with most development of young occurring in the marsupium. Both sexes are

Table 7. Reproductive characteristics of omnivorous furbearers in the southeastern United States.

Species	Breeding Season	Peak birth	Litter size	Pair bond	Estrus Cycle	Litters/ year	Gestation	Delayed implant.	Age at sexual maturity	Citation
Raccoon	Mar.-June (August)	Apr.-May	1-6 $\bar{x}$=2.5	polygamous	polyestrous	1.0	63-73	No	female=1.0 years male (breeds 2)	Johnson 1970 Kaufman 1982 Lotze & Anderson 1979, Nowak & Paradiso 1983
Opossum	Dec.-June	Jan.-July	7-15 $\bar{x}$=7.5	polygamous	polyestrous	1-2	12-15	No	7-9 months	Sealander and Heidt 1990, Gardner 1982
Striped Skunk	Feb.-Mar.	May-Jun.	2-10 $\bar{x}$=6	polygamous	polyestrous	1-2	62-66,	Yes	9-10 months	Rosatte 1987, Godin 1982
Spotted Skunk	Feb.-Mar.	May	1-6 $\bar{x}$=4	polygamous[b]	polyestrous	1-2	45-60[a]	Uncertain Likely Yes	female =8-10 mon. male =5 months	Rosatte 1987

[a] When corrected for delayed implantation.
[b] Some evidence that mated pairs do exist.

capable of breeding within 6-8 months following birth (Reynolds 1952, Jurgelski and Porter 1974). Opossums in the Southeast typically breed from December through February. However, earlier breeding periods have been reported in northern Louisiana (Edmunds et al. 1978). Litter size ranges from 7 to 15 throughout the Southeast (Gardner 1982, Seidensticker et al. 1987).

Skunks.—Similar to most mustelids, striped skunks display delayed implantation and are predominately polyestrous with breeding generally occurring during February and March throughout the southeastern states. Males are polygamous and are capable of breeding multiple females throughout the breeding season. Litter sizes generally range from 5 to 9 with 2 litters possible for some females (Hall and Kelson 1959). These litter sizes are smaller than those of opossums, but larger than litter sizes of raccoons. This larger litter size may adaptively result from high pre-weaning mortality in skunks, a factor less common with raccoons (Rosatte 1987).

It is unclear if delayed implantation exists for the spotted skunk. Rosatte (1987) reported a short delay period (2 weeks); however, Caire et al. (1989) reported that delayed implantation did not occur in Oklahoma. Mead (1968) reported that female spotted skunks entered estrous during March with peak breeding occurring during March and April. Litter sizes range from 3 to 6, averaging 4 young. Some male spotted skunks are sexually mature at 5 to 6 months of age (Mead 1967).

DIET

Raccoons, opossums and skunks are omnivorous, exploiting a wide variety of foods. Dietary patterns of these omnivores vary seasonally and may include fruits, berries, grasses or even carrion. The mild climate, even during winter, and the abundance of prey species, generally affords these species ample food year round.

Raccoon.—Raccoons usually consume similar amounts of plant and animal matter, but the proportion varies seasonally and with availability (Table 8). Plant material includes hard mast, primarily oak acorns, and soft mast such as blackberry, wild grapes, and persimmon. Animal matter consumed is composed of invertebrates, including crayfish and insects. Vertebrate prey species include a variety of mammals such as squirrels, rabbits, rats, mice and moles, and a diversity of birds. Additionally, the raccoon is an efficient predator of eggs of ground-nesting birds. Of particular importance is the predation of nests of game birds by raccoon, especially those of wild turkey and quail. Although the raccoon frequents aquatic habitats, frogs and fishes appear infrequently in diet analyses.

Opossum.—Little published information is available concerning opossum diet in the southeast, with the exception of some research in Texas and Virginia (Table 9). In Texas, mammals, insects and worms dominated opossum diets (Lay 1942, Wood 1954). Similarly, in

Table 8. Composition (percentage occurrence)[a] of diet of raccoon in the southeastern United States.

State	Plant Material: Hard mast	Plant Material: Soft mast	Plant Material: Other	Animal Material: Crustacean	Animal Material: Reptile/amphibian	Animal Material: Invertebrate	Animal Material: Earthworm	Animal Material: Avian	Animal Material: Mammal	Animal Material: Fish	Animal Material: Mollusk	Method	Time Period	N	Citation
Alabama	8.1	67.0	11.3	7.8	0.5	25.0	1.0	1.7	1.1	0.7	1.2	Scat/Stom.		476	Johnson 1970
Louisiana (non-marsh)	6.0	42.4	3.5	56.0	0.0	35.5	0.0	3.0	6.0	11.7	0.0	Scats	Annual	288	Fleming et al.1976
Louisiana (inter-marsh)	0.0	3.0	12.4	79.7	0.0	7.9	0.0	2.7	4.8	26.4	0.0	Scats	Annual	288	Fleming et al.1976
Louisiana (brackish-marsh)	0.0	0.0	7.8	63.3	0.0	28.4	0.0	1.2	0.0	26.0	0.2	Scats	Annual	288	Fleming et al.1976
Mississippi	64.7	24.8	46.7	24.8	11.5	52.4	22.9	2.9	6.8	3.8	5.7	Stomach	Annual	105	O'Hara 1980
Texas	57.4	5.0-10.0	6.1	9.5	5.2	73.8	0.0	1.0	13.9	<1.0	?	Stomach	Annual	53	Wood 1954
	32.3	5.0-10.0	5.2	11.5	0.6	?	0.0	1.0	5.4	<1.0	10.3	Scat	Annual	164	
Texas	51.1	42.1	0.0	61.6	0.0	47.4	0.0	1.3	0.0	3.4	2.1	Scat/stom.	Annual	378	Baker et al. 1945

[a] Expressed as percentage of all scats or stomachs containing that food item. Percentages will not sum to 100% as scats or stomachs may contain more than one food item.

Table 9. Composition of diet of opossum in the southeastern United States.

State	Animal Material: Avian	Animal Material: Mammal	Animal Material: Other vertebrates	Invertebrates	Fruits and plants	Method	N	Citation
Texas[a]	4	7		49	38	Stomach	16	Lay 1942
Texas[a]	4	15	7	25	45	Scat and Stomach	23 25	Wood 1954
Virginia[b]	2	7	1	36	15	Scat	28	Seidensticker et al. 1987

[a] Based on percentage volume of stomach contents, will not sum to 100%.
[b] Based on frequency of occurrence in scats, will not sum to 100%.

Virginia, opossum diets were comprised mostly of invertebrates and fruits (Seidensticker et al. 1987). Some generalizations can be made throughout the Southeast, particularly for seasonal dietary patterns of opossums. During periods of high fruit availability (spring, summer), opossums may subsist almost entirely on locally abundant fruit, such as blackberries or cherries. Insects and their larvae also are consumed during warm seasons. In early fall, persimmons often are preferred by opossums, with the critical period occurring during winter when resources become scarce. Acorns often are greatly used when available during fall and winter (Wood 1954).

Skunks.—Skunks display a highly variable diet throughout their range. However, information on dietary patterns of striped skunks in the southeastern United States is limited. The striped skunk is primarily insectivorous (Wade-Smith and Verts 1982). In Texas, diet was composed mainly of insects and plant material (Patton 1974). Similar dietary patterns have been observed in Virginia and the Carolinas. When insects are unavailable, striped skunks may shift their diet to mice or vegetation (Verts 1967). Striped skunks are known to eat frogs, crayfish, and rodents, prey items that are seasonally abundant.

Although little information is available on diet of spotted skunks in the southeast, some information exists in other parts of its range. Spotted skunks are more carnivorous, preying more on mammals than do striped skunks, with insects being less important in their diet.

Table 10. Home range sizes (ac) of male and female raccoon in the southeastern United States.

			Home range (ac)					
State	**Male**	**N**	**Female**	**N**	**Pooled**	**N**	**Method**	**Citation**
Alabama					121.0-244.0	3		Johnson 1970
Georgia	161	7	96	2			convex	Lotze 1979
Louisiana	324	3	136	2			convex	Fleming 1975
Mississippi	847	30	521	15			convex	Wilson 1996
Tennessee	573	3	331	6			convex	Hardy 1979
Tennessee	902	7	341	11			convex	Taylor 1979
Tennessee	425	9	291	7			convex	Allsbrooks and Kennedy 1980
Tennessee	543	8	375	7			convex	Tabatabai 1988

Table 11. Home range sizes (ac) of male and female opossum in the southeastern United States.

			Home range (ac)					
State	**Male**	**N**	**Female**	**N**	**Pooled**	**N**	**Method**	**Citation**
Georgia	193	2	55	5			minimum area	Allen et al. 1985
Mississippi	139	4	97.24	1			kernel	Wilson 1996
Texas					38.83	29	trap-distance	Lay 1942
Texas					30.88	29	trap-distance	Verts 1963

Spotted skunks also are known to consume corn, grubs, birds, eggs, and fruit (Rosatte 1987, Sealander and Heidt 1990).

HOME RANGE AND HABITAT USE

Home range and habitat use among raccoons, opossums and skunks varies, differing by location, sex and/or age, season, land management and population status. A myriad of factors influence home range, including but not limited to weather patterns, prey availability and habitat conditions. Habitat use may vary by season, a function of habitat availability and quality.

Raccoon.—Home ranges for southeastern raccoons range from approximately 80 ac to 1000 ac (Table 10). Male home ranges are generally larger than those of females, reflecting their polygamous nature and searches for females during the breeding season. Conversely, female home ranges may decrease in response to seasonal resource availability (Gehrt and Fritzell 1997) or maternal responsibilities.

Habitat use has been widely studied for the raccoon in southeastern environments. In general, the raccoon uses mesic and hydric forested environments, more than xeric upland forests. Typically, bottomland hardwood forests or forests adjacent to perennial streams and rivers are most preferred (Minser and Pelton 1982, Leberg and Kennedy 1988). Mature forests are used frequently during spring and summer, presumably because of the female's need for suitable den sites (Atkeson and Hulse 1953, Wilson 1996). Upland sites may be used by raccoons during some seasons, likely because of increased availability of seasonal fruits, such as blackberries (Wilson 1996). Sonenshine and Winslow (1972), studying 2 raccoon populations in Virginia, found distinctly different habitat use patterns, with 1 population using bottomlands and another uplands. Interestingly, the main food consumed by the population using the uplands was corn.

Opossum.—Home range sizes for opossums are generally smaller than those for raccoons. In general, home ranges range from 30 to 193 acres ha for southeastern studies (Table 11). Home ranges are predominately larger for males, particularly during the breeding period, owing to the polygamous mating system in opossums.

Opossums use a variety of habitats in the Southeast including pine forests, bottomland hardwoods, mixed stands, marshlands, and grasslands. In Mississippi, Wilson (1996) reported that opossums were often located in deciduous, mixed pine/hardwood, and older pine forests, often adjacent to water sources. In areas dominated by short rotation pine forests, opossums use all stand types including clearcuts and streamside areas (Chamberlain and Leopold, unpubl. data). In Tennessee, Leberg et al. (1983) reported that opossums used bottomland deciduous stands more than upland forest types.

Skunks.—No published studies of home ranges for striped skunk exist for southeastern states, although there is some limited unpublished data. In forested areas of Mississippi, striped skunks occupied home ranges varying from 144 to 2844 ac (Chamberlain and Leopold, unpubl. data). However, home ranges were considerably smaller for striped skunks in more open, agricultural habitats (Henner and Leopold, unpubl. data).

Striped skunks use a variety of habitats including but not limited to agricultural lands, pine forests, clearcuts, and marsh areas. Information on striped skunk habitat use in the southeastern states is limited. Striped skunks are predominately found in habitats with a high edge component and are seldom found in large timber blocks (Verts 1967). Striped skunks will often use agricultural areas adjacent to timber stands or abandoned agricultural fields where there is food. In Texas, Verts (1967) reported that striped skunks avoided large timber stands and used cropfields and pastures. In a mostly forested area in Mississippi, striped skunks used clearcuts (<4 years old) and openings (Chamberlain and Leopold, unpubl. data). On a Mississippi study area dominated by agriculture, striped skunks were often located along field edges and in dormant or fallow cropfields (Henner and Leopold, unpubl. data). Generally, habitat use and home range patterns are dependent on den site availability. In mountainous areas of Tennessee, Weller and Pelton (1987), found that striped skunks used underground dens and man-made culverts for denning. In Mississippi, skunks may den in brushy ditch banks, log jams or in abandoned agricultural fields (Chamberlain, unpubl. data).

No published information is available on home ranges of spotted skunks in the southeastern United States. Crabb (1948) speculated that spotted skunks were not territorial.

There is little information on specific habitat use patterns of spotted skunks; however, some generalizations can be made. Spotted skunks are known to use a variety of habitats including farmlands, hedgerows, lowlands (Howard and Marsh 1982) and even mountainous areas (Baker and Baker 1975). Spotted skunks also may use a variety of den sites, such as buildings, trees and brushpiles, although some evidence suggests that, unlike striped skunks, spotted skunks may not use permanent dens (Howard and Marsh 1982).

DISEASES AND PARASITES

Diseases and parasites are important components in the ecology of raccoons, opossums, and skunks. Diseases may impact furbearer populations, particularly raccoons. Additionally, these species inhabit urban areas, which increases the need for information on diseases carried by these species. The diseases and parasites detailed are those that are most commonly found for each species, and not a comprehensive list. Much of the material presented below was obtained from Davidson and Nettles (1988).

Raccoon.—Several diseases have been reported for the raccoon in the southeastern United States. The 2 most common are canine distemper and rabies, both of which may reduce local populations. Raccoons infected with rabies often exhibit aimless wandering, paralysis, and a loss of awareness. Occasionally, infected raccoons may become aggressive and attack other objects or humans. Rabies is transmitted through being bitten by an infected animal or exposure to saliva of an infected animal. Rabies is very serious, thus suspected rabies in any animal should be handled in a proper manner. Diagnosis of rabies in raccoons, or any furbearers, requires that the animal be killed, preferably without damage to the brain. If a suspected rabid raccoon is encountered, a wildlife official should be contacted immediately.

The canine distemper virus is highly infectious to raccoons and occurs in raccoons throughout the Southeast. Distemper often occurs at levels classified as outbreaks and may drastically reduce local raccoon populations (Chamberlain et al. 1999). Distemper is transmitted through direct contact with infected animals or their excretia; however, distemper is not infectious to humans.

The roundworm *Baylisascaris procyonis* affects raccoons and is transmitted through feces. Larvae of this nematode are infectious to humans, thus hunters and trappers should use caution when handling or cleaning raccoons; however, reported infections are rare. Other infrequently reported diseases and parasites for raccoon in the Southeast include tularemia, leptospirosis, the protozoan parasite *Trypanosoma*, the tapeworm *Spirometra*, the subcutaneous nematode *Dracunculus insignis*, 2 species of stomach worms (*Gnathostoma procyonis* and *Physaloptera rara*), and the thorny-headed worm *Macracanthorhynchus ingens* (Davidson and Nettles 1988). Trichinosis also has been reported for raccoon, thus given its value for meat, proper cooking is warranted. As with other furbearers, numerous species of ectoparasites including ticks, fleas and lice are common, but rarely reach levels that pose a threat to raccoon populations.

Opossum.—Opossums are susceptible to many parasites and diseases. The natural incidence of rabies in opossums is low, thus opossums should not be considered important reservoirs of the disease and rabies infection within opossum populations is very unlikely (Davidson and Nettles 1988). Tuberculosis and *Pasteurella* (tularemia) are major bacterial diseases occurring in opossums. Opossums also are known carriers of leptospirosis.

Protozoan diseases including *Toxoplasma*, *Trichomonas*, *Sarcocystis*, and *Trypanosoma* are often carried by opossums. *Sarcocystis* infects the intestinal tract and is transmitted through feces, making the protozoan available for intermediate avian hosts. Another protozoan, *Besnoitia*, is similarly passed through feces; however, members of the cat family (Felidae) are definitive hosts. Opossums also are hosts for spotted fever and carry ringworm (Gardner 1982). Opossums are frequently hosts to the nematode *Physaloptera turgida*, a large stomach worm that alone is not considered pathogenic to opossums. However, in large numbers the nematode may contribute to malnutrition.

Similar to other furbearers, opossums are host to numerous species of ectoparasites including ticks, fleas, chiggers and lice. During high stress periods (breeding), infestation by ticks and fleas often becomes severe.

Skunks.—Striped skunks, and to a lesser degree spotted skunks, are a dominant reservoir of rabies in the United States. Due to their often aggressive behavior when infected and their propensity to use urban and suburban areas, skunks are an important source of human exposure to rabies. Skunks also are affected by canine distemper; however, the extent that distemper impacts skunk populations in the Southeast is unclear.

Other diseases that affect skunks include canine hepatitis, a virus that also is infectious to canids. Canine hepatitis is transmitted through direct contact with infected individuals or their excretia. Leptospirosis, a bacteria, frequently infects skunks and is infectious to humans. Most human infections are through contact with infected water, soil, or animals. Skunks are host to a large intestinal roundworm, *Baylisascaris columnaris*, frequently transmitted in feces. The nematode is not considered highly pathogenic to skunks, but may be infectious to humans. Skunks also carry fleas, ticks, lice and mites.

INTERSPECIES INTERACTIONS

Among Furbearers

Home ranges, habitat use, activity patterns, and diet of raccoons, opossums, and skunks overlap wherever these species are sympatric. Because the raccoon is aggressive, it is rarely displaced by other furbearers. The disposition of raccoons, coupled with similar to larger body sizes than opossums and skunks, likely prevents intentional encounters between these species. Although raccoons are infrequently killed by other carnivores, the coyote and bobcat may occasionally kill and consume raccoons. Lotze and Anderson (1979) cite the coyote as a potential predator of raccoon. However, in most instances, it is not advantageous for another predator to risk injury by attacking a raccoon. Thus, intentional encounters between larger carnivores and raccoons are likely rare and situation-specific.

As opossums are generally solitary, confirmed interactions with other furbearers are rare. Several studies have addressed potential interactions between raccoons and opossums, as both species often use similar habitats in the southeast. Seidensticker et al. (1987) reported that raccoons and opossums used different den locations in Virginia. In Tennessee, Kissell and Kennedy (1992) reported that opossums and raccoons did not interact socially and often used different habitat, both spatially and temporally. No published data exists on interactions among other furbearers and opossums; however, current research in Mississippi suggests that opossums rarely interact with other furbearers (bobcat, coyote, gray fox, raccoon) and may avoid other furbearers in overlapping use areas (Chamberlain and Leopold, unpubl. data).

No published information on interactions among skunks and other furbearers exists for the southeastern states. Given the scenting techniques of skunks, aggressive interactions between skunks and other furbearers is likely rare. In Mississippi, research suggests that striped skunks may, to a large extent, overlap home ranges and core use areas with raccoons and other larger furbearers (Chamberlain and Leopold, unpubl. data).

With Other Wildlife Species

Raccoons, opossums, and skunks may impact other wildlife species through depredation of adults or young. Research has shown that these medium-sized furbearers may have an impact on other wildlife, especially on ground-nesting game birds (Balser et al. 1968, Pharris and Goetz 1980, Sargeant et al. 1995). Numerous other studies on raccoons suggest potential impacts on other animal populations, including nests of shorebirds and turtles (Johnson and Rauber 1970), and muskrats (Wilson 1953). Opossums and skunks also predate quail and turkey nests and poults, and in northern parts of its range, striped skunks destroy significant numbers of mallard and blue-winged teal nests. However, the extent to which depredation of nests or young by these furbearers affects and/or limits populations of any wildlife species in the Southeast is unclear.

MANAGEMENT

Management of wildlife populations, particularly furbearers, is challenging, complicated, and involves both state wildlife agencies and the general public. Although larger carnivores usually are the focus of management controversies, furbearers, such as raccoons, generate considerable interest. Thus, management of raccoon populations is often based on issues of recreational opportunities or user group interest. However, rarely is management directed at opossum and skunk populations. For both these species, management usually is in the form of damage control or removal, particularly in urban settings. However, management for any of these species must rely on often unavailable information of population numbers, ideas of public sentiment, and potential effects of various management schemes on furbearer populations.

Censusing

As with most southeastern furbearers, censusing of raccoons, opossums, and skunks is difficult because they are generally solitary, crepuscular or nocturnal, and secretive. Most census procedures rely on indirect counts of animal sign, often to supplement harvest information gathered during legal hunting or trapping seasons.

As with larger furbearers, scent stations have been used to monitor raccoon (Leberg and Kennedy 1987, Gabor et al. 1994) and opossum populations (Conner et al. 1983, Leberg et al. 1983, Nottingham et al. 1989). Raccoon populations also may be monitored and examined using mark-recapture techniques (Moore and Kennedy 1985). Opossum and raccoon populations also have been indexed and monitored using track counts and night counts (spotlight counts) (Johnson and Pelton 1981). In Mississippi, Leopold and Chamberlain (1997) reported that smoked track plates were effective to monitor trends in raccoon and opossum populations, whereas track counts and spotlight counts were generally ineffective. In Florida, Conner et al. (1983) used scent-station indices to monitor trends in raccoons and opossums, whereas Leberg et al. (1983) and Linscombe et al. (1983) used scent-stations in Tennessee and Louisiana, respectively. However, Kocka (1987) and Nottingham et al. (1989) found that scent station procedures were often erratic and could produce unreliable results. In Mississippi, research suggests that a combination of smoke plates and scent-stations may best index raccoon and opossum population levels and monitor trends in abundance (Burton 1998).

Various census techniques have been used to monitor skunk populations or to enumerate relative abundance. Abundance of skunks has been determined using mark-recapture techniques in Virginia (Stout and Sonenshine 1974b). Other techniques including night-lighting, trapper harvest, and road kills have been used to determine relative abundance of skunks in various parts of the United States. Techniques currently used to examine relative abundance of other furbearers may be applicable to monitoring skunk populations. In Mississippi, smoked aluminum track plates and spot-lighting surveys were used to determine presence of striped skunks in bottomland areas (Leopold and Chamberlain 1997). In upland areas of Mississippi, scent-stations may provide seasonal relative abundance information (Burton 1998).

Trapping and Hunting

Raccoons are widely trapped and hunted for sport an their pelts. Raccoons are effectively trapped using live-traps, foot-hold traps, or body gripping kill traps (see Carnivorous furbearers, Table 23). Live-traps require relatively little maintenance compared to foot-hold traps and can be effective in capturing large numbers of raccoons. When using foot-holds, attempts should be made to minimize potential damage to the animal, particularly by using padded-jaw traps or newly developed traps designed to prevent self-inflicted injuries (Hubert et al. 1996). Modifications, including rubber pads on the jaws, chain swivels to minimize limb dislocation, and modified pans to reduce captures of non-target species, have been developed to address animal welfare concerns associated with trapping.

Opossums are attracted to baits and readily enter live-traps. Trapped opossums generally are very docile. Although foot-hold traps can be effective for opossums, generally they are not needed because they require more time to maintain than live-traps and are more likely to harm the animal. However, recent evidence suggests that newly developed foot-hold traps designed to minimize injuries can be very effective and humane for capturing opossums.

Similar to raccoons and opossums, skunks can be easily captured using live-traps baited with sardines or chemical attractants, such as gland lure. Live-traps should be covered with some form of fabric to prevent captured skunks from spraying trappers.

A major point that distinguishes these furbearers from one another is that opossums and skunks are not harvested as intensively as raccoons for their pelts. Thus, fur prices and market fluctuations are less likely to affect opossum and skunk populations to the extent that raccoon populations are affected. Given recent anti-trapping sentiment, coupled with changes in habitat conditions throughout the Southeast, managers are no longer able to rely on trapper harvest to reduce population levels of furbearers, if management goals dictate population reduction. Thus, management schemes for these furbearers must now investigate new techniques, including habitat management schemes to possibly reduce suitable furbearer habitat and thus lower habitat quality and potentially, density. If depredation by these furbearers on game animals is suspected of being problematic, managers should strive to improve habitat quality for game animals, rather than resort to often futile and expensive attempts to control furbearer population levels. However, under any scenario, future management of furbearer populations will require dynamic ideas and development of new techniques to combat ever-changing resource use and public sentiment.

Species

Raccoon.—Raccoons are valued for their fur, although pelt prices vary. Additionally, the raccoon is hunted with dogs for food and sport. As raccoons do depredate eggs and young or ground-nesting birds such as wild turkey, Northern bobwhite, and pheasant, control of raccoon numbers may be important in some circumstances. However, frequently, many of these ground-nesters are capable of maintaining viable populations even with high raccoon populations.

If raccoon population enhancement is the goal, then habitat management should be considered. Habitat management also will ensure viable populations. Forests should be protected, especially bottomland systems. Den trees and mast-producing trees including oaks and beeches are critical for winter survival and should be protected. Aquatic systems such as swamps, marshes and streams are obviously important to raccoons and should be enhanced or protected, especially from pollution. Integrating beaver pond management with raccoon habitat enhancement can be desirable, both from a raccoon and a waterfowl standpoint.

Trapping and hunting are effective in reducing raccoon numbers. Incorporating population control with activities such as raccoon hunting with dogs is desirable as multiple objectives will be achieved: reduction in numbers and recreation. Additionally, removal by hunters may be more effective than trapping, as demonstrated in Alabama (Atkeson and Hulse 1953).

Opossum.—Opossums are not highly valued for their fur. Although not often actively hunted, opossums do provide trapping opportunities for southeastern sportsmen. Trapping is a very effective way to harvest opossums and reduce population levels if warranted. Also, encouraging harvest of opossums by raccoon hunters may provide increased recreational opportunities.

Large-scale population control of opossums is difficult and often impractical given their high reproductive potential. Additionally, as longevity of opossums is generally less than 1 year, potential exists to negatively impact opossum populations through high harvest or control mechanisms. Ensuring viable populations of opossums requires habitat management, similar to management strategies for improving raccoon populations. Forests with deciduous stands intermixed with other habitat types (pine, agriculture, openings) near permanent water sources should be protected.

Skunks.—Skunks have been managed more as a nuisance species than as a furbearer. Therefore, most skunk management has focused on decreasing populations or removing nuisance animals. In some instances this may be warranted, but often it is questionable, as skunks provide many ecological benefits, including control of rodents and insects. Frequently, homeowners in urban and rural areas complain of skunk damage to lawns and even that skunks living under their homes are emitting odors. Skunks can easily be excluded from denning under homes by sealing all openings where skunks could enter foundations or buildings. If already established, skunks can be easily trapped using live-traps. Because skunks are major carriers of rabies, individuals encountering aggressive or odd behaving skunks should immediately contact a wildlife official or game warden.

Where supporting skunk populations is desirable, maintaining suitable habitat is crucial. Maintaining early successional habitats such as fields or other openings, as well as brushy cover is recommended. Availability of den sites may limit skunk populations, thereby providing denning opportunities (brushtops, culverts, etc.) may be necessary. Future research should examine specific habitat and reproductive requirements to better manage skunk populations throughout the Southeast.

SUMMARY

Raccoon, opossum and skunk are key components within southern ecosystems and continue to evolve through complex, dynamic processes in a constantly changing southeastern landscape. In many areas, the abundance of these furbearers has increased due to changes in public sentiment, resource use, and habitat availability. Changes in resource use and user attitudes have created changes in management of these species. Stable or increasing populations of raccoons, opossums, and skunks in many areas may eventually result in increased conflicts. Knowledge of changing ecological requirements for each species will allow natural resource managers to improve decision-making processes regarding these species. As widespread control of any wildlife population is often economically impractical, unjustified, or publicly unacceptable, managers must be proactive in developing effective management tools, and then use them accordingly. Throughout the southeastern United States, harvest of these furbearers will be a major management tool. In some instances, these furbearers may impact other wildlife species, requiring population control through harvest. Similarly, in suburban settings, conflicts with humans and concerns regarding disease transmission may create conditions when control or removal of individual animals is necessary. However, as public sentiment continues to change and land use shifts to more urban situations, management of these southeastern furbearers will continue to evolve and change. Undoubtedly, the southeastern landscape will witness many more sociological, environmental, and political changes that will continue to influence populations of omnivorous furbearers. The success of natural resource professionals in reacting to these changes, managing these species, and ensuring the maintenance of future populations relies on our collective ability to integrate knowledge of species ecology, management alternatives, and user attitude.

ACKNOWLEDGMENTS

We thank the Department of Wildlife and Fisheries and the Forest and Wildlife Research Center at Mississippi State University for funding to complete this chapter. Special thanks to J. Burton, C. Henner, and K. Hodges who provided input on earlier drafts of this manuscript and 2 anonymous reviewers for helpful comments. We greatly appreciate the contributions of the biologists, researchers and technicians that made this chapter possible. This is Forest & Wildlife Research Center Publication Number WF080.

CHAPTER 23

Herbivorous Furbearers

Jeanne Jones and Bruce D. Leopold
Department of Wildlife and Fisheries
Mississippi State University, Mississippi State, MS

Beaver, muskrat, and nutria are common inhabitants of the southeastern United States. These animals are important species due to their production of fur, ecological roles in wetland habitats, and potential economic impacts to agricultural crops, property, and timber. Fur and meat of native muskrats and beaver played a major role in Native American subsistence and the European settlement of North America (Lowery 1974). The importance of the beaver as a furbearer is demonstrated by the fact that many attribute the initial exploration of North America to trappers seeking the beaver for its fur during the 1700s and 1800s. Harvest was so intensive that the beaver was extirpated from many parts of its range by the 1900s, and successful restoration programs were begun. Both species exert important influences in wetland ecosystems through herbivory, burrowing, and in the case of the beaver, creation and expansion of wetland habitats through damming activity.

The nutria, an exotic species from South America, was imported to the west coast of the United States in the late 1800s for commercial fur production. A captive population of nutria was accidentally freed during a hurricane on Avery Island, Louisiana in 1938. As with many non-native organisms, escape led to population establishment and range expansion. In many areas of the southern Gulf Coastal and Atlantic coastal states, nutria continue to expand their range.

All 3 species are semi-aquatic rodents that use similar aquatic and semiaquatic habitats. They utilize natural wetland and riparian systems, as well as manmade impoundments, canals, and channels. Of the 3, the nutria appears most tolerant of polluted, human-altered habitats. As members of the Order Rodentia, these furbearers exhibit potential for high reproductive rates, especially under good habitat conditions where water and food supplies are abundant. Under good habitat conditions, muskrat and nutria inhabiting coastal marshes can attain population levels that cause "eat-outs" of marsh vegetation (Lowery 1974). This phenomena results in the creation of mudflats and open water devoid of vegetation. Several

The beaver once was widespread and its fur valuable enough to inspire exploration in North America. Restoration, reduced trapping, and reduction of predators all probably have led to the return of beavers throughout the South *(Kirtley-Perkins)*.

authors report short and long term changes in wetland vegetation caused by nutria herbivory in Gulf coast marshes of Louisiana (Linscombe and Kinler 1997). In agricultural and timber production areas, these furbearers can cause economic losses through crop depredation, damage to water impoundment structures, and inundation of standing timber.

Predation and harvest are viewed by many land managers and biologists as essential in managing these mammals. Many authors believe that historical losses of large predators, such as the American alligator, exacerbated high population growth of these furbearers (Lowery 1974). In the past 2 decades, lowered fur values caused by changes in the worldwide fur market reduced trapping efforts. Populations of nutria, beaver, and muskrat have increased over much of their southeastern range as a result. Federal and state trapping programs have been implemented to control populations of these animals where damage to property and economic losses occur.

The nutria, an exotic species from South America, is now widespread and expanding in the South.

SPECIES DESCRIPTIONS

The American beaver (Family Castoridae, *Castor canadensis*), muskrat (Family Muridae, *Ondatra zibethicus*), and nutria (Family Capromyidae, *Myocastor coypus*) are members of the order Rodentia. Muskrats are common over most of the Southeast. An identified subspecies, the Louisiana muskrat *(O. z. rivalicius)* inhabits the coastal marshes of Louisiana, southeastern Texas, and southwestern Mississippi (Lowery 1974). The nutria originally introduced to the United States in 1899 was reported by Lowery (1974) to be the subspecies *M. c. bonariensis*.

The adult beaver is the largest rodent of the Southeast, attaining body weights ranging from 24 to 77 lbs. The sexes of beaver are similar in appearance, with some studies reporting slightly larger body sizes in females (Table 1). Large ever-growing incisors, webbed feet, small ears, a split-nail grooming claw on each hind foot, and a dorsally flattened, scaly tail are a few of this mammal's adaptations to aquatic life habits and diet preferences. A tenacious and industrious engineer, the beaver exhibits distinct morphology for cutting and moving trees into lodges and dam structures.

Muskrats resemble a large vole that is adapted to aquatic conditions. The tail is naked, scaled, and flattened vertically. The hind feet exhibit skin folds

Table 1. Morphological characteristics of adult male and female beaver in the southeastern U.S.

State	Age class Sex[a]	Mass (lbs)	Range of Lengths (in) Total body	Tail	Neck	Hind foot	Ear	Sample size	Citation
Alabama	N/A	39.0	40.5	11.3	6.8	1.2	N/A	N/A	Choate et al. 1994
Arkansas[a]	N/A	24.3-77.2	34.5-47.8	9.1-17.3	6.1-7.6	1.3-1.5	N/A	N/A	Sealander and Heidt 1990
Louisiana	Female	N/A	40.8	13.5	6.9	N/A	N/A	2	Lowery 1974
	N/A	33.3	N/A	N/A	N/A	N/A	N/A	82	
Mississippi	N/A	34.0	N/A	N/A	N/A	N/A	N/A	42	Arner et al. 1980
South Carolina	Male	32.4	N/A	N/A	N/A	N/A	N/A	42	Woodward 1977
	Female	33.3	N/A	N/A	N/A	N/A	N/A	46	
South Carolina	Male	34.4	N/A	N/A	N/A	N/A	N/A	9	
	Female	38.8	N/A	N/A	N/A	N/A	N/A	8	Choate et al 1994
Texas	N/A	39.6	45.7	15.8	7.0	N/A	N/A	N/A	Davis and Schmidly 1994
Distribution[b]	N/A	24.3-57.3	34.5-47.8	9.1-17.3	6.1-8.1	0.9-1.1	N/A	N/A	
		24.0-77.2				1.2-1.5			

[a] Range of values given for some measurements rather than averages.

[b] Measurements summarized for species throughout its range.

Table 2. Morphological measurements of muskrats in the southeastern U.S.

State	Age class Sex[a]	Mass (lbs)	Range of Lengths (in) Total body	Tail	Hind foot	Ear	Sample size	Citation
Arkansas	Adults	1.1-4.0	9.0-13.4	7.1-11.6	2.5-3.5	0.6-1.0	N/A	Sealander and Heidt 1990
Louisiana	Adults	N/A	10.2-10.6	7.1-10.1	2.5-3.4	0.6-1.0	50	Lowery 1970
Oklahoma	Adults	N/A	16.1-24.0[b]	N/A	N/A	N/A	N/A	Caire et al. 1989
Texas	Males	2.0[c]	10.9	9.5	N/A	N/A	N/A	Davis and Schmidly 1994
	Females	1.9[c]						
Distribution[d]	Adults	1.1-4.0	9.0-13.4	7.1-11.6	2.5-3.5	0.6-1.0	N/A	Choate et al. 1994
		1.5-3.3	10.0-11.6	7.9-10.0	2.6-3.1	0.8-1.0	N/A	

[a] Values represent adult age class with male and female measurements combined or differentiation between males and females as indicated.
[b] Reported value includes tail length.
[c] Reported value represents sample mean.
[d] Values represent ranges of measurements over the species southeastern distribution based on table references.

between the toes. The fur consists of a thick underlayer and coarse, glossy guard hairs. Pelage coloration is generally dark brown, but may vary from white and silver to tan, brown, and black. Total body length for adults ranges from 18 to 26 inches, with body weight ranging from 1.5 to 3.3 lbs (Table 2). Size and pelage coloration may vary in muskrats according to geographic location and subspecies. Morphological variations reported for the Louisiana muskrat include smaller skull and body sizes and variable pelt coloration (Lowery 1974). In muskrats, the sexes are superficially similar; however, several authors have reported slightly higher body weights in males than in females (Table 2) (Lowery 1974, Davis and Schmidly 1994). Appearance of external genitalia differs between female and male muskrats. Also, female muskrats exhibit a bare area devoid of fur between the vagina and anal opening which is lacking in males.

Nutria resemble beaver in body form and size; however, the scantily haired tail is round and pelage coloration is generally grayish brown. Total body length generally ranges from 33 to 42 inches with adult

Table 3. Morphological measurements of nutria in the southeastern United States.

State	Age class Sex[a]	Mass (lbs)	Range of Lengths (in) Total body	Tail	Hind foot	Ear	Sample size	Citation
Arkansas	Adults	15.4-24.3	19.7-23.6	11.8-17.7	3.9-5.9	0.8-1.2	N/A	Sealander and Heidt 1984
Louisiana	Adults	15.0-16.1	15.0-26.0	N/A	N/A	N/A	35	Atwood 1950
	Female	17.4[b]	25.0	16.5	N/A	N/A		Atwood 1950
	Male	18.1[b]	26.0	17.0	N/A	N/A	N/A	
Louisiana	Adults	13.2[c]	23.5	13.6	5.2	1.1	8	Lowery 1974
	Adults	7.9-20.1	21.1-22.1	11.8-17.7	3.9-5.9	0.8-1.2		
Oklahoma	Adults	15.0-20.1	N/A	N/A	N/A	N/A	N/A	Caire et al. 1989
Texas	Adults	17.6-22.1	17.7-19.7	13.8-15.8	5.1-5.5	N/A	N/A	Davis and Schmidly 1994
Distribution[d]	Adults	7.9-24.3	15.0-26.0	11.8-17.7	3.9-5.9	0.8-1.2	N/A	

[a] Values represent adult age class with male and female measurements combined or differentiation between males and females as indicated. Selected studies report no significant variation between males and females.
[b] Reported value represents largest specimens reported by Atwood (1950).
[c] Reported value represents sample mean.
[d] Values represent ranges of measurements over the species southeastern distribution based on table references.

weights ranging from 8 to 24 lbs (Table 3). The hind feet are webbed with the last toe free. Sexes of the nutria are distinguishable by genitalia and presence or absence of mammary glands and teats. Teats are located on the sides of the body and are visible from above the animal giving rise to the belief that mammae are located on the back (Lowery 1974, Brown 1997).

DISTRIBUTION

Beaver

The beaver, prior to 1940, was extirpated from most of its range because of extensive trapping. Restocking programs in Louisiana, Mississippi, Alabama, Florida, Georgia, Oklahoma, Virginia, Arkansas, and North and South Carolina have led to viable populations in suitable habitat across most of the South (Webster et al. 1985, Miller 1987, Caire et al. 1989, Sealander and Heidt 1990). Today, beaver are found throughout the South except along coastal areas of peninsular Florida south of the Suwannee River (Brown 1997).

Muskrat

The muskrat ranges from the Arctic circle southward through the United States to northern Mexico. This species historically was absent in arid portions of the Southwest, some coastal locales in California and Oregon, and the state of Florida. In the south central United States, muskrats occurred throughout in suitable habitats except the southern portions of Alabama, Georgia, and coastal South Carolina. Highest populations of muskrats were found historically in the coastal marshes of Louisiana, southeast Texas, and southwest Mississippi (Lowery 1974, Choate et al. 1994).

Today muskrats are found in all of the southeastern states. They are most common in the Gulf Coastal Plains of Arkansas, Louisiana, Mississippi, and Alabama. The muskrat is found over most of Oklahoma, with highest abundance occurring in the northeastern corner of the state (Caire et al. 1989). Aquatic habitats of northeastern and south Texas generally support muskrats (Davis and Schmidly 1994). Muskrats inhabit coastal marshes surrounding the Chesapeake Bay and northeastern North Carolina. They are less abundant inland in these states, rare along the coast of southeastern North Carolina, and generally absent in the coastal marshes of South Carolina (Webster et al. 1985). Because the common muskrat has been captured in the Mobile Bay area of Alabama, it possibly inhabits some marshes, ponds, lakes, or streams of the extreme western edge of the Florida Panhandle; however, as of 1997, occurrence had not been verified.

Nutria

The nutria is native to South America where it occurs in coastal areas and along larger rivers from approximately 15° south latitude in southern Brazil, Paraguay, and

Table 4. Reproductive characteristics of beaver, nutria, and muskrat in the southeastern U.S.

Species	Breed season	Peak birth	Litter size	Pair bond	Estrus cycle	Litter/ year	Gestation period	Delayed implant	Age at sexual maturity	Citation
Beaver	Nov-March	Jan-Feb	1-6 Avg=2.4	Monogamous	Polyestrous	1.0	104-111 days Avg=107	No	2 years	Novak 1987
Nutria	Year round	N/A	2-12 Avg=5-6	Polygamous	Polyestrous	2-3 Avg=2	127-132 days Avg=130	No	4-8 months	Atwood 1950 Lowery 1974
Muskrat	Year round	Nov-March	1-13 Avg=3.8	Polygamous	Polyestrous	5-8 Avg=5	22-30 days Avg=28	No	8-10 months	Lay 1945 Lowery 1974

Table 5. Average pelt price and annual harvest (number of animals) of beaver in the southeastern United States from 1970-1991 (Linscombe 1993).

		STATE												
Year	Ave. price	AL	AR	FL	GA	KY	LA	MS	OK	NC	SC	TN	TX	VA
1970-71			538		2444	46	14		89	376				2306
1971-72			512		1417	114	126		82	535				4296
1972-73			1349	6	2596	289	956		661	723			128	4572
1973-74			1437	8	2927	309	472		705	606	4		1071	4307
1974-75	7.06		889	1	3637	269	276		1941	576	0	1640	1302	1640
1975-76	6.49		1008	58	3199	166	207		1003	458	0	31	681	3755
1976-77	9.23		4371	161	4888	681	280	19326	3090	588	0	848	3449	5546
1977-78	7.30	13765	5172	173	5481	382	332	15984	1904	446	306	656	2702	6224
1978-79	8.20	14655	3885	129	5942	438	512	17192	1592	363	329	1239	0	5566
1979-80	15.30	22550	12826	465	7649	1115	2317	19352	2894	776	329	1132	0	13267
1980-81	8.51	9442	8551	613	9802	880	1504	18162	2686	943	407	1094	2193	12059
1981-82	7.43	5503	6819	436	3361	667	2061	14694	1843	1078	570	807	2457	6811
1982-83	4.77	2039	5554	252	1298	474	2106	8236	1512	518	379	515	3239	3081
1983-84	5.34	929	2939	77	966	842	288	6033	830	535	432	350	2613	4821
1984-85	6.56	3394	4745	54	2614	1456	375	9734	2988	604	602	557	2549	3560
1985-86	7.56	3744	6844	27	1642	1372	1115	10247	2658	888	931	630	1066	6904
1986-87	8.75	4049	10527	97	1916	2527	1810	15214	4184	1340	852	2064	4939	6772
1987-88	6.20	3343	8609	210	6233	1633	1274	12952	2950	1379	892	1148	5494	4728
1988-89	4.42	824	4963	9	4159	1211	830	9753	1793	892	1174	398	2847	
1989-90	4.69	216	4396	0	5240	1174	864	8591	1303	1105	689	292	2296	1798
1990-91	4.18	111	1803	0	2535	801	1303	4475	540	401	556	66	3126	2010
1991-92	4.31	95	2167	0	4116	1021	993	5110	923	536	716	225	3562	3887

Bolivia to the Pacific coast in Tierra del Fuego (Osgood 1939). Nutria were introduced on the west coast of the United States as early as 1899. The subspecies, *M. c. bonariensis*, was introduced into Louisiana as a captive, commercial furbearer in 1937. Part of this captive population escaped into marshes of Avery Island, Louisiana during a 1938 hurricane. Subsequently, nutria have become established in wetland habitats of Louisiana and Mississippi (Lowery 1974, Sealander and Heidt 1990, Choate et al. 1994). Natural colonization in Texas was documented in 1946, when a few feral nutria were trapped along the southeast coast. The spread to inland Texas was facilitated by introductions of nutria to 22 counties by 1950 for aquatic plant control. In Oklahoma, nutria were introduced as a potential commercial furbearer in the early 1950s, and by the 1960s nutria were found in the wild near captive populations around Fort Sill (Caire et al. 1989). Introductions also occurred in North Carolina and Virginia (Webster et al. 1985). Colonies of nutria in the northern panhandle of

Table 6. Average price and number of muskrats harvested annually in the southeastern United States from 1970-1991 (Linscombe 1993).

Year	Ave. price	STATE												
		AL	AR	FL	GA	KY	LA	MS	OK	NC	SC	TN	TX	VA
1970-71	0.87		4153		8239	26995	777960		45	89846		19448	0	128991
1971-72	1.17		6135		6960	39510	326513		529	96997			0	146905
1972-73	1.71		8982		10349	50856	346787		926	153369			10108	200543
1973-74	0.86		14834		8980	78141	286087		1395	135266	94		8646	163678
1974-75	2.75		19089		12046	82039	300214		3235	105882	2193	51155	16622	172118
1975-76	3.70		29016		11962	70213	740814		4201	95536	1786	25218	9113	191206
1976-77	4.31		45327		28382	126211	965889	41473	5291	75957		56423	5150	145177
1977-78	3.41	44489	29921		18631	66780	638816	29772	3277	52619	249	35495	4551	141921
1978-79	3.95	40625	33359		19327	62243	445525	20354	2414	55630	595	39568	0	141409
1979-80	6.16	60635	60573		20645	100806	551036	38899	2563	70775	896	39958	0	167803
1980-81	6.36	30094	38148		16830	85644	702474	30185	3182	83269	2069	30234	0	213349
1981-82	3.31	19404	36073		13640	55564	387233	27100	4231	48468	1667	23996	0	110809
1982-83	2.42	12194	37676		7525	56903	321494	16752	3893	39744	2213	40572	0	82038
1983-84	2.35	12437	19911		8008	64808	324330	15749	1237	37806	1580	27133	0	95037
1984-85	2.66	15184	22380		10624	67692	188743	17266	1088	45117	1421	25132	0	25132
1985-86	2.50	12159	25505		4744	58114	71367	10530	1116	26972	921	19103	0	71634
1986-87	3.29	14434	25502		4213	84402	143538	12142	2809	25288	1139	28486	192	72209
1987-88	3.19	14700	23075		4655	79481	163670	9097	2159	25073	911	28823	1063	63464
1988-89	1.80	4946	17010		2608	36146	22193	6853	1214	10187	465	10739	0	0
1989-90	0.79	681	4991		1421	24488	12672	2506	505	5810	386	4477	0	13080
1990-91	0.93	358	3479		1397	8319	2987	681	219	4099	103	1655	0	15561
1991-92	1.67	2117	3773		2235	17123	13071	1256	353	10287	435	7274	0	21961

Florida apparently resulted from the eastern expansion of populations from Louisiana (Atwood 1950). Populations of nutria recorded in southern peninsular Florida probably were a result of escapes and releases from abortive fur farming operations in the mid-1950s (Brown 1975).

The nutria currently is well-established in the West Gulf Coastal Plain and the southern portion of the Mississippi River Delta. Populations of nutria in the Southeast are most concentrated in coastal areas of the Gulf states; however, the nutria's range now extends northwesterly into the eastern two-thirds of Texas, southern Oklahoma, and easterly into Florida and South Carolina. Breeding populations of nutria were reported in Oklahoma by the early 1970s, with distribution occurring currently as scattered populations in southern Oklahoma (Caire et al. 1989). Today, populations in Texas are considered moderately high with predictions of population increases causing eventual overpopulation problems (Davis and Schmidly 1994). Nutria are well-established in Louisiana statewide, with highest abundances occurring in southern Louisiana (Lowery 1974). The nutria occurs in much of Mississippi and Alabama, with highest concentrations being in coastal areas and in major alluvial floodplains of the Mississippi, Alabama, and Tombigbee Rivers. To the north, nutria are colonizing the Arkansas River Valley of Arkansas. Populations in Arkansas and northern portions of Mississippi, Alabama, and Florida are localized and scattered (Brown 1997). Nutria also occur in Atlantic coastal marshes of Georgia, Florida, South Carolina, North Carolina, Virginia, and Maryland (Webster et al. 1985, Brown 1997). This species currently inhabits the Chesapeake Bay and Currituck and Palmico Sounds and appears to be extending its range southward in coastal marshes and inland to freshwater systems in North Carolina (Webster et al. 1985).

DENSITY

Density estimates vary for these furbearers, not only by species, but by geographic location and habitat quality (Palmisano 1972). Estimates of densities may be difficult even at high population levels due to their aquatic

Table 7. Average price and number of nutria harvested annually in the southeastern United States from 1970-1991 (Linscombe 1993).

		STATE												
Year	Ave. price	AL	AR	FL	GA	KY	LA	MS	OK	NC	SC	TN	TX	VA
1970-71			77				1226739			6617				3337
1971-72							1286622			15014				
1972-73			33				1611623			11900			2240	
1973-74			19				1749670			11693			41974	
1974-75	4.83		110				1502617			17070			12197	
1975-76	4.86		92				1525506			10552			6715	4848
1976-77	7.79		1230	18	18		1890853	4308		8115			20010	2137
1977-78	4.81	164	836	2	13		1714083	5692		2577			29795	737
1978-79	4.20	260	925		21		1145084	3164	18	2236			21645	
1979-80	6.78	640	1233	2	117		1300822	7821	11	2663			17973	776
1980-81	8.17	534	2009	16	73		1207050	4765	1	1938			34586	1229
1981-82	4.35	314	1793		1		961471	6692	12	743			21836	93
1982-83	2.53	175	983	3	45		730731	2581	18	874			51080	
1983-84	2.81	142	415		6		881551	2081	36	1774			21179	456
1984-85	3.95	308	487		21		1214600	2292	2	1709			12798	817
1985-86	3.14	92	377		15		761948	9355	3	1194			19162	1101
1986-87	3.40	228	950		3		986014	4199	12	1067			20908	613
1987-88	2.56	105	1448		64		617646	1602	36	2047			21899	1706
1988-89	1.71	4	32		41		223222	1515		1131				
1989-90	2.97		22		6		292760	1017		906			4449	
1990-91	2.52		102		1		134196	378		294			3106	
1991-92	3.12		88				1240229	254		493			4191	

life style and activity patterns. Density estimates and population trends can be ascertained by using indices, such as lodge, burrow, track, or dam counts. Densities may be reported in terms of animals per mile in riparian habitats or animals per acre in impounded habitats.

Beaver

Beaver densities are not derivable in the context of animals/area, but are generally expressed as animals/linear measure of stream or river. However, few southeastern studies have reported or examined beaver densities. For the colonial beaver, density may be expressed as number of colonies/mi^2. In Alabama, Hill et al.(1977) estimated colony saturation in 4 headwaters as 1.2 colonies/1.6 miles of stream. Throughout its distribution, beaver colony densities range from a low of 0.06 colonies per mile in poor habitat in the Soviet Union to as many as 0.78 per mile in New Brunswick, Canada (Novak 1987a). The number of animals in an established colony may range from a low of 4 to 6 individuals consisting of a mated pair with young, to a high of 10 to 12 individuals that include mated pair, offspring, and yearlings (Arner, D. H. pers. commu.).

Muskrat

Studies of muskrats in the Southeast indicated greatest abundance in brackish marshes dominated by vigorous stands of three-cornered sedge (O'Neil 1949). Palmisano (1972) reported that brackish marshes in southeastern Louisiana supported the greatest densities of muskrats, with a range of 25.2 to 107.7 muskrats/100 acres (x = 72 muskrats/100 acres; x = 24 lodges/100 acres). Muskrat numbers per lodge ranged from 1 to 7 in this habitat type, with a mean of 3.5 muskrats per lodge. Freshwater habitats in southeastern Louisiana supported a range of 1.2 to 8.1 muskrats/100 acres (x = 4.8 muskrats/100 acres; x = 1.6 lodges/100 acres) (Palmisano 1972). Poorer habitats of coastal Louisiana support muskrat populations of 1 pair per 400 acres, whereas better quality marsh habitat supports 1 pair per 40 acres (Atwood 1950).

Nutria

Nutria exhibit a broad range of tolerance for various aquatic habitat conditions and may attain high densities in natural and man-made habitats. Brown (1975) reported 10 nutria/acre in a highly eutrophic, sewage lagoon in south Florida, whereas, an adjacent unpolluted pond supported 4.5 nutria/acre. High densities in the sewage lagoon were attributed to a year round, unlimited plant food supply and absence of alligators (Brown 1975). Coastal Louisiana marshes with plant associations of sawgrass, giant cut-grass, southern bulrush, and maidencane can support high nutria populations of 6 active burrows per mile of levee (Atwood 1950). Estimates of one family group (x = 8-9 individuals) for each burrow have been given to interpret burrow count data (Atwood 1950).

HARVEST TRENDS

As with harvest of other furbearers, harvest of beaver, nutria, and muskrat in the southeastern United States reflects great variation during the period 1970 to 1991 (Tables 5-7) (Linscombe 1993). Annual variation in fur harvest varies with the species of interest and may be a function of fur prices, the national and international fur market demand, public sentiment (effectiveness of anti-trapping activities), species ecology (nutria expansion and muskrat decline in the Southeast), and environmental conditions.

Historically, the beaver is one of the South's most harvested furbearers. However, prior to 1989, prices paid for beaver pelts were the lowest of southeastern furbearers (Table 5). Beaver harvest since 1988 has shown declines in all southeastern states, although Georgia, Virginia, and to a greater extent Texas, have had stable harvests. Federally and state supported control programs have been implemented to curtail property, crop, and timber damage from these aquatic rodents (Wade and Ramsey 1984).

The muskrat has been the single most important furbearer in North America in terms of numbers of pelts sold commercially (Tarver et al. 1987). Muskrat comprised 82% of the total fur catch in Louisiana from 1913 to 1960 (Lowery 1974). After 1960, muskrat composition of the total fur catch began declining, and by the late 1980s comprised only 25% of the total fur catch in Louisiana (Tarver et al. 1987). Even with declines, muskrat harvest remains high in good habitat (Table 6).

The highest muskrat fur production and harvest occurred historically in the brackish coastal marshes of Louisiana and southeastern Texas. During peak harvest years, over 50% of the total muskrat harvest for North America came from these marshes (Palmisano 1972).

Changes in marsh habitat quality, reduced trapper effort, and competition from nutria have been cited as reasons for declines in muskrat harvests (Lowery 1974).

Harvest of nutria varies across states (Table 7). Production of nutria pelts exceeded 1 million animals per year in Louisiana from 1970-1981, but declined dramatically during the late 1980s and early 1990s. Pelt prices for nutria were highest during 1977-78 and 1980-81, reaching \$7.79 and \$8.17 per pelt (Table 7).

REPRODUCTION

Nutria and muskrats exhibit reproductive characteristics typical of the order Rodentia. They are generally very prolific, breeding throughout most of the year except in northern portions of the Southeast where prolonged, cold winters occur. Females generally come into estrus soon after giving birth to young; therefore, several litters can be produced in one year. The beaver differs in terms of annual fecundity and mating habits when compared to nutria and muskrat.

Beaver

The beaver reaches sexual maturity at about 2 years of age. Breeding occurs from November through March, with peak births occurring during January and February (Table 4). A mated pair generally produces 1 litter/year that ranges in size from 1 to 6 young/litter (x = 2.4). Gestation exceeds 100 days. Beaver are monogamous in their mating habits and both parents care for the young. Beaver construct complex den sites—lodges and bank dens. Lodges are used for raising young as well as year-round protection. Bank dens may be built in impoundments, rivers, and streams.

Muskrat

In most of the southeastern states, muskrats breed year round, producing 2 to 5 litters annually with 2 to 10 young/litter (x = 6) (Lowery 1974). Kinler et al. (1988) reported that muskrats in coastal Louisiana produce 1 to 7 fetuses/litter (x = 3.54; ± 1.15) and an average of 2.7 litters/breeding female/year. Gestation ranges from 22 to 30 days and females exhibit a post-partum estrus. Gestation periods generally are shorter if females are impregnated prior to initiation of nursing. Young are altricial, but develop rapidly. New-born muskrats have hair in approximately 1 week, at 2 weeks of age their eyes open, and they are weaned at 4 weeks of age. Post-partum mortality in muskrat litters may range from 11% during the first two weeks of life to 41% up to 24 days of age (Kinler et al. 1988). In coastal areas, tidal flooding of lodges may be responsible for early mortality in muskrat litters (Kinler 1986). Sexual maturity and breeding occurs at about 1 year of age. Family groups are housed in muskrat lodges that are built of aquatic vegetation.

Nutria

Nutria breed throughout the year in most of the Southeast. The gestation period ranges from 127 to 132 days (x = 130 days). Litter size ranges from 2 to 12 young. Like muskrats, female nutria exhibit postpartum estrus. Baby nutria are precocial, being born fully furred with eyes open and capable of swimming within hours after birth. Lateral location of teats on females allows nursing of young while in the water. Nutria are weaned when they are 6 to 8 months old. "Juvenile breeding" may occur in nutria as young as 4 months (Brown 1997). Fecundity and production of young has been directly related to food availability in Gulf Coast nutria populations, with food shortage resulting in lower reproductive rates (Atwood 1950).

DIET

The beaver is a strict herbivore, feeding on herbaceous and woody plant material. Muskrats and nutria are considered opportunistic herbivores and omnivores. Primary food items taken by these two species include tubers, roots, stems, and foliage of aquatic plants; however, both species will utilize small amounts of animal foods, such as crayfish, mussels, clams, and animal carrion (Lowery 1974). Beaver and muskrat will cache food in lodges, and nutria may feed on residual vegetation left on feeding platforms from previous feeding periods.

Beaver

Beaver consume woody material (bark and cambium) year-round; however, woody plant material is the primary food item taken during winter months. A minimum of 22 woody perennial plants are used commonly by beaver, including loblolly pine, sweetgum, spruce pine, southern sweetbay, tupelo gum, bald cypress, blue beech, southern red oak, winged sumac, black willow, and cow oak. Roberts and Arner (1981), studying stomach contents in Mississippi, found that 27 herbaceous and 11 woody plant species were consumed by beaver. Prominent herbaceous plants taken by beaver included smartweed (20.0% occurrence), water primrose (12.1% occurrence), numerous grasses (26.7% occurrence), and Japanese honeysuckle (12.1%). Woody plants that were eaten frequently included sweetgum, willow, and pine. In South Carolina, Woodward (1977) found 48 woody tree or shrub species representing 26 families, and 24 herbaceous species representing 15 families were used as food during summer and/or winter. Beaver appear to utilize many woody and herbaceous plant species common to mesic and hydric sites.

Muskrat

Cattails are a major food of muskrats inhabiting freshwater marshes. In coastal brackish marshes, muskrats feed primarily on bulrush and cordgrass. Other consistently utilized foods include rushes, pickerelweed, smartweed, roussea cane, arrowleaf, sweet flag, alligator weed, spike rushes, and numerous aquatic grasses (*Panicum*, *Distichlis*, *Paspalum*, and *Leersia* spp.). Muskrats living in freshwater lakes, flooded rice fields, and bayous feed on the aforementioned freshwater emergents, rice, field grasses, clover, and higher percentages of animal matter, such as freshwater mussels, clams, crayfish, and fish (Lowery 1974).

Nutria

Nutria feed on a diversity of semiaquatic and aquatic vegetation. In coastal areas, nutria have been reported to feed on shellfish (Atwood 1950). Wild rice, lizard's tail, water shield, lotus lily, muskgrass, and bladderwort are important foods in Oklahoma (Caire et al. 1989). These plants, as well as bulrushes, sawgrass, maidencane, water hyacinth, and sedges (Family Cyperaceae), have been reported as major food items in coastal habitats of Louisiana (Atwood 1950). Major foods consumed all year on Mississippi barrier islands were Torpedo grass, sea oats, black needle rush, cattail, and heterotheca. Cattail, black needle rush, and morning glory were utilized heavily during the spring. Summer diets were dominated by sea oats, heterotheca, morning glory, and cordgrass. Fall and winter diets consisted almost exclusively of torpedo grass (Herring 1988).

Nutria also feed extensively on introduced plants, such as water hyacinth and alligator weed. Many early releases of nutria were conducted to control introduced aquatic plants through biological means. In many cases, nutria did not effectively control introduced plants. However, their preference for agricultural crops, including sugar cane, rice, corn, pasture grasses, and vegetable and root crops, caused damage in many areas (Lowery 1974).

HABITAT RELATIONSHIPS

Beaver, nutria, and muskrats utilize natural and man-made aquatic habitats in the southeastern United States. Muskrats and nutria typically occur in both freshwater and brackish water ecosystems, whereas beaver prefer freshwater habitats. Of the 3 species, the muskrat appears to be the most sensitive to habitat changes. Declines in muskrat populations in Louisiana and Texas have been attributed primarily to habitat degradation in coastal marshes resulting from reduction in native plant diversity, exotic plant introductions, and water quality changes. Compared to muskrats, nutria seem to thrive in highly eutrophic habitats where introduced plants are abundant (Brown 1975).

Beaver

Freshwater habitats with ample food resources are considered suitable habitat for beavers. In the Southeast, slow-moving streams and creeks are generally used more readily than fast-moving streams and rivers. Proximity to trees and shrubs that provide a food source is important. However, the beaver is capable of traveling long distances to secure food, including walking long distances on land. Few detailed habitat studies exist for southeastern beaver. Aquatic systems, such as ponds and small lakes with muddy bottoms or meandering streams, are ideal beaver habitat (Novak 1987*a*). Davis and Guynn (1993) studied 2 beaver populations, one associated with lake and one with stream environments. In this study, beaver use of 9 aquatic habitat types was reported, with habitat use varying seasonally with respect to colony location.

Muskrat

Muskrats generally are marsh inhabitants, although inland rivers, streams, canals, lakes, ponds, borrow pits, sloughs, swamps, and oxbows are also used when cover and food resources are present (Brown 1974, Davis and Schmidly 1994). Rice fields are used by muskrats in agricultural areas of the Southeast (Lowery 1974, Sealander and Heidt 1990). Preferred inland habitats of muskrats are freshwater marshes that support clusters of cattails interspersed with bulrushes, sedges, and other herbaceous emergent vegetation. Brackish marshes with good stands of three-square bulrush or cordgrass and stabilized water depths of 6-24 inches constitute optimal muskrat habitat in coastal areas (Lowery 1974, Webster et al. 1985, Davis and Schmidly 1994). In coastal marshes, muskrats typically construct dome-shaped lodges of herbaceous plant materials. Lodges usually are visible in marsh habitats and can be used to index muskrat abundance. Dens and tunnels typically are constructed in banks of freshwater habitats rather than vegetation lodges (Sealander and Heidt 1990). These tunnels may not be apparent due to the location of the opening 6-12 inches below the water's surface.

Nutria

Nutria can be categorized as aquatic to semi-aquatic species due to their preference for wetland edge habitats of swamps, marshes, and shorelines of streams, rivers, and canals in the Southeast (Davis and Schmidly 1994). In their native habitats of Chile and Tierra del Fuego, nutria occur primarily in channels, bays, and estuaries of the mainland and islands (Davis and Schmidly 1994). Habitat types used in the southeastern United States include freshwater and brackish water marshes, swamps, oxbows, rivers, and streams with slack water areas. Nutria construct burrows in earthen structures, such as levees, banks, and terraces. Burrows may be simple, single opening burrows or complex, multi-tunneled structures with several openings. Tunnels normally extend several feet into the bank, but some may exceed 49 feet in length (Wade and Ramsey 1986).

All 3 aquatic herbivorous furbearers have effects on the ecosystems that they inhabit. The beaver has obtained both a bad and a good reputation regarding impacts on the landscape. The beaver's activity of damming watersheds, rivers, and streams to flood forests to access food and aquatic habitat can cause substantial economic impacts on timber production. Arner and DuBose (1979) found that in Mississippi, over 17 million dollars was lost annually because of beaver impounding forest and agricultural lands. Bullock and Arner (1985) found that beaver also impacted non-impounded timber at an approximate cost of $165/acre. Similarly, in South Carolina, increasing beaver populations and the associated damage caused the need for an intensive and extensive beaver management program (Woodward 1977). Potential impacts regarding beaver damage exist throughout the southeastern United States, especially given reduced fur trapping (Miller 1987).

Although the beaver has been linked with timber and agricultural damage through flooding, numerous studies have noted the beneficial aspects of beaver activity. Many landowners and managers view beaver activity as positive due to the creation of wetlands and associated recreational opportunities, such as hunting and fishing (Arner and Dubose 1979, Arner and Hepp 1989). Wetlands created by beaver are beneficial for many reasons, including ground water recharge, increased outdoor recreation, improvement of water quality, aesthetics, slowing of surface water runoff and erosion processes, and creation of habitat for native fish, birds, mammals, reptiles, amphibians, and plants. Specific studies report beaver wetlands as valuable brood habitat for wood ducks, wintering and breeding habitat for waterfowl, fish habitat, and breeding habitat for cavity-nesting birds, such as woodpeckers and prothonotary warblers (Pullen 1967, Lochmiller 1979, Arner and Hepp 1989). Reese and Hair (1976) studied non-game bird use of beaver ponds in South Carolina and found that 92 species of birds representing 31 families were found at beaver pond sites. They attributed high bird diversity to the enhanced structural diversity created by beaver pond environments.

Muskrats can exert influences on coastal marsh vegetation during periods of high population levels and intensive herbivory. With natural or manmade changes, such as burning or saltwater high tides, a kill-off of the climax plant, cordgrass, is followed by dominance of three-cornered bulrush. Historically, when this condition occurs, muskrat numbers increase rapidly, reaching high population levels. Intensive herbivory causes denuding of all marsh vegetation in large areas of the marsh until limited food supplies begin to cause drastic population declines (Lowery 1974). As muskrat densities decline with the onset of food shortages, grazing pressure declines and marsh vegetation may recover over time (Lowery 1974). With extensive herbivory, marsh vegetation may not recover to the original plant cover and diversity (Linscombe and Kinler 1997).

In the past 4 decades, muskrat numbers have been influenced by habitat changes in wetland ecosystems. Since the 1950s, general deterioration of coastal marshes leading to a change in vegetation succession and community composition has favored the introduced nutria instead of the native muskrat.

Nutria, like muskrats, can have a profound effect on vegetation. Marsh "eat-outs" have been reported for coastal marshes where extensive herbivory by nutria has converted marsh landscapes into open water habitat or mudflats (Lowery 1974, Webster et al. 1985). Effects of extensive grazing by nutria have been reported to limit plant succession, alter plant community composition, and reduce availability of selected wildlife food plants (Lowery 1974, Linscombe and Kinler 1997).

HOME RANGE

Beaver

Home ranges for beaver have not been reported in the literature, because movement patterns are linear and are constrained by the boundaries of the aquatic system. In a South Carolina study conducted by Davis and Guynn (1993), areas used by beaver ranged from 27 to 36 acres in size.

Muskrat

Several authors report that muskrats typically remain within 49 feet of their lodge, except during periods of severe food shortages. Chabreck et al. (1989) reported that muskrats in a Louisiana coastal marsh exhibited an average monthly home range of 0.19 acre (± 0.05 acre) and that movement varied considerably among animals. In this study, no differences in movement patterns were detected among seasons or sex-age classes, and temperature and water depth exerted minor influences on movement patterns (Chabreck et al. 1989). In another coastal study, Dell et al. (1983) found muskrats had larger home ranges that averaged 0.28 acre (± 0.08) in size and exhibited greater hourly movements of 112 feet (± 5.9) from lodges. Longer daily movements (more than 230 feet) were generally associated with high water levels (more than 8 inches deep), and dispersals occurred during storm tides in coastal habitats (Dell et al. 1983). Muskrats are generally crepuscular, with greatest activity occurring several hours before sunset to midnight and during early morning (Chabreck et al. 1989).

Nutria

Early studies of nutria movement reported that daily movements seldom exceeded a radius of 200 yards, with maximum home ranges approximating 1200 yd^2 (Coreil 1981). More recent studies report average daily movements of 73 yds/day and home ranges approximating 148 acres in intermediate marsh habitats of southwestern Louisiana (Coreil 1981). Seasonal movements of greater distances have been observed in agricultural areas of rice, corn, and sugar cane, with nutria moving into fields during the growing season and departing following harvest (Wade and Ramsey 1986). Nutria generally exhibit crepuscular and nocturnal activity patterns, but are occasionally observed during the day.

DISEASES AND PARASITES

Beaver

Few studies have investigated diseases and parasites among southeastern beaver. Davidson and Nettles (1988) cite beaver as a host for *Giardia*. This protozoan can be transmitted to humans, but apparently has negligible effects on beaver populations. Waterborne tularemia has been found in northern beaver populations, but has not been reported for southeastern beaver (Davidson and Nettles 1988). Lowery (1974) reported the occurrence of 4 trematodes *(Stichochis subtriquetus, Stephaano-proaoides lawi, Renifer ellipticus*, and *Paraphistomum castori*) and 7 nematodes *(Capillaria hepatica, Travas-sorius americanus, T. rufus, Castor-strongylus castoris, Filaria* sp., *Oxyuris* sp., and *Gongylonema* sp.). Ectopara-sites that were found included 2 arachnids, a mite (*Schizocarpus mingaudi*), a tick *(Dermacentor albipic-tus*), a louse (*Trichoidectes castoris*), and 2 parasitic bee-tles (*Platypsylla castoris* and *Leptinillas validus*) (Lowery 1974).

Muskrat

Parasites of muskrats in Louisiana were studied as early as the 1940s (Lowery 1974). An ectoparasitic mite, *Tetragonyssus spiniger*, was abundant in nests and fur of muskrats. Larvae of the flesh fly, *Sarcophaga* sp., also were found in the fur of muskrats. Muskrats in Louisiana were found to be infested with nymphal stages of the Linguatalid, *Porocephalus crotali*, in visceral and pleural cavities and body musculature. Internal parasites found in muskrats of Texas and Louisiana include 4 nematodes, (*Capillaria hepatica, Rictularia* sp., *Physaloptera* sp., and *Longistriata adunca*), 1 cestode (*Hymenolepis evagina-ta*), and 3 trematodes (*Nudacotyle* sp., *Echinochasmus schwartzi*, and *Paramonostomum crotali*) (Lowery 1974). Protozoan pathogens that infect muskrats are *Giardia ondatrae* and *Trichomonas* (Lowery 1974). Examinations of 36 intestinal tracts of muskrats taken in strip-mine ponds of southern Illinois revealed a trematode (*Quinqueserialis quinqueserialis*) and a cestode (*Monococestus* sp.). Major bacterial diseases include Tyzzer's disease or Errington's disease caused by *Bacillus piliformis*, and tularemia caused by *Francisella tularensis* (Davidson and Nettles 1988). Other diseases reported to infect muskrats are leukemia, coccidiosis, and a fungal infection that is often fatal to the young (Lowery 1974).

Nutria

Nutria in the southern part of Louisiana are host to a number of internal parasites including trematodes (*Echinostoma revolutum, Heterobilharzia americana*, and *Psilostomum* sp.), a cestode (*Anoplocephala* sp.), and nematodes (*Trichostrongylus sigmodontis, Longistriata maldonadoi, Strongyloides myopotami, Trichuris myocastoris*). Eighty to 90% of the nutria in south Louisiana are infected with the nematode *Strongyloides myopotami*. Larvae of this roundworm can penetrate and irritate skin of humans who handle infected nutria, causing a rash known as "nutria or marsh itch" (Lowery 1974). Howerthe et al. (1994) found that nutria in Louisiana tested positive for *Toxoplasma gondii, Chlamydia psittaci*, and *Leptospira* spp.; but no evidence of *Giardia* spp. or *Salmonella* spp. was detected in fecal samples.

INTERSPECIES INTERACTIONS

Beaver

The degree of interaction between beaver and terrestri-al carnivores is generally minimal because of the aquatic nature and feeding habitats of the animals. Otter and beaver interactions are minimal given that they are not competitors for the same food resources, although otter have been implicated as potential preda-tors of beaver. Beaver, by creating or enhancing aquat-ic environments, increase habitats for other aquatic and semi-aquatic furbearers, such as river otter, nutria, mink, and muskrat. If food shortages occur near wet-lands, beaver may travel on ground for food and may be more susceptible to predation by coyote and bobcat. Although coyote and bobcats are cited as predators of beaver, this predation has not been reported to impact beaver populations. Predation of beaver by alligators has been reported by several authors (Arner et al. 1980).

Muskrat

Muskrat are prey for a variety of predators. Animals that prey on muskrats in a general order of importance are mink, raccoons, owls, alligators, ants, marsh hawks, cottonmouth moccasins, bullfrogs, gar, bowfins, snapping turtles, bass, crabs, hogs, domestic dogs, and cats (O'Neil 1949, Lowery 1974, Davis and Schmidly 1994). In habitats where alligators are abun-dant, these reptiles are major predators of muskrats (Lowery 1974). Mink are the major predator of muskrats in marshes of the northern United States. Predation by bullfrogs and ants is generally associated with taking of young animals that are still staying in or near the lodge (O'Neil 1949). Investigations of the imported fireant's *(Solenopsis invicta, S. saevissima)* relationships to young muskrats in Louisiana revealed that there was no relationship between young muskrat presence/absence and fireant occurrence (Newsom et al. 1976).

Nutria

At high population densities, nutria may compete with muskrat for food and space and have displaced muskrats from high ground in marsh habitats (Lowery 1974, Wade and Ramsey 1986). Since nutria exhibit a broader range of environmental tolerance than native muskrats, they may compete with muskrats in degraded marsh habitats (Atwood 1950, Lowery 1974, Brown 1975). Therefore, the interaction of changing habitat conditions along with high nutria populations may limit muskrat populations.

The alligator is the nutria's primary predator in wetlands of the Gulf Coast states. Nutria remains have been found in bald eagle nests around the Chesapeake Bay and in Louisiana. Although adults are generally too large for small to mid-size predators, young nutria are vulnerable to the same predators that take young muskrats, including turtles, gars, large snakes, and birds of prey (Lowery 1974, Webster et al. 1985). Domestic and feral dogs may also prey on nutria (Wade and Ramsey 1986).

MANAGEMENT

Management of the furbearing rodents should be based upon an understanding of their population dynamics, existing population densities, ecological roles, vulnerability of the targeted species to the proposed control measure and excessive harvest, property damage potential, and level of fur harvest expected by local trappers (Wade and Ramsey 1986). Additionally, the attitudes and needs of other stakeholders, including area property owners, recreationists, and the general public, should be considered. The economics of species restoration should be considered in any control program. Although the beaver is now widespread throughout the United States, it was once extirpated from many states, requiring restoration programs for population recovery. In planning control programs, resource managers must consider the impacts of extensive removal and the potential for public support of furbearer conservation due their ecological, commercial, and/or intrinsic values. Flexibility should exist in control programs so that these considerations can be integrated into population management.

Censusing

Estimates of abundance are usually necessary for planning management and control programs. Due to their aquatic and denning life style, beaver, muskrat, and nutria are difficult to observe and count. In some cases, habitat conditions may complicate the abundance surveys for these animals. Most census procedures are based on indirect counts. These are counts that enumerate signs that the animal was present rather than direct observation of the animal. In most cases, indirect counts that allow managers to monitor trends in populations numbers are adequate for effective management.

The primary indirect censusing methods used in southeastern states include lodge or house counts, track counts, burrow counts, interpretation of harvest numbers, or total harvest from small impoundments. State wildlife agencies may use trapper and hunter harvest data, trapper questionnaires, and fur dealer reports. Other techniques that may be used are road mortality samples, spotlight samples, depredation indices, field personnel reports, and controlled harvest.

Beaver.—The most commonly used technique to estimate beaver population size within a wetland is counting beaver lodges and extrapolating to total number of beaver present by multiplying by number of animals/lodge. This variable (beaver/colony) can vary and should be estimated on a site- or region-specific basis. Additionally, beaver in the Southeast tend to build bank dens; therefore, lodge counts may yield low density estimates. Aerial censusing by direct observation or by aerial photography also is useful in censusing beaver colonies (Novak 1987*a*). One problem is determination of active and inactive colony status and estimating the number of individuals in each colony. Criteria for determining activity status, in order of importance, include presence of a food cache, (which is more common with northern populations), presence of dams and resulting high water, fresh cutting on trees and floating limbs, muddy water, and mudded dams and houses (Novak 1987a). The number of individuals per colony is variable, ranging from 5 to 12 animals in the Southeast.

Muskrat.—A survey of lodges or houses is a useful index of changes in muskrat density in coastal marsh ecosystems. Palmisano (1972) reported ranges of 1 to 7 muskrats per lodge, with an average occupancy of 3.2 muskrats per lodge in optimal coastal habitat. Lay (1945) reported that lodge counts performed when vegetation is green are the most effective due to better vis-

Table 8. Recommended harvest methods for beaver, nutria, and muskrat (Hygnstrom et al. 1994).

Species	Livetrap	Snares	Leghold	Suitcase type	Conibear	Chemical	Other
Nutria	Single or Double door 9"x9"x32"	3/32"	No. 2, No.11 double long spring		No. 220 No. 330	 Zinc phosphate	Shooting (night)
Muskrat	Stove-pipe		No. 1, No. 1.5, or No. 2 single or double spring		No. 110	Zinc phosphate	Shooting (early morning)
Beaver	N/A	3/32"	No. 3, No. 4, or No. 5 double spring or coil spring	Yes, for live-trapping	No. 330	None approved	Shooting

ibility. Aerial photographs and aerial strip censuses can be used; however, if lodges are numerous aerial surveys may underestimate densities. Surveys conducted by walking designated strips in high density areas of Texas yielded 7 times greater lodge densities than did aerial surveys conducted at 400 feet elevation (Lay 1945). Stream and pond bank track counts and use of scent stations baited with fatty acid scents (FAS) were used in the surveying of beaver and muskrat populations in North Carolina, Oklahoma, and Virginia (Johnson and Pelton 1981). Johnson and Pelton (1981) reported that track count and FAS station sites should be located more than 1 mile apart.

Nutria.—Presence of feeding platforms constructed by nutria can be used to ascertain occurrence or absence of nutria in aquatic habitats. However, information relating densities to feeding platform occurrence was not available. Burrow counts generally can be used as an index measurement only, because the number of nutria inhabiting each burrow may vary from 1 family group to several generations of family members (Wade and Ramsey 1984). Determining burrow activity status also may be difficult at certain times of the year. In small impoundments, such as sewage lagoons or farm ponds, complete harvest of all nutria is a lethal means to determine animal numbers (Brown 1975). Track count survey methods reported for muskrat and beaver can also be used for determination of nutria occurrence and population trends (Johnson and Pelton 1981).

Distinguishing sign.—Beaver and nutria damage can be similar, because both species commonly burrow into banks, earthen dams, and styrofoam floats of boat houses and docks. In addition, both species are commonly found at the same sites. Because large nutria can be the same size as a small beaver, burrow openings may be similar in size. Observation of animals and track differentiation is recommended to identify species (Wade and Ramsey 1984). Feeding sign and shelter construction also differ among the 3 species. Beaver activity sign includes tree girdling, and dams and lodges comprised of woody material. Nutria generally construct feeding platforms of herbaceous vegetation. Muskrats build vegetation lodges in many habitats. Tracks, scat, and burrow openings of muskrats are generally smaller than those of nutria and beaver. Muskrat burrow openings generally average 6 to 8 inches in diameter. Muskrat and nutria feeding sign in rice fields may be similar in appearance. Therefore, track and scat inspection may be needed for species identification.

Population Management

Managing these rodents generally centers around population management to reduce property, crop, and timber damage. Beaver management may be necessary to reduce inundation of and damage to roads, timber, and farmland. Nutria and muskrat may be controlled to limit crop depredation, herbivory impacts to wetland habitats, and tunneling in levees, spoil banks, and road berms (Wade and Ramsey 1984). Generally, removal by lethal means is the most common technique used. As with most furbearers, control of beaver, muskrat, and nutria through harvest is most effectively accomplished through trapping. There are many types of traps as described by Novak (1987b). Traps that are commonly used to capture furbearing rodents include wire cable snares, leghold, and conibear-type (Table 8). Humane trap modifications have been studied, developed, and recommended to address animal welfare issues (Novak 1987b).

Trapping aquatic furbearers requires expertise that may differ with the targeted species, habitat type, geographic location, climate, and societal norms. A knowledge of animal habits, regulations, and good trapping ethics can enhance trapping efforts and the overall reputation of trapping with the general public.

Due to reduced commercial harvest for fur, nutria and beaver have increased their populations in many areas, resulting in economic losses (Miller 1987). In the

Flooding from beaver dams results in substantial economic loss in the South *(B. Wilson)*.

Southeast, many federal, state, and municipal agencies may be involved with beaver control. Cooperative programs between federal and state agencies are developing to address rodent damage on private and public lands. Numerous publications regarding animal damage control, such as Hygnstrom et al. 1994 and Wade and Ramsey 1984, are available.

Beaver.—Of the southeastern furbearers, the beaver poses the greatest challenge to wildlife managers because of its numerous benefits and its potential to cause damage through flooding. Consequently, a beaver colony may be viewed as an asset because of the wetland environment created, or its activities may be viewed as devastating because of flooding and property damage. Landowners should establish priorities regarding beaver management, weigh the benefits and costs, and then decide if the colony or colonies will be maintained or destroyed.

Beaver are highly vulnerable to intensive harvest due to the high visibility of sign and ease of colony detection. Planning for a sustainable harvest of this animal requires understanding the harvest pressure effect on populations. Studies concerning sustainable levels of harvest in the Southeast are lacking. Studies based on northern beaver populations of Canada and the Soviet Union recommend harvest intensities average from 1 to 1.5 beaver/colony, to as high as 2.5 beaver/colony (Novak 1987*a*).

A variety of methods exists for controlling damage by reducing beaver populations. Methods examined include introducing alligators, poisons, and chemosterilants. Other effective harvest methods include using trained dogs, trapping, and night shooting with spotlights (Hill et al. 1977).

Five non-lethal methods have been developed that prevent the beaver's ability to repair the dam or maintain stable water levels. These are the beaver pipes, three-log drain, wire mesh-culverts, T-culvert guards, and the Clemson beaver pond leveler.

Muskrat.—Muskrat damage is generally not a major problem when population levels are within habitat carrying capacity. However, at high population levels muskrats have been reported to cause alterations to plant communities in Louisiana coastal marshes. Tunneling and burrowing in dams and levees may cause degradation and failure of water impoundment structures in aquaculture ponds, rice fields, recreational lakes, and farm ponds. In agricultural areas, muskrats also feed on rice crops.

Protection of the muskrat's major predators, such as raptors, mink, and alligators, can provide a natural limiting factor on populations. Trapping muskrats for their fur is usually the best control measure. When this is not feasible, other control measures, such as shooting or altering of habitat, may be necessary. Levees may be mowed and fallow rice fields may be burned to concentrate muskrats prior to trapping (Wade and Ramsey 1984). Shooting during early evening and morning may be effective, but trapping is the most common harvest method. Traps used include small cage or "stove pipe" live traps, leghold traps, and small conibear-type traps (Table 8).

Harvest intensity for sustainable muskrat populations has been studied in Gulf Coast marshes. Harvest rates of 2.0 to 3.0 muskrats per lodge were recommended in quality habitat areas and during periods of stable muskrat populations (O'Neil 1949, Palmisano 1972).

Nutria.—Nutria damage is observed commonly in agricultural areas and coastal marsh habitats (Linscomb and Kinler 1997). Nutria will feed extensively on corn, sorghum, sugar cane, rice, vegetable crops, trees and ornamental shrubs (Wade and Ramsey 1984). Economic losses of crops can be extensive at high nutria densities, because each nutria may ingest 2 to 3 pounds of food daily (Wade and Ramsey 1984). Additionally, nutria commonly construct burrows in levees, pond banks, earthen dams and dock floatation materials. Control of nutria densities also may be desired if competition with the native muskrat is perceived to be a localized problem.

Control methods for nutria are similar to those of beaver (Table 8). Due to its large size, native predators may have limited effects on nutria populations; however, dogs and large alligators may prey substantially on adult nutria. Roundworms and liver flukes may cause mortality and localized population declines. Farming practices, such as draining inundated fields, building levees and pond banks with gentle slopes, and reducing cover can also limit nutria habitat. However, population control may still be needed in addition to these factors. Cage-type live traps and leghold traps can be used for live capture. Conibear traps (No. 330 and 220) set at burrow entrances are commonly used for lethal capture. Wire cable snares can also be used to capture nutria. Registered toxic baits can readily reduce population levels (Wade and Ramsey 1984).

SUMMARY

Beaver, muskrat, and nutria are important animals of the Southeast due to their ecological roles, fur values, and potential to cause economic losses. The native muskrat and beaver are important animals of wetland ecosystems. Muskrat adults and young are an important prey species for selected predators, such as mink and alligators. Beaver activities promote development of wetlands and increase habitat for wetland fauna and flora, including waterfowl, nongame birds, aquatic furbearers, reptiles, amphibians, and fish. With recent declines in fur prices and commercial trapping, populations of these aquatic rodents have increased in many areas of the United States, creating some problems with property damage and economic losses (Wade and Ramsey 1984, Miller 1987).

As with most wildlife resource issues, biologists must make management decisions by balancing information about population management needs, species values, attitudes and activity of human stakeholders, and ecological importance of the species in question. This is especially true of the furbearing rodents of the southeastern United States - the beaver, muskrat, and nutria. To reach integrative decisions about these mammals, we must understand their biology, values, and population control implications.

ACKNOWLEDGMENTS

We thank the Department of Wildlife and Fisheries and the Forest and Wildlife Research Center for providing funding to write this chapter. We also thank all of the wildlife professionals who have contributed to our knowledge of furbearers. Special thanks go to Dale Arner and Phil Mastrangelo for providing information and review of this manuscript. This is Forest & Wildlife Research Center Publication Number WF080.

CHAPTER 24

Red-Cockaded Woodpecker

Ralph Costa
U.S. Fish and Wildlife Service
Department of Forest Resources
Clemson University, Clemson, SC

The red-cockaded woodpecker is 1 of 9 *Picoides* native to the United States, and its range overlaps with 2 of those, the hairy woodpecker and the downy woodpecker. The 7 ¼" long red-cockaded woodpecker is larger than the downy woodpecker (5 ¾") and slightly smaller than the hairy woodpecker (7 ½"). Although the red-cockaded woodpecker is similar in size and appearance to the hairy woodpecker, several differences in plumage characteristics make them easily distinguishable. The red-cockaded woodpecker has a black and white barred back, black-flecked flanks, and black bars on its white outer tail feathers; the hairy woodpecker is solid white in these areas. Additionally, the red-cockaded woodpecker has a large white cheek patch, while the hairy woodpecker has a rather broad band of black running through its cheek patch from its eye to its crown. Adult male hairy woodpeckers have relatively large, easily visible, patches of red on each side of the posterior of their heads, while red-cockaded woodpeckers have small red patches of just a few feathers in the same areas. However, these small red patches or, "cockades", are generally hidden under the black plumage of the crown and therefore rarely visible. The concealment of the cockades makes it very difficult to distinguish between male and female red-cockaded woodpeckers in the field. The females of both species lack any red plumage on the head. Nestling (older than 15 days) and fledgling red-cockaded woodpecker males have a red oval crown patch in the center of their black crown; this red patch disappears with the first post fledging molt in the fall. Simultaneously, they acquire their far less conspicuous red cockades similar to adult males (U.S. Fish and Wildlife Service 1985).

Status

The U.S. Department of the Interior identified the red-cockaded woodpecker as a rare and endangered species in 1968 (U.S. Bureau of Sport Fisheries and Wildlife

The red-cockaded woodpecker is a territorial, non-migratory, cooperative breeding species inhabiting the mature southern pine forests of the Southeast. Their territories range in size from 60 to more than 200 acres, depending on population density, stand stocking, and local ecological conditions *(US Forest Service)*.

1968). In 1970, the species was officially listed as endangered (Federal Register 35:16047). With passage of the Endangered Species Act in 1973 (Act), the red-cockaded woodpecker received the protection afforded species listed as endangered under the Act.

The red-cockaded woodpecker Recovery Plan (U.S. Fish and Wildlife Service 1985) states that the recovery goal for the bird is to perpetuate viable populations in the major physiographic provinces and forest types where the species currently exists. Recovery will be achieved when 15 viable populations are established and protected by adequate habitat management programs throughout these major physiographic provinces and forest types. Downlisting to threatened status requires at least 6 viable populations. The Recovery Plan defines a viable population as one containing at least 250 breeding pairs (groups) of red-cockaded woodpeckers. A "group" refers to birds that cooperate to rear the young from a single nest. Groups usually consist of a breeding male and female, and 0 to 4 helpers, usually the male offspring from previous breeding seasons; single bird groups (usually male) are uncommon in healthy populations. The best information available today, indicates that between 310 and 390 groups of potential breeding pairs will be required to achieve a breeding population of 250 breeding pairs (Reed et al. 1993). The U.S. Fish and Wildlife Service (Service) estimates that to support 390 potential breeding pairs, a population should contain between 400 and 500 active clusters because some clusters will harbor non- breeding pairs and others will be occupied by solitary birds (Costa 1995a). A "cluster" is defined as the aggregate of active and/or inactive cavity trees currently (active cluster) or formerly (inactive cluster) occupied by a group of red-cockaded woodpeckers. Clusters range in size from 3 to 20+ acres; most are about 10 acres.

HISTORIC AND CURRENT POPULATION AND DISTRIBUTION

Frost (1993), estimated that prior to European settlement, the southern pine ecosystem covered 92 million acres; 74 million dominated by longleaf pine and 18 million with longleaf pine mixed with other pines and hardwoods. The historical range of the red-cockaded woodpecker was coincident with this ecosystem and extended from southeast Virginia to the southern tip of Florida, west to east Texas, and north to portions of eastern Oklahoma, southeast Missouri, Tennessee, and Kentucky (Jackson 1971) (Fig. 1). Occasional occurrences were also noted for New Jersey, Pennsylvania, Maryland, and Ohio (see Costa and Walker 1995 for references). Prior to European settlement, the red-cockaded woodpecker population may have numbered about 920,000 groups; assuming a density of 100 acres per group, a density observed today in healthy populations. Historic and early 1900 accounts of red-cockaded woodpecker abundance were described variously as fairly common, locally common, common, or abundant (see Costa and Walker 1995 for references).

According to Frost (1993), by 1946 the longleaf pine ecosystem had declined to about 17% of its original range; today only about 3% remains. With the loss of the Southeast's virgin longleaf pine forests, red-cockaded woodpecker numbers declined dramatically. Based on several recent regional surveys, it is estimated that between 4,000 active clusters (1990 data) (James 1995)

The aggregate of cavity trees occupied by a group of red-cockaded woodpeckers is called the cluster. Timber thinnings and prescribed burning are used to maintain clusters in an open park-like condition. Clusters may consist of 1 to more than 20 trees and typically cover about 10 acres *(US Forest Service)*.

Figure 1. **Distribution of Red-cockaded Woodpeckers by county and state.**

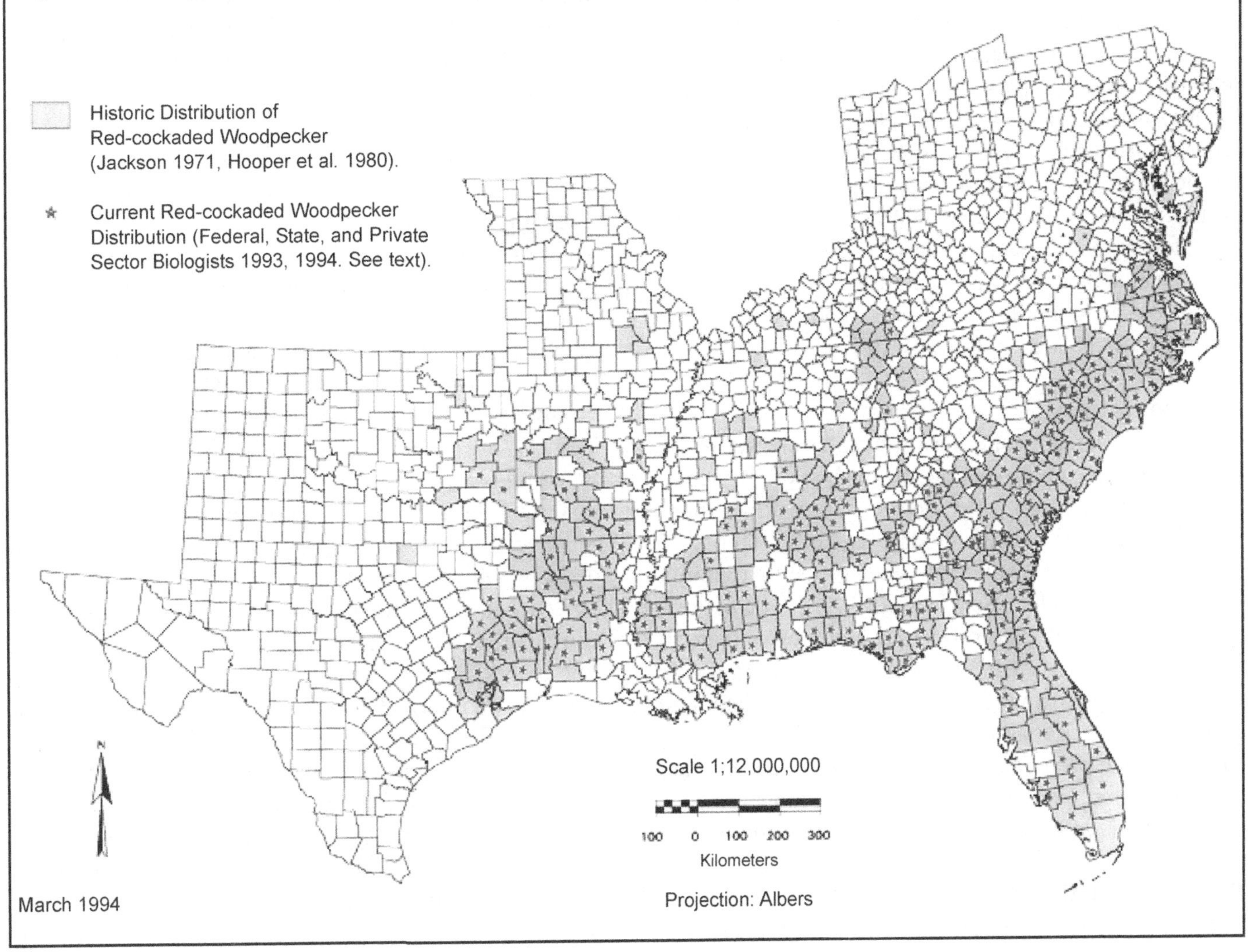

Historic Distribution of Red-cockaded Woodpecker (Jackson 1971, Hooper et al. 1980).

* Current Red-cockaded Woodpecker Distribution (Federal, State, and Private Sector Biologists 1993, 1994. See text).

Scale 1;12,000,000

100 0 100 200 300

Kilometers

March 1994

Projection: Albers

and 4,694 active clusters (1993/1994 data) (Costa and Walker 1995) remain. A 1998 summary of all known populations estimates the range wide population at 4,920 active clusters (unpubl. U.S. Fish and Wildlife Service data 1998). Based on these estimates, and a conservative estimate of the number of groups prior to European settlement, the world's population of red-cockaded woodpeckers has declined approximately 99%.

Red-cockaded woodpeckers currently inhabit a wide variety of habitats in the southeastern United States. They are found in the native slash pine flatwoods of southern Florida, within the Atlantic and Gulf coastal plain longleaf pine forests, north to the pond pine pocossins of northeast North Carolina, loblolly forests of southeastern Virginia, and shortleaf and Virginia pine forests of Kentucky, and west to the pineywoods of east Texas and Ouachita Mountains of Arkansas and Oklahoma.

Federal Populations

Today, red-cockaded woodpeckers are known to occur on 52 federal properties, including 26 national forest units, 14 military installations, 12 national wildlife refuges, 1 national park, and 1 Department of Energy facility. A total of 3,444 active clusters are known on federal property (unpubl. U.S. Fish and Wildlife Service data 1998). The majority (79%; n=41) of these properties have fewer than 100 active clusters; 50% have fewer than 25 active clusters. Only 3 properties have greater than 250 active clusters. With the exception of the very small populations, trends on most federal populations are either stable or increasing.

State Populations

Currently, 43 state properties, in 8 states are known to harbor red-cockaded woodpeckers. Most of the active clusters are found on state forests, state wildlife management areas/game lands or state parks. A total of 507 active clusters are known on state property (unpubl. U.S. Fish and Wildlife Service data 1998). The majority (93%; n=40) of state properties have fewer than 50 active clusters; 84% (n=36) have fewer than 25 active clusters. Only 1 state population is larger than 100 active clusters. Reliable population trend information for most state properties is lacking. While several state populations are known to be increasing, most are considered stable at best and many may be declining.

Private Populations

The total number of private landowners harboring red-cockaded woodpeckers is unknown. Based on the best information currently available, there are approximately 969 active clusters known on private lands in 11 states (Costa and Walker 1995). Of the known private land populations, the vast majority harbor fewer than 25 active clusters. However, there are 4 populations known to exceed 50 active clusters. Two of these large populations, located in the Sandhills of North Carolina and Red Hills of Georgia, are conglomerates of many landowners and number 70 and 179 active clusters, respectively (Carter et al. 1995, Engstrom and Baker 1995).

Across their range, small populations of red-cockaded woodpeckers on private lands continue to decrease and be extirpated (Baker 1983, Carter et al. 1995, James 1995). However, recent implementation of the Service's private lands red-cockaded woodpecker conservation strategy (Costa 1995b) has resulted in population stability, and indeed, population increases in several private land populations. These important and positive trends are expected to continue as additional "no-take" management plans, with accompanying memoranda of agreement, habitat conservation plans, and statewide safe harbor permits are completed and implemented (Costa 1997).

LIFE HISTORY AND ECOLOGY

Breeding Biology

The red-cockaded woodpecker is a territorial, nonmigratory species. It is a cooperative breeder; that is, all members of each group participate in nesting season activities, including incubating eggs, and brooding and feeding nestlings (Lennartz et al. 1987). Typically, each group consists of a breeding pair and up to 4 helpers. Helpers are usually male offspring from previous breeding seasons; they may remain on their natal territory for several years. While it is uncommon for females to serve as helpers, this behavior has been observed in some populations (DeLotelle and Epting 1992). All group members also participate in cavity construction and maintenance, and territorial defense. The composition or demography of a particular group may remain relatively stable over several breeding seasons. However, the group's composition can experience dynamic changes depending on mortality and/or dispersal of group members, and/or the occurrence of similar events on adjacent or nearby territories.

Walters et al. (1988), documented breeding associated behavior and social characteristics of a large population in the Sandhills of North Carolina. The percentages presented in the following discussion represent the annual change observed by Walters et al. (1988) from one breeding season to the next. Female offspring begin dispersing from their natal territory in search of breeding vacancies on nearby territories in early fall, but may remain on the territory until late spring, just prior to the breeding season. Mortality is high for female fledglings, estimated at 68%. Approximately 31% of fledgling females disperse from their natal territory; 92% of those that survive become breeders their first year. Upon acquiring breeding status, about 56% of females tend to remain on their territory. However, about 31% of breeding females disappear each year and about 12% move to another territory.

Male fledglings also experience high annual mortality, estimated at 57% (Walters et al. 1988). While some male fledglings remain on the natal territory as a helper (27%), with the future possibility of inheriting the territory and acquiring breeding status, others (13%) disperse from their natal territory in search of breeding vacancies at adjacent or nearby territories. About 39% of fledgling males that disperse and survive become breeders their first year, while 31% occupy a vacant territory or establish a new territory and remain there as a "solitary" male. Approximately 25% of dispersing male fledglings, called "floaters", continue to explore for a breeding vacancy. Only 3% of fledglings become breeders on their natal territory their first year. Once established as a breeder, 71% of males remain in that status from one breeding season to the next. Although Walters et al. (1998) data represent the best information available on group dynamics, they should be used with caution for other populations because differences in population size, density, and trend can affect group, and therefore population, demography.

Nesting Biology

Red-cockaded woodpeckers typically begin breeding and nesting activity in late March. The breeding female lays her eggs in the breeding males roost cavity; therefore, he incubates the eggs and broods the nestlings at night. During the day, all group members participate in these activities. Although nesting chronology varies across the bird's range, first eggs are normally observed in mid to late April. One egg is laid each day until a clutch of 3 to 5 eggs is complete; incubation begins before the last egg is laid (Ligon 1970) and, therefore, hatching is asynchronous. Hatching occurs following 10 to 12 days of incubation; all group members participate in feeding nestlings. Nestlings fledge 24 to 27 days after hatching. Group members feed fledglings for up to 6 months post-fledging. Renesting may occur if the first nest attempt fails; however, rate of renesting is variable. Only a few instances of double brooding have been observed.

Diet and Foraging Behavior

The diet of red-cockaded woodpecker adults and nestlings is composed primarily of arthropods. Their diet is varied, and includes ants, roaches, spiders, beetles, moths, centipedes and other invertebrates (Hanula and Franzreb 1995, Hess and James 1998). They are also known to eat the fruits and seeds of various plants, including blue berry, poison ivy, sweetbay magnolia,

Red-cockaded woodpeckers forage almost exclusively on live, larger pine trees. They probe beneath and flake off bark, searching for ants, spiders, moths, roaches, beetles, and other invertebrates. Nestlings are fed for 24-27 days at which time they fledge. The breeding pair and helpers will continue to feed the fledglings throughout the summer *(J. Hanula, US Forest Service)*.

Each member of a red-cockaded woodpecker group roosts in its own cavity. Multiple cavities per tree are not uncommon. Cavities take 6 months to more than 3 years to complete. The copious resin flow, produced by the "resin wells" excavated by the red-cockaded woodpeckers, give active cavity trees a candle-like appearance. This resin flow serves as a barrier to tree-climbing rat snakes (*Elaphe* sp.) *(R. Costa USFWS).*

wild grape, wax myrtle, blackgum, and pine (Ligon 1970, Hess and James 1998). The birds hunt for arthropods found on and under the loose bark of living pine trees and within dead limbs on those trees. They will also forage on standing dead pines as long as the bark remains on the snag. They seek prey primarily by probing beneath bark, and scaling or flaking bark off of the bole and limbs. Males typically forage in the crown on live and dead limbs, while females forage primarily on the bole. Their use of hardwood trees as foraging substrate is generally limited and may be related to seasonal abundance of certain arthropods on hardwoods, paucity of suitable pines, and perhaps other factors. They have been observed foraging on oaks, sweetgum, hawthorn, and hickory (Hooper and Lennartz 1981).

HABITAT REQUIREMENTS

Roosting and Nesting Habitat

The red-cockaded woodpecker is the only North American woodpecker that excavates roost and nest cavities in living pine trees. They are known to construct cavities in longleaf, loblolly, shortleaf, slash, pond, Virginia, and pitch pines. The adaptation of using live pines as roosting and nesting sites may have evolved in response to living in a fire-maintained ecosystem where frequent fires, primarily in the growing season, eliminated most standing dead pines relatively quickly (Ligon 1970).

Each member of a group roosts in its own cavity; there may be multiple cavities in a single cavity tree. The aggregate of cavity trees used by a group is called

Cavity trees are typically 80 to 100 years old or older depending on tree species, site, and individual tree characteristics. Many of today's cavity trees are relict trees, for example old turpentine trees, that were not harvested during the early 1900's. Many of these relicts approach or exceed 200 years in age *(R. Costa USFWS).*

Longleaf pine-wiregrass communities are ideal red-cockaded woodpecker nesting and foraging habitat. Pine stands and pine trees of various age classes provide current and future nesting and foraging habitat for red-cockaded woodpeckers. Diverse, herbaceous understory plant communities, a result of prescribed burning, provide a source of abundant arthropod prey *(R. Costa USFWS)*.

a "cluster". Usually, trees chosen for cavity excavation have heartwood decay caused by red heart fungus, which softens the heartwood allowing easier completion of the cavity chamber (Jackson 1977). Cavities require at least 4" to 5" of heartwood to ensure a sap-free environment for roosting and nesting; however, significantly more heartwood (7" to 8") is required to provide for extended use (greater than 5 years) of cavities (Conner and Rudolph 1995). Cavity construction is a long process requiring 1 to 6 or more years to complete (Conner and Rudolph 1995). Conner and Rudolph (1995) suggest that completion time is a function of various factors including tree species, presence of red heart fungus, amount of sapwood, and resinosis rates. Additionally, group size and the number of other suitable cavities available may influence cavity completion rates.

As cavities near completion, red-cockaded woodpeckers chip shallow excavations, called resin wells, around their cavity entrances and on the tree's bole. After many months or years of resin well construction, all the bark around the cavity entrance is removed, exposing the sapwood and forming a resin-covered "plate". Resin flowing from the plate's edge and resin wells on the bole eventually coats much of the tree's surface, giving the cavity tree a candle like appearance and making the tree conspicuous from a distance. Additionally, the birds scale bark off of their cavity trees above and below cavities. These behaviors help protect nests from predation by tree climbing rat snakes, *Elaphe* sp. (Ligon 1970).

While red-cockaded woodpeckers are known to excavate cavities in pines less than 100 years old, most studies indicate they prefer older pines as cavity trees (DeLotelle and Epting 1988, Hooper et al. 1991). The selection of old trees is related to having sufficient heartwood diameter for the cavity chamber (Clark 1992, Conner et al. 1994) and to the presence of red heart fungus to ease cavity excavation (Conner et al. 1994).

Foraging Habitat

Across their range, red-cockaded woodpeckers use pine stands with a wide variety of densities (10 to 100 sq.ft. basal area/acre) to search for prey (Hooper and Harlow 1986, DeLotelle et al. 1987). Typically, quality foraging habitat consists of open, park like pine stands, with little or no hardwood component. However, the birds are known to use pine/hardwood stands as foraging habitat. While in some parts of their range, birds use stands and trees less than 30 years old for foraging, throughout much of their range, they prefer older stands and trees as foraging habitat/substrate (Hooper and Harlow 1986, DeLotelle et al. 1987). They usually prefer trees at least 10" diameter breast height (dbh) and larger (Hooper and Lennartz 1981) and may select the larger of available trees (Engstrom and Sanders 1997).

Federal officials are responsible for providing foraging habitat in quantities sufficient to maintain the health of existing groups and to achieve red-cockaded woodpecker population growth and expansion into unoccupied but suitable habitat. Foraging habitat guidelines to accomplish these objectives are described by Henry (1989). These guidelines were derived from the Recovery Plan and are officially referred to as Guidelines for Preparation of Biological Assessments and Evaluations for Red-cockaded Woodpeckers (Henry 1989) (Bluebook). The Bluebook and the Recovery Plan conclude that 125 acres of well-stocked (60 to 90 sq.ft. basal area/acre), pine and pine-hardwood stands, with over 50% basal area in pines at least 30 years of age (40% over 60 years old) with 24 pines per acre 10" dbh or larger will provide ample foraging substrate. Specifically, federal officials, with some exceptions by property or project, provide at least 8,490 sq.ft. basal area (4" dbh or larger) and 6,350 pine stems 10" dbh or larger for each group of birds within ½ mile of the cluster.

The U.S. Fish and Wildlife Service (1992) recommends that private landowners harboring red- cockaded woodpeckers retain, and manage as appropriate, at least 3,000 sq.ft. basal area of 10" dbh or larger trees at least 25 to 30 years old for each group. Between 10 and 80 sq.ft. basal area/acre should be retained on acres contributing to foraging habitat. Depending on tree diameters, between 2,000 and 5,000 trees would be required to satisfy the basal area guideline. The foraging habitat should be distributed on 60 to 300 acres depending on existing or desired stand density. These Service guidelines provide private landowners with flexibility to pursue timber and other resource management objectives.

HABITAT MANAGEMENT

Roosting and Nesting Habitat

Establishment and/or maintenance of quality red-cockaded woodpecker roosting and nesting habitat requires the production and retention of pine trees 100 to 120+ years old, depending on tree species. Potential cavity trees can be developed by: (1) establishing patches (minimum of 10 acres) of forest exempt from harvesting (recruitment and replacement clusters), (2) retaining trees in perpetuity within seedtree, shelterwood, and unevenaged harvest units, (3) setting minimum rotations of 100 to 120+ years, and/or (4) retaining existing old growth and relict pines within all thinning and regeneration harvest units.

Activities within active clusters that have the potential to harm or damage cavity trees and/or harass or disturb red-cockaded woodpeckers should be avoided, particularly in the nesting season (April 1 to July 31). Such activities may include, but are not limited to, road and utility right of way construction, pesticide use, mineral exploration and/or development, and construction of buildings or other facilities. Timber harvesting and other silvicultural activities such as midstory removal should be conducted outside the nesting season. However, prescribed burning during the nesting season is encouraged provided cavity trees are protected, particularly those that are active. These activities, and any others that may degrade nesting habitat or disturb the birds require Service concurrence to be in compliance with the Act.

Active, recruitment, and replacement clusters should be managed to maintain pine basal area at 50 to 70 sq.ft./acre. Commercial thinnings are the preferred method for managing cluster basal area. Recommended practices for timber harvest operations within clusters include: (1) avoiding logging activities during the nesting season (generally April 1 to July 31), (2) retaining all old growth, relict, and remnant pines, (3) protecting cavity trees from root, bole, and crown damage, (4) minimizing skidding, (5) removing slash, and (6) no log decking/loading.

Hardwood midstory within active clusters has been associated with cluster abandonment (Loeb et al. 1992) and can preclude occupation by red-cockaded woodpeckers in recruitment and replacement clusters. Therefore, it is critical that hardwood midstory be controlled within all clusters. Prescribed burning is the most efficient and ecologically beneficial method to accomplish midstory control. However, mechanical and/or chemical treatments may be required for initial control of midstory if the dbh of the average tree is 4" or larger. Mechanical methods may include chainsawing, drum chopping, or whole tree chipping.

Various chemicals are approved for use in red-cockaded woodpecker habitat to control midstory vegeta-

Prescribed fire is a critical and essential component of red- cockaded woodpecker management and recovery. Fire promotes a diverse understory plant community, is a primary tool for establishing and maintaining healthy longleaf pine forests, and controls the growth of hardwood midstory. Prescribed burning on a 2-5 year rotation is sufficient to accomplish all of the above benefits *(R. Costa, USFWS)*.

tion. These chemicals include the following; trade names are in parentheses: glyphosate (Roundup, Rodeo, Accord), hexazinone (Velpar), imazapyr (Arsenal), and triclopyr (Garlon). All label directions must be followed when applying any chemicals, and cavity trees must be protected from damage. Once larger midstory trees have been eliminated, prescribed fire can be used to maintain an open stand condition. Depending on site conditions, the vegetation to be controlled, and the season of fire, burning may be required on 2 to 5+ year intervals to maintain nesting and foraging habitat.

In addition to fire's value in controlling hardwood midstory development in red-cockaded woodpecker habitat, fire may have other beneficial effects for the birds. James et al. (1997) found that group size and reproductive success, and population density were related to fire history and ground cover composition. Groups inhabiting territories with high percentages of wiregrass and low percentages of woody shrubs, had more adults, produced more young, and had more neighbors. They recommend that in red-cockaded woodpecker habitat a "vigorous prescribed fire regime" be emphasized not only to reduce midstory vegetation, but also to improve other ecosystem processes, that are not fully understood. Since the early 1990s, many managers and researchers have been recommending increased emphasis on burning more during the growing season than in the dormant season, the traditional time of the year to burn.

The absence of suitable cavity trees is known to be the primary limiting factor for red-cockaded woodpecker group formation (Walters et al. 1992). Forest and tree ages throughout much of the birds' range are too young to supply sufficient numbers of potential cavity trees. Costa and Escano (1989) concluded that this paucity of potential cavity trees affects the stability and growth of extant red-cockaded woodpecker groups and populations. Clark (1992), found that the average codominant and dominant longleaf and loblolly pine did not have sufficient heartwood diameter for excavation of red-cockaded woodpecker cavities until they were 90 and 80 years old, respectively. Past forest management practices on both public and private lands did not favor the retention of trees this old. Consequently, until the employment of artificial cavities (Copeyon 1990, Allen 1991), there was limited hope for the species' survival and recovery.

However, after successful experimentation clearly demonstrated that artificial cavities could increase populations (Copeyon et al. 1991), they were used to enhance woodpecker populations (Gaines et al. 1995). In many populations, it will be necessary for the next 10 to 30 years to continue using artificial cavities to provide and/or supplement nesting habitat substrate required by this species (Costa and Escano 1989). While nesting habitat management and improvement have been a critical component of recent red- cockaded woodpecker conservation success stories, these techniques alone are not sufficient to save all populations. More intensive, hands-on programs, such as translocations, are required to save small populations where demographic problems are aggravated by group isolation and habitat and/or landscape fragmentation (Conner and Rudolph 1991).

Foraging Habitat

Commercial timber harvest and/or pre-commercial silvicultural treatments generally are necessary to provide and maintain stand densities that constitute quality foraging habitat. Recommended practices for silvicultural activities in foraging habitat include: (1) retention of old growth, relict, and remnant pines, (2) minimizing damage to residual trees, (3) minimizing rutting, and soil erosion and compaction, and (4) maintenance of open park like stands via prescribed burning.

Providing suitable foraging habitat for red-cockaded woodpeckers over the long-term, not only requires management of the current habitat, but also development of future habitat. Various silvicultural methods can be employed to provide pine regeneration for future foraging and nesting habitat. Both unevenaged and evenaged silvicultural systems have been used to establish and maintain nesting and foraging habitat. Rudolph and Conner (1996) and Engstrom et al. (1996) discuss some of the pros and cons of the two basic systems. Additionally, a detailed analysis of the silvicultural methods commonly used in red-cockaded woodpecker habitat is provided in the Final Environmental Impact Statement for the Management of the Red-cockaded Woodpecker and its Habitat on National Forests in the Southern Region (U.S. Forest Service 1995). The silvicultural system used for any particular stand is dependent upon: (1) agency responsibilities and policies, (2) manager or land owner preference, (3) site conditions, (4) tree species, (5) overstory stand age and structure, (6) existing midstory and understory conditions, and (7) current foraging habitat availability.

Prescribed burning at 2 to 5 year intervals is the most efficient and ecologically sound method for maintaining the open stand conditions preferred by the bird as foraging habitat. However, where most hardwood midstory trees are greater than 4" dbh, an initial mechanical or chemical treatment may be necessary to reduce the midstory to a condition maintainable by fire.

Pine Beetle Suppression and Control

Pine beetle (southern pine beetle, Ips, and black turpentine beetle) infestations can occur within or adjacent to red-cockaded woodpecker nesting or foraging habitat. Timely control is important to minimize habitat loss. Generally, Ips and black turpentine beetles attack individual or very small clumps of trees and do not exhibit significant spot growth; therefore control usually is not required. However, active and expanding southern pine beetle spots should be quickly and aggressively controlled. Control measures include: (1) cut and remove, (2) cut and leave, (3) cut and burn, and (4) cut and spray. Only the fewest number of trees needed to control the spot should be cut. If foraging habitat is limited, trees already killed and vacated by beetles should be retained if possible as high quality, albeit temporary, foraging substrate. Cutting of red-cockaded woodpecker cavity trees, even if infested, must be approved by the Service.

POPULATION MANAGEMENT

Population Surveys

Periodic surveys, at 5 to 10 year intervals, of suitable red-cockaded woodpecker nesting habitat are important for determining changes in population size and trend. Location and status of cavity trees are documented during surveys by walking parallel north-south transects about 100 to 300 feet apart, depending on visibility after leaf fall.

Project Surveys

The purpose of project surveys is to ensure that proposed activities will not adversely affect red-cockaded woodpeckers or their habitat. A 100% survey of the project area and suitable nesting and foraging habitat within ½

Table 1: Species using normal size and enlarged red-cockaded woodpecker cavities.

Birds	Mammals	Reptiles/Amphibians	Invertebrates
Red-bellied woodpecker	Flying squirrel	Gray treefrog	Spider sp.
Red-headed woodpecker	Gray squirrel	Five-lined skink	Honey bee
Pileated woodpecker	Fox squirrel	Broad-headed skink	Wasp sp.
Northern flicker	Evening bat	Gray rat snake	Mud daubers
Great crested flycatcher		Corn snake	Moth sp.
Eastern bluebird		Lizard sp.	Ant sp.
Tufted titmouse			
White-breasted nuthatch			
Brown-headed nuthatch			
Carolina chickadee			
Starling			
Eastern screech owl			
American kestrel			
Wood duck			

From: Jackson 1978, Harlow and Lennartz 1983, Rudolph et al. 1990, Kappes and Harris 1995, Conner et al. 1997b, Phillips and Gault 1997.

mile of the project site is conducted to document the presence of cavity trees and availability of foraging habitat. Generally, project surveys are required if a previous survey has not been conducted within the past year.

Group and Population Monitoring

Most federal, many state, and some private land managers are monitoring all or a sample of their red- cockaded woodpecker groups to determine group and population demographics and health. This monitoring typically is done once each year during the breeding season. Monitoring may include banding adults and nestlings which requires federal and state permits. Additionally, recent dispersal data from banded birds has contributed to our understanding of population demography and genetic viability.

Translocation

Many red-cockaded woodpecker populations are very small and incapable of expanding on their own, even with creation of recruitment clusters via artificial cavities. Translocation, the trapping and relocation of a bird from one cluster, typically its natal territory, to another cluster has become an important conservation program (e.g., Carrie et al. 1999). The recipient cluster may be occupied by a single bird or a group of same sex birds, or it may be unoccupied (Rudolph et al. 1992, Allen et al. 1993, Hess and Costa 1995). The short term goals of translocations are to prevent extirpation of small populations by increasing the number of potential breeding pairs and reducing demographic isolation between groups and subpopulations. The long term goals of translocations are to maintain genetic viability in populations considered non-viable and to increase the rate of growth of selected populations. Translocations generally are limited to juvenile birds. The success of each translocation may be related to various factors, including both the translocated and recipient bird's sex, age, and status (Rudolph et al. 1992, Allen et al. 1993, Costa and Kennedy 1994). All translocations require federal and state permits.

ECOLOGICAL RELATIONSHIPS

Keystone Species

Red-cockaded woodpeckers are the only primary cavity excavator that constructs cavities in living pines in southeastern forests. This adaptation makes the red-cockaded woodpecker a keystone species and a significant contributor to biodiversity in the southern pine ecosystem (Conner et al. 1997a). Red- cockaded woodpeckers construct cavities which persist and are used by a variety of species for a long time. Both normal-size cavities and those enlarged by pileated woodpeckers provide roosting and/or nesting sites for at least 24 other species of vertebrates and numerous invertebrates (Table 1).

Kleptoparasitism

Kleptoparasitism, the usurpation by one species of cavities excavated by individuals of another species (Kappes 1997), of red-cockaded woodpecker cavities, primarily by southern flying squirrels and red- bellied woodpeckers, has been documented. In the Coastal Plain of South Carolina, Harlow and Lennartz (1983) found southern flying squirrels to be the most common occupant, after red-cockaded woodpeckers, of red-cockaded woodpecker cavities; red-bellied woodpeckers were the second most common species. Loeb (1993), studying red-cockaded woodpecker and southern flying squirrel interactions in the Piedmont of Georgia, and Laves (1996) studying the same relationship in the Sandhills of South Carolina, both found southern flying squirrels to be the most common occupants of red-cockaded cavities. Rudolph et al. (1990), examining red-cockaded woodpecker cavities in east Texas, documented southern flying squirrels as the most common occupant, after red-cockaded woodpeckers. In north Florida, Kappes and Harris (1995), found red-bellied woodpeckers and southern flying squirrels to be the most common occupants, respectively. Jackson (1978), studying red-cockaded woodpecker cavities in the coastal plain of South Carolina, central Mississippi, and the Piedmont of Georgia, also documented the most common occupants as red-bellied woodpeckers and southern flying squirrels, respectively.

The impacts of kleptoparasitism on red-cockaded woodpecker productivity and mortality is unclear (e.g., Mitchell et al.1999). Avian and flying squirrel cavity competition [kleptoparasitism] may adversely affect red-cockaded woodpecker nest initiation (Harlow and Lennartz 1983, Loeb and Hooper 1997). Red-bellied woodpeckers (Jackson 1978, Kappes and Harris 1995) and southern flying squirrels can usurp cavities. Southern flying squirrels may adversely impact red-cockaded woodpecker reproduction (Laves 1996) and red-bellied woodpeckers may evict red-cockaded woodpecker nestlings (Jackson 1978).

Distribution and number of snags in red-cockaded woodpecker nesting habitat and their relationship to kleptoparasitism has been examined by several researchers. However, conclusions drawn by these researchers are divergent and the current information on this relationship remains inconclusive. Everhart (1986) concluded that cavity nesting birds preferred red-cockaded woodpecker cavities to snag cavities; and suggested that increasing snag density in clusters would have little effect on red-cockaded woodpecker cavity occupancy. Harlow and Lennartz (1983), investigating the relationship between snag density and several measures of interspecific competition [kleptoparasitism], including the proportion of all cavities occupied by competitors, found weak relationships and insignificant associations between the variables measured. However, Kappes and Harris (1995), suggest that snags may reduce competition [kleptoparasitism] for red-cockaded woodpecker cavities by other cavity nesting species.

The relationships between hardwood midstory and the presence of non red-cockaded woodpecker cavity nesters are not well understood. Kleptoparasitism may increase in red-cockaded woodpecker nesting habitat as a result of hardwood midstory growth. However, there are few, if any studies that clearly explore this relationship. Everhart (1986), concluded that as midstory density increased, cavity nesting bird density decreased. Heiterer (1994), found that southern flying squirrel abundance was greater in stands with a hardwood midstory. Conner et al. (1996) noted that southern flying squirrels' occupancy of red-cockaded woodpecker cavities was independent of the abundance of hardwood midstory vegetation.

Predation

Red-cockaded woodpeckers are preyed upon by rat snakes and probably raptors (Ligon 1970). Flying squirrels have also been implicated as predators of eggs and/or nestlings (Labranche and Walters 1994, Laves 1996). Laves (1996) documented a significant increase in the number of fledglings per nesting group (0.7) when flying squirrels were controlled. In small, at-risk populations, managers may consider using squirrel excluder devices (Montague et al. 1995) and/or squirrel nest boxes (Loeb and Hooper 1997) to minimize the adverse impacts of flying squirrels. Similarly, rat snake predation may be minimized by using snake excluder devices (Neal et al. 1993), particularly in recruitment clusters where new artificial cavities have been installed and there is an insufficient resin barrier to prevent rat snakes from climbing.

In general, because of their expense and monitoring intensity, predator control programs should only be implemented on a cluster basis and for small populations. The use of any predator control device requires Service concurrence and a federal permit.

CONSERVATION OPPORTUNITIES

Federal Lands

The positive population trends on many federal lands are a direct result of recent (mid 1990s to present) attempts to stabilize and grow populations through direct habitat improvement, such as reduction of hardwood midstory and installation of artificial cavities. Additionally, translocations in concert with habitat improvement have been used to enhance smaller populations (Rudolph et al. 1992, Costa and Kennedy 1994, Hess and Costa 1995, Gaines et al. 1995). Recent completion and full implementation of major federal red-cockaded woodpecker recovery and management plans will ensure continued population growth on most federal properties (U.S. Forest Service 1995, U.S. Department of the Army 1996, U.S. Fish and Wildlife Service 1998). Based on existing management plans for federal properties, the potential future population of red-cockaded woodpeckers on federal land is estimated at 12,338 active clusters (unpubl. U.S. Fish and Wildlife Service data 1998).

State Lands

Many red-cockaded woodpecker populations on state lands could be increased if habitat improvement programs, similar to those on federal properties, were implemented. Several state populations are considered critical to the species' recovery. It is particularly important that these populations receive federal and state support for continued and/or more aggressive management of their populations.

Private Lands

Many private landowners have recently (1993 to present) entered into conservation partnerships with the Service, state wildlife agencies, and other cooperators in an effort to either maintain or increase their extant red-cockaded woodpecker populations (Costa 1997). In total, these landowners are, or will be when agreements are finalized, protecting and managing 183,900 acres of habitat for, and 383 groups of, red-cockaded woodpeckers (Costa 1997, unpubl. U.S. Fish and Wildlife Service data 1998). Costa and Edwards (1997), documented various motivations of industrial forest landowners who joined red- cockaded woodpecker conservation partnerships with the Service. Motivations included minimizing compliance risks with the Act, the prestige associated with establishing a conservation agreement, satisfaction in promoting and practicing good wildlife stewardship, and simplifying management by consolidating their population.

The Service's Safe Harbor program (see Costa and Kennedy 1997) is contributing significantly to conservation of red-cockaded woodpeckers on private lands. Under a safe harbor cooperative agreement a landowner agrees to actively maintain suitable habitat for a number of red-cockaded woodpecker clusters equal to the number present (called the "baseline") when the agreement is signed. In turn, the landowner receives a permit authorizing land management actions or changes that may alter occupied habitat for any additional groups, above the baseline number, that may occupy the property in the future as a result of voluntary, beneficial land management practices. Costa and Kennedy (1997) explain how the Safe Harbor program provides multiple conservation and landowner benefits. Benefits include direct habitat improvement and maintenance for all baseline groups, the potential for population increases, and conservation and management of significant local and regional longleaf pine habitat, even if red-cockaded woodpeckers do not occupy the property enrolled in the program. From the landowners perspective, a safe harbor permit removes the fear of future regulatory, legal, and economic consequences associated with additional red-cockaded woodpeckers becoming established on their property.

Private landowners have accepted the challenge of contributing natural and economic resources to further red-cockaded woodpecker conservation through cooperation with public and other private parties pursuing a similar goal, saving an endangered species. Costa and Edwards (1997) conclude that key private land habitat and its associated red-cockaded woodpecker populations can either serve as support populations or contribute to recovery populations and/or other support populations by: (1) increasing their size and stability, (2) providing habitat corridors, and (3) supplying juvenile birds for translocation programs. These private land initiatives may significantly increase the role of private lands in recovery of this species. The involvement of private landowners in the conservation and recovery of the red-cockaded woodpecker is expected to continue and indeed increase.

CHAPTER 25

Bird Communities of Southern Forests

William C. Hunter
US Fish and Wildlife Service
1875 Century Boulevard, Suite 240, Atlanta, GA

James G. Dickson[1]
US Forest Service
Southern Research Station, Nacogdoches, TX

David N. Pashley
American Bird Conservancy
4249 Loudoun Avenue
P.O. Box 249
The Plains, VA

Paul B. Hamel
US Forest Service
Southern Hardwoods Lab
P.O. Box 227 Stoneville, MS

Birds constitute a high-profile group of species that attract a great deal of attention as watchable wildlife. Also, birds are important as indicators of habitat conditions and environmental health. Compared to other groups of animals and plants, birds are relatively conspicuous and can be easily monitored. Available information on bird ecology is substantial, but understanding the management requirements for most nongame bird species lags far behind existing knowledge for managing game species.

The moderate climate and diverse forests across the South support abundant and diverse communities of breeding, wintering, and migrating birds. Bird communities in the South have been shaped and influenced by human beings and the vast land use changes that have taken place. Generally, species associated with old-growth forests have declined with the demise of that habitat, and a few species, such as the Carolina parakeet and passenger pigeon, became extinct as the region was cleared of timber and remaining wildlife was hunted for commercial market. Other species are precariously close to extinction and include the ivory-billed woodpecker and Bachman's warbler. Only the warbler's demise cannot be exclusively tied to events in the Southeast U.S., as habitat loss in Cuban wintering areas also likely contributed to declines (Hamel 1986). Some exotics such as European starlings and native species associated with habitats altered by human beings such

[1]Current Address: School of Forestry, Louisiana Tech University, Ruston, LA

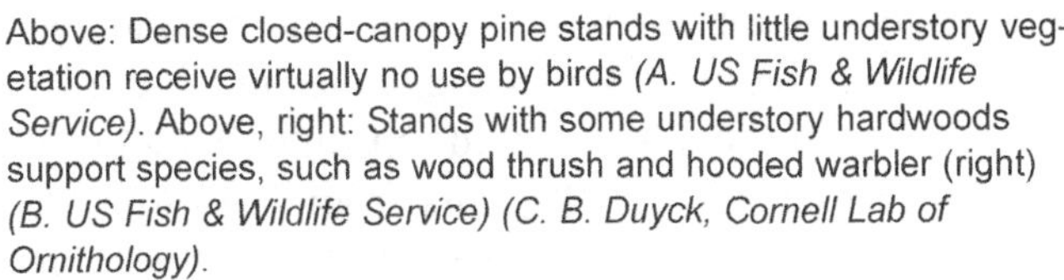

Above: Dense closed-canopy pine stands with little understory vegetation receive virtually no use by birds *(A. US Fish & Wildlife Service)*. Above, right: Stands with some understory hardwoods support species, such as wood thrush and hooded warbler (right) *(B. US Fish & Wildlife Service) (C. B. Duyck, Cornell Lab of Ornithology)*.

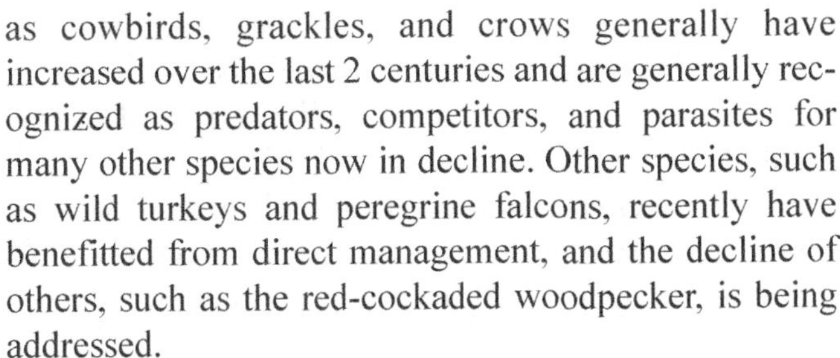

as cowbirds, grackles, and crows generally have increased over the last 2 centuries and are generally recognized as predators, competitors, and parasites for many other species now in decline. Other species, such as wild turkeys and peregrine falcons, recently have benefitted from direct management, and the decline of others, such as the red-cockaded woodpecker, is being addressed.

In this chapter we present information on birds of southern forests, emphasizing species and habitat conditions in need of special management attention throughout the Southeast. Detailed information on individual species can be found in Hamel (1992a). We do not concentrate on game and endangered bird species because information for these species is detailed in individual chapters. Recommendations for habitat management and for the future are presented.

We present first some general concepts regarding bird communities and forest characteristics in the South and then an explanation of how the Partners in Flight prioritization process can be used to guide both management and research priorities. The body of this chapter reviews the status and trends of priority species associated with each of the following habitats found in the South (see physiographic regions in color section): (1) early-successional and shrub-scrub, (2) southern pine, (3) forested wetlands, (4) hardwood-pine mixed forests, (5) central hardwoods, and (6) Appalachian forests. Under each of these subsections, priority species are described and management recommendations are provided. We end this chapter with a discussion of broad trends in landbird populations in the South and a call for caution in using population trends.

Birds and Forest Stands

Bird species distribution and community composition generally are determined by landscape and stand scale habitat conditions. Forest bird communities are associated with foliage layers (MacArthur and MacArthur 1961), foliage volume (Willson 1974), habitat patchiness (Roth 1976), and stand successional stage (Shugart and James 1973, Dickson and Segelquist 1979). The diversity of forest type and stand structure, including age (characteristics that influence bird species occurrences and abundance) are primary determinants of the presence and relative abundance of bird species (Dickson et al. 1993).

In pine stands the hardwood component is the primary determinant of bird community composition (Johnston and Odum 1956, Dickson and Segelquist

1979). Changes to stand structure, such as from tree harvesting, change stand suitability for bird species and communities (Webb et al. 1977, Thompson et al. 1992). Usually in southern pine and hardwood stands bird density and diversity are high in young brushy stands, decrease in dense pole stands as canopies close and shade out understory, and are highest in older stands with distinct vegetation layers. Thus, changes in stand structure and plant species composition through management results in decreases of some species, increases in others, and has little effect on others. This in turn requires determination of which species should receive the most attention in establishing management priorities for defining future desired conditions and allocation of resources accordingly.

Concerns for Southern Forest Birds

The Southeastern landscape has been manipulated by people for millennia (Hamel and Buckner 1998). Since European colonization, impacts of human activities have dominated the landscape. Several physiographic areas formerly dominated by forests (Mississippi Alluvial Plain, much the valley portions of Ridge and Valley, Piedmont, and upper Coastal Plain in South Atlantic and East Gulf states) are now predominantly agricultural. Elsewhere, retirement of agricultural lands has resulted in a widespread recovery of forests (Williams 1989). However, some of these forests may not be suitable for many vulnerable forest bird species. Many of the stands are mid successional, characterized by closed canopies and with little understory and midstory structure. Short-rotation pine monocultures continue to increase in extent. Finally, southern forests generally are increasingly fragmented from recent expansion of residential subdivisions and industrial development accompanying rapid increase in human populations.

From these changes in landscape during the 1900s, 2 overall bird conservation concerns have emerged in recent decades: (1) nearctic-neotropical migratory birds, and (2) grassland birds.

Nearctic-Neotropical Migratory Birds.— Monitoring data indicate recent population declines leading to concern for nearctic-neotropical migratory birds in general (Robbins et al. 1989a,b, 1992). Nearctic-neotropical migrants are those species that breed in temperate areas of North America and winter in the tropics. These reported declines, based on interpretation of Breeding Bird Survey (BBS) data from 1966 to 1987, followed studies showing localized declines of nearctic-neotropical migrants in increasingly urbanized areas and in agriculturally-dominated landscapes, especially in the mid Atlantic and midwest United States (Aldrich and Coffin 1980, Robbins 1980, Blake and Karr 1987, Rappole and McDonald 1994, Robinson et al. 1995, Smith et al. 1996, Latta and Baltz 1997).

These declines were occurring when there was an overall increase in mature forests in eastern North America while tropical forests were being reduced,

Content vs. Context. For bird conservation planning it is important to view the condition of the surrounding landscape as well as the forest stand of interest. There are concerns about bird population viability in heavily fragmented landscapes due to heavy nest predation and parasitism from brown-headed cowbirds (US Fish & Wildlife Service).

Fire historically has been important in maintaining early-successional habitat conditions in older open pine stands.

implying that declines were due to wintering ground effects. However, reasons for the declines of nearctic-neotropical migrants are now understood to be complex and include (1) reduced breeding habitats (perhaps as much in quality as quantity), (2) reduced wintering habitats, (3) increasing threats during migration, (4) predation or competition from other species such as exotics, and (5) possible contaminants (Hagan and Johnston 1992, Finch and Stangel 1993), such as direct exposure to chemicals or indirect effects (global climate change, acid rain, ozone).

Estimated relative densities of representative migratory birds in forest stands of different ages (or stand suitability for bird species) are presented for hardwood forests (Table 1), loblolly-shortleaf pine forests (Table 2), longleaf and slash pine forests (Table 3), and oak-gum-cypress forests (Table 4). These densities may serve as baseline figures for monitoring future population changes.

Grassland Species.—Although this chapter focuses on forest bird species, many species use southern forests that exhibit grassy and shrub-scrub characteristics either through regeneration or disturbances. Many species are particularly associated with fire-maintained forest communities exhibiting grassy or shrub-scrub conditions.

An erroneous, although common, perception has been that declines among nearctic-neotropical migrants involve only forest "area-sensitive" and "forest-interior" species, even though this was never the inference of the authors (Robbins et al. 1989a,b). In fact, many of the nearctic-neotropical migrant species showing the steepest and longest-term declines are grassland and

Table 1. Abundance of nearctic-neotropical migratory birds in central hardwood forests.[a]

Species	Stand age[b]					
	R	S	P	M	G	T
Whip-poor-will	U[c]	U	U	U	U	U
Ruby-throated hummingbird	C	N	N	N	?	N
Acadian flycatcher	N	N	C	A	N	A
Eastern wood-pewee	N	N	U	A	N	A
Eastern phoebe	N	N	U	U	N	U
Great-crested flycatcher	C	C	C	C	C	C
Blue jay	C	C	C	C	C	C
American crow	U	U	U	U	U	U
Carolina wren	C	C	U	N	?	?
Blue-gray gnatcatcher	A	C	C	C	C	C
Eastern bluebird	C	N	N	N	N	N
Wood thrush	U	C	C	C	U	C
Gray catbird	C	C	N	N	?	N
White-eyed vireo	C	C	N	N	?	N
Yellow-throated vireo	N	N	N	U	N	U
Red-eyed vireo	U	U	A	A	U	A
Blue-winged warbler	A	C	N	N	?	N
Golden-winged warbler	C	U	N	N	?	N
Northern parula	N	N	U	C	N	C
Chestnut-sided warbler	C	C	N	N	?	N
Yellow-throated warbler	N	N	U	U	N	U
Pine warbler	N	N	C	C	N	C
Prairie warbler	A	C	N	N	?	N
Black-and-white-warbler	C	C	C	C	C	C
Worm-eating warbler	U	C	C	C	C	C
Ovenbird	U	C	C	C	U	U
Louisiana waterthrush	N	U	C	C	C	C
Common yellowthroat	A	U	N	N	?	N
Kentucky warbler	A	C	U	U	A	C
Hooded warbler	C	C	U	U	C	C
Yellow-breasted chat	A	C	N	N	?	N
Orchard oriole	U	N	N	N	N	N
Summer tanager	C	C	C	A	C	C
Scarlet tanager	U	U	C	A	U	A
Indigo bunting	A	C	U	U	A	C
Eastern towhee	A	U	N	N	C	N
Field sparrow	A	N	N	N	?	N
Brown-headed cowbird	A	C	C	C	C	C
American goldfinch	U	N	N	N	N	N

[a] Data from Dickson et al. (1993)

[b] R = regeneration, S = sapling, P = poletimber, M = mature, G = group selection, T = single tree selection.

[c] A = abundant, C = common or regular, P = present, U = uncommon, N = not present.

Frequent fire promotes grass-forb vegetation important for many species, but some shrub-scrub structure supports associated species, such as prairie warbler and field sparrow *(US Fish & Wildlife Service).*

shrub-scrub associated species. Widespread declines also are seen among temperate migrant and resident grassland and shrub-scrub species (Capel et al. 1994), and have been documented for key game species such as ruffed grouse, northern bobwhite, and American woodcock (see individual chapters). In sum, declining and vulnerable species can be found among all types of habitats as well as having differing migration strategies. These complexities should inhibit generalizations for cause and effect relationships based solely on population trend or grouping of species by either habitat preferences or migration status.

Partners in Flight Prioritization Process

The Partners in Flight Prioritization Process (PIF Process) was developed to help focus conservation efforts on the species or species assemblages most requiring conservation attention (Millsap et al. 1990, Hunter et al. 1993a,b, Carter et al. 2000). The PIF Process is based on a comparative review of those global and local characteristics that may make each species potentially vulnerable, such as relative global abundance and distribution, broad and local level of threat, population trend, and area importance (a measure of relative density within an area compared with other areas within the species' range).

Population trends and some of the other information used to define priority bird species are based on BBS data from southeastern physiographic areas defined by Partners in Flight. Seventeen of these physiographic areas, similar to Bailey's ecoregions (McNab and Avers 1994), include southern forest habitats important for bird conservation.

Table 2. Abundance of nearctic-neotropical migratory birds in loblolly-shortleaf pine forests[a].

Species	Stand age[b]				
	R	S	P	M	O
Whip-poor-will	N[c]	N	N	N	?
Ruby-throated hummingbird	U	U	U	U	U
Acadian flycatcher	N	N	U	C	C
Eastern wood-pewee	N	U	P	C	A
Eastern phoebe	N	N	N	N	?
Great-crested flycatcher	N	N	U	P	C
Blue jay	U	U	C	A	C
American crow	U	U	P	C	C
Blue-gray gnatcatcher	N	N	U	C	A
Eastern bluebird	U	U	N	N	P
Wood thrush	N	N	U	C	A
American robin	N	U	U	U	U
Gray catbird	U	U	N	U	U
White-eyed vireo	U	A	P	U	C
Yellow-throated vireo	N	N	U	A	C
Red-eyed vireo	N	U	C	A	A
Blue-winged warbler	N	N	N	N	N
Golden-winged warbler	N	N	N	N	N
Northern parula	N	N	U	U	C
Chestnut-sided warbler	N	N	N	N	N
Pine warbler	N	N	C	A	A
Prairie warbler	C	A	N	N	U
Black-and-white-warbler	N	U	C	C	C
Worm-eating warbler	N	N	C	C	C
Chuck-will's-widow	U	U	U	U	U
Ovenbird	N	N	U	C	C
Louisiana waterthrush	N	N	N	P	P
Kentucky warbler	N	U	C	P	P
Hooded warbler	N	U	C	A	C
Yellow-breasted chat	C	A	U	N	P
Summer tanager	N	N	U	C	C
Scarlet tanager	N	N	U	U	U
Indigo bunting	N	A	P	U	P
Eastern towhee	N	P	C	C	P
Field sparrow	C	U	N	N	N
Brown-headed cowbird	P	C	P	P	N
American goldfinch	U	U	U	U	U
Blue grosbeak	C	U	N	N	N

[a] Data from Dickson et al. (1993)
[b] R = regeneration, S = sapling, P = poletimber, M = mature, O = oldgrowth.
[c] A = abundant, C = common or regular, P = present, U = uncommon, N = not present.

Table 3. Abundance of nearctic-neotropical migratory birds in longleaf and slash pine forests[a].

Species	Stand age[b]				
	R	S	P	M	O
Longleaf Pine					
Common nighthawk	P[c]	P	U	U	U
Chuck-will's-widow			U	U	U
Eastern wood-pewee			U	C	C
Acadian flycatcher				P	P
Great-crested flycatcher	U	P			
Eastern kingbird			P	P	
Purple martin	U				
Barn swallow	U				
Prairie warbler	C				
Summer tanager		U	U	C	C
Blue grosbeak	P	P			
Slash Pine					
Yellow-billed cuckoo			U	U	U
Ruby-throated hummingbird	C	C			
Eastern wood-pewee			C		
Acadian flycatcher			C		
Great-crested flycatcher		P	C	C	
Eastern kingbird	P				
Bewick's wren			C		
Blue-gray gnatcatcher	P	P			
White-eyed vireo		C			
Yellow-throated vireo		P			
Yellow-throated warbler	C				
Prairie warbler	U	U	U		
Common yellowthroat		C	P	P	P
Yellow-breasted chat		C			
Summer tanager	C		C	C	C
Blue grosbeak	P	P			
Indigo bunting	C	C	P	U	U
Longleaf-Slash Pine					
Osprey				U	U
American swallow-tailed kite			U	U	
Yellow-billed cuckoo	P				
Common nighthawk	P	U	U	U	U
Chuck-will's-widow			U	U	U
Ruby-throated hummingbird	U				
Eastern wood-pewee			U	C	C
Great crested flycatcher	P		U	P	P
Eastern kingbird	U	U	U	U	U
Purple martin	U				
Barn swallow	U				
White-eyed vireo		C	C		
Yellow-throated warbler	U	U	U	U	
Prairie warbler	U	U	U	U	U
Common yellowthroat	U	P	P	C	C
Yellow-breasted chat	U	U			
Summer tanager		U	U	P	P
Blue grosbeak	P	P			
Indigo bunting	C	C	P	U	U

a Data from Dickson et al. (1993)
b R = regeneration, S = sapling, P = poletimber, M = mature, O = old growth.
c A = abundant, C = common or regular, P = present, U = uncommon

Table 4. Nearctic-neotropical migrant breeding bird species present in southeastern oak-gum-cypress forests[a].

Anhinga	Blue-gray gnatcatcher
Green heron	White-eyed vireo
Great blue heron	Yellow-throated vireo
Little blue heron	Red-eyed vireo
Cattle egret[b]	Warbling vireo
Great egret	Black-and-white warbler
Snowy egret	Prothonotary warbler
Tricolored heron	Swainson's warbler
Black-crowned night-heron	Worm-eating warbler
Yellow-crowned night-heron	Bachman's warbler
Wood stork	Northern parula
Glossy ibis	Black-throated green warbler
White ibis	Yellow-throated warbler
Hooded merganser	Cerulean warbler
Swallow-tailed kite	Ovenbird
Mississippi kite	Louisiana waterthrush
Cooper's hawk	Kentucky warbler
Bald eagle	Common yellowthroat[c]
Osprey	Yellow-breasted chat[c]
Purple gallinule	Hooded warbler
Common moorhen	American redstart
Mourning dove[b]	Eastern meadowlark[b]
Yellow-billed cuckoo	Red-winged blackbird
Chimney swift[b]	Brown-headed cowbird[b]
Ruby-throated hummingbird	Orchard oriole
Belted kingfisher	Baltimore oriole
Great-crested flycatcher	Summer tanager
Eastern phoebe[b]	Scarlet tanager
Acadian flycatcher	Blue grosbeak[c]
Eastern wood pewee	Indigo bunting[c]
Barn swallow[b]	Painted bunting[c]
Purple martin[b]	Eastern towhee[c]
Wood thrush	

[a] From Hamel et al. 1982 and Dickson et al 1993.
[b] Associated with human altered non-forest habitat.
[c] Associated with early successional stands.

Based on the PIF process 64 bird taxa are identified as high regional priority species (Table 5, Hunter et al. in prep.). An additional 20 relatively widespread species are considered of moderate regional priority. These species collectively help guide habitat restoration and management objectives. In order to compare relative management priorities among major habitats (see Table 6), we can compare the proportion of all species showing definite and possible declining trends in each habitat type (Table 5) as discussed below.

Table 5. Regional and physiographic area priority levels assigned by the Southeast U.S. Partners in Flight Working Group. E = extremely high priority for physiographic area (total priority score 28-35), H = high priority (total priority score 22-27), M = moderate priority (total priority score 19-21, with high scores for relative abundance and unknown or declining population trends), L = low priority for physiographic area. Species included as of High Regional Priority within the Southeast are those meeting criteria listed for at least high priority within at least 3 physiographic areas for widespread species or for narrowly distributed species these same criteria are met for at least 1 physiographic areas where they occur. Species included as of Moderate Regional Priority within the Southeast are those meeting criteria for at least moderate priority within at least 4 physiographic areas or high priority in 2-3 physiographic areas. Population trend is one of seven factors leading to overall priority scores.

Regional priority species	Physiographic area[a] Priority level and population trend[b]																
	A1	A2	A3	A4	B1	B2	B3	B4	B5	C1	C2	C3	C4	D1	D2	D3	E1
High regional priority																	
Swallow-tailed Kite																	
Southeast U.S. subsp.					E,0			E,0	E,0	E,0				E,-*	E,0		E,-*
Snail Kite																	
Everglades subsp.								E,-	E,-								
Short-tailed Hawk																	
Florida pop.								E,0	E,0								
Crested Caracara																	
Florida pop.								E,-	E,-*								
American Kestrel																	
Southeast U.S. subsp.					E,-			E,-	H,-*	H,-				H,-			
Greater Prairie-Chicken																	
Attwater's subsp.																	E,-*
Sandhill Crane																	
Mississippi subsp.										E,-*							
Florida subsp.					E,0			H,+*		E,0							
Upland Sandpiper		H,-*	H,-*	H,-*													
American Woodcock	H,-	H,-	L,0	L,0	H,-	H,-	L,0	L,-		H,-	L,0	L,0	L,0	H,-	H,-	L,0	H,-
Yellow-billed Cuckoo	L,+	L,+	L,-	M,-*	L,-*	L,0	L,0	L,-*	L,0	H,-*	M,-*	L,+	H,-*	H,-*	H,-*	L,+	M,-
Burrowing Owl																	
Florida subsp.								E,0	E,-								
Short-eared Owl																	
Temperate subsp.	H,-*	L,-*	L,-*	L,0	H,-*	L,-*	L,-*	L,-*	L,-*	L,-*	L,-*	L,-*	L,-*	L,-*	H,-*	H,-*	H,-*
Northern Saw-whet Owl																	
S. Appalachian pop.			E,-				E,-										
Chuck-will's-widow	L,+	L,0	L,0	L,0	L,+	L,+	L,0	L,+	L,0	H,-*	H,-	L,0	L,-	H,-*	L,0	L,+	L,0
Red-headed Woodpecker	L,+*	L,+	L,0	L,-	L,+	L,0	L,0	M,-*		M,-*	L,-*	L,0	H,-*	H,-*	H,-*	H,-*	M,-
Yellow-bellied Sapsucker																	
S. Appalachian pop.			E,-*				E,-*										
Red-cockaded Woodpecker	E,-*				E,-	E,0	E,-*	E,0	E,0	E,-	E,0	E,-*		E,-		E,-*	
Eastern Wood-Pewee	H,-*	L,+	H,-*	H,-*	L,+	M,-	M,-*	L,0		M,-*	M,-*	H,-*	H,-*	H,-*	M,-*	M,-	L,0
Acadian Flycatcher	L,0	L,0	L,+	H,+	L,+*	L,0	H,-*	L,0		L,+*	H,-*	H,-*	L,+	L,+	L,+	H,-*	L,0
Scissor-tailed Flycatcher														H,-	L,0	L,+	H,+
Florida Scrub-Jay								E,-*	E,-*								
Black-capped Chickadee																	
S. Appalachian pop.			H,+	L,0			E,-*										
Red-breasted Nuthatch																	
S. Appalachian pop.			E,0				H,-										
Brown-headed Nuthatch	H,0	H,0			H,-*	H,0	H,0	H,0	H,-*	H,-	H,+			H,+		H,0	
Brown Creeper																	
S. Appalachian pop.			E,0				H,-										

continued

Table 5 continued

Regional priority species	Physiographic area[a]									Priority level and population trend[b]							
	A1	A2	A3	A4	B1	B2	B3	B4	B5	C1	C2	C3	C4	D1	D2	D3	E1
High regional priority																	
Bewick's Wren																	
Appalachian subsp.			E,-*	E,-*	E,-*	E,-*	E,-*				E,-*	E,-*					
Eastern subsp.										E,-*			E,-*	E,-*		E,-	
Winter Wren																	
S. Appalachian pop.			H,+				H,-										
Sedge Wren	H,-*	L,0	L,0	H,0	H,+	L,+		H,+	H,+	H,+				L,+	H,+		H,+
Golden-crowned Kinglet																	
S. Appalachian pop.			H,0				H,-										
Wood Thrush	H,-*	H,-*	H,-*,		L,+	H,-*	H,0	H,-*		L,+	H,-*	H,-*	H,-	L,0	L,0	H,-	L,0
Sprague's Pipit														H,-*			H,-*
Bell's Vireo													H,0	H,0	H,0	H,-	H,0
Yellow-throated Vireo	H,-*	L,+	H,-*	L,+	L,+*	L,+*	H,-*	L,0		L,+	H,-*	H,0	L,+	L,+	L,+	L,0	L,0
Blue-winged Warbler	H,-*	L,0	L,0	L,+*			L,+			L,0	H,-	H,+*		H,-*			L,+
Golden-winged Warbler			E,-*	H,-*			E,-*					E,-					
Northern Parula	L,+	L,+	H,-*	L,0	H,-*	L,+*	L,+	L,+	L,0	L,+*	L,+	L,+	L,0	L,0	H,-*	L,+	L,0
Chestnut-sided Warbler			L,0	L,+		L,0	H,-*				L,0	L,-	L,0			L,0	
Black-throated Blue Warbler			H,0	L,0			H,-					H,0					
Black-throated Green Warbler																	
Atlantic Coastal pop.					E,-*												
Blackburnian Warbler			L,0	L,0			H,-					L,0					
Prairie Warbler																	
Northern subsp.	H,-*	H,+	H,-*	H,-*	H,-	H,-*	H,-	H,-*	H,-*	H,-*	H,-*	H,-*	H,-*	H,-*	L,0	H,-*	
Palm Warbler					M,-*			H,-*	H,-*	M,-*							
Cerulean Warbler	H,0	H,0	E,-*	E,-*	H,0	H,0	H,0			H,0	H,0	E,-*	E,-*	H,0	E,-*	H,-	
Prothonotary Warbler	H,0	L,0	L,0	L,0	L,+*	L,0	L,0	L,0		H,-*	H,0	L,0	L,0	H,-*	H,+	H,-	H,0
Worm-eating Warbler	H,+	H,+	H,+	H,+	H,+	H,0	H,+			H,0	H,0	H,+	H,0	H,0	H,0	H,0	
Swainson's Warbler	H,0		L,0	H,0	H,+*		H,0	E,-		E,0	H,0	E,+	L,0	E,0	E,0	H,0	H,0
Louisiana Waterthrush	H,0	H,+	H,+	H,-	L,+	H,+	H,-*			L,+*	H,-*	H,-*	H,0	H,0	L,0	H,0	
Kentucky Warbler	H,-	H,-	L,+	H,+	L,+*	H,0	H,-*			H,+	H,-*	H,0	H,+	H,-*	H,0	H,0	H,0
Hooded Warbler	L,+	L,+	L,+	L,+	H,-	L,0	H,+	L,0		L,+*	L,0	H,+	L,0	H,-	L,0	L,0	L,0
Canada Warbler			L,+	L,0			H,0					L,0					
Painted Bunting																	
Eastern subsp.					E,-*			E,0	E,-*								
Western subsp.										L,0				L,+	H,-*	L,0	H,-
Dickcissel	L,0	L,0	L,0	L,0	L,0	L,0				L,+	L,0	L,0	H,-*	L,+	L,+	H,-*	H,0
Bachman's Sparrow	H,0	L,0			E,-*	H,-	H,0	E,0	H,0	E,-*	H,0	L,0	L,0	H,0		H,0	
Field Sparrow	M,-*	H,-*	M,-*	H,-*	M,-	H,-*	M,-*			M,-*	M,-*	M,-*	H,-*	L,-*	L,-*	H,-*	L,0
Grasshopper Sparrow																	
Florida subsp.								E,-*	E,-*								
Henslow's Sparrow	H,0	H,0	H,0	H,+	E,-	E,-*		H,-		E,-		H,0	H,0	E,-	H,-		H,-
LeConte's Sparrow					H,+					H,+				H,+	H,+	H,+	H,+
Orchard Oriole	L,+*	L,+	L,0	L,+	L,+	L,+	L,0	L,0		H,-*	H,-*	L,+	L,+	H,-*	H,-*	M,-*	L,+
Red Crossbill																	
S. Appalachian pops.			E,-				E,-				L,0	L,0					

continued

Table 5 continued

Regional priority species	Physiographic area[a] Priority level and population trend[b]																
	A1	A2	A3	A4	B1	B2	B3	B4	B5	C1	C2	C3	C4	D1	D2	D3	E1
Moderate regional priority																	
Northern Harrier	M,-	L,-	L,-	L,-	M,-	L,-	L,-	M,-	M,-	M,-	L,-	L,-	L,0	L,-	M,-	L,0	M,-
Northern Bobwhite	M,-*	M,-*	L,-*	L,-*	M,-*	M,-*	L,-*	M,-*	L,0	M,-*	M,-*	L,-*	M,-*	M,-*	M,-*	M,-*	M,-*
Common Ground-Dove					M,-*	L,0		M,-*	M,-	M,-*				L,0	L,0		
Barn Owl	M,-*	L,0			M,0	L,-*		L,0	M,0	L,0	L,0	L,0	L,0	L,0	L,0	L,0	M,0
Whip-poor-will	L,0	L,-	H,-*	L,+	L,+*	L,0	L,0	L,0	L,0	L,+*	L,0	L,0	H,-*	L,0	L,0	L,+	L,0
Chimney Swift[c]	M,-	L,+	L,+	L,+	L,+	L,+	L,-	L,0		M,-*	L,+	L,+	H,-*	L,+	L,0	L,+	L,+*
Ruby-throated Hummingbird	L,+	L,0	L,0	L,+*	L,+	L,+	M,-*	L,0	L,0	L,+*	M,0	M,0	L,+	M,-	M,0	L,+	L,0
Eastern Kingbird[c]	L,-*	L,-*	L,-*	L,-	L,-	L,-	L,-	L,-*	L,0	M,-*	L,+	L,+	L,+	M,-*	L,-*	L,+	L,0
Carolina Chickadee	M,-*	L,+	L,+	L,+	M,-	M,-	L,-	L,-		M,-*	M,-*	L,+	L,+	M,-	M,-*	M,-	L,+
Blue-gray Gnatcatcher	L,+	L,+*	L,+	M,-	L,+	L,+*	M,-*	L,+	L,0	L,+*	L,+	L,+	M,-	M,-	M,-*	L,+	L,0
Gray Catbird	M,-*	L,+	M,-*	L,+	L,+	L,-*	M,-*	M,-*	M,-*	L,-*	L,-*	M,-*	L,-*	L,0	L,-*	L,-*	L,-*
Brown Thrasher	M,-*	M,-*	M,-*	M,-*	L,+	L,+	L,-	L,+	L,0	L,+	H,-*	L,0	L,+	L,-	L,+	M,-*	L,0
Loggerhead Shrike[c]	L,-*	L,-*	L,-*	L,-*	L,-	L,-*	L,0	H,-*	L,0	M,-*	L,-*	L,0	L,-*	L,-*	L,0	L,-*	L,+
White-eyed Vireo	M,-*	L,+*	L,-*	L,+*	L,+	L,+	L,-	L,+	M,0	L,+*	M,-*	L,+	M,-*	H,-*	H,-*	L,+	L,0
Yellow-throated Warbler	L,-	L,0	L,0	L,+*	H,0	L,+	L,0	L,0	L,0	L,+	H,-*	L,+	L,+*	L,0	L,+	L,0	L,0
Black-and-white Warbler	L,0	L,0	M,-*	L,-	L,+*	L,+	M,-*	L,0	L,0	L,0	L,-*	M,0	L,-*	L,-	L,0	L,-	L,0
Yellow-breasted Chat	L,-	L,+	M,-*	M,-*	L,+*	L,+	L,-*			L,+*	M,-*	M,-*	M,-*	L,+*	M,-*	L,+	L,0
Summer Tanager[c]	L,+	L,+	L,0	L,+	L,+	M,0	L,-	L,0		L,+	H,-*	M,-*	L,+	L,+	L,+	L,+	L,0
Eastern Towhee	M,0	M,-*	M,-*	L,+	M,-*	L,+	L,-	M,-*	L,0	L,+	M,-*	M,-*	M,-*	L,+*	L,+	L,-*	L,0
Lark Sparrow				L,0				L,-*	L,-*	L,-*		L,0	L,-	M,-*	M,-*	M,-*	M,-*
Grasshopper Sparrow																	
Eastern subsp.	L,-*	M,0	M,-*	L,-*	M,-*	L,-	L,0	M,-*	M,-*	M,-*	L,-*	L,0	L,-*	M,-*	M,-*	L,+	M,-*
Rusty Blackbird	M,-*	M,-*	L,-*	L,-*	M,-*	M,-*	L,-*	L,-*	L,-*	M,-*	M,-*	M,-*	M,-*	M,-*	M,-*	M,-*	M,-*

[a]Physiographic areas (PIF Breeding Bird Survey code):
A1=Mid Atlantic Coastal Plain (44)
A2=Mid Atlantic Piedmont (10)
A3=Mid Atlantic Ridge and Valley (12)
A4=Ohio Hills (22)
B1=South Atlantic Coastal Plain (03)
B2=Southern Piedmont (11)
B3=Southern Blue Ridge (23)
B4=Peninsular Florida (02)
B5=Subtropical Florida (01)
C1=East Gulf Coastal Plain (04)
C2=Southern Ridge and Valley (13)
C3=Northern Cumberland Plateau (21)
C4=Interior Low Plateaus (14)
D1=West Gulf Coastal Plain (42)
D2=Mississippi Alluvial Plain (05)
D3=Ozark-Ouachita Highlands (19)
E1=Coastal Prairies (06; all U=upper coast)

[b]Population trends are: +*=definitely (significantly) increasing; +=possibly increasing or stable; 0=trend unclear; -=possibly decreasing; -*=definitely (significantly) decreasing. Most trends are based on the Breeding Bird Survey (see Appendix I) within physiographic areas for breeding species and for wintering species continental-wide data from Breeding Bird Survey or Christmas Bird Counts, as appropriate, were used.

[c]Chimney Swift, Eastern Kingbird, Loggerhead Shrike, and Summer Tanager are included here as species of Moderate Regional Concern by meeting criteria in Table heading by combining physiographic area priority levels reported here with "western" physiographic areas. (E2=Oaks and Prairies, E3=Osage Plains, E4=Rolling Red Plains, E5=Staked and Pecos Plains, E6=Edwards Plateau, E7=South Texas Brushlands, E8=Chihuhuan Desert).

PRIORITY FOREST HABITATS, SPECIES, AND MANAGEMENT RECOMMENDATIONS

Early-Successional Forest and Shrub-Scrub Habitats

Birds associated with early-successional habitats and frequent disturbance fall into 3 broad groups: (1) grassland, (2) early-successional shrub-scrub, and (3) southern pine. Declines are apparent for 24 priority taxa (5 of these are Federally listed) associated with grasslands within this region (Tables 5,6). The largest number of grassland species occur in Peninsular and Subtropical Florida, the Coastal Plain (South Atlantic, East Gulf, and West Gulf), and Coastal Prairies. Only in very few places do remnants of historical prairie community types persist, with most prairie-dependent species now using a combination of both natural and anthropogenic grassland.

As with grassland species, high numbers of shrub-

Table 6. Primary habitat associations and seasonal status among priority landbird species within forested landscapes of the Southeastern U.S. (see Table 5). Most determinations are following Hamel 1992a. R=resident, B=breeding, W=wintering, B,W= refers to species using similar habitat but in different areas between seasons (i.e., highly migratory), lower case (r,b,w)=refers to habitats where species occurs in very low densities but may still prove to be important to that species.

	Major habitat types[a]											
Regional priority species	**Grass**	**Shrub-scrub**		**Southern pine**				**Hardwood-dominated Forests**				
		ES	FE	Sav.	Grass	Shrub	Can.	Forested wetland	Hardwood pine mix	Central hardwoods	Appala. forests[b]	Spruce fir
High regional priority												
Swallow-tailed Kite												
Southeast U.S. subsp.				B				B				
Snail Kite												
Everglades subsp.	R											
Short-tailed Hawk												
Florida pop.				R				R				
Crested Caracara												
Florida pop.	R											
American Kestrel												
Southeast U.S. subsp.	R			R	R		R					
Greater Prairie-Chicken												
Attwater's subsp.	R											
Sandhill Crane												
Mississippi subsp.	R			R								
Florida subsp.	R			R								
Upland Sandpiper	B											
American Woodcock		B,W						B,W	B,W		B	
Yellow-billed Cuckoo								B	B	B	B	
Burrowing Owl												
Florida subsp.	R											
Short-eared Owl												
Temperate subsp.	W											
Northern Saw-whet Owl												
S. Appalachian pop.											b	R
Chuck-will's-widow						B			B			
Red-headed Woodpecker				R			B	B,W		B,W		
Yellow-bellied Sapsucker												
S. Appalachian pop.			B								B	
Red-cockaded Woodpecker				R			R					
Eastern Wood-Pewee							B	B	B	B	B	
Acadian Flycatcher								B	B	B	B	
Scissor-tailed Flycatcher	B			B								
Florida Scrub-Jay		R										
Black-capped Chickadee												
S. Appalachian pop.											b	R
Red-breasted Nuthatch												
S. Appalachian pop.											b	R
Brown-headed Nuthatch				R			R					
Brown Creeper												
S. Appalachian pop.											b	R
Bewick's Wren												
Appalachian subsp.		B,W										

continued

Table 6 continued

Regional priority species	Grass	Shrub-scrub		Southern pine				Hardwood-dominated Forests				
		ES	FE	Sav.	Grass	Shrub	Can.	Forested wetland	Hardwood pine mix	Central hardwoods	Appala. forests[b]	Spruce fir
High regional priority												
Eastern subsp.		B,W										
Winter Wren												
S. Appalachian pop.											b	R
Sedge Wren	W			W	W							
Golden-crowned Kinglet												
S. Appalachian pop.											b	R
Wood Thrush								B	B	B	B	
Sprague's Pipit	W											
Bell's Vireo		B						B				
Yellow-throated Vireo								B		B	B	
Blue-winged Warbler		B										
Golden-winged Warbler		B										
Northern Parula								B	B	B	B	
Chestnut-sided Warbler			B									
Black-throated Blue Warbler											B	
Black-throated Green Warbler												
Atlantic Coastal pop.								B	B			
Blackburnian Warbler											B	B
Prairie Warbler												
Northern subsp.		B				B						
Palm Warbler		W				W						
Cerulean Warbler								B	B	B	B	
Prothonotary Warbler								B				
Worm-eating Warbler								B	B	B	B	
Swainson's Warbler								B	B		B	
Louisiana Waterthrush								B		B	B	
Kentucky Warbler								B	B	B	B	
Hooded Warbler								B	B	B	B	
Canada Warbler											B	B
Painted Bunting												
Eastern subsp.			B,W									
Western subsp.			B			B						
Dickcissel	B											
Bachman's Sparrow	R			R	R							
Field Sparrow	W	R		W	W	R						
Grasshopper Sparrow												
Florida subsp.	R											
Henslow's Sparrow	B,W			W	W							
LeConte's Sparrow	W											
Orchard Oriole			B									
Red Crossbill												
S. Appalachian pops.							R				R	R
Moderate regional priority												
Northern Harrier	W											

Major habitat types[a] span the Grass, Shrub-scrub, Southern pine, and Hardwood-dominated Forests columns.

Table 6 continued

	Major habitat types[a]											
Regional priority species	Grass	Shrub-scrub		Southern pine				Hardwood-dominated Forests				
		ES	FE	Sav.	Grass	Shrub	Can.	Forested wetland	Hardwood pine mix	Central hardwoods	Appala. forests[b]	Spruce fir
Moderate regional priority												
Northern Bobwhite	R	R	R	R	R	R						
Common Ground-Dove		R										
Barn Owl	R			R								
Whip-poor-will						B			B	B	B	
Chimney Swift								B	B	B	B	
Ruby-throated Hummingbird								B		B	B	B
Eastern Kingbird	B			B								
Carolina Chickadee							R	R	R	R	R	
Blue-gray Gnatcatcher			W			W		B	B	B	B	
Gray Catbird			B,W									
Brown Thrasher			B,W									
Loggerhead Shrike	R			R								
White-eyed Vireo			B,W			B		B	B			
Yellow-throated Warbler							B,W	B	B	B	B	
Black-and-white Warbler								B	B	B	B	
Yellow-breasted Chat			B			B						
Summer Tanager							B	B	B	B	B	
Eastern Towhee			B			B						
Lark Sparrow	B,W			W								
Grasshopper Sparrow												
Eastern subsp.	B,W			W	W							
Rusty Blackbird								W				

[a]Grass=Grasslands including prairies, warm-season grasses, regeneration areas and old fields generally 1-5 years after disturbance. ES=early successional habitats in large blocks including bogs, glades, barrens, pocosins, regeneration areas and old fields generaly 6-10 years after disturbance. FE=forest edges typically with early successional habitats for species not typically found in high densities throughout a large habitat patch. Sav.=savannas here specifically refer to longleaf and slash pine savannas, but also may refer to any grassland with non-stocked pine of any species; Grass=here refers to grassy-dominated ground cover in a stocked pine stand; Shrub=here refers to a shrubby component to the pine understory; Can.=canopy here refers to species actually dependent upon mature pine, most with no or little hardwood in the midstory (stands with more hardwood midstory results in bird use more similar to hardwood-pine mix).

[b]Appala. Forests=Appalachian forests include here mature to old-growth northern hardwoods, hemlock-white pine-hardwoods, mixed mesophytic (cove) hardwoods, with various gradations into Appalachian oak (Central Hardwoods) types on drier more exposed sites and into spruce-fir at the highest elevations.

scrub species show widespread declines, with 20 priority species warranting management attention (Tables 5, 6). The federally threatened Florida Scrub-Jay is the highest priority species associated with disturbance regimes. Among non-listed taxa, both the Appalachian and eastern subspecies of Bewick's wren populations are temperate migrants that require conservation attention. Painted buntings, Bell's vireos, and golden-winged warblers are nearctic- neotropical migrants for which conservation attention primarily on their breeding grounds is warranted.

Chestnut-sided and Prairie Warblers.—Some priority shrub-scrub species such as chestnut-sided and prairie warblers are more common today than they were at the turn of the century. However, these species still have relatively small geographic distributions and should receive attention due to the rate at which their shrub-scrub habitat (fire maintained glades, barrens, savannas, etc.) is diminishing. In particular, the prairie warbler appears to have been a species associated primarily with shrub-scrub understories of regularly disturbed longleaf pine, especially in sandhills situations, as well as loblolly-shortleaf pine, and eastern red cedar-pine glades (Nolan 1978). The loss of these habitats through fire suppression appeared to be compensated for by the concurrent increase in old-fields and regeneration of forests through clearcutting. But the overall loss of shrub-scrub habitat in managed landscapes, including the suppression of natural fires is undoubtedly contributing to decline not only of the prairie warbler, but also field sparrow and northern bobwhite (Capel et al. 1994). The reduced disturbance and the overall maturing of forests has reduced populations of the chestnut-sided warbler at mid to high elevations in the Southern Appalachians. Roadside edges, however, presently seem to provide extensive and stable habitat.

Golden-winged Warbler and Bewick's Wren.—The golden-winged warbler, with its southeastern distribution also restricted to the Southern Appalachians, is much more of a specialist, using early-successional habitat generally at elevations between 2,000 and 5,000 feet. There is some question concerning its status. The Appalachian subspecies of the Bewick's wren has declined drastically. We speculate that the decline may be related to changes in landscape patterns where disturbances have diminished especially above 3,000 feet in elevation (see Southern Appalachian forest section). Previously, declines of Appalachian Bewick's wren were thought to be related to expansion of potentially competing house wrens. A more likely explanation is the reduction in number and acreage of small farms and brushpiles combined, followed by increasing amount of mature forest on public lands, with an increase in clean farming and rural housing developments on private lands (Southern Appalachian Assessment 1996). The fact that all Bewick's wren populations east of the Mississippi River are now undergoing steep declines with similar reductions in disturbance-prone habitats may provide a clue to the almost complete loss of the Appalachian populations.

Management Recommendations.—Among priority early-successional species, the presence or absence of up to half of the priority early successional species may be influenced by patch size. The other half of priority species associated with disturbances tend to use narrow forest edges or small forest openings as well as larger openings and are not likely dependent upon habitat patch size (Table 6). Minimum habitat patch size recommendations based on mostly anecdotal evidence and studies in other regions suggest early successional species occur more consistently and have better nesting success in patches greater than 25-50 acres (Rudnicky and Hunter 1993, Thompson and Dessecker 1997).

A frequent management recommendation is to provide narrow shelterbelts (hedgerows), strips on farmland to reduce soil erosion from wind and to provide wildlife habitat. This practice benefits some game species like rabbits and northern bobwhite and some wintering birds, but may function as an "ecological trap" for many breeding birds.

Most importantly, special attention is needed for endangered early-successional shrub-scrub communities. Among these communities are fire-adapted understory vegetation of mature southern pine forests, pitcher plant bogs, cedar-pine glades, and mountain wetlands and similar high-elevation heath balds. Recovering these communities needs to be accomplished in combination with strategies for supporting species presently depending upon old-fields, abandoned farmland, and clearcuts (Capel et al. 1994).

Southern Pine Forests and Pine Savannas

Some of the 18 priority species associated with southern pine forests also show consistent declines among most Southeast physiographic areas (Tables 5,6). In addition to the species included in the discussion of early-successional and shrub species, 2 understory species (Chuck-will's-widow and Whip-poor-will) and 6 species using pines are treated in this section. This discussion here focuses primarily on savannas, sandhills, and flatwoods for species associated with longleaf, shortleaf, slash, and loblolly pines.

The federally endangered Mississippi sandhill crane and red-cockaded woodpecker are the highest priority birds dependent upon southern pine systems. Among the highest regional priority savanna species are Bachman's and Henslow's (winter only) sparrows. Many of the birds for which pine savanna forest is primary habitat also occur in grasslands or shrub-scrub habitat, including the above-mentioned sparrows, northern bobwhite, the southeastern subspecies of American kestrel (requires cavity trees), and loggerhead shrike (requires nest trees). Bachman's and Henslow's sparrows also are associated with longleaf and slash flatwoods where grasses dominate the groundcover.

Extensive patches of shrub-scrub mixed with grasses support prairie warblers, field sparrows, and other moderate regional priority species, especially in longleaf sandhills and loblolly-shortleaf stands. Species dependent on mature open southern pines with few hardwoods include principally the red-cockaded woodpecker, brown-headed nuthatch, and American kestrel (longleaf sandhills). Non-cavity species associated with open pine stands are eastern wood-pewee (high regional priority species), as well as Carolina chickadee and summer tanager (moderate regional priority species).

Many of the highest priority species within the

Early successional stands in largely forested landscapes provide habitat for disturbance dependent species as well as mature forest species requiring edge habitat *(US Fish & Wildlife Service)*.

Southeast are temperate migrant or resident species in addition to nearctic-neotropical migrants, and the former two groups are especially well represented in southern pine communities. For example, the red-cockaded woodpecker and brown-headed nuthatch are permanent residents and are either completely or mostly dependent on healthy and mature southern pine habitats. Among temperate migrants, Henslow's sparrow breeds farther north and winters in southern pines, but not in the tropics. Also Bachman's and field sparrows, the southeastern American kestrel, and the loggerhead shrike also are all temperate migrants. The Prairie Warbler is the only obvious high priority nearctic-neotropical migrant that benefits from fire-maintained pine ecosystems (Nolan 1978). Most of these high priority pine-associated birds thrive best in longleaf habitat in which management favors ground cover that is grassy and herbaceous over that dominated by shrubby fern, palmetto, or gallberry. These conditions are most easily maintained where growing-season burns are conducted. Also, many early-successional species (principally Bachman's and field sparrows, prairie warbler, and perhaps Bewick's wren during winter) can be supported in clearcuts in pine, especially when a grassy dominated groundcover (with scattered hardwood shrub patches) remains (Dickson et al. 1993).

Although appropriate longleaf pine stands can provide the best quality habitats, suitable mature loblolly and shortleaf pines (often mixed with longleaf) provide perhaps the greatest quantity of habitat in the South for brown-headed nuthatch, Bachman's sparrow, field sparrow, prairie warbler, and red-cockaded woodpeckers. The abundance of these birds in these other pine types is dictated by the density of pines and the grass and hardwood component of the stands. These latter factors may be controlled by the season and frequency of burning.

Much of the management of mature southern pines focuses on the red-cockaded woodpecker (covered in separate chapter). However, some management protocols for this species may not satisfy the habitat requirements of other priority pine system species such as the northern bobwhite, brown-headed nuthatch, and Bachman's sparrow (Plentovich et al. 1998b). These species as well as wintering Henslow's sparrows are especially common in longleaf pine habitats with a dense and diverse grassy ground cover (Abrahamson and Hartnett 1990, Myers 1990, Frost 1993). Appropriate management of southern pine forest types can provide optimal habitat for many of these species (Wilson et al. 1995).

Bachman's Sparrow.—The range of Bachman's sparrow, also appropriately called the pinewoods spar-

Open pine savannah with dense ground cover dominated by grasses with some shrubs is excellent habitat for several pine-associated priority species, such as northern bobwhite, Bachman's sparrow, and Henslow's sparrow, shown above left. *(B. Darling, Cornell Lab of Ornithology, US Fish & Wildlife Service.)*

row, probably coincided closely with that of the red-cockaded woodpecker in longleaf and secondarily in shortleaf pine at the time of European colonization. With the wholesale cutting of mature forests in the 1900s it extended its range northward (Brooks 1938, Dunning and Watts 1990), but with the recent maturing of these interior forests its range retracted back to its probable earlier distribution. This species has been listed as state endangered or threatened in several parts of this peripheral range. The migratory habits of Bachman's sparrow are poorly understood, but the more northern breeding populations probably move south in winter to join permanent resident populations in the lower Coastal Plain from North Carolina, south into peninsular Florida, and west to Texas.

Habitat requirements of Bachman's Sparrow include a sparse woody midstory and a high density of grasses and forbs (Dunning and Watts 1990, 1991, Plentovich et al. 1998b). Mature stands of longleaf in this condition are optimal habitat for this species. Suitable conditions are also provided in early- successional habitat such as clearcuts and power line rights-of-way.

Some silvicultural practices provide good quality Bachman's sparrow habitat, while others are detrimental. Long harvest rotations, frequent burning, thinning, retention of some mature and late- successional pines, and less drastic site preparation should favor sparrow populations. Pre-planting site preparation, such as drum chopping, in which all hardwoods are removed probably disfavors Bachman's sparrow because little deadwood is left for the birds' use as song perches (Dunning and Watts 1990). Treatments that leave some bare ground may be important as well, if not for this and other nongame species certainly for northern bobwhite. Clearcuts planted in longleaf pine are suitable habitat for Bachman's Sparrow for 7-8 years, while faster growing loblolly or slash pines usually are suitable for no more than 5 years (Dunning and Watts 1990, Landers et al. 1995).

Distribution of habitat at the landscape scale seems important to this species. Evidence suggests that it is a poor disperser that is unlikely to colonize new sites far from occupied habitat without grassy corridors, such as is often maintained in utility rights-of-way or produced by tornadoes (Dunning et al. 1995). Few Bachman's sparrows were observed in otherwise suitable clearcuts that were widely scattered and isolated within a landscape dominated by agricultural fields and unsuitable forests (Dunning et al. 1995). Use of clearcuts appeared to be greatest where other suitable habitat was nearby.

Henslow's Sparrow.—One of the highest priority birds in eastern North America, Henslow's sparrows, winter primarily in grass and pine habitat in the Coastal Plain. Wintering habitat requirements are somewhat vague, but they seem to be most common in moist to wet grassy savannas and flatwoods. Preliminary results from several studies suggest Henslow's sparrows are most numerous on sites burned during the previous growing season, though birds also occur on sites up to 2 years after dormant season burning (Woodrey and Chandler, unpubl. data). Henslow's sparrow populations may be adversely affected where dormant season burns are predominately used. These and other grassland birds are displaced from sites as dormant season burning occurs (McNair 1998), as also occurs with growing season burns. However, the slow recovery of habitat conditions from dormant (as opposed to growing) season burns and the presumed saturation of other already occupied sites likely reduces overall habitat quality across entire landscapes for wintering grassland-dependent species, especially Henslow's sparrows (McNair 1998, Plentovich et al. 1998a).

Prairie Warbler.—The highest priority nearctic-neotropical migrant associated with pine habitat is the northern (nominate) subspecies of the prairie warbler, a species that presumably did best in pre- settlement fire-maintained pine systems (Nolan 1978). Currently, it typically breeds in early-successional habitat, such as seedling-sapling pine stands and retarded old-field succession. As a result of proliferation of these conditions, the prairie warbler may be more widespread and common than it was before European colonization. However, this and other early-successional specialists have undergone long-term and steep regional population declines during the last 25 years (Table 5,6) despite the abundance of short-rotation pine plantations (early-successional habitat) (Meyers and Johnson 1978, Hunter et al. 1993b).

As with Bachman's sparrow, early-successional habitats used widely by prairie warblers may not be those in which prairie warbler populations historically achieved stable high densities. Prairie warblers also appear to be absent from much of the South Atlantic coastal plain outside of pocosins. This is not easily explained given a higher abundance for this nearctic-neotropical migrant in both mature pine and early-successional habitat, especially southern pines, within the Piedmont and other Coastal Plain physiographic areas.

American Kestrel.—The cavity-nesting American kestrel has greatly declined throughout the Coastal Plain, with a very few remaining in South Carolina and Georgia (including adjacent Piedmont sites above the Fall line) and a small population persisting along the Mississippi Gulf Coast (Collopy 1996). They are found most frequently in longleaf-turkey oak sandhills, sand pine scrub, and pastures with standing snags (Bohall-Wood and Collopy 1986). The bird's decline is attributed to the reduced number of longleaf pine snags left standing in agricultural areas and open pine woods, as well as loss of breeding and foraging habitat to agriculture and urban development (Hoffman and Collopy 1988). However, kestrels readily and successfully use nest boxes and some populations appear to have been stabilized or have even expanded in Florida, South Carolina, and Georgia (Cely and Sorrow 1988, Breen 1995).

Brown-headed Nuthatch.—The brown-headed nuthatch is another cavity-nesting species of potential concern in southern pine systems. This species, though still locally common, is restricted in overall distribution and has shown signs of steep and widespread decline, especially where longleaf pine acreage has declined most (South Atlantic Coastal Plain; Table 5). The trend towards shorter rotations in commercial pine forests also may have reduced habitat suitability because this species nests in cavities in older live pines (often with dead limbs) and pine snags. Lengthened pine rotations on most public lands may compensate for declines associated with shorter rotations underway on most industrial and non- industrial private land.

Recommendations to private landowners may include retention of standing but partially rotted snags, or large limbs on live trees, during thinning operations that also should reduce hardwood midstories, at least temporarily (Wilson and Watts 1999). Regardless of factors leading to vulnerability, specific aspects of this species' habitat requirements merit attention, including local population monitoring and the investigation of the potential use of artificial nests by this species.

Management Recommendations.—Some mature pine stands should be maintained in which measures to control hardwoods and promote grass-forb vegetation, such as burning, are conducted regularly. Growing season burns are particularly effective treatments. Although some nests of low-nesting birds likely would be lost during growing season burns, most birds will renest and long-term effects will greatly outweigh these losses. Also, incentive programs to support development and management of longleaf pine ecosystems on private lands should be developed.

Forested Wetlands and Associated Habitats

A number of nearctic-neotropical migrants reach their highest abundances in mature forested wetlands (Dickson and Warren 1994). Also, these habitats support high densities of wintering birds (Dickson 1978a, b) and are important as migratory stopover sites to a number of species, such as Swainson's and gray-cheeked thrushes,

Hydrology in bottomland hardwoods influences not only forest composition, but also understory density. The more flooded a site, the less understory will be present. Flooded areas favor prothonotary, but drier sites more likely support Swainson's warblers *(US Fish & Wildlife Service).*

and warblers such as Tennessee, black-throated blue warbler, ovenbird, and northern waterthrush (Hamel, Hunter, pers. observ.).

A total of 26 priority species regularly use forested wetlands (Table 6). Surprisingly low percentages of priority species associated with these habitats were found declining during the period covered by the Breeding Bird Survey (Tables 5,6). Only within the West Gulf Coastal Plain, was the number of declining species approaching 50 percent. Despite these overall trends, Smith et al. (1996) speculated that Breeding Bird Survey may be a poor tool to properly characterize population trends for species dependent upon habitats subjected to large scale losses before the survey began. This suggestion may be especially true for mature forested wetlands in the Southeast (and especially within the Mississippi Alluvial Plain) that dwindled significantly during the first part of the 20th century (McWilliams and Rosson 1990).

Populations of some of these species in fact may be stable or increasing today at least in some areas, such as Swainson's warbler in South Atlantic Coastal Plain, but with an almost 30 percent reduction in overall forested wetland acreage during the 1900s, these species are undoubtedly less common today than they were during the 1800s and early 1900s (Sharitz and Mitsch 1993). Regardless of short-term population trends, the most vulnerable breeding species occurring mostly within forested wetland habitats are the swallow-tailed kite, cerulean warbler, and Swainson's warbler. These and other forested wetland- dependent species are treated in detail below.

Swallow-tailed Kite.—The status of the North American breeding subspecies of the swallow-tailed kite in the Southeast is precarious. Total population size for this subspecies is unknown, but estimates are less than 5,000 individuals, or a maximum of 1,150 breeding pairs according to Meyer and Collopy (1990). The breeding range probably has been reduced the most of any still-extant landbird species in eastern North America during the 1900s. The kite probably bred historically in 21 states, but is now known to breed only in

Mature cypress stands which occur on flooded sites support many bird species, a few of which have special affinities for this habitat *(US Fish & Wildlife Service)*.

7 states, with concentrations only in peninsular Florida (Meyer 1990, Meyer and Collopy 1990).

Active management to improve habitat conditions for swallow-tailed kites within existing forested wetland systems and restoration of other systems will improve the outlook for this species. It is estimated that about 100,000 acres of largely forested bottomlands are necessary to support a population of 80-100 kite pairs (Cely and Sorrow 1990). Management in floodplains should emphasize retention of scattered patches of mature and tall (70-90 feet) baldcypress and pine interspersed with open areas for foraging. Openings used by foraging kites in largely forested landscapes can be provided by tree harvesting under a variety of silvicultural techniques. Pre-migratory roost sites in the U.S. may be even more important. Some of these sites support hundreds of birds at one time as they stage before migrating to South America (Meyer 1993).

Cerulean Warbler.—Another nearctic-neotropical migrant with an uncertain and perhaps precarious status in the Southeast's Upper Coastal Plain is the cerulean warbler. The species persists in some numbers in uplands in the southern Appalachians, Cumberland Mountains, and Ozark and Ouachita mountains (Hamel 2000). Present population levels pale in comparison with historical abundance, such as the reference to this species being among the most abundant breeding birds in the Mississippi Alluvial Valley in the early 1900s (Widmann 1907). Known populations persist in forested wetlands along the Roanoke River in North Carolina and in the northern Gulf Coastal Plain (including Mississippi Alluvial Plain) in Tennessee, Kentucky, and Arkansas. Additional populations may persist in forested wetlands in northern Alabama, Mississippi, and Louisiana, but none are known at this time (Rosenberg and Barker 1998). Landscape characteristics were useful predictors of occurrence of the birds in a set of Mississippi Alluvial Valley tracts studied by Hamel et al. (1998), when birds tended to be associated with sites in landscapes with less cropland and more forest. Breeding habitats of cerulean warblers throughout their range are characterized by deciduous forests dominated by tall, large diameter trees and an uneven forest canopy (Hamel 2000). No particular tree species seem to be favored by the birds.

Hamel (1992b; also see Robbins et al. 1992) recommended 10,000-acre tracts of mature forested wetlands to maintain a (potential) source population of cerulean warblers based on his work in western Tennessee. In agriculture-dominated landscapes, such as the Mississippi Alluvial Plain, a more conservative estimate of 20,000 acres may be necessary to support a source population (Mueller et al. 2000). In areas of insufficient habitat, additional habitat patches could be established through improved habitat management or reforestation.

Other Species.—South Atlantic coastal populations of black-throated green warblers are found from the Dismal Swamp in southeastern Virginia south through the Francis Marion National Forest in South Carolina. This species appears to have declined since Hurricane Hugo in 1989 on the Francis Marion where it was formerly common. Mature and late-successional forested wetlands and associated mature upland forests and remnant large pocosin and Carolina bays constitute optimal habitat for this species. Within these habitats, this species is most commonly associated with baldcypress and Atlantic white-cedar, but also can be found in stands of hardwoods and mixed pine-hardwood areas associated with wetlands (Hamel 1981; Hamel 1992a). This warbler appears to be restricted to largely forested areas, so estimates of area needed to support source populations may be similar to those for cerulean warbler, but verification is needed.

Swainson's and prothonotary warblers are forested wetland-associated species ranked highly in the PIF prioritization process. Both species have specific features with which they are associated. Swainson's warblers occur frequently in conjunction with canebrakes, but also with dense understory vegetation approximately 3-12 feet tall that shades a bare ground surface on which they forage, similar to habitat used by American woodcock within forested wetlands. Prothonotary warblers commonly nest in close association with water. Where suitable nest sites are available, the birds apparently have little regard for the particular forest type.

A healthy population (here defined as of at least 500 pairs) of Swainson's warblers may require at least 6,000 acres (10,000 acres in agriculturally-dominated landscapes; Mueller et al. 2000) of mature forested wetlands, with prothonotary warblers requiring at least 4,000 acres (7,000 acres in agriculturally-dominated landscapes). Smaller populations occur in smaller forest patches, but the status of their viability is uncertain.

Tracts large enough to support large and productive populations of swallow-tailed kites, cerulean warblers, Swainson's warblers, and prothonotary warblers should be adequate to support source populations of less area-sensitive associates in mature forested wetlands. Habitat patches too small even for a large population of prothonotary warblers may still benefit some of these other species (Table 6), as well as provide important stopover habitat for birds during migration.

Migratory Stopover Habitats.—Tropical (in Florida) and maritime woodlands (along Gulf and Atlantic coastlines) as well as forested wetlands are very important habitats for migrating and wintering migratory birds. Almost all eastern and many boreal nearctic-neotropical migrants pass through the Southeast, with their survival probably related to the distribution of maritime and tropical woodlands or other forests near the coast (Moore et al. 1993, Moore and Woodrey 1995).

During autumn migrating landbirds "funnel" southward along the South Atlantic coastline (Watts and Mabey 1993). In maritime woods along the Gulf Coast some species stage for a trans-Gulf flight, while other species orient either toward the Peninsular Florida Gulf coast (and the West Indies) or toward the Texas coast (and Mexico). During spring, northward migrating birds by-pass maritime woodlands on fair-weather days for the more extensive inland forested wetlands and other woods. However, during inclement spring weather, Gulf coast maritime woodlands become critically important. These are the first suitable resting and foraging habitat available to exhausted migrants for recuperation (Moore and Kerlinger 1987, Moore et al. 1990).

Thus, a management strategy for nearctic-neotropical migrants using the Gulf coast should include consideration of the extent and condition of both maritime woodlands and inland forested wetlands, particularly along the Chenier Plain where the hiatus between coastal and inland forests is wide (Gosselink et al. 1979). This area of southwestern Louisiana and southeastern Texas is very important for both southward movements of young migrants as well as a safety net for spring migrants that breed throughout eastern North America. Management strategies should also include residential areas, where preferred fruit-bearing trees, shrubs, vines, and water can be provided to stressed migrants.

Riparian Forests.—Southeastern riparian areas include streamside zones, bottomlands, loess bluff oak-hickory forests, hammocks, and mixed mesic hardwoods. Upland riparian habitats may be as important as bottomland habitats for supporting migratory birds.

Riparian forest types deserving special attention are the loess bluff oak-hickory forests and mixed mesic hardwoods. Loess bluffs support remnant oak-hickory forests adjoining remnant stands of forested wetlands in the Mississippi Alluvial Plain, especially in southwestern Mississippi. Some species occurring regularly in rich loess bluff sites, such as Swainson's warblers, are more characteristic of wetland sites. In contrast, remnant oak-hickory stands along Crowley's Ridge (Arkansas and Missouri) and within the Tennessee

Plateau (Upper East Gulf Coastal Plain) are unlikely to support many area-sensitive species without extensive reforestation efforts.

In largely forested landscapes, riparian habitat is important for many species, including some of the most sensitive species that do not inhabit or are found in reduced numbers both in upland forested and fragmented landscapes (Smith 1977). Maintaining mature riparian vegetation along streamsides in intensively managed forests and in agricultural areas is a widespread practice for maintaining stream water quality (National Association of Conservation Districts 1994) and wildlife values (Dickson and Warren 1994). However, a number of questions remain about relationships and management of these zones for wildlife communities, as well as the interactions of economic considerations that temper wildlife management options (Wigley and Melchiors 1994).

Streamside zones often are maintained for nearctic-neotropical migratory birds, many of which are associated with mature forests. In eastern Texas, yellow-throated vireos, hooded warblers, and Acadian flycatchers were virtually absent from streamside zones less than 150 feet wide (Dickson et al. 1995a). Maximum numbers of Acadian flycatchers and Louisiana waterthrushes were found in streamside zones 150-300 feet wide, with a somewhat open understory, adjacent to recently regenerated loblolly pine plantations in coastal plain, piedmont, and Ouachita studies (Dickson et al. 1995a, Tassone 1981, Tappe et al. 1994). Maintaining the width of riparian habitats using the oft-repeated concept that "bigger is better" where feasible perhaps would be an optimum strategy for some precarious species (Dickson and Warren 1994).

The landscape context is a critical issue in consideration of the streamside zone width issue. Riparian zones may be divided into 3 broad categories: (1) streamside zones in managed (usually short- rotation pine) forest stands, (2) riparian forests in agricultural or developed landscapes, and (3) moisture/elevation gradients in largely forested landscapes.

In generally forested landscapes, Acadian flycatchers and Louisiana waterthrushes are more common in narrow riparian zones, becoming rarer with distance from riparian habitats. In similar situations, cerulean and Swainson's warbler are mostly restricted to riparian habitats. Kilgo et al. (1998) found peak densities for most regular species occurred when forest stands were 1/3 mile-wide; and Swainson's warbler, the most area-sensitive species, required 1 mile or more of forest width. The emphasis in this study, was on the ecosystem and not particular streamside zone widths, so timber management could still occur within a mile of the river and Swainson's warbler populations likely would persist as long as the system remains largely forested. In agricultural landscapes, or along major floodplains where much of the surrounding forestland was in short-rotation pine (for example, the Altamaha River in Georgia), maximum numbers of the most area-sensitive species peaked in streamside zones of at least 300 feet in width (Keller et al. 1993, Hodges and Krementz 1996).

It remains unclear whether local implementation of even the wider streamside zones in highly fragmented landscapes would provide suitable or optimal habitat for some vulnerable species. In some areas low reproductive success may be due to high nest parasitism and depredation rates, even in wider patches of high quality riparian habitat. On the other hand, streamside management zones, if widely implemented across a landscape, could be effective in supporting some vulnerable species.

Management Recommendations.—Historical evidence suggests that old-growth southeastern wetland forests were structurally diverse due to break up of stands with age and a variety of disturbance factors influences, such as wind storms and fires. Primarily because of past harvesting, many older riparian stands today tend to be composed of trees of similar diameters, with closed canopies and sparse understories. This habitat condition is not particularly suited to support Swainson's or cerulean warblers. In closed canopy stands, habitat conditions may be enhanced through harvesting operations, such as thinnings, small clearcuts, group selection cuts, and shelterwood cuts. In places such as the Woodbury Tract in South Carolina, it appears Swainson's warblers and other forested wetland species are faring well in the dense understories resulting from recent widespread harvesting, but these conditions likely are short-lived as these stands mature. Swainson's warbler populations also increased in response to natural disturbances to the forest canopy from Hurricane Hugo on the Francis Beidler Forest (Hamel et al. 2000) and in Congaree Swamp National Monument (Hamel 1989), both also in South Carolina.

In addition to promoting dense understories, special efforts are needed to promote and retain large hardwoods with spreading crown and diverse canopy structure within forested wetlands. Some species, such as northern parula, yellow-throated warbler, and especially the cerulean warbler, require mature stands with large trees and complex canopy structure. Cerulean warblers usually occur in the largest stands of mature or late-successional hardwoods (Hamel 1992b, Robbins et al. 1992), now a very rare condition in southeastern bottomlands. However, cerulean warblers can persist in relatively healthy numbers where forests are managed and harvested, as long as a substantial number of large-diameter trees are left after harvesting (Hamel 1992b). Such management appears to produce habitats that mimic the structure of those created by tree fall gaps.

In summary, (1) management of forests should support important diversity components such as variable understories (from cane thickets to openings), diverse age structure (seedlings to mature), and multiple vegetative layers to provide for high priority species. (2) Restoration of special habitats, such as pocosins, Atlantic white-cedar, and maritime woodlands including cheniers and mottes should be a high priority. (3) Enhancement of backyard habitats, such as establishing native fruit-bearing shrubs, vines, and trees as important food for birds, particularly migrants should be encouraged. And, (4) contingent on landowner objectives and costs, recommendations of optimum streamside zone widths for breeding and other birds include:

(a) narrow streamside zones (less than 150 feet) are probably adequate when adjacent lands within the watershed are dominated by mature or maturing forest stands,

(b) moderate to wide zones (150-300 feet) are probably adequate when adjacent lands within the watershed are dominated by short-rotation plantations,

(c) the widest zones (at least 300 feet) would be necessary when adjacent lands within the watershed are dominated by agricultural or developed lands.

Shrub bogs, most prevalent in southeastern Virginia and the eastern Carolinas, provide habitats for a wide diversity of bird species *(US Fish & Wildlife Service).*

Upland Hardwood Forests

Hardwood-Pine Forests.—Much of the Coastal Plain and Piedmont forests not in pure pine or wetlands are in some transitional stage of upland hardwoods and pine (Dickson et al. 1995, Meyers and Johnston 1978). Virtually none of this forest type persists in the South Atlantic Coastal Plain, but is more prevalent in the Piedmont and Gulf Coastal Plain. Of the 17 priority bird species considered to use mixed hardwood-pine forests in lowland physiographic areas, only within the West Gulf Coastal Plain and Southern Ridge and Valley/Southern Cumberland Plateau are declining priority bird species approaching 50 percent (Tables 5,6).

Overall increasing forest acreage and maturity in the Piedmont would suggest greater security for many vulnerable bird species. Breeding Bird Survey trends indicate that very few vulnerable species overall have undergone declines from 1966-1996 in either the Mid-Atlantic or Southern Piedmont physiographic areas. However, wood thrushes and red-eyed vireos have shown consistent declines within patches of mature forests within Piedmont suburban settings, such as Atlanta, GA (Robbins 1980, Terborgh 1989). Furthermore, a number of area-sensitive species (northern parulas, black-throated green warblers, Swainson's warblers, and worm-eating warblers) have population centers in the Southern Blue Ridge and in the South Atlantic Coastal Plain but are absent as breeding species over much of the southern Piedmont today (Hamel 1992a).

Retention is the primary consideration for upland pine-hardwood forests. Regardless of successional stage these forests provide breeding, migratory and winter habitat for many species. Loss of forest to other land uses is likely to result in additional bird declines.

In addition, birds in these forests may be affected by changes in forest composition or by other vertebrate species. For example, very abundant deer in the Piedmont and elsewhere may reduce understory vegetation and negatively affect breeding birds such as hooded warblers (DeCalesta 1994, Leimgruber et al. 1994). Also where hogs are abundant they may severely disrupt conditions for ground- nesting species such as Kentucky warblers.

Piedmont forest patches such as Kennesaw Mountain National Battlefield Park are no doubt important for many transient nearctic-neotropical migrants. Fall migrants orienting towards the South Atlantic coast likely depend on at least one forest patch for resting and foraging. Likewise, many spring migrants orienting northeastward from the Gulf of Mexico to the Southern Appalachians also similarly use Piedmont forests.

Central Hardwood Forests.—The 2 southeastern physiographic areas included within the central hardwood region in the Southeast are the Interior Low Plateaus and Ozarks (the Interior Highlands in part), but this forest type also occurs in the West Gulf Coastal Plain and along the edges and on the ridges of the Mississippi Alluvial Plain. Central hardwoods, or western mesophytic forests, are dominated by oaks and hickories in the east and more so by oak to the west. Of the 18 priority birds using these forest types, declining trends were most pronounced in the Interior Low Plateaus and West Gulf Coastal Plain (both approaching 50 percent), while about 25 percent of these species were declining in the Mississippi Alluvial Plain and the Ozark-Ouachita Highlands (Tables 5,6).

Portions of the Interior Low Plateaus in the states of Kentucky, Tennessee, and Alabama may be limited in capability of supporting healthy populations of most of the vulnerable mature forest species due to variably fragmented landscapes and subsequently lower probabilities for nesting success (Robinson 1992). The continued persistence of many forest birds throughout much of the region perhaps is dependent upon immigration from other mostly forested areas such as the Ozark Highlands (Robinson et al. 1995). The Ozark Highlands of Missouri, Arkansas, and Oklahoma today are the most intact hardwood-dominated forested landscape west of the Southern Appalachians. Thus, the Ozarks appear to support among the healthiest "source" populations where average reproduction results in surplus young emigrating to adjacent areas.

Within the Ozarks, current forestry practices do not appear to be negatively affecting bird populations. Available data indicate that even-aged silviculture, with 100-year rotations, in largely forested areas have little effect on relative abundance of most vulnerable mature forest species, while providing for higher numbers of early-successional species (Thompson et al. 1992). Some mature forest species (black-and-white warblers, worm-eating warblers, Kentucky warblers) were found in higher numbers in even-aged regeneration areas than in passively managed areas officially designated as wilderness. Also, the 3 mature forest species found in lower numbers in the even-aged regeneration areas (red-eyed vireo, pine warbler, scarlet tanager) are doing relatively well throughout most of their ranges in the Southeast.

In largely forested landscapes even-aged silviculture with long rotations and relatively large treatment areas can lead to less forest fragmentation than uneven-aged silviculture with numerous very small patches and frequent stand entry (Thompson et al. 1992). Nevertheless, Thompson (1993) suggests that over the larger Ozark landscape a combination of both uneven-aged and even-aged timber management can provide stability for mature forest species and some early-successional species.

Generally, contiguous and large oak-dominated forest patches are good forest bird habitat when compared to more fragmented landscapes. A recent study by Marquis and Whelan (1995) suggests that healthy bird populations could be important for maintaining healthy oak forests by consumption of herbivorous insects on oak saplings. Therefore, healthy insectivorous bird communities in largely forested landscapes possibly can help to maintain healthier forests.

Management recommendations for upland hardwoods and hardwood-pine forests.—(1) Landscape scale land use patterns should be considered with a goal of maintaining large forest tracts. In large forests, silvicultural options can accommodate timber production and bird communities, including vulnerable mature forest species. (2) Even-aged regeneration with rotations at least 100 years and in relatively large blocks (40-100 acres) can minimize forest fragmentation in largely forested landscapes and support early-successional species. Finally, (3) combining uneven-aged with even-aged regeneration can provide stable habitat for many mature forest breeding species as long as harvest is not excessive.

Appalachian Forests

The Southern Appalachians include some of the most heavily forested regions in the Southeast (Southern Blue Ridge, Northern Cumberland Plateau), but also include some of the most heavily fragmented landscapes (Southern Ridge and Valley/Southern Cumberland Plateau). Effective forest bird conservation in the Southern Appalachians therefore will require not only consideration of forest composition and structure, but also attention to landscape context using measures of percent forest cover in heavily forested areas and forest patch size in more fragmented areas.

Appalachian forests are broadly grouped into (1) spruce-fir-northern hardwoods, (2) hemlock- white pine-hardwoods, (3) mixed mesophytic (cove) hardwoods, and (4) Appalachian oaks and mountain yellow pine. Of the 26 priority species included here, declining trends are most pronounced for the Southern Blue Ridge (exceeding 60 percent) and the Southern Ridge and Valley/Southern Cumberland Plateau (about 50 percent; Tables 5,6). The declines reported from the Southern Blue Ridge appear counterintuitive given that this area is 80 percent forested and suggest that factors other than forest cover may be involved as discussed below in interpreting Breeding Bird Survey and land use patterns.

Spruce-fir-northern hardwoods.—These habitats are found mostly above 3500 feet elevation in the Southern Blue Ridge and at lower elevations in the Allegheny Mountains of West Virginia. As with other forest types, spruce-fir-northern hardwood forests were harvested at about the beginning of the 20th century and regenerated stands present today differ from conditions existing prior to harvest. Generally, spruce was replaced by fir from higher elevations and northern hardwoods from below. Today, with the high percentage of the community in public ownership it would appear that protection of healthy high- elevation biotic communities would be achievable. Nevertheless, spruce-fir communities are threatened by exotic pests, possibly compounded by effects from regional air degradation (White et al. 1993, Rabenold et al. 1998, Nicholas et al. 1999). However, some effective restoration probably is possible, at least for spruce.

As many as 7 species closely associated with spruce-fir-northern hardwood forests are effectively isolated from more northerly and western populations (Table 6). These 7 "endemic" high elevation forest birds are all best classified as short-distance temperate migrants. Among these species, the northern saw- whet owl appears to be the most vulnerable to potential habitat loss (Simpson 1992, Milling et al. 1997), followed by the black-capped chickadee and the red crossbill. Although widespread elsewhere, the owl here occurs as isolated populations that need conservation attention. Northern saw-whet owls respond to nest boxes which may partially mitigate the loss of high-elevation conifers. Also, owls may use other habitat, such as older northern hardwoods and hemlock (Milling et al. 1997).

The suite of bird species of interest found in northern hardwoods is similar to that in spruce-fir-northern hardwood mixes, but red crossbills and northern saw-whet owls are more closely associated with old-growth stands in close proximity to spruce, while more disturbed northern hardwood stands (including high-elevation Appalachian oak) are more likely to support black-billed cuckoo, yellow-bellied sapsucker, and golden-winged warbler. The yellow-bellied sapsucker population isolated in the Southern Blue Ridge is a described subspecies with habitat requirements differing from the other endemic taxa. The sapsucker uses open woodlands (including orchards), forests excessively disturbed by fire, wind damage, and clearcuts where suitable nesting trees are retained.

The importance of early-successional habitats at higher elevations (above 3,000 feet) prior to European colonization remains unclear. However, the likelihood that these habitats were more prevalent prior to European settlement is supported by documented reduction of mountain bogs, balds, savannas, incidence of fire, beaver, and large herbivores in recent times (Delcourt and Delcourt 1997, Buckner and Turrill 1999). Today, only clearcutting and storm damage provide some early successional habitat on a sustainable basis. In addition to high-elevation early-successional habitats supporting the last known Appalachian Bewick's wrens, the decline of both Appalachian yellow-bellied sapsuckers and golden- winged warblers is indicative of that habitat loss in recent decades. Golden-winged warblers in particular are increasingly restricted to elevations between 3,000-5,000 feet with highest densities now apparently in early-successional northern hardwood stands. Large-scale disturbances appear to play an important role in maintaining good habitat conditions (dense grassy-herbaceous layer with scattered saplings) for this species, but opportunities for long-term management may also exist along appropriately maintained powerline rights-of-way, retired agricultural lands, and remaining bogs and bald edges (Confer 1992).

At the other end of the conservation spectrum, the spread of some high-elevation bird species southward appears to correspond with the maturing of some spruce stands, opening of spruce-fir canopies, and understory development. Increases of Swainson's and hermit thrushes as well as magnolia and perhaps yellow-rumped and mourning warblers in recent decades is at least partially attributable to these habitat changes throughout the high-elevation areas within the Southern Appalachians. Black-throated blue, chestnut-sided, and Canada warbler populations are perhaps better stabilized in areas where fir decline is most prevalent but where spruce is still common. At the same time, canopy species such as blackburnian and perhaps black-throated green warblers appear to be in decline, while olive-sided flycatchers now appear to be near extirpation as a breeding species from the Southeast (Simpson 1992, Buckelew and Hall 1994). Unfortunately, most species increasing in the Southern Appalachians are doing relatively well throughout much of their distribution while those species decreasing are generally among the more vulnerable species in the Southeast requiring conservation attention.

Hemlock-White Pine-Hardwood Forests.—Mature hemlock-white pine-hardwood mixes can support local populations of northern parula, black-throated green, blackburnian, and Canada warblers. The first 3 species are obligate canopy species, while the ground nesting Canada warblers are restricted to stands with dense understory (often rhododendron). Blackburnian and Canada warblers are found primarily at the higher elevations. In addition, significant populations of black-throated blue warblers at the higher elevations and Swainson's warblers at the lower elevations (usually below 3,000 feet) also occur in these habitats, and like Canada warblers, both of these species prefer understory thickets.

Groth (1988) provides strong evidence that 2 resident cryptic red crossbill "species" depend upon Southern Appalachian conifers, in particular spruce-fir and hemlock/white pine forests. At least 1 of these types is possibly endemic to the Southern Blue Ridge. Declines in hemlock, white pine, and spruce may be affecting the long-term conservation of at least this crossbill "species."

A few species usually occurring at high-elevations, such as red-breasted nuthatch, winter wren, and golden-crowned kinglet, also occur in pairs or family groups in late successional stands down to elevations of 2,000 feet. Maintenance of existing late-successional hemlock and white pine stands and increasing acreage on public lands may well benefit these as well as more vulnerable birds.

Mixed Mesophytic (Cove) Hardwood Forests.—Mixed mesophytic forests are characteristically found on sites sheltered from frequent disturbances and therefore often include very large trees and a high diversity of both plant and animal species. Cerulean warbler reaches its highest abundance within the Southeast in mixed mesophytic hardwood forests within the Northern Cumberland Plateau and adjacent Ohio Hills physiographic areas. Cerulean warblers are found locally in much lower numbers in mature cove hardwood stands of the Southern Blue Ridge and the Mid Atlantic Ridge and Valley between 1,500 and 4,000 feet elevation, but appear to be increasing in areas where storms or forest management have led to a more open canopy, edges, and retention of large trees. Thus, a key habitat feature is an abundance of very tall trees and well-developed and complex canopy often near edges and on steep terrain, but much more information is needed here to definitively promote key habitat requirements.

Swainson's warblers in the Southern Appalachians are isolated from other populations and occur in different habitats at higher elevations, but as elsewhere, are associated with very dense understories. Most Southern Appalachian Swainson's warbler populations occur below 3,000 feet elevation along streams in mixed mesophytic hardwoods with dense understories, usually dominated by rhododendron. Some occur in lower-elevation mixed hemlock-hardwood stands. Other vulnerable birds that use mixed mesophytic hardwoods as optimal habitat include Acadian flycatchers, black-throated blue warblers, worm-eating warblers, ovenbirds, hooded warblers, and scarlet tanagers.

The prognosis for future health of mixed mesophytic forests would seem optimistic in the publicly protected coves of the Southern Blue Ridge and Mid Atlantic Ridge and Valley. However, much of the mixed mesophytic forests of the Northern Cumberland Plateau and Ohio Hills are in private ownership and are therefore not necessarily secure into the future. Mixed mesophytic sites are very productive and forests can redevelop rapidly after harvest, but much still needs to be learned about the recovery of healthy populations of certain mature forest birds, particularly cerulean warblers, in forested landscapes.

Appalachian Oak-Mountain Yellow Pine Forests.—The Appalachian oak forest is a widespread forest type in the Southeast (Stephenson et al. 1993, Buckner and Turrill 1999). However, several mountain yellow pine communities are highly vulnerable (Table Mountain Pine in particular) due to fire suppression over the last 50 years (Buckner and Turrill 1999). In fact, due to fire suppression practices the nature and future of Appalachian oak may be in some doubt. Nevertheless, the large amount of public lands supporting Appalachian oak forests (about 5 million acres) in the Southern Blue Ridge would suggest future security for those species dependent upon this forest type.

In contrast to the Southern Blue Ridge, the outlook for bird species in Appalachian oak forests in the Southern Ridge and Valley is not as secure. Fragmentation of mature forest here is the highest of any area in the Southern Appalachians. Oak forests remain along narrow ridges, but the wider valleys have been cleared for agriculture and other development. Continuing downward trends among forest birds in the Southern Ridge and Valley perhaps indicate lessening reproductive success of birds breeding in small forest patches due to the increasing negative effects of nest predators and parasites during the last two decades (S. Pearson unpubl. data). There is too little public land in the area to support viable populations of sensitive species.

The situation in the Mid-Atlantic Ridge and Valley is somewhat similar to that in the Southern Ridge and Valley. The oak-dominated ridges of the Mid-Atlantic Ridge and Valley are wider, but the valleys are mostly devoid of forests. These oak forests are being negatively affected by defoliation from the gypsy moth, which is moving from north to south along the Mid Atlantic ridges. Decline of the oak forests may lead to future problems for forest bird communities. Pesticides used to control gypsy moths may remove not only gypsy moth larvae but also many foliage invertebrates important for birds. Other control methods include cutting affected areas, which would favor early-successional bird species over mature forest species. Recent research indicates an integrated approach may be best for controlling gypsy moth defoliation while avoiding severe habitat loss for mature forest birds (Cooper and Marshall 1997).

Management recommendations.—(1) Realize the importance and maintain healthy forests of both spruce-fir and northern hardwoods as best as possible given the problems posed by ecological pests. (2) Conduct land-use planning on public and cooperating private lands with conservation partners, incorporating efforts targeting the needs of species such as golden-winged and cerulean warblers. (3) Develop management plans for corporate forest lands in cooperation with other private and appropriate public entities, with objectives of maintaining healthy forest bird communities compatible with landowner objectives such as profitable timber management. (4) Increase research and monitoring of ecosystems and threats to them, bird communities, and responses of species to habitat management. (5) Promote appropriate silvicultural operations, such as cuttings of hardwood overstory in hemlock stands to allow full hemlock and as well as understory development on appropriate sites. (6) Minimize effects of pesticide and tree-cutting gypsy moth control on mature forest birds by using an integrated approach.

DISCUSSION

Interpreting Bird Population Trends and Land Use Patterns

Current information shows consistent declines in some species (Table 5), sparking concern for their well being. The patterns of bird population change and causes influencing these changes are complex and not easily understood. Our bird survey techniques may be biased, we may not fully understand bird/habitat and landscape scale relationships, there may be historical factors or population phenomena that we do not adequately consider, and we may not yet recognize other factors affecting birds.

The Breeding Bird Survey (BBS) is the standard assessment of occurrence and trends of North American birds, but surveys of breeding birds along roads may not be representative of habitat within landscapes. Trends from BBS data may seem contradictory to the assumption that amount of forest cover is related to population stability among vulnerable species. Some recent interpretations of warbler population trends from BBS data suggest forest birds of the heavily forested Southern Appalachians (especially Southern Blue Ridge) and Ozark-Ouachita Highlands have decreased, while forest species occurring in the highly fragmented Coastal Plain and Mississippi Alluvial Plain physiographic areas are either stable or increasing (James et al. 1992, Smith et al. 1996). But other factors, such as landscape and historical relationships may need to be incorporated in order to properly assess status and trends of bird populations.

Uplands.—Regardless of the forest types involved, many of the upland species of interest are most secure in the physiographic areas with more total forest cover such as the Southern Blue Ridge, Northern Cumberland Plateau, and Ohio Hills. These same species would seem less secure in the Mid Atlantic Ridge and Valley/Allegheny Mountains physiographic areas, and least secure in the Southern Cumberland Plateau/Ridge and Valley, based upon the extent of forest in these regions. Other interior physiographic areas, the Ozark-Ouachita Highlands and the Interior Low Plateaus, where large forested patches alternate with equally large or larger unforested areas, would appear to provide intermediate security overall for vulnerable mature forest species.

Potential contradiction to this assumption is the apparent decline of many bird species in the heavily forested Southern Blue Ridge (James et al. 1992, Hunter et al. 1993b). About a third of all regional priority species (both late and early successional species) are declining, along with 18 percent additional species that are possibly declining (Table 5). A hypothesis proposed by James et al. (1996) is that atmospheric pollution becomes increasingly important as elevation increases by affecting tree growth, insectivore food availability, and reduction of important minerals (such as calcium) necessary for successful reproduction. Another possible factor is the recent expansion of new homes and associated development along roads (and BBS routes) of the region. Yet another factor mentioned earlier is the condition (and not only the amount) of forest, in that the structure of regenerating forests in the Southeast during the last 30 years both eliminates habitat for early successional and minimizes optimal conditions for many mature forest species. A fruitful and relevant line of research topics would be focused on field testing each of these hypotheses (and others).

Also, concluding local cause and effects on individual migratory species based on local (or regional) population trends may be based on high speculation. Regardless of local status, or whether the contributing factors are from breeding habitat, non-breeding habitat, or otherwise, problems persist in all areas for at least some species. For example, cerulean warblers reach their greatest relative abundance in the densely forested Ohio Hills and Northern Cumberland Plateau physiographic areas (Buckelew and Hall 1994), where it has declined over the last 3 decades at rates similar to declines in other physiographic areas. Other widespread species using a greater variety of forested habitats that also are declining across the Southeast include yellow-billed cuckoo, eastern wood-pewee, and wood thrush. Known winter habitat loss for cerulean warblers and wood thrushes may be influencing these widespread declines. Both species, however, are also known to be affected by increasing rates of nest predation and parasitism. Thus, management emphasis should include both breeding and wintering grounds.

Lowlands.—In contrast to upland physiographic areas, lowland physiographic areas generally have fewer nearctic-neotropical migrants showing declines (James et al. 1992, Hunter 1993). However, higher percentages of resident and/or temperate migrants are declining in lowland physiographic areas compared with upland physiographic areas. Decline of species such as red-cockaded woodpecker and northern bobwhite is a reflection of degradation of mature longleaf and grassland ecosystems (Hunter et al. 1994).

Population trends among nearctic-neotropical migrants associated with forested wetlands in lowlands show little consistency. The most extensive losses of these habitats occurred before the initiation of the BBS in 1966. At one time floodplain forests probably covered about 45 million acres in the Southeast. Drainage and clearing of floodplain forests that began in the mid-1800s reduced the total to about 37 million acres remaining by 1952. From 1952 until 1995 during years of the Forest Survey, lowland hardwood forests declined further to about 31 million acres (Dickson and Sheffield, Defining the Forest chapter).

Conclusions

Southern forests are important breeding and wintering habitat for hundreds of bird species, some faring well and some of apparent precarious status. Although the extent of southern forests has remained relatively stable in recent years, continued threats to bird forest habitat remain from a burgeoning human population.

Substantial information needs exist, such as how to interpret population function and how source populations, where reproductive output exceeds mortality, support sink populations, where reproductive output cannot support populations alone. Research to develop this information is necessary as is regionwide monitoring of bird communities.

Recommendations and conclusions herein are based on best information and interpretation at this time. Modifications will be required as more complete information becomes available. Most recommendations are general, and will need to be adapted for local conditions. Also, application of recommendations specific for some bird species should be considered in conjunction with economic considerations, other land uses, and with traditional game and other species in mind. However, with careful and thoughtful planning, many management options based on this information here can be effective for bird conservation in light of these other considerations.

ACKNOWLEDGMENTS

Much of the information and recommendations found in this chapter have been derived from discussions with many dedicated professional and amateur ornithologists and others interested in natural resource management in the Southeast. Most of these discussions have been conducted under the auspices of the Southeast U.S. Partners in Flight Regional Working Group. The authors gratefully thank all involved in Southeast Partners in Flight over the past decade for their insights, opinions, and data and for openly sharing these with us over the years. The many observers conducting Breeding Bird Surveys also made many of the findings here possible. Bruce Peterjohn and John Sauer from U.S.G.S. Biological Resources Division-Patuxent Wildlife Research Center for their advice on the use of these data and Howard Hunt and Mike Staten for their advice and comments on the manuscript.

Appendix 1. Population trend (PT) and population trend data quality (PTDQ) criteria for scoring Breeding Bird Survey data. To determine a PT score, first evaluate PTDQ by checking sample size (n) and statistical significance (P) and choose a trend depending on whether the species is increasing, decreasing, or stable. PDTQ scores are not used in the overall priority score but are important in judging the quality of the trend data.

PT Score	Trend	PTDQ Score	*BBS trend quality* n		P
5 = Significant decrease	Decreasing at or above an average of 1.0% per year	A1 =	≥34	and	≤0.10
			or		
		B1 =	14-33	and	≤0.10
4 = Possible decrease	Decreasing at or above an average of 1.0% per year	C1 =	6-13	and	≤0.10
		or			
		C2 =	≥14	and	0.11-0.35
3 = Trend unknown	Change at or above an average of 1.0% per year	D =	≥14	and	>0.35
3 = Insufficient data	Any trend	E1 =	6-13	and	>0.10
		E2=	1-5	and	any P value
3 = No data	No data	F=	NA	NA	0
2 = Stable or no trend	Trend between -1.0% and +1.0% per year	A2 =	≥34	and	any P value
		or	+		
		B2=	14-33	and	any P value
2 = Possible increase	Increasing at or above an average of 1.0% per year	C1 =	6-13	and	≤0.10
		or	+		
		C2 =	≥14	and	0.11-0.35
1=Significant increase	Increasing at or above an average of 1.0% per year	A1 =	≥34	and	≤0.10+*
		or			
		B1 =	14-33	and	≤0.10
Any score		X=	Based on information other than BBS		

CHAPTER 26

Terrestrial Small Mammals

James G. Dickson[1]
US Forest Service
Southern Research Station, Nacogdoches, TX

A variety of terrestrial small mammals with diverse size, form, geographic range, and ecological niche inhabit southern forests. Some are highly specialized for their environment, such as the semi-aquatic species or fossorial species, such as moles. Some, such as the cotton rat, are widely distributed throughout the region and others highly restrictive in their range and habitat. Because of their secretive and often nocturnal nature, most small mammals are not apparent to the casual observer, but they are prominent in southern forests.

Terrestrial small mammals are integral and important components of southern forest systems. They function as consumers of primary productivity. They consume, distribute, and disperse plant seed, including acorns. They consume large quantities of insects and other arthropods. Also, their subterranean activities aerate soils and they function in dispersing mycorrhizal fungi spores within forests (Maser et al. 1978).

Small mammals are primary prey for many mammals, birds, and reptiles and sustain many vertebrate species on higher trophic levels. As such, small mammals play a substantial role in system energetics and nutrient cycling. Also, small mammals can be important vectors of diseases, such as tularemia, lyme disease, and hantavirus, which can infect humans, livestock, and other species of wildlife. A number of different species inhabit and function in southern forests. In this chapter I cover shrews and moles (Insectivores), and small terrestrial rodents.

INSECTIVORES

Shrews are the smallest mammal, weighing less than an ounce. These Insectivores are very active with a high metabolism and voracious appetite. Their main diet is insects; other invertebrates such as earthworms, sowbugs, and snails; and larger vertebrates. They use burrows of other small mammals and construct burrows of their own. They have a long snout, poor sight and sense of smell, but keen hearing and tactile sense. Owls are among shrew

[1]Current Address: School of Forestry, Louisiana Tech University, Ruston, LA

Small rodents, such as this woodrat, are important components of southern forest systems. They consume primary productivity, and disperse plants and fungi *(J. Dickson)*.

Small mammals are primary prey for many mammals, birds, and reptiles, and sustain many vertebrate species on a higher trophic level *(OK Dept. Wildlife)*.

predators; shrew skulls show up regularly in owl pellets. Several species are found in southern forests.

The southeastern shrew is found throughout the South except the western extremity and along the southern coastal area (Hall 1981). Some specimens have been captured in dry woods, but most have been taken from marshy habitat to moist woods (Sealander and Heidt 1990). They have been documented in some young brushy stands (Table 2) and in some mature stands, particularly in hardwood stands on moist sites (Table 3).

The short-tailed shrew, originally recognized as 1 species (*Blarina brevicauda*), recently has been split into 3 species: *B. brevicauda* in the northeastern part of the region, *B. carolinensis* through the southern portion of the South, and *B. hylophaga* in the midwestern U.S. extending into eastern Oklahoma and northwestern Arkansas. *Blarina* spp. occur regularly throughout the region. Typical habitat of these species is moist woods (Sealander and Heidt 1990). They are very abundant species in the South, commonly inhabiting many different stand types at different stages of stand development from the young brushy stage to maturity (Tables 1,2,3).

The least shrew is distributed throughout the South. It is gregarious, often with several occupying the same nest during winter. It is not a woodland species, but is associated with dense herbaceous vegetation, particularly grasses such as bluestem, bermudagrass, and Johnson grass (Schmidly 1983). It has been documented, apparently in appropriate habitat, in different stand types (Tables 1,2,3).

The water shrew occurs along the Appalachian Mountains from Virginia to northern Georgia (Hall 1981). Appropriately named (*S. palustris*), it occupies moist habitat along pond, stream, and marsh edges. Range of the long-tailed shrew is similar to that of the water shrew.

The smoky shrew occurs in the mountainous central part of the region from central Kentucky to western Virginia and southerly to northeastern Georgia and western South Carolina (Hall 1981). The pygmy shrew occurs along the eastern mountains from northern Virginia to northern Georgia. The swamp short-tailed shrew has been identified along coastal Virginia and North Carolina.

Moles, somewhat larger than shrews, are another Insectivore. They construct extensive tunnels in which they live and are well adapted for their subterranean existence and for digging. Their legs are short and powerful and placement facilitates digging. Their eyes and ears are vestigial and they have a short almost hairless tail (Lowery 1974). Three moles occupy southern forests. The most common and found throughout is the

Table 1. Relative abundance[a] of captures of terrestrial small mammals in 1-year-old stands in the South.

Stand[b]	Cotton Mouse	White-footed Mouse	Golden Mouse	Hispid Cotton Rat	Short-tailed shrew[c]	Least shrew	South-eastern shrew	Eastern Harvest Mouse	Marsh Rice Rat	House Mouse	Eastern Woodrat
1. Pine Plant.-GA		1		2				4		3	
2. Pine Plant.-MS		4		1	5				3	2	
3. Pine regen.-MS	1					2		3			
4. Bottomland hardwood-TX	1								2		3

[a]1=highest abundance, 2=2nd highest, etc.
[b]Citation: 1. Atkeson and Johnson 1979; 2. Perkins et al. 1989; 3. Wolfe and Lohoefener 1983; 4. Dickson et al. unpubl. data
[c]Blarina spp.

Table 2. Relative abundance[a] of captures of terrestrial small mammals in young brushy stands (3-6 years old) in the South.

Stand[b]	Cotton Mouse	White-footed Mouse	Golden Mouse	Hispid Cotton Rat	Short-tailed Shrew[c]	Least shrew	South-eastern Shrew	Eastern Harvest Mouse	Marsh Rice Rat	House Mouse	Eastern Woodrat	Eastern Chipmunk	Other
1. Pine Stand-SC	3			1	4			2					
2. Pine Plant.-SC		3		1				2					
3. Pine Plant.-NC		9	3	1	6	3	8	2	7	5			
4. Pine Plant.-GA		2		1				3		4			
5. Pine Stand-MS	1			2	4	3	6	5					
6. Pine Plant.-MS		4		1	5				2	3			
7. Pine Plant.-TX			3	1				2[d]			4		5[e]
8. Bottoml. Hardw.-TX	2			1	5			3[d]	4		6		
9. Right-of-way-TN		3			2			4				5	1[f]
10. Right-of-way-TN		2			1			4				5	3[f]

[a]1=highest abundance, 2=2nd highest, etc.
[b]Citation: 1.2. Mengak et al. 1989; 3. Mitchell et al. 1995; 4. Atkeson and Johnson 1979; 5. Wolf and Lohoefener 1983; 6. Perkins et al. 1989; 7. Fleet and Dickson 1984; 8. Dickson et al. unpubl. data; 9.10. Johnson et al. 1979.
[c]Blarina spp. [d]Fulvous harvest mouse [e]Black Rat [f]Pine vole

eastern mole. Of more limited range in the eastern mountains is the hairy-tailed mole and in the eastern mountains and along the eastern coast into Florida is the star-nosed mole. Moles feed on a variety of invertebrates in the soil and occasionally plants. They are found in a variety of open and forested habitats; usually in sandy to loamy soil in which they can tunnel easily; they usually do not occupy heavy clay or very rocky soils (Sealander and Heidt 1990).

RODENTS

The eastern chipmunk occurs generally in the central and northwest portion of the region and is mostly absent from the coastal plain (Hall 1981). It is named and noted for storing food in chambers in burrows which it constructs. It often frequents areas with some type of physical structure such as down logs, exposed tree roots, rock outcrops, rock piles, and log piles. Chipmunks are active during the day and seasonally undergo periods of torpor during winter. During winter they awake periodically to feed on their food cache or forage aboveground. Foods include buds, fruits and berries, grain, mushrooms, insects, and small vertebrates and their young or eggs. Acorns and hickory nuts are frequently stored items (Lowery 1974). Chipmunks are commonly captured in mature hardwood and pine stands in Tennessee (Table 3), and appear to be widespread and common in upland stands in the northern central portion of the South.

Table 3. Relative abundance[a] of captures of terrestrial small mammals in mature stands in the South.

Stand[b]	Cotton Mouse	White-footed Mouse	Golden Mouse	Hispid Cotton Rat	Short-tailed Shrew[c]	Least shrew	South-eastern Shrew	Eastern Harvest Mouse	Marsh Rice Rat	House Mouse	Eastern Woodrat	Eastern Chipmunk	Other
1. Pocosin-NC	2	6	1		4		3						5[d]
2. Laurel oak floodplain-GA	1		2		3		7			5	4		6[e]
3. Longleaf/slash-MS	1			3	4	2	4	4					
4. Bayhead-MS	1		3	6	4	4	2				6		
5. Pine-hardw.-MS		1											
6. Pine-hardw.-TX	2			4	3						1		
7. Streamside zone-TX	1		5	6	4			3[e]			2		
8. Bottoml. Hardw.-TX	1		4		3			5[e]			2		5[f]
9. Oak-hickory-TN		3			2							1	
10. Pine-TN		3	5		1							2	4[g]
11. Oak-hickory-TN		1			3							2	
12. Chestnut-oak-TN		1										2	
13. Pine-TN		1	3		4							2	

[a]1=highest abundance, 2=2nd highest, etc.

[b]Citation: 1. Mitchell et al. 1995; 2. Boyd 1976; 3.4. Wolfe and Lohoefener 1983; 5. Perkins et al. 1989; 6. Fleet and Dickson 1984; 7. Dickson and Williamson 1988; 8. Dickson et al. unpubl. data; 9.10. Johnson et al. 1979; 11.12.13. Dueser and Shugart 1978;

[c]Blarina spp. [d]Southern bog lemming [e]Fulvous harvest mouse [f]Marsh rice rat [g]Pine vole

Range of the 13-lined ground squirrel, common throughout the central western U.S., extends only into the western edge of the region (NW Arkansas, NE Oklahoma, SE Texas)(Hall 1981). It is a diurnal, social animal that lives in colonies. They construct and use an extensive burrow system, and hibernate overwinter. Their diet is grass and forbs, insects, and some small vertebrates (Schmidly 1983). Ground squirrel habitat is grassland and they have extended their range easterly recently, apparently as a result of land clearing.

A fossorial rodent of southern forest soils is the pocket gopher. The species is noted for constructing an extensive subterranean burrow system which affords protection from predators and weather extremes. The animal spends most of its life underground and is well designed for that existence. It is a stocky rodent with stout front claws and small eyes. Pocket gophers are usually found in well- drained sandy soils in which they can burrow.

According to Hall (1981) several species of pocket gophers (*Geomys* spp.) occur in southern forests. The range of the plains pocket gopher, typically the midwestern plains, extends easterly into the South into Arkansas and Louisiana. The southeastern pocket gopher occurs from central Florida approximately midway into Georgia and Alabama. Hall (1981) recognizes 3 species of pocket gophers (colonial, Sherman's, Cumberland Island) each with limited range along coastal Georgia.

Range of the hispid pocket mouse, a midwestern plains species, extends easterly into eastern Oklahoma and Texas, and western central Louisiana (Hall 1981). This pouched small mammal feeds mostly on seeds of forbs and grasses which it stores in its underground burrows constructed in soils loose enough for burrowing (Schmidly 1983).

The marsh rice rat occurs throughout the South except western Virginia and North Carolina (Hall 1981). The common and scientific name reflect its propensity to consume rice. It is found in damp, moist habitat such as pond and stream borders and marshy areas; hardly ever frequenting dry upland habitat (Lowery 1974). The species is commonly found in a variety of different stand types and stages of development (Tables 1,2,3), but moist/wet habitat is the key factor. In eastern Texas, none were captured in mesic streamside zones (Dickson and Williamson 1988) or in a young pine plantation or a mature upland hardwood pine stand (Fleet and Dickson 1984).

Harvest mice.—Harvest mice are very small colorful cricetine rodents weighing less than an ounce and scientifically named for their grooved incisors. They construct a baseball-sized nest of plant parts underneath or on the ground, or in grass or shrubs. They are mostly nocturnal and consume forb and grass seed, other plant parts, sometimes grain, and occasionally insects.

Three species of harvest mice are found in the South (Hall 1981). The plains harvest mouse, a species of the midwestern U. S., extends into eastern Oklahoma and the tip of northwestern Arkansas. The eastern harvest mouse occurs throughout the region except the tip of Florida, and predominates in the eastern portion of the region. The fulvous harvest mouse occurs from eastern Mississippi northwesterly through Arkansas and west through the region.

Harvest mice are associated with grass/forb and shrubby vegetation and are found in places such as abandoned fields, pastures, roadsides, and odd places vegetated by plants such as bluestem, Johnson grass, fescue, and honeysuckle (Sealander and Heidt 1990). The eastern harvest mouse predominates in the eastern portion of the region and the fulvous in the western portion. Harvest mice are common and widespread in appropriate habitat and populations often reach high densities. Harvest mice inhabit a wide variety of different stand types. They quickly invade young regeneration stands (Table 1), are very regular and abundant in young brushy stands (Table 2), and are sometimes found in mature stands (Table 3), probably near young stands or in openings where low vegetation has developed.

Peromyscus.—Widespread throughout southern forests are several species of *Peromyscus*. They feed on a variety of vegetative matter including seed and berries, and some insects and other invertebrates (Hall 1981). Several species have somewhat limited range in the South. The deer mouse, a transcontinental northern species, extends into the northern portion of the South,

There are several species of *Peromyscus* spp., which are widespread throughout the South *(H. Williamson)*.

from Virginia south into Georgia and westerly through Arkansas and Oklahoma. It is mostly associated with grass and forb vegetation in dry uplands (Choate et al. 1994). The range of Attwateri's mouse is from central Texas northeast through Oklahoma and easterly through most of northern Arkansas. General habitat of this species with a tufted tail tip is dry rocky outcrops and cedar glades of the Arkansas mountains. In Florida and parts of adjoining states is the old field mouse. It's range is mostly south of the white-footed mouse and apparently supplants it in that region. The old field mouse is usually associated with herbaceous vegetation in dry habitat, such as fallow fields and roadsides. In peninsular Florida is the Florida mouse whose range is mostly south of the old field mouse.

Other *Peromyscus* have wide distribution in the South. The white-footed mouse, a species of eastern U. S., occurs throughout the region except for southern Alabama, Georgia, and South Carolina, and all of Florida. The cotton mouse occupies all of the region, except for an area of eastern Tennessee, most of Virginia, and the northern portion of South Carolina (Hall 1981). These 2 species are probably the most abundant small mammal in southern forests. They are found in forested and sometimes somewhat open areas, often associated with woods' structure such as rocks, down logs, stumps, and logging slash. They are regular and very abundant in a wide variety of different stand types throughout the region from hardwoods of the eastern mountains, to coastal plain pine stands, to bottomland hardwoods. They inhabit stands of all ages including regeneration, young brushy, and mature (Tables 1,2,3). But white-footed and cotton mice are particularly prominent in mature stands. For example, one or the other was the most commonly captured species in 9 of the 13 mature stands comprising Table 3 and were the second most commonly captured species in 2 of the other 4 stands.

There is some question about the taxonomic integrity of the white-footed and cotton mouse where their ranges overlap. Conclusions from early studies were that hybridization did occur but isolation mechanisms were generally effective (McCarley 1954). The cotton mouse was slightly larger and inhabited moist habitat, whereas habitat of the white-footed mouse was dry uplands. But Lowery (1974) concluded that the inverse of the normal habitat relationship occurred in places in Louisiana. They are difficult to differentiate in the field and captures represent a continuum of sizes. Also, only 1 of the species is identified in almost all small mammal studies (Tables 1,2,3,).

The strikingly-colored golden mouse occurs throughout the South except the tip of Florida and coastal Louisiana and Texas (Hall 1981). It is somewhat arboreal, foraging and nesting in trees. Habitat of this species is generally described as forested uplands or lowlands, usually with substantial understory vegetation such as blackberry or cane thickets, or dense vines such as honeysuckle or grape (Sealander and Heidt 1990). The species is found in a variety of pine and hardwood stands and appears to first invade forest stands at the young brushy stage, becoming more prevalent as stands age (Tables 1,2,3). They were the most common species in a north Louisiana pine forest (Shadowen 1963).

The grizzled-appearing hispid cotton rat is found throughout the region except along the northern perimeter of Virginia and Kentucky, and the eastern mountains (Hall 1981). It is active diurnally. The species is associated with grass/forb and shrubby vegetation and usually is very abundant wherever that type of habitat occurs. Goertz (1973) sampled a number of different habitats in northern Louisiana. Cotton rats were captured in cultivated grasslands, broomsedge, broomsedge pond edge, and urban shrub and vines; all grass/forb or shrubby habitat. At high densities cotton rats can cause damage to cultivated crops.

The Hispid cotton rat quickly invades regeneration stands of seedlings and dense low vegetation (Table 1). It is consistently the most abundant of all species in young dense brushy stands throughout the South (Table 2). As stands develop and canopies shade out understory vegetation, cotton rat numbers dwindle in response to the changing habitat suitability (Table 3).

The eastern woodrat, commonly called pack rat because of it's propensity to gather and cache natural and man-made objects, is distributed throughout the region, except for an area along the east coast covering most of Virginia, North Carolina, and central South Carolina; and also the tip of Florida (Hall 1981). It is a nocturnal forager which constructs a large nest or den in trees or on the ground. Nests often are constructed around some kind of physical structure such as an uprooted tree, stump, rocky outcrop, abandoned barn, or human refuse. It feeds mostly on vegetative matter, including mushrooms, twigs, and seeds and berries. Oak acorns are a conspicuous part of their diet. It is found in a variety of different stand types and ages (Tables 1,2,3), but ideal habitat seems to be riparian forests. In the Coastal Plain of eastern Texas, woodrats inhabit a variety of different habitats, including an upland mature pine-hardwood and a young pine plantation, particularly where there were windrows of logging debris (Fleet and Dickson 1984). Also they inhabit mesic streamside zones (Dickson and Williamson 1988), and quickly invade harvested bottomland hardwood sites (Dickson et al. unpublished data). In Mississippi, woodrats were captured only in bayheads, not in upland pine stands (Wolfe and Lohoefener 1983).

Several small microtine rodents occupy southern forests, mostly in the northern portion of the region. These species feed mostly on vegetation, including bark and roots. They develop an extensive runway system above ground in vegetation thick enough to conceal them from predators and also an underground burrow system. Population densities often fluctuate widely.

Gapper's red-backed mouse, found throughout Canada and the northern U.S., extends into the South along the eastern mountains (Hall 1981). The meadow vole is found in the northeast portion of the region into central Georgia. The rock vole occurs throughout northeastern Canada and its range extends southwesterly into the South along the eastern mountains. A species normally associated with midwestern prairies, the prairie vole, extends into the region as far south as central Arkansas and northern Alabama (Hall 1981). In the early part of this century several were captured in the prairies in the vicinity of the Texas/ Louisiana border (Lowery 1974), but none have been found in recent decades. The pine vole occurs throughout the eastern U.S. except along the southern coast, most of Florida, and coastal North Carolina (Hall 1981). The southern bog lemming, a species of northeastern North America, extends into the South along the eastern mountains (Hall 1981).

The meadow jumping mouse is a species of northern North America; but its range extends into the southeast as far south as lower Alabama (Hall 1981). The woodland jumping mouse, a species of northeastern Canada and the U.S., occurs along the eastern mountains into the South. Both species hibernate during winter. Main foods are grass seed, fruits, insects, and fungi. The meadow jumping mouse is associated with herbaceous cover and seems to be especially abundant in dense grass/forb fields in moist habitat such as pond edges and marshes (Choate et al. 1994). The woodland jumping mouse appears to be associated more with forest and forest-field edge than the meadow jumping mouse.

Exotics.—Three species of old world rats and mice; the black rat, Norway rat, and house mouse, have been introduced into the region and occur throughout, usually in association with humans and their habitations, but also elsewhere. All 3 species originated in Asia, and came to North America on ships with early European settlers (Choate et al. 1994). All have naked tails with prominent annulations (Lowery 1974). They have caused immense economic loss from their consumption and damage to human foods.

The house mouse, about the size of a *Peromyscus*, is widespread throughout. They are common in human habitations but feral populations exist also, and populations can reach very high densities (Lowery 1974). They are captured fairly regularly in a variety of young open and brushy forest stands in early developmental stages (Tables 1,2) but not in mature stands (Table 3).

The Norway rat, about the size of a woodrat, is widespread in the South around human habitations and elsewhere, such as rice and cane fields. In Louisiana, Goertz and Long (1973) found them in 5 habitats, most frequently in a zoological park and in occupied urban buildings. The black rat is similar in size and appearance to the Norway rat and is found throughout the South except the northern central portion. It usually inhabits upper parts of buildings, hence its name, roof rat. In northern Louisiana they were found in 6 habitats, most commonly in rural barns with livestock and in areas overgrown with vines (Goertz and Long 1973). Both of these larger species are often associated with human refuse and have been vectors in the transmission of diseases responsible for substantial human mortality in the past in Europe and in places in the United States.

SMALL MAMMALS AND FOREST STANDS

Some small mammal species, such as *Peromyscus*, are widespread throughout the region, occurring in a wide variety of stand habitat types and stages of development. Others, such as the pocket gophers on the islands of Georgia, are restrictive in range. And many of the uncommon species in the South are northern and western species that have only limited range extensions into the South.

Generally, small mammals of southern forests are associated with and respond positively to physical structure such as down logs, debris, and stumps; and to productivity of vegetation close to the ground. Several studies have analyzed relationships of small mammal communities and stand development (Tables 1,2,3). There is a general succession of species in developing forest stands, particularly in stands that are changing rapidly, such as recently regenerated stands. Small mammals quickly invade recently harvested pine and hardwood stands and usually are at their highest abundance in young, rapidly developing stands. In a bottomland hardwood forest in eastern Texas, more than 500 individual animals were captured the first winter after harvesting, even before vegetative growth developed (Dickson et al. unpublished data). And other studies have documented abundant small mammals in very young pine plantations (Atkeson and Johnson 1979), and young northern hardwood stands (Healy and Brooks 1988). Total captures generally were negatively correlated with indicators of mature forest such as tree basal area, and positively correlated with density of low vegetation. *Peromyscus* spp. usually are the earliest invader. *P. gossypinus* or *P. leucopus* were the most abundant small mammal in 3 of 4 very young stands (Table 1). In eastern Texas, harvested bottomland sites were quickly invaded by cotton mice, marsh rice rats, and eastern woodrats.

Relative abundance of small mammals remains very high in young developing stands with dense grass, forbs, and shrubs, and their seeds and fruit. Abundant small mammals have been documented in pine plantations in North Carolina (Mitchell 1995), Georgia (Atkeson and Johnson 1979), and eastern Texas (Fleet and Dickson 1984); and in bottomland hardwoods (Dickson et al. unpublished data).

But small mammal community composition changes quickly in rapidly developing regeneration stands. In the bottomland hardwood study, after the first vegetative growing season (year 2) cotton mice and rice rats, the most abundant species the first year, decreased in captures (Dickson et al. unpublished data). But cotton rats and fulvous harvest mice invaded the clearcuts in response to the development of low, dense vegetation. A somewhat similar situation occurred with small mammal communities in young pine plantations in Georgia (Atkeson and Johnson 1979). White-footed mice quickly invaded pine plantations and were the most abundant small mammal the first year, but by the second year they were mostly supplanted by cotton rats. The small mammal community had shifted from domination by granivores/omnivores to a predominance of herbivores.

As young stands age, their canopies close, and herbaceous and shrubby vegetation is shaded out at about age 7 to 10, habitat suitability for small mammals decreases and small mammal populations decrease. In a series of pine plantations in Georgia (Atkeson and Johnson 1979), captures declined somewhat by planta-

Small mammals, such as this marsh rice rat (above left), are quickly attracted to debris from harvesting (above right), and small mammal populations flourish in the dense vegetative growth which follows (below) *(H. Williamson)*.

tion age 5, but decreased further by age 7 as the pine canopies closed despite increased captures of woodland species. By year fifteen, plantations supported very few small mammals. A similar overview is concluded from trapping in pine plantations in North Carolina (Mitchell et al. 1995). There were more than 3 times the number of small mammals and significantly more species captured in open young pine plantations as were captured in middle-aged closed canopied stands.

Mature forest stands with closed canopies and little herbaceous vegetation usually support a relatively low density of small mammals. In eastern Texas there were about 3 times the number of captures of small mammals in a young clearcut as an adjacent second growth pine-hardwood stand and a similar relationship in Mississippi, where there were abundant small mammals in bedded and herbicided young pine plantations, but virtually none in a mature pine-hardwood forest (Perkins et al. 1989). But openings created by tree fall in mature stands probably attract and benefit small mammals.

Other studies have documented and contrasted small mammal communities in different habitat types. In the Coastal Plain of North Carolina (Mitchell et al. 1995), small mammal abundance and diversity was higher in tall pocosins than in closed-canopy pine plantations, but lower than that in young open pine plantations. In the Coastal Plain of Mississippi more small mammals were captured in hardwood bayheads than in upland longleaf-slash pine stands which were grazed and burned (Wolfe and Lohoefener 1983). In an upland hardwood region of eastern Tennessee, small mammal abundance was higher in pine plantations than rights-of-way (ROW), but lower in a mature oak-hickory forest than ROW's (Johnson et al. 1979).

In a comparison of 3 second-growth forest types in Tennessee, by far the most small mammals were captured in oak-hickory stands, followed by pine stands and chestnut oak stands (Dueser and Shugart 1978). The white-footed mouse was the most frequently captured small mammal, followed by the eastern chipmunk, short-tailed shrew, and golden mouse. In another study in eastern Tennessee (Johnson et al. 1979), small mammal diversity was higher in a pine plantation with a honeysuckle understory than in an oak-hickory forest.

In laurel oak floodplain stands in the Georgia Piedmont, the cotton mouse, golden mouse, short-tailed shrew, woodrat, house mouse, rice rat, and southeastern shrew were found in decreasing order of abundance (Boyd 1976).

MANAGEMENT

Generally, silvicultural activities in which trees are harvested or natural events which create forest openings, which increase ground debris, grass and forbs, and brushy vegetation favor small mammal populations. Small mammals are attracted quickly to recently harvested stands of different types; attracted to the cover and food produced by logging debris and the lush vegetation growth that rapidly follows. In eastern Texas, capture rates were negatively associated with variables reflective of mature forest habitat (leaf ground cover, and basal area of shrubs and trees) and were positively correlated with down woody material and measures of low vegetation. The importance of herbaceous cover to small mammal communities also has been demonstrated elsewhere (for example, Dueser and Shugart 1978, Mitchell et al. 1995). Also, thinning of dense forest stands and the resulting flush of low vegetation growth should benefit small mammals. In North Carolina, more small mammals and a more diverse community was found in thinned pine plantations than in unthinned plantations (Mitchell et al. 1995).

In addition, particular measures may be required for species of concern. Special habitat may need to be protected or managed, and specific species management measures may be necessary.

CHAPTER 27

Bats

Michael J. Harvey
Tennessee Technological University, Cookeville, TN

David A. Saugey
U.S. Forest Service
Ouachita National Forest, Hot Springs, AR

Bats are an important component of southern forest ecosystems. The millions of bats present in southern forests are primarily insectivorous and consume enormous numbers of insects. Twenty species of bats occupy the southeastern United States. Two of these (Jamaican fruit-eating bat, *Artibeus jamaicensis*; Pallas' mastiff bat, *Molossus molossus*) occur only in limited numbers in Florida Keys and will not be covered. The other 18 species inhabit southern forests, although some of their ranges are limited to relatively small geographic areas (Harvey et al. 1999).

Southern forest bats can be lumped into 2 general groups, cave bats and non-cave bats, or tree bats. Cave bats usually inhabit caves during all or part of the year, while non-cave species seldom enter caves. Some species inhabit caves in parts of their range, while in other parts they do not. Ten southern forest species are considered to be cave bats, while the remaining 8 are non-cave species.

Three southern forest cave bat species—the gray bat, the Indiana bat, and Townsend's big-eared bat—are listed as endangered (in danger of extinction throughout all or a significant portion of their range), by the U.S. Fish and Wildlife Service, as well as by most state wildlife agencies. The gray bat and Indiana bat are considered endangered throughout their entire ranges, while only the 2 easternmost subspecies of Townsend's big-eared bat presently are listed as endangered. These are the Ozark big-eared bat and the Virginia big-eared bat.

Three additional southern forest cave bat species have been under review for possible listing as endangered or threatened. These are the southeastern bat, the eastern small-footed bat, and Rafinesque's big-eared bat (Harvey et al. 1999). In addition, Wagner's mastiff bat, a non-cave species found in the United States only in southern Florida, also has been considered for endangered or threatened status (Harvey at al. 1999). Because of recent changes in the federal listing process, the 4 species formerly under review for possible listing as endangered or threatened, are now considered to be of special concern (Bat Conservation International 1999).

Although not listed as endangered or threatened by the U.S. Fish and Wildlife Service, several of the remaining 11 southern forest bat species (especially cave bat species) appear to be declining in numbers.

Hibernation is a critical time of year for bats. Abandoned mines and natural caves provide solitude and protection from the elements for many species. Because virtually all bats of the southeast are insectivorous, they are dependent upon stored fat for energy through the winter months when insect foods are not available. Caves and gated abandoned mines provide undisturbed habitat where bats may overwinter or birth young *(D. Saugey, US Forest Service)*.

Bats have a relatively low rate of reproduction. Most female bats produce only 1 offspring per year, although some species give birth to 3 or 4 babies at a time. Most United States bats breed in autumn, and the females store sperm until the following spring when fertilization takes place. The gestation period lasts only a few weeks, and pups are born in May or June. They develop rapidly, and most are able to fly within 3 to 5 weeks after birth. Bats live relatively long lives for such small animals, some as long as 30 years.

Drastic reductions in bat populations have occurred during recent years in the United States and worldwide (Tuttle 1995). Human disturbance to hibernation and maternity colonies is a major factor in the decline of many bat species. Even well-meaning individuals such as spelunkers (cave explorers) and biologists may cause these disturbances. Hibernating bats arouse from hibernation when disturbed by people entering their caves. When aroused, they use up precious winter fat needed to support them until they feed on insects later in spring. A single arousal probably costs a bat as much energy as it would normally expend in 2 to 3 weeks of hibernation, and frequent arousal may result in starvation. Disturbance to summer maternity colonies is also extremely detrimental. Maternity colonies will not tolerate disturbance, especially when flightless newborn young are present. Baby bats may be dropped or abandoned by parents.

Several animals, including owls, hawks, raccoons, skunks, and snakes prey on bats, yet relatively few animals consume bats as a regular part of their diet. Man seems to be the only animal having significant impact on bat populations. Adverse human impacts include habitat destruction, direct killing, vandalism, disturbance of hibernating and maternity colonies, and the use of pesticides and other chemical toxicants on their food - insects.

Bats, like many other mammals, can contract and transmit rabies, as well as other diseases. Although rabies has been found in many species of bats in the United States, it is relatively uncommon. Rabid bats seldom are aggressive. However, because bats can transmit rabies, they should not be handled, particularly for bats found on the ground, since they may be unhealthy (Brass 1994).

All 18 species of southern forest bats are dependent, to some degree, on forests for shelter, roost sites, and/or foraging areas. Although much is known concerning forest bat species composition, roosting behavior, and habitat use, there is an overall paucity of information concerning specific needs of each bat species. There is much left to be learned concerning how forests should be managed to achieve silvicultural goals, while at the same time providing the best possible habitat for bats as well as for other forest-dwelling wildlife species (Marcot 1996, Lacki 1996).

In the past decade the use of miniature radio transmitters attached to bats began to provide insight into habitat preference, foraging activities, and movements, that were difficult to obtain just a few years earlier using conventional means (mist nets/wing bands) (Kunz 1988). Although a number of published studies are available from across the country regarding the use of forested habitats by bats, additional research in the South will have to be conducted with bats before definitive relationships between forest structure and species of bats are truly known. Many of the available studies have been conducted in areas where the terrain, forest types, elevation, rainfall, etc., are very different from those present in southern forests, and although generalities may be drawn from the evidence presented, specific application may not be plausible (Barclay and Brigham 1996). For this reason, many of the comments regarding management activities and their impacts on bats and the specific relationships of bats in southern forests are general in nature because there is a paucity of forest management information.

An endangered gray bat with attached radio transmitter. Radiotelemetry has allowed us to learn about bat movements and habitat use *(D. Saugey, US Forest Service).*

Timber management (harvest and post-harvest silvicultural activities) is probably the single most important activity on southern forest lands that has the potential to impact bats and their habits (Pierson 1998, Barclay and Brigham 1996). Timber harvest and follow-up activities typically occur simultaneously at a number of locations on managed forests. The resulting habitat matrix consists of stands of trees of different ages, types and heights—a diverse and dynamic ecosystem where change is constant. Areas exempted from management activities such as wilderness or areas of special designation provide different, older habitat.

Timber harvests affect bat habitat significantly. The following methods are basic types of timber harvests in southern forests and an assessment of their effects on bat habitat. Use of the clearcut harvest method on federal land has declined in recent years and has been completely halted on some national forests. However, extensive clearcutting during the 1960's and 1970's has resulted in vast stands of even- aged timber which may not be suitable for use by bats, particularly bole and cavity users, since these stands do not provide the cavities and bark characteristics preferred by these niche users (Pierson 1998).

This harvest method will usually eliminate roosting opportunities for bats for a number of years until replacement trees of suitable size and species are again available. Use of clearcut stands for roosting will likely occur as follows: foliage roosting species will return first as trees attain suitable height and crown development; bole roosting species will follow as tree diameters increase and bark characteristics occur that allow for roosting beneath sloughing bark. Cavity roosting species may never be able to use young stands if the rotation age for harvest occurs at a frequency that precludes trees reaching a stage where cavities develop. Preharvest considerations beneficial to bats (and many other species of wildlife) include the retention of all existing cavity trees and snags, creation of large snags where none exist naturally (by chemical injection or

Cavity trees, particularly hardwoods, provide important refugia from harsh environmental conditions and places to rear young with some degree of protection. A silver-haired bat flew from a roost beneath peeling shortleaf pine bark and entered this cavity when a winter storm brought sleet and snow *(D. Saugey, US Forest Service)*.

Loss of old cavity trees probably has negatively affected bats. This pure pine habitat fragment in what was once a mixed hardwood-pine ecosystem has little to offer southeastern bats *(D. Saugey, US Forest Service)*.

mechanical girdling), and the designation of significant streamside zones where the presence of hardwoods affords an opportunity to manage for cavity development and retention (Ouachita National Forest 1990).

Clearcuts increase opportunities for foraging by bats. The flush of herbaceous vegetation growth where trees once shaded the ground results in increased insect populations, which provide significant food sources for various species of bats. The interior of clearcuts may be avoided; bats prefer to forage along forest edges, which offer some protection from predators such as owls (Krusic et al. 1996, Barclay and Brigham 1998).

Seedtree and shelterwood harvests open the harvested stand, which creates good foraging opportunities for bats by reducing clutter within the stand. Retention of habitat components important to bats, as in the clearcut, would apply in these harvest methods as well.

If tree species are retained that are known to be cavity prone, then this suitable habitat component can be grown with the stand of desirable crop trees to ensure it is available to bats in the distant future. However, if during harvest, cavity prone trees are not retained, then foraging and roosting habitat for foliage and bole roosting species may be provided, but not cavity trees for cavity roosting bats.

The planning and execution of cultural treatments is the second most important activity that has the potential to dramatically and immediately impact bats and their habitats, with effects lasting for decades. It is typically during cultural activities when snags and cavity trees, both very important habitat components for bats, are eliminated from the harvested stand. Cultural treatments are often performed by contractors who may treat large acreages. It is extremely important that the planned retention of habitat components is conveyed verbally and in contract specifications to ensure their retention. Failure to do so will mean selecting against cavity roosting species and may result in local extirpation of these bats due to a lack of suitable habitat which, from a cumulative perspective, may result in loss of viability for some forest populations (Nietro et al. 1985, Kulhavy and Conner 1986).

Fire has been a natural force in southern forest ecosystems for a long time. Some of the effects of fire on bats and their habitats are beneficial while others may be detrimental. Beneficial aspects would include the reduction of leaf litter, removal of small understory and midstory trees and shrubs (vegetative clutter—as it relates to foraging), and regeneration of herbaceous plants. The openings created by the removal of small shrubs and trees allow for additional sunlight on the forest floor, growth of herbaceous ground cover, and enhanced insect populations which are potential food sources for bats. The gaps created in the forest canopy reduce the clutter beneath the forest canopy, which may provide additional areas for foraging.

Cavities provide important structural habitat components, particularly for forest colonial bats. Tree wounds resulting from fires on cavity-prone trees may initiate the process of cavity development in living trees, which ultimately may be used by bats. In addition, abandoned woodpecker cavities in snags created by fire may provide additional cavity roosts for small groups and individual bats, but snags used by bats may be felled by fire if their bases burn through, resulting in the loss of cavities or roosting sites under exfoliating bark. More rarely, living cavity trees may be killed by very intense fire. However, prescribed fires are usually of low intensity.

Recent findings indicate some woodland tree dwelling bat species may hibernate in a variety of locations, including leaf litter, in woody debris, and within rock crevices (Barclay and Brigham 1996). Others hibernate beneath exfoliating bark and within cavities of dead and living trees. Prescribed fire would appear to jeopardize bats hibernating on the ground during winter when they are in torpor and slow to arouse. However, anecdotal observations of bat activity in prescribed burns on the Ouachita National Forest and elsewhere suggest bats rarely succumb to prescribed fire. During prescribed burns, red bats often have been observed lying on top of the leaf litter, flapping their wings in an attempt to raise body temperature in order to fly. These bats usually exhibited this behavior long before fire was near, apparently aroused by the scent of smoke (Moorman et al. 1999, Saugey et al. 1989). Radiotelemetry of red bats confirmed the use of mixed pine-hardwood leaf litter as a hibernation site where the red color of this bat's fur blended with the colors of cast deciduous leaves (Saugey et al. 1998). Although on occasion bats may be killed by prescribed fire, the positive ecological aspects of burning outweigh the direct mortality, which probably is insignificant.

Streamside zones are usually retained and provide forested habitat along streams. These zones often contain cavity trees or potential cavity trees, or sometimes recently dead trees with loose bark, both of which serve as roost sites.

Ponds located in forested and open habitat conditions provide an extremely important resource for forest bats. Most average less than 1 acre in size and many are constructed along ridgetops and other locations within habitats where water is scarce. They serve not only as an important source of drinking water for bats, but also provide breeding sites and act as attractants for insects which are eaten by bats. They also provide gaps in the forest canopy where bats can fly easily (Wilhide et al. 1998).

SPECIES ACCOUNTS

Information in the following species accounts was taken from Harvey et al. (1999), and does not contain additional citations. Because of the brief and general nature of the accounts, the authors of that publication did not cite or reference the numerous authors and publications from which they obtained much of the information presented in the accounts.

Gray Bat (*Myotis grisescens*) — Endangered

Gray bats weigh 0.3 - 0.4 ounce and have a wingspan of 11-12 inches. Distribution in the South includes mainly the cave regions of Alabama, Arkansas, Kentucky, and Tennessee, but a few occur in northwestern Florida, western Georgia, northeastern Oklahoma, northeastern Mississippi, western Virginia, and western North Carolina. Distribution within the range was always patchy, but populations have become more fragmented and isolated over the past 3 decades.

The gray bat population was estimated to be about 2,250,000 in 1970; however, in 1976 a census of 22 important colonies in Alabama and Tennessee revealed an average decline of more than 50%. Due to protective measures taken at high priority colony sites in the late 1970s and throughout the 1980s, declines at those sites have been arrested and those populations are now stable or increasing. The present population is estimated to number over 1,500,000. Because about 95% of these bats hibernate in only 10 caves, 2 in Tennessee, 3 in Missouri, 3 in Arkansas, and 1 each in Alabama and Kentucky, gray bats are extremely vulnerable to destruction.

Gray bats are cave residents year-round, but usually occupy different caves in summer and winter. Few have been found roosting outside caves. They hibernate primarily in deep vertical caves with large rooms acting as cold-air traps (42-52°F). In summer, females form maternity colonies of a few hundred to many thousands of individuals, often in large caves containing streams. Maternity colonies occur in caves that, because of their configuration, trap warm air (58-77°F) or provide restricted rooms or domed ceilings capable of trapping body heat from bat clusters. Males and non-reproductive females form bachelor colonies in summer. Because of their specific habitat requirements, fewer than 5% of available caves are suitable for gray bats.

Gray bats primarily forage over water of rivers and lakes. Moths, beetles, flies, mosquitos, mayflies, and other insects are important in their diet. Mating occurs in September and October. Females hibernate immediately after mating, followed by males. Females store sperm through winter and become pregnant after emerging from hibernation. One baby is born, in late May or early June, and begins to fly within 20-25 days of birth. Lifespan may exceed 14-15 years.

Gray bat populations are concentrated in only a few caves, most of which are located in forested areas. These caves and adjacent forest constitute critical habitat for the species. Therefore, it is recommended that management activities adjacent to these caves be designed to maintain or enhance gray bat habitat within a 0.5 mile zone of gray bat caves.

Although there is limited information available, forests are apparently important to gray bats. When gray bats emerge from their caves to forage, they usually fly in the protection of forest canopy en route to rivers or reservoirs. They often go considerably out of their way in order to use forest cover. Especially during weather extremes, such as cold periods in spring, gray bats may forage in forested areas near their caves, and newly volant gray bats are poor fliers and often spend several nights foraging in forested areas near their caves before venturing farther away. Forest cover also provides convenient resting sites and protection from predators and wind.

Indiana Bat (*Myotis sodalis*) — Endangered

Indiana bats weigh about 0.3 ounce and have a wingspan of 10-11 inches. Distribution in the South includes Kentucky, Tennessee, northern Arkansas, eastern Oklahoma, western Virginia, eastern Alabama, western Georgia, northwestern Florida, and western North Carolina. Distribution is associated with major cave regions and areas north of cave regions, such as parts of Iowa, Illinois, Indiana, Ohio, and Michigan. The present total population is estimated at fewer than 400,000 with more than 85% hibernating at only 9 locations—2 caves and a mine in Missouri, 3 caves in Indiana, and 3 caves in Kentucky. This species continues to decline, despite protection and recovery efforts. Estimates at major hibernacula indicated a 35% population decline from 1983 -1989.

Indiana bats usually hibernate in large dense clusters of up to several thousand individuals in sections of the hibernation cave where temperatures average 38-43°F and with relative humidities of 66-95%. They hibernate from October to April, depending on climatic conditions. Females depart hibernation caves before males and arrive at summer maternity roosts in mid-May. Summer roosts are usually located under exfoliating bark of dead trees or, less frequently, in cavities. The summer roost of adult males often is near maternity roosts, but where most spend the day is unknown. Others remain near the hibernaculum, and a few males are found in caves during summer. Between early August and mid-September, Indiana bats arrive near their hibernation caves and engage in swarming and mating activity. Swarming at cave entrances continues into mid-to-late October. During this time, fat reserves are built up for hibernation.

Females eat soft-bodied insects when pregnant, moths when lactating, and moths, beetles, and hard-bodied insects after lactation. Males also eat a variety of insects. One baby is born, in June, and is raised under loose tree bark, primarily in wooded, streamside habitat. Lifespans of nearly 14 years have been documented.

Indiana bat hibernating populations are concentrated in only a few caves, most of which are located in forested areas, and these caves and adjacent forested areas constitute critical habitat for the species. Therefore, it is recommended that management activities within a 0.5 mile buffer zone of Indiana bat caves and within 0.5 mile of known Indiana bat summer non-cave roost sites be designed to maintain or enhance Indiana bat habitat.

Since Indiana bats may roost during summer in tree cavities or under the exfoliating bark of snags or live shagbark hickories, these should be conserved in areas where Indiana bats occur.

Townsend's Big-eared Bat
(*Corynorhinus townsendii*) — Endangered

Townsend's big-eared bats weigh 0.3-0.5 ounce and have a wingspan of 12-13 inches. Distribution in the South consists of 2 small, isolated populations—the Virginia big-eared bat, found in eastern Kentucky, western Virginia, eastern West Virginia, and western North Carolina; the Ozark big-eared bat is found in eastern Oklahoma and northwestern Arkansas. Only these 2 subspecies are listed as endangered; additional populations occur in the West. The total Virginia big-eared bat population numbers about 15,000, while only about 1,700 Ozark big-eared bats are known to exist.

These bats hibernate in caves or mines where the temperature is 54°F or less, but usually above freezing.

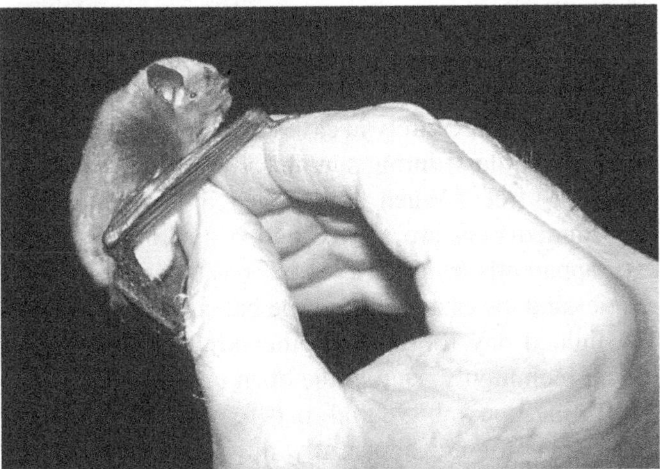

Southeastern bat, a species of concern. Above: Orange color phase. Top: Hibernating cluster of southeastern bats from an abandoned mine in the Ouachita Mountains. This species, which once used cavities of large trees, now frequently uses man-made structures. Maternity colonies outside of Florida are rarely encountered and the species seems to have a spotty distribution, often closely associated with cave regions *(D. Saugey, US Forest Service)*.

Hibernation sites in caves often are near entrances in well-ventilated areas. If temperatures near entrances become extreme, they move to more thermally stable parts of the cave. They hibernate in clusters of a few to more than 100 individuals. During hibernation, the long ears may be erect or coiled. Solitary bats sometimes hang by only 1 foot. Maternity colonies usually are located in relatively warm parts of caves. During the maternity period, males apparently are solitary. Where most males spend the summer is unknown. No long-distance migrations are known. Like many other bats, they return year after year to the same roost sites.

Townsend's big-eared bats are believed to feed entirely on moths. Mating begins in autumn and continues into winter, sperm are stored during winter, and fertilization occurs shortly after arousal from hibernation. One baby is born, in June. Bat babies are large at birth, weighing nearly 25% as much as their mother. They can fly in 2.5-3 weeks and are weaned by 6 weeks. Lifespan may be 16 or more years.

Virginia and Ozark big-eared bat populations are concentrated in only a few caves, most of which are located in forested areas. These caves and adjacent forest constitute critical habitat for the species. Therefore, it is recommended that management activities adjacent to these caves be designed to maintain or enhance Townsend's big-eared bat habitat within a 0.5 mile zone of these caves.

Southeastern Bat (*Myotis austroriparius*) — Special Concern

Southeastern bats weigh 0.2-0.3 ounce and have a wingspan of 10-11 inches. Distribution in the South includes Kentucky, Tennessee, Louisiana, Mississippi, Alabama, Georgia, South Carolina, northern Florida, southeastern North Carolina, southern Arkansas, northeastern Texas, and southeastern Oklahoma.

Caves are favorite roosting sites, although buildings and other shelters sometimes are used. Maternity colonies comprised of thousands of individuals inhabit caves. Throughout much of the South, these bats reside in buildings and hollow trees, but in the northern part of their range they roost primarily in caves. In winter, they leave the maternity caves and take up residence in small groups at outdoor sites.

Predators include opossums, snakes, and owls, but by destruction of roosting sites and killing of these bats, humans are the major threat to the species. Southeastern bats usually are associated with bodies of water, over which they feed. They forage low, close to the water's surface. Various insects are consumed. Mating time is unknown, but about 90% of pregnant females bear twins, in late April or mid-May. The birth of twins is unique to their genus in the United States; all others usually produce only one baby. Clusters of babies often are separate from adult females during the day. Young bats can fly when 5-6 weeks old. Although once common, populations of the southeastern bat have decreased significantly.

Eastern Small-footed Bat (*Myotis leibii*) — Special Concern

Eastern small-footed bats weigh about 0.1 ounce and have a wingspan of 8-10 inches. Distribution in the South includes Kentucky, Tennessee, northern Arkansas, eastern Oklahoma, western Virginia, western North Carolina, northern Alabama, and northern Georgia. This is one of the smallest bats in the United States. It is uncommon throughout most of its range.

Eastern small-footed bats hibernate in caves or mines and are among the hardiest of cave bats. Their tolerance for cold, relatively dry places for hibernation is remarkable for such a small bat. They are among the last bats to enter caves in autumn and often hibernate near cave or mine entrances where temperatures drop below freezing and humidity is relatively low. Several have been found hibernating in cracks in cave floors and under rock slabs in quarries and elsewhere. In summer, they often inhabit buildings and caves; a small summer colony was found behind a sliding door of a barn. Nursery colonies of up to 20 bats in buildings have been reported. They often fly repeated patterns within 3 feet of the floor of a cave or crevice, hang up on the wall, and then fly again.

Eastern small-footed bats emerge to forage shortly after sunset, and fly slowly and erratically, usually 3-10 feet above the ground. Apparently, they fill their stomachs within an hour. They consume flies, mosquitos, true bugs, beetles, ants, and other insects. One baby is born, in late spring or early summer. Lifespan is unknown.

Rafinesque's Big-eared Bat (*Corynorhinus rafinesquii*) — Special Concern

Rafinesque's big-eared bats weigh 0.3-0.5 ounce and have a wingspan of 10-12 inches. Distribution includes all of the South, except northwestern Arkansas and northern Virginia. This species is uncommon over most of its range, and may be the least known of all bats in the South. In the northern part of its range, it hibernates in caves, mines, or similar habitats, including cisterns and wells. In contrast, Rafinesque's big-eared bats usually are not found in caves during winter in the more southern parts of their range. Maternity colonies consist of a few to several dozen adults. They usually are found in abandoned buildings, sometimes in rather well-lighted areas and more rarely in caves and mines. Males generally are solitary during summer, roosting in buildings or hollow trees. When approached in summer, these bats immediately are alerted and begin to wave their ears, apparently trying to keep track of the intruder. This species and the eastern pipistrelle bat choose more open and lighted day roosts than other kinds of bats. Both species commonly hang in the open in plain sight.

A cluster of Rafinesque's big-eared bats hibernating in an abandoned water well. Abandoned water wells and cisterns provide limited, cave-like, environmentally-stable hibernation sites in regions where caves and abandoned mines are not available *(D. Saugey, US Forest Service)*.

Rafinesque's big-eared bats emerge late in the evening to forage; apparently they do not forage at twilight. Their flight is agile. Moths and other night-flying insects are eaten. One baby is born, in late May or early June in the northern part of the range and about mid-May in the South. The young shed their milk teeth in mid-July and reach adult size by August or early September.

Wagner's Mastiff Bat (*Eumops glaucinus*) — Special Concern

Wagner's Mastiff bats weigh 1.1-1.7 ounces and have a wingspan of about 20 inches. Distribution within the United States includes only southern Florida, where it is apparently rare.

Although these bats are known to occur in cities as well as in forested areas, foraging and roosting habits and long-term requirements are unknown. In Florida, favorite daytime roosts are under the shingles of Spanish-tile roofs, but some have been found in shafts of leaves of royal palms, in low shrubbery, in places where there are dense tropical flowers and shrubs. One colony was in a cavity in a longleaf pine! At any time during the year, juveniles, adult males, and adult females may occur in the same roost. Unlike most other free-tailed bats, which need to drop 25 or more feet from a roost before they can fly, Wagner's Mastiff bat can take flight from horizontal surfaces.

These bats leave their roost after dark and seldom fly below 30 feet. Their loud, piercing calls can be heard for some distance, and once a person recognizes this call, it can easily be differentiated from other nighttime sounds. They do not migrate. The diet includes beetles, flies, mosquitos, true bugs, moths, and other insects. One baby is born, during summer.

Little Brown Bat (*Myotis lucifugus*)

Little brown bats weigh 0.3-0.5 ounce and have a wingspan of 9-11 inches. Distribution in the South includes Tennessee, Virginia, Kentucky, eastern Oklahoma, northwestern Arkansas, western North Carolina, northern Alabama, and northern Georgia. This species is one of the most common bats throughout much of the northern United States and Canada, but is scarce or only locally common in the South.

The little brown bat usually hibernates in caves and mines. During summer, it often inhabits buildings, usually rather hot attics, where females form nursery colonies of hundreds or even thousands of individuals. Where most males spend the summer is unknown, but they likely are solitary and scattered in a variety of roost types. Colonies usually are close to a lake or stream.

This species seems to prefer to forage over water, but also forages among trees in rather open areas. When foraging, it may repeat a hunting pattern around houses or trees. They eat insects, including gnats, crane flies, beetles, wasps, and moths. Insects usually are captured with a wing tip, immediately transferred into a scoop formed by the forwardly curled tail and interfemoral membrane, and then grasped with the teeth. Mating occurs in autumn, but also may occur during the hibernation period. One baby is born, in May, June, or early July. When the mother is at rest during the day, she keeps the baby beneath a wing. Lifespan may be more than 20 years.

Northern Long-eared Bat (*Myotis septentrionalis*)

Northern long-eared bats weigh 0.2-0.3 ounce and have a wingspan of 9-10 inches. Distribution in the South includes Kentucky, eastern Tennessee, northwestern Arkansas, eastern Oklahoma, western Virginia, western North Carolina, eastern Alabama, western Georgia, and northwestern Florida. This species is common over much of its range.

Northern long-eared bats hibernate in parts of caves and mines that are relatively cool, moist, and where the air is still. In summer, they roost by day in a variety of shelters, including buildings and under tree bark and shutters, but they commonly use caves as night roosts. Northern long-eared bats seem much more solitary in their habits than other members of their genus, and they generally are found singly or in small groups containing up to 100 individuals. Although they frequently hang in the open, they seem to prefer tight crevices and holes. Sometimes only the nose and ears are visible, but they can be distinguished from most other members of their genus by their longer ears and long pointed tragus.

These bats forage mainly on forested hillsides and ridges rather than in streamside and floodplain forests. They consume a variety of small night-flying insects. Presumably most mating occurs in autumn prior to hibernation. Apparently small nursery colonies are formed in June and July where pregnant females give birth to one baby. Mothers may be able to retrieve their young that fall from roost sites. Lifespan may be more than 18 years.

Big Brown Bat (*Eptesicus fuscus*)

Big brown bats weigh 0.5-0.7 ounce and have a wingspan of 13-16 inches. Distribution includes all of the South, except southern Florida. It is common throughout most of its range.

These bats are closely associated with humans and are familiar to more people in the United States than is any other species of bat. Most summer roosts are located in attics, barns, bridges, or other man-made structures, where colonies of a few to several hundred individuals gather to form maternity colonies. They move into caves, mines, and other underground structures to

Interactions between bats and humans typically occur when maternity colonies invade occupied buildings. Shown is a colony of big brown bats in the attic of a home. A colonial species, this bat likely used large hollow trees when they were readily available but has learned to utilize man-made structures *(D. Saugey, US Forest Service).*

hibernate only during the coldest weather. Where most of these bats winter remains unknown.

They emerge at dusk and fly a steady, nearly straight course at a height of 20-30 feet en route to foraging areas. Its large size and steady flight make it readily recognizable. Apparently, some individuals use the same foraging area repeatedly. After feeding, they fly to night roosts to rest, such as garages, breezeways, and porches of houses. These bats consume beetles, ants, flies, mosquitos, mayflies, stoneflies, and other insects. Mating occurs in autumn and winter, females store sperm, and fertilization takes place in spring. In the eastern United States, big brown bats usually bear twins, in early June. In the western United States, usually only one baby is born each year.

Eastern Pipistrelle (*Pipistrellus subflavus*)

Eastern pipistrelle bats weigh 0.2-0.3 ounce and have a wingspan of 8-10 inches. Distribution includes all of the South, except southern Florida. It is common throughout its range.

Caves, mines, and rock crevices are used as hibernation sites in winter, and occasionally as night roosts in summer. These bats rarely occupy buildings, and apparently most roost in trees in summer. This species inhabits more caves in eastern North America than any other species of bat, usually hanging singly in warmer parts of the cave. An individual may occupy a precise spot in a cave on consecutive winters.

This bat emerges from its daytime retreat early in the evening. It is a weak flier and so small that it may be mistaken for a large moth. Eastern pipistrelle bats usually are solitary, although occasionally in late summer 4 or 5 will appear about a single tree. The flight is erratic and the foraging area is small. It often forages over waterways and forest edges and eats moths, beetles, mosquitos, true bugs, ants, and other insects. Mating occurs in autumn, sperm are stored during winter, and fertilization takes place in spring. These bats usually bear twins in late spring or early summer. Babies are born hairless and pink with eyes closed, and they are capable of making clicking sounds that may aid their mothers in locating them. They grow rapidly and can fly within a month.

Evening Bat (*Nycticeius humeralis*)

Evening bats weigh 0.3-0.5 ounce and have a wingspan of 10-11 inches. Distribution includes all of the South. Although less common throughout most of its range, it is one of the most common bats throughout the southern coastal states.

This species usually inhabits tree cavities or buildings in summer. In the South, it may share roosts with the Brazilian free-tailed bat. It almost never enters caves, although it sometimes joins bats swarming at certain cave entrances in late summer. Maternity colonies in buildings sometimes contain hundreds of individuals. Smaller colonies may occur behind the loose bark of dead pines and in hollow cypress trees. Winter habitat is almost completely unknown, but evening bats accumulate large reserves of fat in autumn, sufficient for either hibernation or a long migration.

A number of silver-haired bats were tracked to peeling bark on the boles of shortleaf pine during winter hibernation in the Ouachita National Forest *(D. Saugey, US Forest Service)*.

This species forages early and flies a slow and steady course. Heavy rain and cold temperatures retard activity, and females nursing babies return to the roost periodically to care for their offspring. It consumes a variety of small insects. Usually 2 babies are born, sometime between mid-May and mid-June. As with most other species of bats, birth is by breech presentation. After the babies are born, they grasp a nipple within 5-8 minutes. Newborn are pink, except for slightly darker feet, membranes, ears, and lips; their skin is so transparent that the viscera can be seen. Lifespan is greater than 5 years.

Silver-haired Bat (*Lasionycteris noctivagans*)
Silver-haired bats weigh 0.3-0.4 ounce and have a wingspan of 11-12 inches. Distribution includes all of the South, except Florida and the coastal regions of other Gulf Coast states. This bat is relatively uncommon throughout much of its range, especially in the southern United States.

A typical day roost is under loose tree bark, but these bats have been found in woodpecker holes and bird nests. Although they may occupy any kind of building, they favor open sheds, garages, and outbuildings rather than enclosed attics. During migration, they may be encountered in a variety of other shelters including piles of wood material. Silver-haired bats are rather common locally during about a 2-week migration period in April in Kentucky and Tennessee. Autumn migration is spread over a longer period and these bats seem less common. They hibernate in trees, buildings, rock crevices, and similar protected shelters.

This species emerges earlier than most bats and is easily recognized in flight; it is one of the slowest flying bats in North America. It forages over woodland ponds and streams at heights up to 25 feet and sometimes flies repeatedly over the same circuit. Silver-haired bats consume insects, including moths, true bugs, flies, mosquitos, termites, and beetles. Babies apparently are raised in the northern tier of states and northward into Canada. Most females apparently give birth to twins in June or early July.

Hoary Bat (*Lasiurus cinereus*)
Hoary bats weigh 0.9-1.1 ounces and have a wingspan of 14-16 inches. This is the most widespread bat in the Americas, occurring in most of southern Canada and southward through most of South America. It also occurs in Hawaii (where it is the only native land mammal), Iceland, Bermuda, and the Dominican Republic. Although relatively common throughout most of North America, the Hawaiian subspecies, Hawaiian hoary bat, is considered endangered. Distribution includes all of the South, except southern Florida.

These are large, heavily furred bats. They spend summer days concealed in the foliage of trees, where they choose a leafy site well-covered above, but open from beneath, generally 10-20 feet above the ground, and usually at the edge of a clearing. In late summer, they may wander into caves; many of these never find their way out. Because they rarely enter buildings and spend the daylight hours well concealed, they seldom are encountered by humans. Northern populations make long seasonal migrations to and from warmer winter habitats. The sexes apparently are segregated throughout most of the summer range; males are uncommon in the eastern United States at this time.

Hoary bats may fly during late afternoon on warm days in winter. Their swift and direct flight pattern and large size make them readily identifiable on the wing in most parts of their range. Moths, true bugs, mosquitos,

One of the largest woodland bats in the southeast, the hoary bat weighs in at about an ounce. Virtually nothing is known of habitat use or preferences of this species *(D. Saugey, US Forest Service)*.

other insects, and occasionally other bats may be captured as food. Hoary bats bear 2 babies, in mid-May, June, or early July. The young cling to the mother through the day, but are left clinging to a twig or leaf while she forages at night.

Eastern Red Bat (*Lasiurus borealis*)
Eastern red bats weigh 0.3-0.5 ounce and have a wingspan of 11-13 inches. Distribution includes all of the South, except the Florida peninsula. It is common throughout most of its range.

Eastern red bats spend daylight hours hanging in foliage of trees. They usually hang by one foot, giving them the appearance of dead leaves. Although these bats seldom enter caves for any distance, they often swarm about cave entrances in autumn. In colder parts of their range, they may migrate south in winter or hibernate in hollow trees or leaf litter. These bats are almost completely furred, except for the ears and parts of the wings, and they can respond to subfreezing temperatures by increasing their metabolism. Predators include several kinds of birds, especially blue jays.

Although the red bat is considered one of the most common species throughout the southeast, virtually nothing is known about populations. It commonly roosts in deciduous trees where it appears as a dead, curled leaf on small, outer branches. Red bats hibernate in mixed pine and hardwood leaf litter where they are well camouflaged *(D. Saugey, US Forest Service)*.

Eastern red bats emerge early in the evening, and often fly on warm winter afternoons. They forage regularly over the same territory on successive nights. They commonly feed beneath street lights. Eastern red bats consume moths, crickets, flies, mosquitos, true bugs, beetles, cicadas, and other insects. Eastern red bats mate in flight during August and September, sperm is stored over winter, and females give birth to 1 to 4 babies (average is 3.2), during late spring or early summer. They are born hairless, with the eyes closed, and they cling to the fur of their mother with their teeth, thumbs, and feet.

Seminole Bat (*Lasiurus seminolus*)
Seminole bats weigh 0.3-0.5 ounce and have a wingspan of 12-13 inches. Distribution in the South includes Louisiana, Mississippi, Alabama, Georgia, Florida, South Carolina, North Carolina, southeastern Virginia, southern Tennessee, Arkansas, and eastern Texas. It is common throughout most of its range.

Seminole bats frequently roost in Spanish moss, and also beneath loose bark, in clumps of foliage, and in caves. These bats often select roost sites in moss hanging on the southwestern exposure of trees. The height of Spanish moss roost sites occupied by Seminole bats is variable, but is high enough for the bats to drop into the unobstructed space beneath when initiating flight.

These are the most common bats seen flying in the evening throughout much of the southern United States.

They fly during all seasons, even on warm evenings in mid-winter. Seminole bats emerge early in the evening from daytime roosts and usually feed at treetop level. The flight is direct and usually rather swift. They consume true bugs, flies, mosquitos, beetles, crickets, and other insects, which usually are captured around and in tree canopies. One to 4 babies are born, during late spring or early summer. Like several other species, Seminole bats apparently wander extensively during late summer after the young are weaned.

Northern Yellow Bat (*Lasiurus intermedius*)
Northern yellow bats weigh 0.5-1.1 ounces and have a wingspan of 14-16 inches. Distribution in the South includes Florida, southeastern Texas, southern Louisiana, southern Mississippi, southern Alabama, southeastern South Carolina, eastern North Carolina, and southeastern Virginia. It is relatively common throughout most of its range.

These bats typically inhabit wooded areas in the vicinity of permanent water. In the southern United States, the distribution of northern yellow bats nearly coincides with that of Spanish moss where they often roost and bear their young. A single oak tree, draped with Spanish moss, may harbor several of these bats. In some parts of Florida, it is the most abundant bat. Northern yellow bats are somewhat colonial, especially females during the nursing season. As with other bats, it is doubtful if the mother ever carries her babies while foraging, but mothers may carry them when they are flushed from their day roosts. In June-August, when the babies have begun to fly, they form evening feeding aggregations with adult females; males rarely are present in these aggregations, and are believed to be solitary and scattered at this time of year.

Northern yellow bats usually forage 15-25 feet above the ground over open areas with few shrubs and only scattered clumps of trees, or along the edge of forests. Grassy areas, such as airports, open pastures, golf courses, and edges of lakes, are favored. True bugs, flies, mosquitos, beetles, and other insects are important components of the diet. Mating occurs in autumn and winter. Two to 4 babies are born in May or June.

Brazilian Free-tailed Bat (*Tadarida brasiliensis*)
Brazilian free-tailed bats weigh 0.4-0.5 ounce and have a wingspan of 12-14 inches. Distribution is in the southern United States and southward through Mexico and Central America into northern South America. Habitat of Brazilian free-tailed bats differs in various parts of the United States. In the Southwest, they primarily are cave bats that migrate long distances into Mexico to winter. During summer, about 20,000,000 bats of this species occupy Bracken Cave near San Antonio, Texas; this is the largest concentration of mammals in the world. Their distribution in the South includes Florida, Louisiana, eastern Texas, southern Arkansas, southern Mississippi, southern Alabama, southern Georgia, and southern South Carolina. The subspecies found in the southeastern United States, Le Conte's free-tailed bat, is only locally common. The subspecies inhabiting the southwestern United States in summer, the Mexican free-tailed bat, is present in very large numbers. It has been estimated that more than 100,000,000 are present in Texas alone.

In the South, this species does not occur in caves; it is present only in man made structures; it does not migrate great distances (if at all), and few colonies larger than a few hundred individuals are known. They often select hot attics as roosts; young bats seem to be able to tolerate higher temperatures than adults. High temperatures in roosts appear to be important for rapid growth of young bats.

Brazilian free-tailed bats usually feed on small moths and beetles. One baby is born, in late spring or early summer. Birth occurs with the mother hanging head downward. Newborn are hairless, but have all their milk teeth. Mothers can locate their own young among the thousands of babies in a colony.

CONCLUSIONS

The many species of bats are important components of southern forests. Several species are endangered or of special concern. Special measures are merited to help conserve bats. Bat maternity and hibernaculum sites should be protected. Consideration of bats, particularly those of concern, should be incorporated into forest management. And research should be developed to help understand and manage bats more effectively.

CHAPTER 28

Reptiles and Amphibians

J. Whitfield Gibbons and Kurt A. Buhlmann
Savannah River Ecology Laboratory
University of Georgia, Aiken, SC

The southern United States contains forest habitats in great diversity, including upland and bottomland hardwood forests, pine flatwoods, and cypress-tupelo gum swamps, that are of vital importance to a variety of species. Among the permanent residents of southern forests, the herpetofauna, comprising the reptiles and amphibians, rival all other vertebrate groups in biodiversity.

Although the most diverse and abundant 2 classes of terrestrial vertebrates in the region, reptiles and amphibians have traditionally received minimal attention from a wildlife management perspective (Gibbons 1988) and have seldom been the focus of wildlife management practices. Most wildlife management guides have had little information on herpetofaunal communities, and few universities have emphasized their importance in wildlife programs. Nonetheless, reptiles and amphibians are becoming recognized as meaningful components of forest wildlife communities that are deserving of management consideration.

Traditional wildlife and fisheries management is perceived as being at a crossroads (Muth et al. 1998). Whereas traditional wildlife objectives emphasized production of game species and management of their habitat for human use, other important objectives began to emerge almost three decades ago that focused on nongame species, biodiversity, landscape-level ecology, conservation, and the role of all plants and animals as ecosystem components. Within this framework of ecological communities and ecosystems, the importance of reptiles and amphibians has become recognized. Our goal is to introduce forest herpetofauna of the southern United States and provide an overview of their ecology, habitat requirements, and problems, and suggest proactive wildlife management and conservation activities that will benefit reptiles and amphibians.

DISTRIBUTION AND ABUNDANCE

The southeastern region has the richest herpetofaunal biodiversity found in the United States. More than 460 species are native to the United States and Canada, of which more than half (approximately 272; Table 1) occur in some portion of the area prescribed for this book as the southern United States (eastern Oklahoma, eastern Texas, Louisiana, Mississippi, Alabama, Georgia, Florida, South Carolina, North Carolina, Virginia, Tennessee, Arkansas, and Kentucky). Excluding the 16 species of amphibians and 36 of reptiles whose geographic ranges technically enter the southeastern United States (east of the 100th meridian) but whose primary ranges are in the western or midwestern United States, 116 amphibians and 104 reptiles can be considered as southern species of herpetofauna (Table 1). Most of these 220 species can be classified as directly dependent on forests during part or all of their life cycle, although some may be considered indirectly dependent due to having only a peripheral association with forested, terrestrial habitats.

With the exception of the lizards, which are more abundant in the West, each of the other classes or subclasses of U.S. reptiles (snakes, turtles, crocodilians) and amphibians (salamanders, frogs and toads) reach their highest species diversity in the southeastern region. The snakes reach their highest diversities in southern forests and their peripheral habitats, such as rivers, streams, and isolated wetlands (Mount 1975). More turtle species are known to occur in the southeastern United States than anywhere else in the world (Iverson 1992), 23 species being known from Alabama alone (Lydeard and Mayden 1995). The greatest diversity of salamanders in the United States occurs in the southern Appalachian region (Pough et al. 1998).

Thus, approximately half or more of all species in most U.S. families of herpetofauna are indigenous to the southern United States, and many species are actually endemic. Enhancing the level of concern and attention for the environmental welfare and conservation of reptiles and amphibians should be in the best interest of southern forest ecosystems.

Public Perceptions of Forest Herpetofauna

A common query from the general populace about various species of herpetofauna and the need for the conservation of a particular one is, "What good is it?" The reason a standard answer cannot be given is because anyone who views wildlife only from the perspective of what immediate benefits can be derived from the species (food, medicine, clothing, or sports hunting) is unlikely to see the need for protecting any aspect of the environment that does not contribute directly to that purpose in most instances. Most of today's ecologists and wildlife managers realize that the interconnectedness of habitats and species within an ecosystem provides an importance to each that may be undetermined, yet still exists.

Aside from the ethical grounds of the sanctity of all species and the importance of maintaining natural levels of species diversity, some herpetofauna have traits that people should find as compelling reasons for their conservation. The rodent-eating habits of many species of snakes, including rattlesnakes, results in the consumption of high numbers of mice and rats, a justification of the value of snakes in rodent control. Amphibians are quantitatively important in forest ecosystems (Pough et al. 1998). In a Hubbard Brook study, red-backed salamanders more efficiently converted energy to animal biomass and provided more energy to the food chain than either birds or mammals (Burton and Likens 1975). Some turtles are known to be efficient scavengers in aquatic systems, reducing the levels of decaying fish and other organisms. And, of course, frogs are noted for consuming large quantities of insects, many of which might be noxious to humans.

Despite the former lack of support for herpetofauna, the positive interest shown by many naturalists and the general public in some or all members of the herpetofauna has burgeoned in recent years. Awareness of the complexity and intrigue that can be found in communities of reptiles and amphibians has heightened considerably. Hence, one of the greatest contributions of forest herpetofauna as a group may be the fascinating, interesting, and appealing array of animals that can be enjoyed by the people of the southeastern United States who take the time and make the effort to learn about them.

CATEGORIES OF FOREST-INHABITING REPTILES AND AMPHIBIANS

Although some southern herpetofauna spend their entire lifetime in the forest itself and are therefore directly influenced by forest conditions, many others live in peripheral habitats (rivers, caves, marshes) and, although the effect may be less immediate, these also can be affected by the conditions of surrounding or upstream forest habitat. That is, the wooded habitat (which may consist of hardwoods, pine, or both) has essential components for maintaining sustainable popu-

Table 1. Amphibians and reptiles native to the southern United States (as defined in book). Common names are those that have been standardly used or ones used regionally. Species whose geographic ranges technically enter the southeastern United States east of the 100th meridian but whose primary ranges are in the western or mid-western United States are indicated by an asterisk (*). Numbers preceding species names indicate the herpetofaunal group (see text) to which the species is assigned, as follows:

Group 1 – species that are permanent residents of forested terrestrial habitats.
Group 2 – species for which the forest habitat is essential for part of their life cycle.
Group 3 – semi-aquatic species that use forests as corridors between other used habitats.
Group 4 –species whose primary habitat is peripheral to the forest.

	Class AMPHIBIA	Common Name	Group Number
Order Caudata-Salamanders			
Proteidae	*Necturus alabamensis*	Alabama waterdog	4
Proteidae	*Necturus beyeri*	Gulf Coast waterdog	4
Proteidae	*Necturus lewisi*	Neuse River waterdog	4
Proteidae	*Necturus maculosus*	mudpuppy	4
Proteidae	*Necturus punctatus*	dwarf waterdog	4
Cryptobranchidae	*Cryptobranchus alleganiensis*	hellbender	4
Amphiumidae	*Amphiuma means*	two-toed amphiuma	4
Amphiumidae	*Amphiuma pholeter*	one-toed amphiuma	4
Amphiumidae	*Amphiuma tridactylum*	three-toed amphiuma	4
Sirenidae	*Pseudobranchus striatus*	dwarf siren	4
Sirenidae	*Siren intermedia*	lesser siren	4
Sirenidae	*Siren lacertina*	greater siren	4
Ambystomatidae	*Ambystoma annulatum*	ringed salamander	2
Ambystomatidae	*Ambystoma barbouri*	streamside salamander	2
Ambystomatidae	*Ambystoma cingulatum*	flatwoods salamander	2
Ambystomatidae	*Ambystoma jeffersonianum*	Jefferson's salamander	2
Ambystomatidae	*Ambystoma mabeei*	Mabee's salamander	2
Ambystomatidae	*Ambystoma maculatum*	spotted salamander	2
Ambystomatidae	*Ambystoma opacum*	marbled salamander	2
Ambystomatidae	*Ambystoma talpoideum*	mole salamander	2
Ambystomatidae	*Ambystoma texanum*	small-mouthed salamander	2
Ambystomatidae	*Ambystoma tigrinum*	tiger salamander	2
Salamandridae	*Notophthalmus meridionalis*	black-spotted newt	*
Salamandridae	*Notophthalmus perstriatus*	striped newt	2
Salamandridae	*Notophthalmus viridescens*	red-spotted newt	2
Plethodontidae	*Aneides aeneus*	green salamander	4
Plethodontidae	*Desmognathus aeneus*	seepage salamander	1
Plethodontidae	*Desmognathus apalachicolae*	Apalachicola salamander	1
Plethodontidae	*Desmognathus auriculatus*	southern dusky salamander	1
Plethodontidae	*Desmognathus brimleyorum*	Ouachita dusky salamander	1
Plethodontidae	*Desmognathus imitator*	imitator salamander	1
Plethodontidae	*Desmognathus monticola*	seal salamander	1
Plethodontidae	*Desmognathus ochrophaeus*	mountain dusky salamander	1
Plethodontidae	*Desmognathus fuscus*	dusky salamander	1
Plethodontidae	*Desmognathus quadramaculatus*	black-bellied salamander	4
Plethodontidae	*Desmognathus santeetlah*	Santeetlah dusky salamander	4
Plethodontidae	*Desmognathus welteri*	Black Mountain salamander	1
Plethodontidae	*Desmognathus wrighti*	pigmy salamander	1
Plethodontidae	*Eurycea aquatica*	brownback salamander	2
Plethodontidae	*Eurycea bislineata*	northern two-lined salamander	2
Plethodontidae	*Eurycea cirrigera*	southern two-lined salamander	2
Plethodontidae	*Eurycea guttolineata*	three-lined salamander	2
Plethodontidae	*Eurycea junaluska*	Junaluska salamander	2
Plethodontidae	*Eurycea longicauda*	long-tailed salamander	2
Plethodontidae	*Eurycea lucifuga*	cave salamander	2
Plethodontidae	*Eurycea multiplicata*	many-ribbed salamander	2
Plethodontidae	*Eurycea nana*	San Marcos salamander	*
Plethodontidae	*Eurycea neotenes*	Texas salamander	*
Plethodontidae	*Eurycea quadridigitata*	dwarf salamander	2
Plethodontidae	*Eurycea tridentifera*	Comal blind salamander	*
Plethodontidae	*Eurycea tynerensis*	Oklahoma salamander	2
Plethodontidae	*Eurycea wilderae*	Blue Ridge two-lined salamander	2
Plethodontidae	*Gyrinophilus palleucus*	Tennessee cave salamander	4
Plethodontidae	*Gyrinophilus porphyriticus*	spring salamander	2
Plethodontidae	*Haideotriton wallacei*	Georgia blind salamander	4
Plethodontidae	*Hemidactylium scutatum*	four-toed salamander	1
Plethodontidae	*Leurognathus marmoratus*	shovelnose salamander	4

Table 1 continued

	Class AMPHIBIA	Common Name	Group Number
Plethodontidae	*Phaeognathus hubrichti*	Red Hills salamander	1
Plethodontidae	*Plethodon aureolus*	Tellico salamander	1
Plethodontidae	*Plethodon caddoensis*	Caddo Mountain salamander	1
Plethodontidae	*Plethodon dorsalis*	zigzag salamander	1
Plethodontidae	*Plethodon fourchensis*	Fourche Mountain salamander	1
Plethodontidae	*Plethodon glutinosus (complex)*	slimy salamander	1
Plethodontidae	*Plethodon hoffmani*	Valley and Ridge salamander	1
Plethodontidae	*Plethodon hubrichti*	Peaks of Otter salamander	1
Plethodontidae	*Plethodon jordani*	Jordan's salamander	1
Plethodontidae	*Plethodon kentucki*	Cumberland Plateau salamander	1
Plethodontidae	*Plethodon ouachitae*	Rich Mountain salamander	1
Plethodontidae	*Plethodon petraeus*	Pigeon Mountain salamander	1
Plethodontidae	*Plethodon punctatus*	Cow Knob salamander	1
Plethodontidae	*Plethodon richmondi*	ravine salamander	1
Plethodontidae	*Plethodon serratus*	southern redback salamander	1
Plethodontidae	*Plethodon shenandoah*	Shenandoah salamander	1
Plethodontidae	*Plethodon teyahalee*	southern Appalachian salamander	1
Plethodontidae	*Plethodon websteri*	Webster's salamander	1
Plethodontidae	*Plethodon wehrlei*	Wehrlei's salamander	1
Plethodontidae	*Plethodon welleri*	Weller's salamander	1
Plethodontidae	*Plethodon yonahlossee*	Yonahlossee salamander	1
Plethodontidae	*Pseudotriton montanus*	mud salamander	2
Plethodontidae	*Pseudotriton ruber*	red salamander	2
Plethodontidae	*Stereochilus marginatus*	many-lined salamander	4
Plethodontidae	*Typhlomolge rathbuni*	Blanco blind salamander	*
Plethodontidae	*Typhlomolge robusta*	Texas blind salamander	*
Plethodontidae	*Typhlotriton spelaeus*	grotto salamander	4
Order Anura —Frogs and toads			
Pelobatidae	*Scaphiopus bombifrons*	Plains spadefoot toad	*
Pelobatidae	*Scaphiopus couchii*	Couch's spadefoot toad	*
Pelobatidae	*Scaphiopus holbrooki*	eastern spadefoot toad	2
Bufonidae	*Bufo americanus*	American toad	2
Bufonidae	*Bufo debilis*	green toad	*
Bufonidae	*Bufo houstonensis*	Houston toad	2
Bufonidae	*Bufo punctatus*	red-spotted toad	*
Bufonidae	*Bufo quercicus*	oak toad	2
Bufonidae	*Bufo speciosus*	Texas toad	*
Bufonidae	*Bufo terrestris*	southern toad	2
Bufonidae	*Bufo valliceps*	Gulf Coast toad	2
Bufonidae	*Bufo woodhousii*	Woodhouse's toad	2
Bufonidae	*Bufo fowlerii*	Fowler's toad	2

	Class AMPHIBIA	Common Name	Group Number
Hylidae	*Acris crepitans*	northern cricket frog	2
Hylidae	*Acris gryllus*	southern cricket frog	2
Hylidae	*Hyla andersonii*	pine barrens treefrog	2
Hylidae	*Hyla avivoca*	bird-voiced treefrog	2
Hylidae	*Hyla chrysoscelis*	Cope's gray treefrog	2
Hylidae	*Hyla cinerea*	green treefrog	2
Hylidae	*Hyla femoralis*	pine woods treefrog	2
Hylidae	*Hyla gratiosa*	barking treefrog	2
Hylidae	*Hyla squirella*	squirrel treefrog	2
Hylidae	*Hyla versicolor*	gray treefrog	2
Hylidae	*Pseudacris brachyphona*	mountain chorus frog	2
Hylidae	*Pseudacris brimleyi*	Brimley's chorus frog	2
Hylidae	*Pseudacris clarkii*	spotted chorus frog	*
Hylidae	*Pseudacris crucifer*	spring peeper	2
Hylidae	*Pseudacris nigrita*	southern chorus frog	2
Hylidae	*Pseudacris ocularis*	little grass frog	2
Hylidae	*Pseudacris ornata*	ornate chorus frog	2
Hylidae	*Pseudacris streckeri*	Strecker's chorus frog	2
Hylidae	*Pseudacris triseriata*	striped chorus frog	2
Hylidae	*Smilisca baudinii*	Mexican treefrog	*
Microhylidae	*Gastrophryne carolinensis*	eastern narrow-mouthed toad	2
Microhylidae	*Gastrophryne olivacea*	Great Plains narrow-mouthed toad	*
Microhylidae	*Hypopachus variolosus*	sheep toad	*
Ranidae	*Rana areolata*	crawfish frog	2
Ranidae	*Rana berlandieri*	Rio Grande leopard frog	*
Ranidae	*Rana capito*	gopher frog	2
Ranidae	*Rana catesbeiana*	bullfrog	2
Ranidae	*Rana clamitans*	green frog; bronze frog	2
Ranidae	*Rana grylio*	pig frog	4
Ranidae	*Rana heckscheri*	river frog	2
Ranidae	*Rana okaloosae*	Florida bog frog	4
Ranidae	*Rana palustris*	pickerel frog	2
Ranidae	*Rana sylvatica*	wood frog	2
Ranidae	*Rana utricularia*	southern leopard frog	2
Ranidae	*Rana virgatipes*	carpenter frog	2

	Class REPTILIA	Common Name	Group Number
Order Crocodilia — Crocodilians			
Alligatoridae	*Alligator mississippiensis*	American alligator	3
Alligatoridae	*Crocodylus acutus*	American crocodile	4

Table 1 continued

	Class REPTILIA	Common Name	Group Number
Order Chelonia —Turtles			
Chelydridae	*Chelydra serpentina*	common snapping turtle	3
Chelydridae	*Macroclemys temminckii*	alligator snapping turtle	4
Kinosternidae	*Kinosternon baurii*	striped mud turtle	2
Kinosternidae	*Kinosternon flavescens*	yellow (Illinois) musk turtle	*
Kinosternidae	*Kinosternon subrubrum*	eastern mud turtle	2
Kinosternidae	*Sternotherus carinatus*	razorback musk turtle	4
Kinosternidae	*Sternotherus depressus*	flattened musk turtle	4
Kinosternidae	*Sternotherus minor*	loggerhead musk turtle	4
Kinosternidae	*Sternotherus odoratus*	stinkpot	3
Emydidae	*Chrysemys picta*	painted turtle	3
Emydidae	*Clemmys guttata*	spotted turtle	3
Emydidae	*Clemmys insculpta*	wood turtle	2
Emydidae	*Clemmys muhlenbergii*	bog turtle	3
Emydidae	*Deirochelys reticularia*	chicken turtle	2
Emydidae	*Graptemys barbouri*	Barbour's map turtle	4
Emydidae	*Graptemys caglei*	Cagle's map turtle	*
Emydidae	*Graptemys ernsti*	Ernst's map turtle	4
Emydidae	*Graptemys flavimaculata*	yellow-blotched map turtle	4
Emydidae	*Graptemys geographica*	common map turtle	4
Emydidae	*Graptemys gibbonsi*	Gibbons' map turtle	4
Emydidae	*Graptemys kohnii*	Mississippi map turtle	4
Emydidae	*Graptemys nigrinoda*	black-knobbed map turtle	4
Emydidae	*Graptemys oculifera*	ringed map turtle	4
Emydidae	*Graptemys pseudogeographica*	false map turtle	4
Emydidae	*Graptemys pulchra*	Alabama map turtle	4
Emydidae	*Graptemys versa*	Texas map turtle	*
Emydidae	*Malaclemys terrapin*	diamondback terrapin	4
Emydidae	*Pseudemys alabamensis*	Alabama red-bellied turtle	4
Emydidae	*Pseudemys concinna*	river cooter	4
Emydidae	*Pseudemys floridana*	Florida cooter	3
Emydidae	*Pseudemys peninsularis*	peninsula cooter	4
Emydidae	*Pseudemys nelsoni*	Florida red-bellied turtle	4
Emydidae	*Pseudemys rubriventris*	red-bellied turtle	4
Emydidae	*Pseudemys texana*	Texas river cooter	*
Emydidae	*Terrapene carolina*	eastern box turtle	1
Emydidae	*Terrapene ornata*	ornate box turtle	1
Emydidae	*Trachemys scripta*	slider turtle	3
Testudinidae	*Gopherus berlandieri*	Texas tortoise	*
Testudinidae	*Gopherus polyphemus*	gopher tortoise	1
Trionychidae	*Apalone ferox*	Florida softshell turtle	4

	Class REPTILIA	Common Name	Group Number
Trionychidae	*Apalone mutica*	smooth softshell turtle	4
Trionychidae	*Apalone spinifera*	spiny softshell turtle	4
Order Squamata — Snakes and lizards			
Suborder Amphisbaenia			
Amphisbaenidae	*Rhineura floridana*	Florida worm lizard	1
Suborder Lacertilia — Lizards			
Polychridae	*Anolis carolinensis*	green anole (chameleon)	1
Phrynosomatidae	*Cophosaurus texanus*	Texas earless lizard	*
Phrynosomatidae	*Holbrookia lacerata*	spot-tailed earless lizard	*
Phrynosomatidae	*Holbrookia propinqua*	keeled earless lizard	*
Phrynosomatidae	*Phrynosoma cornutum*	Texas horned lizard	4
Phrynosomatidae	*Sceloporus grammicus*	mesquite lizard	*
Phrynosomatidae	*Sceloporus olivaceus*	Texas spiny lizard	*
Phrynosomatidae	*Sceloporus serrifer*	blue spiny lizard	*
Phrynosomatidae	*Sceloporus undulatus*	eastern fence lizard	1
Phrynosomatidae	*Sceloporus woodi*	Florida scrub lizard	1
Crotaphytidae	*Crotaphytus collaris*	collared lizard	*
Crotaphytidae	*Crotaphytus reticulatus*	reticulated collared lizard	*
Teiidae	*Cnemidophorus gularis*	Texas spotted whiptail	*
Teiidae	*Cnemidophorus sexlineatus*	six-lined racerunner	4
Scincidae	*Eumeces anthracinus*	coal skink	1
Scincidae	*Eumeces egregius*	mole skink	1
Scincidae	*Eumeces fasciatus*	five-lined skink	1
Scincidae	*Eumeces inexpectatus*	southeastern five-lined skink	1
Scincidae	*Eumeces laticeps*	broadheaded skink	1
Scincidae	*Eumeces obsoletus*	Great Plains skink	*
Scincidae	*Eumeces septentrionalis*	prairie skink	*
Scincidae	*Eumeces tetragrammus*	four-lined skink	*
Scincidae	*Neopseps reynoldsi*	sand skink	1
Scincidae	*Scincella lateralis*	ground skink	1
Anguidae	*Ophisaurus attenuatus*	slender glass lizard	1
Anguidae	*Ophisaurus compressus*	island glass lizard	1
Anguidae	*Ophisaurus mimicus*	mimic glass lizard	1
Anguidae	*Ophisaurus ventralis*	eastern glass lizard	1
Suborder Serpentes — Snakes			
Colubridae	*Arizona elegans*	glossy snake	*
Colubridae	*Carphophis amoenus*	eastern worm snake	1
Colubridae	*Carphophis vermis*	western worm snake	*
Colubridae	*Cemophora coccinea*	scarlet snake	1
Colubridae	*Clonophis kirtlandii*	Kirtland's water snake	*
Colubridae	*Coluber constrictor*	racer	1
Colubridae	*Coniophanes imperialis*	black-striped snake	*

Table 1 continued

	Class REPTILIA	Common Name	Group Number
Colubridae	*Diadophis punctatus*	ringneck snake	1
Colubridae	*Drymarchon corais*	indigo snake	1
Colubridae	*Drymobius margaritiferus*	speckled racer	*
Colubridae	*Elaphe guttata*	corn snake	1
Colubridae	*Elaphe obsoleta*	rat snake	1
Colubridae	*Farancia abacura*	mud snake	3
Colubridae	*Farancia erytrogramma*	rainbow snake	3
Colubridae	*Ficimia streckeri*	Mexican hooknose snake	*
Colubridae	*Heterodon nasicus*	western hognose snake	*
Colubridae	*Heterodon platyrhinos*	eastern hognose snake	1
Colubridae	*Heterodon simus*	southern hognose snake	1
Colubridae	*Hypsiglena torquata*	Texas night snake	*
Colubridae	*Lampropeltis calligaster*	mole kingsnake	4
Colubridae	*Lampropeltis getula*	common kingsnake	1
Colubridae	*Lampropeltis triangulum*	scarlet kingsnake	1
Colubridae	*Leptodeira septentrionalis*	cat-eyed snake	*
Colubridae	*Leptotyphlops dulcis*	Texas blind snake	*
Colubridae	*Masticophis flagellum*	coachwhip	1
Colubridae	*Nerodia clarkii*	salt marsh snake	4
Colubridae	*Nerodia cyclopion*	western green water snake	3
Colubridae	*Nerodia erythrogaster*	red-bellied water snake	2
Colubridae	*Nerodia fasciata*	southern banded water snake	3
Colubridae	*Nerodia floridana*	eastern green water snake	3
Colubridae	*Nerodia rhombifer*	diamond-backed water snake	3
Colubridae	*Nerodia sipedon*	northern water snake	3
Colubridae	*Nerodia taxispilota*	brown water snake	4
Colubridae	*Opheodrys aestivus*	rough green snake	1
Colubridae	*Opheodrys vernalis*	smooth green snake	*
Colubridae	*Pituophis melanoleucus*	pine snake	1
Colubridae	*Regina alleni*	striped crawfish snake	4
Colubridae	*Regina grahamii*	Graham's crawfish snake	4
Colubridae	*Regina rigida*	glossy crawfish snake	3
Colubridae	*Regina septemvittata*	queen snake	4
Colubridae	*Rhadinaea flavilata*	pine woods (yellow-lipped) snake	1
Colubridae	*Salvadora grahamiae*	patchnose snake	*
Colubridae	*Seminatrix pygaea*	black swamp snake	3
Colubridae	*Sonora semiannulata*	ground snake	*
Colubridae	*Stilosoma extenuatum*	short-tailed snake	1
Colubridae	*Storeria dekayi*	brown snake	1
Colubridae	*Storeria occipitomaculata*	red-bellied snake	1
Colubridae	*Tantilla coronata*	southeastern crowned snake	1
Colubridae	*Tantilla gracilis*	flat-headed snake	*
Colubridae	*Tantilla nigriceps*	plains black-headed snake	*
Colubridae	*Tantilla oolitica*	rim rock crowned snake	4
Colubridae	*Tantilla relicta*	Florida crowned snake	1
Colubridae	*Thamnophis marcianus*	checkered garter snake	*
Colubridae	*Thamnophis proximus*	western ribbon snake	3
Colubridae	*Thamnophis sauritus*	eastern ribbon snake	3
Colubridae	*Thamnophis sirtalis*	eastern garter snake	1
Colubridae	*Tropidoclonion lineatum*	lined snake	*
Colubridae	*Virginia striatula*	rough earth snake	1
Colubridae	*Virginia valeriae*	smooth earth snake	1
Elapidae	*Micrurus fulvius*	eastern coral snake	1
Viperidae (=Crotalidae)	*Agkistrodon contortrix*	copperhead	1
Viperidae (=Crotalidae)	*Agkistrodon piscivorus*	cottonmouth	3
Viperidae (=Crotalidae)	*Crotalus adamanteus*	eastern diamondback rattler	1
Viperidae (=Crotalidae)	*Crotalus atrox*	western diamondback rattler	*
Viperidae (=Crotalidae)	*Crotalus horridus*	timber rattler (canebrake)	1
Viperidae (=Crotalidae)	*Sistrurus catenatus*	massasagua	*
Viperidae (=Crotalidae)	*Sistrurus miliarius*	pigmy rattlesnake	1

lations both of species that are forest inhabitants and others that are not.

The quality of forest ecosystems influences the ecology of most if not all species of riverine turtles, permanently aquatic salamanders, and cave salamanders. For example, map turtles, cooter turtles, flattened musk turtles, and hellbender salamanders that are restricted to streams and rivers still can be affected by the condition of the riparian forests, which act as a buffer to increased sedimentation and channelization, changes in water temperature, availability of basking sites, and chemical pollutants (Nickerson and Mays 1973, Dodd et al. 1988, Buhlmann and Vaughan 1991). Management or development of riparian forests becomes an especially important consideration for some species of map turtles whose global distributions are restricted to single river systems in the Gulf Coastal Plain. A relationship between forest habitat quality and species that are

The river frog is an inhabitant of floodplain swamp forests in the southeastern United States. The spiny softshell turtle (insert) is a riverine species whose habitat quality is determined by the condition of the riparian forest *(K. Buhlmann)*.

The Savannah River floodplain forest on the Georgia-South Carolina line provides habitat for many species of amphibians and reptiles including brown water snakes, cottonmouths, river frogs, bird-voiced treefrogs, and three-lined salamanders *(K. Buhlmann)*.

restricted to non-forested terrestrial habitats, such as grasslands or arid areas with sparse vegetation, is less likely to be found.

Reptiles and amphibians dependent on southern forests can be partitioned further into species that are permanent residents of forested terrestrial habitats (Herpetofaunal Group 1) and species for which the forest habitat is essential for part of their life cycle (Herpetofaunal Group 2; Table 1). Further divisions are Herpetofaunal Group 3 (semi-aquatic species that use forests as corridors and pathways to or between other habitats such as isolated wetlands) and Herpetofaunal Group 4 (species whose primary habitat is peripheral to the forest but influenced by it). As with many classification schemes, a gradient exists so that clear dichotomies are not always evident between some categories and the assignment of some species becomes subjective.

Group 1 includes the great diversity of salamander species in the genus *Plethodon* (more than 20) occurring in moist forested habitats, primarily in mountain forests, where they may reproduce and live their entire lives within a small area (Buhlmann et al. 1988; Kramer et al. 1993). Within Group 2 are salamanders, such as tiger salamanders and others in the genus *Ambystoma* that must return to water for egg-laying but can nonetheless be classified as near-permanent forest residents as the adults remain terrestrial for all but the breeding period (Semlitsch 1983, Stine 1984); however, the larvae are aquatic for several months (Semlitsch 1987, deMaynadier and Hunter 1995). Also included in Group 2 are many frog species, such as narrow-mouthed toads and spadefoot toads. Adults may spend only one to a few days around water in mating activities, lay eggs that hatch within a day, and produce tadpoles that metamorphose into froglets within 2 weeks, at which time the young toads move into the forest (Dodd 1995, 1996).

Species that spend as much or more of their life in the water as in the forest, but for which the terrestrial period is essential, are placed in Group 3. Chicken turtles and mud turtles, which use terrestrial habitat for nesting and for winter dormancy (Burke and Gibbons 1995, Buhlmann 1995, 1998) while spending the warmer months in small wetlands, are examples.

Group 4 includes species such as the Tennessee cave salamander whose primary habitat is a cave ecosystem within a forested landscape and the green salamander that occurs on shaded, moist sandstone cliffs kept cool by forest habitat.

Although species in Group 1 and 2 are directly dependent on forest ecosystems during all or most of their lives, those in Group 3 and 4 can also be affected by peripheral forest habitat conditions. The vital impor-

Above left: Cave entrances within forest stands provide habitats for cave salamanders (right). In cave regions, such as the Cumberland Plateau, mixed hardwood forests provide suitable microhabitat conditions that allow for movement of individuals and connectivity of populations *(K. Buhlmann)*.

tance of the linkages between forests and embedded habitats such as isolated wetlands, caves, rock faces or crevices, and streams cannot be overemphasized in gauging the value of forests to reptiles and amphibians (Wynn et al. 1988; Buhlmann et al. 1993; Buhlmann 1998).

Above left: Siltation of streams from inappropriate land use practices can impact streamside amphibians. These impacts can occur in surface and underground (cave) systems *(K. Buhlmann)*. Above right: Amphibians are doubly susceptible to landscape impact because they require both terrestrial and aquatic habitats.Good water quality is required by amphibian larvae, such as the tiger salamander illustrated. Appropriate forest cover with suitable microhabitat conditions is required by the adults. *(K. Buhlmann)*.

FOREST HERPETOFAUNA IN MAJOR PHYSIOGRAPHIC REGIONS

Mountains

The southern Appalachian Mountains harbor an extraordinarily high species diversity of salamanders, primarily within the family Plethodontidae (Pough et al. 1998). In addition to the small home ranges of individual salamanders, several of the species have restricted geographic ranges. Several mountain tops within the region contain endemic species (Wynn 1991, Pague 1991). For example, the Peaks of Otter salamander is found only along a 5-mile stretch of ridgetop in Botetourt and Bedford counties, Virginia (Kramer et al. 1993, Sattler and Reichenbach 1998), and the Cow Knob salamander occurs along a 25-mile stretch above 2400 feet in the George Washington National Forest along the Virginia-West Virginia state line (Buhlmann et al. 1988). Weller's salamander, named for a young biologist, W. H. Weller, who died in a fall from Grandfather Mountain shortly after collecting the first specimens of the species that he had discovered, occurs in high elevation remnant spruce forests on several high mountains in North Carolina and Virginia (Pague 1991). The

The Cow Knob salamander is endemic to a 25-mile stretch of ridgetop along the Virginia-West Virginia line, where it occurs primarily above 2400 ft and is most abundant in mature hardwoods and old growth hemlock stands *(K. Buhlmann).*

In the southern Appalachians, red spruce and balsam fir forests are glacial relicts that occur only on the highest mountain peaks. These forests are threatened by acid precipitation and exotic insects. Wellers salamander is an endemic species that occurs in association with this forest type (K. Buhlmann).

Pigeon Mountain salamander is known only from the mixed hardwood-pine forests and cave entrances on Pigeon Mountain in northwest Georgia (Wynn et al. 1988).

Besides the high diversity of salamander species, the forested mountain regions of the southern United States harbor an abundance of frogs, such as wood frogs, green frogs, and mountain chorus frogs as well as reptiles, including worm snakes, copperheads, ring-neck snakes, bog turtles, and coal skinks. In the southern United States, bog turtles are found in wet meadows of the Blue Ridge mountain physiographic region (Buhlmann et al. 1997, Herman and Tryon 1997).

Piedmont

The Piedmont contains many species of reptiles and amphibians, all of which occur in one or both of the adjacent mountain and coastal plain physiographic regions. Although no species is endemic to the Piedmont, the Red Hills salamander is restricted to a Piedmont-like habitat (the Red Hills formations of Alabama) in the Coastal Plain, comprising cool, moist, forested ravines (Mount 1975). Piedmont forests often seem herpetofaunally depauperate, due in part to a combination of the ecological requirements of the animals and past agricultural and forestry practices in the region. Most forest-dwelling reptiles and amphibians are fossorial, requiring deep, moist soils in association with surface cover, such as woody debris or rock outcrops.

With the exception of beaver ponds, Piedmont physiography is also limited in the variety and abundance of wetland habitats that are characteristic of the Coastal Plain. In particular, isolated seasonal wetlands that are of critical importance to many reptile and amphibian species in the South, are rare in the Piedmont. Consequently, although Piedmont forests provide important habitat for some reptiles and amphibians, the biodiversity levels are often below that found in other regions in the South.

Coastal Plain

The South's overall reptile and amphibian species diversity is greatest by far in the Atlantic and Gulf Coastal Plains. The longleaf pine/wiregrass community, cypress-gum swamps, isolated wetlands, and mixed hardwood-pine habitats have long been recognized for their abundance of herpetofauna (Ditmars 1939, Kauffeld 1957, Gibbons and Semlitsch 1991, Gibbons et al. 1997). The species diversities of snakes and turtles that are characteristically high in the Southeast reach their highest levels in the Coastal Plain (Lydeard and Mayden 1995).

In contrast to the mountains, which are noted for their diversity of plethodontid salamanders, the coastal plain forests provide habitat for numerous ambystomatid salamander species, including tiger, spotted, marbled, mole, and flatwoods salamanders. Flatwoods salamanders are found in the longleaf pine-wiregrass

Left: The southern hognose snake is a declining species of xeric southern forests *(D. Scott)*.

A gopher tortoise burrow in a longleaf pine habitat *(T. Tuberville)*. Gopher tortoise (insert upper right).

Below: Natural longleaf pine forests are some of the most diverse habitats botanically and also provide habitat for many amphibians and reptiles including gopher tortoises, indigo snakes, flatwood salamanders, legless lizards (inset), and diamondback rattlesnakes *(T. Tuberville)*.

ecosystem where small flatwoods ponds and cypress domes are present in the landscape (Means et al. 1996, Palis 1997). In even greater abundance are the many species of treefrogs, toads, and other frogs. Pine barrens treefrogs occur at intermittent locations in coastal plain forests from Alabama to New Jersey where acidic seepage bogs that are required for breeding habitat are also present (Means and Longden 1976).

Some of the rare amphibian species in Group 2, such as the flatwoods salamander and gopher frog, are strongly dependent on suitable forest ecosystems to maintain sustainable populations. Although the quality of forest habitat is critical to these amphibians, of equal importance is the condition of seasonal wetlands and their locations within the forest matrix. The need for protection of these wetlands within forested landscapes is unquestionably one of the most vital aspects of forest management in a consideration of biodiversity of reptiles and amphibians.

The classical longleaf pine-wire grass community is noted as the ideal habitat for gopher tortoises (Guyer and Bailey 1993) and supports numerous other species such as the mole skink, glass lizards, scarlet snake, pine snake, and coachwhip snake. The cypress-gum swamps are home to rainbow snakes, mud snakes, western green water snakes, and striped crawfish snakes, all of which are also able to persist in other wetland habitats but which thrive in swamp forest ecosystems.

HISTORICAL DISTRIBUTION, ABUNDANCE, AND THREATS OF HERPETOFAUNAL HABITAT

Today's landscape is vastly different from that at the time of European settlement 400 years ago. Numerous naturalists described the North American fauna and flora during the period from the early 1700s to mid-1800s (Adler 1979). Although descriptions of natural landscapes are available from early botanists, specific information on the abundances and habitats of reptiles and amphibians is sparse. Even into the twentieth century, as with many groups of animals without commercial significance, writings on the herpetofauna of North America were largely descriptive taxonomy with the minimal information on population levels, being primarily anecdotal (McIlhenny 1935, Ditmars 1936, Dellinger and Black 1938, Cagle 1953, Martof 1956). Many of the early historical statements of population trends were based on anecdotal observations and impressions. Aside from references to American alligators (McIlhenny 1935, Ditmars 1936), early naturalists provided few references to perceived population levels of other non-game animals. However, Ditmars (1939) did note the decline in snake populations in Florida due to the increase in "motor roads" and the spread of fires.

Recently developed survey techniques have documented that many reptiles and amphibians are more abundant and widespread than previously believed (Gibbons et al. 1997), leading to a better understanding of their habitats, behavior, and potential environmental threats.

Most terrestrial and aquatic ecosystems on the landscape of the southeastern United States have historically undergone a progressive alteration of habitats. Among the more dramatic changes have been those in the fire-maintained longleaf pine communities, which once dominated much of the Coastal Plain. The virgin forests of oaks, hickories, yellow poplar, and pine as well as wetlands and open savannas described by Bartram (1791) give testimony to the modification of vast reaches of forest habitats from Alabama to the Carolinas. Bottomland hardwood and bald cypress forests bordered all coastal plain rivers. Although mountainous regions of the Blue Ridge and Cumberland Plateau are once again forested, the loss of American chestnut (chestnut-blight fungus), the current declines of spruce and fir (acid precipitation and exotic insects) and of hemlocks and oak (gypsy moths and other exotic insects) have and will likely continue to alter the composition and dynamics of the herpetofaunal assemblages of those regions.

Presumably, all of these forest habitats originally supported viable populations of reptiles and amphibians, and those remaining today still do. However, the forest habitats of pre-settlement times have been greatly reduced from their former sizes and composition. For example, longleaf pine-wiregrass habitats have declined to less than 10% of their original land area (Frost et al. 1986), much of the previously forested lands now being agricultural or urban. Bottomland hardwood forests in the floodplains of southern rivers have also been progressively altered through conversion to agriculture and diking for flood control (Sharitz and Mitsch 1993), contributing to a 69% loss of the bottomland forests throughout the continental United States since European settlement (Gosselink and Lee 1989). The original extent of southern bottomland hardwood forests is estimated to have been 17.7 million acres compared to the current extent of 6.6 million acres.

Associated with the disruption of forest habitats has been the modification or elimination of many of the natural wetlands of the Coastal Plain that have been filled, drained, or become isolated in a fragmented landscape that was formerly forested. The destruction or severe alteration of forest wetlands has presumably had a major negative impact on populations of the majority of reptile and amphibian species indigenous to the Southeast.

Oak-hickory-loblolly pine forests of the Georgia Piedmont have undergone extensive harvesting (Skeen et al. 1993), a century of cotton and tobacco planting, short-term timber rotation, and urbanization. Original topsoil has been lost following farming, logging, and regional soil practices, resulting in erosion of red clay subsoil into streams and rivers (Trimble 1973, Buhlmann and Gibbons 1997).

Although not always directly a consequence of logging or forest clearing activities, the runoff, siltation, and pollution imposed on southern streams, rivers, and other wetlands has presumably had a major, albeit it unmeasured, impact on the herpetofauna. The ditching and draining of mountain bogs and fens in the Appalachian region associated with farming and cattle grazing (Herman and Tryon 1997) have affected critical habitat for some species such as the bog turtle. The replacement of gravel and clear waters with mud bottoms and silt in Piedmont streams has presumably taken a toll on the abundance and distribution of stream salamanders. Although documentation will never be available, the destruction and modification of the original natural habitats of North America undoubtedly resulted in a loss of biodiversity among reptiles and amphibians. The challenge today is to curtail any further losses through proper stewardship of remaining habitats.

SAMPLING AND MONITORING FOREST HERPS

The diversity of techniques in sampling for herpetofaunal species in a region is dictated in part by the number of species that inhabit it. Because of the differing behavioral patterns and microhabitats among the many species of herpetofauna, some techniques are applicable to only a single species, sometimes within a specific habitat or location. Therefore, a thorough review of sampling techniques currently in use for monitoring and

Top right: Red efts are the terrestrial juvenile stage of the aquatic red-spotted newt. Efts may take up to seven years to mature before they return to the wetland to breed. Right: Red salamanders live in forested streamside riparian zones and the aquatic larvae require silt-free water. Below: Swamp forest *(K. Buhlmann).*

Above: Many amphibians and reptiles that inhabit seasonal wetlands require upland forest as well. These species likely decline when buffers are not provided. Left, adult barking treefrogs inhabit forests that surround isolated wetlands where breeding occurs. Bottom left: Mud snakes are secretive snakes of swamp forests *(K. Buhlmann).*

assessing population levels or simply determining presence/absence of reptiles and amphibians is beyond the scope of this chapter. An extensive list of references is available that refer to the development of new techniques within the last two decades or modifications of old techniques, most of which are covered in several summary works (Jones 1986, Gibbons 1990, Heyer et al. 1994).

Among the most commonly used techniques for herpetofauna in forest habitats are standard hand-collecting, the use of drift fences and pitfall traps or funnel traps, coverboards, and aquatic traps for semi-aquatic or aquatic species (Gibbons and Semlitsch 1981, Buhlmann et al. 1988, Gibbons 1990, Dodd 1991, 1992, Buhlmann et al. 1993, Grant et al. 1994, Mitchell et al. 1997). Sampling effectiveness can be influenced significantly by daily, seasonal, or annual weather conditions, local or regional habitat variability, and the competence of the investigator. Therefore, simply documenting species presence at a site often requires repeated sampling in different seasons and years. Because no single technique is suitable for all species, knowledge of a variety of sampling approaches is necessary to achieve a thorough assessment of biodiversity within a region or even a localized habitat.

PROBLEMS FACING FOREST HERPETOFAUNA (See Photographs).

The general problems faced by reptiles and amphibians in southern forests are similar to those confronted by herpetofauna in many regions of the world. Environmental impacts from human activities, difficulties in assessing problems because of the challenge in monitoring some populations, characteristics of the animals themselves, and negative or neutral public attitudes about conservation needs all have operated in the past to the detriment of reptile and amphibian populations.

Critical Biological Characteristics

A variety of ecological and life history traits among reptiles and amphibians make them more susceptible to certain activities to which forests are subjected. The traits are diverse among southern herpetofauna and could greatly influence the response of species communities to forest manipulation.

Life History, Demography, and Longevity

A critical life history characteristic of many reptile and amphibian species is that they take longer to mature and have life spans far longer than typical game species of mammals and birds. Among the examples of long-lived herpetofauna are the tiny red eft salamanders, the intermediate life stage between larval and adult newts (Group 2) that may take more than 7 years to reach maturity (Gill 1978). Some turtles that are dependent on forest habitat, including box turtles (Group 1) and snapping turtles (Group 3) take more than 10 years to reach maturity (Congdon et al. 1994; Ernst et al. 1994). In contrast, deer may begin reproducing between 0.5 and 1.5 years of age and normally have a lifespan of less than 10 years (Smith 1991). Hence, a typical deer herd might go through 2 or more generations from the time a female newt, box turtle, or snapping turtle is born until she lays her first eggs. The annual adult survivorship values for several long-lived turtle species have been modeled and have been found to be in excess of 80% (Gibbons 1990). A level of 90% adult survivorship coupled with high survivorship of juveniles is necessary to maintain stable populations for some turtle species (Congdon et al. 1993).

Managing for sustainable populations of long-lived, late-maturing species, such as most turtles and many other reptiles and amphibians, requires different strategies than for short-lived, rapid turnover species. Using the approach of sustainable harvest is unlikely to be suitable for many if not most species of herpetofauna, a point that has been documented for box turtles and snapping turtles (Buhlmann 1996, Galbraith et al. 1997).

Spatial Ecology on a Landscape Level

Unlike North American mammals and birds that have widespread distribution patterns, many species of herpetofauna have geographic ranges that are restricted, at least to certain physiographic regions. Some salamanders in Group 1 can be considered glacial relicts that were isolated on mountain tops that retained northern climates and are now associated with relict-type forests. Likewise, some frog species, such as the pine barrens tree frog and Houston toad in Group 2 and the Florida bog frog (Group 4) are known from small, isolated populations throughout their ranges, which are greatly restricted for the latter two. Included among the reptiles that have relatively small geographic ranges are the short-tailed snake (Group 1) of Florida and the flattened musk turtle (Group 4) of Alabama. All of these species could be directly or indirectly affected by conditions of surrounding forests. Other Group 1 species living permanently in southern forest habitat and having disjunct populations are the pine woods snake, coal skink, and Webster's salamander.

A distinction from most mammals and birds with sizable geographic ranges is that many disjunct populations of herpetofauna are so distantly removed from the nearest population of the species that recolonization following extirpation would be unlikely. However, in some situations, the landscape can change too rapidly for forest-dwelling herpetofauna. For example, sites with short-term rotation of timber, urban development, or agricultural activities may not be able to be recolonized from recently altered sites nearby if the latter sites have not yet recovered herpetofaunally themselves.

Mobility and Dispersal

Many birds and mammals have been documented to respond favorably to habitat alterations that produce early successional habitats. Also, providing a managed diversity of habitat types within a landscape can increase species diversity of neotropical migrants and other songbirds (Opdam 1991). However, for many sedentary species of herpetofauna, population presence is determined by the long-term persistence of certain specific, and often natural, habitats within the landscape. For example, ambystomatid salamanders that use southern forest habitats in their adult stage can only persist if unrestricted movement is possible to an isolated wetland located within dispersal range of individuals. In addition, the dynamics of hydrology, which can be greatly influenced by commercial development or agricultural activities in surrounding forests, may render essential seasonal wetlands inhospitable in certain years, affecting many reptiles and amphibians. Therefore, the long-term persistence of certain herpetofauna may depend on the availability of alternative breeding sites and appropriate travel habitat between them. In these situations, reptile and amphibian populations can truly be viewed as metapopulations (Opdam

1991) within the landscape, to which source-sink models (Pulliam 1988) apply.

The home range of many of the smaller species of herpetofauna is minute compared to that characteristic of larger, more mobile vertebrates. For example, some salamanders and small snakes are poor dispersers in that they are adapted to travel only short distances in response to habitat alteration. The possibility exists, although it is untested, that some populations are so small that a major land alteration could conceivably extirpate a population from a region. For example, conversion of land to agriculture, pasture, reservoirs, suburbs, or urban areas in the past has resulted in elimination of extensive forest habitats, associated wetlands, and their attendant herpetofaunal populations. Conceivably, even entire species with restricted geographic ranges could have been forced to extinction if the rate of forest removal was rapid and vast enough to preclude dispersal to similar habitats.

In general, high herpetofaunal biodiversity on the landscape is due to the long-term presence and persistence of certain habitats and not to the prevalence of species that occupy early successional, disturbed habitats. However, some Group 1 and Group 2 herpetofauna, such as fence lizards, racers, and southern toads, appear to be rapid colonizers that respond favorably to disturbances. Nonetheless, as indicated above, many species of herpetofauna in isolated populations have low mobility. Hence, the scale and speed of habitat alterations can be critical in determining the persistence and sustainability of herpetofaunal communities.

Habitat Loss and other Environmental Impacts

Threats to forest herpetofauna come from several quarters as a result of environmentally negative impacts that can potentially occur from improper forest management, damming of streams and rivers to form reservoirs, conversion of forests for agriculture, and urban and suburban development. Replacement of native trees and shrubs with monoculture crops, housing developments, malls and shopping centers, and industrial complexes has resulted in erosion and runoff in addition to the removal of natural shelter. Although few documented records are available, it is intuitive that certain environmental impacts, especially elimination of natural habitats, has reduced numbers and population sizes of some species.

For example, commercial development, forestry operations, and agricultural activities over the past two centuries have had major impacts on the woodland and wetland habitats in the mountains, Piedmont, and Coastal Plain of the southern United States. Although documented evidence for the previous century is virtually unobtainable, the major modifications in the affected land areas have indisputably resulted in concomitant major changes in herpetofaunal populations. Agricultural and urban interests have understandably focused on crop productivity and municipal expansion but, with few exceptions, a consequence has been reduction in or elimination of native herpetofaunal wildlife. The total effect of farming and commercial development practices on reptiles and amphibians of once-forested regions in the South can only be speculated upon but has unquestionably been extensive.

The loss of microhabitats has been suggested as causing declines in Northwest amphibians that disappear from forests after logging of old-growth (Welsh 1990), a phenomenon that may apply to southern forests as well. Destruction of soil structure by disking, windrows, and furrows during some forestry operations has not been carefully assessed with long-term studies, but presumably these would have negative impacts on the majority of forest herpetofauna that live in underground burrows or beneath ground litter. The loss of refugia in underground root systems in some managed pine plantations is also considered to be a major environmental disruption of the life style of some snake species such as the eastern diamondback rattlesnake (Steve Bennett, pers. comm.). The retention of microhabitat features such as snags and coarse woody debris is highly valuable in habitat restoration efforts for reptiles and amphibians but is unlikely to prevent declines of herpetofauna on intensively disturbed sites.

Roads also have had a negative impact on almost all species of reptiles and amphibians, as well as many other wildlife species, in two demonstrable ways, one direct and the other more subtle. First is the direct road kill mortality associated with highways through productive forest habitat. Highways are probably the greatest single cause of mortality in box turtles (Mitchell 1994). Amphibian mortality is intensified when a heavily traveled road separates the adults of Group 2 species from the forest they live in and the wetland they require for breeding. Secondly, a more multifarious impact of road construction occurs on a long-term basis through fragmentation of habitats. A decline in populations of large snakes is believed to be due to the ever-increasing network of roads that fragments forest habitat into smaller and smaller parcels.

Fragmentation and isolation of habitats may preclude or limit dispersal and migratory movements (Noss 1987). Reducing functional habitat size likely reduces

The isolation of several Carolina bays in an agricultural landscape likely impairs movement and dispersal abilities of wetland herpetofauna. Spotted turtles (inset) are known to use the bottomland forest swamps (lower portion of photo) as well as the Carolina bays (center of photo) when water is seasonally available. A road between the bays also restricts movements *(K. Buhlmann)*.

Due to seasonal variability in hydroperiod among ponds in a sinkhole complex, all ponds are necessary to insure the long-term persistence of the tiger salamander (inset) population at this site. Although encroachment of development is a threat here, forest management activities that consider buffers and corridors could prevent the isolation of ponds in the landscape *(K. Buhlmann)*.

the number of species present in an area simply because smaller habitats support fewer species (MacArthur and Wilson 1967; Wyman 1990). When natural stochastic events cause extirpation of local populations (Pechmann et al. 1991), they may later become reestablished by dispersing individuals that emigrate from source populations (Pulliam 1988), but only if appropriate landscape connections are left to other source habitats. In contrast to birds, which are capable of flying to new habitat, most salamanders and small, fossorial snakes cannot crawl through a large deforested area to reach other suitable forest habitat. Therefore, large scale forest clearing, with heavy soil impact (disking, wind-rowing, chopping) can be presumed to reduce population sizes at some level. Low population sizes would be prolonged through habitat fragmentation. If declines or extirpation of herpetofaunal populations present on a site occur, population sizes will not be rebuilt quickly in a fragmented landscape.

A plethora of other environmental impacts can affect herpetofaunal communities in forests, most not being specific to reptiles and amphibians but affecting all components of wildlife communities. For example, the reduction of pH in aquatic habitats due to atmospheric deposition of sulfuric and nitric acids has been implicated in the declines of amphibians (Wyman 1988, 1990) as well as the decline of high elevation spruce forests (Schulze 1989), the habitat of several salamanders endemic to the Appalachians. The difficulties of documenting the effects of non-point source toxic chemicals unequivocally is well known, but some herpetofaunal populations, particularly amphibians, have undoubtedly been affected by industrial effluents and broadscale applications of pesticides and herbicides. Likewise, heavy metals and other toxic chemicals released in industrial activities can affect forest-dwelling reptiles and amphibians. The abnormal mouth morphology as a consequence of power plant fly ash residues on tadpoles is clear documentation of an impact on Group 2 forest species that require wetlands for breeding (Rowe et al. 1996).

Contamination by high levels of arsenic, cadmium, and selenium has been observed in semi- aquatic turtles and snakes (Justin D. Congdon pers. comm.). The overuse of herbicides and pesticides as by-products of farming has presumably had severe impacts on herpetofauna in the past, although field measurements are rarely available.

The invasion of introduced exotics can sometimes be detrimental to native species. Fire ants in particular have been implicated in the reduction in numbers of terrestrial egg-laying reptiles (Mount 1986). Finally, some species of forest-dwelling reptiles and amphibians suffer direct losses due to intentional killing (snakes), use as fish bait (salamanders), and capture for the pet trade. The introduction of fish into small, isolated wetlands disrupts the ecology of those systems that can cause declines in the amphibian fauna.

None of the above mentioned environmental impacts is likely to operate singly to eliminate an entire species in a region. Yet, the collective effect of these activities, although not easily measured, unquestionably results in a gradual but widespread decline in herpetofaunal biodiversity.

A small seasonally flooded wetland left isolated in the landscape by clearcutting activities without terrestrial habitat buffers or corridors to other nearby wetlands. Such land management likely causes local extinctions of amphibian and reptile species that require both seasonal wetlands and surrounding upland forests in their annual activity cycle. The chicken turtle lives in seasonal wetland habitats where it feeds on odonate larvae and crayfish. Chicken turtles leave the wetland during drying conditions and seek underground refugia in upland forests, usually 150-500 ft from the wetland edge. *(K. Buhlmann).*

Lack of Ecological Knowledge

A predominant problem faced by herpetofauna not only in southern forests but worldwide is that most species are not recognized by environmental managers, urban developers, farmers, politicians, the general public, and even some biologists as being species of concern. This problem is exacerbated for land managers, foresters, and commercial developers of southern forests, as well as for the herpetofaunal inhabitants themselves, because of the hidden biodiversity phenomenon. Reptiles and amphibians are in most instances highly secretive and often difficult to capture without special techniques. Therefore, the basic step of documenting the presence of a particular species in a habitat can be extremely difficult, particularly if the species is rare or has a primarily fossorial lifestyle that keeps it underground and out of sight most of its life.

Evidence exists that species diversity in a habitat or region can be much higher than documented, even after concentrated survey efforts (Gibbons et al. 1997). Thus, habitat alteration or destruction may occur with no awareness of the effect on herpetofauna. A study based on more than 3 decades of intensive survey efforts and on the capture of more than one million reptiles and amphibians on the 300-square-mile Savannah River Site (SRS) in South Carolina (Gibbons et al. 1997) exemplifies this problem. For, despite extensive survey and monitoring efforts, the herpetofaunal distribution and abundance patterns for the site are only partially known. Thorough surveys of this nature have not been conducted in the vast majority of forest habitats in the southern United States, and therefore knowledge of what species actually inhabit specific areas is extremely meager.

Unfortunately so little is known about the life history and ecology of most species of forest herpetofauna that recommendations for the best ways to provide protection are based mostly on speculation. For example, even the long-term impact of clear-cutting forested areas is poorly understood, although some investigators have documented short-term responses of amphibians at particular sites (Petranka et al. 1993, Sattler and Reichenbach 1998) and comparisons among different-aged pine stands have been made (Bennett et al. 1980). Yet, the interpretations remain equivocal.

RECOMMENDATIONS FOR ENHANCING HERPETOFAUNAL BIODIVERSITY IN SOUTHERN FORESTS

Habitat

Amphibian and reptile communities should be considered in land management decisions. Although information on habitat relationships is incomplete for many species, sensitive reptile and amphibian species depend on essential habitat features. Attributes of forest structure that are requirements for most amphibians and reptiles in forest communities, such as ground cover, should be taken into account in land or forest manipulations.

Numerous forest management approaches, such as prescribed burns, fire lanes, and clearcutting, are in use, but most are given minimal consideration to the herpetofaunal communities that will be affected. The ditching of wetlands, if not totally destructive, at least alters the hydroperiod and hence the composition of species that can use the wetland (Pechmann et al. 1989). Replacing natural wetlands with man-made mitigation ponds has not been demonstrated in most situations to result in habitat improvements for the herpetofaunal assemblages originally present. Although some common species of reptiles and amphibians (slider turtles, racers, southern toads, bullfrogs) adapt readily to man-made habitats such as farm ponds and fields, the majority of southern reptiles and amphibians do not.

The damming of streams to form reservoirs has had a major effect on eliminating herpetofaunal species and other stream organisms (Nickerson and Mays 1973, Mitchell 1994) by replacing riffle habitats with lakes managed for large predatory fish. And, clearly, any commercial development that replaces forest habitat with asphalt, housing, shopping centers and other products of urban sprawl has been detrimental to entire forest communities.

One previously mentioned contrast between larger mammals and birds versus reptiles and amphibians is that the majority of southern herpetofauna do not make long-range migratory movements overland. Most terrestrial travel is limited to short trips between woodland sites and wetlands in many species for purposes of breeding, egg laying, or hibernation. Hence, wetland buffers and habitat corridors would enhance productivity of numerous species of reptiles and amphibians in a high species diversity region such as the southern United States. The importance of leaving extensive terrestrial buffer zones around forest wetlands has been clearly demonstrated (Burke and Gibbons 1995, Buhlmann 1998, Semlitsch 1998, Semlitsch and Bodie 1998). McWilliams and Bachmann (1988) stated, "the primary management objective [for an ambystomatid salamander species] should be to preserve ephemeral woodland ponds and adjacent terrestrial habitat favorable for larval and adult survival." Semlitsch and Bodie (1998) argued that small isolated wetlands, especially those smaller than current regulations protect, are extremely valuable for maintaining biodiversity.

Likewise, although some conflicting results were detected, Beier and Noss (1998), in a comprehensive review of the effectiveness of corridors for conservation management, concluded that connected landscapes are preferable to fragmented ones. They also suggested that those who would destroy the remnants of connectivity should bear the burden of proving that their activities do not cause declines in populations. Clearly this is one aspect of conservation ecology where additional rigorously conducted studies are required, especially for reptiles and amphibians. Providing safe passage under roadways for reptiles and amphibians that migrate between habitats has been implemented with varying success (Jackson and Tyning 1989). The design of experiments that seek to determine the validity of corridors are presented in Inglis and Underwood (1992).

Although virtually all southern forests have been altered from their original states of half a millennium ago, many of the features critical to most reptiles and amphibians still remain to some degree. An emphasis on maintaining these critical features in forest habitats, or restoring them where possible in some situations, is the most basic habitat management approach for assuring the continuance of intact herpetofaunal assemblages.

Wildlife Researchers and Managers

In contrast to many traditional game species that have either increased or stabilized due to wildlife management activities of the past 100 years, reptile and amphibian populations are generally on the decline, and the loss of some species has possibly occurred but gone undetected. Yet, with the exception of endangered or threatened species, forest management programs do not characteristically manage for high herpetofaunal biodiversity.

Developing a single habitat management plan for the 220 species of reptiles and amphibians indigenous to forests and forest peripheries of the southern United States is not feasible. However, understanding the status of knowledge concerning herpetofaunal responses could greatly enhance a land manager's abilities to make decisions regarding habitat manipulations. For example, the convention of relocating individuals from populations where habitat is to be destroyed has not been demonstrated to be an effective or appropriate means of achieving conservation goals for herpetofauna (Dodd and Seigel 1991).

Special efforts to train professional wildlife managers in the field of herpetology would develop an awareness of the distribution patterns, habitat requirements, and behavior of herpetofauna in a region. A stronger emphasis on herpetofaunal studies in university wildlife departments would serve to diminish this problem of lack of information. A land manager with a background in herpetology and sensitive to herpetofauna could effectively implement specific programs for declining species, conservation of critical habitats such as isolated wetlands and their peripheries, and protection of migration routes during key periods of seasonal activity such as nesting by turtles or movement to wetlands by amphibians.

Increased Research Efforts

Modern wildlife biologists are becoming aware of how specific some of the habitat requirements are for individual species of herpetofauna. Like game species, to develop a suitable land management plan, each species or lifestyle grouping of reptiles or amphibians must be considered independently of others, an approach that may be impractical in some situations. To acquire the necessary understanding for the best management practices and alterations of Southern forests, extensive and intensive research will be necessary on the ecology, life history, and general biology of herpetofaunal species and communities. Thus, more specific habitat information is currently needed on forest species of special concern, such as the flatwoods salamander, striped newt, and gopher frog among the amphibians, and the southern hognose snake, pine woods snake, and pine snake among the reptiles. Also needed is general ecological information on various herpetofaunal assemblages associated with particular habitats, such as herpetofauna that use isolated wetlands, streamside riparian zones, or turkey oak sandhills communities.

Although a variety of herpetofaunal surveys in southern forest habitats has been conducted, some species are recorded infrequently and in nearly all regions of high biodiversity additional long-term sampling will reveal the presence of species not previously reported from the area despite the use of a wide variety of monitoring techniques. Yet such an understanding is essential to developing land management programs that affect the species present and can only be accomplished with research programs dedicated to reaching a fuller understanding of the environmental relationships among the herpetofauna and the forests they live in.

At this time, recommendations on how various forest management approaches can have impacts on particular species must rely on general limited information about how such species use forest systems, often based on studies of related species. Additional field research and experiments will reveal that some forest management practices have significantly less impact on the herpetofaunal community than do others. For example, silvicultural techniques such as thinning and hand planting would be less destructive than clearcutting and intense site preparation, a situation in which environmental gains must be weighed against economic losses. The development and testing of models that balance community environmental impacts against economic gains and losses would be of great service to the forest products industry, to managers of public lands, to conservationists interested in herpetofauna, and to many reptiles and amphibians themselves.

Public Education

Public attitudes must become more positive about reptiles and amphibians if broadscale conservation efforts are to be successful for forest herpetofauna. The attitudes and perceptions of the public about particular species or groups of species is often the most influential factor operating for or against conservation efforts. Negative attitudes toward snakes, particularly venomous species, are strong in many regions, although the true danger of many species may be greatly overrated (Gibbons and Dorcas 1998). A redirection of negative or passive public attitude toward snakes and other reptiles and amphibians is being made in many parts of the South through environmental education programs, and a turning of public opinion about the importance of such animals in forest ecosystems appears possible.

Herpetofauna as a group need public support, and wildlife biologists with a knowledge of reptiles and amphibians will be an important force in providing the local and regional education needed. Cooperative partnerships between herpetologists, wildlife and conservation professionals, state and federal agencies, the forest products industry, commercial development and industrial interests, the pet trade, agriculturists, and local communities will be necessary to bring about a full shift in attitudes about reptiles and amphibians. Such partnerships may result in proactive changes that are in the best interest of this beleaguered group of animals.

CONCLUSIONS

Modification of current forest management, agricultural, and land development practices may be necessary to assure the long-term environmental welfare of some species of forest-living reptiles and amphibians in the southern United States. Suitable changes in land management tactics toward southern forest ecosystems on a broad scale can help avoid the possibility of actual extinction of some species of herpetofauna and the certainty of a retraction in geographic range and general decline in abundance of others. The following suggestions are provided as guidelines for maintaining and enhancing the natural biodiversity of native reptiles and amphibians.

1. Develop and implement conservation and management plans for forest ecosystems that include a focus on species and assemblages of reptiles and amphibians. Emphasis should also be concentrated on communities within the forest habitat such as isolated wetlands, streamside riparian zones, sandhill uplands, and bogs that are critical for survival and reproduction.

2. Increase field research on herpetofauna to develop a better understanding of the ecological requirements of species and communities. Topics on which research is deficient include effects of pollutants and acid precipitation on aquatic amphibians, collection for the pet trade, introduction of exotic species, timing of forest management activities, and the use of buffers and corridors.

3. Increase the emphasis in traditional wildlife programs on studies of the ecology, evolutionary theory, and conservation biology of herpetofauna. Some natural history traits of many herpetofauna (delayed maturity, greater longevity, and limited mobility and dispersal within the landscape) differ from those of most game species on which traditional wildlife and forest management plans are based.

4. Develop a public attitude that extends to private land owners, land managers, agriculturists, and land developers that reptiles and amphibians are significant and important components of forest ecosystems and that the availability of suitable habitat is essential. Emphasize that successful short-term conservation of most species will require inventorying, protecting (through cooperative, incentive-based management plans with landowners), and in some cases restoring remaining natural areas. The success of long-term management strategies will require establishing effective buffers for these habitats and connecting them with other natural areas on the landscape.

Acknowledgments

Manuscript preparation was aided by Financial Assistance Award Number DE-FC09-96SR18546 from the U. S. Department of Energy to the University of Georgia Research Foundation and Savannah River Ecology Laboratory. We thank David E. Scott and Tracey D. Tuberville for providing photographs not taken by KAB. This article supports the PARC (Partnership for Amphibian and Reptile Conservation) effort to promote education about reptiles and amphibians.

CHAPTER 29

Resolving Wildlife Conflicts

Rick D. Owens
U.S. Department of Agriculture, Wildlife Services, Raleigh, NC

In this book we discuss various aspects of wildlife management, principally population enhancement and conservation. Natural resource managers have been successful in increasing production of many wildlife species and elevating public consciousness of the need to appreciate and protect wildlife and its habitats. Unfortunately, this has coincided with increased human populations and increased human-wildlife contacts and conflicts.

Anytime human activities come into contact with wildlife, there is the potential for conflict. These conflicts are diverse, affecting production of food and fiber as well as protection of property, human health and safety, and other natural resources. Human values are highly individualistic and what are negative experiences to some people are positive to others.

Wildlife damage management is defined as the alleviation of damage or other problems caused by or related to the presence of wildlife and is an integral component of wildlife management. The need for effective and environmentally sound wildlife damage management is rising dramatically, as is the public scrutiny these activities receive. This, along with heightened political interest, is the result of five major trends that can be expected to continue through the coming years including: 1) increasing suburban development which intrudes upon wildlife habitat; 2) population expansion of some adaptable wildlife species; 3) shift in public attitudes toward the welfare of animals; 4) increasing media interest in wildlife issues; and 5) advances in wildlife science and technology.

Natural resource managers are presented with the challenge of understanding and resolving the various aspects of negative human-wildlife interactions. As well, we must be able to effectively communicate to the public at large the whats, whys, and hows of wildlife damage management and be able to determine and apply the most practical and effective damage resolution

Wildlife interactions with humans frequently result in conflicts ranging from minor nuisances to significant damage *(USDI Fish and Wildlife Service)*.

technology. The resolution of these conflicts is necessary to ensure that positive values toward wildlife are maintained by individuals and our society as a whole.

Two important concepts to consider in evaluating and resolving wildlife damage problems are biological carrying capacity and wildlife acceptance capacity (Decker and Purdy 1988). Biological carrying capacity relates to factors of environmental resistance limiting wildlife populations including the quantity, quality, and distribution of food, cover, and water. Wildlife acceptance capacity (often referred to as cultural carrying capacity) reflects the maximum wildlife population level in an area that is acceptable to people. Wildlife managers traditionally have viewed wildlife management largely from the context of biological carrying capacity. However, wildlife acceptance capacity is often critical in assessing how wildlife damage management may affect public opinion and political processes. The threshold of wildlife damage acceptance is a primary limiting factor in determining the wildlife acceptance capacity. For any given damage situation, there will be varying acceptance thresholds by those directly, as well as indirectly, affected by the damage. Wildlife management agencies must develop and implement programs that will achieve the goal of managing wildlife. These programs must be compatible with habitat carrying capacity and society's interests or the agencies' images will be tarnished and credibility will be lost (Doig 1995).

My objectives in this section are to provide an overview of wildlife-human conflicts associated with southern forest wildlife and to discuss principles and processes related to development and implementation of effective wildlife damage management strategies.

Feeding of wildlife by humans often exacerbates conflicts *(P. Mastrangelo)*.

Substantial economic loss results from flooding from beaver dams and beaver feeding *(P. Mastrangelo)*.

DAMAGE

If a tree fell in the forest and nobody heard it, would it make a noise? Similarly, without people, would there be wildlife damage? It is our presence and diverse values that determine "damage." Without natural resource managers' values to protect plant diversity and maintain healthy populations of deer, there would be no need to manage overpopulations of deer to prevent habitat destruction and prevent starvation; without society's values to protect human life whenever possible, there would be no need to prevent aircraft and automobile collisions with wildlife; and without the need to produce food crops and associated economic benefits, wildlife damage to agriculture would not exist. Human values and perceptions toward wildlife and associated conflicts are highly diverse and vary with species, space, time, and numerous other situational factors.

The following is a brief overview of the diversity of damage associated with southern forest wildlife relative to economics, human health and safety, and natural resources.

Economics

Conover et al. (1995) assessed the potential cost of wildlife problems in the United States in terms of economic losses and human illnesses, injuries, and fatalities and concluded that little is known about the magnitude of damage or problems caused by wildlife. This literature review determined that few data exist on: 1) actual rather than perceived economic losses to agriculture and forestry, 2) the incidence of many human diseases for which wildlife may serve as a vector or reservoir to the pathogen, 3) frequency of and damage from deer-vehicle and bird-aircraft collisions, and 4) damage to rural and urban households. They were able to estimate, within the confines of existing data, economic losses approaching $3 billion annually.

Probably the most significant economic losses in the South can be attributed to 2 species, beaver and white-tailed deer. However, there is a paucity of current data. In 1986, Federal and State land management agencies and most of the large forest industries in 16 southern states were surveyed to determine the extent of damage caused by wildlife species to southern forests in the previous 12-month period (Miller 1987). The total acreage owned, managed, or reported by respondents accounted for approximately 31% of the commercial forests in those states. Estimated damage from all wildlife species totaled $11.2 million with beaver and white-tailed deer responsible for $10.2 and $0.4 million of these losses, respectfully. Thus, total losses for all commercial forests in those states from all species may have approached $36 million with beaver losses totaling near $32.9 million and deer near $1.4 million. The high monetary cost of beaver damage is reflected in losses reported by property owners and agencies to the U.S. Department of Agriculture's Wildlife Services program (Table 1). In Mississippi, North Carolina, and South Carolina, reported economic losses to all resources from 1994-1996 totaled $23 million with timber losses accounting for approximately one-half of this figure. These USDA figures do not represent statewide losses but are reflective only of losses reported by landowners and agencies requesting assistance from that agency.

Timber damage caused by beaver has been estimated at $8.6 million annually in Mississippi (Arner and Dubose 1982), $2.2 million annually in Alabama (Hill 1976), $45 million in Georgia (Godbee and Price 1975), and $14.5 million in Louisiana in 1993 (Fowler et al. 1994). Landowners in North Carolina reported $2.35 million to beaver damage in 1983 with individual losses up to $400,000 (Woodward et al. 1985). Leland and

Table 1. Economic losses (thousand $) in Mississippi, North Carolina, and South Carolina caused by beavers as reported to the U.S. Department of Agriculture, 1994-1996.

			Water			
State	Timber	Roadways	Control[a]	Crops	Other[b]	Total
Mississippi	2,662	2,272	630	632	231	6,430
N. Carolina	4,796	2,236	2,169	438	299	9,938
S. Carolina	4,904	942	–	377	522	6,745
Total	12,362	5,453	2,799	1,447	1,052	23,113

[a] Ditches, dams, levees.

[b] Septic systems, water treatment facilities, landscape plantings, etc.

Large concentrations of fish-eating birds can result in significant aquaculture losses *(USDA Wildlife Services).*

Hoagland (1993) reported beaver-related damages in Oklahoma averaged $690,158 annually. In 1994, beaver impounded 14,000 acres of bottomland hardwoods on the Delta National Forest in Mississippi, resulting in a $1.25 million timber loss in addition to threatening valuable wildlife habitat and adjacent cotton acreage.

Deer browsing can alter plant species composition, abundance, and distribution. Notable impacts are reduced height growth (Marquis and Brenneman 1981) as well as seedling mortality (Gottshalk 1987).

Wildlife damage to agricultural production was estimated at $591 million in 1994 (A. Wywialowski, U.S. Dep. Agric., unpubl. data). The USDA National Agricultural Statistics Service conducted a nationwide survey of farmers to assess the extent of wildlife damage to agricultural resources and found 58% of the respondents reporting wildlife-caused losses of some agricultural commodity with deer being the species primarily cited. Data showed damage to be highly variable among states with deer damage increasing from 1989 to 1994. In the 9-state southeastern reporting region (Alabama, Arkansas, Florida, Georgia, Louisiana, Mississippi, North Carolina, South Carolina, and Tennessee), deer damage to field crops in 1994 was reported by 25.3% of the respondents.

Deer browsing can also be problematic in residential areas where ornamental trees, shrubs, and flowers can be extensively damaged. Commercial plant nurseries sometimes receive severe damage from deer due to browsing or antler rubbing. Browsing impacts to forest, agriculture and urban resources vary by habitat type, deer density, location, time of year, and weather. Also, rodents such as voles, rats, nutria, and beaver can adversely impact forestry production due to feeding or dam building.

Predation to livestock and poultry by coyotes, bears, and vultures can be locally significant. West Virginia Extension Service survey data for 1995-1996 indicated that coyote predation to livestock totaled $605,000 and bear predation totaled $73,000. Livestock predation by vultures (primarily black) was reported to USDA Wildlife Services at approximately $131,000 in Virginia during the same period. Vultures can also cause extensive damage to property by pulling and tearing roofing shingles, window caulking, and vinyl upholstery in boats. Property damage by vultures has also been reported to USDA as sometimes exceeding $200,000/year in Florida and Georgia.

Wildlife-vehicle collisions are extensive. Conover et al. (1995) estimated 726,000 auto-deer collisions nationwide annually. Multiplied by a mean property damage loss of $1,577 as estimated from deer-auto collision costs in Michigan, New York, Pennsylvania, Utah, and West Virginia, this produces a damage esti-

Collisions between wildlife and automobiles or airplanes can cause human death and extensive property damage *(USDI Fish and Wildlife Service).*

Table 2. Estimated property losses from deer-auto collisions.

State	No. deer killed/year[a]	Damage costs($)[b]
Arkansas	3,901	6,151,877
Georgia	50,000	78,850,000
Kentucky	5,677	8,952,629
Louisiana	3,500	5,519,500
N. Carolina	8,000	12,616,000
Oklahoma	495	780,615
S. Carolina	3,689	5,817,553
Virginia	3,427	5,404,379
Total	78,689	124,092,553

[a] Highest yearly figure used from 1982-1991 deer mortality data reported by Romin and Bissonette 1996.

[b] Calculated at $1,577 per collision as estimated by Conover et al. 1995.

mate of approximately $1.1 billion annually. A survey by Romin and Bissonette (1996) of 50 state wildlife agencies indicated an upward trend in auto-deer collisions from 1982-1991. In 8 southern states an annual mortality of nearly 79,000 animals was reported (Table 2). When multiplied by Conover's et al. (1994) estimated cost of $1,577 vehicle damage per collision, this yields an annual damage estimate of $124 million in these 8 states. This is supported by estimates from Georgia where the Georgia Farm Bureau Insurance Company insures approximately 4% of Georgia motorists. In 1994, 3,313 deer-related auto insurance claims were reported for a net loss value of $4.6 million.

Wildlife collisions with aircraft also result in significant economic losses. In 1992-1996, wildlife strikes cost the U.S. civil aviation industry an estimated $216 million/year in direct monetary losses and over 406,000 hours/year of aircraft down time (Cleary et al. 1997). Birds were involved in 97% of reported strikes and mammals in 3%. Gulls, blackbirds, waterfowl, doves, and raptors were the most commonly struck bird groups, and deer and coyotes the most commonly struck mammals. Most bird strikes occurred between July and October, during the day, when aircraft were on approach or during take- off, and below 100 feet above ground level. Most mammal strikes occurred in the fall, at night, and during landing.

Human Health and Safety

In addition to economic losses resulting from wildlife collisions with automobiles and aircraft, such incidents can result in harm to human life. Conover et al. (1995) estimated 29,000 human injuries and 220 people killed annually from deer-automobile collisions. The Federal Aviation Administration reports that, since 1960, 20 civil aircraft have been destroyed and 95 civilian lives lost in the U.S. as a direct result of wildlife-aircraft strikes, and military crashes from 1985-1997 have resulted in 23 military aircraft lost and 33 personnel killed.

There are numerous diseases transmissible from wildlife to humans (Table 3). These can be transmitted directly from animal bites or through contact with body fluids and tissue through skinning, necropsying or other handling of wildlife. Indirect transmission may result from biting and sucking by arthropods such as ticks, fleas, and mosquitoes (McLean 1994). There are 7 human diseases nationally reported to the U.S. Centers for Disease Control and Prevention for which wildlife may serve as vectors or reservoirs. Of these, 5 diseases were reported in the Southeast in 1995 with a total of 685 cases of wildlife disease-related illnesses (Table 4). Plague and trichinosis were not reported (U.S. Dep. Health and Human Serv. 1995).

Blackbird, starling, crow, and vulture roosts and egret and heron rookeries in urban environments create nuisances and/or potential health hazards due to objectionable odors and the accumulation of droppings and feathers. Droppings sometimes create a favorable environment for growth of the fungal organism responsible for the respiratory disease, histoplasmosis.

Physical injuries also result from bites or attacks by wildlife. Conover et al. (1995) estimated that about 35,000 people are bitten in the U.S. annually by wildlife, predominantly by rodents, snakes, skunks and

Table 3. Some important wildlife diseases that may affect humans in the Southeast.[a]

Disease	Method of transmission	Wildlife hosts
Rabies	Animal bite and scratches	Striped skunk, raccoon, foxes, bats, other mammals
Anthrax	Contact with infected animals	Deer, bison, other hoofed mammals
Hantavirus	Aerosol, animal bite	Deer mouse, other wild and commensal rodents
Leptospirosis	Urine contamination, ingestion	Commensal and wild rodents, rabbits, foxes, skunks, raccoon, opossum
Brucellosis	Contamination, ingestion	Wild swine, elk, bison
Rat-bite fever	Animal bite	Commensal rodents
Salmonellosis	Ingestion of food contaminated with feces	Rodents, wild birds, pet reptiles
Ornithosis (Psittacosis)	Inhalation of contaminated air	Parrots, pigeon, waterfowl, herons, egrets
Histoplasmosis	Inhalation of spores	None, grows in soil enriched by feces under bird and bat roosts
Cryptococcosis	Inhalation is suspected	None, grows in feces-enriched soil
Trichinosis	Ingestion of uncooked meat	Wild swine, bear, carnivores, commensal rodents
Toxoplasmosis	Ingestion of uncooked meat, fecal contamination(feces)	All mammals and birds (tissue), Bobcats
Ascarid roundworm	Ingestion of nematode eggs	Raccoon
Alveolar hydatid disease	Ingestion of tapeworm eggs from feces	Red fox, coyote, arctic fox, wolves
Tularemia	Contamination from skinning animals, tick, biting insects	Rabbits, hares, muskrat, beaver, other mammals
Rocky Mountain spotted fever	Tick	Wild rodents, rabbits, hares, carnivores
Human monocytic ehrlichiosis	Tick	Deer, possibly other mammals
Human granulocytic ehrlichiosis	Tick	Wild rodents (white-footed mouse), possibly other rodents and mammals
Lyme disease	Tick	Wild rodents (*Peromyscus* spp., chipmunks), raccoon, deer, rabbits, birds
Babesiosis	Tick	Wild rodents (white-footed mouse, meadow vole)
St. Louis encephalitis	Mosquito	Birds, rodents
Eastern equine encephalitis	Mosquito	Birds, bats
Western equine encephalitis	Mosquito	Birds, rodents
Louse-borne typhus	Body louse, animal contact	Flying squirrel
Flea-borne (murine) typhus	Rat flea	Commensal rats, wild rodents, opossum
Plague	Contamination from skinning animals, flea	Wild rodents

[a] From McLean 1994 and W.R. Davidson pers. commun.

foxes. About 10-16 human fatalities/year occur as the result of these bites with venomous snakes being primarily responsible. These incidents will likely become more common in the future due to increasing human-wildlife interactions and the public's desire to touch and "bond" with wildlife.

Natural Resources

Deer can negatively impact plant and animal communities. Miller and Bratton (1992) identified 36 families and 98 species of threatened or endangered plants disturbed by deer browsing and grazing. High deer densities can affect habitat quality and reduce songbird species richness and abundance (DeCalesta 1994) and possibly have long-term impacts on woody vegetation communities which cannot be reversed by reducing deer densities (Stromayer and Warren 1997). Deer overabundance can also result in deterioration of deer herd health, reduction in reproduction, and increase in parasitism and disease (Kroll et al. 1986).

Beaver can alter local environments and adversely impact habitats and wildlife species of special concern. In Louisiana, beaver activities negatively impact the threatened Louisiana pearlshell (*Margaritifera hembeli*), a freshwater clam which requires clear, fast flowing, highly oxygenated water. Beaver dams built below

Winter blackbird roosts, which may contain millions of birds, are a nuisance and may be a health hazard due to histoplasmosis fungus associated with bird droppings *(USDI Fish and Wildlife Service)*.

Table 4. Reported cases of 5 human diseases in the Southeast for which wildlife may serve as a vector or reservoir.[a]

State	Brucellosis	Lyme disease	Psittacosis	Rabies[b]	Rocky Mtn. spotted fever
Alabama	-	12	-	(150)	3
Arkansas	4	11	-	(52)	31
Florida	2	17	1	1(248)	7
Georgia	1	14	5	(294)	9
Kentucky	-	16	-	(28)	16
Louisiana	-	9	-	(54)	2
Mississippi	-	17	-	(9)	32
N. Carolina	3	84	3	(466)	150
S. Carolina	1	17	3	(125)	37
Tennessee	-	28	1	(98)	32
Virginia	-	55	1	(459)	34
Total	11	306	14	1(1,983)	353

[a] U. S. Dep. Health and Human Serv. 1995.

[b] Figures in parenthesis denote animal cases.

pearlshell colonies slow water flow and cause water temperatures to rise, thereby reducing dissolved oxygen necessary for mussel survival. Similarly, in the Southern Appalachians, beaver impoundments negatively impact brown trout through elevated water temperatures, reduced dissolved oxygen, and lower pH (Barnes 1993). In Alabama, beaver-caused flooding is detrimental to the endangered Alabama canebrake pitcher plant (*Sarracenia rubra alabamensis*). Bottomland, mast-producing hardwoods in green tree reservoirs can also be severely impacted by beaver activities. Gnawing, girdling, and extended flooding can cause direct mortality or reduction in vigor. Nutria damage to planted bald cypress seedlings has been as high as 100% in Louisiana (Conner and Toliver 1987). Cotton and rice rats can be a limiting factor in efforts to direct-seed willow oak in bottomland hardwood habitat.

Wildlife damages are often evaluated based on regional or statewide averages. However, average losses do not accurately reflect the impacts on individuals

Beaver dams may be breached by hand, explosives, or heavy machinery (USDA Wildlife Services).

who may suffer no losses or on others whose losses may be catastrophic (Miller 1987, Wade 1987). While problems may be relatively minor on a large scale, damage is not evenly distributed and local impacts may be severe. Each situation should be evaluated to determine the extent and magnitude of the problem and the most practical and effective damage management strategies.

MANAGEMENT APPROACHES

The alleviation of wildlife damage is misunderstood and is commonly viewed as either lethal or non-lethal control of wildlife. However, there are many approaches to be considered in developing damage management strategies. Management approaches have been recently described in detail by Dolbeer et al. (1994) and Hyngstrom et al. (1994). Wildlife damage management can best be described as three basic actions: 1) management of the resource being negatively affected, 2) management of the wildlife responsible for, or associated with, damage, or 3) physical separation of the two.

Resource management includes alteration of cultural practices such as animal husbandry or crop selection, other habitat modification, and alteration of human behavior. Management of the wildlife species includes behavior alteration through harassment or scaring and population manipulation through translocation or lethal removal. Physical separation may consist of fencing, netting, or other barriers. The most effective approach to resolving wildlife damage problems is to integrate the use of several methods, either simultaneously or sequentially. The integrated pest management (IPM) approach, as applied in wildlife management, is the integration and application of practical methods of prevention and control to reduce damage by wildlife while minimizing harmful effects of control measures on humans, other species, and the environment (U.S. Dep. Agric. 1994).

The following description of methods is modified from the U.S. Department of Agriculture's *Animal Damage Control Program, Environmental Impact Statement* (1994). A more complete description of control methods by species and supply sources is provided in detail in *Prevention and Control of Wildlife Damage* (Hygnstrom et al., eds. 1994) published cooperatively by the University of Nebraska Cooperative Extension

Service, U.S. Department of Agriculture and the Great Plains Agricultural Council.

Resource Management

Resource management includes a variety of practices that may be employed by the resource manager to prevent or reduce wildlife damages or conflicts. Implementation of these practices is appropriate when the potential for damage can be reduced without significantly increasing the cost of production or diminishing the resource manager's ability to achieve management and production goals. These management approaches are usually implemented by the resource manager.

Animal Husbandry.—This general category includes modifications in the level of care and attention given to livestock, shifts in the timing of breeding and birth, selection of less vulnerable livestock species to be produced, and the introduction of human custodians or guarding animals to protect livestock.

Crop Selection and Planting Schedules.—The choice of crops and the time of planting have a direct bearing on the potential for depredation losses as some crops are less prone to depredation than others. Crops planted for early or late harvest may have a high potential for wildlife depredation due to the lack of alternate food sources. The composition of native wildlife and their feeding preferences should be considered prior to final selection of crops for production. If migratory wildlife species are involved, it may be possible to regulate the time of planting to reduce or eliminate the availability of vulnerable crops. If altered planting schedules are not feasible, selection of damage-resistant varieties may be possible. Other management approaches include removal of slash and planting large seedlings immediately after logging to reduce rabbit damage potential; planting or encouraging plant species preferred by deer to improve habitat and reduce the likelihood of browsing damage to commercially grown trees; decreasing cover and foods adjacent to sugar cane to suppress the carrying capacity for rodents; use of tree species or varieties that are generally resistant to damage by animals; and use of bird-resistant hybrids of corn and sorghum.

Human Behavior Modification.—The alteration of human behavior and activities can often resolve conflicts between humans and wildlife. The elimination of feeding of wildlife in parks and residential areas can reduce the wildlife's dependence upon humans. At airports where there is the potential for wildlife-aircraft collisions, flight patterns and other operations could be changed to reduce the safety risks.

Different electric and non-electric fences have been developed to exclude deer from areas (USDA Wildlife Services).

Physical Exclusion

Physical exclusion methods restrict the access of wildlife to areas where contact with human activities would be undesirable. These methods provide a means of appropriate and effective prevention of wildlife damage in many situations and are usually implemented by the resource manager.

Fencing.—Fences are widely used to prevent damage to livestock, farm crops, and forest plantings caused by such species as coyotes, deer, elk, and rabbits. Wire fencing of varying design (woven, single/multiple strand) and mode of operation (electric, nonelectric) can be effective dependent upon the individual circumstances. "Fences" of wind-rowed trees have been used to exclude white-tailed deer from newly planted, bottomland hardwood plantations.

Sheathing.—Hardware cloth, solid metal flashing, or other materials may be used to protect trees or to block entrances to gardens, dwellings, or other areas. Tree protectors are often used as protection from bears, beavers, or porcupines. A mixture of paint and sand applied to tree trunks may prevent gnawing by beavers. Entrance barricades of various kinds are used to exclude such animals as opossums, raccoons, skunks, squirrels, and starlings from dwellings and storage areas.

Netting, Porcupine Wire, and Wire Grids.—Wire and plastic netting are also used to exclude a variety of birds and mammals from specific objects or areas such as crops, roadways, nurseries, poultry operations, and other areas. Plastic mesh seedling tubes are widely used in reforestation efforts to protect newly planted seedling trees from hares, rabbits, pocket gophers, deer, and elk. Strips of sharp wire or metal spikes are placed on building ledges to exclude pigeons, sparrows, and many other birds. Aquacultural depredation by fish-eating birds may be managed by totally enclosing ponds and raceways with netting or through the use of overhead wire or kevlar lines suspended horizontally in a crisscross pattern. Grid wires over park lakes have inhibited access by urban Canada geese.

Wildlife Management

Wildlife management is directed at moving or removing wildlife, or making the habitat unsuitable for their presence. Direct, hands-on management of wildlife may be conducted by the professional wildlife specialist or resource owner depending on legal constraints, expertise, or other factors.

Habitat Management.—Just as habitat management is an integral part of other wildlife management programs, it also plays an important role in wildlife damage control. The type, quality, and quantity of habitat are directly related to the wildlife that are produced. Therefore, habitat can be managed to favor or not favor certain wildlife species. Habitat management is frequently used to address bird- aircraft strikes by eliminating nesting, roosting, loafing, and feeding sites in the vicinity of airport operations. Large urban blackbird and starling roosts which develop in the fall and winter can be dispersed by removing roost trees or selectively thinning the stands. Vole damage to fruit orchards can sometimes be alleviated by reducing vole numbers through eliminating or reducing grass cover. Pocket gopher damage to forest plantations may be minimized through selective cutting rather than clear-cutting and by weed and grass control. The architectural designs of buildings or other public spaces can often be modified to address wildlife damage situations. The elimination of ledges and similar external structures will preclude use by pigeons for roosting and nesting. Selecting species of trees and shrubs that are not attractive to wildlife can reduce the likelihood of potential damage to residential areas, parks, and other public spaces.

Limitations of habitat management as a method of controlling wildlife damage are determined by the characteristics of the species involved, the nature of the damage, economic feasibility, and other factors. Legal constraints may exist which preclude altering particular habitats.

Lure Crops/Alternate Foods.—When depredation cannot be avoided by careful crop selection or modified planting schedules, lure crops or an alternative food source can sometimes be used to mitigate damages. Frightening devices may be necessary in protected fields and wildlife should not be disturbed in lure crop areas.

Frightening Devices.—The success of frightening devices depends on animals' fears and subsequent aversion to offensive stimuli. Persistent effort is usually required to effectively apply frightening techniques as animals can easily become habituated to these devices. Animals frightened from one area may become a problem elsewhere. Frightening techniques include the use of electronic distress and alarm calls, propane exploders, pyrotechnics, lights, water sprays, helium-filled balloons, and reflective mylar tape. Trained dogs may be used to chase deer from orchards and nurseries and Canada geese from public facilities and private residences. The use of these noise-making and visual stimuli is most effective when used collectively, rather than individually, and often must be augmented by limited shooting.

Chemical Repellents.—These are compounds that prevent consumption of food items or use of an area and function by producing an undesirable taste, odor or feel. The reaction of different animals to a chemical formulation varies, and there may be variations in repellency among different habitat types. Grease-like paste repellents are sprayed or applied with a caulking gun to window sills, ledges, or similar perches to repel birds around structures. Methyl anthranilate (ReJeX-iT®) is a grape-flavored food additive which, when added to food or water, acts as a sensory repellent to birds such as gulls and Canada geese. The avian frightening agent, 4-aminopyridine (Avitrol®), is a toxic chemical used to repel flocking birds such as blackbirds, starlings, gulls, and crows. Birds ingesting the chemical usually die, but in the process emit distress calls and fly erratically. It is applied so only a few individuals ingest the treated food

The body-gripping conibear trap is used extensively to control beaver populations *(USDA Wildlife Services)*.

items but their behavior negatively impacts remaining members of the flock. Capsaicin (red pepper) is used to repel some mammals such as rodents and bears. Several repellents are registered for use in repelling deer and elk. Chemical repellents are strictly regulated and suitable repellents are not available for many wildlife species or damage situations.

Relocation.—There are a number of devices and methods which may be used to capture and restrain a variety of wildlife for relocation to other areas. Cage traps are usually made from wood, wire, or sheet metal and function by animals entering and becoming enclosed in the device. These include a variety of designs such as the box trap, culvert trap, "suitcase" trap, Australian crow trap, and many others. Netting may be dropped or propelled from overhead structures or aircraft to entangle deer and elk or may be held stationary to capture these animals driven into it. Leghold traps are the most versatile and widely used tool for capturing animals such as coyote, bobcat, mountain lion, fox, raccoon, muskrat, and nutria. Body snares made of wire or cable are most frequently used to capture coyotes, beaver, and otter. Spring-loaded foot snares are used to capture mountain lions and grizzly and black bears.

Tranquilizing drugs, which are strictly regulated, are used to immobilize animals and are applied orally or by injection. Injection of mammals may be by hand-held syringes, pole syringes or jab sticks, projected darts or capture guns, and blowguns. The orally-administered drug, alpha-chloralose, has limited use in capturing waterfowl, coots, and pigeons.

Lethal Methods.—The capture-and-relocation methods previously discussed can also be used as capture-and-kill methods. There are also specialized quick-kill traps which are available for a limited number of species. Conibear traps are used mostly to capture muskrat, nutria, and beaver in shallow water or underwater traps. Snap traps are used to remove mice or rats from buildings. Spring-powered harpoon traps and scissor-like traps are set in active tunnels or burrows to capture moles or pocket gophers.

Shooting may be labor intensive, but can be selective for target species. Removal of beaver and deer by night shooting can be effective in reducing damage in many situations. This technique may also be used to supplement bird harassment when birds adapt and no longer shy from scaring efforts.

Denning is the practice of seeking out the dens of coyotes or foxes and destroying the young, adults, or both to stop or prevent depredations on livestock. The removal of pups will often stop depredations even though the adults are not taken. Egg and nest destruction is used to control or limit the growth of a bird population in a specific area or to move the birds elsewhere. This can be used to limit population growth of Canada geese in urban areas, eliminate rooftop nesting by gulls, and move cattle egret nesting colonies from airports.

Table 5. Wildlife damage control methods and applications for selected wildlife species in the Southeast.[a]

Control method[b]	Beaver	Deer	Black bear	Coyote	Blackbird
Resource management					
Animal husbandry			X	X	
Night penning			X	X	
Shed lambing				X	
Time of breeding			X	X	
Move livestock			X	X	
Change livestock class			X	X	
Herding			X	X	
Guarding animals			X	X	
Crop types/schedules					
Time of planting				X	X
Time of harvest				X	X
Crop type/variety		X	X	X	X
Human behavior modification					
Stop feeding wildlife		X	X	X	
Alter aircraft schedules					X
Physical exclusion					
Fencing	X	X	X	X	
Sheathing	X	X	X		
Netting					X
Porcupine wire, Nixalite®					X
Wire grids					X
Storage containers			X		
Wildlife management					
Habitat management					
Modify vegetation					X
Eliminate standing water					X
Thin/remove roost					X
Close garbage dump			X		X
Manipulate water level	XX				
Remove dam	XX				
Lure crops/alternate foods					
Grain piles					X
Sacrificial crops					X
Sacrificial livestock				X	
Frightening devices					
Electronic distress					XX
Propane exploders		X	X	X	XX
Pyrotechnics			X		XX
Lights			X	X	
Water spray devices					XX
Strobe siren			XX	XX	
Eye spot balloons					XX
Effigies/scarecrows				X	X
Chemical repellents					
Odor	X	X			
Tactile (Tanglefoot®)					X
Frightening (Avitrol®)					X
Relocation					
Leghold traps	XX			XX	
Cage traps	XX	XX	XX	XX	XX
Snares					
Neck/body	XX			XX	
Foot/leg			XX	XX	
Lethal					
Conibear trap	XX				
Denning				XX	
Shooting					
Calling			XX	XX	
Spotlighting	XX	XX		XX	
Shooting on sight	XX	XX	XX	XX	XX
Hunting dogs					
Tracking/trailing			XX	XX	
Decoy dogs				XX	
Chemical toxicants					
Sodium cyanide				XXX	
Sodium fluoroacetate				XXX	
Gas cartridge				XX	
DRC-1339					XXX

[a] Modified from Slate et al. 1994

[b] X = primarily used by resource owners; XX = used by resource owners and wildlife damage management specialists; XXX = used only by licensed wildlife damage management specialists

Several toxic chemicals have been developed to control wildlife damage. The proper placement, size, type of bait, and time of year are keys to selectivity and successful control. Vertebrate pesticides are generally not species specific and their use may be hazardous unless used with care and by knowledgeable personnel. Some of these chemical compounds and target wildlife species are anticoagulants (rodents), fumigants (burrowing rodents and moles), and toxicants including zinc phosphide (rodents), strychnine (pocket gophers), sodium cyanide (coyotes, foxes), sodium fluoroacetate (coyotes), and Starlicide® (starlings, blackbirds, pigeons, gulls, crows). The use of pesticides not approved by the Environmental Protection Agency is illegal.

Table 5 illustrates control methods potentially applicable to managing damage associated with beavers,

Figure 1. Wildlife damage management decision model. Decision-making requires a step-wise thought process.

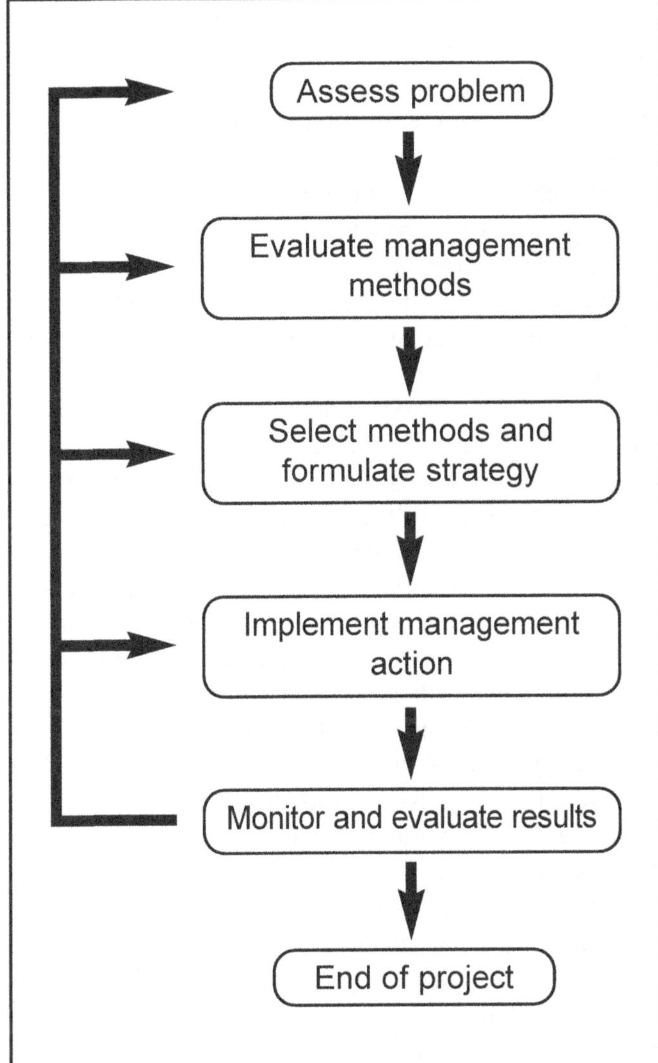

black bears, blackbirds, coyotes and white-tailed deer. The species-methods groupings are representative of the variability of damage techniques among species. All of these methods have limitations dependent upon the circumstances of the individual situations.

DECISION-MAKING PROCESS

It is human nature to desire quick-fix, cookbook solutions to problems, and the resolution of wildlife- related problems is no exception. However, wildlife damage management decision-making is complex and requires a step-wise thought process to arrive at solutions which are both effective and practical. Because each situation is unique, management strategies must be tailored to the specific problem at hand. Such decisions cannot be based solely on economics, but must also include biological, physical, social, and legal considerations. The resultant management strategies and actions should therefore be environmentally cost-effective (Owens and Slate 1992).

Wildlife managers, like other professionals such as medical doctors, follow a similar approach to decision-making (Fig. 1). The following discussion will assist the resource manager or property owner in determining what methods and approaches are appropriate in resolving wildlife damage problems. This wildlife damage management decision-making process has been previously described by Slate et al. (1992) and U.S. Dep. of Agric. (1994).

Problem Assessment

Immediate attention is given to determining the species responsible for the damage as well as the type, extent, and magnitude of damage. We must determine present and future environmental impacts in the absence of control actions. If left unaddressed, what will be the biological impacts? Will there be unacceptable habitat degradation? What will economic losses be? What are the sociopolitical implications? Will there be legal liability for damages if no action is taken? The seriousness of the problems must be determined so relative comparisons can be made of management options potentially applicable to the particular situation. We must also consider pertinent aspects of the damage history. Is this a recurring problem or is it a single episode? What control actions, if any, have been previously implemented? What were the results?

Methods Evaluation

After completing the problem assessment, potentially available methods must be evaluated to determine their practicality. Conceptually, this component of decision-making consists of a series of legal, administrative, and environmental screens for each potential method (Fig. 2). The result is a list of methods which may be considered further in formulating control strategies.

Legal and Administrative Considerations.—Wildlife damage management methods are subject to various legal and administrative authorities. For example, a method may be legal in one state but not in another or may be legal only in portions of a state such as not being allowed in areas heavily populated by humans. Application of the method may be restricted to specially trained, wildlife damage management personnel. Specific authorization may be required from state and federal regulatory agencies. The status of the target species (state or federally listed threatened or endangered) or the presence of such listed species in the area

Figure 2. Wildlife damage management methods evaluation and screening. Numerous legal, administrative, and environmental considerations must be made in determining methods that are practical and environmentally cost-effective.

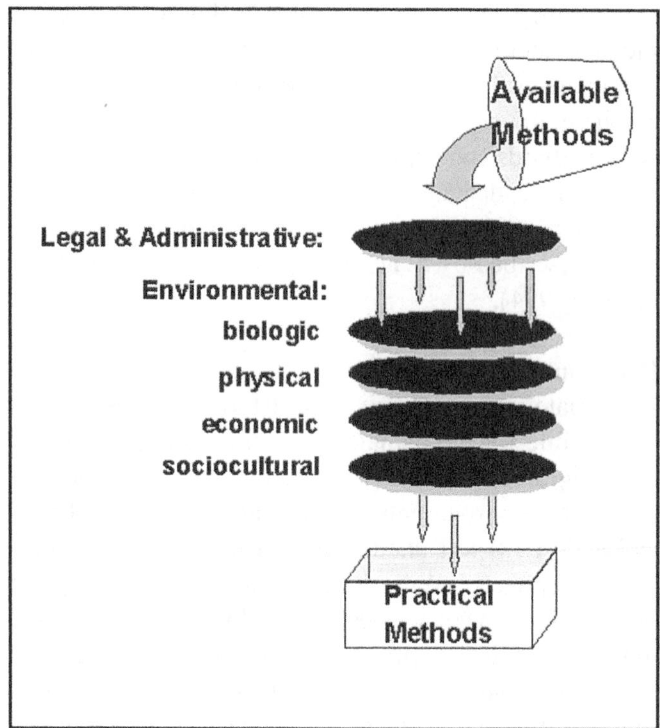

where control activities are planned could preclude the use of a method. Key questions to answer for each method include: Is it legally and administratively permissible to use this method on this species within the state? Is it permissible to use this method to address this specific type of damage? Is it permissible to use this method at this specific site or are there restrictions because of land class, land use patterns, or presence of specially protected species?

Environmental Considerations.—The methods that have made it through the evaluation screening at this point are further evaluated with regard to pertinent aspects of the biologic, physical, sociocultural, and economic environments. This is an analysis of the relative environmental cost- effectiveness of the methods. A general question to be considered is: What are the positive or negative short-or long-term direct, indirect, or cumulative environmental effects of using or not using this method?

Important questions to be addressed for the biologic environment include: Is the target species abundant or rare? Could species or habitats of special concern be affected? Are there special behavioral traits of the target species such as daily or seasonal movement patterns that require consideration? Could the method affect biological diversity?

Important questions to be addressed for the physical environment include: What effect would local weather or climatic patterns have on the use of the method? What effect would soil, water, air, elevation, or other physical habitat features have on the use of the method? What effect would the method have on soil, water, and air quality? What health and safety risks would be posed with, or without, the method being used?

Important questions to be addressed for the economic environment include: Would the use of the method be likely to reduce damage? Does the magnitude of the damage warrant the cost of applying the method?

Evaluating methods relative to the sociocultural environment frequently presents the greatest challenge because of differences in human attitudes toward wildlife species, wildlife damage management methods, and the resources damaged by wildlife. In spite of the difficulties associated with evaluating methods in the sociocultural environment, societal values are important in decision-making and deserve consideration in methods evaluation similar to the other environmental factors. Some important sociocultural issues to consider include: What are the perceptions regarding the humaneness of the method? How acceptable are the method's risks to nontarget species to the resource manager as well as the general public? How acceptable to the resource owner as well the general public are the method's effects on the target animal?

This evaluation of potentially available methods should result at this point in the identification of several practical methods. However, it is possible to determine that no practical method exists for this particular situation. This would result in no action being recommended or taken. Additionally, monetary compensation for wildlife damage is sometimes legislatively mandated. However, compensation does not address the problem.

Strategy Formulation

Control methods which have been determined to be practical are formulated into a control strategy based on considerations of available expertise, legal constraints on methods users, costs, and relative effectiveness. In determining the sequence or combination of methods to be applied and who will apply them, preference is usually given to practical nonlethal methods. However, this does not mean that nonlethal methods must always be applied as a first response to each problem. There may be situations where the use of lethal methods alone is the most appropriate strategy.

Expertise.—Resource management and physical exclusion methods are usually applied by the resource owner or affected party. Some wildlife management methods also may be applied by the resource owner. However, effective application of many of these methods often requires personnel with special expertise in wildlife damage management. The availability of expertise may influence the balance of direct, hands-on management provided by the resource owner and wildlife damage management specialists. Effective solutions to many damage problems require the resource owner to integrate his/her management activities with direct control services provided by a wildlife damage management specialist. Professional damage management assistance may be available from state or federal wildlife management agencies or private wildlife damage control businesses.

Legal Constraints.—Methods were previously screened to determine which methods were legally permissible for the problem. Here in the strategy formulation, it is necessary to determine legal constraints on who may use the method. For example, restricted-use pesticides cannot be used by persons who are not trained, certified applicators. Also, Environmental Protection Agency label restrictions on specific pesticides may limit their use to specific groups or agencies.

Costs.—Economic cost-effectiveness is an obvious goal in wildlife damage management. However, the costs of implementing wildlife damage management cannot be considered independently from the damage problem, probable environmental impacts, and other strategy considerations. A lack of funds may restrict the resource owner from using the most practical method or hiring special expertise adequate to solve the problem. Overriding social concerns may preclude the use of the most cost-effective method. For example, the use of pyrotechnic frightening devices in and around urban areas to reduce damage by birds may not be feasible because of noise intolerance by the local public.

Relative Effectiveness.—Effectiveness of a method or combination of methods must take into account the variables discussed above, and very importantly, the ability of the methods to reduce damage. Ideally, the method or methods selected should produce maximum damage resolution with minimal negative environmental impacts.

Implementation

The management strategy may be implemented by the resource owner, professional wildlife damage management personnel, or both. Wildlife management agencies are a source of technical assistance in the form of advice, recommendations, information, or materials. In some instances, direct control assistance by wildlife agency personnel may be available. For example, U.S. Department of Agriculture Wildlife Services personnel may provide management assistance on a reimbursable basis, dependent on the species involved and services requested. Private companies may be available also. Direct control by appropriately trained personnel should be employed when actions may affect sensitive species or areas or involve certain hazardous materials.

Evaluation

Regardless who implements the control strategy, routine monitoring is necessary to determine when to terminate the actions. If the implemented strategy is not effective, a continuation of the strategy or reevaluation may be necessary as represented by the feedback loop shown in Fig. 1.

FUTURE

Wildlife damage management is about finding "balance" between the needs of people and needs of wildlife. This is extremely challenging as nature has no balance, but rather, is in continual flux. Wildlife damage must be managed because of this natural imbalance, shifting societal needs, and other dynamic environmental influences.

As mentioned earlier, there will be increasing suburban development which intrudes upon and modifies wildlife habitat, and a resultant population expansion of some adaptable wildlife species. Public attitudes will continue to shift toward the welfare of animals and media interest in wildlife issues will increase. This will increasingly result in the paradox of greater protection of wildlife with little or no consideration for responsible management of human-wildlife conflicts. Wildlife damage management decision-making will become more complex due to increased public scrutiny and associated political interest. Natural resource managers must adapt to these changes.

Public concerns for animal welfare, as well as other natural resource protection issues, will place increasing pressures on forest and wildlife managers in the South to develop, communicate, and implement effective and practical solutions to managing wildlife problems. Animal welfare and animal rights activists will attempt to change wildlife management philosophy and practice to conform to their respective beliefs. Natural resource managers and agencies must be futuristic and innovative to be successful. Wildlife management actions cannot be successfully implemented independent of public scrutiny and involvement.

It must be communicated to the public the whats, whys, whos, and hows of wildlife damage and the environmental cost-effectiveness of various corrective measures which are available, practical and effective. The public must understand that wildlife damage management decisions are the result of a complex assessment process and that each situation is unique, as are the solutions to that problem. This will require that alliances be developed with customers and stakeholders. Citizen participation through community meetings, stakeholder working groups, surveys, or other means should be used to create educational opportunities, improve agency image as being responsive to stakeholder needs, and lead to more acceptable, if not universally embraced, decisions and actions to solve management problems (Stout et al. 1993).

Management strategies must be developed and implemented which balance the needs of people with needs of wildlife. The failure to develop, communicate, and implement such strategies will diminish the professional credibility, and effectiveness, of wildlife management.

CHAPTER 30

Wildlife Recreation

H. Ken Cordell
USDA Forest Service
Southern Research Station, Athens, GA

John C. Bergstrom, R. Jeff Teasley, and Jeremy Thomas
University of Georgia, Agriculture & Applied Economics, Athens, GA

Southern U.S. forests contribute to sustaining and adding quality to human life in many important ways. From before, during, and continuing now well after early European settlement of the South, native and immigrant populations in the South have lived in, off of and with forests as a major feature of their landscape. One of the important ways people benefit from the forests of the South is through outdoor recreation. In this paper we focus on wildlife recreation as one of the major uses of southern forests using the 1995 National Survey on Recreation and the Environment (NSRE) as the primary source of data. We also examine demographic trends and shifts in the recreational role of wildlife and seek a resource management interpretation of these trends.

The NSRE was developed by a partnership of federal agencies and the private sector to assess trends in outdoor recreation participation nationwide and across all the regions of the country (Cordell et al. 1998). The survey included questions on nearly 90 different types of outdoor recreation pursuits, including wildlife activities. In our discussion of the wildlife recreation activities included in the NSRE, estimates of participation in both nonconsumptive and consumptive activities are presented. All estimates are for participation occurring during a 12-month period in 1994-95 by people 16 years or older. Before we focus attention on wildlife-based outdoor recreation activities, however, we will first take a look at the overall social and outdoor contexts and trends in the South within which wildlife is a highly valued recreational resource.

THE SOCIAL AND OUTDOOR RECREATION CONTEXTS FOR SOUTHERN WILDLIFE

The Social Context

The social context of the South has been changing dramatically over the last few decades, as it has in the rest of the Nation, except more dramatically so. Growth of population, land use shifts, urbanization, expanding minority populations, a thriving economy, rising environmental sentiments, and shifts in property ownership, among many other changes, have put forest and wildlife management in a much different context than at any other time in this region's history (Cordell et al. 1998). Some of the more salient changes are reviewed below.

Population Growth.—Since 1970, the population of the South has grown to almost 87 million, an increase of nearly 31 million, up 54% in barely more than 25 years. Population in the states of South Carolina, Georgia and Florida, the southeastern coastal states, grew fastest among the southern subregions at 87.3%. The South's population growth was second fastest among the major regions of the United States, exceeded only by the West. This region's population gain was in part due to net domestic immigration, contributing around 380,000 new residents between the 1980s and the middle 1990s. The South was the only region in the country with a net gain from migration.

Urban Growth.—Much of the growth of the region's population occurred in the ever expanding urban areas, leaving a number of rural counties with declining population (Cordell et al. 1998). One hundred and sixty four counties in the South have had over 100% growth since 1970. Of these fast growing counties, almost 73% are metropolitan counties (MSA, Metropolitan Statistical Area). Of the remaining nonmetro counties with substantial gains in population, most were either adjacent to counties that are MSAs, or they were in high natural amenity areas such as the Southern Appalachians, the Ozarks, or the Atlantic coast (Economic Research Service, 1997).

Economic Growth.—Income has been changing in the South, along with population. Income changes are important, because as incomes rise or fall, so do consumption of goods and services, participation in outdoor recreation, savings, government tax revenues, and people's lifestyles. Real per capita income in the South in 1980 was $11,453; by 1998, it was $13,184—a rise of a little over 15% in 18 years (English and Gentle, 1998). This is moderate growth, below that of other regions. However, the income growth that has occurred in the South has resulted in the Nation's largest decline in percentage of people living in poverty of any of the U. S. regions. In looking at changing incomes in the South, we found that an increasingly larger share of total wage earner income is going to women and minorities, a shift that is changing the distribution of consumer "voting" power and demand for outdoor recreation.

Sustaining growth of its economy and income are very much dependent on the region's productive diversity. Measured as a ratio of the number of viable economic sectors relative to the maximum number of sectors possible, the South experienced growth in economic diversity of almost 18% between 1982 and 1992 (English and Beavers in press). This rate of diversification was slightly higher than the national average between 1982 and 1992, which was just over 17%.

Environmental Attitudes.—Contrary to popular beliefs, research has shown that environmental attitudes vary little across the regions of the country (Christiansen and Arcury 1992). Looking broadly at Americans' environmental attitudes is usually a good representation of attitudes held in any particular region, or state. In the South and across the nation, environmental concern among the citizenry rose rapidly in the 1960s (Dunlap 1991). By the early 1990s, this environmental concern expressed in opinion surveys, including concerns over the natural environment, had attained an all time high. Opinion surveys of residents in Alabama and the Mid-South conducted in 1992 provided direct evidence that the environmental values and opinions of southerners closely resemble those of the broader American public (Bliss et al. 1994). Three-quarters of southern respondents agreed with the statement, "Private property rights should be limited if necessary to protect the environment." Fewer than one quarter agreed that, "Forest owners have the right to do as they please with their forests, regardless of what it does to the environment." Southern forest land owners themselves share the public's concerns about the environment. In opinion surveys, they expressed feeling that clearcutting and use of herbicides should be regulated where necessary to protect environmental values, while seeking a balance between protecting the environment and protecting the rights of property owners. Only 2% of the American public in the mid- 1990s indicated they were not supportive of the environmental movement (Times Mirror 1994). Ninety percent feel there is a need to strike a balance between economic progress and environmental protection.

Changing Landownership.—Another important change in the South is ownership of private rural land (Cordell et al. 1998). Of private land owners, steadily increasing proportions do not live on the land (absentees) and owners express an increasingly wide range of reasons for owning. In a recent survey of land owners of 10 or more acres (Teasley et al. 1998), the estimated regionwide percentage of owners who are absentee was 56.2%. The reasons owners gave for owning rural land

Hiking is popular southwide *(US Forest Service).*

included having personal recreation opportunities (43%), raising livestock for sale (42%), investing to eventually sell (39%), growing landscaping shrubbery for sale (31%), providing recreation opportunities for others (31%), enjoying one's own personal green space (27%), being able to live in a rural setting (25%), renting dwellings for profit (25%), and using the land as a tax shelter (20%). Eight percent indicated owning to provide habitat for wildlife, and 3% indicated growing timber for sale as reasons.

Land owners resemble other southerners in the U.S., generally by the environmental attitudes they profess. In a survey of southern landowners (Teasley et al. 1998), nearly 77% strongly agreed with the statement, "The balance of nature is very delicate, so we must try to limit economic growth that exploits nature." This attitude of seeking balance was held equally strongly by resident as well as absentee owners. And, when asked what they intend to emphasize on their land, 38% indicated improvement of the natural conditions, while about 27% indicated earning income. About 32% were undecided about what to emphasize.

Recreational Access to Private Land.—Recreation demand continues to grow and private owners have responded with a gradual and steady closure of access to all but persons they know or to a lesser extent to persons to whom they lease (Teasley et al. 1998). In the South, 41% of owners with 10 or more acres post an average of 238 acres. Reasons for posting include, "To know who is on the property" (40% of those who post), "To keep out persons not having permission" (40%), and "To keep hunters out" (32%). About 80% of southern owners expect to post the same acreage in the future, but 15% indicate they plan to post more. Mostly, the persons allowed on their land are limited to members of the owner's household, immediate family, friends, or others they know personally. A relatively low percentage of private landowners (just over 7%) lease to outside individuals, clubs or groups for hunting or other recreation. This figure does not include private industrial land (such as owned by timber companies) that may be leased for recreation. Additionally, some private landowners in our survey sample may not have reported leasing activity for privacy and nondisclosure reasons. Thus, when industrial landowners and nonindustrial landowners who may not have reported leasing activity are included, the total number of private landowners who lease land for recreation may be greater than 7%.

The Outdoor Context

When examining outdoor recreation in the South, it is informative to compare this region with other regions. In the first section below, we briefly provide some of those comparisons. In the second section below, we begin to focus on wildlife-based recreation by comparing it with other forms of outdoor recreation.

Comparison of Outdoor Recreation Participation Rates Among Regions.—Across the 4 major regions of the country (North, South, Rocky Mountains/Great Plains, and Pacific Coast), there are few differences in participation among the broad types of outdoor recreation activities, including trail, street, and road-based activities such as hiking or driving for pleasure, individual sports such as tennis, team sports (softball, etc.), spectator sports, boating, swimming, and social activities such as family gatherings out of doors (Cordell et al. 1998). Regardless of differences in climate, landscapes, the nature of opportunities, and population size and culture, participation percentages for these types of activities are quite similar across the 4 regions.

The activity types (groupings of similar activities) for which there are marked regional differences include viewing and learning activities (including wildlife viewing and bird watching), snow and ice activities, camping, hunting, fishing, and outdoor adventure activities (for example, rock climbing or white water canoeing) (Cordell et al. 1998). These activity types are directly dependent on the nature of the resources and settings available. Thus differences among regions in resources and settings are obviously major reasons for the regional differences we observed.

Regional differences in participation percentages are especially pronounced for snow and ice activities, camping, and outdoor adventure activities (for example, rock climbing). For snow and ice activities, participation percentages in activities such as skiing is highest in the North, including the Great Lakes area, and as one might expect, lowest in the South. Regional differences in participation in outdoor adventure activities show the 2 western regions (Rocky Mountain/Great Plains and the Pacific Coast) with 48 and 45% of the population participating in one or more adventure activities, while in the eastern regions (the North and the South), 35 and 33% participate.

Smaller regional differences were found for the viewing, hunting, and fishing types of participation (Cordell et al. 1998). For viewing activities, the region with the smallest percentage of people 16 or older participating is the South with 74%; the highest is the Rocky Mountain/Great Plains region with 80%. Differences in hunting participation are most pronounced between the Rocky Mountain/Great Plains region, at 13%, and the Pacific Coast region, at 5.5%. The region with the highest percentage participating in fishing is the South (32%), and the region with the lowest percentage is the Pacific Coast (24%). Prominent examples of particular activities with highly noticeable differences in regional participation include visiting prehistoric sites, primitive area camping, hiking, backpacking, mountain climbing, and off-road vehicle driving. The pattern of regional differences for specific activities is very much like the patterns summarized above for groupings of similar activities—participation is generally higher in the 2 western regions and lower in the 2 eastern regions.

The Relative Importance of Wildlife-Based Recreation in the South.—Table 1 indicates in 2 ways the relative importance of wildlife-based outdoor recreation in the South. The first is the percentage of the population which participates and the second is average number of participation days per year. Shown in Table 1 are activities in which 20% or more of the South's population of persons 16 or older participate, in descending order. Walking is by far the most popular outdoor activity in the South, as it is in the nation. Walking is followed by sightseeing, attending sporting events, picnicking, and pool swimming, all of which have participation rates greater than 40%. Activities with the largest average number of days per person per year include walking (almost 110 days per year), birdwatching (97.5), wildlife viewing (40.4), biking (39.5), and pool swimming (31.3).

Hunting has long been an important tradition to southerners *(US Forest Service)*.

Wildlife- and fish-related activities, including wildlife viewing, birdwatching, and freshwater fishing (which includes warmwater fishing) have participation rates in the 20-percent range. An important point from Table 1 is that 2 wildlife-related activities are among the most popular of all outdoor recreational activities in the

Table 1. Outdoor recreational activities in which 20% or more of the population 16 or older in the South participate, 1994-95.[a]

Activity	Percentage of population participating	Average days per participant per year
Walking	64.3	109.8
Sightseeing	54.3	17.9
Attending outdoor sporting events	47.9	[b]
Picnicking	44.8	8.6
Pool swimming	46.8	31.3
River/lake/ocean swimming	37.3	17.6
Attending outdoor concerts	31.3	[b]
Wildlife viewing	28.9	40.4
Running/jogging	27.3	[b]
Freshwater fishing	26.2	20.4
Birdwatching	26.2	97.5
Biking	24.6	39.5
Motorboating	24.4	19.0
Warmwater fishing	24.3	20.2

[a] Cordell, H.K., R.J. Teasley, J.C. Bergstrom, and C. Betz. National Survey on Recreation and the Environment Weighted Data Sets. Environmental Resources Assessment Group, Department of Agricultural and Applied Economics, The University of Georgia, and Outdoor Recreation and Wilderness Assessment Unit (SRS-4901), USDA Forest Service (afterwards cited as Cordell et al. 1997).

[b] Day of participation not collected for these activities.

South, and they are among the activities with the highest levels of participation in terms of days per year.

The relative importance of hunting is shown in Table 2. Participation rates for the 3 types of hunting, big game, small game, and migratory birds, are within the 2-to-8% range. Migratory bird hunting is the least popular of these 3 hunting activities with a rate comparable to such activities as sailing and rock climbing. Off-road driving, catch-and-release fishing, fish viewing, salt water fishing, and hiking are more popular than hunting in average number of days per participant among the activities shown in Table 2. Days of participation in hunting per year are substantially less than days per year for the 2 non-consumptive wildlife activities shown in Table 1, birdwatching and wildlife viewing.

While the estimates shown in Tables 1 and 2 indicate a relatively wide distribution in participation rates for wildlife-related recreation in the south, they also point out that wildlife-related recreation is an important component of the outdoor lifestyles of southerners. The importance of wildlife-related recreation to the participants themselves is reflected in the number of trips they take away from home for these activities. Annually, participants in the South take an average of 12.7 trips for wildlife viewing, 7.6 for bird watching, and 9.5, 7.7, and 5.2 for big-game, small-game, and migratory bird hunting, respectively.

In addition to benefitting those who personally participate in wildlife-related recreational activities, these forms of outdoor activities also contribute to the jobs and incomes of other people as a result of trip-related expenditures. The major categories of expenditures associated with wildlife recreation trips include gas, souvenirs, food, lodging, guide books, equipment, land leasing, licenses, stamps, tags, and permits. Total annual expenditures on these items on the part of hunting and wildlife viewing participants in southern states are shown in Table 3.

The expenditures shown in Table 3, as well as expenditures in other outdoor recreation activities, can represent an important injection of money into state or regional economies. For example, when a hunter or a wildlife viewer fills up their car with gas at a local service station, the jobs and incomes of the service station owner and employees are directly supported. Further, the multiplier effects associated with hauling and delivering more gasoline to be sold by the local service station can result in much wider economic impacts throughout the southern region, including workers at refineries and distribution centers. As well, hunting license fees support state game and fish commissions

Table 2. Outdoor recreational activities in which less than 20% of the population 16 or older in the South participate, 1994-95.[a]

Activity	Percentage of population participating	Average days per participant per year
Hiking	18.6	17.2
Developed camping	17.2	10.8
Off-road driving	14.7	24.3
Fish viewing	13.7	19.7
Saltwater fishing	13.4	18.3
Water skiing	9.4	10.9
Catch and release fishing	9.0	20.3
Coldwater fishing	8.0	9.2
Big game hunting	8.0	15.7
Small game hunting	7.9	13.0
Canoeing	6.6	4.2
Backpacking	5.9	6.9
Downhill skiing	5.5	4.2
Sailing	3.8	7.2
Rock climbing	2.9	3.5
Migratory bird hunting	2.5	7.0
Kayaking	1.1	8.8

[a] Cordell et al. 1997.

Table 3. Expenditures by state resident participants in the South for wildlife-related recreation, 1996. (Population 16 years old and older: expenditures in thousands of dollars.)

State	Activity	
	Hunting	Wildlife viewing
Arkansas	$541,732	$181,835
Alabama	$536,753	$277,292
Florida	$471,602	$1,557,719
Georgia	$858,437	$942,890
Kentucky	$342,811	$352,076
Louisiana	$637,004	$262,246
Mississippi	$501,561	$185,552
North Carolina	$561,891	$578,573
South Carolina	$350,233	$316,693
Tennessee	$824,891	$384,854
Texas	$1,340,335	$1,578,678
Virginia	$428,794	$781,840

[a] From U.S. Fish and Wildlife Service 1997. 1996 National Survey of Fishing, Hunting, and Wildlife-Associated Recreation: State Overview. USDI, Fish and Wildlife Service, Arlington, VA. 115 pp.

(agencies) and the many conservation activities these agencies routinely undertake.

Another source of wildlife-related economic impacts in the south are the activities of citizen conservation organizations. Organizations such as the National Wild Turkey Federation, National Wildlife Federation, Quail Unlimited, Ducks Unlimited, and Trout Unlimited have combined memberships in the south numbering in the thousands of people. Members of these organizations, for example, contribute time and money to wildlife management projects. These expenditures result in economic impacts in addition to the impacts of expenditures on wildlife-related recreational activities such as birdwatching, hunting, and fishing. The National Private Landowners Survey, the results of which are the focus of this chapter, did not address participation in conservation or environmental organizations. The activities and impacts of members of these organizations is an interesting area for future research.

Unlike many of the nonwildlife-related recreational activities listed in Tables 1 and 2, wildlife- related recreational activities are directly dependent on the conditions of forest ecosystems, as discussed in other chapters of this book. Maintenance of healthy forest ecosystems is, therefore, essential to providing continued opportunities for wildlife-related recreation and support for income and jobs in the South.

In the next sections of this chapter, wildlife viewing, birdwatching, and hunting are described in more detail, as are the people in the South who participate in these activities.

WILDLIFE VIEWING AND BIRDWATCHING

The nonconsumptive wildlife recreational activities we cover are wildlife viewing and birdwatching. As indicated in Table 1, 28.9% of the population in the South participated in wildlife viewing and 26.2% in birdwatching.

The characteristics of participants and their households in the South who engage in wildlife viewing and birdwatching are compared below. Also shown are comparisons of percentages participating by demographic strata nationally and in the South.

The race, gender, and age distributions of wildlife viewers, nationally and for the South, are shown in Table 4. As with other wildlife-related activities, the vast majority of participants in wildlife viewing are Caucasian. However, much unlike hunting, larger percentages are female and in age groups over 40 years. Compared with wildlife viewers, larger percentages of birdwatchers are African-American, female, and over age 50. Smaller percentages of birdwatchers are under age 30. Overall, however, there are few differences between percentages of wildlife viewers and bird watchers by demographic category when comparing the South with the nation.

About one-third of wildlife viewing and birdwatching participants in the South are college graduates (Table 5). Another 27% are high school graduates, while a slightly larger percentage had completed at least some college. The $25,000 to $50,000 income range is

Bird watching is a popular and growing activity in the South (C. Gelb, The Nature Conservancy).

Table 4. Percentages in the South age 16 or older participating in wildlife viewing and birdwatching by race, gender, and age, 1994-95.[a]

Demographic	National		South	
	Wildlife viewing	Birdwatching	Wildlife viewing	Birdwatching
Race				
Caucasian	88.2	86.3	86.4	83.9
African-American	6.4	8.4	9.8	12.6
Hispanic	0.7	0.8	0.3	0.5
Others	4.6	4.5	3.5	3.0
Gender				
Male	48.2	43.9	49.6	43.6
Female	51.8	56.1	50.4	56.4
Age				
16-24	15.8	10.5	17.3	12.4
25-29	11.5	8.7	11.9	9.0
30-39	25.7	23.1	24.5	22.2
40-49	19.9	20.6	19.7	19.8
50-59	11.9	13.8	11.8	13.5
60+	15.2	23.3	14.9	23.4

[a]Cordell et al., 1997.

Table 5. Percentages in the South age 16 or older participating in wildlife viewing and birdwatching by education and income, 1994-95.[a]

Demographic	National		South	
	Wildlife viewing	Birdwatching	Wildlife viewing	Birdwatching
Education				
College graduate	33.3	34.6	31.9	33.3
Some college	30.9	30.1	28.7	30.1
Completed high school	27.2	27.7	29.7	27.1
Some high school	8.4	7.6	9.6	9.6
Income				
Less than $15,000	7.3	8.9	7.8	9.3
$15,000-25,000	14.0	16.0	13.7	14.8
$25,000-50,000	40.7	39.0	40.0	37.2
$50,000-75,000	21.6	20.4	22.0	23.2
$75,000-100,000	9.7	9.1	10.2	9.4
More than $100,000	6.6	6.5	6.2	6.2

[a]Cordell et al. 1997.

the most frequently reported income for both wildlife viewers and birdwatchers. Slightly larger percentages of wildlife viewers are in this income range. The next most frequent income categories are the $50,000 to $75,000 range, between 22% and 23% for the South for the 2 activities, and the $15,000 to $25,000 range, between 14% and 15% (Table 5).

Table 6. Percentage in the South age 16 or older participating in wildlife viewing and birdwatching by household characteristic, 1994-95.[a]

Demographic	National		South	
	Wildlife viewing	Birdwatching	Wildlife viewing	Birdwatching
Number of vehicles				
0-1	21.6	25.7	20.0	24.4
2	42.9	42.9	43.5	44.0
3 or more	35.5	31.4	35.9	31.3
Number in household				
1	13.7	16.1	12.0	15.3
2	33.3	37.4	35.2	38.3
3	20.0	17.9	21.5	18.3
4	19.7	17.0	20.4	18.8
5 or more	13.3	11.7	10.9	9.3
Household members 16 and over				
1	15.6	16.7	13.7	15.4
2	58.8	61.0	60.9	62.6
3 or more	25.6	22.3	25.4	22.0
Household members 6 and under				
0	55.9	59.9	54.4	58.6
1 or more	44.1	40.1	45.6	41.4
Family members				
1	14.3	15.6	11.8	13.6
2	32.2	37.0	34.9	38.7
3	20.2	18.5	22.2	19.7
4 or more	33.3	28.9	31.1	28.0

[a]Cordell et al. 1997.

Table 6 describes the characteristics of households in which 1 or more members are wildlife viewers. Again, percentages are shown for the nation and for the South. About 44% of wildlife viewer households in the South have 2 cars, and about 36% own 3 or more cars. The most frequent number of persons in southern wildlife viewer households is 2. Birdwatchers tend to have somewhat fewer vehicles in the household, are slightly more frequently in smaller households, and more frequently have no members 6 years or under. This is very similar to the patterns shown nationally in Table 6.

Over one-half of wildlife viewer households have at least 2 persons age 16 or over, less than the percentage of bird watchers. Over 50% of wildlife viewer and bird-watcher households have no members age 6 or under. The number of immediate family members within wildlife viewer households is relatively evenly distributed between 1 and 4 family members, with one-member households representing the lowest frequency. For

Table 7. Percentages in the South age 16 or older participating in wildlife viewing and birdwatching by employment status, 1994-95.[a]

Demographic	National		South	
	Wildlife viewing	Birdwatching	Wildlife viewing	Birdwatching
Employment				
Full-time	56.1	51.1	56.6	50.1
Homemaker	7.5	8.5	8.1	9.1
Not employed	2.9	2.9	3.1	3.1
Part-time	13.2	12.3	10.3	9.8
Retired	13.8	20.3	14.2	21.5
Student	6.4	4.8	7.8	6.4

[a]Cordell et al. 1997.

birdwatcher households, smaller percentages have one other family member, while a larger percentage has 2 other family members in the household. With regard to employment status, just over 50% of birdwatchers in the South are full-time workers and around 9% are homemakers (Table 7). Higher percentages of birdwatchers are retired.

In Table 8, other outdoor activities are listed in which wildlife viewers and birdwatchers participate, for the nation and for the South. Larger percentages of wildlife viewers appear to participate in other nonconsumptive outdoor activities, rather than in consumptive ones. These nonconsumptive viewing activities include birdwatching, fish viewing, and nature study. Other activities enjoyed by wildlife viewers include hiking, camping (developed and primitive), and freshwater (including warmwater) fishing. Birdwatchers differ in that smaller percentages hunt or fish (except for catch and release), smaller percentages hike, camp, ride horses, or canoe; but larger percentages of birdwatchers also view wildlife other than birds.

Table 8. Percentage of wildlife viewers and birdwatchers in the South age 16 or older by other outdoor recreation activities in which they participate, 1994-95.[a]

Demographic	National		South	
	Wildlife viewing	Birdwatching	Wildlife viewing	Birdwatching
Big game hunting	12.2	7.8	13.7	7.6
Small game hunting	10.5	7.2	12.7	7.6
Migratory bird hunting	3.7	2.8	4.5	3.6
Freshwater fishing	35.9	31.9	38.9	34.3
Saltwater fishing	13.2	12.4	20.2	18.9
Warmwater fishing	30.2	27.1	36.5	32.3
Coldwater fishing	16.2	13.4	12.6	10.3
Anadromous fishing	7.3	6.5	6.0	6.2
Catch/release fishing	11.9	16.9	14.0	20.2
Birdwatching	57.9	100.0	58.8	100.0
Wildlife viewing	100.0	66.9	100.0	64.8
Fish viewing	29.8	28.8	30.7	29.3
Nature study	50.0	26.9	49.7	24.8
Hiking	39.4	34.5	33.2	29.1
Orienteering	4.7	4.1	4.5	3.5
Backpacking	13.1	10.3	10.3	7.9
Developed camp	32.2	26.0	28.3	22.0
Primitive camp	23.2	17.8	20.3	14.7
Horseback riding	11.4	8.7	12.7	9.4
Canoeing	12.5	10.6	11.7	8.3
Kayaking	2.2	2.0	2.0	1.9

[a]Cordell et al. 1997.

Table 9. Percentage and millions of participants and average days of participation per year in hunting activities in the South, 1994-95.[a]

Type of hunting	% of population	Millions participating	Average days per participant per year
Big game	8.0	5.5	15.7
Small game	7.9	5.4	13.0
Migratory bird	2.5	1.7	7.0
Any hunting	10.6	7.3	13.4

[a]Cordell et al. 1997.

HUNTING

Hunting, as covered by the NSRE, includes big game, small game, and migratory bird hunting by persons 16 years and older. Based on the NSRE, 8.0% of the population in southern states participated in big game hunting, 7.9% participated in small game hunting, and 2.5% participated in migratory bird hunting. These percentages, as well as total number of hunting participants in the South, are shown in Table 9. As indicated in Table 9, 7.3 million people in the South participate in hunting, including big game hunters (5.5 million), small game hunters (5.4 million), and migratory bird hunters (1.7 million). Almost equal proportions participate in big game and small game hunting, but a much smaller proportion participate in migratory bird hunting. Across all 3 hunting activities, 10.6% reported participating one or more times during the 1994-95 survey period, somewhat higher than the 9.3% shown for the nation.

Table 10 examines some of the demographic characteristics of people who hunt in the South, compared with national percentages. Most hunting participants are

Table 10. Percentages of persons 16 years or older nationally and in the South participating in hunting by race, gender, and age, 1994-95.[a]

Hunters	National	South
Race		
Caucasian	92.0	90.2
African-American	4.0	7.9
Hispanic	1.0	0.5
Others	3.1	1.3
Gender		
Male	84.9	84.2
Female	15.1	15.8
Age		
16-24	24.3	29.6
25-29	14.3	13.3
30-39	26.0	23.9
40-49	15.9	15.8
50-59	10.7	9.4
60 and over	8.7	8.0

[a]Cordell et al. 1997.

Table 11. Percentages of hunters 16 years or older nationally and in the South by education and income, 1994-95.[a]

Hunters	National	South
Education		
College graduate	21.1	18.0
Some college	29.8	27.6
Completed high school	34.1	33.6
Some high school	14.9	20.5
Income		
Less than $15,000	4.4	4.7
$15,000 - 25,000	13.5	16.7
$25,000 - 50,000	36.9	32.4
$50,000 - 75,000	17.2	15.1
$75,000 - 100,000	6.9	7.5
Greater than $100,000	4.1	5.0
Refused, don't know, not available	17.0	18.8

[a]Cordell et al. 1997.

Table 12. Percentages of household nationally and the South having at least one member who hunts by household characteristic, 1994-95.[a]

Hunters	National	South
Number of vehicles		
0-1	12.9	12.1
2	41.8	42.6
3 or more	45.3	46.4
Household members		
1	13.2	11.3
2	28.0	26.8
3	22.9	25.4
4	21.2	23.1
5 or more	14.8	13.5
Household members 16 and over		
1	14.0	12.6
2	57.1	54.0
3	28.9	33.4
Household members 6 and under		
0	52.5	55.6
1 or more	47.5	44.4
Family members		
1	13.4	11.4
2	26.9	25.7
3	23.6	25.4
4 or more	36.1	37.5

[a]Cordell et al. 1997.

Caucasian, although other races or ethnicities also are represented. The gender of hunters in the South is mostly male at nearly 85%. As well, most southern hunters (about 2/3) are below 40 years of age, with 30-39 years being the most frequent age reported. There is also a relatively large proportion of hunters in the 16-24 age category, larger than the national proportion in this age group. The proportions in other age ranges who hunt substantially decrease after age 49.

Table 11 indicates that the education of about 54% of hunters in the South is at or below the high school level. Eighteen percent of hunters in the South have completed college, and 28% have completed some college. The income category with the highest percentage of hunters is between $25,000 and $50,000 (Table 11).

Table 12 describes general characteristics of households in the South in which one or more members (family, boarders, roommates) is a hunter. Most households with a hunting member own 2 or 3 vehicles, and only a relatively small percentage own 1 or no vehicles. The majority of hunter households have only 2 to 3 members, although 4 and 5-member households combined constitute about 37% of all households with someone who hunts. Within these households, the majority have 2 members 16 or over, while almost one-third of them had 3 and under one-fifth had only 1. About 55% of the households with hunters have no members under the age of 6. The most frequent num-

Table 13. Percentage of hunters 16 years or older nationally and in the South by employment status, 1994-95.[a]

Hunters	National	South
Employment Status		
Full-time	69.6	66.5
Homemaker	2.4	2.4
Not employed	2.4	2.9
Part-time	9.9	10.4
Retired	7.3	6.7
Student	8.3	11.1

[a]Cordell et al. 1997.

Table 14. Percentages of hunters nationally and in the South participating in other outdoor recreation activities, 1994-95.[a]

Activity	National	South
Big game hunting	56.6	55.9
Small game hunting	51.7	55.3
Migratory bird hunting	17.0	17.6
Freshwater fishing	62.3	64.0
Saltwater fishing	20.1	28.2
Warmwater fishing	53.7	60.7
Coldwater fishing	30.4	23.0
Anadromous fishing	13.8	10.5
Catch/release fishing	20.0	21.1
Birdwatching	29.8	25.9
Wildlife viewing	50.7	47.4
Fish viewing	21.4	21.1
Nature study	34.8	32.2
Hiking	36.3	31.1
Orienteering	5.7	5.4
Backpacking	16.1	13.6
Developed camping	36.6	34.6
Primitive camping	37.5	35.7
Horseback riding	14.8	17.7
Canoeing	15.7	14.2
Kayaking	2.1	2.0

[a]Cordell et al. 1997.

ber of immediate family members in hunter households is 4.

About two-thirds of hunters in the South are employed full-time. About 11% are students; 7% are retired; 2% are homemakers; and another 10% work part-time (Table 13). Table 14 shows the frequency with which hunters participate in recreational activities other than hunting. Some of the more popular other outdoor activities among hunters are warmwater fishing, wildlife viewing, primitive camping, developed camping, nature watching, hiking, and birdwatching.

SOME FURTHER COMPARISONS AND CONCLUDING REMARKS

Birds, mammals and other terrestrial wildlife continue to be important to the recreational experiences of many in the South. In this chapter we have examined the role of wildlife in outdoor recreation by looking at participation in viewing wildlife, birdwatching, and various forms of hunting. Data from the National Survey on Recreation and the Environment and from previous national surveys have shown a significant shift in this role. This shift is characterized primarily as a rise in popularity of nonconsumptive wildlife viewing and birdwatching, relative to that of hunting. Very likely this shift has been strongly influenced by the rapidly changing demographic makeup and lifestyles of the population of the South—increasingly urban and increasingly detached from the land.

The relationship between shifting demographics and shifts in wildlife recreation are indicated by looking at differences in the demographics of consumptive and nonconsumptive wildlife recreationists. While there were some demographic differences between people who engage in wildlife viewing and those who birdwatch (namely higher percentages of birdwatchers are African-American, female, and over 50), hunters differed even more. Higher percentages of those who hunt than those who watch wildlife or birds were white, nearly double the percentage were male, and higher percentages were under 30. In addition to these differences, smaller percentages of hunters than wildlife or bird watchers had attended college, smaller percentages had incomes over $50,000 per year and higher percentages lived in households of 3 or more. Larger percentages of mostly-male hunters than either wildlife viewers or birdwatchers were employed full-time (they are younger), and much smaller percentages were homemakers. Much larger percentages of birdwatchers were part-time employed or retired than either wildlife viewers or hunters. It follows from the above differences that demographic trends in the South toward better educated, higher income, smaller household, and more ethnically diverse populations are likely contributing significantly to our observed shifts from consumptive to nonconsumptive recreational uses of wildlife.

In addition to demographic shifts, growing detachment from working on or having direct contact with the "land" — the natural environment, is also a likely cause

People seek to reconnect with nature in many different ways *(US Forest Service).*

of the trend from hunting toward nonconsumptive forms of wildlife recreation. Population growth in the South has been startlingly large. Especially in Florida, Georgia, some parts of Texas, and northern Virginia, this growth is transforming the landscape rapidly and permanently. In some parts of the region, urban growth is accelerating, drastically transforming forests and open habitat as well. This growth is fed by the proliferation of highways, more fuel-efficient automobiles, mass transit systems and the declining necessity to work at a centralized work place.

More people living in ever expanding metropolitan areas assures increasing generational detachment from the "land". Detachment, that is, from having regular, direct contact with the out-of-doors, and certainly void of traditional rural lifestyles, where hunting was a traditional part of that lifestyle. For example, it is not unusual for many, if not most people of the 1990s, to start their day by leaving their air conditioned homes through attached garages with automatic door openers and driving in their air conditioned vehicle to their work-place garage through which they enter their workplace to spend the day in an air conditioned office environment. Throughout the day, many never feel the warm rays of the sun nor the cooling breezes of night fall.

For many of us who have lived the 1990s and are thinking of life in the new millennium, wildlife, wildlands, forests, and wilderness can seem remote and full of mystery. Strangely, this remoteness and mystery seems to have resulted in more, not less concern for nature and wildlife. A growing concern for nature and wildlife is reflected in polls that show most people being supportive of the environment and of the laws set up to protect it. This environmental concern is reinforced, it seems, by people's seeking to reconnect with the out-of-doors through outdoor recreation, including wildlife recreation, especially nonconsumptive wildlife recreation. For most, going back to the rural lifestyles of generations past is not possible, but for most, outdoor recreation is possible.

Given these trends, one might ask how we as natural resource managers and scientists might work more effectively with the public to maintain a significant place for forests and wildlife in this fast changing region. One clue to finding ways to work more effectively may lay in research showing that most people support the environment, even at the expense of economic growth. Whether people literally would make sacrifices in economic growth in favor of improving the environment is a good question, but they have clearly stated a willingness to do so. And perhaps the literalness of people's expressed attitudes and values doesn't matter all that much. Perhaps, as the authors believe, what matters more is that people have a concern for maintaining a healthy natural environment. This concern for nature seems to offer one avenue for working more effectively with the public to reestablish a connection with the "land".

Very much in harmony with growing environmental sentiments, is the popularity of outdoor recreation, especially the popularity of and desire to learn about wildlife-based outdoor recreation. The desire to learn as a part of outdoor recreation is indicated by the popularity of viewing/learning activities, including wildlife viewing and bird watching. Ours and others' research has shown repeatedly that outdoor recreation is as motivated by a desire to learn as it is by a desire to have fun. Widespread sentiments toward protecting our environment, the overall popularity of outdoor recreation and wildlife-based recreation, and recreation participants' desire to learn seem to offer an unparalleled opportunity to help people reconnect with their natural environment and to provide information that may help them better understand what is happening to it. Better understanding relationships between human activity, development, population dynamics and the natural environment may open new avenues and ideas for having economic growth while at the same time caring for the natural resources of the region.

Outdoor recreation is a part of most people's lives whether they live in cities or in the country. With little or no coaxing, people seek information and learning opportunities as they recreate. Participation and exposure to unbiased, science-based information can be a very important way for people across a broad spectrum of demographic strata to learn about nature, environmental changes and wildlife. A challenge to wildlife and other natural resource managers in the future will be to find ways to keep wildlife, including birds and nontraditional forms such as reptiles, a part of outdoor recreational experiences and provide information and learning opportunities along the way. Innovation and opportunism are characteristics of the American way. It is our challenge to be innovative in exploring the connections between outdoor recreation and environmental education as one way, maybe a critical path, to helping brighten the future of forests and wildlife in the South.

CHAPTER 31

Conclusions

James G. Dickson[1]
US Forest Service
Southern Research Station, Nacogdoches, TX

In this chapter I recapture some of the salient points of the book, and offer some recommendations. Most of the material is taken from individual chapters of the book and readers are referred to appropriate chapters for more detailed information.

PEOPLE

Since arriving in the South over 10,000 years ago, humans have had profound effects on the land and its wildlife. In recent years these impacts on southern ecosystems have increased as a direct result of the human population; and its growth and influence on natural resources. About 100 million people now live in the South. In the last 25 years, the human population of South Carolina, Georgia, and Florida has about doubled. This burgeoning human population has tremendous demands on and profound effects on the land. People need places to live, and food and fiber; but also want wilderness and wildlife.

The very nature of the people is changing too. What once was a rural population is now an urban and suburban population. More than two-thirds of the people reside in metropolitan areas in each of the 13 southeast-

[1]Current Address: School of Forestry, Louisiana Tech University, Ruston, LA

In the South today the human population is burgeoning and predominantly urban *(T. Holbrook)*.

ern States, except Kentucky, Mississippi, and Arkansas (U.S. Dep. Commerce 1995). Over the last several decades, populations in some rural counties have even dropped. Southerners who once were closely tied to the land and its capability, find themselves out of touch with the land. Although this trend probably will continue, many people still have a heritage and ties to the land. Hunting still is important to many who live in the South as well as to the region's economy. For example, about one-third of the nation's duck hunters and almost half of the total number of ducks harvested comes from the South. Although fewer people hunt today, the opportunity to hunt still is important. In addition, a wide array of southerners are interested in wildlife, and enjoy related activities such as wildlife viewing (See Chapter 30, Wildlife Recreation).

Also, our technological advances have increased our capacity to affect southern forest systems. The axe, fire brand, and plow are virtually gone. Now, large-scale changes to the landscape are being wrought by machines that dig coal, construct shopping malls, and dam rivers to form reservoirs. Also, there has been misuse of some chemicals, such as pesticides. And the long-term effects of some effluents remain largely unknown.

LAND

The southern landscape always has been in a state of flux; changing in response to both natural and anthropogenic forces. Forests have dominated the South for thousands of years, although they have undergone profound changes. During the glacial period southern forests underwent drastic changes in response to climatic shifts. Historically and recently, wind storms, insects, and diseases have played a significant role in shaping these forests. And humans have substantially changed the landscape. For example, the once vast cypress forests were cut to provide decay-resistant wood for houses, boats, and other products. The once extensive bottomlands of the Mississippi Valley were cleared and replaced by row crops. The forests of the South today have been molded by a wide variety of forces for a very long time.

Data from the last half century have shown that the total area of forestland in the South has remained relatively constant. Although some land that was cleared is being restored to forest, the future forest land base probably will decrease with the increased demands of a growing human population. Also, even with the increases in young pine plantations, southern forests have aged somewhat in the last 50 years. However, with increasing utilization of young hardwoods and pines, aging of southern forests is not expected to continue, except on public land.

Currently, there are some programs such as the Conservation Reserve and Wetland Reserve which support the restoration of bottomland to forest. Also, there is some effort, particularly on Federal land, to restore longleaf pine and other mature upland ecosystems.

Several exotic and other pests may threaten natural systems and native species of the South. Some historic and current examples illustrate. The American chestnut once was a dominant tree of the Appalachian Mountains, but was eliminated by the chestnut blight. The health of today's oak forests is diminished by the gypsy moth. The balsam wooly adelgid threatens the Fraser fir forests high in the Blue Ridge Mountains. Dogwoods, which are important aesthetically as well as for wildlife food, are threatened by dogwood anthracnose. Chinese tallow tree is invading and dominating prairie and bottomland ecosystems. The imported fire ant certainly negatively affects some species of native fauna, such as the northern bobwhite (Mueller et al. 1999). And wild hogs compete with native species for hard mast during years of shortage, and may adversely affect sensitive ecosystems by their rootings and wallows.

WILDLIFE AND WILDLIFE HABITAT

There are hundreds of species of southern wildlife, and no general statement can describe their status or role in southern ecosystems. In a broad sense, wildlife communities are associated with and have changed in response to habitat changes, and sometimes other factors. Migratory species depend on and are influenced by breeding and wintering habitat often disjunct and quite different from their southern habitat. Some neotropical migratory birds that have suffered recent population declines probably are negatively affected by loss of forested wintering habitat in the tropics. Also, wintering duck populations in the South are greatly affected by breeding habitat conditions in the northern prairie pothole region, which may vary year to year depending on land use, precipitation, and other factors.

The importance of habitat to vertebrate communities is illustrated by the wildlife habitat relationships of mature bottomland hardwoods. Southern bottoms are important wintering waterfowl habitat. Acorns are an important winter food; and oak detritus and invertebrates are nutritionally important for prebreeding wood ducks and mallards. Also, southern bottomlands support high densities of wintering birds that breed further north (Dickson 1978); as well as provide important breeding habitat for a wide variety of birds, including several species of concern, such as the prothonotary warbler, Swainson's warbler, and swallow-tailed kite.

Some recent changes in wildlife populations appear to be associated with the aging of southern forests and the loss of early-successional habitat due to clean farming and improved pasture. Rabbits, ruffed grouse, northern bobwhites, prairie warblers, Bachman's sparrows and other species associated with herbaceous habitat have declined in recent years. Bobwhites and quail hunting have declined since the 1940s. Bird dogs, once a common southern sight, are rarely seen now. The whistle of the bobwhite has been replaced by the gobble of the wild turkey.

With settlement and the exploitation of natural resources, a few species, such as the passenger pigeon and the Carolina parakeet, have become extinct. Other

In recent decades, species associated with early-successional habitat generally have declined. For example, the whistle of the northern bobwhite has been replaced by the gobble of the wild turkey (J. Dickson).

The wild turkey—What an amazing wildlife success story, the return of America's bird throughout the South, and the rest of forested North America *(D. Baumann).*

species, however, have benefitted from our efforts to restore and manage them. Populations of several game species, such as white-tailed deer, black bear, wild turkey, and wood duck were drastically reduced, and extirpated from vast areas. But they have been restored and now thrive in appropriate habitat throughout the region. Deer are found in every county in the South. Black bear range continues to expand, and populations increase where there are large blocks of suitable habitat. The number of bears in the South has increased six-fold over the last 30 years.

Also in recent years, there have been successes with some nongame species of concern. Restrictions on pesticides, active management, and also probably reservoirs and their fish populations have benefitted osprey and bald eagles. In mature pine habitat, red-cockaded woodpeckers are benefitting from habitat management and specific measures such as artificial cavity inserts and translocations. River otter now play where they have been absent for a long time. And in marsh systems alligators are faring well again. Many of these species have proven far more resilient and adaptable than once thought.

People/wildlife interactions are common now and are likely to increase as the human population and suburbia expand. In the South today, beaver dams and flooding are widespread, deer are eating yard plants, bears are feeding at garbage dumps and bird feeders, and alligators are showing up in swimming pools. It seems ironic that state agencies that were restoring key species such as deer a few decades ago, now are working to resolve people/wildlife conflicts with some of these same species. Resolving conflicts can be particularly difficult because of the emotional and widely divergent views held by the public regarding the control of nuisance wildlife.

Species that are expected to fare well in the future are those that are widely adapted to human- altered con-

It seem ironic that wildlife managers, who a few decades ago were restoring species, now are resolving people-wildlife conflicts *(USDA Wildlife Services).*

ditions, such as the ubiquitous coyote, raccoon, rock dove, and mockingbird. On the other hand, there is concern for species that have limited distribution, such as forest interior species, may have population viability problems, or be otherwise imperiled, such as the swallow-tailed kite and Swainson's warbler. Also, there is concern for the probable declines of some species of vertebrate groups, such as bats, amphibians, and reptiles, for which our information is sparse.

THE FUTURE

For the future, particular efforts will be necessary to restore natural systems that have been decimated and to protect and manage sensitive systems that are threatened. Managers need to address and emphasize ecosystem integrity rather than individual species. However, specific management measures may be necessary to create or maintain desired conditions, or to control forest diseases, and insect and vertebrate pests.

We need more complete information to manage southern wildlife effectively. We know little about the status or trends of many species, or even the life history of some. Long-term monitoring and research will foster understanding of ecosystems' function, and better management of forest communities and species.

The beaver and its activities often are at odds with man's land use objectives.

There is concern for some species that are limited in distribution or are otherwise imperiled, such as this swallow-tailed kite *(Temple-Inland Corp.)*.

State and Federal wildlife agencies deal with fragmented and polarized users. To be successful in the future these agencies will have to receive public support from a broader constituency. It is easy for people to associate with individual animals. But generating excitement for wildlife populations or habitat is not so easy. Wildlife agencies must generate enthusiastic support of the public interested in the nonconsumptive aspects of wildlife and develop from them a sound financial and political base.

Although obvious challenges lie ahead in our efforts to maintain forest systems and their wildlife communities, all is not gloomy. Although most southerners no longer live in rural areas, many still are interested in wildlife. We have reforested much of the South. We have had some successes in managing wildlife where we have identified and addressed problems. We have restored primary game and some imperiled nongame species. And our southern forest systems and wildlife communities remain very resilient.

Common and Scientific Names of Animals in Text

Common Name	Scientific Name
MAMMALS	
MARSUPIALS	
FAMILY DIDELPHIDAE	
Virginia opossum	*Didelphis virginiana*
INSECTIVORES	
FAMILY SORICIDAE	
Southeastern shrew	*Sorex longirostris*
Water shrew	*Sorex palustris*
Smoky shrew	*Sorex fumeus*
Long-tailed shrew	*Sorex dispar*
Pygmy shrew	*Microsorex hoyi*
Northern short-tailed shrew	*Blarina brevicauda*
Southern short-tailed shrew	*Blarina carolinensis*
Elliot's short-tailed shrew	*Blarina hylophaga*
Swamp short-tailed shrew	*Blarina telemalestes*
Least shrew	*Cryptotis parva*
Hairy-tailed mole	*Parascalops breweri*
Eastern mole	*Scalopus aquaticus*
Star-nosed mole	*Condylura cristata*
BATS	
FAMILY VESPERTILIONIDAE	
Eastern small-footed bat	*Myotis leibii*
Little brown bat	*Myotis lucifugus*
Indiana bat	*Myotis sodalis*
Southeastern bat	*Myotis austroriparius*
Gray bat	*Myotis grisescens*
Northern long-eared bat	*Myotis septentrionalis*
Silver-haired bat	*Lasionycteris noctivagans*
Eastern pipistrelle	*Pipistrellus subflavus*
Big brown bat	*Eptesicus fuscus*
Northern yellow bat	*Lasiurus intermedius*
Eastern red bat	*Lasiurus borealis*
Seminole bat	*Lasiurus seminolus*
Hoary bat	*Lasiurus cinereus*
Evening bat	*Nycticeius humeralis*
Rafinesque's big-eared bat	*Corynorhinus rafinesquii*
Townsend's big-eared bat	*Corynorhinus townsendii*
FAMILY MOLOSSIDAE	
Brazilian free-tailed bat	*Tadarida brasiliensis*
Wagner's mastiff bat	*Eumops glaucinus*
EDENTATES	
FAMILY DASYPODIDAE	
Nine-banded armadillo	*Dasypus novemcinctus*
LAGOMORPHS	
FAMILY LEPORIDAE	
Marsh rabbit	*Sylvilagus palustris*
Eastern cottontail	*Sylvilagus floridanus*
Swamp rabbit	*Sylvilagus aquaticus*
Appalachian cottontail	*Sylvilagus obscurus*
Snowshoe rabbit	*Lepus americanus*
Black-tailed jackrabbit	*Lepus californicus*
RODENTS	
FAMILY SCIURIDAE	
Eastern chipmunk	*Tamias striatus*
Squirrel	*Sciurus* spp.
Gray squirrel	*Sciurus carolinensis*
Fox squirrel	*Sciurus niger*
Red squirrel	*Tamiasciurus hudsonicus*
Southern flying squirrel	*Glaucomys volans*
Northern flying squirrel	*Glaucomys sabrinus*
FAMILY GEOMYIDAE	
Pocket gophers	*Geomys, Thomomys* spp.
Southern pocket gopher	*Thomomys umbrinus*
FAMILY CASTORIDAE	
Beaver	*Castor canadensis*
FAMILY MURIDAE	
Marsh rice rat	*Oryzomys palustris*
Harvest mice	*Reithrodontomys* spp.
Deer mice	*Peromyscus* spp.

Common Name	Scientific Name
White-footed mouse	*Peromyscus leucopus*
Cotton mouse	*Peromyscus gossypinus*
Golden mouse	*Ochrotomys nuttalli*
Eastern woodrat	*Neotoma floridana*
Voles	Microtines
Woodchuck	*Marmota monax*
Muskrat	*Ondatra zibethicus*
Louisiana muskrat	*O.z. rivalicius*
Black rat	*Rattus rattus*
Norway rat	*Rattus norvegicus*
House mouse	*Mus musculus*
FAMILY ZAPODIDAE	
Meadow jumping mouse	*Zapus hudsonius*
FAMILY CAPROMYIDAE	
Nutria	*Myocastor coypus*
	M.c bonariensis
CARNIVORES	
FAMILY CANIDAE	
Coyote	*Canis latrans*
Wolf	
Gray wolf	*Canis lupus*
Red wolf	*Canis rufus*
Fox	
Red fox	*Vulpes vulpes*
Gray fox	*Urocyon cinereoargenteus*
FAMILY URSIDAE	
Black bear	*Ursus americanus*
FAMILY PROCYONIDAE	
Raccoon	*Procyon lotor*
FAMILY MUSTELIDAE	
Weasel	
Least weasel	*Mustela nivalis*
Long-tailed weasel	*Mustela frenata*
Mink	*Mustela vison*
Badger	*Taxidea taxus*
Skunk	
Eastern spotted skunk	*Spilogale putorius*
Striped skunk	*Mephitis mephitis*
River otter	*Lutra canadensis*
FAMILY FELIDAE	
Mountain lion	*Felis concolor*
Texas mountain lion	*Felis concolor stanleyana*
Florida panther	*Felis concolor coryi*
Bobcat	*Lynx rufus*
EVEN-TOED UNGULATES	
FAMILY SUIDAE	
Wild pig	*Sus scrofa*
FAMILY CERVIDAE	
Elk	*Cervus elaphus*
White-tailed deer	*Odocoileus virginianus*

BIRDS

Common Name	Scientific Name
Cormorant	*Phalacrocorax spp.*
Anhinga	*Anhinga anhinga*
Great blue heron	*Ardea herodias*
Great egret	*Ardea alba*
Snowy egret	*Egretta thula*
Little blue heron	*Egretta caerulea*
Tricolored heron	*Egretta tricolor*
Cattle egret	*Bubulcus ibis*
Striated heron	*Butorides striatus*
Black-crowned night-heron	*Nycticorax nycticorax*
Yellow-crowned night-heron	*Nyctanassa violacea*
White ibis	*Eudocimus albus*
Glossy ibis	*Plegadis falcinellus*
Wood stork	*Mycteria americana*
Greater white-fronted goose	*Anser albifrons*
Lesser white-fronted goose	*Anser erythropus*
Snow goose	*Chen caerulescens*
Ross' goose	*Chen rossii*
Canada goose	*Branta canadensis*
Trumpeter swan	*Cygnus buccinator*
Wood duck	*Aix sponsa*
Gadwall	*Anas strepera*
American wigeon	*Anas americana*
American black duck	*Anas rubripes*
Mallard	*Anas platyrhynchos*
Mottled duck	*Anas fulvigula*
Blue-winged teal	*Anas discors*
Northern shoveler	*Anas clypeata*
Northern pintail	*Anas acuta*
Green-winged teal	*Anas crecca*

Common Name	Scientific Name
Canvasback	*Aythya valisineria*
Redhead	*Aythya americana*
Ringed-necked duck	*Aythya collaris*
Greater scaup	*Aythya marila*
Lesser scaup	*Aythya affinis*
White-winged scoter	*Melanitta fusca*
Oldsquaw	*Clangula hyemalis*
Bufflehead	*Bucephala albeola*
Common goldeneye	*Bucephala clangula*
Hooded merganser	*Lophodytes cucullatus*
Common merganser	*Mergus merganser*
Red-breasted merganser	*Mergus serrator*
Ruddy duck	*Oxyura jamaicensis*
Osprey	*Pandion haliaetus*
Swallow-tailed kite	*Elanoides forficatus*
Mississippi kite	*Ictinia mississippiensis*
Bald eagle	*Haliaeetus leucocephalus*
Northern harrier	*Circus cyaneus*
Sharp-shinned hawk	*Accipiter striatus*
Cooper's hawk	*Accipiter cooperii*
Red-shouldered hawk	*Buteo lineatus*
Broad-winged hawk	*Buteo platypterus*
Red-tailed hawk	*Buteo jamaicensis*
Golden eagle	*Aquila chrysaetos*
American kestrel	*Falco sparverius*
Merlin	*Falco columbarius*
Peregrine falcon	*Falco peregrinus*
Ruffed grouse	*Bonasa umbellus*
Wild turkey	*Meleagris gallopavo*
Eastern wild turkey	*Meleagris gallopavo silvestris*
Florida wild turkey	*Meleagris gallopavo osceola*
Rio Grande wild turkey	*Meleagris gallopavo intermedia*
Northern bobwhite	*Colinus virginianus*
Black-throated bobwhite	*Colinus nigrogularis*
Crested bobwhite	*Colinus cristatus*
Purple gallinule	*Porphyrula martinica*
Common moorhen	*Gallinula chloropus*
Sandhill crane	*Grus canadensis*
Common snipe	*Gallinago gallinago*
Eurasian woodcock	*Scolopax rusticola*
American woodcock	*Scolopax minor*
Rock dove	*Columba livia*
Mourning dove	*Zenaida macroura*
Passenger pigeon	*Ectopistes migratorius*
Carolina parakeet	*Conuropsis carolinensis*
Yellow-billed cuckoo	*Coccyzus americanus*
Barn owl	*Tyto alba*
Eastern screech owl	*Otus asio*
Great horned owl	*Bubo virginianus*
Barred owl	*Strix varia*
Short-eared owl	*Asio flammeus*
Unspotted saw-whet owl	*Aegolius ridgwayi*
Common nighthawk	*Chordeiles minor*
Chuck-will's-widow	*Caprimulgus carolinensis*
Whip-poor-will	*Caprimulgus vociferus*
Chimney swift	*Chaetura pelagica*
Ruby-throated hummingbird	*Archilochus colubris*
Belted kingfisher	*Ceryle alcyon*
Red-headed woodpecker	*Melanerpes erythrocephalus*
Red-bellied woodpecker	*Melanerpes carolinus*
Yellow-bellied sapsucker	*Sphyrapicus varius*
Downy woodpecker	*Picoides pubescens*
Hairy woodpecker	*Picoides villosus*
Red-cockaded woodpecker	*Picoides borealis*
Northern flicker	*Colaptes auratus*
Pileated woodpecker	*Dryocopus pileatus*
Ivory-billed woodpecker	*Campephilus principalis*
Eastern wood-pewee	*Contopus virens*
Acadian flycatcher	*Empidonax virescens*
Eastern phoebe	*Sayornis phoebe*
Great crested flycatcher	*Myiarchus crinitus*
Eastern kingbird	*Tyrannus tyrannus*
Loggerhead shrike	*Lanius ludovicianus*
White-eyed vireo	*Vireo griseus*
Bell's vireo	*Vireo bellii*
Yellow-throated vireo	*Vireo flavifrons*
Warbling vireo	*Vireo gilvus*
Red-eyed vireo	*Vireo olivaceus*
Blue jay	*Cyanocitta cristata*
Florida scrub-jay	*Aphelocoma coerulescens*
American crow	*Corvus brachyrhynchos*
Purple martin	*Progne subis*
Barn swallow	*Hirundo rustica*
Carolina chickadee	*Poecile carolinensis*
Black-capped chickadee	*Poecile atricapillus*
Tufted titmouse	*Baeolophus bicolor*
Red-breasted nuthatch	*Sitta canadensis*
White-breasted nuthatch	*Sitta carolinensis*
Brown-headed nuthatch	*Sitta pusilla*
Brown creeper	*Certhia americana*
Carolina wren	*Thryothorus ludovicianus*
Bewick's wren	*Thryomanes bewickii*
Winter wren	*Troglodytes troglodytes*
Golden-crowned kinglet	*Regulus satrapa*
Ruby-crowned kinglet	*Regulus calendula*

Common Name	Scientific Name
Blue-gray gnatcatcher	*Polioptila caerulea*
Eastern bluebird	*Sialia sialis*
Gray-cheeked thrush	*Catharus minimus*
Swainson's thrush	*Catharus ustulatus*
Hermit thrush	*Catharus guttatus*
Wood thrush	*Hylocichla mustelina*
American robin	*Turdus migratorius*
Gray catbird	*Dumetella carolinensis*
Brown thrasher	*Toxostoma rufum*
European starling	*Sturnus vulgaris*
Bachman's warbler	*Vermivora bachmanii*
Blue-winged warbler	*Vermivora pinus*
Golden-winged warbler	*Vermivora chrysoptera*
Tennessee warbler	*Vermivora peregrina*
Northern parula	*Parula americana*
Chestnut-sided warbler	*Dendroica pensylvanica*
Yellow-rumped warbler	*Dendroica coronata*
Black-throated green warbler	*Dendroica virens*
Blackburnian warbler	*Dendroica fusca*
Yellow-throated warbler	*Dendroica dominica*
Pine warbler	*Dendroica pinus*
Prairie warbler	*Dendroica discolor*
Cerulean warbler	*Dendroica cerulea*
Black-and-white warbler	*Mniotilta varia*
American redstart	*Setophaga ruticilla*
Prothonotary warbler	*Protonotaria citrea*
Worm-eating warbler	*Helmitheros vermivorus*
Swainson's warbler	*Limnothlypis swainsonii*
Ovenbird	*Seiurus aurocapillus*
Northern waterthrush	*Seiurus noveboracensis*
Louisiana waterthrush	*Seiurus motacilla*
Kentucky warbler	*Oporornis formosus*
Common yellowthroat	*Geothlypis trichas*
Hooded warbler	*Wilsonia citrina*
Wilson's warbler	*Wilsonia pusilla*
Canada warbler	*Wilsonia canadensis*
Yellow-breasted chat	*Icteria virens*
Summer tanager	*Piranga rubra*
Scarlet tanager	*Piranga olivacea*
Eastern towhee	*Pipilo erythrophthalmus*
Bachman's sparrow	*Aimophila aestivalis*
Chipping sparrow	*Spizella passerina*
Field sparrow	*Spizella pusilla*
Lark sparrow	*Chondestes grammacus*
Grasshopper sparrow	*Ammodramus savannarum*
Henslow's sparrow	*Ammodramus henslowii*
Song sparrow	*Melospiza melodia*
Lincoln's sparrow	*Melospiza lincolnii*
Swamp sparrow	*Melospiza georgiana*
White-throated sparrow	*Zonotrichia albicollis*
White-crowned sparrow	*Zonotrichia leucophrys*
Dark-eyed junco	*Junco hyemalis*
Blue grosbeak	*Guiraca caerulea*
Indigo bunting	*Passerina cyanea*
Painted bunting	*Passerina ciris*
Dickcissel	*Spiza americana*
Red-winged blackbird	*Agelaius phoeniceus*
Eastern meadowlark	*Sturnella magna*
Brown-headed cowbird	*Molothrus ater*
Orchard oriole	*Icterus spurius*
Baltimore oriole	*Icterus galbula*
Purple finch	*Carpodacus purpureus*
Red crossbill	*Loxia curvirostra*
Pine siskin	*Carduelis pinus*

REPTILES AND AMPHIBIANS

Common Name	Scientific Name
American Alligator	*Alligator mississippiensis*
Gray treefrog	*Hyla versicolor*
Bullfrog	*Rana catesbeiana*
Snapping turtle	*Chelydra serpentina*
Five-lined skink	*Eumeces fasciatus*
Broadhead skink	*Eumeces laticeps*
Eastern cottonmouth	*Agkistrodon piscivorus*
Corn snake	*Elaphe guttata*
Rat snake	*Elaphe obsoleta*
Gray rat snake	*Elaphe obsoleta spiloides*

Common Name	Scientific Name	Common Name	Scientific Name
INVERTEBRATES			
Ant	Hymenoptera	Spider	Araneida
Beetle	Coleoptera	Ticks	
Biting midges	*Culicoides* spp.	Black-legged tick	*Ixodes scapularis*
Butterfly	Lepidoptera	Lone star tick	*Amblyomma americanum*
Centipede	Chilopoda	Wasp	Hymenoptera
Crayfish	Decapoda	Worms	
Earthworm	Opisthopera	Arterial worm	*Elaeophora schneideri*
Fly	Diptera	Exotic hookworm	*Ancylostoma pluridentatum*
Gypsy moth	*Lymantria dispar*		
Liver fluke	*Fascioloides magna*	Large stomach worm	*Haemonchus contortus*
Millipede	Diplopoda	Lungworm	*Dictyocaulus viviparus*
Moth	Lepidoptera	Meningeal worm	*Parelaphostrongylus tenuis*
Southern pine beetle	*Dendroctonus frontalis*	Muscle worm	*Parelaphostrongylus*

Common and Scientific Names of Plants in Text

Common Name	Scientific Name
Alabama supplejack	*Berchemia scandens*
Alfalfa	*Medicago sativa*
Alligator weed	*Alternanthera philoxeroides*
Alyceclover	*Alysicarpus vaginalis*
American beautyberry	*Callicarpa americana*
Arrowleaf	*Sagittaria* spp.
Ash, white	*Fraxinus americana*
Aspen	*Populus* sp.
Aster	*Aster* spp.
Bald cypress	*Taxodium distichum*
Basswood, white	*Tilia heterophylla*
Bedstraw	*Galium* spp.
Beech, American	*Fagus grandifolia*
Beggarticks	*Bidens frondosa*
Beggar weeds	*Desmodium* spp.
Bermuda grass	*Cynodon* spp.
Birch	*Betula* sp.
Blackberry	*Rubus* spp.
Blackgum	*Nyssa sylvatica*
Black bayberry	*Myrica heterophylla*
Black cherry	*Prunus serotina*
Black locust	*Robinia pseudoacacia*
Black walnut	*Juglans nigra*
Black willow	*Salix nigra*
Bladderwort	*Utricularia* spp.
Blue beech	*Carpinus caroliniana*
Blueberry	*Vaccinium* spp.
Bluestem	*Andropogon* spp.
Broomsedge	*Andropogon virginicus*
Little	*Andropogon scoparius*
Buckeye	*Aesculus* spp.
Buckwheat tree	*Cliftonia monophylla*
Bulrush	*Scirpus* spp.
Olney bulrush	*Scirpus olneyii*
Southern bulrush	*Scirpus californicus*
Bush clovers	*Lespedeza virginica*
Cane	*Arundinaria* spp.
Carolina cranesbill	*Geranium carolinianum*
Carolina jessamine	*Gelsemium sempervirens*
Cattail	*Typha* spp.
Narrowleaf cattail	*Typha angustifolia*
Cherry	*Prunus* spp.
Chestnut, American	*Castanea dentata*
Chinese privet	*Ligustrum sinense*
Cocklebur	*Xanthium* spp.
Coralberry (Indiancurrant)	*Symphoricarpos orbiculatus*
Cottonweed	*Froelichia* spp.
Cottonwood, eastern	*Populus deltoides*
Cowpeas	*Vigna unguiculata*
Crabgrass	*Digitaria* spp.
Cranesbill	*Geranium carolinianum*
Crotons	*Croton* spp.
Curtis dropseed	*Sporobolus curtissii*
Day flower	*Commelina* spp.
Deers-tongue	*Trilisa odoratissima*
Devil's walkingstick	*Aralia spinosa*
Dewberry	*Rubus* spp.
Dogwood	*Cornus* spp.
Flowering dogwood	*Cornus florida*
Roughleaf dogwood	*Cornus drummondii*
Dove weeds	*Croton* spp.
Elm	*Ulmus* spp.
American elm	*Ulmus americana*
Winged elm	*Ulmus alata*
Fescue	*Festuca* spp.
Fir	*Abies* sp.
Foxtail	*Alopecurus* spp.
Fringetree	*Chionanthus virginicus*
Galax	*Galax* spp.
Gallberry	*Ilex glabra*
Large (or sweet)	*Ilex coriacea*
Giant cut-grass	*Zizaniopsis miliacea*
Goldenrod	*Solidago* spp.
Gopher-apple	*Chrysobalanus oblongifolius*
Grape	*Vitis* spp.
Grasses	
Bahia grass	*Paspalum notatum*
Bermudagrass	*Cynodon dactylon*
Bluegrass	*Poa* spp.

Common Name	Scientific Name
Bull grass	*Paspalum boscianum*
Cordgrass, marshhay	*Spartina patens*
Foxtail	*Seteria* spp.
Muskgrass	*Chara* spp.
Orchardgrass	*Dactylis glomerata*
Torpedo grass	*Panicum repens*
Wiregrass	*Spartina patens*
Greenbrier	*Smilax* spp
Ground nut	*Apios americana*
Hackberry	*Celtis* spp.
Hawthorn	*Crataegus* spp.
Hazel, beaked	*Corylus cornuta*
Hemlock, eastern	*Tsuga canadensis*
Hemp	*Cannabis sativa*
Heterotheca	*Heterotheca submaxillaris*
Hickory	*Carya* spp.
Bitternut	*Carya cordiformis*
Mockernut	*Carya tomentosa*
Pignut	*Carya glabra*
Shagbark	*Carya ovata*
Water	*Carya aquatica*
Hog peanut	*Amphicarpa bracteata*
Holly	*Ilex* spp.
Dahoon	*Ilex cassine*
Deciduous	*Ilex decidua*
Myrtle	*Ilex myrtifolia*
Yaupon	*Ilex vomitoria*
Honeysuckle	*Lonicera* spp.
Japanese	*Lonicera japonica*
Hophornbeam, eastern	*Ostrya virginiana*
Hornbeam, American	*Carpinus caroliniana*
Horseweed	*Conyza* spp.
Huckleberry	*Gaylussacia* spp.
Indiangrass	*Sorghastrum* spp.
Jewel-weeds	*Impatiens* spp.
Johnson grass	*Sorghum halepense*
Laurel, mountain	*Kalmia latifolia*
Lambsquarter	*Chenopodium album*
Lespedeza	*Lespedezas* spp.
Common lespedeza	*Lespedeza striata*
Korean clover	*Lespedeza stipulacea*
Sericea	*Lespedeza cuneata*
Bicolor	*Lespedeza bicolor*
Lotus, American	*Nelumbo lutea*
Lyonia	*Lyonia* spp.
Maidencane	*Panicum hemitomon*
Magnolia, sweetbay	*Magnolia virginiana*
Mallow	*Malvaviscus* spp.
Maple	*Acer* spp.
Red maple	*Acer rubrum*
Sugar maple	*Acer saccharum*
Marshpurslane	*Lugwigia* spp.
Milk Peas	*Galactia* spp.
Morning glory	*Ipomoea* spp.
	Ipomoea imbricata
	Ipomoea stolonifera
Mountain laurel	*Kalmia latifolia*
Mustards	*Brassica* spp.
Nightshades	*Solanum* spp.
Norway spruce	*Picea abies*
Oak	*Quercus* spp.
Black oak	*Quercus velutina*
Blackjack oak	*Quercus marilandica*
Bur oak	*Quercus macrocarpa*
Cherrybark oak	*Quercus falcata*
Chestnut oak	*Quercus montana*
Chinkapin oak	*Quercus muhlenbergii*
Cow oak	*Quercus michauxii*
Laurel oak	*Quercus laurifolia*
Northern red oak	*Quercus rubra*
Nuttall oak	*Quercus nuttallii*
Overcup oak	*Quercus lyrata*
Pin oak	*Quercus palustris*
Post oak	*Quercus stellata*
Scarlet oak	*Quercus coccinea*
Southern red oak	*Quercus falcata*
Swamp white oak	*Quercus bicolor*
Water oak	*Quercus nigra*
White oak	*Quercus alba*
Willow oak	*Quercus phellos*
Oats	*Avena* spp.
Palmetto	*Serenoa repens*
Panicum	*Panicum* spp.
Partridgeberry	*Mitchella repens*
Partridgepea	*Cassia fasciculata*
Paspalums	*Paspalum* spp.
Paw Paw	*Asimina triloba*
Pecan	*Carya illinoensis*
Peppervine	*Ampelopsis arborea*
Persimmon, common	*Diospyros virginiana*
Pickerelweed	*Pontederia cordata*
Pigweed	*Amaranthus* spp.
Pine	*Pinus* spp.
Loblolly pine	*Pinus taeda*
Longleaf pine	*Pinus palustris*
Pitch pine	*Pinus rigida*
Pond pine	*Pinus serotina*
Ponderosa pine	*Pinus ponderosa*

Common Name	Scientific Name
Sand pine	*Pinus clausa*
Shortleaf pine	*Pinus echinata*
Slash pine	*Pinus elliottii*
Spruce pine	*Pinus glabra*
Virginia pine	*Pinus virginiana*
White pine	*Pinus strobus*
Plum	*Prunus* spp.
Poison Ivy	*Toxicodendron radicans*
Pokeweed	*Phytolacca americana*
Pondweed	*Potamogeton* spp.
Pond cypress	*Taxodium ascendens*
Poor Joe	*Diodia teres*
Poplar, yellow	*Liriodendron tulipifera*
Pricklypoppies	*Argemone* spp.
Privet	*Ligustrum* spp.
Pussytoe	*Antennaria* spp.
Ragweed	*Ambrosia* spp.
Rattan vine	*Berchemia scandens*
Red bay	*Persea borbonia*
Redbud, eastern	*Cercis canadensis*
Redcedar, eastern	*Juniperus virginiana*
Red mulberry	*Morus rubra*
Rhododendron	*Rhododendron* spp.
Rice cutgrass	*Leersia oryzoides*
Rose	Rosaceae
Roussea cane	*Phragmites communis*
Rush	*Juncus* spp.
Black needle	*Juncus romerianus*
Nut rush	*Scleria* spp.
Rye	*Secale cereale*
Saltbush	*Avicennia* spp.
Sassafras	*Sassafras albidum*
Sawgrass, Jamaica	*Cladium jamaicensis*
Saw palmetto	*Serenoa* spp.
Sea oats	*Uniola paniculata*
Sedges	*Carex* spp.
Serviceberry	*Amelanchier* spp.
Sesbania	*Sesbania* spp.
Smartweed	*Polygonum* spp.
Smooth bidens	*Bidens laevis*
Sorghum	*Sorghum* spp.
Sourwood	*Oxydendrum arboreum*
Southern sweetbay	*Magnolia virginiana*
Southern wildrice, giant	*Zizaniopsis miliacea*
Spanish moss	*Tillandsia usneoides*
Spikerush	*Eleocharis* spp.
Spurred butterfly pea	*Centrosema virginianum*
Squawroot	*Conophilis americana*
St. Andrews cross	*Hypericum hypericoides*
Strawberry	*Fragaria* spp.
Sugarberry	*Celtis laevigata*
Sumac	*Rhus* spp.
Flameleaf (or shining) sumac	*Rhus copallina*
Sunflower	*Helianthus* spp.
Swamp cyrilla	*Cyrilla racemiflora*
Sweetclovers	*Melilotus* spp.
Sweetgum, American	*Liquidambar styraciflua*
Sweetleaf	*Symplocos tinctoria*
Sweet flag	*Acorus* spp.
Sweet pepperbrush	*Clethra* spp.
Switch cane	*Arundinaria gigantea*
Sycamore	*Platanus occidentalis*
Tallowtree	*Sapium*
Thistle	*Cirsium* spp.
Three-seeded mercuries	*Acalypha* sp.
Tickclovers	*Desmodium* spp.
Trumpet creeper	*Campsis radicans*
Tupelo	*Nyssa* spp.
Blackgum	*Nyssa sylvatica*
Water tupelo	*Nyssa aquatica*
Swamp tupelo	*Nyssa biflora*
Vervains	*Verbena* spp.
Vetch	*Vicia* spp.
Viburnum	*Viburnum* spp.
Mapleleaf	*Viburnum acerifolium*
Possumhaw	*Viburnum nudum*
Waterlily	Nymphaea
Watermelon	*Citrullus vulgaris*
Water hyacinth	*Eichhornia crassipes*
Water locust	*Gleditsia aquatica*
Watershield	*Brasenia* spp.
Schreber	*Brasenia schreberi*
Waxmyrtle	*Myrica* spp.
Southern wax myrtle	*Myrica cerifera*
Wheat	*Triticum aestivum*
White clover	*Trifolium repens*
White spruce	*Picea glauca*
Willow, black	*Salix nigra*
Wild beans	*Strophostyles* spp.
Wintergreen	*Gaultheria procumbens*
Wiregrass	*Aristida stricta*
Common witch hazel	*Hamamelis virginiana*
Wood sorrels	*Oxalis stricta*
Yaupon holly	*Ilex vomitoria*
Yellow jessamine	*Gelsemium sempervirens*

Literature Cited

Ables, E. D. 1975. Ecology of the red fox in America. Pages 216-236 in M. W. Fox Ed. The wild canids: their systematics, behavioral ecology and evolution. Van Norstrand Reinhold Co., New York, NY.

Abraham, K. F., R. L. Jefferies, R. F. Rockwell, and C. D. MacInnes. 1996. Why are there so many white geese in North America? Pages 79-92 in J. T. Ratti, ed. Proc. 7th Int. Waterfowl Symp., Ducks Unlimited, Inc., Memphis, TN.

Abrahamson, W. G., and D. C. Hartnett. 1990. Pine flatwoods and dry prairies. Pages 103-149 in R. L. Myers and J. J. Ewel, eds. Ecosystems of Florida. Univ. Central Florida Press, Orlando.

Adam, M. D., M. J. Lacki, and T. G. Barnes. 1994. Foraging areas and habitat use of the Virginia big-eared bat in Kentucky. J. Wildl. Manage. 58:462-469.

Adams, W. V., G. E. Sanford, E. E. Roth, and L. L. Glasgow. 1964. Nighttime capture of striped skunks in Louisiana. J. Wildl. Manage. 28:368-373.

Adler, K. 1979. A brief history of herpetology in North America before 1900. Society for the Study of Amphibians and Reptiles, Athens, Ohio, Herpetological Circular No. 8. 40pp.

Aldrich, J. W. 1946. The United States races of the bob-white. Auk 63:493-508.

Aldrich, J. W. 1993. Classification and distribution. Pages 47-54 in T. S. Baskett, M. W. Sayre, R. E. Tomlinson, and R. E. Mirarchi, eds. Ecology and management of the mourning dove. Stackpole Books, Harrisburg, PA.

Aldrich, J. W., and R. W. Coffin. 1980. Breeding bird populations from forest to suburbia after thirty-seven years. Am. Birds. 34:3-7.

Alisauskas, R. T., and C. D. Ankney. 1992. The cost of egg laying and its relationship to nutrient reserves in waterfowl. Pages 30-61 in B. D. J. Batt, A. D. Afton, M. G. Anderson, C. D. Ankney, D. H. Johnson, J. A. Kadlec, and G. L. Krapu, eds. The ecology and management of breeding waterfowl. Univ. Minnesota Press, Minneapolis.

Allen, A. A. 1984. Habitat suitability index models: eastern cottontail. USDI Fish and Wildl. Serv. FWS/OBS-82/10.66. 23pp.

Allen, A. A. 1985. Habitat suitability index models: swamp rabbit. USDI Fish and Wildl. Serv. Biol. Rep. 82(10.107). 20pp.

Allen, C. H., R. L. Marchinton, and W. M. Lentz. 1985. Movement, habitat use, and denning of opossums in the Georgia Piedmont. Am. Midl. Nat. 113:408-412.

Allen, D. H. 1991. An insert technique for constructing artificial red-cockaded woodpecker cavities. USDA For. Serv. Gen. Tech. Rep. SE-73. 19pp.

Allen, D. H., K. E. Franzreb, and R. F. Escano. 1993. Efficacy of translocation strategies for red-cockaded woodpeckers. Wildl. Soc. Bull. 21:155-159.

Allen, D. L. 1942. Populations and habits of the fox squirrel in Allegan County, Michigan. Am. Midl. Nat. 27:338-339.

Allen, S. L. 1982. Habitat preferences of cottontail rabbits on an intensive farm and a traditional farm. Proc. Annu. Conf. Southeast. Assoc. Fish and Wildl. Agencies 36:614-626.

Allen, T. F. H., and T. B. Starr. 1982. Hierarchy: perspectives for ecological complexity. Univ. Chicago Press, Chicago, IL.

Allsbrooks, D. W., and M. L. Kennedy. 1980. Movement patterns of raccoons (Procyon lotor) in western Tennessee. J. Tenn. Acad. Sci. 55:15-19.

Alvarez, K. 1993. Twilight of the panther. Myakka River Pub., Sarasota, FL. 501pp.

Amend, S. R. 1969. Progress report on Carolina Sandhills mourning dove studies. Proc. Annu. Conf. Southeast. Assoc. Game and Fish Comm. 23:191-201.

Anderson, B. F., and M. R. Pelton. 1977. Movements, home range, and cover use: factors affecting the susceptibility of cottontails to hunting. Proc. Annu. Conf. Southeast. Assoc. Fish and Wildl. Agencies 31:525-535.

Anderson, D. R. 1997. Corridor use, feeding ecology, and habitat relationships of black bears in a fragmented landscape in Louisiana. M.S. Thesis, Univ. Tennessee, Knoxville, TN. 123pp.

Anderson, S. J., and C. P. Stone. 1993. Snaring to control feral pigs (Sus scrofa) in a remote Hawaiian rainforest. Biological Conserv. 63:195-201.

Annand, E. M., and F. R. Thompson, III. 1997. Forest bird response to regeneration practices in central hardwood forests. J. Wildl. Manage. 61:159-171.

Armitage, K. B., and K. S. Harris. 1982. Spatial patterning in sympatric populations of fox and gray squirrels. Am. Midl. Nat. 108:389-397.

Arner, D. H., and G. Hepp. 1989. Beaver pond wetlands: a southern perspective. Pages 117-128 in L. Smith, R. Pederson, and R. Kaminski, eds. Habitat management for migrating and wintering waterfowl. Texas Tech Univ. Press, Lubbock, TX.

Arner, D. H., and J. S. DuBose. 1979. The impact of the beaver on the environment and economics in the southeastern United States. Int. Congr. Game Biol. 14:241-247.

Arner, D. H., C. Mason, and C. J. Perkins. 1980. Practicality of reducing a beaver population through the release of alligators. In J. A. Chapman and D. Pursley, eds. Worldwide Furbearer Conf. Proc. 3:1799-1805.

Arthur, S. C. 1931. The fur animals of Louisiana. Louisiana Dept. Conserv. Bull. 18. 444pp.

Asdell, S. A. 1964. Patterns in mammalian reproduction, 2nd ed.

Cornell Univ. Press, Ithaca, NY. 670pp.

Askins, R. A., J. F. Lynch, and R. Greenberg. 1990. Population declines in migratory birds in eastern North American. Current Ornith. 7:1-57.

Atkeson, T. D., and A. S. Johnson. 1979. Succession of small mammals on pine plantations in the Georgia piedmont. Am. Midl. Nat. 101:385-392.

Atkeson, T. Z., and D. C. Hulse. 1953. Trapping versus night hunting for controlling raccoons and opossums within sanctuaries. J. Wildl. Manage. 17:159-162.

Atwood, E. L. 1950. Life history of nutria, or coypu, in coastal Louisiana. J. Wildl. Manage. 14:249-265.

Audubon, J. J., and J. Bachman. 1851. The viviparous quadrupeds of North America, Volume 2. New York, NY. 334pp.

Babb, J. G., and M. L. Kennedy. 1988. Home range of the coyote in western Tennessee. Proc. Annu. Conf. Southeast. Assoc. Fish and Wildl. Agencies. 42:443-447.

Baber, D. W. and B. E. Coblenz. 1986. Density, home range, habitat use, and reproduction in feral pigs on Santa Catalina island. J. Mamm. 67:512-525.

Bailey, R. G. 1998. Ecoregions map of North America. USDA For. Serv. Misc. Pub. No. 1548. 10pp.

Bailey, R. G., P. E. Avers, T. King, W. H. McNab, eds. 1994. Ecoregions and subregions of the United States (map). U.S. Geological Survey, Washington, DC.

Baker, R. H., and M. W. Baker. 1975. Montane habitat used by the spotted skunk (Spilogale putorius) in Mexico. J. Mamm. 56:671-673.

Baker, R. H., C. C. Newman, and F. Wilke. 1945. Food habits of the raccoon in eastern Texas. J. Wildl. Manage. 9:45-48.

Baker, W. W. 1983. Decline and extirpation of a population of red-cockaded woodpeckers in northwest Florida. Pages 44-45 in D. A. Wood, ed. Red-cockaded Woodpecker Symp. II Proceedings. Florida Game and Fresh Water Fish Comm., Tallahassee, FL.

Balser, D. S., H. H. Dill, and H. K. Nelson. 1968. Effect of predator reduction on waterfowl nesting success. J. Wildl. Manage. 32:669-682.

Barbour, R. W., and W. H. Davis. 1969. Bats of America. Univ. Kentucky Press, Lexington. 286pp.

Barbour, R. W., and W. H. Davis. 1974. Mammals of Kentucky. Univ. Kentucky Press, Lexington. 322pp.

Barclay, R. M. R. 1991. Population structure of temperate zone insectivorous bats in relation to foraging behavior and energy demand. J. Anim. Ecol. 60:165-178.

Barclay, R. M. R., and R. M. Brigham, eds. 1996. Bats and forests symposium, October 19-21, 1995, Victoria, British Columbia. Research Branch, Ministry of Forests, Victoria. 292pp.

Barclay, R. M. R., and R. M. Brigham. 1998. Hide and seek: in search of forest bats. Bats 16(1): 3-7.

Barden, L. S. 1977. Self-maintaining populations of Pinus pungens Lam. In the southern Appalachian Mountains. Castanea 42:316-323.

Barden, L. S. 1997. Historic prairies in the Piedmont of North and South Carolina, USA. Nat. Areas J. 17:149-152.

Barkalow, F. S., Jr., R. B. Hamilton, and R. F. Soots, Jr. 1970. The vital statistics of an unexploited gray squirrel population. J. Wildl. Manage. 34:489-500.

Barnes, J. A. 1993. Impact of beaver (Castor canadensis carolinensis) on trout habitat on the Chauga River drainage in South Carolina. M. S. Thesis, Clemson Univ., Clemson, SC. 76pp.

Baron, J. S. 1979. Vegetation damage by feral hogs on Horn Island, Gulf Islands National Seashore, Mississippi. M. S. Thesis, Univ. Wisconsin, Madison. 122pp.

Barone, M. A., M. E. Roelke, J. Howard, J. L. Brown, A. E. Anderson, and D. E. Wildt. 1994. Reproductive characteristics of male Florida panthers: comparative studies from Florida, Texas, Colorado, Latin America, and North American zoos. J. Mamm. 75:150-162.

Barrett, R. H. 1978. The feral hog on the Dye Creek Ranch, California. Hilgardia 46:283-355.

Barrett, R. H. 1983. Smoked aluminum track plots for determining furbearer distribution and relative abundance. California Fish and Game 69:188-190.

Bartholomew, R.M. 1967. A study of the winter activity of bobwhites through the use of radio telemetry. Occas. Papers C.C. Adams center for Ecol. Studies No. 17. 25pp.

Bartram, W. 1791. Travels through North and South Carolina, Georgia, East and West Florida, the Cherokee Country. Mark Van Doren, ed. Dover Publ., Inc., New York, NY. 414pp.

Baskett, R. K. 1993. Shooting field management. Pages 495-506 in T. S. Baskett, M. W. Sayre, R. E. Tomlinson, and R. E. Mirarchi, eds. Ecology and management of the mourning dove. Stackpole Books, Harrisburg, PA.

Baskett, T. S. 1993. Biological evaluation of the call-count survey. Pages 453-468 in T. S. Baskett, M. W. Sayre, R. E. Tomlinson, and R. E. Mirarchi, eds. Ecology and management of the mourning dove. Stackpole Books, Harrisburg, PA.

Baskett, T. S., and M. W. Sayre. 1993. Characteristics and importance. Pages 1-6 in T. S. Baskett, M. W. Sayre, R. E. Tomlinson, and R. E. Mirarchi, eds. Ecology and management of the mourning dove. Stackpole Books, Harrisburg, PA.

Baskett, T. S., M. W. Sayre, R. E. Tomlinson, and R. E. Mirarchi, eds. 1993. Ecology and management of the mourning dove. Stackpole Books, Harrisburg, PA. 567pp.

Baskin, J.M., and C.C. Baskin. 1986. Distribution and geographical/evolutionary relationships of cedar glade endemics in southeastern United States. Assoc. of Southeast. Biologists Bull. 3:138-154.

Baskin, J.M., and C.C. Baskin. 1989. Cedar glade endemics in Tennessee, and a review of their autecology. Journal of the Tenn. Acad. Sci. 64:63-74.

Baskin, J.M., C.C. Baskin, and E.W. Chester. 1994. The Big Barrens Region of Kentucky and Tennessee: further observations and considerations. Castanea 59:226-254.

Bat Conservation International, Inc. 1999. Bats in eastern woodlands. 243pp.

Batzli, G. O. 1977. Population dynamics of the white-footed mouse in floodplain and upland forests. Am. Midl. Nat. 97:18-32.

Baumann, D. P., Jr., W. E. Mahan, and W. E. Rhodes. 1996. Effects of Hurricane Hugo on the Francis Marion National Forest wild turkey population. Proc. National Wild Turkey Symp. 7:55-60.

Baumgartner, F. M. 1944. Bobwhite quail populations on hunted vs. protected areas. J. of Wildl. Manage. 8:259-260.

Baxter, W.L., and C. W. Wolfe. 1972. The interspersion index as a technique for evaluation of bobwhite quail habitat. Pages 158-165 in J. A. Morrison and J. C. Lewis, eds. Proc. First National Bobwhite Quail Symp. Oklahoma State Univ., Stillwater, OK.

Beach, R. 1993. Depredation problems involving feral hogs. Pages 67-75 in C. W. Hanselka and J. F. Cadenhead, eds. Feral Swine:

A Compendium for Resource Managers. Texas Agric. Ext. Serv., Kerrville, TX.

Beasom, S. L. 1974a. Intensive short-term predator removal as a game management tool. Trans. N. Amer. Wildl. and Nat. Resour. Conf. 39:230-240.

Beasom, S. L. 1974b. Relationships between predator removal and white-tailed deer net productivity. J. Wildl. Manage. 38:854-859.

Beauchamp, W. D., T. D. Nudds, and R. G. Clark. 1996. Duck nest success declines with and without predator management. J. Wildl. Manage. 60:258-264.

Becker, H. N., R. C. Belden, T. Breault, M. J. Burridge, W. B. Frankenberger, and P. Nicoletti. 1978. Brucellosis in feral swine in Florida. J. Amer. Vet. Med. Assoc. 173:1181-1182.

Beeman, L. E., and M. R. Pelton. 1977. Seasonal foods and feeding ecology of black bears in the Smoky Mountains. Proc. Internat. Conf. Bear Res. and Manage. 3:141-147.

Beier, P., and R. F. Noss. 1998. Do habitat corridors provide connectivity? Conserv. Biol. 12:1241-1252.

Bekoff, M. 1977. Canis latrans. Mammalian Species. Amer. Soc. Mamm. 79:1-9.

Bekoff, M. 1984. Coyote. Pages 447-459 in J.A. Chapman and G.A. Feldhamer, eds. 1983. Wild mammals of North America. Johns Hopkins Univ. Press, Baltimore, MD.

Belden, R. C. 1976. Wallows of the European wild hog in the mountains of east Tennessee. J. Tenn. Acad. Sci. 51:91-93.

Belden, R. C., and B. W. Hagedorn. 1993. Feasibility of translocating panthers into northern Florida. J. Wildl. Manage. 57:388-397.

Belden, R. C., and M. R. Pelton. 1975. European wild hog rooting in the mountains of east Tennessee. Proc. Annu. Conf. Southeast. Assoc. Fish and Wildl. Agencies 29:665-671.

Belden, R. C., and W. B. Frankenberger. 1977. A portable root-door hog trap. Proc. Annu. Conf. Southeast. Assoc. Fish and Wildl. Agencies 31:123-125.

Belden, R. C., and W. B. Frankenberger. 1990. Biology of a feral hog population in south central Florida. Proc. Annu. Conf. Southeast. Assoc. Fish and Wildl. Agencies 44:231-249.

Bell, B. K., Dancak, and P. J. Zwank. 1985. Range, movements, and habitat use by bobwhites in Southeastern Louisiana Pinelands. Proc. Annu. Conf. Southeast. Assoc. Fish and Wildl. Agencies 39:512-519.

Bellrose, F. C. 1980. Ducks, geese and swans of North America. 3rd ed. Stackpole Books, Harrisburg, PA. 540pp.

Bellrose, F. C., and D. J. Holm. 1994. Ecology and management of the wood duck. Stackpole Books, Harrisburg, PA. 588pp.

Bendel, P. R., and G. D. Therres. 1994. Movements, site fidelity and survival of Delmarva fox squirrels following translocations. Am. Midl. Nat. 132:227-233.

Bennett, S. H., J. W. Gibbons, and J. Glanville. 1980. Terrestrial activity, abundance and diversity of amphibians in differently managed forest types. Am. Midl. Nat. 103:412-416.

Bennitt, R. 1951. Some aspects of Missouri quail and quail hunting 1938-1948. Missouri Conserv. Comm. Tech. Bull. 2, Jefferson City. 51pp.

Best, L. B., and D. F. Stauffer. 1980. Factors affecting nesting success in riparian bird communities. Condor 82:149-158.

Bidwell, T. G., S. R. Tulley, A. D. Peoples, and R. E. Masters. 1991. Habitat appraisal guide for bobwhite quail. Okla. Coop. Extension Serv. Circ. E-904. 11pp.

Bigler, W. J., G. L. Hoff, W. H. Hemmert, J. A. Tomas, and H. T. Janowski. 1977. Trends in brucellosis in Florida: an epidemiological review. Amer. J. Epidemiol. 105:245.

Blackburn, W. E., J. P. Kirk, and J. E. Kennamer. 1975. Availability and utilization of summer foods by eastern wild turkey broods in Lee County, Alabama. Proc. National Wild Turkey Symp. 3:86-96.

Blair, R. M. 1982. Growth and nonstructural carbohydrate content of southern browse species as influenced by light intensity. J. Range Manage. 35:756-760.

Blair, R. M., and D. P. Feduccia. 1977. Midstory hardwoods inhibit deer forage in loblolly pine plantations. J. Wildl. Manage. 41:677-684.

Blair, R. M., and H. G. Enghardt. 1976. Deer forage and overstory dynamics in a loblolloy pine plantation. J. Range Manage. 29:104-108.

Blair, R. M., H. L. Short, and E. A. Epps, Jr. 1977. Seasonal nutrient yield and digestibility of deer forage from a young pine plantation. J. Wildl. Manage. 41:667-676.

Blake, J. G., and J. R. Karr. 1987. Breeding birds of isolated woodlots: area and habitat relationships. Ecology 68:1724-1734.

Blanton, K. M., and E. P. Hill. 1989. Coyote use of white-tailed deer fawns in relation to deer density. Proc. Annu. Conf. Southeastern Assoc. Fish and Wildl. Agencies 43:470-478.

Bliss, J. C., S. K. Nepal, R. T. Brooks, Jr., and M. D. Larsen. 1994. Forestry community or granfalloon? J. For. 92:6-10.

Blockstein, D. E., and D. Westmoreland. 1993. Reproductive strategy. Pages 105-116 in T. S. Baskett, M. W. Sayre, R. E. Tomlinson, and R. E. Mirarchi, eds. Ecology and management of the mourning dove. Stackpole Books, Harrisburg, PA.

Blymyer, M. J., and H. S. Mosby. 1977. Deer utilization of clearcuts in southwestern Virginia. Sou. J. Appl. For. 1:10-13.

Boag, D. A., and K. M. Sumanik. 1969. Characteristics of drumming sites selected by ruffed grouse in Alberta. J. Wildl. Manage. 33:621-628.

Bock, C. E., and J. H. Bock. 1992. Response of birds to wildfire in native versus exotic Arizona grassland. Southwest. Nat. 37:73-81.

Boggus, T. G., and R. M. Whiting, Jr. 1982. Effects of habitat variables on foraging of American woodcock wintering in east Texas. Pages 148-153 in T. J. Dwyer and G. L. Storm, tech. coords. Woodcock ecology and management. USDI Fish and Wildl. Serv., Wildl. Res. Rep. 14.

Bohall-Wood, P. G., and M. W. Collopy. 1986. Abundance and habitat selection of two American Kestrel subspecies in north-central Florida. Auk 103:557-563.

Bouffard, S., and D. Hein. 1978. Census methods for eastern gray squirrels. J. Wildl. Manage. 42:550-557.

Bourne, W. 1991. The art and science of dove-field management. Southern Outdoors 39(5):48-49, 51-53.

Boyce, S.G., and W.H. Martin. 1993. The future of the terrestrial communities of the southeastern United States. Pages 339-366 in W.H. Martin, S.G. Boyce, and A.C. Echternacht, eds. Biodiversity of the southeastern United States: upland terrestrial communities. John Wiley & Sons, New York, NY.

Boyd, H. E. 1976. Biological productivity in two Georgia swamps. Ph.D. Thesis, Univ. Tennessee, Knoxville, TN. 98pp.

Boyd, R. A. 1990. Population density and habitat utilization of ruffed grouse in the southern Appalachians. M.S. Thesis, Univ. Tennessee, Knoxville, TN. 95pp.

Brack, V., and R. K. LaVal. 1985. Food habits of the Indiana bat in Missouri. J. Mamm. 66:308-315.

Bradley, L. C., and D. B. Fagre. 1988. Movements and habitat use by coyotes and bobcats on a ranch in southern Texas. Proc. Annu. Conf. Southeast. Assoc. Fish and Wildl. Agencies 42:411-430.

Brakhage, D. H. 1990. Techniques currently used for monitoring wood duck populations. Pages 201-203 in L. H. Fredrickson, G. V. Burger, S. P. Havera, D. A. Graber, R. E. Kirby, and T. S. Taylor, eds. Proc. 1988 N. Am. Wood Duck Symp., St. Louis, MO.

Brandenburg, D. M. 1996. Effects of roads on behavior and survival of black bears in coastal North Carolina. M.S. Thesis, Univ. Tennessee, Knoxville, TN. 131pp.

Brass, D.N. 1994. Rabies in bats: natural history and public health implications. Livia Press, Ridgefield, CT. 335pp.

Bratton, S. P. 1974. An integrated ecological approach to the management of European wild boar (Sus scrofa) in GRSM. Manage. Rep. No. 3, Uplands Field Res. Lab, Great Smoky Mountains National Park, Gatlinburg, TN. 42pp.

Bratton, S. P. 1977. The effect of the European wild boar on the flora of the Great Smoky Mountains National Park. Pages 47-52 in G. W. Wood, ed. Research and management of wild hog populations. Belle Baruch Forest Science Inst. of Clemson Univ., Georgetown, SC.

Braun, C. E., N. J. Silvy, T. S. Baskett, and R. E. Tomlinson. 1993. Research and management needs. Pages 507-513 in T. S. Baskett, M. W. Sayre, R. E. Tomlinson, and R. E. Mirarchi, eds. Ecology and management of the mourning dove. Stackpole Books, Harrisburg, PA.

Breen, T. F. 1995. The use of American Kestrel (Falco sparverius) nest boxes by American Kestrels and other secondary cavity nesting birds in south Georgia. M.S. Thesis, Georgia Southern Univ., Statesboro, GA.

Brennan, L. A. 1991. How can we reverse the northern bobwhite population decline? Wildl. Soc. Bull. 19:544-555.

Brennan, L. A. 1993. Strategic plan for quail management and research in the United States: issues and strategies. Pages 170-171 in K. E. Church and T. V. Dailey, eds. Quail III: National Quail Symp. Kansas Dep. Wildl. and Parks, Pratt.

Brennan, L. A., and G. A. Hurst. 1995. Summer foods of northern bobwhite in eastern Mississippi: implications for habitat management. Proc. Annu. Conf. Southeast. Assoc. Fish and Wildl. Agencies 49:516-524.

Britt, T. L. 1971. Studies of woodcock on the Louisiana wintering ground. M.S. Thesis, Louisiana State Univ., Baton Rouge, LA. 105pp.

Brooks, M. 1938. Bachman's Sparrow in the north-central portion of its range. Wilson Bull. 50:86-109.

Brown, B. W., and G. O. Batzli. 1984. Habitat selection by fox and gray squirrels: a multivariate analysis. J. Wildl. Manage. 48:616-620.

Brown, B. W., and G. O. Batzli. 1985. Field manipulations of fox and gray squirrel populations: how important is interspecific competition? Can. J. Zool. 63:2134-2140.

Brown, L. 1975. Ecological relationships and breeding biology of nutria (Myocastor coypus) in the Tampa, Florida area. J. Mamm. 56:928-930.

Brown, L. N. 1997. Mammals of Florida. Winward Publishing, Inc., Miami, FL. 224pp.

Brown, L. W. 1997. A guide to the mammals of the southeastern United States. Univ. Tennessee Press, Knoxville. 236pp.

Brown, N. C., and J. S. Bethel. 1958. Lumber. John Wiley & Sons, 2nd ed. New York, NY. 371pp.

Brownlee, W. C. 1977. Status of the bobcat (Lynx rufus) in Texas. Sp. Rep. Texas Parks and Wildl. Dept., Austin, TX. 20pp.

Bruggink, J. G. 1997. American woodcock harvest and breeding population status, 1997. USDI Fish and Wildl. Serv., Laurel, MD. 14pp.

Bruna, J. 1951. Kentucky rabbit investigation. Proc. Annu. Conf. Southeast. Assoc. Game and Fish Comm. 5:421-437.

Buckelew, A. R., Jr., and G. A. Hall. 1994. The West Virginia breeding bird atlas. Univ. Pittsburgh Press, Pittsburgh, PA. 215pp.

Buckner, E. R., and N. L. Turrill. 1999. Fire and Southern Appalachian ecosystem management. In J. Peine, ed. Ecosystem management for sustainability principles and practices. St. Lucie Press, Boca Raton, FL.

Buckner, J. L., and J. L Landers. 1980. A forester's guide to wildlife management in southern industrial pine forests. International Paper Co., Southlands Experimental Forest. Bainbridge, GA. 16pp.

Buhlmann, K. A. 1995. Habitat use, terrestrial movements, and conservation of the turtle, Deirochelys reticularia in Virginia. J. Herp. 29:173-181.

Buhlmann, K. A. 1996. Legislation and conservation. Herp. Rev. 27:54-55.

Buhlmann, K. A. 1998. Ecology, terrestrial habitat use, and conservation of a freshwater turtle assemblage inhabiting a seasonally fluctuating wetland with emphasis on the life history of Deirochelys reticularia. Ph.D. Dissertation, Univ. Georgia, Athens, GA. 176pp.

Buhlmann, K. A., and J. W. Gibbons. 1997. Imperiled aquatic reptiles of the southeastern United States: historical review and current conservation status. Pages 201-232 in G. W. Benz and D. E. Collins, eds. Aquatic Fauna in Peril: The Southeastern Perspective. Southeast Aquatic Research Institute, Lenz Design and Communications, Decatur, GA.

Buhlmann, K. A., and M. R. Vaughan. 1991. Ecology of the turtle, Pseudemys concinna in the New River, West Virginia. J. Herp. 25:72-78.

Buhlmann, K. A., C. A. Pague, J. C. Mitchell, and R. B. Glasgow. 1988. Forestry operations and terrestrial salamanders: Techniques in a study of the Cow Knob salamander, Plethodon punctatus. Pages 38-44 in Management of Amphibians, Reptiles, and Small Mammals in North America. USDA For. Serv. Gen. Tech. Rep. RM-166.

Buhlmann, K. A., J. C. Mitchell, and C. A. Pague. 1993. Amphibian and small mammal abundance and diversity in saturated forested wetlands and adjacent uplands of southeastern Virginia. Pages 1-7 in S. D. Eckles, A. Jennings, A. Spingarn and C. Wienhold, eds. Proc. Workshop on Saturated Forested Wetlands in the Mid-Atlantic Region: the State of the Science, Annapolis, MD.

Buhlmann, K. A., J. C. Mitchell, and M. G. Rollins. 1997. New approaches for the conservation of bog turtles, Clemmys muhlenbergii, in Virginia. Pages 359-363 in J. Van Abbema, ed. Proc. Conservation and Management of tortoises and freshwater turtles. Am. Mus. Nat. Hist., NY.

Buller, R. J. 1975. Redistribution of waterfowl: influence of water, protection, and feed. Proc. 1st Int. Waterfowl Symp. 1:143-154.

Bullock, J. 1993. Cooperation benefits bears. Tree farmer. Sept./Oct.:12-13.

Bullock, J. F., and D. H. Arner. 1985. Beaver damage to nonimpounded timber in Mississippi. Sou. J. App. For. 9:137-140.

Bump, G., R. W. Darrow, F. C. Edminster, and W. F. Crissey. 1947. The ruffed grouse: life history, propagation, management. New York State Conserv. Dep. 915pp.

Burdette, D. 1995. The southern forests: a legacy of nations. Alabama's treasured forests. Fall:27,30,31.

Burdette, D. 1996a. The southern forests, Part 2: 1800-1850. Alabama's treasured forests. Winter:22-23.

Burdette, D. 1996b. The southern forests, Part 3: 1850-1930. Alabama's treasured forests. Spring:26-27.

Burger, L. W., Jr., D. A. Miller, and R. I. Southwick. 1999. Economic impact of northern bobwhite hunting in the southeastern United States. Wildlife Soc. Bull. 27:1010-1018.

Burger, L. W., Jr., D. C. Sisson, H. L. Stribling, and D. W. Speake. 1998. Northern bobwhite survival and cause-specific mortality on an intensively managed plantation in Georgia. Proc. Annu. Conf. Southeast. Assoc. Fish and Wildl. Agencies. 52:174-190.

Burger, L. W., Jr., E. W. Kurzejeski, L. D. Vangilder, T. V. Dailey, and J. H. Shultz. 1994a. Effects of harvest on population dynamics of upland birds: are bobwhite the model? Trans. N. Amer. Wildl. and Nat. Resour. Conf. 59:466-476.

Burger, L. W., Jr., M. R. Ryan, E. W. Kurzejeski, and T. V. Dailey. 1994c. Factors affecting the habitat value of Conservation Reserve Program lands for northern bobwhite in northern Missouri. Pages 142-156 in M.R. Dicks, ed. Proceedings of the NCT-163 Post Conservation Reserve Program land use conference. 10-11 January. Denver, CO. Great Plains Agricultural Policy Center, Oklahoma State University.

Burger, L. W., Jr., M. R. Ryan, T. V. Dailey, and E. W. Kurzejeski. 1994b. Temporal patterns in cause-specific mortality of northern bobwhite in northern Missouri. Proc. Annu. Conf. Southeast. Assoc. Fish and Wildl. Agencies 48:208-219.

Burger, L. W., Jr., M. R. Ryan, T. V. Dailey, and E. W. Kurzejeski. 1995b. Reproductive strategies, success, and mating systems of northern bobwhite in northern Missouri. J. Wildl. Manage. 59:417-426.

Burger, L. W., Jr., T. V. Dailey, E. W. Kurzejeski, and M. R. Ryan. 1995a. Seasonal and annual survival and cause-specific mortality of northern bobwhite in northern Missouri. J. Wildl. Manage. 59:401-410.

Burk, J. D., G. A. Hurst, D. R. Smith, B. D. Leopold, and J. G. Dickson. 1990. Wild turkey use of streamside management zones in loblolly pine plantations. National Wild Turkey Symp. 6:84-89.

Burke, V. J., and J. W. Gibbons. 1995. Terrestrial buffer zones and wetland conservation: a case study of freshwater turtles in a Carolina bay. Cons. Biol. 9:1365-1369.

Burroughs, A. L., R. Holdenreid, D. S. Longanecker, and K. F. Meyer. 1945. A field study of latent tularemia in rodents with a list of all known naturally infected vertebrates. J. Infect. Dis. 76:115-119.

Burton, J. G. 1998. Population estimates and indices for selected medium-sized carnivores in central Mississippi. M.S. Thesis, Mississippi State Univ., Mississippi State, MS. 213pp.

Burton, T. M., and G. E. Likens. 1975. Energy flow and nutrient cycling in salamander populations in the Hubbard Brook Experimental Forest. Ecology 56:1068-1080.

Buss, I. O., H. Mattison, and F. M. Kozlik. 1947. The bobwhite quail in Dunn County, Wisconsin. Wis. Conserv. Bull. 12:6-13.

Cagle, F. R. 1953. The status of the turtle Graptemys oculifera (Baur). Zoologica 38:137-144.

Cahalane, V. H. 1947. Mammals of North America. The Macmillan Co., New York, NY. 682pp.

Cain, M. D. 1996. Hardwood snag fragmentation in a pine-oak forest of southeastern Arkansas. Am. Midl. Nat. 136:72-83.

Caire, W., J. D. Tyler, B. P. Glass, and M. A. Mares. 1989. Mammals of Oklahoma. Univ. Oklahoma Press, Norman. 566pp.

Callahan, E. V., R. D. Drobney, and R. L. Clawson. 1997. Selection of summer roosting sites by Indiana bats (Myotis sodalis) in Missouri. J. Mamm. 78:818-825.

Campo, J. J., and G. A. Hurst. 1980. Soft mast production in young loblolly pine plantations. Proc. Annu. Conf. Southeast. Assoc. Fish and Wildl. Agencies 34:470-475.

Campo, J. J., W. G. Swank, and C. R. Hopkins. 1989. Brood habitat use by eastern wild turkeys in eastern Texas. J. Wildl. Manage. 53:479-482.

Canadian Wildlife Service, and USDI Fish and Wildlife Service. 1986. North American waterfowl management plan. USDI Fish and Wildlife Serv., Washington, DC. 31pp.

Cantrell, M. A. 1989. Characteristics of a managed raccoon population in east Tennessee with an emphasis on summer dog training and fall harvest. M.S. Thesis, Univ. Tennessee, Knoxville, TN. 140pp.

Capel, S., B. Carmichael, M. Gudlin, and D. Long. 1994. Wildlife needs assessment: Southeast Region. A report for the Wildlife Management Inst., Washington, DC. 16pp.

Carley, C. J. 1975. Activities and findings of the Red Wolf Recovery Program from late 1973 to July 1, 1975. USDI Fish and Wildl. Serv., Albuquerque, NM. 215pp.

Carley, C. J., and J. L. Mechler. 1983. An experimental reestablishment of red wolves (Canis rufus) on the Tennessee Valley Authority's Land Between the Lakes. USDI Fish and Wildl. Serv., Asheville, NC. 72pp.

Carter, J. H., III, J. R. Walters, and P. D. Doerr. 1995. Red-cockaded woodpeckers in the North Carolina Sandhills: a 12-year population study. Pages 259-269 in D. L. Kulhavy, R. G. Hooper, and R. Costa, eds. Red-cockaded woodpecker: recovery, ecology and management. Stephen F. Austin State Univ., Nacogdoches, TX.

Carter, M. F., W. C. Hunter, D. N. Pashley, and K.V. Rosenberg. 2000. Setting conservation priorities for landbirds in the United States: The Partners in Flight Approach. Auk 117:541-548.

Carrie, N. R., R. N. Conner, D. C. Rudolph, and D. K. Carrie. 1999. Reintroduction and postrelease movements of red-cockaded woodpecker groups in eastern Texas. J. Wildl. Manage. 63:824-832.

Casteel, D. A. 1966. Nest building, parturition, and copulation in the cottontail rabbit. Am. Midl. Nat. 75:160-167.

Causey, M. K., J. Roboski, and G. Horton. 1974. Nesting activities of the American woodcock (Philohela minor Gmelin) in Alabama. Pages 5-12 in J. H. Jenkins, chairman. Proc. Fifth American Woodcock Workshop, Athens, GA.

Causey, M. K., M. K. Hudson, and T. P. Mack. 1987. Breeding activity of American woodcock in Alabama as related to temperature. Proc. Annu. Conf. Southeast. Assoc. Fish and Wildl. Agencies 41:373-377.

Cely, J. E., and D. P. Ferral. 1995. Status and distribution of the red-cockaded woodpecker in South Carolina. Pages 470-476 in D. L. Kulhavy, R. G. Hooper, and R. Costa, eds. Red-cockaded woodpecker: recovery, ecology and management. Stephen F. Austin State Univ., Nacogdoches, TX.

Cely, J. E., and J. A. Sorrow. 1988. American kestrel and common barn-owl nest box use in South Carolina. Nongame and Heritage Trust Publication No. 2. South Carolina Wildl. and Marine Resour. Dept.

Cely, J. E., and J. A. Sorrow. 1990. The American swallow-tailed kite in South Carolina. South Carolina Wildlife and Marine Resources Department No 1. 160pp.

Chabreck, R. H., J. E. Holcombe, R. G. Linscombe, and N. E. Kinler. 1982. Winter foods of river otters from saline and fresh environments in Louisiana. Proc. Annu. Conf. Southeast. Assoc. Fish and Wildl. Agencies 36:473-483.

Chabreck, R. H., P. D. Keyser, D. A. Dell, and R. G. Linscombe. 1989. Movement patterns of muskrats in a Louisiana coastal marsh. Proc. Annu. Conf. Southeast. Assoc. Fish and Wildl. Agencies 43:437-443.

Chamberlain, M. J., D. A. Miller, B. D. Leopold, and G. A. Hurst. 1996. Predation rates on wild turkey hens in a hardwood bottomland forest and a mixed forest in Mississippi. Proc. Annu. Conf. Southeast. Assoc. Fish and Wildl. Agencies 50:428-435.

Chamberlain, M. J., K. M. Hodges, B. D. Leopold, and T. S. Wilson. 1999. Survival and cause-specific mortality of adult raccoons in central Mississippi. J. Wildl. Manage. 63:880-888.

Chester, E. W., B. E. Wofford, J. M. Baskin, and C. C. Baskin. 1997. A floristic study of barrens on the southwestern Pennyroyal Plain, Kentucky and Tennessee. Castanea 62:161-171.

Choate, J. R., J. K. Jones, Jr., and C. Jones. 1994. Handbook of mammals of the south-central states. Louisiana State Univ. Press, Baton Rouge, LA. 304pp.

Chomel, B. B. 1993. The modern epidemiological aspects of rabies in the world. Comp. Imm., Micro., and Infect. Dis. 16:11-20.

Christensen, N. L. 1979. The xeric sandhill and savanna ecosystems of the southeastern Atlantic Coastal Plain, U.S.A. Pages 246-262 in H. Lieth and E. Landolt, eds. Contributions to the knowledge of flora and vegetation in the Carolinas. Proc. of the 16th Int. Phytogeographic Excursion (IPE), 1978. Veroffentlichungen des Geobotanischen Institutes der Eidg. Techn. Hochschule, Stiftung Rubel, Zurich, Switzerland.

Christensen, N. L. 1981. Fire regimes in southeastern ecosystems. Pages 112-136 in H. A. Mooney, T. M. Bonnicksen, N. L. Christensen, J. E. Lotan and W. A. Reiners, eds. Fire regimes and ecosystem properties. USDA For. Serv. Gen. Tech. Rep. WO-26. 594pp.

Christensen, N. L. 1988. Vegetation of the southeastern Coastal Plain. Pages 117-363 in M.G. Barbour and W.D. Billings, eds. North American Terrestrial Vegetation. Cambridge University Press, Cambridge, U.K.

Christianson, E. H., and T. A. Arcury. 1992. Regional diversity in environmental attitudes, knowledge and policy: the Kentucky River authority. Human Organization 51:99-108.

Church, K. E., J. R. Sauer, and S. Droege. 1993. Population trends of quails in North America. Pages 44-54 in K. E. Church and T. V. Dailey, eds. Quail III: National Quail Symp. Kansas Dep. Wildl. and Parks, Pratt.

Clark, A., III. 1992. Heartwood formation in loblolly and longleaf pines for red-cockaded woodpecker nesting cavities. Proc. Annu. Conf. Southeast. Assoc. Fish and Wildl. Agencies 46:79-87.

Clark, B. K., J. B. Bowles, and B. S. Clark. 1987. Summer habitat of the endangered Indiana bat in Iowa. Amer. Midl. Nat. 118:32-39.

Clark, B. S., D. M. Leslie, Jr., and T. S. Carter. 1993. Foraging activity of adult female Ozark big-eared bats (Plecotus townsendii ingens) in summer. J. Mamm. 74:422-427.

Clark, D. R., Jr. 1981. Bats and environmental contaminants; a review. USDI Fish & Wildl. Serv. Spec. Sci. Rep. Wildl. No. 235. 27pp.

Clark, J. D., D. L. Clapp, K. G. Smith, and T. B. Wigley. 1991. Black bear damage and landowner attitudes toward bears in Arkansas. Proc. Annu. Conf. Southeast. Assoc. Fish and Wildl. Agencies 45:208-217.

Clark, J. D., T. Hon, K. D. Ware, and J. H. Jenkins. 1987. Methods for evaluating abundance and distribution of river otters in Georgia. Proc. Annu. Conf. Southeast. Assoc. Fish and Wildl. Agencies 41:358-364.

Clark, W. R., and R. D. Andrews. 1982. Review of population indices applied in furbearer management. Pages 11-22 in G. C. Sanderson, ed. Midwest furbearer management. Proc. 43rd Mid-west Conf., KS.

Clawson, R. 1987. Indiana bats: down for the count. Endangered Species Technical Bull. 22:9-11.

Cleary, E. C., S. E. Wright, and R. A. Dolbeer. 1997. Wildlife strikes to civil aircraft in the United States 1992-1996. DOT/FAA/AS/97-3. Fed. Aviation Adm. Office of Airport Safety and Standards, Washington, DC. 30pp.

Colin, W. F. 1957. Alabama squirrel investigations. Alabama Dept. of Cons., Montgomery. Final Rep. W-25-R. 83pp.

Collopy, M. W. 1996. Southeastern American Kestrel. Pages 212-218 in Rodgers, et al, eds. Rare and Endangered Biota of Florida, Vol V. Birds. Univ. Press of Florida, Gainesville.

Confer, J. L. 1992. Golden-winged Warbler Vermivora chrysoptera. Pages 369-383 in K. J. Schneider and D. M. Pence, eds. Migratory nongame birds of management concern in the Northeast. USDI Fish and Wildlife Service, Newton Corner, MA.

Congdon, J. D., A. F. Dunham, and R. C. Van Loben Sels. 1993. Delayed sexual maturity and demographics of Blanding's turtles (Emydoidea blandingii): implications for conservation and management of long-lived organisms. Cons. Biol. 7:826-833.

Congdon, J. D., A. F. Dunham, and R. C. Van Loben Sels. 1994. Demographics of common snapping turtles (Chelydra serpentina): implications for conservation and management of long-lived organisms. Am. Zool. 34: 397-408.

Conley, R. H., V. G. Henry, and G. H. Matschke. 1972. Final report for the European hog research project W-34. Tenn. Game and Fish Comm., Nashville, TN. 259pp.

Conner, L. M., and B. D. Leopold. 1996. Bobcat habitat use on multiple spatial scales. Proc. Annu. Conf. Southeast. Assoc. Fish and Wildl. Agencies 50:622-631.

Conner, L. M., B. D. Leopold, and K. J. Sullivan. 1992. Bobcat home range, density, and habitat use in east-central Mississippi. Proc. Annu. Conf. Southeast. Assoc. Fish and Wildl. Agencies 46:147-158.

Conner, M. C., R. F. Labisky, and D. R. Progulske, Jr. 1983. Scent-station indices as measures of population abundance for bobcats, raccoons, gray foxes and opossums. Wildl. Soc. Bull. 11:146-152.

Conner, R. N. 1978. Snag management for cavity nesting birds. Pages 120-128 in R. M. DeGraaf, tech. coord. Proc. of the Workshop. Management of Southern Forests for Nongame Birds. USDA For. Serv., Gen. Tech. Rep. SE-14.

Conner, R. N., and C. S. Adkisson. 1975. Effects of clearcutting on the diversity of breeding birds. J. For. 73:781-785.

Conner, R. N., and D. C. Rudolph. 1989. Red-cockaded woodpecker colony status and trends on the Angelina, Davy Crockett, and Sabine National Forests. USDA For. Serv. Res. Paper SO-250. 15pp.

Conner, R. N., and D. C. Rudolph. 1991. Forest habitat loss, fragmentation, and red-cockaded woodpecker populations. Wilson Bull. 103:446-457.

Conner, R. N., and D. C. Rudolph. 1995. Excavation dynamics and use patterns of red-cockaded woodpecker cavities: relationships with cooperative breeding. Pages 343-352 in D. L. Kulhavy, R. G. Hooper, and R. Costa, eds. Red-cockaded woodpecker: recovery, ecology and management. Center for Applied Studies in Forestry, College of Forestry, Stephen F. Austin State Univ., Nacogdoches, TX.

Conner, R. N., and D. C. Rudolph, and L. H. Bonner. 1995. Red-cockaded woodpecker population trends and management on Texas national forests. J. Field Ornithol. 66:140-151.

Conner, R. N., and D. C. Rudolph, D. Saenz, and R. R. Schaefer. 1994. Heartwood, sapwood, and fungal decay associated with red-cockaded woodpecker cavity trees. J. Wildl. Mange. 58:728-734.

Conner, R. N., D. C. Rudolph, D. Saenz, and R. N. Coulson. 1997a. The red-cockaded woodpecker's role in the southern pine ecosystem, population trends and relationships with southern pine beetles. Texas J. Sci. 49:139-154.

Conner, R. N., and D. C. Rudolph, D. Saenz, and R. R. Schaefer. 1996. Red-cockaded woodpecker nesting success, forest structure, and southern flying squirrels in Texas. Wilson Bull. 108:697-711.

Conner, R. N., D. C. Rudolph, D. Saenz, and R. R. Schaefer. 1997b. Species using red-cockaded woodpecker cavities in eastern Texas. Bull. Texas Ornith. Soc. 30:11-16.

Conner, W. H., and J. R. Toliver. 1987. The problem of planting Louisiana swamplands when nutria (Myocastor coypu) are present. Proc. East. Wildl. Damage Control Conf. 3:42-49.

Connolly, G. E. 1978a. Predators and predator control. Pages 369-394 in J. L. Schmidt and D.L. Gilbert, eds. Big game of North America: ecology and management. Stackpole Books, Harrisburg, PA.

Connolly, G. E. 1978b. Predator control and coyote populations: a review of simulation models. Pages 327-345 in M. Bekoff, ed. Coyotes: biology, behavior and management. Academic Press, New York, NY.

Connolly, G. E. 1992. Coyote damage to livestock and other resources. Pages 161-169 in A. H. Boer, ed. Ecology and management of the eastern coyote. Symp. on the Eastern coyote. New Brunswick, Canada. November 1991.

Conover, M. R., W. C. Pitt, K. K. Kessler, T. J. DuBow, and W. A Sanborn. 1995. Review of human injuries, illnesses, and economic losses caused by wildlife in the United States. Wildl. Soc. Bull. 23:407-414.

Conroy, M. J., R. G. Olderwald, and T. L. Sharik. 1982. Forage production and nutrient concentrations in thinned loblolly pine plantations. J. Wildl. Manage. 46:716-727.

Conti, J. A. 1993. Diseases, parasites and contaminants. Pages 205-224 in T. S. Baskett, M. W. Sayre, R. E. Tomlinson, and R. E. Mirarchi, eds. Ecology and management of the mourning dove. Stackpole Books, Harrisburg, PA.

Cook, W. J. 1982. Biochemical, hematological, and pathological observations of black bears in the Smoky Mountains. M.S. Thesis, Univ. Tennessee, Knoxville, TN. 125pp.

Cook, W. J., and M. R. Pelton. 1979. Selected infections and parasitic diseases of black bears in the Great Smoky Mountains National Park. Proc. Eastern Workshop on Black Bear Res. and Manage. 4:120-124.

Cooley, L. S. 1983. Winter food habits and factors influencing the winter diet of river otter in north Florida. M.S. Thesis, Univ. Florida, Gainesville, FL. 50pp.

Cooper, R. J., and M. R. Marshall. 1997. A land manager's guide to simultaneously managing gypsy moth and forest bird populations: preliminary efforts. Univ. Georgia, Athens, GA.

Cooper, W. J., Jr., and T. E. Terrill. 1990. The American South: A History. A. A. Knopf, New York, NY. 835pp.

Cope, J. B., and S. R. Humphrey. 1977. Spring and autumn swarming behavior in the Indiana bat, Myotis sodalis. J. Mamm. 58:93-95.

Cope, J. B., A. R. Richter, and R. S. Mills. 1974. Concentration of the Indiana bat, Myotis sodalis, in Wayne county, Indiana. Proc. Indiana Acad. Sci. 83:482-484.

Copeland, J. D. 1989. White-tailed deer forage, plant species composition, and pine seedling growth on 1- and 2-year-old loblolly pine plantations site-prepared by mechanical and chemical methods. M.S. Thesis, Mississippi State Univ., Mississippi State, MS. 48pp.

Copeyon, C. K. 1990. A technique for constructing cavities for the red-cockaded woodpecker. Wildl. Soc. Bull. 18:303-311.

Copeyon, C. K., J. R. Walters, and J. H. Carter, III. 1991. Induction of red-cockaded woodpecker group formation by artificial cavity construction. J. Wildl. Manage. 55:549-556.

Cordell, H. K., B. L. McDonald, B. Lewis, M. Miles, J. Martin, and J. Bason. 1996. United States of America. Pages 215-235 in G. Cushman, A. J. Veal, and J. Zuzanek, eds. World leisure participation: free time in the global village. CAB International, Oxford, England.

Cordell, H. K., B. L. McDonald, R. J. Teasley, J. C. Bergstrom, J. Martin, J. Bason, and V. L. Leeworthy. 1999. Outdoor Recreation Participation Trends. Pages 219-321 in Outdoor Recreation in American Life: A National Assessment of Demand and Supply Trends. Sagamore Publishing, Champaign, IL.

Cordell, H. K., J. C. Bliss, C. Y. Johnson, and M. Fly. 1998. Voices from Southern Forests. Pages 332-347 in Trans. 63rd N. Am. Wildl. & Nat. Resour. Conf.

Cordes, C. L. 1965. Home range and movements of the eastern gray squirrel, Sciurus carolinensis carolinensis Gmelin, in Wake County, North Carolina. M. S. Thesis, North Carolina State Univ., Raleigh. 58pp.

Cordes, C. L., and F. S. Barkalow, Jr. 1972. Home range and dispersal in North Carolina gray squirrel population. Proc. Annu. Conf. Southeast. Assoc. Fish and Wildl. Agencies 26:124-135.

Coriel, P. D. 1981. Habitat preferences, movements, and activities of nutria in a southwestern Louisiana intermediate marsh area. M. S. Thesis, Louisiana State Univ., Baton Rouge, LA. 68pp.

Costa, R. 1995a. Biological opinion on the U.S. Forest Service environmental impact statement for the management of the red-cockaded woodpecker and its habitat on national forests in the southern region. USDI Fish and Wildl. Serv., Clemson, SC. 192pp.

Costa, R. 1995b. Red-cockaded woodpecker recovery and private lands: a conservation strategy responsive to the issues. Pages 67-74 in D. L. Kulhavy, R. G. Hooper, and R. Costa, eds. Red-cockaded woodpecker: recovery, ecology and management. Stephen F. Austin State Univ., Nacogdoches, TX.

Costa, R. 1997. The U.S. Fish and Wildlife's red-cockaded woodpecker private lands conservation strategy: an evaluation. Endangered Species Update 14:40-44.

Costa, R., and E. Kennedy. 1994. Red-cockaded woodpecker translocations 1989-1994: state-of-our-knowledge. Pages 74-81 in Annu. Proc. Am. Zoo and Aquar. Assoc. Zoo Atlanta, Atlanta, GA.

Costa, R., and E. T. Kennedy. 1997. An incentive program to enhance conservation of longleaf pine and red-cockaded woodpeckers on private land: the case of safe harbor. Pages 30-33 in J.S. Kush, compiler. Proc. First Longleaf Alliance Conf.: Longleaf Pine: A Regional Perspective of Challanges and Opportunities. The Longleaf Alliance, Auburn, AL.

Costa, R., and J. L. Walker. 1995. Red-cockaded woodpecker. Pages 86-89 in E. T. LaRoe, G. S. Farris, C. E. Puckett, and others, eds. Our living resources: a report to the nation on the distribution, abundance, and health of U.S. plants, animals, and ecosystems. U.S. Natl. Biol. Serv., Washington, DC.

Costa, R., and J. W. Edwards. 1997. Cooperative conservation agreements for managing red-cockaded woodpeckers on industrial forest lands: what are the motivations? Pages 111-124 in R. Johnson, ed. Proc. symposium on the economics of wildlife resources on private lands. Auburn University, Auburn, AL.

Costa, R., and R. Escano. 1989. Red-cockaded woodpecker: status and management in the southern region in 1986. USDA For. Serv. Tech. Pub. R8-TP12. 71pp.

Cote, I. M., and W. J. Sutherland. 1997. The effectiveness of removing predators to protect bird populations. Conservation Biology. 11:395-405.

Crabb, W. D. 1948. The ecology and management of the prairie spotted skunk in Iowa. Ecol. Monogr. 18:201-232.

Crampton, L. H. 1991. Bat abundance and distribution in northern Alberta mixedwood stands of different seral stages. Bat Res. News 35:95-96.

Crawford, B. A., M. R. Pelton, and K. G. Johnson. 1993. Techniques to monitor relative abundance of coyotes in east Tennessee. Proc. Annu. Conf. Southeast. Assoc. Fish and Wildl. Agencies 47:62-70.

Criddle, S. 1947. A nest of the least weasel. Can. Field-Nat. 61:69.

Croker, T. C., Jr. 1987. Longleaf pine: a history of man and a forest. USDA For. Serv. Rep. R8-FR7. Atlanta, GA. 37pp.

Cross, S. P. 1985. Responses of small mammals to forest riparian perturbations. Pages 269-275 in R. R. Johnson et al., tech. coords. Riparian ecosystems and their management: reconciling conflicting use. USDA For. Serv. Gen. Tech. Rep. RM-120.

Crossett, R. L., II, and C. L. Elliott. 1991. Winter food habits of red foxes and coyotes in central Kentucky. Proc. Annu. Conf. Southeast. Assoc. Fish and Wildl. Agencies 45:97-103.

Crouch, L. C. 1983. Movements of and habitat utilization by feral hogs at the Savannah River Plant, South Carolina. M.S. Thesis, Clemson University, SC. 69pp.

Crum, J. M. 1977. Some parasites of black bears (Ursus americanus) in the southeastern Unites States. M. S. Thesis, Univ. Georgia, Athens, GA. 76pp.

Cubbage, F. W., and C. H. Flather. 1993. Forested wetland area and distribution. J. For. 91:35-40.

Cunham, C. D., and O. L. Loucks. 1984. Catastrophic windthrow in the presettlement forests of Wisconsin. Ecology 65:803-809.

Cunningham, E. R. 1962. A study of the eastern raccoon on the Atomic Energy Commission Savannah River Plant. M. S. Thesis, Univ. Georgia, Athens, GA. 55pp.

Curtis, P. D., B. S. Mueller, P. D. Doerr, and C. F. Robinette. 1988. Seasonal survival of radio-marked northern bobwhite quail from hunted and non-hunted populations. Biotelem. X: Int. Radio-telem. Symp. 10:263-275.

Curtis, P. D., T. L. Sharpe, and P. D. Doerr. 1990. Early summer diet of male northern bobwhite in the North Carolina sandhills. Proc. Annu. Conf. Southeast. Assoc. Fish and Wildl. Agencies 44:250-259.

Curtis, P. D., T. L. Sharpe, P. D. Doerr, and T. DeVos. 1993. Potential polygamous breeding behavior in northern bobwhite. Pages 55-63 in K. E. Church and T. V. Dailey, eds. Quail III: National Quail Symp. Kansas Dep. Wildl. and Parks, Pratt.

Dahl, T. E. 1990. Wetland losses in the United States 1780's to 1980's. USDI Fish and Wildl. Serv., Washington, DC. 13pp.

Dalla-Tea, F., and E. J. Jokela. 1991. Needlefall, canopy light interception, and productivity of young intensively managed slash and loblolly pine stands. For. Sci. 37:1298-1313.

Darveau, M., P. Beauchesne, L. Belanger, J. Huot, and P. Larue. 1995. Riparian forest strips as habitat for breeding birds in boreal forest. J. Wildl. Manage. 59:67-78.

Davidson, W. R., and E. J. Wentworth. 1992. Population influences: diseases and parasites. Pages 101-118 in J. G. Dickson, ed. The wild turkey: biology and management. Stackpole Books, Harrisburg, PA.

Davidson, W. R., and G. L. Doster. 1997. Health characteristics and white-tailed deer population density in the Southeastern United States. Pages 164-184 in W. J. McShea, H. B. Underwood, and J. H. Rappole, eds. The science of overabundance: deer ecology and population management. Smithsonian Institution Press, Washington, DC.

Davidson, W. R., and V. F. Nettles. 1988. Field manual of wildlife diseases in the southeastern United States. Southeast. Coop. Dis. Study. Univ. Georgia, Athens, GA. 309pp.

Davidson, W. R., K. E. Kellogg, and G. L. Doster. 1982a. An overview of disease and parasitism in Southeastern bobwhite Quail. Pages 57-63 in F. Schitoskey, Jr., E. C. Schitoskey, and L. G. Talent., eds. Proc. Second National Bobwhite Symp. Oklahoma State Univ., Stillwater, OK.

Davidson, W. R., K. E. Kellogg, and G. L. Doster. 1982b. Avian pox infections in Southeastern bobwhites: historical and recent information. Pages 64-73 in F. Schitoskey, Jr., E. C. Schitoskey, and L. G. Talent., eds. Proc. Second National Bobwhite Symp. Oklahoma State Univ., Stillwater, OK.

Davis, D. S. 1993. Feral hogs and disease: implications for humans and livestock. Pages 84-87 in C. W. Hanselka and J. F. Cadenhead, eds. Feral Swine: A Compendium for Resource Managers. Texas Agric. Ext. Serv., Kerrville, TX.

Davis, J. R., and D. C. Guynn, Jr. 1993. Activity and habitat utilization of beaver colonies in South Carolina. Proc. Annu. Conf. Southeast. Assoc. Fish and Wildl. Agencies 47:299-310.

Davis, J. W., and R. C. Anderson. 1971. Parasitic diseases of wild mammals. Iowa State Univ. Press, Ames. 364pp.

Davis, M. B. 1996. Extent and Distribution. Pages 18-32 in M.B. Davis, ed., Eastern old-growth forests. Island Press, Washington, DC.

Davis, W. B., and D. J. Schmidly. 1994. The mammals of Texas. Texas Parks and Wildl. Press, Austin, TX. 338pp.

Davis, W. S. 1981. Aging, reproduction and winter food habits of bobcat (Lynx rufus) and river otter (Lutra canadensis) in Mississippi. M.S. Thesis, Mississippi State Univ., Mississippi State, MS. 41pp.

De Bellevue, E. B. 1976. Hendry County: an agricultural district in a wetland region. South Florida Study. Center for Wetlands, Univ. Florida, Gainesville, FL.

DeCalesta, D. S. 1971. A literature review on cottontail feeding habits. Special Rep. No. 25. Colorado Division of Game, Fish and Parks, Fort Collins. 15pp.

DeCalesta, D. S. 1994. Effect of white-tailed deer on songbirds within managed forests in Pennsylvania. J. Wildl. Manage. 58:711-718.

Decker, D. J., and K. G. Purdy. 1988. Toward a concept of wildlife acceptance capacity in wildlife management. Wildl. Soc. Bull. 16:53-57.

DeFazio, J. T., Jr., A. E. Stone, and R. J. Warren. 1988. Effects of tebuthiuron site preparation on white-tailed deer habitat. Wildl. Soc. Bull. 16:12-18.

Degner, R. L. 1989. Economic importance of feral swine in Florida. Pages 39-41 in N. Black, ed. Proc. Feral Pig Symp., Orlando, FL. Livestock Conserv. Inst., Madison, WI.

Dekker, D. 1983. Denning and foraging habits of red foxes, Vulpes vulpes, and their interaction with coyotes, Canis latrans, in Central Alberta, 1972-1981. Can. Field-Nat. 97:303-306.

Delcourt, H. R., and P. A. Delcourt. 1974. Primeval magnolia-holly-beech climax in Louisiana. Ecology 55:638-644.

Delcourt, H. R., and P. A. Delcourt. 1997. Pre-Columbian Native American use of fire on southern Appalachian landscapes. Conserv. Biol. 11:1010-1014.

Dell, D. A., R. H. Chabreck, and R. G. Linscombe. 1983. Spring and summer movements of muskrats in a Louisiana coastal marsh. Proc. Annu. Conf. Southeast. Assoc. Fish and Wildl. Agencies 37:210-218.

Dellinger, S. C., and J. D. Black. 1938. Herpetology of Arkansas. Occasional Paper. Univ. Arkansas Museum, Fayetteville, AR. 16:1-47.

Delnicki, D., and K. J. Reinecke. 1986. Midwinter food use and body weights of mallards and wood ducks in Mississippi. J. Wildl. Manage. 50:43-51.

DeLotelle, R. S., and R. J. Epting. 1988. Selection of old trees for cavity excavation by red-cockaded woodpeckers. Wilson Bull. 16:48-52.

DeLotelle, R. S., and R. J. Epting. 1992. Reproduction of the red-cockaded woodpecker in central Florida. Wilson Bull. 104:285-294.

DeLotelle, R. S., R. J. Epting, and J. R. Newman. 1987. Habitat use and territory characteristics of red-cockaded woodpeckers in central Florida. Wilson Bull. 99:202-217.

DeMaso, S. J., A. D. Peoples, S. A. Cox, E. S. Parry. 1997. Survival of northern bobwhite chicks in western Oklahoma. J. Wildl. Manage. 61:846-853.

DeMaynadier, P. G., and M. L. Hunter, Jr. 1995. The relationship between forest management and amphibian ecology: a review of the North American literature. Environ. Rev. 3:230-261.

DeSelm, H.R. 1989. The barrens of Tennessee. J. Tenn. Acad. Sci. 64:89-95.

DeSelm, H.R. 1994. Tennessee barrens. Castanea 59:214-225.

DeSelm, H.R., and N. Murdock. 1993. Grass-dominated communities. Pages 87-141 in W.H. Martin, S.G. Boyce, and A.C. Echternacht, eds. Biodiversity of the southeastern United States: upland terrestrial communities. John Wiley & Sons, New York, NY.

DeVan, R. 1982. The ecology and life history of the long-tailed weasel (Mustela frenata). Ph.D. Thesis, Univ. Cincinnati, OH. 300pp.

DeVos, T., and B. S. Mueller. 1993. Reproductive ecology of northern bobwhite in north Florida. Pages 83-90 in K. E. Church, and T. V. Dailey, eds. Quail III: National Quail Symp. Kansas Dep. Wildl. and Parks, Pratt.

Dickson, J. G. 1978a. Seasonal bird populations in a mature bottomland hardwood forest in south central Louisiana. J. Wildl. Manage. 42:875-883.

Dickson, J. G. 1978b. Forest bird communities of the bottomland hardwoods. Pages 66-73 in R. M. DeGraaf, tech. coord. Proc. of the Workshop: Management of Southern Forests for Nongame Birds. USDA For. Serv. Gen. Tech. Rep. SE-14.

Dickson, J. G. 1981. Effects of forest burning on songbirds. Pages 67-72 in G. W. Wood, ed. Prescribed fire and wildlife in southern forests. Belle Baruch For. Sci. Inst., Clemson Univ., SC.

Dickson, J. G. 1985. USDA Forest Service: management, research, and cooperative forestry for multiple benefits. Trans. N. Amer. Wildl. and Natur. Resour. Conf. 50:215-220.

Dickson, J. G. 1988. Bird communities in oak-gum-cypress forests. Pages 51-62 in J. A. Jackson, ed. Bird Conservation 3. Int. Council for Bird Preservation, Univ. Wisconsin Press, Madison.

Dickson, J. G. 1990. Oak and flowering dogwood production for eastern wild turkeys. Proc. National Wild Turkey Symp. 6:90-95.

Dickson, J. G., and C. A. Segelquist. 1979. Breeding bird populations in pine and pine-hardwood forests in Texas. J. Wildl. Manage. 43:549-555.

Dickson, J. G., and J. C. Huntley. 1987. Riparian zones and wildlife in southern forests: the problem and squirrel relationships. Pages 37-39 in J. G. Dickson and O. E. Maughan, eds. Managing Southern Forests for Wildlife and Fish — A Proceedings. USDA For. Serv. Gen. Tech. Rep. SO-65.

Dickson, J. G., and J. H. Williamson. 1988. Small mammals in streamside management zones in pine plantations. Pages 375-378 in R. C. Szaro, K. E. Severson, and D. R. Patton, tech. coords. Proc. of the Symp. Management of Amphibians, Reptiles, and Small Mammals in North America. USDA Forest Service Gen. Tech. Rep. RM-166.

Dickson, J. G., and M. L. Warren, Jr. 1994. Wildlife and fish communities of eastern riparian forests. Pages 1-31 in Riparian Ecosystems in the Humid U. S.: Functions, Values, and Management. National Assoc. Conserv. Dist., Washington, DC.

Dickson, J. G., F. R. Thompson, III, R. N. Conner, and K. E. Franzreb. 1993. Effects of silviculture on Neotropical migratory birds in central and southeastern oak pine forests. Pages 374-

385 in D. M. Finch, P. W. Stangel, eds. Status and Management of Neotropical Migratory Birds. USDA For. Serv., Gen. Tech. Rep. RM-229.

Dickson, J. G., F. R. Thompson, III, R. N. Conner, and K. E. Franzreb. 1995c. Silviculture in central and southeastern oak-pine forests. Pages 245-268 in T. E. Martin and D. M. Finch, eds. Ecology and management of neotropical migratory birds. Oxford Univ. Press, New York, NY.

Dickson, J. G., J. H. Williamson, and R. N. Conner. 1995b. Longevity and bird use of hardwood snags created by herbicides. Proc. Annu. Conf. Southeast. Assoc. Fish and Wildl. Agencies 49:332-339.

Dickson, J. G., J. H. Williamson, R. N. Conner, and B. Ortego. 1995a. Streamside zones and breeding birds in eastern Texas. Wildl. Soc. Bull. 23:750-755.

Dickson, J. G., R. N. Conner, and J. H. Williamson. 1980. Relative abundance of breeding birds in forests in the Southeast. Sou. J. Appl. For. 4:174-179.

Dickson, J. G., R. N. Conner, and J. H. Williamson. 1983. Snag retention increases bird use of a clear-cut. J. Wildl. Manage. 47:799-804.

Dickson, J. G., R. N. Conner, and J. H. Williamson. 1993. Neotropical migratory bird communities in a developing pine plantation. Proc. Annu. Conf. Southeast. Assoc. Fish and Wildl. Agencies 47:439-446.

Diefenbach, D. R., M. J. Conroy, R. J. Warren, W. E. James, L. A. Baker, and T. Hon. 1994. A test of the scent-station survey technique for bobcats. J. Wildl. Manage. 58:10-17.

Dijak, W. D., and F. R. Thompson, III. 2000. Landscape and edge effects on the distribution of mammalian predators in Missouri. J. Wildl. Manage. 64:209-216.

Dimmick, R. W. 1968. A study of bobwhite nesting on the Ames Plantation. Tenn. Farm Sci. 68:8-9.

Dimmick, R. W. 1974. Populations and reproductive effort among bobwhites in western Tennessee. Proc. Annu. Conf. Southeast. Assoc. Game and Fish Comm. 28:594-602.

Dimmick, R. W., F. E. Kellogg, and G. L. Doster. 1982. Estimating bobwhite population size by direct counts and the Lincoln index. Pages 13-18 in F. Schitoskey, Jr., E. C. Schitoskey, and L. G. Talent, eds. Proc. Second National Bobwhite Symp. Oklahoma State Univ., Stillwater.

Ditmars, R. L. 1936. The reptiles of North America. Doubleday, Doran, and Co., New York, NY. 476pp.

Ditmars, R. L. 1939. A field book of North American snakes. Doubleday, Doran, and Co., New York, NY. 305pp.

Dixon, K. R. 1982. Mountain lion. Pages 711-727 in J. A. Chapman and G. A Feldhamer, eds. Wild mammals of North America. Johns Hopkins Univ. Press, Baltimore, MD.

Dixon, K. R., M. A. Horner, S. R. Anderson, W. D. Henriques, D. Durham, and R. J. Kendall. 1996. Northern bobwhite habitat use and survival on a South Carolina plantation during winter. Wildl. Soc. Bull. 24:627-635.

Dodd, C. K., Jr. 1992. Biological diversity of a temporary pond herpetofauna in north Florida sandhills. Biodiv. Conserv. 1:125-142.

Dodd, C.K., Jr. 1995. Reptiles and amphibians in the endangered longleaf pine ecosystem. Pages 129-131 in E.T. Laroe, G.S. Farris, C.E. Puckett, P.D. Doran, and M.J. Mac, eds. Our living resources: a report to the nation on the distribution, abundance, and health of U.S. plants, animals, and ecosystems. USDI, National Biological Service, Washington, DC.

Dodd, C. K., Jr. 1995. The ecology of a sandhills population of the eastern narrow-mouthed toad, Gastrophryne carolinensis, during a drought. Bull. Florida Mus. Nat. Hist. 38, Pt. I:11-41.

Dodd, C. K., Jr. 1996. Use of terrestrial habitats by amphibians in the sandhill uplands of north-central Florida. Alytes 14:42-52.

Dodd, C. K., Jr., and R. A. Seigel. 1991. Relocation, repatriation, and translocation of amphibians and reptiles: are they conservation strategies that work? Herpetologica 47:336-350.

Dodd, C. K., Jr., K. M. Enge, and J. N. Stuart. 1988. Aspects of the biology of the flattened musk turtle, Sternotherus depressus in northern Alabama. Bull. Florida Mus. Nat. Hist. Biol. Sci. 34:1-64.

Doebel, J. H., and B. S. McGinnes. 1974. Home range and activity of a gray squirrel population. J. Wildl. Manage. 38:860-867.

Doig, H. E. 1995. Agency challenges in managing urban deer. Pages 171-175 in J. B. McAninch, ed. Urban Deer: A Manageable Resource? Proc. 1993 Symp. North Central Section, The Wildl. Soc.

Dolan, P. G., and D. C. Carter. 1977. Glaucomys volans. Mammalian Species Number 78. Am. Soc. of Mamm. 6pp.

Dolbeer, R. A., N. R. Holler, and D. W. Hawthorne. 1994. Identification and control of wildlife damage. Pages 474-506 in T. A. Bookhout, ed. Research management techniques for wildlife and habitats. The Wildl. Soc., Bethesda, MD.

Dolton, D. D. 1993. The call-count survey: historic development and current procedures. Pages 233-252 in T. S. Baskett, M. W. Sayre, R. E. Tomlinson, and R. E. Mirarchi, eds. Ecology and management of the mourning dove. Stackpole Books, Harrisburg, PA.

Dolton, D. D., and G. W. Smith. 1997. Mourning dove breeding population status, 1997. USDI Fish and Wildl. Serv., Laurel, MD. 21pp.

Dolton, D. D., and G. W. Smith. 1999. Mourning dove breeding population status, 1999. U.S. Fish and Wildl. Serv., Laurel, MD. 28pp.

Donovan, T. M., F. R. Thompson III, J. Faaborg, and J. Probst. 1995a. Reproductive success of migratory birds in habitat sources and sinks. Conserv. Biol. 9:1380-1395.

Donovan, T. M., P. W. Jones, E. M. Annand, and F. R. Thompson, III. 1997. Variation in local-scale edge effects: mechanisms and landscape context. Ecology 78:2064-2075.

Donovan, T. M., R. H. Lamberson, A. Kimber, F. R. Thompson III, and J. Faaborg. 1995b. Modeling the effects of habitat fragmentation on source and sink demography of neotropical migrant birds. Conserv. Biol. 9:1396-1407.

Drobney, R. D. 1980. Reproductive bioenergetics of wood ducks. Auk 97:480-490.

Drobney, R. D., and L. H. Fredrickson. 1979. Food selection by wood ducks in relation to breeding status. J. Wildl. Manage. 43:109-120.

Dueser, R. D., and H. H. Shugart, Jr. 1978. Microhabitats in a forest-floor small mammal fauna. Ecology 59:89-98.

Dugger, B. D., K. M. Dugger, and L. H. Fredrickson. 1994. Hooded merganser. In A. Poole, P. Stettenheim, and F. Gill, eds. The birds of North America. Philadelphia Acad. Nat. Sci., Washington, DC.

Dunlap, R. E. 1991. Trends in public opinion toward environmental issues: 1965-1990. Soc. & Nat. Resour. 4:285-312.

Dunning, J. B., and B. D. Watts. 1990. Regional differences in habitat occupancy by Bachman's Sparrow. Auk 107:463-472.

Dunning, J. B., and B. D. Watts. 1991. Habitat occupancy by Bachman's Sparrow in the Francis Marion National Forest before and after Hurricane Hugo. Auk 108:723-725.

Dunning, J. B., B. J. Danielson, and H. R. Pulliam. 1992. Ecological processes that affect populations in complex landscapes. Oikos 65:169-175.

Dunning, J. B., Jr., R. Borgella, Jr., K. Clements, and G. K. Meffe. 1995. Patch isolation, corridor effects, and colonization by a resident sparrow in a managed pine woodland. Conserv. Biol. 9:542-550.

Dyer, J. M., and R. B. Hamilton. 1977. Analysis of several site components of diurnal woodcock habitat in southern Louisiana. Proc. Woodcock Symp. 6:51-62.

Dyess, J. G., M. K. Causey, and H. L. Stribling. 1994. Effects of fertilization on production and quality of Japanese honeysuckle. Sou. J. Appl. For. 18:68-71.

Eagle, T. C., and J. S. Whitman. 1987. Mink. Pages 614-624 in M. Novak, J. A. Baker, M. E. Obbard, and B. Malloch, eds. Wild furbearer management and conservation in North America. Ontario Trappers Assoc., North Bay.

Early, J. O., J. C. Roetheli, and G. R. Brewer. 1974. An economic study of predation in the Idaho range sheep industry, 1970-71 production cycle. Idaho Ag. Res. Rep. No. 182. Univ. Idaho, Moscow, ID.

Eason, T. H. 1995. Weights and morphometrics of black bears in the southeastern United States. M.S. Thesis, Univ. Tennessee, Knoxville, TN. 132pp.

Eastridge, R., and J. D. Clark. 1998. An experimental repatriation of black bears into the Big South Fork area of Kentucky and Tennessee. Final Rep. Tennessee Wildl. Res. Agency, Nashville. 132pp.

Economic Research Service. 1997. Nonmetro population growth rebound of the 1990's continues, but at a slower rate. Pages 46-51 in Rural conditions and trends. USDA Economic Res. Serv., Washington, DC.

Eddleman, W.R., K.E. Evans, and W.H. Elder. 1980. Habitat characteristics and management of Swainsons warbler in southern Illinois. Wild. Soc. Bull. 8:228-233.

Edmunds, R. M., J. W. Goertz, and G. Linscombe. 1978. Age ratios, weights, and reproduction of the Virginia opossum in north Louisiana. J. Mamm. 59:884-885.

Edwards, D. A., Jr. 1996. Ecological relationships among bobcats, coyotes, and gray foxes in central Mississippi. M.S. Thesis, Mississippi State Univ., Mississippi State, MS. 182pp.

Edwards, J. W., and D. C. Guynn, Jr. 1995. Nest characteristics of sympatric populations of fox and gray squirrels. J. Wildl. Manage. 59:103-110.

Edwards, J. W., D. C. Guynn, Jr., and M. R. Lennartz. 1989. Habitat use by southern fox squirrel in coastal South Carolina. Proc. Annu. Conf. Southeast. Assoc. Fish and Wildl. Agencies 43:337-345.

Edwards, J. W., D. G. Heckel, and D. C. Guynn, Jr. 1998. Niche overlap in sympatric populations of fox and gray squirrels. J. Wildl. Manage. 62:354-363.

Ehrlich, P. R., D. S. Dobkin, and D. Wheye. 1992. Birds in jeopardy. Stanford Univ. Press, Stanford, CA. 259pp.

Eiler, J. H., W. G. Wathen, and M. R. Pelton. 1989. Reproduction in black bears in the southern Appalachian mountains. J. Wildl. Manage. 53:353-360.

Elkins, G. M. 1996. Law enforcement issues related to baiting regulations and moist-soil management. Pages 178-181 in J. T. Ratti, ed. 7th Int. Waterfowl Symp. Ducks Unlimited, Inc. Memphis, TN.

English, D. B. K., and P. Gentle. 1998. Economic dimensions of the SEELA study. USDA Forest Service, Pacific Northwest Res. Stn.

English, D. B. K., and R. M. Beavers. In Press. Economic trends in the U. S. In H. K. Cordell, ed. Footprints on the land. Sagamore Publ., Champaign, IL.

Engstrom, R. T., and F. J. Sanders. 1997. Red-cockaded woodpecker foraging ecology in an old-growth longleaf pine forest. Wilson Bull. 109:203-217.

Engstrom, R. T., and W. W. Baker. 1995. Red-cockaded woodpecker on Red Hills hunting plantations: inventory, management, and conservation. Pages 489-493 in D. L. Kulhavy, R. G. Hooper, and R. Costa, eds. Red-cockaded woodpecker: recovery, ecology and management. Stephen F. Austin State Univ., Nacogdoches, TX.

Engstrom, R. T., L. A. Brennan, W. L. Neel, R. M. Farrar, S. T. Lindeman, W. K. Moser, and S. M. Hermann. 1996. Silvicultural practices and red-cockaded woodpecker management: a reply to Rudolph and Conner. Wildl. Soc. Bull. 24:334-338.

Erlinge, S. 1975. Feeding habits of the weasel Mustela nivalis in relation to prey abundance. Oikos 26:378-384.

Ernst, C. H., J. E. Lovich, and R. W. Barbour. 1994. Turtles of the United States and Canada. Smithsonian Inst. Press, Washington DC. 578pp.

Errington, P. L. 1934. Vulnerability of bobwhite populations to predation. Ecology 15:110-127.

Errington, P. L. 1936. Food habits of the weasel family. J. Mamm. 17:406-407.

Errington, P. L. 1943. An analysis of mink predation upon muskrats in north-central United States. Pages 797-924 in Res. Bull. 320. Iowa Agric. Exp. Stn.

Errington, P. L., and F. N. Hamerstrom, Jr. 1935. Bobwhite winter survival on experimentally shot and unshot areas. Iowa State Coll. J. Sci. 9:625-639.

Evans, K. E., and R. N. Conner. 1979. Snag management. Pages 214-225 in R. M. DeGraaf and K. E. Evans, tech. coord. Management of North Central and Northeastern Forests for Nongame Birds. Proc. Workshop, USDA For. Serv. Gen. Tech. Rep. NC-51.

Everett, D. D., D. W. Speake, and W. K. Maddox. 1980. Natality and mortality of a north Alabama wild turkey population. Proc. National Wild Turkey Symp. 4:117-126.

Everett, D. D., Jr., D. W. Speake, and W. K. Maddox. 1985. Habitat use by wild turkeys in northwest Alabama. Proc. Annu. Conf. Southeast. Assoc. Fish and Wildl. Agencies 39:479-488.

Everhart, S. H. 1986. Avian interspecific utilization of red-cockaded woodpecker cavities. Ph.D. Thesis, North Carolina State Univ., Raleigh. 113pp.

Ewel, K. C. 1990. Swamps. Pages 281-323 in R.L. Myers and J.J. Ewel, eds, Ecosystems of Florida. University of Central Florida Press, Orlando, FL.

Ewel, K. C. 1998. Pondcypress swamps. Pages 405-420 in M.G. Messina and W.C. Conner, eds. Southern Forested Wetlands. Lewis Publishers, New York, NY.

Exum, J. H., J. A. McGlincy, D. W. Speake, J. L. Buckner, and F. M.

Stanley. 1985. Evidence against dependence upon surface water by turkey hens and poults in southern Alabama. Proc. National Wild Turkey Symp. 5:83-89.

Exum, J. H., J. A. McGlincy, D. W. Speake, J. L. Buckner, and F. M. Stanley. 1987. Ecology of the eastern wild turkey in an intensively managed pine forest in southern Alabama. Tall Timbers Res. Stn. Bull. 23. 70pp.

Exum, J. H., R. W. Dimmick, and B. L. Deardon. 1982. Land use and bobwhite populations in an agricultural system in west Tennessee. Pages 6-12 in F. Schitoskey Jr., E. C. Schitoskey, and L. G. Talent, eds. Proc. Second National Bobwhite Quail Symp. Oklahoma State Univ., Stillwater, OK.

Faaborg, J., M. Brittingham, T. Donovan, and J. Blake. 1992. Habitat fragmentation in the temperate zone: a perspective for managers. Pages 331-338 in Finch, D. M. and P. W. Stangel, eds. Status and management of neotropical migratory birds. USDA For. Serv. Gen. Tech. Rep. RM-229.

Faaborg, J., M. Brittingham, T. Donovan, and J. Blake. 1995. Habitat fragmentation in the temperate zone. Pages 357-380 in T. E. Martin and D. M. Finch, eds. Ecology and management of neotropical migratory birds. Oxford Univ. Press, New York, NY.

Fagerstone, K. A. 1987. Black-footed ferret, long-tailed weasel, short-tailed weasel, and least weasel in North America. Pages 548-573 in M. Novak, J. A. Baker, M. E. Obbard, and B. Malloch, eds. Wild furbearer management and conservation in North America. Ontario Trappers Assoc., North Bay.

Feeback, D., and J.O. Luken. 1992. Proper transplanting method in restoration of canebrakes (Kentucky). Restoration and Management Notes 10:195.

Ferrell, R. E., D. C. Morizot, J. Horn, and C. J. Carley. 1980. Biochemical markers in a species endangered by introgression: The red wolf. Biochem. Gen. 18:39-47.

Fies, M. L., I. L. Kenyon, and J. V. Gwynn. 1992. Effects of changing landuse patterns on bobwhite quail habitat in Virginia. Virginia J. Sci. 23:143-155.

Fischer, R. A., and N. R. Holler. 1991. Habitat use and relative abundance of gray squirrels in southern Alabama. J. Wildl. Manage. 55:52-59.

Fleet, R. R., and J. G. Dickson. 1984. Small mammals in two adjacent forests stands in East Texas. Pages 264-269 in W. C. McComb, ed. Proc. Workshop on Management of Nongame Species and Ecological Communities. Univ. Kentucky, Lexington, KY.

Fleming, D. M. 1975. Movement patterns of the coastal marsh raccoon in Louisiana and notes on its life history. M. S. Thesis, Louisiana State Univ., Baton Rouge, LA. 90pp.

Fleming, D. M., A.W. Palmisano, and T. Joanen. 1976. Food habits of coastal marsh raccoons with observations of alligator nest predation. Proc. Ann. Conf. Southeast. Assoc. Fish and Wildl. Agencies 30:348-357.

Flyger, V., and J. E. Gates. 1982a. Fox and gray squirrels. Pages 209-229 in J. A. Chapman and G. A. Feldhamer, eds. Wild mammals of North America: biology, management, and economics. Johns Hopkins Univ. Press, Baltimore, MD.

Flyger, V., and J. E. Gates. 1982b. Pine squirrels. Pages 230-238 in J. A. Chapman and G. A. Feldhamer, eds. Wild mammals of North America: biology, management, and economics. Johns Hopkins Univ. Press, Baltimore, MD.

Folkerts, G.W. 1997. Citronelle ponds: little-known wetlands of the central Gulf Coastal Plain, USA. Nat. Areas J. 17:6-16.

Folkerts, G.W. 1982. The gulf coast pitcher plant bogs. Am. Scientist 70:260-267.

Foote, A. L. 1984. Home range, movements and habitat utilization of gray foxes in eastern Louisiana. M.S. Thesis, Louisiana State Univ., Baton Rouge, LA. 91pp.

Forman, R. T. T., and M. Godron. 1986. Landscape ecology. John Wiley and Sons, New York, NY.

Forrester, D. J., M. G. Spalding, and J. B. Wooding. 1993. Demodiosis in black bears (Ursus americanus) from Florida. J. Wildl. Dis. 19:136-138.

Foti, T.L., and S.M. Glenn. 1991. The Ouachita Mountain landscape at the time of settlement. Pages 49-66 in D. Henderson and L.D. Hedrick, eds. Restoration of old-growth forests in the Interior Highlands of Arkansas and Oklahoma: Proceedings of a Conference, Winrock Int., Morrilton, AR.

Fowler, J. F., S. Verma, and T. Delphin. 1994. An impact assessment of beaver damage in Louisiana during 1993. La. Coop. Ext. Serv., Baton Rouge, LA. 19pp.

Fox, J. R., and M. R. Pelton. 1977. An evaluation of control techniques for the European wild hog in the Great Smoky Mountains National Park. Pages 53-66 in G. W. Wood, ed. Research and management of wild hog populations. Belle Baruch Forest Science Inst. of Clemson Univ., Georgetown, SC.

Fox, S., and R. A. Mickler, eds. 1995. Impact of air pollutants on southern pine forests. Springer-Verlag, New York, NY. 513pp.

Foy, M. K. 1984. Seasonal movement, home range, and habitat use of river otter in southeastern Texas. M.S. Thesis, Texas A&M Univ., College Station, TX. 101pp.

Franklin, J. F., and R. T. T. Forman. 1987. Creating landscape patterns by forest cutting: ecological consequences and principles. Landscape Ecol. 1:5-18.

Fredrickson, L. H. 1980. Management of lowland hardwood wetlands for wildlife: problems and potential. Trans. N. Am. Wildl. and Nat. Resour. Conf. 45:376-386.

Fredrickson, L. H., and D. L. Batema. 1993. Greentree reservoir handbook. Gaylord Memorial Laboratory Wetland Manage. Ser. No. 1. Univ. Missouri-Columbia, Puxico, MO.

Fredrickson, L. H., and J. L. Hansen. 1983. Second broods in wood ducks. J. Wildl. Manage. 47:320-326.

Fredrickson, L. H., and M. E. Heitmeyer. 1988. Waterfowl use of forested wetlands of the southern United States: an overview. Pages 307-323 in M. W. Weller, ed. Waterfowl in Winter - A Symposium. Univ. Minnesota Press, Minneapolis.

Fredrickson, L. H., and R. D. Drobney. 1979. Habitat utilization by postbreeding waterfowl. Pages 119-130 in T. A. Bookhout, ed. Waterfowl and wetlands - an integrated review. N. Cent. Sect., The Wildl. Soc., Madison, WI.

Fredrickson, L. H., and T. S. Taylor. 1982. Management of seasonally flooded impoundments for wildlife. USDI Fish and Wildl. Serv. Resour. Publ. 148. Washington, DC.

Freemark, K. E., J. B. Dunning, S. J. Hejl, and J. R. Probst. 1995. A landscape ecology perspective for research, conservation, and management. Pages 381-427 in T. E. Martin and D. M. Finch, eds. Ecology and management of neotropical migratory birds. Oxford Univ. Press, New York, NY.

Friend, M. E. 1987. Field guide to wildlife diseases. U.S. Fish and Wildl. Serv. Resour. Publ. 167. Washington, DC.

Fritts, S. H. 1973. Age, food habits and reproduction of the bobcat (Lynx rufus) in Arkansas. M.S. Thesis, Univ. Arkansas,

Fayetteville, AR. 80pp.

Fritts, S. H., and J. A. Sealander. 1978. Diets of bobcats in Arkansas with special reference to age and sex differences. J. Wildl. Manage. 42:533-539.

Fritzell, E. K. 1987. Gray fox and island gray fox. Pages 408-420 in M. Novak, J. A. Baker, M. E. Obbard, and B. Malloch, eds. Wild furbearer management and conservation in North America. Ministry of Natural Resources, Ontario.

Fritzell, E. K., and K. J. Haroldson. 1982. Urocyon cinereoargenteus. Mammalian Species. Amer. Soc. Mamm. 189:1-8.

Frost, C. C. 1993. Four centuries of changing landscape patterns in the longleaf pine ecosystem. Pages 17-43 in S. M. Hermann, ed. The Longleaf Pine Ecosystem: Ecology, Restoration, and Management. Proc. Tall Timbers Fire Ecol. Conf., No. 18. Tall Timbers Res. Stn., Tallahassee, FL.

Frost, C. C. 1995. Presettlement fire regimes in southeastern marshes, peatlands, and swamps. Pages 39-60 in S. I. Cerulean and R. T. Engstrom, eds. Fire in Wetlands: A Management Perspective. Proc. Tall Timbers Fire Ecol. Conf., No. 19. Tall Timbers Res. Stn., Tallahassee, FL.

Frost, C. C. 1998. Presettlement fire frequency regimes of the United States: a first approximation. Tall Timbers Fire Ecol. Conf. Proc. 20:70-81.

Frost, C. C., J. Walker, and R. K. Peet. 1986. Fire-dependent savannas and prairies of the Southeast: original extent, preservation status and management problems. Pages 348-357 in D. L. Kulhavy and R. N. Conner, eds. Wilderness and natural areas in the eastern United States: a management challenge. Center for Applied Studies, School of Forestry, Stephen F. Austin St. Univ., Nacogdoches, TX. 416pp.

Gabor, T. M., R. E. Kissell, Jr., D. A. Elrod, and R. E. Lizotte, Jr. 1994. Factors affecting scent station visitation rates of raccoons and bobcats. Proc. Annu. Conf. Southeast. Assoc. Fish and Wildl. Agencies 48:182-190.

Gaines, G. D., K. E. Franzreb, D. H. Allen, K. Laves, and W. L. Jarvis. 1995. Red-cockaded woodpecker management on the Savannah River Site: a management/research success story. Pages 81-88 in D. L. Kulhavy, R. G. Hooper, and R. Costa, eds. Red-cockaded woodpecker: recovery, ecology and management. Center for Applied Studies in Forestry, College of Forestry, Stephen F. Austin State Univ., Nacogdoches, TX.

Galbraith, D. A., R. J. Brooks, and G. P. Brown. 1997. Can management intervention achieve sustainable exploitation of turtles? Pages 186-194 in J. Van Abbema, ed. Proc. Conservation and Management of tortoises and freshwater turtles. Am. Mus. Nat. Hist., New York, NY.

Gardner, A. L. 1982. Virginia opossum. Pages 3-36 in J. A. Chapman and G. A. Feldhamer, eds. Wild mammals of North America: biology, management, and economics. Johns Hopkins Univ. Press, Baltimore, MD.

Garner, N. P. 1986. Seasonal movements and habitat preferences of bears (Ursus americanus) in Shenandoah National Park, Virginia. M.S. Thesis, Virginia Tech, Blacksburg, VA. 104pp.

Garshelis, D. L., and M. R. Pelton. 1980. Activity of black bears in the Great Smoky Mountains National Park. J. Mamm. 61:8-19.

Garshelis, D. L., and M. R. Pelton. 1981. Movements of black bears in the Great Smoky Mountains National Park. J. Wildl. Manage. 45:912-925.

Gehrt, S. D., and E. K. Fritzell. 1997. Sexual differences in home ranges of racoons. J. Mamm. 78:921-931.

Geier, A. R., and L. B. Best. 1980. Habitat selection by small mammals of riparian communities: evaluating effects of habitat alterations. J. Wildl. Manage. 44:16-24.

Gese, E. M., O. J. Rongstad, and W. R. Mytton. 1989. Population dynamics of coyotes in southeastern Colorado. J. Wildl. Manage. 53:174-181.

Gibbons, J. W. 1988. The management of amphibians, reptiles and small mammals in North America: the need for an environmental attitude adjustment. Pages 4-10 in Management of Amphibians, Reptiles, and Small Mammals in North America. USDA For. Serv. Gen. Tech. Rep. RM-166.

Gibbons, J. W. 1990. Life History and Ecology of the Slider Turtle. Smithsonian Institution Press, Washington, DC. 368pp.

Gibbons, J. W., and M. E. Dorcas. 1998. Cottonmouth: overrated warrior of the Coastal Plain. Natural History magazine. November:56-57.

Gibbons, J. W., and R. D. Semlitsch. 1981. Terrestrial drift fences with pitfall traps: an effective technique for quantitative sampling of animal populations. Brimleyana 7:1-16.

Gibbons, J. W., and R. D. Smelitsch. 1991. Guide to the Reptiles and Amphibians of the Savannah River Site. University of Georgia Press. Athens. 131pp.

Gibbons, J. W., et al. 1997. Perceptions of species abundance, distribution, and diversity: lessons from four decades of sampling on a government-managed reserve. Environmental Manage. 21:259-268.

Gibson, T.C. 1983. Competition, disturbance, and the carnivorous plant community in the southeastern United States. Ph.D. Diss. University of Utah, Salt Lake City.

Gill, D. E. 1978. The metapopulation ecology of the red-spotted newt, Notophthalmus viridescens (Rafinesque). Ecol. Monogr. 48:145-166.

Gipson, P. S. 1974. Food habits of coyotes in Arkansas. J. Wildl. Manage. 38:848-853.

Gipson, P. S., and J. A. Sealander. 1972. Home range and activity of the coyote (Canis latrans frustror) in Arkansas. Proc. Annu. Conf. Southeast. Assoc. Game and Fish Comm. 26:82-95.

Giuliano, W. M., C. L. Elliott, and J. D. Sole. 1993. Seasonal changes in abundance of Kentucky cottontails. Trans. Ky. Acad. Sci. 54:22-27.

Glasgow, L. L. 1958. Contributions to the knowledge of the ecology of the American woodcock, Philohela minor (Gmelin), on the wintering range in Louisiana. Ph.D. Thesis, Texas A&M Univ., College Station, TX. 158pp.

Glass, S. L. 1991. Ecology and population dynamics of raccoons in east Tennessee. M. S. Thesis, Univ. Tennessee, Knoxville, TN. 200pp.

Glitzenstein, J.S., W.J. Platt, and D.R. Streng. 1995. Effects of fire regime and habitat on tree dynamics in north Florida longleaf pine savannas. Ecol. Monogr. 56:243-258.

Godbee, J., and T. Price. 1975. Beaver damage survey. Ga. For. Comm., Macon, GA. 24pp.

Godin, A. J. 1983. Striped and hooded skunks. Pages 674-687 in J. A. Chapman and G. A. Feldhamer, eds. Wild mammals of North America: biology, management, and economics. Johns Hopkins Univ. Press, Baltimore, MD.

Goertz, J. W., and R. C. Long. 1973. Habitats of five species of rat in Louisiana. Amer. Midl. Nat. 90:460-465.

Goertz, J. W., R. M. Dawson, and E. E. Mowbray. 1975. Response to nest boxes and reproduction by Glaucomys volans in northern Louisiana. J. Mamm. 56:933-939.

Goldman, E. A. 1944. Classification of wolves. Pages 389-636 in S. P. Young and E. A. Goldman, eds. The Wolves of North America. Am. Wildl. Inst., Washington, DC.

Goldsmith, D. M. 1981. The ecology and natural history of striped skunks in the Cades Cove Campground, Great Smoky Mountains National Park. M. S. Thesis, Univ. Tennessee, Knoxville, TN. 77pp.

Golley, F. B. 1962. Mammals of Georgia: a study of their distribution and functional role in the ecosystem. Univ. Georgia Press, Athens. 218pp.

Goodrum, P. 1949. Status of bobwhite quail in the United States. Trans. N. Amer. Wildl. Conf. 1:481-486.

Goodwin, G. C. 1977. Cherokees in transition: a study of changing culture and environment prior to 1775. Univ. Chicago, Dep. of Geog. Res. Pap. No. 181.

Gordon, K. L., and D. H. Arner. 1976. Preliminary study using chemosterilants for control of nuisance beaver. Proc. Annu. Conf. Southeast. Assoc. Fish and Wildl. Agencies 30:463-465.

Goss, L. J. 1948. Species susceptibility to the viruses of Carre and feline enteritis. Am. J. Vet. Res. 9:65.

Gosselink, J. G., and L. C. Lee. 1989. Cumulative impact assessment in bottomland hardwood forests. Wetlands 9: 89-174.

Gosselink, J. G., C. L. Cordes, and J. W. Parsons. 1979. An ecological characterization study of the Chenier Plain coastal ecosystem of Louisiana and Texas. 3 vols. USDI Fish and Wildl. Serv. FWS/OBS-78/9 through 78/11.

Gottshalk, K. W. 1987. Effects of deer on oak regeneration following thinning and clear-cutting in central Pennsylvania. Page 2 in Proc. Symp. Deer, For., and Agric. Soc. Amer. For., Warren, PA.

Grand, J. B., and R. E. Mirarchi. 1988. Habitat use by recently fledged mourning doves in eastcentral Alabama. J. Wildl. Manage. 53:153-157.

Grand, J. B., R. R. Hitchcock, and R. E. Mirarchi. 1984. Mortality of nestling and fledgling Mourning doves in east central Alabama. J. Ala. Acad. Sci. 55:131.

Grant, B. W., K. L. Brown, G. W. Ferguson, and J. W. Gibbons. 1994. Changes in amphibian biodiversity associated with 25 years of pine forest regeneration: implications for biodiversity management. Pages 355-366 in F. J. B. S. K. Majumdar, J. E. Lovich, J. F. Schalles, and W. E. Miller, eds. Biological Diversity: Problems and Challenges. Pennsylvania Acad., PA.

Grasman, B. T., and E. C. Hellgren. 1993. Phosphorus nutrition in white-tailed deer: nutrient balance, physiological responses, and antler growth. Ecology 74:2279-2296.

Graves, H. B., and K. L. Graves. 1977. Some observations on biobehavioral adaptations of swine. Pages 103-110 in G. W. Wood, ed. Research and management of wild hog populations. Belle Baruch Forest Science Inst. of Clemson Univ., Georgetown, SC.

Greenberg, C. H. In Press. Dynamics of acorn production by five species of southern Appalachian oaks. In W. J. Meshea and W. M. Healy, eds. Oak forest ecosystems; ecology and management for wildlife. Smithsonian Inst. Press.

Greenwood, R. J., A. B. Sargeant, D. H. Johnson, L. M. Cowardin, and T. L. Shaffer. 1995. Factors associated with duck nest success in the prairie pothole region of Canada. Wildl. Monogr. 128:1-57.

Greg, L. 1984. Population ecology of woodcock in Wisconsin. Wisconsin Dep. Nat. Resour., Tech. Bull 144. 51pp.

Gregory, J. F. 1987. Food habits and preferences of American woodcock wintering in young pine plantations of east Texas. M.S. Thesis, Stephen F. Austin State Univ., Nacogdoches, TX. 70pp.

Greslin, H. G., Jr. 1970. A radio-tracking study of home range, movements, and habitat uses of the fox squirrel (Sciurus niger) in east Texas. M. S. Thesis, Texas A&M Univ., College Station, TX. 118pp.

Griffith, M. A., and T. T. Fendley. 1982. Influence of density on movement behavior and home range size of adult bobcats on the Savannah River Plant, South Carolina. Pages 261-275 in S. D. Miller and D. D. Everett, eds. Cats of the world: biology, conservation, and management. Proc. 2nd Int. Symp. National Wildl. Fed.

Grindal, S. D. 1994. Impacts of forest harvesting on the foraging ecology of bats in southern British Columbia. Bat Res. News 35:100.

Grossman, D.H., D. Faber-Langendoen, A.S. Weakley, M. Anderson, P. Bourgeron, R. Crawford, K. Goodin, S. Landaal, K. Metzler, K. Patterson, M. Myne, M. Reid, and L. Sneddon. 1998. International Classification of Ecological Communities: Terrestrial Vegetation of the United States. Volume I. The National Vegetation Classification System: Development, status, and applications. The Nature Conservancy, Arlington, VA.

Grossman, D.H., K.L. Goodin, and C.L. Reuss, eds. 1994. Rare plant communities of the conterminous United States. The Nature Conservancy, Arlington, VA. 620 pp.

Groth, J. G. 1988. Resolution of cryptic species in Appalachian red crossbills. The Condor 90:745-760.

Grue, C. E., R. R. Reid, and N. J. Silvy. 1983. Correlation of habitat variables with mourning dove call counts in Texas. J. Wildl. Manage. 47:186-195.

Gudlin, M. J., and R. W. Dimmick. 1984. Habitat utilization by ruffed grouse transplanted from Wisconsin to west Tennessee. Pages 75-88 in W.L. Robinson, ed. Ruffed grouse management: state of the art in the early 1980's. North Central Section The Wildlife Society. 181pp.

Guenther, D. D. 1980. Home range, social organization, and movement patterns of the bobcat, Lynx rufus, from spring to fall in south-central Florida. M.S. Thesis, Univ. S. Florida, Tampa, FL. 66pp.

Gullion, G. W. 1984. Managing northern forests for wildlife. The Ruffed Grouse Society. 72pp.

Gullion, G. W. 1988. Effect of hunting on a ruffed grouse population. 50th Midwest Fish & Wildl. Conf., Columbus, OH. 31pp.

Guo, Y., B. R. Lockhart, and T. T. Ku. 1998. Effect of nitrogen and phosphorous fertilization on growth in a sweetgum plantation in southeastern Arkansas. Sou. J. Appl. For. 22:163-168.

Guthery, F. S. 1986. Beef, brush and bobwhites: Quail management in cattle country. Golden Banner Press, Inc. Corpus Christi, TX. 182pp.

Guthery, F. S.. 1997. A philosophy of habitat management for northern bobwhites. J. Wildl. Manage. 61:291-301.

Guthery, F. S., and R. L. Bingham. 1992. On Leopold's principle of edge. Wildl. Soc. Bull. 20:340-344.

Guthery, F. S., and W. P. Kuvlesky, Jr. 1998. The effect of multiple-brooding on age ratios of quail. J. Wildl. Manage. 62:540-549.

Guyer, C., and M. A. Bailey. 1993. Amphibians and reptiles of longleaf pine communities. Pages 139-158 in S. M. Hermann, ed.

The Longleaf Pine Ecosystem: Ecology, Restoration, and Management. Proc. of the Tall Timbers Fire Ecology Conference. Tall Timbers, Tallahassee, FL.

Ha, J. C. 1983. Food supply and home range in the fox squirrel (Sciurus niger). M. A. Thesis, Wake Forest Univ., Winston-Salem, NC. 32pp.

Hale, P. E., A. S. Johnson, and J. L. Landers. 1982. Characteristics of ruffed grouse drumming sites in Georgia. J. Wildl. Manage. 46:115-123.

Hall, E. R. 1951. American weasels. Univ. Kansas Publ., Mus. Nat. Hist. 4:1-466.

Hall, E. R. 1981. The mammals of North America. 2nd ed. John Wiley and Sons, New York, NY. 1181pp.

Hall, E. R., and K. R. Kelson. 1959. The mammals of North America. Vol. 2. The Ronald Press Co., New York, NY. 537pp.

Hall, H. M. 1946. Woodcock ways. Oxford Univ. Press, New York, NY. 84pp.

Hall, H. T. 1973. An ecological study of the bobcat in southern Louisiana. M.S. Thesis, Louisiana State Univ., Baton Rouge, LA. 132pp.

Hall, H. T., and J. D. Newsome. 1976. Summer home ranges and movements of bobcats in bottomland hardwoods of southern Louisiana. Proc. Annu. Conf. Southeast. Assoc. Game and Fish Comm. 30:427-436.

Hall, J. S. 1962. A life history and taxonomic study of the Indiana bat, Myotis sodalis. Reading Public Mus. And Art Gallery, Sci. Publ. 12:1-68.

Halls, L. K., and R. Alcaniz. 1968. Browse plants yield best in forest openings. J. Wildl. Manage. 32:185-186.

Hamel, P. B. 1981. A hierarchical approach to avian community structure. Ph.D. Thesis, Clemson Univ., Clemson, SC. 323pp.

Hamel, P. B. 1986. Bachman's warbler, a species in peril. Smithsonian Institution Press, Washington, DC.

Hamel, P. B. 1989. Breeding birds of Congaree Swamp National Monument. Pages 617-628 in R. R. Sharitz and J. W. Gibbons, eds. Freshwater Wetlands and Wildlife, CONF-8603101, DOE Symp. Series No. 61, USDOE Office of Scientific and Technical Information, Oak Ridge, TN.

Hamel, P. B. 1992a. Land manager's guide to the birds of the South. The Nature Conservancy, Southeastern Region. Chapel Hill, NC. 437pp.

Hamel, P. B. 1992b. Cerulean warbler Dendroica cerulea. Pages 385-400 in K. J. Schneider and D. M. Pence, eds. Migratory nongame birds of management concern in the northeast. USDI Fish and Wildl. Serv., Newton Corner, MA. 400pp.

Hamel, P. B. 2000. Cerulean warbler status assessment. USDI Fish and Wildl. Serv., Ft. Snelling, MN.

Hamel, P. B., and E. R. Buckner. 1998. So how far could a squirrel travel in the treetops? A prehistory of the southern forest. Trans. N. Amer. Wildl. and Nat. Res. Conf. 63:309-315.

Hamel, P. B., R. J. Cooper, and W. P. Smith. 1998. The uncertain future for Cerulean warblers in the Mississippi Alluvial Valley. Pages 95-108 in Proc. Delta Conf., 13-16 August 1996, Memphis, TN. USDA Nat. Resour. Cons. Serv., Madison, WI.

Hamel, P. B., H. E. LeGrand, Jr., M. R. Lennartz, and S. A. Gauthreaux, Jr. 1982. Bird-habitat relationships on southeastern forest land. USDA For. Serv. Gen. Tech. Rep. SE-22. 417pp.

Hamel, P. B., N. L. Brunswig, M. R. Dawson, and M. Staten. 2000. Lying in wait for Partners in Flight: Some experiences in southeastern bottomlands. Proc. Partners in Flight International Workshop, Cape May, NJ, 1-5 October 1995. Cornell Laboratory of Ornithology, Ithaca, NY.

Hamilton, R. J., and R. L. Marchinton. 1980. Denning and related activities of black bears in the coastal plains of North Carolina. Proc. International Conf. Bear Res. and Manage. 4:121-126.

Hamilton, W. H., Jr. 1943. The mammals of the eastern United States. Comstock Publ. Co., Inc., New York, NY. 432pp.

Hamrick, W. J., and J. R. Davis. 1971. Summer food items of juvenile wild turkeys. Proc. Ann. Conf. Southeast. Assoc. Game and Fish Comm. 25:85-89.

Handley, C. O. 1931. The food and feeding habits of bobwhites. Pages 113-157 and 509-521 in H. L. Stoddard, ed. The bobwhite quail: its habits, preservation, and increase. Charles Schribner's Sons. New York, NY. 559pp.

Handley, C. O., Jr. 1991. Mammals. Pages 539-616 in K. Terwilliger, ed. Virginia's Endangered Species. Proc. Symp. McDonald and Woodward Pub. Co., Granville, OH.

Handley, C. O., Jr., and C. P. Patton. 1947. Wild mammals of Virginia. Comm. Game and Inland Fisheries. Richmond, VA. 220pp.

Hanson, R. P. and L. Karstad. 1959. Feral swine in the southeastern United States. J. Wildl. Manage. 23:64-75.

Hanula, J. L., and K. E. Franzreb. 1995. Arthropod prey of nestling red-cockaded woodpeckers in the upper coastal plain of South Carolina. Wilson Bull. 107:485-495.

Harcombe, P.A., J.S. Glitzenstein, R.G. Knox, S.L. Orzell, and E.L. Bridges. 1993. Vegetation of the longleaf pine region of the West Gulf Coastal Plain. Tall Timbers Fire Ecol. Conf. Proc. 18:83-104.

Hardesty, J. L., K. E. Gault, and H. F. Percival. 1997. Ecological correlates of red-cockaded woodpecker (Picoides borealis) foraging preference, habitat use, and home range size in northwest Florida (Eglin Air Force Base). Florida Coop. Fish and Wildl. Res. Unit, Univ. Florida, Gainesville. Final Rep. Work Order 99. 80pp.

Hardin, E.D., and D.L. White. 1989. Rare vascular plant taxa associated with wiregrass (Aristida stricta) in the southeastern United States. Nat. Areas J. 9: 234-245.

Hardy, G. H. 1979. Movement ecology of resident raccoons in east Tennessee. M. S. Thesis, Univ. Tennessee, Knoxville, TN. 82pp.

Harlow, R. F., and A. T. Doyle. 1990. Food habits of southern flying squirrels (Glaucomys volans) collected from re-cockaded woodpecker (Picoides borealis) colonies in South Carolina. Am. Midl. Nat. 124:187-191.

Harlow, R. F., and D. C. Guynn, Jr. 1987. Foods, food habits and food habits analysis studies of white-tailed deer. Dept. For., Clemson Univ., Clemson, SC. 179pp.

Harlow, R. F., and M. R. Lennartz. 1977. Foods of nestling red-cockaded woodpeckers in coastal South Carolina. Auk 94:376-377.

Harlow, R. F., and M. R. Lennartz. 1983. Interspecific competition for red-cockaded woodpecker cavities during the breeding season in South Carolina. Pages 41-43 in D. A. Wood, ed. Red-cockaded woodpecker symposium II proceedings. Fla. Game and Fresh Water Fish Commiss., Tallahassee, FL.

Harlow, R. F., B. A. Sanders, J. B. Whelan, and L. C. Chappel. 1980. Deer habitat on the Ocala National Forest: improvement through forest management. Sou. J. Appl. For. 4:98-102.

Harmon, M. E. 1982. The fire history of the westernmost portion of Great Smoky Mountains National Park. Bull. Torrey Bot. Club 109:74-79.

Harmon, M. E. 1984. Survival of trees in low intensity fires in Great Smoky Mountain National Park. Ecology 75: 796-802.

Harmon, M.E., S. P. Bratton, and P. S. White. 1983. Disturbance and vegetation response in relation to environmental gradients in the Great Smoky Mountains. Vegetatio 55:129-139.

Harris, L. D. 1984. The fragmented forest; island biogeography theory and the preservation of biotic diversity. Univ. Chicago Press, Chicago, IL. 211pp.

Harrison, D. J., J. A. Bissonette, and J. Sherburne. 1989. Spatial relationships between coyotes and red foxes in eastern Maine. J. Wildl. Manage. 53:181-185.

Harrod, J.C., M.E. Harmon, and P.S. White. In press. Post-fire succession and twentieth century vegetation change on xeric southern Appalachian sites. J. Veg. Science.

Harrod, J.C., P.S. White, and M.E. Harmon. 1998. Changes in xeric forests in western Great Smoky Mountains, National Park, 1936-1995. Castanea 63:346-360.

Harshbarger, T. J., and J. L. Buckner. 1971. Quail foods in Georgia flatwoods. Georgia For. Resour. Pap. 68. 5pp.

Harvey, M. J. 1978. Status of the endangered bats Myotis sodalis, M. grisescens, and Plecotus townsendii ingens in the southern Ozarks. Pages 221-223 in D. E. Wilson and A. L. Garner, eds. Proc. 5th Int. Bat Res. Conf. Texas Tech Univ. Press, Lubbock, TX.

Harvey, M. J., J. S. Altenbach, and T.L. Best. 1998. Bats of the United States. Arkansas Game and Fish Comm., Little Rock, AR. 64pp.

Harvey, M. J., J. S. Altenbach, and T.L. Best. 1999. Bats of the United States. Arkansas Game and Fish Commission, Little Rock, AR. 64pp.

Hayne, D. W., and P. H. Geissler. 1977. Hunted segments of the mourning dove population: movement and importance. Southeast. Assoc. Game and Fish Comm. Tech. Bull. 3. 152pp.

Haynes, R. J., R. J. Bridges, S. W. Gard, T. M. Wilkins, and H. R. Cook, Jr. 1995. Bottomland hardwood forest reestablishment efforts of the U.S. Fish and Wildlife Service: southeastern region. Pages 322-334 in J.C. Fischenich, C.M. Lloyd, and M.R. Palermo, eds. Proc. Nat. Wetland Engineering Workshop. Tech. Rep. WRP-RE-8. U.S. Army Corps of Engineers, Waterways Exp. Stat., Vicksburg MS.

Hayssen, V., A. van Tienhoven, and A. van Tienhoven. 1993. Asdell's patterns of mammalian reproduction: a compendium of species-specific data. Cornell Univ. Press, Ithaca, NY. 1023pp.

Haywood, J. D., and R. E. Thill. 1995. Long-term responses of understory vegetation on a highly erosive Louisiana soil to fertilization. USDA For. Serv. Res. Note SO-382. 6pp.

Healy, W. M., and J. E. Welsh. 1992. Evaluating line transects to monitor gray squirrel populations. Wildl. Soc. Bull. 20:83-90.

Healy, W. M., and R. T. Brooks. 1988. Small mammal abundance in northern hardwood stands in West Virginia. J. Wildl. Manage. 52:491-496.

Heidt, G. A. 1970. The least weasel (Mustela nivalis Linnaeus): developmental biology in comparison with other North American Mustela. Michigan State Univ. Mus. Publ., Biol. Ser. 4:227-282.

Heiterer, A. J. 1994. Effects of hardwood midstory on utilization of southeastern pine forests by southern flying squirrels, Glaucomys volans. M.S. Thesis, Clemson Univ., Clemson, SC. 69pp.

Heitmeyer, M. E. 1985. Wintering strategies of female mallards related to dynamics of lowland hardwood wetlands in the Upper Mississippi Delta. Ph.D. Thesis, Univ. Missouri-Columbia, Columbia, MO. 378pp.

Heitmeyer, M. E. 1988a. Protein costs of the prebasic molt of female mallards. Condor 90:263-266.

Heitmeyer, M. E. 1988b. Body composition of female mallards in winter in relation to annual cycle events. Condor 90:669-680.

Heitmeyer, M. E., and L. H. Fredrickson. 1981. Do wetland conditions in the Mississippi Delta hardwoods influence mallard recruitment? Trans. N. Am. Wildl. Nat. Resour. Conf. 46:44-57.

Heitmeyer, M. E., and L. H. Fredrickson. 1990a. Abundance and habitat use of woods in the Mingo Swamp of southeastern Missouri. Pages 99-109 in L. H. Fredrickson, G. V. Burger, S. P. Havera, D. A. Graber, R. E. Kirby, and T. S. Taylor, eds. Proc. 1988 N. Am. Wood Duck Symp., St. Louis, MO.

Heitmeyer, M. E., and L. H. Fredrickson. 1990b. Fatty acid composition of wintering female mallards in relation to nutrient use. J. Wildl. Manage. 54:54-61.

Heitmeyer, M. E., and P. A. Vohs, Jr. 1984. Characteristics of wetlands used by migrant dabbling ducks in Oklahoma, USA. Wildfowl 35:51-60.

Heitmeyer, M. E., L. H. Fredrickson, and G. F. Krause. 1989. Water and habitat dynamics of the Mingo Swamp in southeastern Missouri. USDI Fish and Wildl. Serv., Fish and Wildl. Res. No. 6., Washington, DC. 26pp.

Heitmeyer, M. E., P. J. Caldwell, B. D. J. Batt, and J. W. Nelson. 1996. Waterfowl conservation and biodiversity in North America. Pages 125-138 in J.T. Ratti, ed. Proc. 7th Int. Waterfowl Symp., Ducks Unlimited, Inc., Memphis, TN.

Heller, S. P., and T. T. Fendley. 1982. Bobcat habitat on the Savannah River Plant, South Carolina. Pages 415-423 in S. D. Miller and D. D. Everett, eds. Cats of the World: Biology, Conservation and Management. Proc. 2nd Int. Symp. National Wildl. Fed.

Hellgren, E. C. 1993. Biology of feral hogs (Sus scrofa) in Texas. Pages 50-58 in C. W. Hanselka and J. F. Cadenhead, eds. Feral Swine: A Compendium for Resource Managers. Texas Agric. Ext. Serv., Kerrville, TX.

Hellgren, E. C., and M. R. Vaughan. 1990. Range dynamics of black bears in Great Dismal Swamp, Virginia - North Carolina. Proc. Annu. Conf. Southeast Assoc. Fish and Wildl. Agencies 44:268-278.

Hellgren, E. C., and M. R. Vaughan. 1994. Conservation and management of isolated black bear populations in the southeastern coastal plain of the United States. Proc. Annu. Conf. Southeast. Assoc. Fish and Wildl. Agencies 48:276-285.

Hellgren, E. C., M. R. Vaughan, and D. F. Stauffer. 1991. Macrohabitat use by black bears in a southeastern wetland. J. Wild. Manage. 55:442-448.

Henke, S. E., and F. C. Bryant. 1999. Effects of coyote removal on the faunal community in western Texas. J. Wildl. Manage. 63:1066-1081.

Henry, J. D. 1996. Red fox: the catlike canine. Smithsonian Institution Press, Washington, DC. 174pp.

Henry, V. G. 1969. Predation on dummy nests of ground-nesting birds in the southern Appalachians. J. Wildl. Manage. 33:169-172.

Henry, V. G. 1989. Guidelines for preparation of biological assessments and evaluations for the red-cockaded woodpecker. USDI Fish and Wildl. Serv., Southeast Region, Atlanta, GA. 13pp.

Henry, V. G. 1991. Endangered and threatened wildlife and plants; determination of experimental population status for an introduced population of red wolves in North Carolina and Tennessee. Federal Register 56(213):56325-56334.

Henry, V. G. 1995. Endangered and threatened wildlife and plants; final rule for nonessential experimental populations of red wolves in North Carolina and Tennessee. Federal Register 60(71):18940-18948.

Henry, V. G., and R. H. Conley. 1972. Fall foods of European wild hogs in the southern Appalachians. J. Wildl. Manage. 36:854-860.

Hensley, M. A., and J. E. Fisher. 1975. Effects of intensive gray fox control on population dynamics of rodents and sympatric carnivores. Proc. Annu. Conf. Southeast. Assoc. Game and Fish Comm. 29:694-705.

Herman, D. W., and B. W. Tryon. 1997. Land use, development, and natural succession and their effects on bog turtle habitat in the southeastern United States. Pages 364-371 in J. Van Abbema, ed. Proc. Conservation and Management of tortoises and freshwater turtles. Am. Mus. Nat. Hist., New York, NY.

Herring, R. E. 1988. The food habits of raccoons, eastern cottontails, and nutria on Horn Island. M. S. Thesis, Mississippi State Univ., Mississippi State, MS. 75pp.

Hess, C. A., and F. C. James. 1998. Diet of the red-cockaded woodpecker in the Apalachicola National Forest. J. Wildl. Manage. 62:509-517.

Hess, C., and R. Costa. 1995. Augmentation from the Apalachicola National Forest: the development of a new management technique. Pages 385-388 in D. L. Kulhavy, R. G. Hooper, and R. Costa, eds. Red-cockaded woodpecker: recovery, ecology and management. Center for Applied Studies in Forestry, College of Forestry, Stephen F. Austin State Univ., Nacogdoches, TX.

Heuer, E. T., Jr. and H. R. Perry, Jr. 1976. Squirrel and rabbit abundances in the Atchafalaya Basin, Louisiana. Proc. Annu. Conf. Southeast. Assoc. Fish and Wildl. Agencies 30:552-559.

Heyward, F. 1939. The relation of fire to stand composition of longleaf pine forests. Ecology 20:287-304.

Hill, E. P. 1972. Litter size in Alabama cottontails as influenced by soil fertility. J. Wildl. Manage. 36:1199-1209.

Hill, E. P. 1976. Control methods for nuisance beaver in the southeastern United States. Proc. Vertebr. Pest Control Conf. 7:85-98.

Hill, E. P. 1986. Wilderness management: a perspective on furbearers. Pages 36-43 in D. L. Kulhavy and R. N. Conner, eds. Wilderness and natural areas in the eastern United States: a management challenge. Stephen F. Austin State Univ., Nacogdoches, TX.

Hill, E. P., and E. J. Jones. 1986. Coyote control in the eastern United States. Miss. Coop. Exten. Serv. Publ. No. 1509. 8pp.

Hill, E. P., D. N. Lasher, and R. B. Roper. 1977. A review of techniques for minimizing beaver and white-tailed deer damage in southern hardwoods. Proc. Symp. Sou. Hardwood. 2:79-93.

Hill, E. P., P. W. Sumner, and J. B. Wooding. 1987. Human influences on range expansion of coyotes in the southeast. Wildl. Soc. Bull. 15:521-524.

Hill, J. E., and J. D. Smith. 1984. Bats: a natural history. Univ. Texas Press, Austin, TX. 243pp.

Hillestad, H. O. 1973. Movements, behavior, and nesting ecology of the wild turkey in eastern Alabama. Pages 109-123 in G. C. Sanderson and H. C. Schultz, eds. Wild turkey management: current problems and programs. The Missouri Chapter of The Wildlife Society and Univ. Missouri Press, Columbia.

Hillestad, H. O., and D. W. Speake. 1970. Activities of wild turkey hens and poults as influenced by habitat. Proc. Annu. Conf. Southeast. Assoc. Game and Fish Comm. 24:244-251.

Hodges, M. F., Jr., and D. G. Krementz. 1996. Neotropical migratory breeding bird communities in riparian forests of different widths along the Altamaha River, Georgia. Wilson Bull. 108:496-506.

Hoerath, J. D., and M. K. Causey. 1991. Seasonal diets of coyotes in western central Alabama. Proc. Annu. Conf. Southeast. Assoc. Fish and Wildl. Agencies 45:91-96.

Hoffman, M. L., and M. W. Collopy. 1988. Historical status of the American Kestrel (Falco sparverius paulus) in Florida. Wilson Bull. 100:91-107.

Hohman, W. L., R. D. Pritchert, R. D. Pace III, D. W. Woolington, and R. Helm. 1990. Influence of ingested lead on body mass of wintering canvasbacks. J. Wildl. Manage. 54:211-215.

Hollifield, B. K., and R. W. Dimmick. 1995. Arthropod abundance relative to forest management practices benefitting ruffed grouse in the southern Appalachians. Wildl. Soc. Bull. 23:756-764.

Holman, J. A. 1961. Osteology of living and fossil New World quails (Aves, Galliformes). Bull Florida State Mus. Biol. Sci. 6:131-233.

Holzman, S., M. J. Conroy, and J. Pickering. 1992. Home range, movements, and habitat use of coyotes in south-central Georgia. J. Wildl. Manage. 56:139-146.

Hon, T., D. P. Belcher, B. Mullis, and J. R. Monroe. 1978. Nesting, brood range and reproductive success of an insular turkey population. Proc. Ann. Conf. Southeast. Assoc. Fish and Wildl. Agencies 32:137-149.

Hone, J., and H. Pedersen. 1980. Changes in a feral pig population after poisoning. Proc. Vert. Pest Conf. 9:176-182.

Hone, J., and W. Atkinson. 1983. Evaluation of fencing to control feral pig movement. Aust. Wildl. Res. 10:499-505.

Hooper, R. G., A. F. Robinson, Jr., and J. A. Jackson. 1980. The red-cockaded woodpecker: notes on life history and management. USDA For. Serv. Gen. Rep. SA-GR 9. 8pp.

Hooper, R. G., and M. R. Lennartz. 1981. Foraging behavior of the red-cockaded woodpecker in South Carolina. Auk 98:321-334.

Hooper, R. G., and R. F. Harlow. 1986. Forest stands selected by foraging red-cockaded woodpeckers. USDA For. Serv. Res. Pap. SE-259. 10pp.

Hooper, R. G., M. R. Lennartz, and H. D. Muse. 1991. Heart rot and cavity tree selection by red-cockaded woodpeckers. J. Wildl. Manage. 55:323-327.

Hornocker, M. G. 1969. Defensive behavior in bighorn sheep. J. Mamm. 50:128.

Horton, G. I., and M. K. Causey. 1979. Woodcock movements and habitat utilization in central Alabama. J. Wildl. Manage. 43:414-420.

Horton, G. I., and M. K. Causey. 1982. Association among woodcock brood members after brood breakup. Pages 71-74 in T. J. Dwyer and G. L. Storm, tech. coords. Woodcock ecology and management. U.S. Fish and Wildl. Serv., Wildl. Res. Rep. 14.

Howard, W. E., and R. E. Marsh. 1982. Spotted and hog-nosed skunks. Pages 664-673 in J. A. Chapman and G. A. Feldhamer, eds. Wild mammals of North America: biology, management, and economics. Johns Hopkins Univ. Press, Baltimore, MD.

Howe, T. D., F. J. Singer, and B. B. Ackerman. 1981. Forage relationships of European wild boar invading northern hardwood forests. J. Wildl. Manage. 45:748-754.

Howerthe, E. W., A. J. Reeves, M. R. McElveen, and F. W. Austin. 1994. Survey for selected diseases in nutria (Myocaster coypus) from Louisiana. J. Wildl. Diseases 30:450-453.

Hubbard, M. W., E. E. Klaas, and D. L. Garner. 2001. Factors influencing wild turkey poult survival in south-central Iowa. Proc. National Wild Turkey Symposium 8:(in press).

Hubert, G. F., L. L. Hungerford, G. Proulx, R. D. Bluett, and L. Bowman. 1996. Evaluation of two restraining traps to capture raccoons. Wildl. Soc. Bull. 24:699-708.

Huff, M. H. 1977. The effect of the European wild boar (Sus scrofa) on the woody vegetation of the gray beech forest in the Great Smoky Mountains. U.S. National Park Serv. Res./Resource Manage. Rep. 18. 63pp.

Hughes, R.H. 1966. Fire ecology of canebrakes. Tall Timbers Fire Ecol. Conf. Proc. 5:149-158.

Humphrey, S. R. 1975. Nursery roosts and community diversity of Nearctic Bats. J. Mamm. 56:321-346.

Humphrey, S. R. 1978. Status, winter habitat, and management of the endangered Indiana bat, Myotis sodalis. Florida Scientist 41:65-76.

Humphrey, S. R., A. R. Richter, and J. B. Cope. 1977. Summer habitat and ecology of the endangered Indiana bat, Myotis sodalis. J. Mamm. 58:334-346.

Humphrey, S. R., and T. L. Zinn. 1982. Seasonal habitat use by river otters and everglades mink in Florida. J. Wildl. Manage. 46:375-381.

Hunter, M. L., Jr. 1990. Wildlife, forests, and forestry; principles of managing forests for biological diversity. Prentice-Hall, Englewood Cliffs, NJ. 370pp.

Hunter, W. C. 1993. How much management emphasis should Nearctic-neotropical migrants receive in the Southeast? Proc. Annu. Conf. Southeast. Assoc. Fish and Wildl. Agencies 47:428-438.

Hunter, W. C., A. J. Mueller, and C. L. Hardy. 1994. Managing for red-cockaded woodpeckers and neotropical migrants-is there a conflict? Proc. Annu. Conf. Southeast. Assoc. Fish and Wildl. Agencies 48:383-394.

Hunter, W. C., D. N. Pashley, and R. E. F. Escano. 1993b. Nearctic-neotropical migratory landbird species and their habitats of special concern within the Southeast Region. Pages 159-171 in D. M. Finch and P. W. Stangel, eds. Status and management of neotropical migratory birds. USDA For. Serv. Gen. Tech. Rep. RM-229.

Hunter, W. C., M. F. Carter, D. N. Pashley, and K. Barker. 1993a. The partners in flight species prioritization scheme. Pages 109-119 in D. M. Finch and P. W. Stangel, eds. Status and management of neotropical migratory birds. USDA For. Serv. Gen. Tech. Rep. RM-229.

Huntley, J. C. 1986. Wilderness areas: impact on gray and fox squirrels. Pages 54-61 in D. L. Kulhavy and R. N. Conner, eds. Wilderness and natural areas in the eastern United States: a management challenge. Stephen F. Austin State Univ., Nacogdoches, TX.

Hunyadi, B. W. 1984. Ruffed grouse restoration in Missouri. Pages 21-35 in W. L. Robinson, ed. Ruffed grouse management: state of the art in the early 1980's. North Central Section, The Wildlife Society. 181pp.

Hurst, G. A. 1972. Insects and bobwhite quail brood habitat management. Pages 65-82 in J. A. Morrison and J. C. Lewis, eds. Proc. First National Bobwhite Quail Symp. Oklahoma State Univ., Stillwater, OK.

Hurst, G. A. 1992. Foods and feeding. Pages 66-83 in J. G. Dickson, ed. The wild turkey: biology and management. Stackpole Books, Harrisburg, PA.

Hurst, G. A., and B. D. Stringer, Jr. 1975. Food habits of wild turkey poults in Mississippi. Proc. National Wild Turkey Symp. 3:76-85.

Hurst, G. A., and J. G. Dickson. 1992. Eastern turkey in southern pine-oak forests. Pages 265-285 in J. G. Dickson, ed. The wild turkey: biology and management. Stackpole Books, Harrisburg, PA.

Hurst, G. A., and P. M. Blake. 1987. Plant species composition following hexazinone treatment-site preparation. Proc. Annu. Meeting South. Weed Sci. Soc. 40:194.

Hurst, G. A., and W. E. Palmer. 1988. Vegetative responses to hexazinone for site prep. Proc. Annu. Meet. South. Weed Sci. Soc. 41:210.

Hurst, G. A., J. J. Campo, and M. B. Brooks. 1982. Effects of precommercial thinning and fertilizing on deer forage in a loblolly pine plantation. South. J. Appl. For. 6:140-144.

Hurst, G. A., L. W. Burger, Jr., and B. D. Leopold. 1996. Predation and galliforms: an old issue revisited. Trans. N. Amer. Wildl. and Nat. Resour. Conf. 61:61-66.

Hurst, G. A., R. C. Warren, and M. Y. Grant. 1979. Nesting box trails on clearcut pine plantations. Sailia 1:46-51.

Hygnstrom, S. E., R. M. Timm, and G. E. Larson, eds. 1994. Prevention and control of wildlife damage. Univ. Nebraska Coop. Ext. Serv., Lincoln and USDA and Great Plains Ag. Council. Vol. 1-2. Non-paginated.

Ice, G. G., D. W. Schmedding, and J. P. Shepard. 1998. State restrictions and initiatives to restrict the use of silvicultural chemicals: what we know and need to know. Pages 303-325 in Proceedings 1998 NCASI Northeast Regional Meeting. National Council for Air and Stream Improvement, Inc. (NCASI) Research Triangle Park, NC.

Irwin, K. M., M. L. Duryea, and E. L. Stone. 1998. Fall-applied nitrogen improves performance of 1-0 slash pine nursery seedlings after outplanting. South. J. Appl. For. 22:111-116.

Iverson, J. B. 1992. A revised checklist with distribution maps of the turtles of the world. Earlham College, privately published, Richmond, IN. 363pp.

Jackson, J. A. 1971. The evolution, taxonomy, distribution, past populations, and current status of the red-cockaded woodpecker. Pages 4-29 in R. L. Thompson, ed. Ecology and management of the red-cockaded woodpecker. U.S. Bureau of Sport Fish. and Wildl. and Tall Timbers Res. Sta., Tallahassee, FL.

Jackson, J. A. 1974. Gray rat snakes versus red-cockaded woodpeckers: predator-prey adaptations. Auk 91:342-347.

Jackson, J. A. 1977. Red-cockaded woodpeckers and pine red heart disease. Auk 94:160-163.

Jackson, J. A. 1978a. Competition for cavities and red-cockaded woodpecker management. Pages 103-112 in S. A. Temple, ed.

Endangered birds: management techniques for the preservation of threatened species. Univ. Wisconsin Press, Madison.

Jackson, J. A. 1978b. Predation by a gray rat snake on red-cockaded woodpecker nestlings. Bird-banding 49:187-188.

Jackson, D. L., and H. A. Jacobson. 1987. Population ecology of the bobcat (Felis rufus) in managed southern forest ecosystem. Proc. Southeast. Assoc. Fish and Wildl. Agencies 35:261-272.

Jackson, J. R., G. A. Hurst, and E. A. Gluesing. 1987. Abundance and selection of invertebrates by northern bobwhite chicks. Proc. Annu. Conf. Southeast. Assoc. Fish and Wildl. Agencies 41:303-310.

Jackson, S. D., and T. F. Tyning. 1989. Effectiveness of drift fences and tunnels for moving spotted salamanders, Ambystoma maculatum, under roads. Pages 93-99 in T. E. S. Langton, ed. Amphibians and Roads. ACO Polymer Products Ltd., London.

Jacobson, H. A. 1984. Relationships between deer and soil nutrients in Mississippi. Proc. Annu. Conf. Southeast. Assoc. Fish and Wildl. Agencies 38:1-12.

Jacobson, H. A. 1994. Feeding behavior. Pages 192-198 in D. Gerlach, S. Atwater, and J. Schnell, eds. Deer. Stackpole Books, Mechanicsburg, PA.

Jacobson, H. A., and D. C. Guynn, Jr. 1995. A primer. Pages 81-102 in K. V. Miller and R. L. Marchinton, eds. Quality whitetails: the why and how of quality deer management. Stackpole Books, Mechanicsburg, PA.

Jacobson, H. A., D. C. Guynn, Jr., and E. J. Hackett. 1979. Impact of the botfly on squirrel hunting in Mississippi. Wildl. Soc. Bull. 7:46-48.

James, F. C. 1995. The status of the red-cockaded woodpecker in 1990 and the prospect for recovery. Pages 439-451 in D. L. Kulhavy, R. G. Hooper, and R. Costa, eds. Red-cockaded woodpecker: recovery, ecology and management. Stephen F. Austin State Univ., Nacogdoches, TX.

James, F. C., C. A. Hess, and D. Kufrin. 1997. Species-centered environmental analysis: indirect effects of fire history on red-cockaded woodpeckers. Ecol. Appl. 7:118-129.

James, F. C., C. E. McCulloch, and D. A. Wiedenfeld. 1996. New approaches to the analysis of population trends in land birds. Ecology 77:13-27.

James, F. C., D. A. Wiedenfeld, C. E. McCulloch. 1992. Trends in breeding populations of warblers: declines in the southern highlands and increases in the lowlands. Pages 43-56 in J. M. Hagan III and D. W. Johnston, eds. Ecology and conservation of nearctic-neotropical migrant landbirds. Smithsonian Institution Press, Washington, DC.

Jodice, P. G. R. 1992. Activity and diet of an urban population of big cypress fox squirrels. J. Wildl. Manage. 56:685-692.

Jodice, P. G. R., and S. R. Humphrey. 1993. Movement patterns of translocated big cypress fox squirrels (Sciurus niger avicennia). Fl. Scientist 56:1-6.

Johnson, A. S. 1970. Biology of the raccoon in Alabama. Bull. 402. Agric. Exp. Stn. Auburn Univ., Auburn, AL. 148pp.

Johnson, K. G. 1978. Den ecology of black bears (Ursus americanus) in the Great Smoky Mountains National Park. M.S. Thesis, Univ. Tennessee, Knoxville, TN. 107pp.

Johnson, A. S. 1987. Pine plantations as wildlife habitat: a perspective. Pages 12-18 in J. G. Dickson and O. E. Maughan, eds. Managing southern forests for wildlife and fish. USDA For. Serv. Gen. Tech. Rep S0-65.

Johnson, E. F., and E. L. Rauber. 1970. Control of raccoons with rodenticides. Proc. Annu. Conf. Southeast. Assoc. Game and Fish Comm. 24:277-281.

Johnson, F. A., C. T. Moore, W. L. Kendall, J. A. Dubovsky, D. F. Caithamer, J. R. Kelley, and B. K. Williams. 1997. Uncertainty and the management of mallard harvests. J. Wildl. Manage. 61:202-216.

Johnson, K. G., and M. R. Pelton. 1981. A survey of procedures to determine relative abundance of furbearers in the southeastern United States. Proc. Annu. Conf. Southeast. Assoc. Fish and Wildl. Agencies 35:261-272.

Johnson, K. G., R. W. Duncan, and M. R. Pelton. 1982. Reproductive biology of European wild hogs in the Great Smoky Mountains National Park. Proc. Annu. Conf. Southeast. Assoc. Fish and Wildl. Agencies 36:552-564.

Johnson, R. C., and M. K. Causey. 1982. Use of longleaf pine stands by woodcock in southern Alabama following prescribed burning. Pages 120-125 in T. J. Dwyer and G. L. Storm, tech. coords. Woodcock ecology and management. U.S. Fish and Wildl. Serv., Wildl. Res. Rep. 14.

Johnson, T. G., and D. P. Stratton. 1998. Historic trends of timber product output in the south. Resour. Bull. SRS-32.

Johnson, W. C., R. K. Schreiber, and R. L Burgess. 1979. Density of small mammals in a powerline right-of-way and adjacent forest in East Tennessee. Am. Midl. Nat. 101:231-235.

Johnston, D. W., and E. P. Odum. 1956. Breeding bird populations in relation to plant succession on the Piedmont of Georgia. Ecology 37:50-62.

Jokela, E. J., and S. C. Stearns-Smith. 1993. Fertilization of established pine stands: effects of single and split nitrogen treatments. South. J. Appl. For. 17:135-138.

Jones, K. B. 1986. Amphibians and reptiles. Pages 267-290 in A. Y. Cooperrider, R. J. Boyd, and H. R. Stuart, eds. Inventory and Monitoring of Wildlife Habitat. USDI Bureau of Land Manage. Serv. Center, Denver, CO.

Jordan, D. B. 1990. A proposal to issue endangered species permits to capture select Florida panthers (Felis concolor coryi) for the establishment of a captive population. Draft Environmental Assessment. U.S. Fish and Wildl. Serv., Gainesville, FL. 66pp.

Jordan, D. B. 1991. A proposal to establish a captive breeding population of Florida panthers. Final Suppl. Environ. Impact Statement. U.S. Fish and Wildl. Serv., Atlanta, GA. 65pp.

Jordan, D. B. 1994. Final preliminary analysis of some potential Florida panther population reestablishment sites. Final Rep., USDI Fish and Wildl. Serv., University of Florida. 11pp. with enclosures. Gainesville, FL. 11pp.

Jordan, J. S. 1971. Yield from an intensively hunted population of eastern fox squirrels. USDA For. Serv. Res. Pap. NE-186. 10pp.

Jurgelski, W., Jr., and M. E. Porter. 1974. The opossum (Didelphis virginiana) as a biomedical model. III. Breeding the opossum in captivity: methods. Lab. Anim. Sci. 24:412-425.

Kabat, C., and D. R. Thompson. 1963. Wisconsin quail, 1834-1962: population dynamics and habitat management. Wisconsin Conserv. Dep. Tech. Bull. 30. Madison. 136pp.

Kaminski, R.M., and E.A. Gluesing. 1987. Density- and habitat-related recruitment in mallards. J. Wildl. Manage. 51:141-148.

Kammermeyer, K. E., and R. Thackston. 1995. Habitat management and supplemental feeding. Pages 129-154 in K.V. Miller and R. L. Marchinton, eds. Quality whitetails: the why and how of quality deer management. Stackpole Books, Mechanicsburg, PA.

Kantola, A. T. 1986. Fox squirrel home range and mast crops in Florida. M. S. Thesis, Univ. Florida, Gainesville. 68pp.

Kantola, A. T., and S. R. Humphrey. 1990. Habitat use by Sherman's fox squirrel (Sciurus niger shermani) in Florida. J. Mamm. 71:411-419.

Kappes, J. J., Jr. 1997. Defining cavity-associated interactions between red-cockaded woodpeckers and other cavity-dependent species: interspecific competition or cavity kleptoparasitism? Auk 114:778-780.

Kappes, J. J., Jr, and L. D. Harris. 1995. Interspecific competition for red-cockaded woodpecker cavities in the Apalachicola National Forest. Pages 389-393 in D. L. Kulhavy, R. G. Hooper, and R. Costa, eds. Red-cockaded woodpecker: recovery, ecology and management. Center for Applied Studies in Forestry, College of Forestry, Stephen F. Austin State Univ., Nacogdoches, TX.

Kartesz, J.T. 1994. Synonymized checklist of the vascular flora of the United States, Canada, and Greenland. Second edition. Timber Press, Portland, OR.

Kartesz, J.T. and C. A. Meacham. 1999. Synthesis of the North American Flora, Version 1.0. North Carolina Botanical Garden, Chapel Hill, NC.

Kasbohm, J. W., M. R. Vaughan, and J. G. Kraus. 1994. Black bear harvest and nuisance behavior in response to gypsy moth infestation. Proc. Annu. Conf. Southeast. Assoc. Fish and Wildlife Agencies 48:261-269.

Kasbohm, J. W., M. R. Vaughan, and J. G. Kraus. 1996. Effects of gypsy moth infestations on black bear reproduction and survival. J. Wildl. Manage. 60:408-415.

Kasbohm, J. W., M. R. Vaughan, and J. G. Kraus. 1997. Black bear home range dynamics and movement patterns during a gypsy moth infestation. Ursus 10:259-267.

Kassinis, N. I., and F. S. Guthery. 1996. Flight behavior of northern bobwhites. J. Wildl. Manage. 60:581-585.

Kauffeld, C. 1957. Snakes and snake hunting. Hanover House, Garden City, NY. 266pp.

Kaufmann, J. H. 1982. Raccoon and allies. Pages 567-585 in J. A. Chapman and G.A. Feldhamer, eds. Wild mammals of North America. Johns Hopkins Univ. Press, Baltimore, MD.

Kay, C. E. In Press. Aboriginal overkill: the role of Native Americans in structuring western ecosystems. Oxford Univ. Press.

Keeler, E. W. 1978. Some aspects of the natural history of the raccoon (Procyon lotor) in Cades Cove, The Great Smoky Mountains National Park. M. S. Thesis, Univ. Tennessee, Knoxville. 81pp.

Keller, C. M. E., C. S. Robbins, and J. S. Hatfield. 1993. Avian communities in riparian forests of different widths in Maryland and Delaware. Wetlands 13:137-144.

Kellogg, F. E., and G. L. Doster. 1972. Diseases and parasites of the bobwhite. Pages 233-267 in J. A. Morrison and J. C. Lewis, eds. Proc. First National Bobwhite Quail Symp. Oklahoma State Univ., Stillwater.

Kellogg, F. E., G. L. Doster, E. V. Komarek. 1972. The one quail per acre myth. Pages 15-20 in J. A. Morrison and J. C. Lewis, eds. Proc. First National Bobwhite Quail Symp. Oklahoma State Univ., Stillwater.

Kellogg, F. E., G. L. Doster, and L. L. Williamson. 1970. A bobwhite density greater than one bird per acre. J. Wildl. Manage. 34:249-254.

Kennamer, J. E., J. R. Gwaltney, and K. R. Sims. 1980. Habitat preferences of eastern wild turkeys on an area intensively managed for pine in Alabama. Proc. National Wild Turkey Symp. 4:240-245.

Kennamer, J. E., and M. C. Kennamer. 1996. Status and distribution of the wild turkey in 1994. Proc. National Wild Turkey Symp. 7:203-211.

Kennamer, J. E., M. C. Kennamer, and R. Brenneman. 1992. History. Pages 6-17 in J. G. Dickson, ed. The wild turkey: biology and management. Stackpole Books, Harrisburg, PA.

Kennamer, M. C., R. E. Brenneman, and J. E. Kennamer. 1992. Guide to the American wild turkey. National Wild Turkey Fed., Edgefield, SC. 149pp.

Kennelly, J. J. 1978. Coyote reproduction. Pages 73-93 in M. Bekoff, ed. Coyotes: biology, behavior and management. Academic Press, New York, NY.

Kennelly, J. J., and J. D. Roberts. 1969. Fertility of coyote-dog hybrids. J. Mamm. 50:830-831.

Keppie, D. M., and R. M. Whiting, Jr. 1994. American woodcock (Scolopax minor). In A. Poole and F. Gill, eds. The birds of North America, No. 100. The Academy of Natural Sciences, Philadelphia, PA; The American Ornithologists' Union, Washington, DC.

Keys, J., Jr., C.Carpenter, S.Hooks, F.Koenig, W.H.McNab, W.E. Russell, M-L. Smith. 1995. Ecological units of the eastern United States -first approximation (map and booklet of map unit tables). USDA, Forest Service Tech. Publ. R8-TP 21. Atlanta, GA.

Kight, J. 1960. An ecological study of the bobcat, Lynx rufus (Schreber), in west-central South Carolina. M.S. Thesis, Univ. Georgia, Athens. 52pp.

Kilgo, J. C., R. A. Sargent, B. R. Chapman, and K. V. Miller. 1998. Effect of stand width and adjacent habitat on breeding bird communities in bottomland hardwoods. J. Wildl. Manage. 62:72-83.

King, C. M. 1975. The home range of the weasel, (Mustela nivalis) in an English woodland. J. Anim. Ecol. 44:639-668.

King, S. L., H. L. Stribling, and D. Speake. 1991. Cottontail rabbit initial responses to prescribed burning and cover enhancement. J. Alabama Academy of Science 62:178-188.

Kinler, J. Q. 1986. Muskrat reproduction and the effect of tidal flooding in Louisiana. M. S. Thesis. Louisiana State Univ., Baton Rouge. 90pp.

Kinler, J. Q., R. H. Chabreck, N. W. Kinler, and G. Linscombe. 1988. Mortality estimates of muskrat litters in a Louisiana coastal marsh. Proc. Annu. Conf. Southeast. Assoc. Fish and Wildl. Agencies 42:376-381.

Kirkland, G. L., Jr. 1978. Initial responses of small mammals to clearcutting of Pennsylvania hardwood forests. Proc. Pennsylvania Academy of Science 52:21-23.

Kirkpatrick, C. 1950. Crow predation on nestling cottontails. J. Mamm. 31:322-327.

Kirkpatrick, R. L., J. L. Coggin, H. S. Mosby, and J. O. Newell. 1976. Parturition times and litter sizes of gray squirrels in Virginia. Proc. Annu. Conf. Southeast. Assoc. Game and Fish Comm. 30:541-545.

Kissel, R. E., Jr., and M. L. Kennedy. 1992. Ecological relationships of co-occurring populations of opossums and raccoons in Tennessee. J. Mamm. 73:808-813.

Kitchings, J. T., and J. D. Story. 1979. Home range and diet of bobcats in eastern Tennessee. Pages 47-52 in Proc. Bobcat Res. Conf. Front Royal, Virginia. 137pp.

Kitchings, J. T., and J. D. Story. 1984. Movements and dispersal of bobcats in east Tennessee. J. Wildl. Manage. 48:957-961.

Klimstra, W. D., and J. L. Roseberry. 1975. Nesting ecology of the bobwhite in southern Illinois. Wildl. Monogr. 41. 37pp.

Klimstra, W. D., and V. C. Ziccardi. 1963. Night-roosting habitat of bobwhites. J. Wildl. Manage. 27:202-214.

Knowlton, F. F. 1972. Preliminary interpretations of coyote population mechanics with some management implications. J. Wildl. Manage. 36:369-383.

Kocka, D. M. 1987. An evaluation of population estimators, densities, and scent station indices of a raccoon population in east Tennessee. M. S. Thesis, Univ. Tennessee, Knoxville. 153pp.

Kolenosky, G. B., and S. M. Strathearn. 1987. Black bear. Pages 443-454 in M. Novak, J. A. Baker, M. E. Obbard, and B. Malloch, eds. Wild furbearer management and conservation in North America. Ministry of Natural Resources, Ontario.

Komarek, E. V. 1974. Effects of fire on temperate forests and related ecosystems: southeastern United States. Pages 251-277 in T. T. Kozlowski and C. E. Ahlgren, eds. Fire and Ecosystems. Academic Press, New York, NY.

Koprowski, J. L. 1994a. Sciurus carolinensis. Mammalian Species Number 480. Am. Soc. Mamm. 9pp.

Koprowski, J. L. 1994b. Sciurus niger. Mammalian Species Number 479. Am. Soc. Mamm. 9pp.

Korschgen, L. J. 1981. Foods of fox and gray squirrels in Missouri. J. Wildl. Manage. 45:260-266.

Korte, P. A., and L. H. Fredrickson. 1977. Loss of Missouri's lowland hardwood ecosystem. Trans. N. Am. Wildl. Nat. Resour. Conf. 42:31-41.

Kramer, P., N. Reichenbach, M. Hayslett, and P. Sattler. 1993. Population dynamics and conservation of the peaks of otter salamander, Plethodon hubrichti. J. Herp. 27:431-435.

Krementz, D. G., J. T. Seginak, D. R. Smith, and G. W. Pendleton. 1994. Survival rates of American woodcock wintering along the Atlantic coast. J. Wildl. Manage. 58:147-155.

Krementz, D. G., J. T. Seginak, D. R. Smith, and G. W. Pendleton. 1995. Habitat use at night by wintering American woodcock in coastal Georgia and Virginia. Wilson Bull. 107:686-697.

Kroll, J. C., P. J. Behrman, and W. D. Goodrum. 1986. Twenty-seven years of overbrowsing: implications in white-tailed deer management. Pages 6-7 in The 9th Annu. Meeting of the Southeast Deer Study Group. Gatlinburg, TN.

Kroll, J. C., and R. M. Whiting. 1977. Discriminate function analysis of woodcock winter habitat in east Texas. Proc. Woodcock Symp. 6:63-71.

Krusic, R.A., M. Yamasaki, C.D. Neefus, and P.J. Perkins. 1996. Bat habitat use in the White Mountain National Forest. J. Wildl. Manage. 60:625-631.

Kubisiak, J. F. 1985. Ruffed grouse habitat relationships in aspen and oak forests of central Wisconsin. Wisconsin Dep. Nat. Resour. Tech. Bull. No. 151. 22pp.

Kubisiak, J. F. 1985. Ruffed grouse harvest levels and population characteristics in central Wisconsin. Wisconsin Dep. Nat. Resour. Res. Rep. No. 136. 24pp.

Kuchler, A.W. 1964. Potential natural vegetation of the conterminous United States, map and accompanying manual. Am. Geographical Soc., New York, NY. 116 p.

Kulhavy, D.L., and R.N. Conner, eds. 1986. Wilderness and natural areas in the eastern United States: a management challenge. Center for Applied Studies, School of Forestry, Stephen F. Austin State University, Nacogdoches, TX. 416pp.

Kunz, T.H., ed. 1988. Ecological and behavioral methods for the study of bats. Smithsonian Institution Press, Washington, DC. 533pp.

Kurta, A., J. Kath, E. L Smith, R. Foster, M. Orick, and R. Ross. 1993. A maternity roost of the endangered Indiana bat (Myotis sodalis) in an unshaded, hollow, sycamore tree (Platanus occidentalis). Amer. Midl. Nat. 130:405-407.

Kurta, A., D. King, J. A Teramino, J. M. Stribley, and K. J. Williams. 1993. Summer roosts of the endangered Indiana bat (Myotis sodalis) on the northern edge of its range. Amer. Midl. Nat. 128:132-138.

Kurta, A., and K. J. Williams. 1994. Thermal aspects of Indiana bats roosting in trees. Bat Res. News 35:104.

Kurz, J. C. and R. L. Marchinton. 1972. Radiotelemetry studies of feral hogs in South Carolina. J. Wildl. Manage. 36:1240-1248.

Labranche, M. S., and J. R. Walters. 1994. Patterns of mortality in nests of red-cockaded woodpeckers in the Sandhills of south-central North Carolina. Wilson Bull. 106:258-271.

Labranche, M. S., J. R. Walters, and K. S. Laves. 1994. Double brooding in red-cockaded woodpeckers. Wilson Bull. 106:403-408.

Lacki, M.J. 1996. The role of research in conserving bats in managed forests. Pages 39-48 in R. M. R. Barkley and R. M. Brigham, eds. Bats and forests Symp. October 19-21, 1995, Victoria, British Columbia. Research Branch, British Columbia Ministry of Forests, Victoria.

Lacki, M. J., M. D. Adam, and L. G. Shoemaker. 1994. Observations on seasonal cycle, population patterns and roost selection in summer colonies of Plecotus townsendii virginianus in Kentucky. Amer. Midl. Nat. 131:34-42.

Lacki, M. J., and R. A. Lancia. 1983. Changes in soil properties of forest rooted by wild boar. Proc. Annu. Conf. Southeast. Assoc. Fish and Wildl. Agencies 37:228-236.

Lair, H. 1985. Length of gestation in the red squirrel, Tamiasciurus hudsonicus. J. Mamm. 66:809-810.

Land, D. 1994. Florida panther population dynamics in southwest Florida. Pages 71-81 in Proc. Florida Panther Conference. USDI Fish and Wildl. Serv. Pub., Fort Myers, FL.

Landers, J. L. 1987. Prescribed burning for managing wildlife in southeastern pine forests. Pages 19-27 in J. G. Dickson, ed. Managing Southern Forests for Wildlife and Fish: A Proceedings. USDA Forest Service Gen. Tech. Rep. SO-65.

Landers, J. L., R. J. Hamilton, A. S. Johnson, and R. L. Marchinton. 1979. Foods and habitat of black bears in southeastern North Carolina. J. Wildl. Manage. 43:143-153.

Landers, J. L., and A. S. Johnson. 1976. Bobwhite quail food habits in the southeastern United States with a seed key to important foods. Tall Timbers Res. Sta. Misc. Pub. No. 4. 90pp.

Landers, J. L., D. H. Van Lear, and W. D. Boyer. 1995. The longleaf pine forests of the Southeast: requiem or renaissance? J. For. 93:39-44.

Lariviere, S., and M. Pasitschniak-Arts. 1996. Vulpes vulpes. Mammalian Species. Amer. Soc. Mamm. 537:1-11.

Lariviere, S., and L. R. Walton. 1997. Lynx rufus. Mammalian Species. Amer. Soc. Mamm. 563:1-8.

Latham, R. M. 1952. The fox as a factor in the control of weasel populations. J. Wildl. Manage. 16:516-517.

Latta, S. C., and M. E. Baltz. 1997. Population limitation in neotropical migratory birds: Comments. Auk 114:754-762.

Laubhan, M. K., and L. H. Fredrickson. 1993. Integrated wetland management: concepts and opportunities. Trans. N. Am. Wildl. Nat. Resour. Conf. 58:323-334.

Lauhachinda, V. 1978. Life history of the river otter in Alabama with emphasis on food habits. Ph.D. Thesis, Auburn Univ., Auburn, AL. 169pp.

Lauhachinda, V., and E. P. Hill. 1977. Winter food habits of river otters from Alabama and Georgia. Proc. Annu. Conf. Southeast. Assoc. Fish and Wildl. Agencies 31:246-253.

LaVal, R. K., R. L. Clawson, M. L. LaVal, and W. Caire. 1977. Foraging behavior and nocturnal activity patterns of Missouri bats, with special emphasis on the endangered species Myotis grisescens and Myotis sodalis. J. Mamm. 58:592-599.

Laves, K. 1996. Effects of southern flying squirrels, Glaucomys volans, on red-cockaded woodpecker, Picoides borealis, reproductive success. M.S. Thesis, Clemson Univ., Clemson, S.C. 75pp.

Lay, D. W., and W. P. Taylor. 1943. Wildlife aspects of cutover pine woodland in eastern Texas. J. For. 41:446-448.

Lay, D. W. 1942. Ecology of the opossum in eastern Texas. J. Mamm. 23:147-159.

Lay, D. W. 1945. Muskrat investigations in Texas. J. Wildl. Manage. 9:56-76.

Leberg, P. L., and M. L. Kennedy. 1987. Use of scent-station methodology to assess raccoon abundance. Proc. Annu. Conf. Southeast. Assoc. Fish and Wildl. Agencies 41:394-403.

Leberg, P. L., and M. L. Kennedy. 1988. Demography and habitat relationships of raccoons in western Tennessee. Proc. Annu. Conf. Southeast. Assoc. Fish and Wildl. Agencies 42:272-282.

Leberg, P. L., M. L. Kennedy, and R. A. VanDen Bussche. 1983. Opossum demography and scent-station visitation in western Tennessee. Proc. Annu. Conf. Southeast. Assoc. Fish and Wildl. Agencies 37:34-40.

Lee, J. M. 1994. Habitat ecology of the northern bobwhite on Copiah County Wildlife Management Area. M.S. Thesis, Mississippi State Univ., Mississippi State. 107pp.

Lee, R. M., III, and M. L. Kennedy. 1986. Food habits of the coyote in Tennessee. Proc. Annu. Conf. Southeast. Assoc. Fish and Wildl. Agencies 40:364-372.

Lehmann, V. W. 1984. Bobwhites in the Rio Grande Plain of Texas. Texas A&M Press, College Station. 371pp.

Leidolf, A., and S. McDaniel. 1998. A floristic study of black prairie plant communities at Sixteen Section Prairie, Oktibbeha County, Mississippi. Castanea 63:51-62.

Leimgruber, P., W. J. McShea, and J. H. Rappole. 1994. Predation on artifical nests in large forest blocks. J. Wildl. Manage. 58:254-260.

Leland, B., and J. W. Hoagland. 1993. A summary of beaver damage and harvest in Oklahoma. Page unnumbered in J. W. Hoagland, ed. Proc. 11th Midwest and 7th Southeast. Furbearer Workshops. Oklahoma Dep. Wildl. Conserv., Oklahoma City, OK.

Lennartz, M. R., R. G. Hooper, and R. F. Harlow. 1987. Sociality and cooperative breeding of red-cockaded woodpeckers (Picoides borealis). Behav. Ecol. Sociobiol. 20:77-88.

Leopold, A. 1933. Game management. Charles Schribner's Sons, New York, NY. 481pp.

Leopold, A. 1966. A Sand County Almanac. Oxford University Press. New York, NY. 269pp.

Leopold, A. S. 1945. Sex and age ratios among bobwhite quail in southern Missouri. J. Wildl. Manage 9:30-34.

Leopold, B. D., and G. A. Hurst. 1994. Experimental designs for assessing impacts of predators on gamebird populations. Trans. N. Amer. Wildl. and Nat. Res. Conf. 59:477-487.

Leopold, B. D., and M. J. Chamberlain. 1997. Program for monitoring vertebrate abundance on the Mississippi delta lands (Twin Oaks and Mahannah Wildlife Management Areas). Proj. Compl. Rep. U.S. Army Corps. of Engineers. 62pp.

Leverett, R. 1996. Definitions and history. Pages 3-17 in M.B. Davis, ed. Eastern Old-Growth Forests. Island Press, Washington, DC.

Lewis, E., G. L. Hoff, W. J. Bigler, and M. B. Jefferies. 1975. Public health and the urban gray squirrel. J. Wildl. Dis. 11:502-504.

Lewis, J. C. 1993. Foods and feeding ecology. Pages 181-204 in T. S. Baskett, M. W. Sayre, R. E. Tomlinson, and R. E. Mirarchi, eds. Ecology and management of the mourning dove. Stackpole Books, Harrisburg, PA.

Ligon, J. D. 1970. Behavior and breeding biology of the red-cockaded woodpecker. Auk 87:255-278.

Ligon, J. D., P. B. Stacey, R. N. Conner, C. E. Bock, and C. S. Adkisson. 1986. Report of the American Ornithologists' Union Committee for the conservation of the red-cockaded woodpecker. Auk 103:848-855.

Lindsay, M.M., and S.P. Bratton. 1979. Grassy balds of the Great Smoky Mountains: their history and flora in relation to potential management. Env. Manage. 3: 417-430.

Linscombe, G. 1993. U.S. Fur harvest (1970-1992) and fur value (1974-1992) statistics by state and region. Fur Resour. Comm., Internat. Assoc. Fish and Wildl. Agencies. Washington, DC. Non-paginated.

Linscombe, G., and N. Kinler. 1997. A survey of vegetation damage caused by nutria herbivory in the Barataria and Terrebonne Basins. Louisiana Dep. Wildl. and Fisheries, Baton Rouge, LA. 14pp.

Linscombe, G., N. Kinler, and R. J. Aulerich. 1982. Mink. Pages 629-643 in J. A. Chapman and G. A. Feldhamer, eds. Wild mammals of North America: biology, management and economics. Johns Hopkins Univ. Press, Baltimore, MD.

Linscombe, G., N. Kinler, and V. Wright. 1983. An analysis of scent station response in Louisiana. Proc. Annu. Conf. Southeast. Assoc. Fish and Wildl. Agencies 37:190-200.

Linzey, D. W. 1998. The mammals of Virginia. McDonald & Woodward Publ. Company, Blacksburg, VA. 459pp.

Linzey, D. W., and A. Z. Linzey. 1979. Growth and development of the southern flying squirrel (Glaucomys volans volans). J. Mamm. 60:615-620.

Lipscomb, D. J. 1989. Impacts of feral hogs on longleaf pine regeneration. Sou. J. Appl. For. 13:177-181.

Littauer, G. A. 1993. Control techniques for feral hogs. Pages 139-148 in C. W. Hanselka and J. F. Cadenhead, eds. Feral Swine: A Compendium for Resource Managers. Texas Agric. Ext. Serv., Kerrville, TX.

Litvaitis, J. A., and D. J. Harrison. 1989. Bobcat-coyote niche relationships during a period of coyote population increase. Can. J. Zool. 1180-1188.

Litvaitis, J. A., and J. H. Shaw. 1980. Coyote movements, habitat use, and food habits in southwestern Oklahoma. J. Wildl. Manage. 44:62-68.

Liu, X. 1995. Survival, movements, and habitat selection of relocated and resident northern bobwhite in East Texas. Ph.D. Thesis. Stephen F. Austin State University. Nacogdoches, TX. 132pp.

Lochmiller, R. L. 1979. Use of beaver ponds by southeastern woodpeckers in winter. J. Wildl. Manage. 43:263-266.

Lochmiller, R. L., M. R. Vestey, and J. C. Boren. 1993. Relationship between protein nutritional status and immunocompetence in northern bobwhite chicks. Auk 110:503-510.

Loeb, S. C. 1993. Use and selection of red-cockaded woodpecker cavities by southern flying squirrels. J. Wildl. Manage. 57:329-335.

Loeb, S. C. 1996. Effectiveness of flying squirrel excluder devices on red-cockaded woodpecker cavities. Proc. Annu. Conf. Southeast. Assoc. Fish and Wildl. Agencies 50:303-311.

Loeb, S. C., and R. G. Hooper. 1997. An experimental test of interspecific competition for red-cockaded woodpecker cavities. J.Wildl. Manage. 61:1268-1280

Loeb, S. C., and R. G. Hooper. 1997. Effectiveness of nest boxes for reducing use of red-cockaded woodpecker cavities by other vertebrates. Page 398 in J. L. Haymond, D. D. H. a. W. R. H., eds. Hurricane Hugo: South Carolina forest land research and management related to the storm. USDA For. Serv. Gen. Tech. Rep. SRS-5.

Loeb, S. C., and N. D. Moncrief. 1993. The biology of fox squirrels (Sciurus niger) in the southeast: a review. Pages 1-19 in J. W. Edwards and P. A. Tappe, eds. Proc. Second Symp. on Southeast. Fox Squirrel, Sciurus niger. Virginia Museum of Natural History, Spec. Pub. No. 1.

Loeb, S. C., W. D. Pepper, and A. T. Doyle. 1992. Habitat characteristics of active and abandoned red-cockaded woodpecker colonies. South. J. Appl. For. 16:120-125.

Logan, T. J., A. C. Eller, Jr., R. Morrell, D. Ruffner, and J. Sewell. 1993. Florida panther habitat preservation plan - south Florida population. Florida Panther Interagency Comm. Rep. Tallahassee, FL.

Lord, R. D. 1961. A population study of the gray fox. Amer. Midl. Nat. 66:87-109.

Losito, M. P., and R. E. Mirarchi. 1991. Summertime habitat use and movements of hatching-year mourning doves in northern Alabama. J. Wildl. Manage. 55:137-146.

Losito, M. P., R. E. Mirarchi, and G. A. Baldassarre. 1990. Summertime activity budgets of hatching-year mourning doves. Auk 107:18-24.

Lotze, J. H. 1979. The raccoon (Procyon lotor) on St. Catherines Island, Georgia. Amer. Mus. Nov. No. 2664. 25pp.

Lotze, J. H., and S. Anderson. 1979. Procyon lotor. Mammalian Species. Amer. Soc. Mamm. 119:1-8.

Lovell, C. D. 1996. Bobcat, coyote, and gray fox micro-habitat use and interspecific relationships in a managed forest in central Mississippi. M.S. Thesis, Mississippi State Univ., Mississippi State. 162pp.

Lovell, C. D., B. D. Leopold, and C. C. Shropshire. 1998. Trends in Mississippi predator populations,1980-1995. Wildl. Soc. Bull. 26:552-556.

Lowery, G. H., Jr. 1974. The mammals of Louisiana and its adjacent waters. Louisiana State Univ. Press, Baton Rouge. 565pp.

Lucas, E. G. 1977. Feral hogs – problems and control on National Forest lands. Pages 17-21 in G. W. Wood, ed. Research and management of wild hog populations. Belle Baruch Forest Science Inst. of Clemson Univ., Georgetown, SC.

Lucash, C. F., and B. A. Crawford. 1995. Reestablishment of red wolves in the southern Appalachian mountains, January 1, 1994 to December 31, 1994. USDI Fish and Wildl. Serv., Atlanta, GA. 14pp.

Lustig, L. W., and V. Flyger. 1975. Observations and suggested management practices for the endangered Delmarva fox squirrel. Proc. Annu. Conf. Southeast. Assoc. Game and Fish Comm. 29:433-440.

Lydeard, C., and R. L. Mayden. 1995. A diverse and endangered aquatic ecosystem of the southeastern United States. Cons. Biol. 9: 800-805.

Lydeard, C., M. L. Kennedy, and E. P. Hill. 1988. Taxonomic assessment of coyotes and domestic dogs in the southeastern United States. Proc. Annu. Conf. Southeast. Assoc. Fish and Wildl. Agencies 42:513-519.

Lynch, J. 1951. Woodcock in south Louisiana during the freeze of January-February, 1951. Pages 3-9 in J. W. Aldrich, compiler. Investigations of woodcock, snipe and rails in 1951. U.S. Fish and Wildl. Serv. and Canadian Wildl. Serv., Spec. Sci. Rep. - Wildl. 14. 58pp.

MacArthur, R. H. 1972. Geographical ecology: patterns in the distribution of species. Harper and Row, New York, NY.

MacArthur, R. H., and E. O. Wilson. 1963. An equilibrium theory of insular biogeography. Evolution 17:373-387.

MacArthur, R. H., and E. O. Wilson. 1967. The theory of island biogeography. Princeton Univ. Press, Princeton, NJ. 203pp.

MacArthur, R. H., and J. W. MacAuthur. 1961. On bird species diversity. Ecology 37:50-62.

MacDonald, P. O., W. E. Frayer, and J. K. Clauser. 1979. Documentation, chronology, and future projections of bottomland hardwood habitat loss in the lower Mississippi Alluvial Plain. Vol. I. Basic Rep., USDI Fish and Wildl. Serv. Ecol. Serv., Vicksburg, MS. 133pp.

Maddrey, R. C. 1995. Morphology, reproduction, food habits, crop depredation, and mortality of black bears on the Neuse-Pamlico peninsula, North Carolina. M. S. Thesis, Univ. Tennessee, Knoxville. 149pp.

Madson, J. 1963. The cottontail rabbit. 2nd edition. Olin Mathieson Corp. East Alton, IL. 55pp.

Madson, J. 1978. The mourning dove. Winchester Press, East Alton, IL. 114pp.

Maehr, D. S. 1984. Distribution of black bears in eastern North America. Page 74 in D. S. Maehr and J. R. Brady, eds. Proc. 7th Eastern Workshop on Black Bear Management and Research. Florida Game and Fresh Water Fish Comm., Gainesville, FL.

Maehr, D. S. 1990. The Florida panther and private lands. Conserv. Biol. 4:167-170.

Maehr, D. S., and J. R. Brady. 1986. Food habits of bobcats in Florida. J. Mamm. 67:133-138.

Mahan, W. 1978. Mourning dove. Pages 3-15 in V. Bevill, W. Mahan, T. Strange, eds. Game on your land - Part 1. Small game and wood duck. S. Carolina Wildl. Marine Res. Dept., Columbia, SC.

Mangrum, J. W. 1994. Evaluation of four attractants as indices of relative abundance of wildlife with emphasis on bobcats. M.S. Thesis, Mississippi State Univ., Mississippi State. 161pp.

Manley, S. W. 1994. Evaluation of old-field habitat manipulations for breeding northern bobwhites. M.S. Thesis, Mississippi State Univ., Mississippi State. 109pp.

Marchinton, R. L., and D. H. Hirth. 1984. Behavior. Pages 129-168 in L. K. Halls, ed. White-tailed deer: ecology and management. Stackpole Books, Harrisburg, PA.

Marcot, B. G. 1996. An ecosystem context for bat management: a case study of the Interior Columbia River Basin, U.S.A. Pages 19-36 in R. M. R. Barclay and R. M. Brigham, eds. Bats and forests Symp., October 19-21, 1995. Victoria, British Columbia. Research Branch, British Columbia Ministry of Forests, Victoria.

Marquis, D. A., and R. Brennan. 1981. The impact of deer on forest vegetation in Pennsylvania. USDA For. Serv. Gen. Tech. Rep. NE-65.

Marquis, D. A., and R. Jacobs. 1989. Principles of managing stands. Pages 6.01-1 - 6.01-6 in F.B. Clark and J.G. Hutchinson, eds. Central Hardwood Notes. USDA For. Serv., St. Paul, MN.

Marquis, R. J., and C. J. Whelan. 1995. Insectivorous birds increase growth of white oak through consumption of leaf-chewing insects. Ecology 75:2007-2014.

Marsden, H. M., and T. S. Baskett. 1958. Annual mortality in a banded bobwhite population. J. Wildl. Manage. 22:414-419.

Marshall, A. D. 1969. Spring and summer movements and home ranges of bobcats in the coastal plain of South Carolina. M.S. Thesis, Univ. Georgia, Athens. 52pp.

Marshall, A. D., and J. H. Jenkins. 1966. Movements and home ranges of bobcats as determined by radio-tracking in the upper coastal plain of west-central South Carolina. Proc. Annu. Conf. Southeast. Assoc. Game and Fish Comm. 20:206-214.

Martin, E. M., and P. I. Padding. 1996. Preliminary estimates of waterfowl harvest and hunter activity in the United States during the 1995 hunting season. U.S. Fish and Wildl. Serv. Office Migratory Bird Manage. Admin. Rep. - July, 1996. U.S. Fish Wildl. Serv., Laurel, MD.

Martin, F. W., and J. R. Sauer. 1993. Population characteristics and trends in the Eastern Management Unit. Pages 281-304 in T. S. Baskett, M. W. Sayre, R. E. Tomlinson, and R. E. Mirarchi, eds. Ecology and management of the mourning dove. Stackpole Books, Harrisburg, PA.

Martin, F. W., R. S. Pospahala, and J. D. Nichols. 1979. Assessment and population management of North American migratory birds. Pages 187-239 in J. Cairns, G. P. Patil, and W. E. Waters, eds. Environmental biomonitoring, assessment, prediction and management - certain case studies and related quantitative issues. Stat. Ecol. Serv., Vol. II, International Coop. Publ. House, Fairland, MD.

Martin, S. W., R. L. Bailey, and E. J. Jokela. 1999. Growth and yield predictions for lower Coastal Plain slash pine plantations fertilized at mid-rotation. South. J. Appl. For. 23:39-45.

Martin, W.H., S.G. Boyce, and A.C. Echternacht, eds. 1993a. Biodiversity of the southeastern United States: lowland terrestrial communities. John Wiley & Sons, New York, NY. 502 p.

Martin, W.H., S.G. Boyce, and A.C. Echternacht, eds. 1993b. Biodiversity of the southeastern United States: upland terrestrial communities. John Wiley & Sons, New York, NY. 373p.

Martinson, R. K., J. W. Holten, and G. K. Brakhage. 1961. Age criteria and population dynamics of the swamp rabbit in Missouri. J. Wildl. Manage. 25:271-280.

Maser, C., J. H. Trappe, and R. A. Nussbaum. 1978. Fungal-small mammal interrelationships with emphasis on Oregon coniferous forests. Ecology 59:799-809.

Masterson, R. A., H. W. Stegmiller, M. A. Parsons, C. C. Croft, and C. B. Spencer. 1971. California encephalitis: an endemic puzzle in Ohio. Health Lab. Sci. 8:89-96.

Mastrangelo, P. M. 1995. Beaver damage management in the southeast: a cooperative effort. Pages 22-31 in C.L. Brown, ed. Proc. of the 1995 Joint Fur Res. Workshop.

Matschke, G. H. 1964. The influence of oak mast on European wild hog reproduction. Proc. Annu. Conf. Southeast. Assoc. Game and Fish Comm. 18:35-39.

Matschke, G. H. 1965. Predation by European wild hogs on dummy nests of ground-nesting birds. Proc. Annu. Conf. Southeast. Assoc. Game and Fish Comm. 19:154-156.

Mayer, J. J., and I. L. Brisbin, Jr. 1988. Sex identification of Sus scrofa based on canine morphology. J. Mamm. 69:408-412.

Mayer, J. J., and I. L. Brisbin, Jr. 1991. Wild pigs in the United States: their history, comparative morphology, and current status. Univ. Georgia Press, Athens. 313pp.

Mayer, J. J., and I. L. Brisbin, Jr. 1993. Distinguishing feral hogs from introduced wild boar and their hybrids: a review of past and present efforts. Pages 28-49 in C. W. Hanselka and J. F. Cadenhead, eds. Feral Swine: A Compendium for Resource Managers. Texas Agric. Ext. Serv. Kerrville, TX.

Mayer, J. J., and I. L. Brisbin, Jr. 1995. Feral swine and their role in the conservation of global livestock genetic diversity. Pages 175-179 in R. D. Crawford, E. E. Lister, and J. T. Buckley, eds. Proc. 3rd Global Conf. on Conservation of Domestic Animal Genetic Resour. Rare Breeds International, Warwickshire, England, U.K.

McCabe, R. E., and T. R. McCabe. 1984. Of slings and arrows: an historical retrospection. Pages 19-72 in L. K. Halls, ed. White-tailed deer: ecology and management. Stackpole Books, Harrisburg, PA.

McCarley, W. H. 1954. The ecological distribution on *Peromyscus leucopus* species group in eastern Texas. Ecology 35:375-379.

McCarley, W. H., and C. J. Carley. 1979. Recent changes in the distribution and status of wild red wolves Canis rufus. End. Sp. Rep. No. 4, U.S. Fish and Wildl. Serv., Albuquerque, NM. 38pp.

McComb, W. C., and G. A. Hurst. 1987. Herbicides and wildlife in southern forests. Pages 28-36 in J. G. Dickson and O. E. Maughan, eds. Managing Southern Forests for Wildlife and Fish: A Proceedings. USDA For. Serv. Gen. Tech. Rep. SO-65.

McComb, W. C., and R. L. Rumsey. 1982. Response of small mammals to forest clearings created by herbicides in the central Appalachians. Brimleyana 8:121-134.

McCord, C. M., and J. E. Cardoza. 1984. Bobcat and lynx. Pages 728-766 in J. A. Chapman and G. A. Feldhamer. Wild mammals of North America. Johns Hopkins Univ. Press, Baltimore, MD.

McDaniel, J. C. 1963. Otter population study. Proc. Ann. Conf. Southeast. Assoc. Game and Fish Comm. 17:163-168.

McDonald, J. S., and K. V. Miller. 1993. A history of white-tailed deer restocking in the United States. Quality Deer Manage. Assoc., Res. Publ. 93-1. 109pp.

McIlhenny, E. A. 1935. The alligator's life history. Christopher Publishing House, Boston, MA. 177pp.

McKeever, S. 1959. Relative abundance of twelve southeastern mammals in six vegetative types. Amer. Midl. Naturalist 62:222-226.

McLean, P. K., and M. R. Pelton. 1990. Some demographic comparisons of wild and panhandler bears in Great Smoky Mountains. Int. Conf. Bear Res. and Manage. 8:105-112.

McLean, R. G. 1994. Wildlife diseases and humans. Pages A25-41 in S. E. Hygnstrom, R. M. Timm, and G. E. Larson, eds. Prevention and control of wildlife damage. Univ. Nebraska Coop. Ext. Serv., Lincoln and USDA and Great Plains Agric. Council. Vol. 1-2.

McManus, J. J. 1974. Didelphis virginiana. Mamm. Species. Amer. Soc. Mamm. 40:1-6.

McNab, W. H., and P. E. Avers, comps. 1994. Ecological subregions of the United States: section descriptions. USDA For. Serv. Publ. WO-WSA-5, Washington, DC.

McNair, D. B. 1998. Response of Henslow's Sparrows and Sedge Wrens to a dormant-season prescribed fire. Florida Field Nat. 26:46-47.

McRae, W. A., J. L. Landers, J. L. Buckner, and R. C. Simpson. 1979. Importance of habitat diversity in bobwhite management. Proc. Annu. Conf. Southeast. Assoc. Fish and Wildl. Agencies 33:127-135.

McWilliams, S. R., and M. D. Bachmann. 1988. Using life history and ecology as tools to manage a threatened salamander species. J. Iowa Acad. Sci. 95:66-71.

McWilliams, W. H., and J. F. Rosson, Jr. 1990. Composition and vulnerability of bottomland hardwood forests of the Coastal Plain Province in the south central United States. For. Ecol. Manage. 33/34:485-501.

Mead, R. A. 1967. Age determination in the spotted skunk. J. Mamm. 48:606-616.

Mead, R. A. 1968. Reproduction in eastern forms of the spotted skunk (genus Spilogale). J. Zool. (London) 156:119-136.

Mead, R. A. 1981. Delayed implantation in mustelids, with special emphasis on the spotted skunk. J. Reprod. Fert. Suppl. 29:11-24.

Meadows, J. S., and J. D. Hodges. 1995. Biotic agents of stress in the South. Pages 244-280 in S. Fox and R. A. Mickler, eds. Impact of air pollutants on southern pine forests. Springer-Verlag, New York, NY.

Means, D. B., and C. J. Longden. 1976. Aspects of the biology and zoogeography of the pine barrens treefrog, Hyla andersonii, in northern Florida. Herpetologica 32:117-130.

Means, D. B., J. G. Palis, and M. Baggett. 1996. Effects of slash pine silviculture on a Florida population of flatwoods salamander. Cons. Biol. 10:426-437.

Mebus, C. A. 1989. Potential role of feral pigs in the spread of foreign animal diseases. Pages 34-36 in N. Black, ed. Proc. Feral Pig Symp., Orlando, FL. Livestock Conserv. Inst., Madison, WI.

Mech, L. D. 1984. Predators and Predation. Pages 189-200 in L. K. Halls, ed. White-tailed deer: ecology and management. Stackpole Books, Harrisburg, PA.

Melchiors, M. A. 1991. Wildlife management in southern pine regeneration systems. Pages 391-420 in M. L. Duryea, and P. M. Dougherty, eds. Forest regeneration manual. Kluwer Academic Publishers, Boston, MA.

Melquist, W. E., and A. E. Dronkert. 1987. River Otter. Pages 627-641 in M. Novak, J. A. Baker, M. E. Obbard, and B. Malloch, eds. Wild furbearer management and conservation in North America. Ministry of Natural Resources, Ontario.

Melquist, W. E., and M. G. Hornocker, 1979. Methods and techniques for studying and censusing river otter populations. Univ. Idaho. For., Wildl. and Range. Exp. Stn., Tech. Rep. 8:1-17.

Mengel, R. M. 1971. A study of coyote-dog hybrids and implications concerning hybridization in Canis. J. Mamm. 52:316-336.

Messina, M. G., and W. H. Conner, eds. 1998. Southern forested wetlands: ecology and management. Lewis Publ. Co., Washington, DC. 616pp.

Metzler, R., and D. W. Speake. 1985. Wild turkey poult mortality rates and their relationship to brood habitat structure in northeast Alabama. Proc. National Wild Turkey Symp. 5:103-111.

Meyer, K. D. 1990. Kites. Pages 38-49 in Proc. Southeast Raptor Management Symp. and Workshop. National Wildl. Fed., Washington, DC.

Meyer, K. D. 1993. Communal roosts of the American swallow-tailed kite in Florida: Habitat associations, critical sites, and a technique for monitoring population status. Draft Final Report. Florida Game and Fresh Water Fish Comm., Tallahassee, FL. 97pp.

Meyer, K. D., and M. W. Collopy. 1990. Status, distribution, and habitat requirements of the American swallow-tailed kite (Elanoides forficatus) in Florida. Draft Final Report. Florida Game and Fresh Water Fish Commission, Tallahassee, FL. 137pp.

Meyers, J. M., and A. S. Johnson. 1978. Bird communities associated with succession and management of loblolly-shortleaf pine forests. Pages 50-65 in R. M. DeGraaf, tech. coord. Proc. of the Workshop: Management of Southern Forests for Nongame Birds. USDA For. Serv. Gen. Tech. Rept. SE-14. Asheville, NC.

Mickler, R. A. 1995. Southern pine forests of North America. Pages 19-57 in S. Fox and R. A. Mickler, eds. Impact of air pollutants on southern pine forests. Springer-Verlag, New York, NY.

Miller, D. L., and M. K. Causey. 1985. Food preferences of American woodcock wintering in Alabama. J. Wildl. Manage. 49:492-496.

Miller, J. E. 1987. Assessment of wildlife damage on southern forests. Pages 48-53 in J. G. Dickson and E. O. Maughan, eds. Managing Southern Forests for Wildlife and Fish: A Proceedings. USDA For. Serv. Gen. Tech. Rep. SO-65.

Miller, J. E. 1993. A national perspective on feral swine. Pages 9-16 in C. W. Hanselka and J. F. Cadenhead, eds. Feral Swine: A Compendium for Resource Managers. Texas Agric. Ext. Serv., Kerrville, TX.

Miller, J. E., and B. D. Leopold. 1992. Population influences: predators. Pages 119-128 in J. G. Dickson, ed. The wild turkey: biology and management. Stackpole Books, Harrisburg, PA.

Miller, K. V., and B. R. Chapman. 1995. Responses of vegetation, birds, and small mammals to chemical and mechanical site preparation. Pages 146-148 in R. E. Gaskin, and J. A. Zabkiewicz, compilers. Popular summaries from second international conference on forest vegetation management. FRI Bulletin No. 192. New Zealand For. Res. Inst., Rotorua, New Zealand.

Miller, K. V., and J. J. Ozoga. 1997. Density effects on deer sociobiology. Pages 136-150 in W. J. McShea, H. B. Underwood, and J. H. Rappole, eds. The science of overabundance: deer ecology and population management. Smithsoinian Institution Press, Washington, DC.

Miller, K. V., and J. S. Witt. 1991. Impacts of forestry herbicides on wildlife. Pages 795-800 in S. S. Coleman, and D. G. Neary, compilers and eds. Proc. Sixth Biennial Southern Silvicultural Res. Conf. USDA For. Serv. Gen. Tech. Rep. SE-70.

Miller, S. D. 1980. The ecology of the bobcat in south Alabama.

Dissertation, Auburn Univ., Auburn, AL. 156pp.

Miller, S. D., and D. W. Speake. 1978. Prey utilization by bobcats on quail plantations in southern Alabama. Proc. Annu. Conf. Southeast. Assoc. Fish and Wildl. Agencies 32:100-111.

Miller, S. D., and D. W. Speake. 1979. Progress report: demography and home range of the bobcat in south Alabama. Bobcat Res. Conf. Natl. Wildl. Fed. Sci. Tech. Ser. 6:123-124.

Miller, S. G., S. P. Bratton, and J. Hadidian. 1992. Impacts of white-tailed deer on endangered and threatened vascular plants. Nat. Areas J. 12:67-74.

Milling, T. C., M. P. Rowe, B. L. Cockerel, T. A. Dellinger, J. B. Bailes, and C. E. Hill. 1997. Population densities of northern saw-whet owls in degraded boreal forests of the southern Appalachians. Pages 272-285 in J. R. Duncan, D. H. Johnston, and T. H. Nicholls, eds. Biology and Conservation of owls of the northern hemisphere. USDA For. Serv. Gen. Tech. Rep. NC-190.

Millsap, B. A., J. A. Gore, D. E. Runde, and S. I. Cerulean. 1990. Setting priorities for the conservation of fish and wildlife species in Florida. Wildl. Monogr. 111:1-57.

Minser, W. G., and M. R. Pelton. 1982. Impact of hunting on raccoon populations and the management implications. Agric. Exp. Stn., Univ. Tennessee Bull. No. 612. 32pp.

Mirarchi, R. E. 1993a. The crop gland. Pages 117-128 in T. S. Baskett, M. W. Sayre, R. E. Tomlinson, and R. E. Mirarchi, eds. Ecology and management of the mourning dove. Stackpole Books, Harrisburg, PA.

Mirarchi, R. E. 1993b. Energetics, metabolism and reproductive physiology. Pages 143-160 in T. S. Baskett, M. W. Sayre, R. E. Tomlinson, and R. E. Mirarchi, eds. Ecology and management of the mourning dove. Stackpole Books, Harrisburg, PA.

Mirarchi, R. E. 1993c. Growth, maturation and molt. Pages 129-142 in T. S. Baskett, M. W. Sayre, R. E. Tomlinson, and R. E. Mirarchi, eds. Ecology and management of the mourning dove. Stackpole Books, Harrisburg, PA.

Mirarchi, R. E., and T. S. Baskett. 1994. Mourning dove (Zenaida macroura). In A. Poole and F. Gill, eds. The Birds of North America, No. 117. Philadelphia: the Academy of Natural Sciences; Washington, DC.: The American Ornithologists' Union.

Mitchell, J. C. 1994. The Reptiles of Virginia. Smithsonian Inst. Press, Washington, DC. 352pp.

Mitchell, J. C., S. C. Rinehart, J. F. Pagels, K. A. Buhlmann, and C. A. Pague. 1997. Factors influencing amphibian and small mammal assemblages in central Appalachian forests. For. Ecol.Manage. 96:65-76.

Mitchell, L. R., L. D. Carlile, and C. R. Chandler. 1999. Effects of southern flying squirrels on nest success of red-cockaded woodpeckers. J. Wildl. Manage. 63:538-545.

Mitchell, M. S., K. S. Karriker, E. J. Jones, and R. A. Lancia. 1995. Small mammal communities associated with pine plantation management of pocosins. J. Wildl. Manage. 59:875-881.

Mock, K. E., T. C. Theimer, D. L. Greenburg, and P. Keim. 2001. Conservation of genetic diversity within and among subspecies of wild turkey. Proc. National Wild Turkey Symp.8:(in press).

Montague, W. G., J. C. Neal, J. E. Johnson, and D. A. James. 1995. Techniques for excluding southern flying squirrels from cavities of red-cockaded woodpeckers. Pages 401-409 in D. L. Kulhavy, R. G. Hooper, and R. Costa, eds. Red-cockaded woodpecker: recovery, ecology and management. Center for Applied Studies in Forestry, College of Forestry, Stephen F. Austin State Univ., Nacogdoches, TX.

Moore, D. W., and M. L. Kennedy. 1985. Factors affecting response of raccoons to traps and populations size estimation. Am. Midl. Nat. 81:192-197.

Moore, F. R., S. A. Gauthreaux, Jr., P. Kerlinger, and T. R. Simons. 1993. Stopover habitat: management implications and guidelines. Pages 58-69 in D. M. Finch and P. W. Stangel, eds. Status and management of neotropical migratory birds. USDA For. Serv. Gen. Tech. Rep. RM-229.

Moore, F. R., and P. Kerlinger. 1987. Stopover and fat deposition by North American wood-Warblers (Parulinae) following spring migration over the Gulf of Mexico. Oecologia 74:47-54.

Moore, F. R., P. Kerlinger, T. R. Simons. 1990. Stopover on a Gulf coast barrier island by spring trans-Gulf migrants. Wilson Bulletin 102:487-500.

Moore, F. R., and M. S. Woodrey. 1995. Stopover habitat and its importance in the conservation of landbird migrants. Proc. Annu. Conf. Southeast. Assoc. Fish and Wildl Agencies 47:447-459.

Moore, G. C. and G. R. Parker. 1992. Colonization by the eastern coyote (Canis latrans). Pages 23-37 in A.H. Boer, ed. Ecology and management of the eastern coyote. Symp. on the Eastern Coyote. New Brunswick, Canada.

Moorhead, K.K., and I.M. Rossell. 1998. Southern mountain fens. Pages 379-403 in M.G. Messina and W.C. Conner, eds., Southern Forested Wetlands. Lewis Publishers, New York, NY.

Moorman, C. E., K. R. Russell, M. A. Menzel, S. M. Lohr, J. E. Ellenberger, and D. H.Van Lear. 1999. Bats roosting in deciduous leaf litter. Bat Res. News 40:74.

Morrison, D. W., R. M. Edmunds, G. Linscombe, and J. W. Goertz. 1981. Evaluation of specific scent station variables in north-central Louisiana. Proc. Annu. Conf. Southeast. Assoc. Fish and Wildl. Agencies 35:281-291.

Morrison, M. L., and E. C. Meslow. 1983. Impacts of forestry herbicides on wildlife: toxicity and habitat alteration. Trans. N. Amer. Wildl. and Nat. Resour. Conf. 48:175-185.

Mosby, H. S. 1949. The present status and the future outlook of the eastern and Florida wild turkeys. Trans. N. Amer. Wildl. Conf. 14:346-354.

Mosby, H. S. 1969. The influence of hunting on the population dynamics of a woodlot gray squirrel population. J. Wildl. Manage. 33:59-73.

Mosby, H. S., and C. O. Handley. 1943. The wild turkey in Virginia: its status, life history and management. Virginia Comm. of Game and Inland Fish., Richmond, VA. 281pp.

Mosby, H. S., R. L. Kirkpatrick, and J. O. Newell. 1977. Seasonal vulnerability of gray squirrels to hunting. J. Wildl. Manage. 41:284-289.

Mount, R. H. 1975. The reptiles and amphibians of Alabama. Agricultural Exp. Stn., Auburn Univ., Auburn, AL. 347pp.

Mount, R. H. 1986. Southern Hognose Snake, Heterodon simus (Linnaeus). Pages 34-35 in R. H. Mount, ed. Vertebrate Animals of Alabama in Need of Special Attention. Alabama Ag. Exp. Stn., Auburn Univ., Auburn, AL. 124pp.

Mueller, B.S., W. R. Davidson, J. B. Atkinson, Jr. 1993. Survival of northern bobwhite infected with avian pox. Pages 79-82 in K. E. Church and T. V. Dailey, eds. Quail III: National Quail Symp. Kansas Dep. Wildl. and Parks, Pratt.

Mueller, J. M., C. B. Dabbert, S. Demarais, and A. R. Forbes. 1999.

Northern bobwhite chick mortality caused by red imported fire ants. J. Wildl. Manage. 63:1291-1298.

Mueller, A. J., D. J. Twedt, and C. R. Loesch. 2000. Development of management objectives for breeding birds in the Mississippi Allusial Valley. Pages 12-17 in Strategies for bird conservation: The Partners in Flight planning process. Proc. 3rd Partners in Flight workshop. 1995. Cape May, NJ.

Murdock, N.A. 1994. Rare and endangered plants and animals of southern Appalachian wetlands. Water, Air and Soil Pollution 77:324-329.

Murdy, W.H. 1968. Plant speciation associated with granite outcrop communities of the southeastern Piedmont. Rhodora 70:394-407.

Murphy, D. W., and F. R. Thompson. 1993. Breeding chronology and habitat of the American woodcock in Missouri. Pages 12-18 in J. R. Longcore and G. F. Sepik, eds. Eighth Woodcock Symp. U. S. Fish and Wildl. Serv., Biol. Rep. 16.

Murray, N. L., and D. F. Stauffer. 1995. Nongame bird use of habitat in central Appalachian riparian forests. J. Wildl. Manage. 59:78-88.

Muth, R. M., D. A. Hamilton, J. F. Organ, D. J. Witter, M. E. Mather, and J. J. Daigle. 1998. The future of wildlife and fisheries policy and management : assessing attitudes and values of wildlife and fisheries professionals. Trans. N. Amer. Wildl. and Nat. Resour. Conf. 63:604-627.

Myers, R.L. 1990. Scrub and high pine. Pages 150-193 in R.L. Myers and J.J. Ewel, eds. Ecosystems of Florida. University of Central Florida Press, Orlando, FL.

Mykytka, J. M., and M. R. Pelton. 1990. Management strategies for Florida black bears based on home range composition. Intenat. Conf. Bear Res. and Manage. 8:161-167.

Nassar, J.R., W.E. Cohen, and C.R. Hopkins. 1993. Waterfowl habitat management handbook for the lower Mississippi River Valley. Miss. Coop. Ext. Serv., Mississippi State Univ., Mississippi State 15pp.

Natl. Assoc. Conserv. Dist. 1994. Riparian ecosystems in the humid U.S.: functions, values, and management. Washington, DC. 553pp.

Neal, J. C., W. G. Montague, and D. A. James. 1993. Climbing by black rat snakes on cavity trees of red-cockaded woodpeckers. Wildl. Soc. Bull. 21:160-165.

Nedbal, M. A., R. L. Honeycutt, S. G. Evans, R. M. Whiting, Jr., D. R. Dietz. 1997. Northern bobwhite restocking in east Texas: a genetic assessment. J. Wildl. Manage. 61:854-863.

Nelson, A. L. 1933. A preliminary report on the winter food of Virginia foxes. J. Mamm. 14:40-43.

Nelson, R. D., H. Black, Jr., R. E. Radtke, and J. Mumma. 1983. Wildlife and fish management in the Forest Service: a goal oriented approach. Trans. N. Amer. Wildl. and Natur. Resour. Conf. 48:87-95.

Nestler, R. B., W. W. Bailey, and H. E. McClure. 1942. Protein requirements of bobwhite quail chicks for survival, growth, and efficiency of feed utilization. J. Wildl. Manage. 6:185-193.

Nettles, V. F. 1989. Disease of wild swine. Pages 16-18 in N. Black, ed. Proc. Feral Pig Symp., Orlando, FL. Livestock Conserv. Inst., Madison, WI.

Newling, C.J. 1990. Restoration of bottomland hardwood forests in the lower Mississippi Valley. Restor. Manage. Notes 8:23-28.

Newsom, J. D. 1984. Coastal Plain. Pages 367-380 in L.K. Halls, ed. White-tailed deer ecology and management. Stackpole Books, Harrisburg, PA.

Newsom, J. D., H. R. Perry, and P. E. Schilling. 1976. Fire ant-muskrat relationships in Louisiana coastal marshes. Proc. Annu. Conf. Southeast. Assoc. Fish and Wildl. Agencies 30:414-418.

Nicholas, N., C. Eager, and J. Peine. 1999. Threatened ecosystem: high elevation spruce-fir forest. Pages 431-454 in J. D. Peine, ed. Ecosystem management for sustainability. Lewis Publ., Boca Raton, FL.

Nichols, J. D., and R. E. Tomlinson. 1993. Analyses of banding data. Pages 269-280 in T. S. Baskett, M. W. Sayre, R. E. Tomlinson, and R. E. Mirarchi, eds. Ecology and management of the mourning dove. Stackpole Books, Harrisburg, PA.

Nichols, J. D., K. J. Reinecke, and J. E. Hines. 1983. Factors affecting the distribution of mallards wintering in the Mississippi Alluvial Valley. Auk 100:932-946.

Nicholson, W. S., and E. P. Hill. 1984. Mortality in gray foxes from east-central Alabama. J. Wildl. Manage. 48:1429-1432.

Nickerson, M. A., and C. E. Mays. 1973. The hellbenders: North American "Giant Salamanders." Milwaukee Pub. Mus. Milwaukee, WI. 106pp.

Nietro, B., V. Binkley, S. Cline, R. Mannan, B. Marcot, D. Taylor, and F. Wagner. 1985. Pages 129-159 in E. R. Brown, ed. Management of wildlife and fish habitats in forests of western Oregon and Washington. USDA Forest Serv., Publication R6-F&WL – 192-1985.

Nixon, C. M., R. W. Donohoe, and T. Nash. 1974. Overharvest of fox squirrels from two woodlots in Ohio. J. Wildl. Manage. 38:67-80.

Nixon, C. M., S. P. Havera, and L. P. Hansen. 1980. Initial response of squirrels to forest changes associated with selection cutting. Wildl. Soc. Bull. 8:298-306.

Nixon, C. M., S. P. Havera, and L. P. Hansen. 1986. Demographic characteristics of an unexploited population of fox squirrels (Sciurus niger). Can. J. Zool. 64:512-521.

Nixon, C. M., M. W. McClain, and R. W. Donohoe. 1975. Effects of hunting and mast crops on a squirrel population. J. Wildl. Manage. 39:1-25.

Nolan, V., Jr. 1978. The ecology and behavior of the prairie warbler Dendroica discolor. Ornith. Monogr. 26. 595pp.

Norman, G. W., and R. L. Kirkpatrick. 1984. Foods, nutrition, and condition of ruffed grouse in southwestern Virginia. J. Wildl. Manage. 48:183-187.

Noss, R. F. 1987. Protecting natural areas in fragmented landscapes. Nat. Areas J. 7:2-13.

Noss, R.F., E.T. LaRoe III, and J.M. Scott. 1995. Endangered ecosystems of the United States: a preliminary assessment of loss and degradation. National Biological Service, Biological Report 28. 58 p.

Nottingham, B. G., K. G. Johnson, and M. R. Pelton. 1989. Evaluation of scent-station surveys to monitor raccoon density. Wildl. Soc. Bull. 17:29-35.

Nottingham, B. G., K. G. Johnson, J. W. Woods, and M. R. Pelton. 1982. Population characteristics and harvest relationships of a raccoon population in east Tennessee. Proc Annu. Conf. Southeast. Assoc. Fish and Wildl. Agencies 36:691-700.

Novak, M. 1987a. Beaver. Pages 282-312 in M. Novak, J. A. Baker, M. E. Obbard, and B. Malloch, eds. Wild furbearer management and conservation in North America. Ministry of Natural Resour., Ontario.

Novak, M. 1987b. Traps and trap research. Pages 943-969 in M. Novak, J. A. Baker, M. E. Obbard, and B. Malloch. eds. Wild furbearer management and conservation in North America. Ministry of Natural Resour., Ontario.

Nowak, R. M. 1979. North American Quaternary Canis. Mus. Nat. Hist. Univ. of Kansas. Monogr. 6. 154pp.

Nowak, R. M., and J. L. Paradiso. 1983. Walker's mammals of the world, Vol. II. Johns Hopkins Univ. Press, Baltimore, MD. 1362pp.

Obbard, M. E., J. G. Jones, R. Newman, A. Booth, A. J. Satterwaite, and G. Linscombe. 1987. Furbearer harvests in North America. In M. Novak, J. A. Baker, M. E. Obbard, and B. Malloch, eds. Wild furbearer management and conservation in North America. Ontario Ministry of Natural Resour., Ontario Trappers Assoc., North Bay, Ontario.

O'Brien, S. J., M. E. Roelke, N. Yuhki, K. W. Richards, W. E. Johnson, W. L. Franklin, A. E. Anderson, O. L. Bass, Jr., R. C. Belden, and J. S. Mantenson. 1990. Genetic introgression within the Florida panther, Felis concolor coryi. Nat. Geog. Res. 6:485-494.

O'Hara, M. P. 1980. A comparative study of raccoons from the Mississippi Delta and east-central Mississippi. M. S. Thesis, Mississippi State Univ., Mississippi State. 126pp.

Okoniewski, J. C., and R. E. Chambers. 1984. Coyote vocal response to an electronic siren and human howling. J. Wildl. Manage. 48:217-222.

O'Neil, T. 1949. The muskrat in the Louisiana coastal marshes. Louisiana Dep. Wildl. and Fisheries, Baton Rouge, LA. 152pp.

Opdam, P. 1991. Metapopulation theory and habitat fragmentation: a review of holarctic breeding bird studies. Landscape Ecol. 5:93-106.

Osgood, W. H. 1939. The mammals of Chile. Zool. Ser. Field Mus. Nat. Hist. 30pp.

Ouachita National Forest. 1990. Amended land and resource management plan. USDA Forest Service, Hot Springs, Arkansas.

Outcalt, K. W., and C.E. Lewis. 1990. Response of wiregrass (Aristida stricta) to mechanical site preparation. In L.C. Duever and R.F. Noss, eds., Proceedings of Symposium on Wiregrass Biology and Management, October 13, 1988, Valdosta, GA. KBN Engineering and Applied Sciences, Gainesville, FL.

Owen, C. N. 1976. Food habits of wild turkey poults (Meleagris gallopavo silvestris) in pine stands and fields and the effects of mowing hayfield edges on arthropod populations. M.S. Thesis, Mississippi State Univ., Mississippi State, MS. 62pp.

Owens, R. D., and D. Slate. 1992. Economics and effectiveness of control methods: fact and fiction. Proc. East. Wildl. Damage Control Conf. 5:24-27.

Ozoga, J. J., L. J. Verme, and C. S. Bienz. 1982. Parturition behavior and territoriality in white-tailed deer: impact on neonatal mortality. J. Wildl. Manage. 46:1-11.

Pague, C. A. 1991. Weller's salamander, Plethodon welleri. Pages 442-443 in K. Terwilleger, ed. Virginia's Endangered Species. McDonald and Woodward, Blacksburg, VA.

Pais, R. C., S. A. Bonney, and W. C. McComb. 1988. Herpetofaunal species richness and habitat associations in an eastern Kentucky forest. Proc. Annu. Conf. Southeast. Assoc. Fish and Wildl. Agencies 42:448-455.

Palis, J. G. 1997. Distribution, habitat, and status of the flatwoods salamander (Ambystoma cingulatum) in Florida, USA. Herp. Nat. Hist. 5:53-65.

Palmer, W. E, K. M. Puckett, J. A. Anderson, and P. T. Bromely. 1998. Effects of foliar insecticides on survival of northern bobwhite quail chicks. J. Wildl. Manage. 62:1565-1573.

Palmer, W. E., G. A Hurst, B. D. Leopold, and D. C. Cotton. 1991. Body weights and sex ratios for the swamp rabbit in Mississippi. J. Mamm. 72:620-622.

Palmisano, A. W. 1971. Louisiana's fur industry. Commercial Wildl. Work Unit Rep. of Louisiana Wildl. and Fisheries Comm. to U. S. Army Corps of Eng., New Orleans District. Mimeogr.

Palmisano, A. W. 1972. The distribution and abundance of muskrats (Ondatra zibethicus) in relation to vegetative types in Louisiana coastal marshes. Proc. Annu. Conf. Southeast. Assoc. Fish and Wildl. Agencies 26:160-177.

Parker, R. R. 1934. Recent studies of tick-borne diseases made at the United States Public Health Service Laboratory at Hamilton, Montana. Proc. Fifth Pacific Sci. Congr. B5:3367.

Parmalee, P. W. 1953. Hunting pressure and its effect on bobwhite quail populations in east-central Texas. J. Wildl. Manage. 17:341-345.

Paton, P. 1994. The effect of edge on avian nest success: how strong is the evidence? Conserv. Biol. 7:618-622.

Patton, R. F. 1974. Ecological and behavioral relationships of the skunks of Trans Pecos, Texas. Ph.D. Thesis, Texas A&M Univ., College Station. 193pp.

Payeur, J. B. 1989. Feral swine: a potential threat to domestic cattle and swine. Pages 19-33 in N. Black, ed. Proc. Feral Pig Symp., Orlando, FL. Livestock Conserv. Inst., Madison, WI.

Payne, J. L., D. R. Young, and J. F. Pagels. 1989. Plant community characteristics associated with the endangered northern flying squirrel, Glaucomys sabrinus, in the southern Appalachians. Am. Midl. Nat. 121:285-292.

Pearlstine, L. G., L. A. Brandt, W. M. Kitchens, and F. J. Mazzotti. 1995. Impacts of citrus development on habitats of southwest Florida. Conserv. Biol. 9:1020-1032.

Pechmann, J. H. K., D. E. Scott, J. W. Gibbons, and R. D. Semlitsch. 1989. Influence of wetland hydroperiod on diversity and abundance of metamorphosing juvenile amphibians. Wetlands Ecol. Manage. 1:3-11.

Pechmann, J. H. K., D. E. Scott, R. D. Semlitsch, J. P. Caldwell, L. J. Vitt, and J. W. Gibbons. 1991. Declining amphibian populations: the problem of separating human impacts from natural fluctuations. Science 253:892-895.

Peet, R. K., and D.J. Allard. 1993. Longleaf pine vegetation of the southern Atlantic and eastern Gulf coast regions: a preliminary classification. Tall Timbers Fire Ecol. Conf. Proc. 18:45-81.

Pelham, P. H., and J. G. Dickson. 1992. Physical characteristics. Pages 32-45 in J. G. Dickson, ed. The wild turkey: biology and management. Stackpole Books, Harrisburg, PA.

Pelton, M. R. 1982. Black bear. Pages 504-514 in J.A. Chapmanand G.A. Feldhamer, eds. Wild mammals of North America: biology, management, and economics. John Hopkins Univ. Press, Baltimore, MD.

Pelton, M. R. 1989. The impacts of oak mast on black bears in the southern Appalachians. Pages 7-11 in C.E. McGee, ed. Proc. Southern Appalachian Mast Management Workshop. USDA Forest Service and Dep. For., Wildl. and Fisheries, Univ. Tennessee, Knoxville.

Pelton, M. R., L. E. Beeman, and D. C. Eagar. 1977. Den selection by black bears in the Great Smoky Mountains National Park. Internat. Conf. Bear Res. and Manage. 4:149-151.

Pelton, M. R., A. B. Coley, T. H. Eason, D. L. D. Martinez, J. A Pedersen, F. T. van Manen, and K. M. Weaver. 1994. American black bear conservation action plan. IUCN/SSC Bear Specialist Group. Tech. Report #.

Pelton, M. R., and J. H. Jenkins. 1971. Productivity of Georgia cottontails. Proc. Annu. Conf. Southeast. Assoc. Game and Fish Comm. 25:261-268.

Pelton, M. R., and R. G. Nichols. 1972. Status of the black bear (Ursus americanus) in the Southeast. Proc. East. Black Bear Workshop. 1:18-23.

Pelton, M. R., and F. T. van Manen. 1994. Distribution of black bears in North America. Proc. East. Black Bear Workshop. 12:133-138.

Pelton, M. R., and F. T. van Manen. 1996. Benefits and pitfalls of long-term research: a case study of black bears in Great Smoky Mountains National Park. Wildl. Soc. Bulletin 24:443-450.

Pelton, M. R., and F. T. van Manen. 1997. Status of black bears in the Southeast. Proc. Int. Trade of Bear Parts. 2:31-44.

Pence, D. B., and L. A. Windberg. 1994. Impact of a sarcoptic mange epizootic on a coyote population. J. Wildl. Manage. 58:624-633.

Peoples, J. C., D. C. Sisson, and D. W. Speake. 1995. Mortality of wild turkey poults in coastal plain pine forests. Proc. Annu. Conf. Southeast. Assoc. Fish and Wildl. Agencies 49:448-453.

Peoples, J. C., D. C. Sisson, and D. W. Speake. 1996. Wild turkey brood habitat use and characteristics in coastal plain pine forests. Proc. National Wild Turkey Symp. 7:89-96.

Perkins, C. J., G. A. Hurst, and E. R. Roach. 1989. Relative abundance of small mammals in young loblolly pine plantations. Pages 589-591 in Proc. 5th Biennial Southern Silvicultural Research Conference. USDA For. Serv. Gen. Tech Rep SO-74.

Peterson, J. R., and J. M Perkins. 1994. Maternity roost distribution on a managed forest, as determined by mist-netting. Bat Res. News 35:110.

Petranka, J. W., M. E. Eldridge, and K. E. Haley. 1993. Effects of timber harvesting on southern Appalachian salamanders. Conserv. Biol. 7:363-370.

Pettingill, O. S., Jr. 1977. Reflections on early woodcock research. Proc. Woodcock Symp. 6:25-27.

Pharris, L. 1983. A different drummer for Arkansas. Arkansas Game & Fish 14:10-11.

Pharris, L. D., and R. C. Goetz. 1980. An evaluation of artificial wild turkey nests monitored by automatic cameras. Proc. National Wild Turkey Symp. 4:108-116.

Phillips, L. F., Jr., and K. E. Gault. 1997. Predation of red-cockaded woodpecker young by a corn snake. Florida Field Nat. 25:67-68.

Phillips, M. K. 1994. Reestablishment of red wolves in the Alligator River National Wildlife Refuge, North Carolina. September 14, 1987, to September 30, 1992. Red Wolf Manage. Series Tech. Rep. No. 10, USDI Fish and Wildl. Serv., Atlanta, GA. 28pp.

Phillips, M. K., and V. G. Henry. 1992. Comments on red wolf taxonomy. Conserv. Biol. 6:596-599.

Phillips, M. K., R. Smith, V. G. Henry, and C. Lucash. 1995. Red wolf reintroduction program. Pages 157-168 in L. N. Carbyn, S. H. Fritts, and D. R. Seip, eds. Ecology and conservation of wolves in a changing world. Can. Circumpolar Inst., Univ. Alberta, Edmonton.

Pierson, E. D. 1998. Tall trees, deep holes, and scarred landscapes: conservation biology and North American bats. Pages 309-325 in T. H. Kunz and P. A. Racey, eds. Bat biology and conservation. Smithsonian Institution Press, Washington, DC.

Platt, S.G., and C.G. Brantley. 1993. Switchcane: propagation and establishment in the southeastern United States. Restoration and Manage. 11:134-137.

Platt, S.G., and C.G. Brantley. 1997. Canebrakes: an ecological and historical perspective. Castanea 62:8-21.

Plentovich, S. M., J. W. Tucker, Jr., N. R. Holler, and G. E. Hill. 1998b. Enhancing Bachman's sparrow habitat via management of red-cockaded woodpeckers. J. Wildl. Manage. 62:347-354.

Plentovich, S. M., N. R. Holler, and G. E. Hill. 1998a. Site fidelity of wintering Henslow's sparrows. J. Field Ornith. 69:486-490.

Pollock, K. H., C. T. Moore, W. R. Davidson, F. E. Kellogg, and G. L. Doster. 1989. Survival rates of bobwhite quail based on band recovery analysis. J. Wild. Manage. 53:1-6.

Porath, W. R., and P. A. Vohs, Jr. 1972. Population ecology of the ruffed grouse in northeastern Iowa. J. Wildl. Manage. 36:793-802.

Poteet, M. L., R. E. Thill, R. M. Whiting, Jr., and R. L. Rayburn. 1996. Deer use of riparian zones and adjacent pine plantations in Texas. Proc. Annu. Conf. Southeast. Assoc. Fish and Wildl. Agencies 50:541-549.

Pough, F. H., R. M. Andrews, J. E. Cadle, M. L. Crump, A. H. Savitzky, and K. D. Wells. 1998. Herpetology. Prentice Hall, Upper Saddle River, NJ. 577pp.

Powell, D. S., J. L. Faulkner, D. R. Darr, Z. Zhu, and D. W. MacCleery. Forest resources of the United States, 1992. USDA Forest Service Gen. Tech Rep. RM-234. 132pp.

Powers, J. S. 1993. Fox squirrel home range and habitat use in the southeastern Coastal Plain. M. S. Thesis, Auburn Univ., Auburn, AL. 93pp.

Prestwood, A. K., J. F. Smith, and J. Brown. 1971. Lungworms in white-tailed deer of the southeastern United States. J. Wildl. Dis. 7:149-154.

Probst, J. R., and J. Weinrich. 1993. Relating Kirtland's warbler population to changing landscape composition and structure. Landscape Ecology 8:257-271.

Progulske, D. R. 1952. The bobcat and its relation to prey species in Virginia. M.S. Thesis, Virginia Polytechnic Inst., Blacksburg, VA. 135pp.

Progulske, D. R. 1955. Game animals utilized as food by bobcats in the southern Appalachians. J. Wildl. Manage. 19:249-253.

Progulske, D. R., Jr. 1982. Spatial distribution of bobcats and gray foxes in eastern Florida. M.S. Thesis, Univ. of Florida, Gainesville. 63pp.

Puckett, K. M., W. E. Palmer, P. T. Bromley, J. R. Anderson, Jr., and L. T. Sharpe. 1995. Bobwhite nesting ecology and modern agriculture: a management experiment. Proc. Annu. Conf. Southeast. Assoc. Fish and Wildl. Agencies 49:505-516.

Pullen, T. M., Jr. 1967. Some effects of beaver (Castor canadensis) and beaver pond management on the ecology and utilization of fish populations along warm-water streams in Georgia and South Carolina. Ph.D. Thesis, Univ. Georgia, Athens. 84pp.

Pulliam, H. R. 1988. Sources, sinks, and population regulation. Amer. Nat. 132:652-661.

Pulliam, H. R., and J. B. Danielson. 1991. Sources, sinks, and habitat selection: a landscape perspective on population dynamics.

Amer. Nat. 137:S50-S66.

Pursglove, S. R., Jr. 1973. Some parasites and diseases of the American woodcock, Philohela minor (Gmelin). Ph.D. Thesis, Univ. Georgia, Athens. 221pp.

Putnam, J. A., G. M. Furnival, and J. S. McKnight. 1960. Management and inventory of southern hardwoods. USDA For. Serv., Agric. Handb. 181. U.S. Government Printing Office, Washington, DC. 102pp.

Quarterman, E., M.P. Burbanck, and D.J. Shure. 1993. Rock outcrop communities: limestone, sandstone, and granite. Pages 35-86 in W.H. Martin, S.G. Boyce, and A.C. Echternacht, eds. Biodiversity of the southeastern United States: upland terrestrial communities. John Wiley & Sons, New York, NY.

Queeny, E. M. 1946. Prairie wings. Schiffer Publ. Ltd., Exton, PN. 256pp.

Quick, H. F. 1951. Notes on the ecology of weasels in Gunnison County, Colorado. J. Mamm. 32:281-290.

Rabenold, K. N., P. T. Fauth, B. W. Goodner, J. A. Sadowski, and P. G. Parker. 1998. Response of avian communities to disturbance by an exotic insect in spruce-fir forests of the Southern Appalachians. Conserv. Biol. 12:177-189.

Ransome, D. B., and T. P. Sullivan. 1997. Food limitation and habitat preference of Glaucomys sabrinus and Tamiasciurus hudsonicus. J. Mamm. 78:538-549.

Raphael, M. G., C. A. Taylor, and R. H. Barrett. 1986. Smoked aluminum track stations record flying squirrel occurrence. USDA For. Serv. Res. Note PSW-384.

Rappole, J. H., and M. V. McDonald. 1994. Cause and effect in population declines of migratory birds. Auk 111:652-660.

Raybourne, J. W. 1987. The black bear: home in the highlands. Pages 105-117 in H. Kallman, C. P. Agee, W. R. Goforth, J. P. Linduska, eds. Restoring America's wildlife: 1937-1987. USDI Fish & Wildl. Serv., USGPO, Washington, DC.

Rebertus, A.J., G.B. Williamson, and W.J. Platt. 1993. Impacts of temporal variation in fire regime on savanna oaks and pines. Pages 215-225 in S.M. Hermann, ed. The longleaf pine ecosystem: ecology, restoration and management. Proc. of the Tall Timbers Fire Ecology Conf. 18, Tall Timbers Research Station, Tallahassee, FL.

Reed, J. M., J. R. Walters, T. E. Emigh, and D. E. Seaman. 1993. Effective population size in red-cockaded woodpeckers: population and model differences. Conserv. Biol. 7:302-308.

Reese, K. P., and J. D. Hair. 1976. Avian species diversity in relation to beaver pond habitats in the Piedmont region of South Carolina. Proc. Annu. Conf. Southeast. Assoc. Fish and Wildl. Agencies. 30:437-447.

Reeves, H. M. 1993. Mourning dove hunting regulations. Pages 429-448 in T. S. Baskett, M. W. Sayre, R. E. Tomlinson, and R. E. Mirarchi, eds. Ecology and management of the mourning dove. Stackpole Books, Harrisburg, PA.

Reeves, H. M., and R. E. McCabe. 1993. Historical perspective. Pages 7-46 in T. S. Baskett, M. W. Sayre, R. E. Tomlinson, and R. E. Mirarchi, eds. Ecology and management of the mourning dove. Stackpole Books, Harrisburg, PA.

Reeves, H. M., R. E. Tomlinson, and J. C. Bartonek. 1993. Population characteristics and trends in the Western Management Unit. Pages 341-376 in T. S. Baskett, M. W. Sayre, R. E. Tomlinson, and R. E. Mirarchi, eds. Ecology and management of the mourning dove. Stackpole Books, Harrisburg, PA.

Reinecke, K. J., R. M. Kaminski, D. J. Moorhead, J. D. Hodges, and J. R. Nassar. 1989. Mississippi Alluvial Valley. Pages 203-247 in L. M. Smith, R. L. Pederson, and R. M. Kaminski, eds. Habitat management for migrating and wintering waterfowl in North America. Texas Tech. Univ. Press, Lubbock.

Reynolds, H. C. 1952. Studies on the reproduction in the opossum (Didelphis virginiana). Univ. California Publ. Zool. 52:223-284.

Rhodes, M. N. 1989. Effects of exploitation on population parameters of fox squirrels and gray squirrels: a hunting experiment and computer model. Ph. D. Thesis, Univ. Missouri, Columbia. 156pp.

Rice, S. M., F. S. Guthery, G. S. Spears, and J. S. DeMaso. 1993. A precipitation-habitat model for northern bobwhite on semiarid rangeland. J. Wildl. Manage. 57:92-102.

Richardson, C. J., and J. W. Gibbons. 1993. Pocosins, Carolina bays, and mountain bogs. Pages 257-310 in W. H. Martin, S. G. Boyce, and A. C. Echternacht, eds. Biodiversity of the southeastern United States, lowland terrestrial communities. John Wiley and Sons, Inc. New York, NY.

Richardson, D. M., and D. L. Smith. 1992. Hardwood removal in red-cockaded woodpecker colonies using a shear V-blade. Wildl. Soc. Bull. 20:428-433.

Richardson, D. M., and J. Stockie. 1995. Response of a small red-cockaded woodpecker population to intensive management at Noxubee National Wildlife Refuge. Pages 98-105 in D. L. Kulhavy, R. G. Hooper, and R. Costa, eds. Red-cockaded woodpecker: recovery, ecology and management. Stephen F. Austin State Univ., Nacogdoches, TX.

Richter, A. R., and R. F. Labisky. 1985. Reproductive dynamics among disjunct white-tailed deer herds in Florida. J. Wildl. Manage. 49:964-971.

Ridley, T. R., G. L. Chapman, and S. C. Loeb. 1997. Southern flying squirrel displaces a red-cockaded woodpecker from its cavity. Chat 61:112-115.

Riege, D. A. 1991. Habitat specialization and social factors in distribution of red and gray squirrels. J. Mamm. 72:152-162.

Riley, G. A., and R. T. McBride. 1972. A survey of the red wolf Canis rufus. USDI Spec. Scient. Rep., Wildl. No.162. Washington, DC. 15pp.

Ringelman, J.K., W.R. Eddleman, and H.W. Miller. 1989. High Plains reservoirs and sloughs. Pages 311-340 in L.M. Smith, R.L. Pederson, and R.M. Kaminski, eds. Habitat management for migrating and wintering waterfowl in North America. Texas Tech. Univ. Press, Lubbock.

Robbins, C. S. 1979. Effect of forest fragmentation on bird populations. Pages 198-212 in R. M. DeGraaf and K. E. Evans, eds. Management of northcentral and northeastern forests for nongame birds. USDA For. Serv. Gen. Tech. Rep. NC-51.

Robbins, C. S. 1980. Effect of forest fragmentation on breeding bird populations in the Piedmont of the mid-Atlantic region. Am. Nat. 33:31-36.

Robbins, C. S., D. K. Dawson, and B. A. Dowell. 1989a. Habitat area requirements of breeding birds of the middle Atlantic states. Wildl. Monogr. 103:1-34.

Robbins, C. S., J. R. Sauer, R. S. Greenberg, and S. Droege. 1989b. Population declines in North American birds that migrate to the Neotropics. Proc. National Acad. Sci. 86:7658-7662.

Robbins, C. S., J. W. Fitzpatrick, and P. B. Hamel. 1992. A warbler in trouble: Dendroica cerulea. Pages 549-561 in J. M. Hagan

III and D. W. Johnston, eds. Ecology and conservation of neotropical migrant landbirds. Smithsonian Institution Press, Washington, DC.

Robbins, L.E., and R.L. Myers. 1992. Seasonal effects of prescribed burning in Florida: a review. Tall Timbers Research, Inc. Misc. Publ. No. 8. Tallahassee, FL. 96 pp.

Robel, R. J. 1993. Symposium wrap-up:what is missing? Pages 156-158 in K. E. Church, and T. V. Dailey, eds. Quail III: National Quail Symp. Kansas Dep. Wildl. and Parks, Pratt.

Roberts, T. H., and D. H. Arner. 1981. Food habits of beaver in east-central Mississippi. J. Wildl. Manage. 48:1414-1419.

Roberts, T. H., and R. W. Dimmick. 1978. Distribution and breeding chronology of woodcock in Tennessee. Proc. Annu. Conf. Southeast. Assoc. Fish and Wildl. Agencies 32:8-16.

Roberts, T. H., E. P. Hill, and E. A. Gluesing. 1984. Woodcock utilization of bottomland hardwoods in the Mississippi delta. Proc. Annu. Conf. Southeast. Assoc. Fish and Wildl. Agencies 38:137-141.

Robertson, P. A., and A. A. Rosenberg. 1988. Harvesting gamebirds. Pages 177-201 in P. J. Hudson and M. R. W. Rands, eds. Ecology and management of game birds. Blackwell Scientific Publishing, Ltd. Oxford.

Robicheaux, B. L. 1978. Ecological implications of variably spaced ditches on nutria in a brackish marsh, Rockefeller Refuge, Louisiana. M.S. Thesis, Louisiana State Univ., Baton Rouge. 50pp.

Robinette, C. F., and P. D. Doerr. 1993. Survival of northern bobwhite on hunted and nonhunted study areas in the North Carolina Sandhills. Pages 74-78 in K. E. Church and T. V. Dailey, eds. Quail III: National Quail Symp. Kansas Dep. Wildl. and Parks, Pratt.

Robinson, S. K. 1988. Reappraisal of the costs and benefits of habitat heterogeneity for nongame wildlife. Trans. N. Amer. Wildl. and Nat. Res. Conf. 53:145-155.

Robinson, S. K. 1992. Population dynamics of breeding birds in a fragmented Illinois landscape. Pages 408-418 in J. M. Hagan and D. W. Johnston, eds. Ecology and conservation of neotropical migrant landbirds. Smithsonian Institution Press, Washington, DC.

Robinson, S. K., and D. S. Wilcove. 1994. Forest fragmentation in the temperate zone and its effect on migratory songbirds. Bird Conserv. Int. 4:233-249.

Robinson, S. K., F. R. Thompson III, T. M. Donovan, D. R. Whitehead, and J. Faaborg. 1995. Regional forest fragmentation and the nesting success of migratory birds. Science 267:1987-1990.

Roblee, K. L. 1987. The use of the T-culvert guard to protect road culverts from plugging damage by beavers. Proc. Eastern Wildl. Damage Control Conf. 3:25-33.

Roboski, J. C., and M. K. Causey. 1981. Incidence, habitat use, and chronology of woodcock nesting in Alabama. J. Wild. Manage. 45:793-797.

Rodgers, R. D. 1981. Factors affecting ruffed grouse drumming counts in southwestern Wisconsin. J. Wildl. Manage. 45:409-418.

Roelke, M. E., J. S. Martenson, and J. J. O'Brien. 1993. The consequences of demographic reduction and genetic depletion in the endangered Florida panther. Current Biol. 3:340-350.

Rogers, M. E., L. K. Halls, and J. G. Dickson. 1990. Deer habitat in the Ozark forests of Arkansas. USDA Forest Service Res. Pap. SO-259. 17pp.

Rolley, R. E. 1987. Bobcat. Pages 670-681 in M. Novak, J. A. Baker, M. E. Obbard, and B. Malloch. eds. Wild furbearer management and conservation in North America. Ministry of Natural Resources, Ontario.

Rolley, R. E. 1983. Behavior and population dynamics of bobcats in Oklahoma. Ph.D. Thesis, Oklahoma State Univ., Stillwater. 109pp.

Romin, L. A., and J. A. Bissonette. 1996. Deer-vehicle collisions: status of state monitoring activities and mitigation efforts. Wildl. Soc. Bull. 24:276-283.

Roosevelt, T. 1908. In the Louisiana Canebrakes. Scribners Magazine. (Reprinted by Louisiana Wild. and Fish. Comm. 1962). Wild. Education Bull. 59. 11pp.

Rosatte, R. C. 1987. Striped, spotted, hooded, and hog-nosed skunk. Pages 599-613 in M. Novak, J. A. Baker, M. E. Obbard, and B. Malloch, eds. Wild Furbearer Management and Conservation in North America. Ontario Ministry of Natural Resour., Ontario Trappers Assoc., North Bay.

Rose, G. B. 1977. Mortality rates of tagged adult cottontail rabbits. J. Wildl. Manage. 41:511-514.

Roseberry, J. L. 1964. Some response of bobwhite to snow cover in southern Illinois. J. Wildl. Manage. 28:244-249.

Roseberry, J. L. 1979. Bobwhite population responses to exploitation: real and simulated. J Wildl. Manage. 43:285-305.

Roseberry, J. L. 1993. Bobwhite and the "new" biology. Pages 16-20. in K. E. Church and T. V. Dailey, eds. Quail III: National Quail Symp. Kansas Dep. Wildl. and Parks, Pratt.

Roseberry, J. L., and W. D. Klimstra. 1984. Population ecology of the bobwhite. Southern Illinois Univ. Press, Carbondale. 259 pp.

Roseberry, J. L., B. G. Peterjohn, and W. D. Klimstra. 1979. Dynamics of an unexploited bobwhite population in deteriorating habitat. J. Wildl. Manage. 43:306-315.

Rosenberg, K. V., and S. E. Barker. 1998. Cerulean Warbler Atlas Project Southeast Interim Report. Unpublished Report submitted to USDA Fish and Wildl. Serv., Atlanta, GA. 7pp.

Rosene, W. 1969. The bobwhite quail: Its life and management. Rutgers Univ. Press, New Brunswick, NJ. 418pp.

Rostlund, E. 1957. The myth of a natural prairie belt in Alabama: an interpretation of historical records. Annals of the Assoc. of Amer. Geographers 47:392-411.

Roth, R. R. 1976. Spatial heterogeneity and bird species diversity. Ecology 57:773-782.

Roughton, R. D., and M. W. Sweeny. 1982. Refinements in scent-station methodology for assessing trends in carnivore populations. J. Wildl. Manage. 46:217-229.

Rowe, C. L., O. M. Kinney, A. P. Fiori, and J. D. Congdon. 1996. Oral deformities in tadpoles (Rana catesbeiana) associated with coal ash deposition: effects on grazing ability and growth. Freshwater Biol. 36:723-730.

Roy, M. S., E. Geffen, D. Smith, and R. K. Wayne. 1996. Molecular genetics of pre-1940 red wolves. Conserv. Biol. 10:1413-1424.

Rucker, R. A., M. L. Kennedy, G. A. Heidt, and M. J. Harvey. 1989. Population density, movements, and habitat use of bobcats in Arkansas. Southwest. Nat. 34:101-108.

Rucker, R. A., and R. Tumlinson. 1985. Biology of the bobcat in Arkansas. Final Report. Fed. Aid. Wildl. Restor. Proj. No. W-56-24, Study No. XV. 225pp.

Rudis, V. A., and J. B. Tansey. 1995. Regional assessment of remote forests and black bear habitat from forest resource surveys. J. Wildl. Manage. 59:170-180.

Rudnicky, T. C., and M. L. Hunter, Jr. 1993. Reversing the fragmentation perspective: effects of clearcut size and bird species richness in Maine. Ecol. Applications 3:357-366.

Rudolph, D. C., and R. N. Conner. 1996. Red-cockaded woodpeckers and silvicultural practice: is uneven-aged silviculture preferable to even-aged? Wildl. Soc. Bull. 24:330-333.

Rudolph, D. C., R. N. Conner, and J. Turner. 1990. Competition for red-cockaded woodpecker roost and nest cavities: effects of resin age and entrance diameter. Wilson Bull. 102:23-36.

Rudolph, D. C., R. N. Conner, D. K. Carrie, and R. R. Shaefer. 1992. Experimental reintroduction of red-cockaded woodpeckers. Auk 109:914-916.

Rudolph, D. C., and J. G. Dickson. 1990. Streamside zone width and amphibian and reptile abundance. Southwest. Nat. 35:472-476.

Rusch, D. H, J. C. Wood, and G. G. Zenner. 1996. The dilemma of giant Canada goose management. Pages 72-78 in J. T. Ratti, ed. Proc. 7th International Waterfowl Symp., Ducks Unlimited, Inc., Memphis, TN.

Russell, D. M. 1974. The dove shooter's handbook. Winchester Press, New York, NY. 256pp.

Russell, D. M. 1993. Hunting in the South. Pages 449-558 in T. S. Baskett, M. W. Sayre, R. E. Tomlinson, and R. E. Mirarchi, eds. Ecology and management of the mourning dove. Stackpole Books, Harrisburg, PA.

Sadler, K. C. 1993a. Other natural mortality. Pages 225-230 in T. S. Baskett, M. W. Sayre, R. E. Tomlinson, and R. E. Mirarchi, eds. Ecology and management of the mourning dove. Stackpole Books, Harrisburg, PA.

Sadler, K. C. 1993b. Mourning dove harvest. Pages 449-558 in T. S. Baskett, M. W. Sayre, R. E. Tomlinson, and R. E. Mirarchi, eds. Ecology and management of the mourning dove. Stackpole Books, Harrisburg, PA.

Samuel, D. E., and B. B. Nelson. 1984. Foxes. Pages 475-490 in J. A. Chapman, and G. A. Feldhamer, eds. Wild mammals of North America. Johns Hopkins Univ. Press, Baltimore, MD.

Samuel, W. M. 1994. The parasites and diseases of whitetails. Pages 233-235 in D. Gerlach, S. Atwater, and J. Schnell, eds. Deer. Stackpole Books, Mechanicsburg, PA.

Sanders, O. T. 1978. An evaluation of bear sanctuaries. Proc. East. Black Bear Workshop. 4:278-297.

Sanderson, G. C. 1980. Conservation of waterfowl. Pages 43-58 in F. C. Bellrose, ed. Ducks, geese and swans of North America. Stackpole Books, Harrisburg, PA.

Sanderson, G. C., and F. C. Bellrose. 1969. Wildlife habitat management of wetlands. Suppl. Dos An. Acad. Brasil. Cienc. 41:153-204.

Sanderson, G. C., and F. C. Bellrose. 1986. A review of the problem of lead poisoning in waterfowl. Ill. Nat. Hist. Surv. Spec. Publ. No. 4. 34pp.

Sanderson, H. R. 1975. Den-tree management for tree squirrels. Wildl. Soc. Bull. 3:125-131.

Sanderson, H. R., W. M. Healy, J. C. Pack, J. D. Gill, and J. W. Thomas. 1975. Gray squirrel habitat and nest-tree preference. Proc. Annu. Conf. Southeast. Assoc. Game and Fish Comm. 29:609-616.

Sargeant, A. B., S. H. Allen, and J. O. Hastings. 1987. Spatial relations between sympatric coyotes and red foxes in North Dakota. J. Wildl. Manage. 51:285-293.

Sargeant, A. B., and D. H. Raveling. 1992. Mortality during the breeding season. Pages 396-422 in B. D. J. Batt, A. D. Aften, M. G. Anderson, C. D. Ankney, D. H. Johnson, J. A. Kadlec, and G. L. Krapu, eds. Ecology and management of breeding waterfowl. Univ. Minnesota Press, Minneapolis.

Sargeant, A. B., M. A. Sovada, and T. L. Shaffer. 1995. Seasonal predator removal relative to hatch rate of duck nests in waterfowl production areas. Wildl. Soc. Bull. 23:507-513.

Sargeant, A. B., G. A. Swanson, and H. A. Doty. 1973. Selective predation by mink, Mustela vison, on waterfowl. Am. Midl. Nat. 89:208-214.

Sasse, D. B., and P. J. Pekins. 1994. The summer roosting behavior of bats on the White Mountain National Forest. Bat Res. News 35:113-114.

Sattler, P., and N. Reichenbach. 1998. The effects of timbering on Plethodon hubrichti: short-term effects. J. Herp. 32:399-404.

Sauer, J. R., and S. Droege. 1990. Wood duck population trends from the North American breeding bird survey. Pages 225-231 in L. H. Fredrickson, G. V. Burger, S. P. Havera, D. A. Graber, R. E. Kirby, and T. S. Taylor, eds. Proc. 1988 N. Am. Wood Duck Symp., St. Louis, MO.

Sauer, J. R., J. E. Hines, G. Gough, I. Thomas, and B. G. Peterjohn. 1997. The North American Breeding Bird Survey Results and Analysis. Version 96.4. Patuxent Wildlife Research Center, Laurel, MD

Saugey, D. A., D. R. Heath, and G. A. Heidt. 1989. The bats of the Ouachita Mountains. Proc. Arkansas Acad. Science 43:71-77.

Saugey, D. A., R. L. Vaughn, B. G. Crump, and G. A. Heidt. 1998. Notes on the natural history of Lasiurus borealis in Arkansas. J. Arkansas Acad. Science 52:92-98.

Sawyer, D. T., and T. T. Fendley. 1994. Seasonal habitat use by gray foxes on the Savannah River site. Proc. Annu. Conf. Southeast. Assoc. Fish and Wildl. Agencies 48:162-172.

Sawyer, S. L., and R. K. Rose. 1985. Homing and ecology of the southern flying squirrel, Glaucomys volans in southeastern Virginia. Am. Midl. Nat. 113:238-244.

Sayre, M. W., and N. J. Silvy. 1993. Nesting and production. Pages 81-104 in T. S. Baskett, M. W. Sayre, R. E. Tomlinson, and R. E. Mirarchi, eds. Ecology and management of the mourning dove. Stackpole Books, Harrisburg, PA.

Sayre, M. W., T. S. Baskett, and R. E. Mirarchi. 1993. Behavior. Pages 161-180 in T. S. Baskett, M. W. Sayre, R. E. Tomlinson, and R. E. Mirarchi, eds. Ecology and management of the mourning dove. Stackpole Books, Harrisburg, PA.

Schafale, M.P., and A.S. Weakley. 1990. Classification of the natural communities of North Carolina, third approximation. North Carolina Natural Heritage Program. North Carolina Dep. Env., Health, and Nat. Resources, Raleigh.

Schemnitz, S. D. 1980. Wildlife management techniques manual. The Wildlife Society, Washington, DC. 686pp.

Schmidly, D. J. 1983. Texas mammals east of the Balcones Fault zone. Texas A&M Univ. Press, College Station. 400pp.

Schmidly, D. J. 1986. Wilderness preserves and small mammals in the eastern United States. Pages 44-48 in D. L. Kulhavy and R. N. Conner, eds. Wilderness and natural areas in the eastern United States: a management challenge. Stephen F. Austin State Univ., Nacogdoches, TX.

Schnell, J. H. 1964. A mink exterminates an insular cotton rat population. J. Mamm. 45:305-306.

Schoeneberger, P. 1995. Soils, geomorphology, and land use of the southeastern United States. Pages 58-82 in S. Fox and R. A. Mickler, eds. Impact of air pollutants on southern pine forests. Springer- Verlag, New York, NY.

Schorger, A. W. 1944. The quail in early Wisconsin. Trans. Wisconsin Acad. Sci., Arts, and Letters. 36:77-103.

Schroeder, R. L. 1985. Habitat suitability models: northern bobwhite. Biol. Rep. 82 (10.104) U.S. Fish. And Wildl. Serv., Washington, D. C. 32pp.

Schulze, E. D. 1989. Air pollution and forest decline in a spruce (Picea abies) forest. Science 244:776-783.

Scott, C. D., and M. R. Pelton. 1975. Seasonal food habits of the European wild hog in the Great Smoky Mountains National Park. Proc. Annu. Conf. Southeast. Assoc. Fish & Wildl. Agencies 29:585-593.

Scott, V. E. 1979. Bird responses to snag removal in ponderosa pine. J. For. 77:26-28.

Scott, V. E., K. E. Evans, D. R. Patton, and C. P. Stone. 1977. Cavity-nesting birds of North American forests. USDA For. Serv. Agric. Handb. 511, 112pp.

Seal, U. S., R. C. Lacy, and Workshop Participants. 1992. Genetic management strategies and population viability of the Florida panther. USDI Fish and Wildl. Serv. Rep. to the Cons. Breeding Specialist Group, Species Survival Comm., IUCN, Apple Valley, MN.

Sealander, J. A. 1943. Winter food habits of mink in southern Michigan. J. Wildl. Manage. 7:411-417.

Sealander, J. A. 1979. A guide to Arkansas mammals. River Road Press, Conway, AR. 313pp.

Sealander, J. A., and G. A. Heidt. 1990. Arkansas mammals: their natural history, classification, and distribution. Univ. Arkansas Press, Fayetteville. 308pp.

Seidensticker, J., M. A. O'Connell, and A. J. T. Johnsingh. 1987. Virginia opossum. Pages 247-261 in M. Novak, J. A. Baker, M. E. Obbard, and B. Malloch, eds. Wild Furbearer Management and Conservation in North America. Ontario Ministry of Natural Resour., Ontario Trappers Assoc., North Bay.

Seiss, R. S. 1989. Reproductive parameters and survival rates of wild turkey hens in east-central Mississippi. M. S. Thesis, Mississippi State Univ., Mississippi State. 99pp.

Seiss, R. S., P. S. Phalen, and G. A. Hurst. 1990. Wild turkey nesting habitat and success rates. Proc. National Wild Turkey Symp. 6:18-24.

Semlitsch, R. D. 1983. Terrestrial movements of an eastern tiger salamander, Ambystoma tigrinum. Herp. Rev. 14:112-113.

Semlitsch, R. D. 1987. Relationship of pond drying to the reproductive success of the salamander Ambystoma talpoideum. Copeia 1987:61-69.

Semlitsch, R. D. 1998. Biological delineation of terrestrial buffer zones for pond-breeding amphibians. Conserv. Biol. 12:1113-1119.

Semlitsch, R.D., and J.R. Bodie. 1998. Are small, isolated wetlands expendable? Cons. Biology 12:1129-1133.

Sermon, W. O., and D. W. Speake. 1987. Production of second broods by northern bobwhites. Wilson Bull. 99:285-286.

Servello, F. A., and R. L. Kirkpatrick. 1987. Regional variation in the nutritional ecology of ruffed grouse. J. Wildl. Manage. 51:749-770.

Sexton, O. J. 1990. Replacement of fox squirrels by gray squirrels in a suburban habitat. Am. Midl. Nat. 124:198-205.

Shadowen, H. E., 1963. A live-trap study of small mammals in Louisiana. J. Mamm. 44:103-108.

Sharitz, R.R., and C. A. Gresham. 1998. Pocosins and Carolina bays. Pages 343-377 in M.G. Messina and W.C. Conner, eds. Southern Forested Wetlands. Lewis Publishers, New York, NY.

Sharitz, R. R., and W. J. Mitsch. 1993. Southern floodplain forests. Pages 311-372 in W. H. Martin, S. G. Boyce, and A. C. Echternacht, eds. Biodiversity of the southeastern United States, lowland terrestrial communities. John Wiley and Sons, Inc. New York, NY.

Shaw, J. H. 1975. Ecology, behavior, and systematics of the red wolf Canis rufus. Ph.D. Thesis, Yale Univ., New Haven, CT. 99pp.

Shea, S. M., and J. S. Osborne. 1995. Poor quality habitats. Pages 193-209 in K. V. Miller and R. L. Marchinton, eds. Quality whitetails: the why and how of quality deer management. Stackpole Books, Mechanicsburg, PA.

Sheffield, R. M., and J. G. Dickson. 1998. The South's forest land - on the hot seat to provide more. Proc. N. Amer. Wildl. and Natural Res. Conf: 63:316-331.

Sheffield, S. R., and H. H. Thomas. 1997. Mustela frenata. Mammalian Species. Amer. Soc. Mamm. 570:1-9.

Sheldon, W. G. 1949. Reproductive behavior of foxes in New York State. J. Mamm. 30:236-246.

Sheldon, W. G. 1971. The book of the American woodcock. Univ. Massachusetts Press, Amherst. 277pp.

Shoop, C. R., and C. A. Ruckdeschel. 1990. Alligators as predators on terrestrial mammals. Amer. Midl. Nat. 124:407-412.

Shropshire, C. C. 1996. History, status, and habitat components of black bears in Mississippi. Ph.D. Thesis, Mississippi State Univ., Mississippi State. 295pp.

Shugars, J. C. 1986. Harvest analysis of a Maryland gray squirrel population. Proc. Annu. Conf. Southeast. Assoc. Fish and Wildl. Agencies 40:382-388.

Shugart, H. H., Jr, and D. James. 1973. Ecological succession of breeding bird populations in northwestern Arkansas. Auk 90:62-77.

Silver, H., and W. T. Silver. 1969. Growth and behavior of the coyote-like canid of northern New England with observations on canid hybrids. Wildl. Mono. 17:1-41.

Simpson, M. B., Jr. 1992. Birds of the Blue Ridge Mountains. Univ. North Carolina Press, Chapel Hill. 354pp.

Simpson, R. C. 1972. A study of bobwhite quail nest initiation dates, clutch sizes, and hatch sizes in southwestern Georgia. Pages 199-204 in J. A. Morrison and J. C. Lewis, eds. Proc. First National Bobwhite Quail Symp. Oklahoma State Univ., Stillwater.

Simpson, R. C. 1976. Certain aspects of the bobwhite quail's life history and population dynamics in southwest Georgia. Georgia Dep. Nat. Resour., Game and Fish Div. Tech. Bull. WL1. Atlanta, GA. 117pp.

Singer, F. C., D. K. Otto, A. R. Tipton, and C. P. Hable. 1981. Home ranges, movements, and habitat use of European wild boar in Tennessee. J. Wildl. Manage. 45:343-353.

Singer, F. J., W. T. Swank, and E. E. C. Clebsch. 1982. Some ecosystem responses to European wild boar rooting in a deciduous forest. Res./Resour. Manage. Rep. No. 54, U.S. Dep. Int., National Park Service, SERO, Atlanta, GA. 31pp.

Skeen, J. N., P. D. Doerr, and D. H. Van Lear. 1993. Chapter 1: oak-hickory-pine forests. Pages 1-35 in W. H. Martin, S. G. Boyce, and A. C. Echternacht, eds. Biodiversity of the southeastern United States: Upland Terrestrial Communities. John Wiley and Sons, Inc., New York, NY.

Slate, D., R. Owens, G. E. Connolly, and G. Simmons. 1992. Decision making for wildlife damage management. Trans. N. Am. Wildl. Nat. Resour. Conf. 57:51-62.

Small, C.J., and T.R. Wentworth. 1998. Characterization of montane cedar-hardwood woodlands in the Piedmont and Blue Ridge Provinces of North Carolina. Castanea 63:241-261.

Smith, C. C. 1968. The adaptive nature of social organization in the genus of tree squirrels Tamiasciurus. Ecol. Monogr. 38:31-63.

Smith, D. M. 1962. The practice of silviculture. John Wiley and Sons, New York, NY. 552pp.

Smith, D. M. 1986. The practice of silviculture. John Wiley and Sons, New York, NY. 51pp.

Smith, H. C., N. I. Lamson, and G. W. Miller. 1989. An aesthetic alternative to clearcutting? Deferment cutting in eastern hardwoods. J. For. 87:14-18.

Smith, H. M., Jr. 1981. Parasites of wild swine (Sus scrofa) in the southeastern United States. M.S. Thesis, Univ. Georgia, Athens. 126pp.

Smith, K. G. 1977. Distribution of summer birds along a forest moisture gradient in an Ozark watershed. Ecology 58:810-819.

Smith, K. G., and J. D. Clark. 1994. Black bears in Arkansas: characteristics of a successful translocation. J. Mamm. 75:309-320.

Smith, N. B., and F. S. Barkalow, Jr. 1967. Precocious breeding in the gray squirrel. J. Mamm. 48:328-330.

Smith, R. A., and M. L. Kennedy. 1983. Taxonomic status of the coyote in Tennessee. Proc. Annu. Conf. Southeast. Assoc. Fish and Wildl. Agencies 37:219-227.

Smith, T. R., and M. R. Pelton. 1989. Home ranges and movements of black bears in a bottomland hardwood forest in Arkansas. Int. Conf. Bear Res. and Manage. 8:213-218.

Smith, W. P. 1991. Odocoileus virginianus. Mammalian Species 388:1-13.

Smith, W. P., and R. D. Teitelbaum. 1986. Habitat use by eastern wild turkey hens in southeastern Louisiana. Proc. Ann. Conf. Southeast. Assoc. Fish and Wildl. Agencies 40:405-415.

Smith, W. P., P. B. Hamel, and R. P. Ford. 1996. Mississippi Alluvial Valley forest conversion: implications for Eastern North American avifauna. Proc. 1993 Annu. Conf. Southeast. Assoc. Fish and Wildl. Agencies 47:460-469.

Sole, J. 1991. Kentucky Department of Fish & Wildlife Resources current ruffed grouse projects - Summary. 8pp.

Sole, J. D. 1994. Assessing swamp rabbit distribution in Kentucky. Proc Annu. Conf. Southeast. Assoc. Fish and Wildl. Agencies 48:145-151.

Sonenshine, D. E., D. M. Lauer, T. C. Walker, and B. L. Elisberg. 1979. The ecology of Glaucomys volans in Virginia. Acta Theriologica 24:363-377.

Sonenshine, D. E., and G. F. Levy. 1981. Vegetative associations affecting Glaucomys volans in Central Virginia Phytosociology, flying squirrel, forest area. Acta Theriologica 26:359-371.

Sonenshine, D. E., and E. L. Winslow. 1972. Contrasts in distribution of raccoons in two Virginia localities. J. Wildl. Manage. 36:838-847.

Soulliere, G. J. 1990. Review of wood duck nest-cavity characteristics. Pages 153-162 in L. H. Fredrickson, G. V. Burger, S. P. Havera, D. A. Graber, R. E. Kirby, and T. S. Taylor, eds. Proc. 1988 N. Am. Wood Duck Symp., St. Louis, MO.

Southern Appalachian Man and The Biosphere (SAMAB). 1996. The Southern Appalachian Assessment (SAA) Terrestrial Tech. Rep. Rep. 5 of 5. USDA For. Serv., Southern Region, Atlanta, GA.

Soutiere, E. C., and E. G. Bolen. 1972. Role of fire in mourning dove nesting ecology. Proc. Ann. Tall Timbers Fire Ecol. Conf. 12:277-288.

Speake, D. W., T. E. Lynch, W. J. Fleming, G. A. Wright, and W. J. Hamrick. 1975. Habitat use and seasonal movements of wild turkeys in the Southeast. Proc. National Wild Turkey Symp. 3:122-130.

Spears, G. S., F. S. Guthery, S. M. Rice, S. J. DeMaso, and B. Zaiglin. 1993. Optimum seral stage for northern bobwhite as influenced by site productivity. J. Wildl. Manage. 57:805-811.

Stafford, S. K., and R. W. Dimmick. 1979. Autumn and winter foods of ruffed grouse in the southern Appalachians. J. Wildl. Manage. 43:121-127.

Stalkneslit, D. E., V. F. Nettles, G. A. Erickson, and D. A. Jessup. 1986. Antibodies to vesicular stomatitis in populations of feral swine in the United States. J. Wildl. Dis. 22:320-325.

Stamps, R. T., and P. D. Doerr. 1977. Reproductive maturation and breeding of woodcock in North Carolina. Proc. Woodcock Symp. 6:185-190.

Stanford, J. A. 1972. Bobwhite quail population dynamics: relationships of weather, nesting, production patterns, fall populations characteristics, and harvest. Pages 115-139 in J. A. Morrison and J. C. Lewis, eds. Proc. First National Bobwhite Quail Symp. Oklahoma State Univ. Stillwater.

Stapper, R. J., D. L. Rakestraw, D. B. Fagre, and N. J. Silvy. 1989. A comparison of scent-station surveys and track counts for monitoring furbearers. Proc. Annu. Conf. Southeast. Assoc. Fish and Wildl. Agencies 43:452-459.

Stauffer, D. F., and L. B. Best. 1980. Habitat selection by birds of riparian communities: evaluating effects of habitat alterations. J. Wildl. Manage. 44:1-15.

Steele, M. A. 1998. Tamiasciurus hudsonicus. Mammalian Species Number 586. Am. Soc. Mamm. 9pp.

Steen, H. K. 1976. The U.S. Forest Service, a history. Univ. Washington Press, Seattle. 346pp.

Stegeman, L. J. 1938. The European wild boar in the Cherokee National Forest, Tennessee. J. Mamm. 19:279-290.

Stephenson, S. L., A. N. Ash, and D. F. Stauffer. 1993. Appalachian oak forests. Pages 255-304 in W. H. Martin, S. G. Boyce, and A. C. Echternacht, eds. Biodiversity of the southeastern United States, upland terrestrial communities. John Wiley and Sons, New York.

Still, H. R., Jr., and D. P. Baumann, Jr. 1990. Wild turkey nesting ecology on the Francis Marion National Forest. Proc. National Wild Turkey Symp. 6:13-17.

Stine, C. J. 1984. The life history and status of the eastern tiger salamander, Ambystoma tigrinum tigrinum (Green) in Maryland. Bull. Maryland Herp. Soc. 20:65-108.

Stoddard, H. L. 1931. The bobwhite quail: its habits, preservation, and increase. Charles Scribner's Sons, New York, NY. 559pp.

Stoddard, H. L. 1963. Maintenance and increase of the eastern wild turkey on private lands of the coastal plain of the deep southeast. Tall Timbers Res. Sta. Bull. 3. 49pp.

Stoll, R. J., Jr., and M. W. McClain. 1988. Body weights of Ohio ruffed grouse (Bonasa umbellus). Ohio J. Sci. 88:126-131.

Stoll, R. J., Jr., M. W. McClain, R. L. Boston, and G. P. Honchul.

1979. Ruffed grouse drumming site characteristics in Ohio. J. Wildl. Manage. 43:324-333.

Storm, G. L., and W. M. Tzilkowski. 1982. Furbearer population dynamics: a local and regional management perspective. Pages 69-90 in G. C. Sanderson, ed. Midwest furbearer management. Proc. 43rd Mid-west Conf., KS.

Story, J. D., W. J. Galbraith, and J. T. Kitchings. 1982. Food habits of bobcats in eastern Tennessee. J. Tennessee Acad. Sci. 57:29-32.

Stout, I.J., and W.R. Marion. 1993. Pine flatwoods and xeric pine forest of the southern (lower) Coastal Plain. Pages 373-446 in W.H. Martin, S.G. Boyce, and A.C. Echternacht, eds. Biodiversity of the southeastern United States: lowland terrestrial communities. John Wiley & Sons, New York, NY.

Stout, I. J., and D. E. Sonenshine. 1974a. Ecology of an opossum population in Virginia, 1963-69. Acta Theriol. 19:235-245.

Stout, I. J., and D. E. Sonenshine. 1974b. A striped skunk population in Virginia, 1963-69. Chesapeake Sci. 15:14-145.

Stout, R. J., R. C. Stedman, D. J. Decker, and B. A. Knuth. 1993. Perceptions of risk from deer-related vehicle accidents: implications for public preferences for deer herd size. Wildl. Soc. Bull. 21:237-249.

Stransky, J. J., and L. K. Halls. 1980. Fruiting of woody plants affected by site preparation and prior land use. J. Wildl. Manage. 44:258-263.

Stransky, J. J., and R. D. Harlow. 1981. Effects of fire on deer habitat in the Southeast. Pages 135-142 in G. W. Wood, ed. Prescribed fire and wildlife in southern forests. Belle Baruch For. Sci. Inst., Clemson Univ., SC.

Stratton, D.A., and P.S. White. 1982. Grassy balds of Great Smoky Mountains National Park: vascular plant floristics, rare plant distributions, and an assessment of the floristic data base. USDI NPS Research/Resource Management Report SER-58. Southeast Regional Office, Atlanta, GA. 33 p.

Strausberg, S., and W.A. Hough. 1997. The Ouachita and Ozark-St. Francis National Forests: a history of the lands and USDA Forest Service tenure. Gen. Tech. Rep. SO-121. 45pp.

Straw, J. A., Jr., D. G. Krementz, M. W. Olinde, and G. F. Sepik. 1994. American woodcock. Pages 97-114 in T. C. Tacha and C. E. Braun, eds. Migratory shore and upland game bird management in North America. Int. Assoc. Fish and Wildl. Agencies, Washington, DC.

Stribling, H. L., and W. B. Mikel. 1991. Cooking Alabama's wild game. Ala. Coop. Ext. Serv. Publ. No. HE-587. 83pp.

Stromayer, K. A. K., and R. J. Warren. 1997. Are overabundant deer herds in the eastern United States creating alternate stable states in forest plant communities? Wildl. Soc. Bull. 25:227-234.

Stys, E. D., and B. D. Leopold. 1993. Reproductive biology and kitten growth of captive bobcats in Mississippi. Proc. Annu. Conf. Southeast. Assoc. Fish and Wildl. Agencies 47:80-89.

Suchy, W. J., and R. J. Munkel. 1993. Breeding strategies of the northern bobwhite in marginal habitat. Pages 69-73 in K. E. Church and T. V. Dailey, eds. Quail III: National Quail Symp. Kansas Dep. Wildl. and Parks, Pratt.

Sullivan, E. G. 1956. Gray fox reproduction, denning, range and weights in Alabama. J. Mamm. 37:346-351.

Sullivan, K. J. 1995. Diel activity and movement patterns of adult bobcats in central Mississippi. M.S. Thesis, Mississippi State Univ., Mississippi State. 60pp.

Sumner, P. W. 1984. Movements, home range, and habitat use by coyotes in east Mississippi and West Alabama. M.S. Thesis, Mississippi State Univ., Mississippi State. 104pp.

Sumner, P. W., and E. P. Hill. 1980. Scent-stations as indices of abundance in some furbearers of Alabama. Proc. Annu. Conf. Southeast. Assoc. Fish and Wildl. Agencies 34:572-583.

Sumner, P. W., E. P. Hill, and J. B. Wooding. 1984. Activity and movements of coyotes in Mississippi and Alabama. Proc. Annu. Conf. Southeast. Assoc. Fish and Wildl. Agencies 38:174-181.

Sutter, R.D., and R. Kral. 1994. The ecology, status, and conservation of two non-alluvial wetland communities in the south Atlantic and eastern Gulf coastal plain, USA. Biological Conserv. 68: 235-243.

Svendsen, G. E. 1982. Weasels. Pages 613-628 in J. A. Chapman and G. A. Feldhamer, eds. Wild mammals of North America: biology, management, and economics. Johns Hopkins Univ. Press, Baltimore, MD.

Swanson, D. A., J. C. Pack, C. I. Taylor, D. Samuel, and P. W. Brown. 1996. Selective timber harvesting and wild turkey reproduction in West Virginia. Proc. Wild Turkey Symp. 7:81-88.

Sweeney, J. M. 1970. Preliminary investigation of a feral hog (Sus scrofa) population on the Savannah River Plant, SC. M.S. Thesis, Univ. Georgia, Athens. 58pp.

Sweeney, J. M., and J. R. Sweeney. 1982. Feral Hog. Pages 1099-1113 in J. A. Chapman and G. A. Feldhammer eds. Wild mammals of North America: biology, management, and economics. Johns Hopkins Univ. Press, Baltimore, MD.

Tabatabai, F. R. 1988. Ecology of the raccoon (Procyon lotor) in Tennessee. Ph.D. Thesis, Memphis State Univ., Memphis. 188pp.

Tanner, J. T. 1942. The Ivory-billed Woodpecker. National Audubon Soc. Resour. Pap. No. 1. National Audubon Soc., New York, NY. 111pp.

Tapley, J., R. Abernethy, J. E. Kennamer, and W. M. Healy. 2001. Status of wild turkey hunting in North America. Proc. National Wild Turkey Symp. 8:(in press).

Tappe, P. A., R. E. Thill, M. A. Melchoirs, and T. B. Wigley. 1994. Wildlife values of streamside management zones in the Ouachita Mountains, Arkansas. Pages 122-138 in Riparian ecosystems in the humid U.S.: functions, values, and management. National. Assoc. Conserv. Dist., Washington, DC.

Tappe, P. A., and R. M. Whiting, Jr. 1989. Correlation of woodcock counts with habitat types in eastern Texas. Proc. Annu. Conf. Southeast. Assoc. Fish and Wildl. Agencies 43:346-349.

Tarver, J., G. Linscombe, and N. Kinler. 1987. Fur animals, alligator, and the fur industry in Louisiana. La. Dep. Wildl. and Fisheries, Baton Rouge, LA. 74pp.

Tassone, J. F. 1981. Utility of hardwood leave strips for breeding birds in Virginia's central Piedmont. M.S. Thesis, Virginia Polytechnic Inst. and State Univ., Blacksburg. 83pp.

Taulman, J. F., K. G. Smith, and R. E. Thill. 1998. Demographic and behavioral responses of southern flying squirrels to experimental logging in Arkansas. Ecol. Appl. 8:1144-1155.

Taylor, C. I. 1979. Movements, activities, and survival of translocated raccoons in east Tennessee. M. S. Thesis, Univ. Tennessee, Knoxville. 178pp.

Taylor, C. J. 1973. Present status and habitat survey of the Delmarva fox squirrel (Sciurus niger cinereus) with a discussion of reasons for its decline. Proc. Annu. Conf. Southeast.

Assoc. Game and Fish Comm. 27:278-289.

Taylor, J. D. 1996. Northern bobwhite habitat use and reproductive success in managed old field habitats in Mississippi. M.S. Thesis, Mississippi State University, Mississippi State. 103pp.

Taylor, J. D., and L. W. Burger, Jr., 1997. Reproductive effort and success of northern bobwhite in Mississippi. Annu. Conf. Southeast Assoc. Fish and Wildlife Agencies 51:329-341.

Taylor, J. D., and L. W. Burger, Jr. 2000. Habitat use of breeding bobwhite in managed oldfield habitats in Mississippi. Quail IV: Fourth National Quail Symp. 4:7-15.

Taylor, J. D., L. W. Burger, Jr., S. W. Manley, and L. A. Brennan. 2000. Seasonal survival and cause-specific mortality of northern bobwhite in Mississippi. Quail IV: Fourth National Quail Symp. 4:103-107.

Taylor, J. S., and F. S. Guthery. 1994a. Daily movements of northern bobwhite broods in Southern Texas. Wilson Bull. 106:148-150.

Taylor, J. S., and F. S. Guthery. 1994b. Components of northern bobwhite brood habitat in southern Texas. The Southwestern Natural. 39:73-77.

Taylor, R. 1991. The feral hog in Texas. Texas Parks and Wildlife Dep., Austin, TX. 19 pp.

Taylor, W. P., and D. W. Lay. 1944. Ecological niches occupied by rabbits in eastern Texas. Ecology 25:120-121.

Teasley, R. J., J. C. Bergstrom, H. K. Cordell, S. J. Zarnoch, and P. Gentle. 1999. Private Lands and Outdoor recreation in the United States. Pages 183-218 in H. K. Cordell, Principal Investigator. Outdoor recreation in American life: a national assessment of demand and supply trends. Sagamore Publ., Champaign, IL.

Temple, S. A. 1986. Predicting impacts of habitat fragmentation on forest birds: a comparison of two models. Pages 301-304 in J. Verner, M. L. Morrison, and C. J. Ralph, eds. Wildlife 2000: modeling habitat relationships of terrestrial vertebrates. Univ. Wisconsin Press, Madison.

Temple, S. A., and J. R. Cary. 1988. Modeling dynamics of habitat-interior bird populations in fragmented landscapes. Conserv. Biol. 2:340-347

Tennessee Wildlife Resources Agency. 1996. Wildlife Research Report. Small Game Harvest Report. TWRA Tech. Rep. 96-1. 51pp.

Terborgh, J. 1989. Where have all the birds gone? Princeton Univ. Press, Princeton, NJ. 207pp.

Thackston, R. E., P. E. Hale, A. S. Johnson, and J. J. Harris. 1982. Chemical composition of mountain-laurel leaves from burned and unburned sites. J. Wildl. Manage. 46:492-496.

Theberge, J. B., and C. H. R. Wedeles. 1989. Prey selection and habitat partitioning in sympatric coyote and fox populations, southwest Yukon. Can. J. Zool. 67:1285-1290.

Thomas, D. W. 1988. The distribution of bats in different ages of Douglas-fir forests. J. Wild. Manage. 52:619-626.

Thomas, D. W., M. Dorais, and J. M. Bergeron. 1990. Winter energy budgets and cost of arousals for hibernating little brown bats (Myotis lucifugus). J. Mamm. 71:475-479.

Thompson, F. R., III. 1993. Simulated responses of a forest-interior bird population to forest management options in central hardwood forests of the United States. Conserv. Biol. 7:325-333.

Thompson, F. R., III. 1994. Temporal and spatial patterns of breeding brown-headed cowbirds in the Midwestern United States. Auk 111:979-990.

Thompson, F. R., III., and D. R. Dessecker. 1997. Management of early-successional communities in central hardwood forests: with special emphasis on the ecology and management of oaks, ruffed grouse, and forest songbirds. USDA For. Serv. Gen. Tech. Rep. NC-195.

Thompson, F. R., III, W. D. Dijak, T. G. Kulowiec, and D. A. Hamilton. 1992. Effects of even-aged forest management on breeding bird densities. J. Wildl. Manage. 56:23-29.

Thompson, F. R., III., and E. K. Fritzell. 1988. Ruffed grouse winter roost site preference and influence on energy demands. J. Wildl. Manage. 52:454-460.

Thompson, F. R., III., J. R. Probst, and M. G. Rapheal. 1995. Impacts of silviculture: overview and management recommendations. Pages 201-219 in T. E. Martin and D. M. Finch, eds. Ecology and management of neotropical migratory birds. Oxford Univ. Press, New York, NY.

Thompson, F. R., III., S. K. Robinson, T. M. Donovan, J. Faaborg, D. R. Whitehead, D. R. Larsen. 2000. Biogeographic, landscape, and local factors affecting cowbird abundance and host parasitism levels. In T. Cook, S. K. Robinson, S. I. Rothstein, S. G. Sealy, and J. N. M. Smith, eds. Ecology and management of cowbirds. Univ. Texas Press, Austin.

Thompson, F. R., III., S. K. Robinson, D. R. Whitehead, J. D. Brawn. 1996. Management of central hardwood landscapes for the conservation of migratory birds. Pages 117-143 in F. R. Thompson, III, ed. Management of midwestern landscapes for the conservation of neotropical migratory birds. USDA For. Serv. Gen. Tech. Rep. NC-187.

Thompson, R. L. 1977. Feral hogs on national wildlife refuges. Pages 11-15 in G. W. Wood, ed. Research and management of wild hog populations. Belle Baruch Forest Science Inst. of Clemson Univ., Georgetown, SC.

Thurmond, D. P., and K. V. Miller. 1994. Small mammal communities in streamside management zones. Brimleyana 21:125-130.

Times Mirror. 1994. From anxiety toward action: a status report on conservation in 1994. Times Mirror Magazines, Washington, DC. 58pp.

Tisdell, C. A. 1982. Wild pigs: environmental pest or economic resource? Pergamon Press, New York, NY. 445pp.

Tomialojc, L. 1991. Characteristics of old growth in the Bialowieza Forest, Poland. Nat. Areas J. 11:7-18.

Tomlinson, R. E. 1993. Migration. Pages 57-80 in T. S. Baskett, M. W. Sayre, R. E. Tomlinson, and R. E. Mirarchi, eds. Ecology and management of the mourning dove. Stackpole Books, Harrisburg, PA.

Tomlinson, R. E., D. D. Dolton, R. R. George, and R. E. Mirarchi. 1994. Mourning dove. Pages 5-26 in T. C. Tacha and C. E. Braun, eds. Migratory Shore and Upland Game Bird Management in North America. Internat. Assoc. Fish and Wildl. Agencies. Washington, DC.

Tomlinson, R. E., and J. H. Dunks. 1993. Population characteristics and trends in the Central Management Unit. Pages 305-340 in T. S. Baskett, M. W. Sayre, R. E. Tomlinson, and R. E. Mirarchi, eds. Ecology and management of the mourning dove. Stackpole Books, Harrisburg, PA.

Toweill, D. E., and J. E. Tabor. 1984. River Otter. Pages 688-703 in J. A. Chapman and G. A. Feldhamer, eds. Wild mammals of North America. Johns Hopkins Univ. Press, Baltimore, MD.

Towne, C. W., and E. N. Wentworth. 1950. Pigs from cave to cornbelt. Univ. Oklahoma Press, Norman. 305pp.

Trapp, G. R., and D. L. Hallberg. 1975. Ecology of the gray fox (Urocyon cinereoargenteus): a review. Pages 164-178 in M. W. Fox, ed. The wild canids: their systematics, behavioral ecology and evolution. Van Nostrand Reinhold Co., New York, NY.

Trettin, C. C., W. M. Aust, and J. Wisniewski, eds. 1995. Wetlands of the interior southeastern U.S. Kluwer Academic Publishers, Boston, MA.

Trimble, S. W. 1973. A geographic analysis of erosive land use on the Southern Piedmont 1700-1970. Ph.D. Thesis, Univ. Georgia, Athens. 176pp.

Truett, J. C., and D. W. Lay. 1984. Land of bears and honey: a natural history of east Texas. Univ. Texas Press, Austin. 176pp.

Tucker, R. L. 1987. Home range size and habitat use of gray foxes on the Copiah County wildlife management area in Mississippi. Ph.D. Thesis, Mississippi State Univ., Mississippi State. 104pp.

Tucker, R. L., and H. A. Jacobson. 1986. Survival, natality, and exploitation of foxes in Mississippi. Compl. Rep. Fed. Aid. Wildl. Restor. Proj. W-48-Study XIII. 85pp.

Turner, M. G. 1989. Landscape ecology: the effect of pattern on process. Annu. Rev. of Ecol. and Systematics 20:171-197.

Turrill, N.L., E.R. Buckner, and T.A. Waldrop. 1997. Pinus pungens Lam. (Table Mountain pine): a threatened species without fire? Pages 301-306 in J.M. Greenlee, ed. Proceedings—Fire effects of rare and endangered species and habitats conference, Nov. 13-16, 1995. Couer d' Alene, Idaho. International Association of Wildland Fire, Fairfield, WA.

Tuttle, M. D. 1979. Status, causes of decline, and management of endangered gray bats. J. Wildl. Manage. 43:1-17.

Tuttle, M. D. 1995. Saving North America's beleaguered bats. National Geographic 188(2):37-57.

U.S. Bureau of Sport Fisheries and Wildlife. 1968. Rare and endangered fish and wildlife of the United States. U.S. Bureau of Sport Fish. and Wildl., Washington, D.C. Resource Publ. 34

U.S. Congress. 1976. National Forest Management Act. Public Law 94-588, 90 Statute 2949.

U.S. Department of Agriculture. 1981. Wildlife habitat management handbook: southern region. FSH 2609.23R. USDA For. Serv., Atlanta, GA. Pagination by chapter.

U.S. Department of Agriculture. 1991. Agricultural Statistics 1991. U.S. Govt. Printing Office, Washington, D.C. 524pp.

U.S. Department of Agriculture. 1992. Wild pigs hidden danger for farmers and hunters. Ag. Information Bull. 620. 7pp.

U.S. Department of Agriculture. 1994. Agricultural statistics. U. S. Government Printing Office, Washington, DC.

U.S. Department of Agriculture. 1994. Animal damage control final environmental impact statement. USDA, Washington, DC. Vol. 1-3.

U.S. Department of Commerce. 1995. Statistical abstracts of the United States 1995. U.S. Government Printing Office, Washington, DC.

U.S. Department of Health and Human Services. 1995. Summary of notifiable diseases. Centers for Disease Control and Prevention Morbidity and Mortality Weekly Report 44(53):4-9.

U.S. Department of the Army. 1996. Management guidelines for the red-cockaded woodpecker on army installations. U.S. Army, Pentagon, Washington, DC. 32pp.

U.S. Fish and Wildlife Service. 1985. Red-cockaded woodpecker recovery plan. U.S. Fish and Wildl. Serv., Southeast Reg., Atlanta, Ga. 88pp.

U.S. Fish and Wildlife Service. 1992. Draft red-cockaded woodpecker procedures manual for private lands. U.S. Fish and Wildl. Serv., Southeast Reg., Atlanta, GA. 12pp.

U.S. Fish and Wildlife Service. 1997. Endangered and threatened wildlife and plants. 50 CFR 17.11 & 17.12. Special Reprint. USDI, Fish and Wildlife Service, Washington, DC.

U.S. Fish and Wildlife Service. 1998. Strategy and guidelines for the recovery and management of the red-cockaded woodpecker and its habitats on national wildlife refuges. U.S. Fish and Wildl. Serv., Southeast Reg., Atlanta, GA. 51pp.

U.S. Forest Service. 1995. Final environmental impact statement for the management of the red-cockaded woodpecker and its habitat on national forests in the southern region. U.S. For. Serv. Manage. Bull. R8-MB 73 (3 volumes). 407pp and appendices.

Umber, R. W., and L. D. Harris. 1974. Effects of intensive forestry on succession and wildlife in Florida sandhills. Proc. Southeast. Assoc. Game and Fish Comm. 28:686-693.

Urban, D. 1972. Aspects of bobwhite quail mobility during spring through fall months. Pages 194-199 in J. A. Morrison and J. C. Lewis, eds. Proc. First National Bobwhite Quail Symp. Oklahoma State Univ. Stillwater.

USDA Forest Service. 1969. A forest atlas of the south. Sou. For. Exp. Stn., New Orleans, LA. Southeast. For. Exp. Stn., Asheville, NC. 27pp.

USDA Forest Service. 1984. Pesticide background statements, Vol 1: Herbicides. USDA For. Serv. Agr. Handbook No. 633.

USDA Forest Service. 1988. The South's fourth forest: alternatives for the future. For. Resour. Rep. 24. 512pp.

USDA Forest Service. 1995. Final environmental impact statement for the management of the red-cockaded woodpecker and its habitat on national forests in the southern region. USDA For. Serv. Manage. Bull. R8-MB 73 (3 volumes). 407pp and appendices.

USDA Forest Service. 1995. The Forest Service program for forest and rangeland resources: a long-term strategic plan. USDA For. Serv., Washington, DC.

USDI Fish and Wildlife Service. 1985. Red-cockaded woodpecker recovery plan. U.S. Fish and Wildl. Serv., Southeast Reg., Atlanta, Ga. 88pp.

USDI Fish and Wildlife Service. 1987. Florida panther recovery plan. Prepared by the Florida Panther Interagency Committee for the U.S. Fish and Wildl. Serv., Atlanta, GA. 75pp.

USDI Fish and Wildlife Service. 1989. Red wolf recovery plan. U.S. Fish and Wild. Serv., Atlanta, GA. 99pp.

USDI Fish and Wildlife Service. 1990. Red wolf recovery plan. Atlanta, GA. 110pp.

USDI Fish and Wildlife Service. 1992. Draft red-cockaded woodpecker procedures manual for private lands. U.S. Fish and Wildl. Serv., Southeast Reg., Atlanta, GA. 12pp.

USDI Fish and Wildlife Service. 1992. Genetic management strategies and population viability of the Florida panther (Felis concolor coryi). Workshop Proc., 21-22 October, Yulee, FL. 27pp.

USDI Fish and Wildlife Service. 1995. Louisiana black bear recovery plan. 52 pp. mimeo.

USDI Fish and Wildlife Service. 1997. 1996 National Survey of Fishing, Hunting, and Wildlife-Associated Recreation: State Overview. USDI Fish and Wildl. Serv., Arlington, VA. 115pp.

USDI Fish and Wildlife Service. 1998. Strategy and guidelines for the recovery and management of the red-cockaded woodpecker and its habitats on national wildlife refuges. U.S. Fish and

Wildl. Serv., Southeast Reg., Atlanta, GA. 51pp.

USDI Fish and Wildlife Service. 1998. Waterfowl population status, 1998. USDI, Fish and Wildl. Serv., Washington, DC.

Van Doren, M., ed. 1928. The travels of William Bartram. Dover Publications, New York, NY. 414pp.

Van Horne, B. 1983. Density as a misleading indicator of habitat quality. J. Wildl. Manage. 47:893-901.

Vance, D. R. 1976. Changes in land-use and wildlife populations in southeastern Illinois. Wildl. Soc. Bull. 4:11-15.

Vance, D. R., and J. A. Ellis. 1972. Bobwhite populations and hunting on Illinois public hunting areas. Pages 165-173 in J. A. Morrison, and J. C. Lewis, eds. Proc. First National Bobwhite Symp. Oklahoma State Univ., Stillwater.

Vangilder, L. D. 1996. Survival and cause specific mortality of wild turkeys in the Missouri Ozarks. Proc. National Wild Turkey Symp. 7:21-31.

Vangilder, L. D. 1992. Population dynamics. Pages 144-164 in J. G. Dickson, ed. The wild turkey: biology and management. Stackpole Books, Harrisburg, PA.

Vangilder, L. D., and D. A. Hamilton. 1992. Furbearer populations, animal rights and wild turkey production. Missouri Dept. Conserv., Columbia, MO. 36pp.

Vangilder, L. D., M. W. Hubbard, and D. A. Hasenbeck. 2001. Reproductive ecology of eastern wild turkey hens in the Missouri Ozarks. Proc. National Wild Turkey Symp. 8:(in press).

Van Manen, F. T., B. A. Crawford, and J. D. Clark. 2000. Predicting red wolf release success in the southeastern United States. J. Wildl. Manage. 64:895-902.

Vaughan, M. R., and M. R. Pelton. 1995. Black bears in North America. Pages 100-103 in E. T. LaRoe, G. S. Farris, C. E.Puckett, P. D. Doran, and M. J. Mac, eds. Our living resources. USDI - National Biol. Serv., Washington, DC.

Verme, L. J., and D. E. Ullrey. 1984. Physiology and nutrition. Pages 91-118 in L. K. Halls, ed. White-tailed deer: ecology and management. Stackpole Books, Harrisburg, PA.

Verts, B. J. 1963. Movements and populations of opossums in a cultivated area. J. Wildl. Manage. 27:127-129.

Verts, B. J. 1967. The biology of the striped skunk. Univ. Illinois Press, Urbana. 218pp.

Voigt, D. R., and B. D. Earle. 1983. Avoidance of coyotes by red fox families. J. Wildl. Manage. 47:852-857.

Vose, J.M., W.T. Swank, B.D. Clinton. 1997. Using fire to restore pine-hardwood ecosystems in the southern Appalachians of North Carolina. Pages 149-154 in J.M. Greenlee, ed. Proceedings—Fire effects of rare and endangered species and habitats conference, Nov. 13-16, 1995. Couer d' Alene, Idaho. Internat. Association of Wildland Fire, Fairfield, WA

Wade, D. A. 1987. Economics of wildlife production and damage control on private lands. Pages 154-163 in D. J. Decker and G. R. Goff, eds. Valuing wildlife: economic and social perspectives. Westview Press, Boulder, CO.

Wade, D. A., and C. W. Ramsey. 1986. Identifying and managing aquatic rodents in Texas: beaver, nutria, and muskrats. Texas Ag. Ext. Serv. Texas A&M Univ., College Station. 45pp.

Wade-Smith, J., and B. J. Verts. 1982. Mephitis mephitis. Mamm. Species. Amer. Soc. Mamm. 73:1-7.

Wagner, G. D., and E. P. Hill. 1994. Evaluation of southeastern coyote diets during the wild turkey reproductive season. Proc. Ann. Conf. Southeast. Assoc. Fish and Wildl. Agencies 38:173-181.

Wahlenberg, W. G. 1946. Longleaf pine. Charles Lathrop Pack Forestry Foundation, Washington, D.C. 429pp.

Wakely, P. C. 1954. Planting the southern pine. USDA For. Serv. Agric. Mono. No. 18. 233 pp.

Walker, J. 1998. Ground layer vegetation in longleaf pine landscapes: an overview for restoration and management. Pages 2-13 in J.S. Kush, ed. Proceedings of the Longleaf Pine Ecosystem Restoration Symposium, Society for Ecological Restoration Annual International Conference, November 12-15, 1997. Longleaf Alliance Report No. 3. Auburn University School of Forestry, Auburn, AL.

Walker, J.L., and B.P. Van Eerden. 1996. Relationships between disturbance history and vegetation in Carolina sandhills. Bull. Ecol. Soc. of America 77:465.

Walker, L. C. 1991. The southern forest. Univ. Texas Press, Austin. 322pp.

Walker, W. A., and M. K. Causey. 1982. Breeding activity of American woodcock in Alabama. J. Wildl. Manage. 46:1054-1057.

Walters, J. R., C. K. Copeyon, and J. H. Carter, III. 1992. Test of the ecological basis of cooperative breeding in red-cockaded woodpeckers. Auk 109:90-97.

Walters, J. R., P. D. Doerr, and J. H. Carter, III. 1988. The cooperative breeding system of the red-cockaded woodpecker. Ethology 78:275-305.

Warburton, G. S. 1984. An analysis of a black bear sanctuary in western North Carolina. M.S. Thesis, North Carolina State Univ., Raleigh. 121pp.

Warburton, G. S., and R. A. Powell. 1985. Movements of black bears on the Pisgah National Forest. Proc. Annu. Conf. Southeast. Assoc. Fish and Wildl. Agencies 39:351-361.

Warburton, G. S., R. C. Maddrey, and D. W. Rowe. 1993. Characteristics of black bear mortality on the coastal plain of North Carolina. Proc. Annu. Conf. Southeast. Assoc. Fish and Wildl. Agencies 47:276-286.

Ware, S., C. Frost, and P. D. Doerr. 1993. Southern mixed hardwood forest: The former longleaf pine forest. Pages 447-494 in W. H. Martin, S. G. Boyce, and A. C. Echternacht, eds. Biodiversity of the southeastern United States: lowland terrestrial communities. John Wiley and Sons, New York, NY.

Warren, R. J., and C. R. Ford. 1997. Diets, nutrition, and reproduction of feral hogs on Cumberland Island, Georgia. Proc. Annu. Conf. Southeast. Assoc. Fish and Wildl. Agencies 51:285-296.

Warren, R. C., and G. A. Hurst. 1980. Squirrel densities in pine-hardwood forests and streamside management zones. Proc. Annu. Conf. Southeast. Assoc. Fish and Wildl. Agencies 34:492-498.

Warren, R. C., and G. A. Hurst. 1981. Ratings of plants in pine plantations as white-tailed deer food. Miss. Agric. and For. Exp. Stn., Infor. Bull. 18. Starkville, MS. 14pp.

Waters, R. E. 1983. How to attract doves for hunting. U.S. Soil Conserv. Serv., Auburn, AL. 16pp.

Wayne, R. K., and S. M. Jenks. 1991. Mitochondrial DNA analysis implying extensive hybridization of the endangered red wolf, Canis rufus. Nature 351:565-568.

Weakley, A.S., K.D. Patterson, S. Landaal, M. Pyne, and others, compilers. 1998. International Classification of Ecological Communities: Terrrestrial Vegetation of the Southeastern United States. Working Draft of March 1998. The Nature Conservancy, Southeast Regional Office, Chapel Hill, NC. 689 pp.

Weaver, K. M., and M. R. Pelton. 1992. Denning ecology of black bears in a bottomland hardwood forest in Louisiana. Int. Conf. Bear Res. and Manage. 9:427-433.

Weaver, K. M., D. K. Tabberer, L. U. Moore, Jr., G. A. Chandler, J. C. Posey, and M. R. Pelton. 1990. Bottomland hardwood forest management for black bears in Louisiana. Proc. Annu. Conf. Southeast. Assoc. Fish and Wildl. Agencies 44:342-350.

Webb, D.H., H.R. DeSelm, and W.M. Dennis. 1997. Studies of prairie barrens of northwestern Alabama. Castanea 62:173-184.

Webb, W. L., D. F. Behrend, and B. Saisorr. 1977. Effect of logging on songbird populations in a northern hardwood forest. Wildl. Monogr. 55:6-35.

Webster, W. D., J. F. Parnell, and W. C. Biggs, Jr. 1985. Mammals of the Carolinas, Virginia and Maryland. Univ. North Carolina Press, Chapel Hill. 255pp.

Weeks, H. P., Jr. 1995. Mineral supplementation and antler production. Pages 155-168 in K. V. Miller and R. L. Marchinton, eds. Quality whitetails: the why and how of quality deer management. Stackpole Books, Mechanicsburg, PA.

Weigl, P. D. 1978. Resource overlap, interspecific interactions and the distribution of the flying squirrels, Glaucomys volans and G. sabrinus. Am. Midl. Nat. 100:83-96.

Weigl, P. D., and D. W. Osgood. 1974. Study of the northern flying squirrel, Glaucomys sabrinus, by temperate telemetry. Am. Midl. Nat. 92:482-486.

Weigl, P. D., M. A. Steele, L. J. Sherman, J. C. Ha, and T. L. Sharpe. 1989. The ecology of the fox squirrel (Sciurus niger) in North Carolina: implications for survival in the southeast. Tall Timbers Res. Sta. Bull. No. 24. 93pp.

Weller, D. M. G., and M. R. Pelton. 1987. Denning characteristics of striped skunks in Great Smoky Mountains National Park. J. Mamm. 68:177-179.

Weller, J. R. 1995. Food habits of the red wolf (Canis rufus) on Horn Island, Mississippi. M.S. Thesis, Univ. Southern Mississippi, Hattiesburg. 82pp.

Wells-Gosling, N., and L. R. Heaney. 1984. Glaucomys sabrinus. Mammalian Species Number 229. Am. Soc. Mamm. 8pp.

Welsh, H. H., Jr. 1990. Relictual amphibians and old-growth forests. Conserv. Biol. 4:309-319.

Wentworth, J. M., A. S. Johnson, P. E. Hale, and K. E. Kammermeyer. 1992. Relationships of acorn abundance and deer herd characteristics in the southern Appalachians. Sou. J. Appl. For. 19:5-8.

Wharton, C. H. 1977. The natural environments of Georgia. Georgia Dept. of Nat. Resour. 227pp.

Wharton, C. H., W. M. Kitchens, E. C. Pendleton, and T. W. Sipe. 1982. The ecology of bottomland hardwood swamps in the southeast: a community profile. USDI Fish and Wildl. Serv. FWS/OBS - 81/37. 133pp.

Wheeler, R. J., Jr. 1948. The wild turkey in Alabama. Montgomery: Alabama Dep. of Conserv. Bull. 12. 92 pp.

Whitaker, J., R. B. Fredrick, and T. L. Edwards. 1987. Home range size and overlap of eastern Kentucky bobcats. Proc. Annu. Conf. Southeast. Assoc. Fish and Wildl. Agencies 41:417-423.

White, L. D., L. D. Harris, J. E. Johnston, and D. G. Milchunas. 1975. Impact of site preparation on flatwoods wildlife habitat. Proc. Southeast. Assoc. Game and Fish Comm. 29:347-353.

White, P. S., E. Buckner, J. D. Pittillo, and C. V. Cogbill. 1993. High-elevation forests: spuce-fir forests, northern hardwoods forest, and associated communities. Pages 305-338 in W. H. Martin, S. G. Boyce, and A. C. Echternacht, eds. Biodiversity of the southeastern United States, upland terrestrial communities. John Wiley and Sons, New York, NY.

White, P.S.(ed.). 1984. The Southern Appalachian Spruce-Fir Ecosystem: its biology and threats. USDI, National Park Service, Research/Resources Management Rep. SER-71. 268 pp.

White, P.S., and R.D. Sutter. 1998. Southern Appalachian grassy balds: lessons for management and regional conservation. Pages 375-396 in J.D. Peine, ed. Lucie Press, Delray Beach, FL.

White, P.S., and J.L. Walker. 1997. Approximating nature's variation: selecting and using reference information in restoration ecology. Restoration Ecol. 5:338-349.

White, P.S., and R.D. White. 1996. Old-growth oak and oak-hickory forests. Pages 178-198 in M.B. Davis, ed. Eastern Old-Growth Forests. Island Press, Washington, DC.

White, P.S., S.P. Wilds, and G.A. Thunhorst. 1998. Southeast. Pages 255-314 in M.J. Mac, P.A. Opler, C.E. Puckett Haecker, and P.D. Doran, eds. Status and trends of the nation's biological resources. 2 vol. USDI, US Geological Survey, Reston, VA.

Whitehead, G. K. 1993. The Whitehead encyclopedia of deer. Swan Hill Press, Shrewsbury, England. 597pp.

Whiting, R. M., and T. G. Boggus. 1982. Breeding biology of American woodcock in east Texas. Pages 132-138 in T. J. Dwyer and G. L. Storm, tech. coords. Woodcock ecology and management. USDI Fish and Wildl. Serv., Wildl. Res. Rep. 14.

Whiting, R. M., R. R. George, M. K. Causey, and T. H. Roberts. 1985. February hunting of American woodcock: breeding implications. Pages 309-317 in S. L. Beasom and S. F. Roberson, eds. Game harvest management. Caesar Kleberg Wildl. Res. Inst., Kingsville, TX.

Widmann, O. 1907. Preliminary catalog of the birds of Missouri. Trans. Acad. Sci. St. Louis, 17:1-296.

Wiens, J. A., J. T. Rotenberry, and B. Van Horne. 1986. A lesson in the limitations of field experiments: shrubsteppe birds and habitat alteration. Ecology 67:365-376.

Wigley, T. B., and M. A. Melchiors. 1994. Wildlife habitat and communities in streamside management zones: a literature review for the eastern United States. Pages 100-121 in Riparian ecosystems in the humid U.S.: functions, values, and management. Nat. Assoc. Conserv. Dist., Washington, DC.

Wiley, E. N., II, and M. K. Causey. 1987. Survival of American woodcock chicks in Alabama. J. Wildl. Manage. 51:583-586.

Wilhide, J. D., M. J. Harvey, V. R. McDaniel, and V. E. Hoffman. 1998. Highland pond utilization by bats in the Ozark National Forest. J. Arkansas Acad. Science 52:110-112.

Williams, C.E. 1998. History and status of Table Mountain pine-pitch pine forests of the Southern Appalachian Mountains (USA). Nat. Areas J. 17:81-90.

Williams, C.E., and W.C. Johnson. 1992. Factors affecting recruitment of Pinus pungens in the southern Appalachian Mountains. Canadian J. of For. Res. 22:878-887.

Willson, M. F. 1974. Avian community organization and habitat structure. Ecology 55:1017-1029.

Wilson, C. W., R. E. Masters, and G. A. Bukenhofer. 1995. Breeding bird response to pine-grassland community restoration for red-cockaded woodpeckers. J. Wildl. Manage. 59:56-67.

Wilson, K. A. 1953. Raccoon predation on muskrats near Currituck, North Carolina. J. Wildl. Manage. 17:113-119.

Wilson, K. A. 1959. The otter in North Carolina. Proc. Annu. Conf. Southeast. Assoc. Game and Fish Comm. 13:267-277.

Wilson, M. D., and B. D. Watts. 1999. Response of brown-headed nuthatches to thinning of pine plantations. Wilson Bull. 111:56-60.

Wilson, T. S. 1996. Raccoon and opossum home ranges, movements and habitat use in a managed forest of central Mississippi. M. S. Thesis, Mississippi State Univ., Mississippi State. 132pp.

Wiseman, D. S., and J. C. Lewis. 1981. Bobwhite use of habitat in tallgrass rangeland. Wildl. Soc. Bull. 9:248-255.

Wiser, S.K. 1994. High elevation cliffs and outcrops of the southern Appalachians: vascular plants and biogeography. Castanea 59:85-116.

Witmer, G. W., and D. S. DeCalesta. 1986. Resource used by unexploited bobcats and coyotes in Oregon. Can. J. Zool. 64:2333-2338.

Wobeser, G.A. 1981. Diseases of wild waterfowl. Plenum Press, New York, NY. 300pp.

Wolfe, J. L., and R. Lohoefener. 1983. The small mammal fauna of a longleaf-slash pine forest in southern Mississippi. J. Miss. Acad. Science 28:37-47.

Wood, G. W. 1986. Influences of forest fertilization on South Carolina deer forage quality. Sou. J. Appl. For. 10:203-206.

Wood, G. W., and R. H. Barrett. 1979. Status of wild pigs in the United States. Wildl. Soc. Bull. 7:237-246.

Wood, G. W., R. H. Barrett, D. C. Mathews, and J. R. Sweeney. 1992. Feral hog control efforts on a coastal South Carolina plantation. Proc. Annu. Conf. Southeast. Assoc. Fish and Wildl. Agencies 46:167-178.

Wood, J. E. 1954. Food habits of furbearers of the upland post oak region of Texas. J. Mamm. 35:406-415.

Wood, J. E. 1958. Age structure and productivity of a gray fox population. J. Mamm. 39:74-86.

Wood, J. E., D. E. Davis, and E. V. Komarek. 1958. The distribution of fox populations in relation to vegetation in southern Georgia. Ecology 39:160-162.

Wooding, J. B. 1984. Coyote food habits and the spatial relationship of coyotes and red foxes in Mississippi and Alabama. M.S. Thesis, Mississippi State Univ., Mississippi State. 43pp.

Wooding, J. B., and J. R. Brady. 1987. Black bear road kills in Florida. Proc. Annu. Conf. Southeast. Assoc. Fish and Wildl. Agencies 41:438-442

Wooding, J. B., J. A. Cox, and M. R. Pelton. 1994. Distribution of black bears in the southeastern coastal plain. Proc. Annu. Conf. Southeast. Assoc. Fish and Wildl. Agencies 48:270-275.

Wooding, J. B., and T. S. Hardisky. 1994. Home range, habitat use, and mortality of black bears in north-central Florida. Int. Conf. Bear Res. and Manage. 9:349-356.

Wooding, J. B., E. P. Hill, and P. W. Sumner. 1984. Coyote food habits in Mississippi and Alabama. Proc. Ann. Conf. Southeast. Assoc. Fish and Wildl. Agencies 38:182-188

Wooding, J. B., N. L. Hunter, and T. S. Hardisky. 1988. Trap and release apiary-raiding black bears. Proc. Annu. Conf. Southeast. Assoc. Fish and Wildl. Agencies 42:333-336.

Woodward, D. K. 1977. Status and ecology of the beaver (Castor canadensis carolinensis) in South Carolina with emphasis on the Piedmont Region. M. S. Thesis, Clemson Univ., Clemson, SC. 208pp.

Woodward, D. K., R. B. Hazel, and B. P. Gaffney. 1985. Economic and environmental impacts of beaver in North Carolina. Proc. East. Wildl. Damage Control Conf. 2:89-96.

Woolner, F. 1974. Timberdoodle! A thorough, practical guide to the American woodcock and to woodcock hunting. Crown Publ., Inc., New York, NY. 168pp.

Wyman, R. L. 1988. Soil acidity and moisture and the distribution of amphibians in five forests of southcentral New York. Copeia 1988:394-399.

Wyman, R. L.. 1990. What's happening to the amphibians? Conserv. Biol. 4:350-352.

Wynn, A. H. 1991. Shenandoah salamander, Plethodon shenandoah. Pages 439-442 in K. Terwilleger, ed. Virginia's Endangered Species. McDonald and Woodward, Blacksburg, VA.

Wynn, A. H., R. Highton, and J. F. Jacobs. 1988. A new species of rock-crevice dwelling Plethodon from Pigeon Mountain, Georgia. Herpetologica 44:135-143.

Yates, S. W., D. C., Sisson, H. L. Stribling, and D. W. Speake. 1995. Northern bobwhite brood habitat use in southern Georgia. Proc. Annu. Conf. Southeast. Assoc. Fish and Wildl. Agencies 49:498-504.

Yoho, N.S., and R. W. Dimmick. 1972. Habitat utilization by bobwhite quail during winter. Pages 90-99. in J. A. Morrison, and J. C. Lewis, eds. Proc. First National Bobwhite Symp. Oklahoma State Univ., Stillwater.

Yoho, N. S., and V. G. Henry. 1972. Foods of the gray fox (Urocyon cinereoargenteus) on European wild hog (Sus scrofa) range in east Tennessee. J. Tenn. Acad. Sci. 47:77-79.

Young, G. L., B. L. Karr, B. D. Leopold, and J. D. Hodges. 1995. Effect of greentree reservoir management on Mississippi bottomland hardwoods. Wildl. Soc. Bull. 23:525-531.

Young, S. P. 1958. The bobcat in North America. Stackpole Books, Harrisburg, PA. 193pp.

Young, S. P., and H. H. T. Jackson. 1951. The clever coyote. Wildlife Management Institute. 411pp.

Zartman, C.E., and J.D. Pitillo. 1998. Spray cliff communities of the Chattooga Basin. Castanea 63:217-240.

Zielinski, W. J. 1995. Track plates. Pages 67-89 in W. J. Zielinski, and T. E. Kucera, eds. American marten, fisher, lynx, and wolverine: survey methods for their detection. USDA For. Serv. Gen. Tech. Rep. PSW-GTR-157.

Zim, H. S., and H. M. Smith. 1953. Reptiles and amphibians. Golden Press, New York, NY. 160pp.

Zutter, B. R., and J. H. Miller. 1998. Eleventh-year response of loblolly pine and competing vegetation to woody and herbaceous plant control on a Georgia flatwoods site. Sou. J. Appl. For. 22:88-95.

Zygmont, S. M., V. F. Nettles, E. B. Shotts, W. A. Carmen, and B. O. Blackburn. 1982. Brucellosis in wild swine: A serologic and bacteriologic survey in the southeastern United States and Hawaii. J. Am. Vet. Med. Assoc. 181:1285-1287.

Index

Made in the USA
Middletown, DE
24 February 2024